Praise for the Reformation Commentary on Scripture

"Protestant reformers were fundamentally exegetes as much as theologians, yet (except for figures like Luther and Calvin) their commentaries and sermons have been neglected because these writings are not available in modern editions or languages. That makes this new series of Reformation Commentary on Scripture most welcome as a way to provide access to some of the wealth of biblical exposition of the sixteenth and seventeenth centuries. The editor's introduction explains the nature of the sources and the selection process; the intended audience of modern pastors and students of the Bible has led to a focus on theological and practical comments. Although it will be of use to students of the Reformation, this series is far from being an esoteric study of largely forgotten voices; this collection of reforming comments, comprehending every verse and provided with topical headings, will serve contemporary pastors and preachers very well."

Elsie Anne McKee, *Archibald Alexander Professor of Reformation Studies and the History of Worship, Princeton Theological Seminary*

"This series provides an excellent introduction to the history of biblical exegesis in the Reformation period. The introductions are accurate, clear and informative, and the passages intelligently chosen to give the reader a good idea of methods deployed and issues at stake. It puts precritical exegesis in its context and so presents it in its correct light. Highly recommended as reference book, course book and general reading for students and all interested lay and clerical readers."

Irena Backus, *Professeure Ordinaire, Institut d'histoire de la Réformation, Université de Genève*

"The Reformation Commentary on Scripture is a major publishing event—for those with historical interest in the founding convictions of Protestantism, but even more for those who care about understanding the Bible. As with IVP Academic's earlier Ancient Christian Commentary on Scripture, this effort brings flesh and blood to 'the communion of saints' by letting believers of our day look over the shoulders of giants from the past. By connecting the past with the present, and by doing so with the Bible at the center, the editors of this series perform a great service for the church. The series deserves the widest possible support."

Mark A. Noll, *Francis A. McAnaney Professor of History, University of Notre Dame*

"For those who preach and teach Scripture in the church, the Reformation Commentary on Scripture is a significant publishing event. Pastors and other church leaders will find delightful surprises, challenging enigmas and edifying insights in this series, as many Reformational voices are newly translated into English. The lively conversation in these pages can ignite today's pastoral imagination for fresh and faithful expositions of Scripture."

J. Todd Billings, *Gordon H. Girod Research Professor of Reformed Theology, Western Theological Seminary*

"The reformers discerned rightly what the church desperately needed in the sixteenth century—the bold proclamation of the Word based on careful study of the sacred Scriptures. We need not only to hear that same call again for our own day but also to learn from the Reformation how to do it. This commentary series is a godsend!"

Richard J. Mouw, *President Emeritus, Fuller Theological Seminary*

"Like the Ancient Christian Commentary on Scripture, the Reformation Commentary on Scripture does a masterful job of offering excellent selections from well-known and not-so-well-known exegetes. The editor's introductory survey is, by itself, worth the price of the book. It is easy to forget that there were more hands, hearts and minds involved in the Reformation than Luther and Calvin. Furthermore, encounters even with these figures are often limited to familiar quotes on familiar topics. However, the Reformation Commentary helps us to recognize the breadth and depth of exegetical interests and skill that fueled and continue to fuel faithful meditation on God's Word. I heartily recommend this series as a tremendous resource not only for ministry but for personal edification."

Michael S. Horton, *J. G. Machen Professor of Systematic Theology and Apologetics, Westminster Seminary, California*

"The Reformation was ignited by a fresh reading of Scripture. In this series of commentaries, we contemporary interpreters are allowed to feel some of the excitement, surprise and wonder of our spiritual forebears. Luther, Calvin and their fellow revolutionaries were masterful interpreters of the Word. Now, in this remarkable series, some of our very best Reformation scholars open up the riches of the Reformation's reading of the Scripture."

William H. Willimon, *Professor of the Practice of Christian Ministry, Duke Divinity School*

"The Reformation Scripture principle set the entirety of Christian life and thought under the governance of the divine Word, and pressed the church to renew its exegetical labors. This series promises to place before the contemporary church the fruit of those labors, and so to exemplify life under the Word."

John Webster, *Chair of Systematic Theology, University of Aberdeen*

"Since Gerhard Ebeling's pioneering work on Luther's exegesis seventy years ago, the history of biblical interpretation has occupied many Reformation scholars and become a vital part of study of the period. The Reformation Commentary on Scripture provides fresh materials for students of Reformation-era biblical interpretation and for twenty-first-century preachers to mine the rich stores of insights from leading reformers of the sixteenth century into both the text of Scripture itself and its application in sixteenth-century contexts. This series will strengthen our understanding of the period of the Reformation and enable us to apply its insights to our own days and its challenges to the church."

Robert Kolb, *Professor Emeritus, Concordia Theological Seminary*

"The multivolume Ancient Christian Commentary on Scripture is a valuable resource for those who wish to know how the Fathers interpreted a passage of Scripture but who lack the time or the opportunity to search through the many individual works. This new Reformation Commentary on Scripture will do the same for the reformers and is to be warmly welcomed. It will provide much easier access to the exegetical treasures of the Reformation and will hopefully encourage readers to go back to some of the original works themselves."

Anthony N. S. Lane, *Professor of Historical Theology and Director of Research, London School of Theology*

"This volume of the RCS project is an invaluable source for pastors and the historically/biblically interested that provides unparalleled access not only to commentaries of the leading Protestant reformers but also to a host of nowadays unknown commentaters on Galatians and Ephesians. The RCS is sure to enhance and enliven contemporary exegesis. With its wide scope, the collection will enrich our understanding of the variety of Reformation thought and biblical exegesis."

Sigrun Haude, *Associate Professor of Reformation and Early Modern European History, University of Cincinnati*

"The Reformation Commentary on Scripture series promises to be an 'open sesame' to the biblical exegesis, exposition and application of the Bible that was the hallmark of the Reformation. While comparisons can be odious, the difference between Reformation commentary and exposition and much that both preceded and followed it is laid bare in these pages: whereas others write about the Bible from the outside, Reformation exposition carries with it the atmosphere of men who spoke and wrote from inside the Bible, experiencing the power of biblical teaching even as they expounded it. . . . This grand project sets before scholars, pastors, teachers, students and growing Christians an experience that can only be likened to stumbling into a group Bible study only to discover that your fellow participants include some of the most significant Christians of the Reformation and post-Reformation (for that matter, of any) era. Here the Word of God is explained in a variety of accents: German, Swiss, French, Dutch, English, Scottish and more. Each one vibrates with a thrilling sense of the living nature of God's Word and its power to transform individuals, churches and even whole communities. Here is a series to anticipate, enjoy and treasure."

Sinclair Ferguson, *Senior Minister, First Presbyterian Church, Columbia, South Carolina*

"I strongly endorse the Reformation Commentary on Scripture. Introducing how the Bible was interpreted during the age of the Reformation, these volumes will not only renew contemporary preaching, but they will also help us understand more fully how reading and meditating on Scripture can, in fact, change our lives!"

Lois Malcolm, *Associate Professor of Systematic Theology, Luther Seminary*

"Discerning the true significance of movements in theology requires acquaintance with their biblical exegesis. This is supremely so with the Reformation, which was essentially a biblical revival. The Reformation Commentary on Scripture will fill a yawning gap, just as the Ancient Christian Commentary did before it, and the first volume gets the series off to a fine start, whetting the appetite for more. Most heartily do I welcome and commend this long overdue project."

J. I. Packer, *Retired Board of Governors Professor of Theology, Regent College*

"There is no telling the benefits to emerge from the publication of this magnificent Reformation Commentary on Scripture series! Now exegetical and theological treasures from Reformation era commentators will be at our fingertips, providing new insights from old sources to give light for the present and future. This series is a gift to scholars and to the church; a wonderful resource to enhance our study of the written Word of God for generations to come!"

Donald K. McKim, *Executive Editor of Theology and Reference, Westminster John Knox Press*

"Why was this not done before? The publication of the Reformation Commentary on Scripture should be greeted with enthusiasm by every believing Christian—but especially by those who will preach and teach the Word of God. This commentary series brings the very best of the Reformation heritage to the task of exegesis and exposition, and each volume in this series represents a veritable feast that takes us back to the sixteenth century to enrich the preaching and teaching of God's Word in our own time."

R. Albert Mohler Jr., *President, The Southern Baptist Theological Seminary*

"Today more than ever, the Christian past is the church's future. InterVarsity Press has already brought the voice of the ancients to our ears. Now, in the Reformation Commentary on Scripture, we hear a timely word from the first Protestants as well."

Bryan Litfin, *Professor of Theology, Moody Bible Institute*

"I am delighted to see the Reformation Commentary on Scripture. The editors of this series have done us all a service by gleaning from these rich fields of biblical reflection. May God use this new life for these old words to give him glory and to build his church."

Mark Dever, *Senior Pastor, Capitol Hill Baptist Church, and President of 9Marks.org Ministries*

"Monumental and magisterial, the Reformation Commentary on Scripture, edited by Timothy George, is a remarkably bold and visionary undertaking. Bringing together a wealth of resources, these volumes will provide historians, theologians, biblical scholars, pastors and students with a fresh look at the exegetical insights of those who shaped and influenced the sixteenth-century Reformation. With this marvelous publication, InterVarsity Press has reached yet another plateau of excellence. We pray that this superb series will be used of God to strengthen both church and academy."

David S. Dockery, *President, Union University*

"Detached from her roots, the church cannot reach the world as God intends. While every generation must steward the scriptural insights God grants it, only arrogance or ignorance causes leaders to ignore the contributions of those faithful leaders before us. The Reformation Commentary on Scripture roots our thought in great insights of faithful leaders of the Reformation to further biblical preaching and teaching in this generation."

Bryan Chapell, *chancellor and professor of practical theology, Covenant Theological Seminary*

"After reading several volumes of the Reformation Commentary on Scripture, I exclaimed, 'Hey, this is just what the doctor ordered—I mean Doctor Martinus Lutherus!' The church of today bearing his name needs a strong dose of the medicine this doctor prescribed for the ailing church of the sixteenth century. The reforming fire of Christ-centered preaching that Luther ignited is the only hope to reclaim the impact of the gospel to keep the Reformation going, not for its own sake but to further the renewal of the worldwide church of Christ today. This series of commentaries will equip preachers to step into their pulpits with confidence in the same living Word that inspired the witness of Luther and Calvin and many other lesser-known Reformers."

Carl E. Braaten, *cofounder of the Center for Catholic and Evangelical Theology*

REFORMATION COMMENTARY ON SCRIPTURE

NEW TESTAMENT
VI

ACTS

EDITED BY
ESTHER CHUNG-KIM
AND TODD R. HAINS

GENERAL EDITOR
TIMOTHY GEORGE

ASSOCIATE GENERAL EDITOR
SCOTT M. MANETSCH

IVP Academic
An imprint of InterVarsity Press
Downers Grove, Illinois

InterVarsity Press
P.O. Box 1400, Downers Grove, IL 60515-1426
World Wide Web: www.ivpress.com
E-mail: email@ivpress.com

InterVarsity Press® is the book-publishing division of InterVarsity Christian Fellowship/USA®, a movement of students and faculty active on campus at hundreds of universities, colleges and schools of nursing in the United States of America, and a member movement of the International Fellowship of Evangelical Students. For information about local and regional activities, write Public Relations Dept., InterVarsity Christian Fellowship/USA, 6400 Schroeder Rd., P.O. Box 7895, Madison, WI 537077895, or visit the IVCF website at <www.intervarsity.org>.

Excerpts from The Acts of the Apostles, 2 vols., translated by John W. Fraser and W. J. G. McDonald, are copyright © 1965–1966 by Wm. B. Eerdmans Publishing Co. www.eerdmans.com. Used by permission. All rights reserved.

Excerpts from The Book of Concord, 2nd ed., edited by Robert Kolb and Timothy J. Wengert, are copyright © 2000 by Augsburg Fortress Publishers. www.augsburgfortress.org. Used by permission. All rights reserved.

Excerpts from The Confession of 1535, 2nd ed., translated by C. Daniel Crews, are copyright © 2007 by Moravian Archives. moravianarchives.org. Used by permission. All rights reserved.

Excerpts from Luther's Works, vol. 58, Sermons V, are copyright © 2010 by Concordia Publishing House. cph.org. Used by permission. All rights reserved.

Excerpts from Paraphrase on the Acts of the Aposteles, edited by John J. Bateman and translated by Robert D. Sider, are copyright © 1995 by University of Toronto Press. utpress.utoronto.ca. Used by permission. All rights reserved.

Excerpts from Balthasar Hubmaier: Theologian of Anabaptism, edited and translated by H. Wayne Pipkin and John H. Yoder, are copyright © 1989 by Herald Press, Scottdale, PA 15683. Used by permission.

Excerpts from The Writings of Dirk Philips, 1504–1568, edited and translated by Cornelius J. Dyck, William E. Keeney and Alvin J. Beachy, are copyright © 1992 by Herald Press, Scottdale, PA 15683. Used by permission.

Excerpts from Peter Riedemann's Confession of Faith, edited and translated by John J. Friesen, are copyright © 1999 by Herald Press, Waterloo, ON N2L 6H7. Used by permission.

Excerpts from Jörg Maler's Kunstbuch, edited by John D. Rempel, are copyright © 2010 by Pandora Press. pandorapress.com. Used by permission. All rights reserved.

Map of Paul's Journeys in The Bible and Holy Scriptures conteyned in the Old and Newe Testament (Geneva: Rouland Hall, 1560), no pagination, map is inserted between 53v and 54r; Henry E. Huntington Library and Art Collection (Early English Books Online, STC [2nd ed.] / 2093).

Image of Demetrius's Silver Medal in John Downame, ed., Annotations upon All the Books of the Old and New Testament (London: Evan Tyler, 1657), LLL2v; Christ Church (University of Oxford) Library (Early English Books Online, Wing [2nd ed., 1994] / D2064.)

This publication contains The Holy Bible, English Standard Version®, copyright © 2001 by Crossway, a publishing ministry of Good News Publishers. The ESV® text appearing in this publication is reproduced and published by cooperation between Good News Publishers and InterVarsity Press and by permission of Good News Publishers. Unauthorized reproduction of this publication is prohibited.

The Holy Bible, English Standard Version (ESV) is adapted from the Revised Standard Version of the Bible, copyright Division of Christian Education of the National Council of the Churches of Christ in the U.S.A. All rights reserved.

English Standard Version®, ESV® and ESV® logo are tradmarks of Good News Publishers located in Wheaton, Illinois. Used by permission.

Design: Cindy Kiple
Images: Wooden cross: iStockphoto

The Protestant Church in Lyon: The Protestant Church in Lyon, called "The Paradise" at Bibliotheque Publique et Universitaire, Geneva, Switzerland, Erich Lessing/Art Resource, NY.

ISBN 978-0-8308-2969-9 (print)
ISBN 978-0-8308-9568-7 (digital)

Printed in the United States of America ∞

Library of Congress Cataloging-in-Publication Data
A catalog record for this book is available from the Library of Congress.

P	27	26	25	24	23	22	21	20	19	18	17	16	15	14	13	12	11	10	9	8	7	6	5	4	3	2	1
Y	37	36	35	34	33	32	31	30	29	28	27	26	25	24	23	22	21	20	19	18	17	16	15	14			

Reformation Commentary on Scripture
Project Staff

Project Editor
Brannon Ellis

Managing Editor
Benjamin M. McCoy

Copyeditor
Linda Triemstra

Editorial Assistant
Claire VanderVelde

Assistants to the General Editors
Gail Barton
B. Coyne
Le-Ann Little

Design
Cindy Kiple

Design Assistant
Beth Hagenberg

Content Production
Kirsten Pott
Maureen G. Tobey
Jeanna L. Wiggins

Proofreader
Nina Rynd Whitnah

Print Coordinator
Jim Erhart

InterVarsity Press

Publisher
Robert A. Fryling

Associate Publisher, Editorial
Andrew T. Le Peau

Associate Editorial Director
James Hoover

Production Manager
Anne Gerth

CONTENTS

ACKNOWLEDGMENTS

In his commentary on Acts 17, Heinrich Bullinger writes, "Teaching is a wonderful art to the souls of listeners." This book has heightened my awareness of the many teachers who have contributed to my development as a scholar. Not only did the work of translation remind me of my language teachers of Hebrew, Greek, Latin, German and French but also of those who expected me to exercise those skills in the pursuit of greater understanding of another time and place. This journey has brought me to the Reformation of the sixteenth century, which I seek to understand through the lens of biblical interpretation. Thanks to David Steinmetz who introduced the history of biblical interpretation as a way to study Christian history and who continues to be a conversation partner. I also wish to thank the project editors: Joel Scandrett for the invitation to join the series, Michael Gibson for his blog updates and willingness to listen, and Brannon Ellis for his solution-oriented responses. In addition, the general editor, Timothy George, and associate general editor, Scott Manetsch, have provided the necessary leadership to coordinate such a series. Great thanks goes to my coeditor, Todd Hains, who contributed his valuable perspective to produce a more balanced, more thorough and all-around better volume.

Since the initial stages of research, accruing the sources to complete this book has not been a simple process. Therefore I appreciate the detective work involved in compiling the available print or more often digital sources done by student assistants Kirsten Gerdes and Kerry Moller. Special thanks goes to student assistants Jennifer Smith and Andy Yost who helped with Latin translations, as well as two classics professors, Amy Alexander and Kirk Summers, whose assistance with further additions allowed me to finish this project in a timely manner. The libraries and staff at the Honnold Library, Huntington Library, Luther Seminary, Princeton Theological Seminary and the Meeter Center at Calvin College have also been quite helpful for accessing manuscripts and other research materials. Various colleagues of Reformation studies have provided motivation, knowingly or unknowingly, including Richard Muller, who helped me find several elusive sixteenth-century sources; Beth Kreitzer, who offered practical advice on how to get started; and John Thompson, whose intellectual enthusiasm for his work and contribution to the series was contagious. I am also grateful for the support of my institution, Claremont McKenna College, especially the Dean's Faculty Summer Research Fellowship, which enabled me to make significant progress on this book.

I must acknowledge the support of my husband, Steven, whose vicarious interest in this book project meant reduced vacations and greater responsibility in family matters. Nathan, my nine-year-old, said he was proud of me because I was "working so hard on my book" and helped me to retrieve a couple of paragraphs that disappeared in a computer glitch. Eli, my five-year-old, who likes reading books, could finally understand that I was writing one of those, but with more pages and no pictures. Finally, to my parents, Sungman and Grace Chung, who first taught me to read the Bible in English and Korean, I dedicate this volume.

Esther Chung-Kim

With this project complete I am pointedly aware of my gratitude for the Triune God's grace. Without the aid and experience of a host of folks this volume would not have turned out nearly so well as it has. I would like to thank first my coeditor, Esther Chung-Kim, whose deep convictions about justice and equality have made this volume much more than an antiquarian nicety—merely what dead people said about the Bible three hundred or four hundred years ago. I owe many thanks—perhaps some meals—to the cheerful and industrious IVP representatives, especially Dr. Timothy George and Andy Le Peau, who have worked so diligently on this series. Claire VanderVelde patiently endured our many edits. Dr. Kirk Summers and Amy Alexander bolstered this volume with their Latin expertise. Dr. Brannon Ellis has been a steadfast and merciful shepherd of this project. Through his deft editing and clever wordsmithing this commentary has gained clarity, coherence and charm. I am deeply grateful for his ability to understand "the heart of the matter," his encouragement and his manifold expertise.

My doctoral advisor, Dr. Scott Manetsch, has been a cavernous cistern of encouragement and challenge—even willing to help with my Latin and to translate some French. He models a compassionate pastoral heart for all his students, reminding us that *all* people—whether we agree with them or not—are made in the image of God. I am deeply indebted to this mentor at Trinity Evangelical Divinity School (TEDS). Speaking of TEDS, I would like to thank Dr. David Pao and the participants of his spring 2013 Acts seminar for putting up with a historian in their midst and teaching me so much about the details and nuances of contemporary New Testament scholarship. They have influenced and improved this volume in ways seen and unseen.

My family has loved me through this project, tolerating my quasi-nonstop chatter about it. Thank you, Mom and Dad, for encouraging me to pursue historical theology and for instructing me in the life-giving waters of Scripture. I have benefited from dialogue with and support from my siblings and their spouses (not to mention all their rambunctious children): Laura and Matt, and Andrew and Karen. Most importantly my dear and delightful wife, Veronica—who listens to my rambling thoughts, consoles me and questions my assumptions (remember, "the candle people"?)—has endured my odd hours, my forgetful eating and my many eccentricities. Without your love, grace and empathy I could not have finished this editorial race.

Todd R. Hains

ABBREVIATIONS

ANF	*The Ante-Nicene Fathers*. 10 vols. Edited by Alexander Roberts and James Donaldson. Buffalo, NY: Christian Literature, 1885-1896. Accessible online at ccel.org.
BCP 1549	*The Book of Common Prayer* (1549). In *The Two Liturgies, AD 1549 and AD 1552*. Edited by Joseph Ketley, 9-158. Cambridge: Cambridge University Press, 1844.
BoC	*The Book of Concord: The Confessions of the Evangelical Lutheran Church*. Edited by Robert Kolb and Timothy J. Wengert. Translated by Charles Arand et al. Minneapolis: Fortress, 2000.
Boh 1535	*Bohemian Confession of 1535*. Edited by C. Daniel Crews. Digital copy online at moravianarchives.org.
Boh 1575	*Bohemian Confession of 1575*. Edited by C. Daniel Crews. Digital copy online at moravianarchives.org.
BNP	Brill's New Pauly: Encyclopedia of the Ancient World. Edited by Hubert Cancik and Helmuth Schneider. 20 vols. Leiden: Brill, 2002–2011.
BRN	Bibliotheca Reformatoria Neederlandica. 10 vols. Edited by S. Cramer and F. Pijper. The Hague: Martinus Nijhoff, 1903–1914. Digital copy online at babel.haithtrust.org.
BSLK	*Die Bekenntnisschriften der evangelisch-lutherischen Kirche*. 12th ed. Göttingen: Vandenhoeck & Ruprecht, 1998.
CHB	*Cambridge History of the Bible*. 3 vols. Cambridge: Cambridge University Press, 1963–1970.
CNTC	*Calvin's New Testament Commentaries*. 12 vols. Edited by D. W. Torrance and T. F. Torrance. Grand Rapids, MI: Eerdmans, 1959–1972.
CO	*Ioannis Calvini Opera quae supersunt omnia*. 59 vols. Corpus Reformatorum 29-88. Edited by G. Baum, E. Cunitz and E. Reuss. Brunswick and Berlin: C. A. Schwetschke, 1863–1900. Digital copies online at archive-ouverte.unige.ch/Calvin.
Creeds	Philip Schaff. *The Creeds of Christendom: With a Critical History and Notes*. 3 vols. New York: Harper & Row, 1877; reprint, Grand Rapids, MI: Baker, 1977. Accessible online at ccel.org.
CRR	Classics of the Radical Reformation. 12 vols. Waterloo, ON, and Scottdale, PA: Herald Press, 1973–2010.
CWE	*Collected Works of Erasmus*. 86 vols. planned. Toronto: University of Toronto Press, 1969–.

DMBI	*Dictionary of Major Biblical Interpreters*. Edited by Donald K. McKim. Downers Grove, IL: InterVarsity Press, 2007.
DNB	Dictionary of National Biography. Edited by Leslie Stephen and Sidney Lee. 63 vols. London: Smith, Elder, and Co., 1885–1900.
EEBO	Early English Books Online. Subscription database online at eebo.chadwyck.com.
LB	*Desderii Erasmi Roterodami Opera Omnia*. 10 vols. Edited by Jean LeClerc. Leiden: Van der Aa, 1704–1706; reprint, Hildesheim: Georg Olms, 1961–1962. Digital copy online at babelhaithtrust.org.
LCC	Library of Christian Classics. 26 vols. Edited by John Baillie et al. Philadelphia: Westminster, 1953–1966.
LW	*Luther's Works [American edition]*. 82 vols. planned. St. Louis: Concordia; Philadelphia: Fortress, 1955–1986; 2009–.
LWA	*Luthers Werke in Auswahl*. 8 vols. Edited by Otto Clemen et al. Berlin: Walter de Gruyter, 1912–1933.
𝔐	Majority text, which for Acts includes the following witnesses: L, 81, 323, 614, 945, 1175, 1241, and 1505.
MO	*Philippi Melanthonis Opera quae supersunt omnia*. 28 vols. Corpus Reformatorum 1-28. Edited by C. G. Bretschneider. Halle: C. A. Schwetschke, 1834–1860. Digital copies online at archive.org and books.google.com.
MWA	*Melancthons Werke in Auswahl [Studienausgabe]*. Edited by Robert Stupperich. 7 vols. Gütersloh: C. Bertelsmann, 1951–1975.
NDB	Neue Deutsche Biographie. 28 vols. projected. Berlin: Duncker & Humblot, 1953-. Accessible online at deutsche-biographie.de.
NPNF	A Select Library of the Nicene and Post-Nicene Fathers of the Christian Church. 28 vols. in two series, denoted as NPNF and NPNF². Edited by Philip Schaff et al. Buffalo, NY: Christian Literature, 1887–1894. Several reprints; also accessible online at ccel.org.
OER	Oxford Encyclopedia of the Reformation. 4 vols. Edited by Hans J. Hillerbrand. New York: Oxford University Press, 1996.
PRDL	Post Reformation Digital Library. Online database at prdl.org.
QGT	Quellen zur Geschichte der Täufer. 18 vols. Leipzig: M. Heinsius; Gütersloh: Gerd Mohn, 1930–. The first two volumes are under the series title Quellen zur Geschichte der Wiedertäufer.
r, v	Some early books are numbered not by page but by folio (leaf). Front and back sides (pages) of a numbered folio are indicated by *recto* (r) and *verso* (v), respectively.
WA	*D. Martin Luthers Werke, Kritische Gesamtausgabe: [Schriften]*. 73 vols. Weimar: Hermann Böhlaus Nachfolger, 1883–2009. Digital copies online at archive.org.
WABr	*D. Martin Luthers Werke, Kritische Gesamtausgabe: Briefwechsel*. 18 vols. Weimar: Hermann Böhlaus Nachfolger, 1930–1983.

WADB	*D. Martin Luthers Werke, Kritische Gesamtausgabe: Deutsche Bibel.* 12 vols. Weimar: Böhlaus Nachfolger, 1906–1961.
WATR	*D. Martin Luthers Werke, Kritische Gesamtausgabe: Tischreden.* 6 vols. Weimar: Hermann Böhlaus Nachfolger, 1912-1921. Digital copies online at archive.org.
ZSW	*Huldreich Zwinglis Sämtliche Werke.* 14 vols. Corpus Reformatorum 88-101. Edited by E. Egli et al. Berlin: C. A. Schwetschke, 1905-59; reprint Zürich: Theologischer Verlag Zürich, 1983. Digital access via Institut für Schweizerische Reformationsgeschichte at irg.u3h.ch.

BIBLE TRANSLATIONS

ESV	English Standard Version
KJV	King James Version
LXX	Septuagint
NKJV	New King James Version
NRSV	New Revised Standard Version
Vg	Vulgate

A GUIDE TO USING THIS COMMENTARY

Several features have been incorporated into the design of this commentary. The following comments are intended to assist readers in making full use of this volume.

Pericopes of Scripture

The scriptural text has been divided into pericopes, or passages, usually several verses in length. Each of these pericopes is given a heading, which appears at the beginning of the pericope. For example, the first pericope in the commentary on Acts is "1:1-11 The Promise of the Spirit and the Ascension." This heading is followed by the Scripture passage quoted in the English Standard Version (ESV). The Scripture passage is provided for the convenience of readers, but it is also in keeping with Reformation-era commentaries, which often followed the patristic and medieval commentary tradition, in which the citations of the reformers were arranged according to the text of Scripture.

Overviews

Following each pericope of text is an overview of the Reformation authors' comments on that pericope. The format of this overview varies among the volumes of this series, depending on the requirements of the specific book(s) of Scripture. The function of the overview is to identify succinctly the key exegetical, theological and pastoral concerns of the Reformation writers arising from the pericope, providing the reader with an orientation to Reformation-era approaches and emphases. It tracks a reasonably cohesive thread of argument among reformers' comments, even though they are derived from diverse sources and generations. Thus, the summaries do not proceed chronologically or by verse sequence. Rather, they seek to rehearse the overall course of the reformers' comments on that pericope.

We do not assume that the commentators themselves anticipated or expressed a formally received cohesive argument but rather that the various arguments tend to flow in a plausible, recognizable pattern. Modern readers can thus glimpse aspects of continuity in the flow of diverse exegetical traditions representing various generations and geographical locations.

Topical Headings

An abundance of varied Reformation-era comment is available for each pericope. For this reason we have broken the pericopes into two levels. First is the verse with its topical heading. The reformers' comments are then focused on aspects of each verse, with topical headings summarizing the essence of the individual comment by evoking a key phrase, metaphor or idea. This feature provides a bridge by which modern readers can enter into the heart of the Reformation-era comment.

Identifying the Reformation Authors, Texts and Events

Following the topical heading of each section of comment, the name of the Reformation commentator is given. An English translation (where needed) of the reformer's comment is then provided. This is immediately followed by the title of the original work rendered in English.

Readers who wish to pursue a deeper investigation of the reformers' works cited in this commentary will find full bibliographic detail for each reformation title provided in the bibliography at the back of the volume. Information on English translations (where available) and standard original-language editions and critical editions of the works cited is found in the bibliography. The Biographical Sketches section provides brief overviews of the life and work of each commentator, and each confession or collaborative work, appearing in the present volume (as well as in any previous volumes). Finally, a Timeline of the Reformation offers broader context for people, places and events relevant to the commentators and their works.

Footnotes and Back Matter

To aid the reader in exploring the background and texts in further detail, this commentary utilizes footnotes. The use and content of footnotes may vary among the volumes in this series. Where footnotes appear, a footnote number directs the reader to a note at the bottom of the right-hand column, where one will find annotations (clarifications or biblical cross references), information on English translations (where available) or standard original-language editions of the work cited.

Where original-language texts have remained untranslated into English, we provide new translations. Where there is any serious ambiguity or textual problem in the selection, we have tried to reflect the best available textual tradition. Wherever current English translations are already well rendered, they are utilized, but where necessary they are stylistically updated. A single asterisk (*) indicates that a previous English translation has been updated to modern English or amended for easier reading. We have standardized spellings and made grammatical variables uniform so that our English references will not reflect the linguistic oddities of the older English translations. For ease of reading we have in some cases removed superfluous conjunctions.

GENERAL INTRODUCTION

The Reformation Commentary on Scripture (RCS) is a twenty-eight-volume series of exegetical comment covering the entire Bible and gathered from the writings of sixteenth-century preachers, scholars and reformers. The RCS is intended as a sequel to the highly acclaimed Ancient Christian Commentary on Scripture (ACCS), and as such its overall concept, method, format and audience are similar to the earlier series. Both series are committed to the renewal of the church through careful study and meditative reflection on the Old and New Testaments, the charter documents of Christianity, read in the context of the worshiping, believing community of faith across the centuries. However, the patristic and Reformation eras are separated by nearly a millennium, and the challenges of reading Scripture with the reformers require special attention to their context, resources and assumptions. The purpose of this general introduction is to present an overview of the context and process of biblical interpretation in the age of the Reformation.

Goals

The Reformation Commentary on Scripture seeks to introduce its readers to the depth and richness of exegetical ferment that defined the Reformation era. The RCS has four goals: the enrichment of contemporary biblical interpretation through exposure to Reformation-era biblical exegesis; the renewal of contemporary preaching through exposure to the biblical insights of the Reformation writers; a deeper understanding of the Reformation itself and the breadth of perspectives represented within it; and a recovery of the profound integration of the life of faith and the life of the mind that should characterize Christian scholarship. Each of these goals requires a brief comment.

Renewing contemporary biblical interpretation. During the past half-century, biblical hermeneutics has become a major growth industry in the academic world. One of the consequences of the historical-critical hegemony of biblical studies has been the privileging of contemporary philosophies and ideologies at the expense of a commitment to the Christian church as the primary reading community within which and for which biblical exegesis is done. Reading Scripture with the church fathers and the reformers is a corrective to all such imperialism of the present. One of the greatest skills required for a fruitful interpretation of the Bible is the ability to listen. We rightly emphasize the importance of listening to the voices of contextual theologies today, but in doing so we often marginalize or ignore another crucial context—the community of believing Christians through the centuries. The serious study of Scripture requires more than the latest

Bible translation in one hand and the latest commentary (or niche study Bible) in the other. John
L. Thompson has called on Christians today to practice the art of "reading the Bible with the
dead."[1] The RCS presents carefully selected comments from the extant commentaries of the Reformation as an encouragement to more in-depth study of this important epoch in the history of
biblical interpretation.

Strengthening contemporary preaching. The Protestant reformers identified the public preach-
ing of the Word of God as an indispensible means of grace and a sure sign of the true church.
Through the words of the preacher, the living voice of the gospel *(viva vox evangelii)* is heard. Luther famously said that the church is not a "pen house" but a "mouth house."[2] The Reformation in
Switzerland began when Huldrych Zwingli entered the pulpit of the Grossmünster in Zurich on
January 1, 1519, and began to preach a series of expositional sermons chapter by chapter from the
Gospel of Matthew. In the following years he extended this homiletical approach to other books
of the Old and New Testaments. Calvin followed a similar pattern in Geneva. Many of the commentaries represented in this series were either originally presented as sermons or were written
to support the regular preaching ministry of local church pastors. Luther said that the preacher
should be a *bonus textualis*—a good one with a text—well-versed in the Scriptures. Preachers in
the Reformation traditions preached not only about the Bible but also from it, and this required
more than a passing acquaintance with its contents. Those who have been charged with the office
of preaching in the church today can find wisdom and insight—and fresh perspectives—in the
sermons of the Reformation and the biblical commentaries read and studied by preachers of the
sixteenth century.

Deepening understanding of the Reformation. Some scholars of the sixteenth century prefer
to speak of the period they study in the plural, the European Reformations, to indicate that many
diverse impulses for reform were at work in this turbulent age of transition from medieval to
modern times.[3] While this point is well taken, the RCS follows the time-honored tradition of
using Reformation in the singular form to indicate not only a major moment in the history of
Christianity in the West but also, as Hans J. Hillerbrand has put it, "an essential cohesiveness in
the heterogeneous pursuits of religious reform in the sixteenth century."[4] At the same time, in
developing guidelines to assist the volume editors in making judicious selections from the vast
amount of commentary material available in this period, we have stressed the multifaceted character of the Reformation across many confessions, theological orientations and political settings.

Advancing Christian scholarship. By assembling and disseminating numerous voices from
such a signal period as the Reformation, the RCS aims to make a significant contribution to the
ever-growing stream of Christian scholarship. The post-Enlightenment split between the study

---

[1] John L. Thompson, *Reading the Bible with the Dead* (Grand Rapids: Eerdmans, 2007).
[2] WA 10,2:48.
[3] See Carter Lindberg, *The European Reformations*, 2nd ed. (Malden, MA: Wiley-Blackwell, 2010).
[4] Hans J. Hillerbrand, *The Division of Christendom* (Louisville, KY: Westminster John Knox, 2007), x. Hillerbrand has also edited the
standard reference work in Reformation studies, *OER*. See also Diarmaid MacCulloch, *The Reformation* (New York: Viking, 2003),
and Patrick Collinson, *The Reformation: A History* (New York: Random House, 2004).

of the Bible as an academic discipline and the reading of the Bible as spiritual nurture was foreign to the reformers. For them the study of the Bible was transformative at the most basic level of the human person: *coram deo*.

The reformers all repudiated the idea that the Bible could be studied and understood with dispassionate objectivity, as a cold artifact from antiquity. Luther's famous Reformation break-through triggered by his laborious study of the Psalms and Paul's letter to the Romans is well known, but the experience of Cambridge scholar Thomas Bilney was perhaps more typical. When Erasmus's critical edition of the Greek New Testament was published in 1516, it was accompanied by a new translation in elegant Latin. Attracted by the classical beauty of Erasmus's Latin, Bilney came across this statement in 1 Timothy 1:15: "Christ Jesus came into the world to save sinners." In the Greek this sentence is described as *pistos ho logos*, which the Vulgate had rendered *fidelis sermo*, "a faithful saying." Erasmus chose a different word for the Greek *pistos—certus*, "sure, certain." When Bilney grasped the meaning of this word applied to the announcement of salvation in Christ, he tells us that "Immediately, I felt a marvellous comfort and quietness, insomuch as 'my bruised bones leaped for joy.'"[5]

Luther described the way the Bible was meant to function in the minds and hearts of believers when he reproached himself and others for studying the nativity narrative with such cool unconcern:

> I hate myself because when I see Christ laid in the manger or in the lap of his mother and hear the angels sing, my heart does not leap into flame. With what good reason should we all despise ourselves that we remain so cold when this word is spoken to us, over which everyone should dance and leap and burn for joy! We act as though it were a frigid historical fact that does not smite our hearts, as if someone were merely relating that the sultan has a crown of gold.[6]

It was a core conviction of the Reformation that the careful study and meditative listening to the Scriptures, what the monks called *lectio divina*, could yield transformative results for *all* of life. The value of such a rich commentary, therefore, lies not only in the impressive volume of Reformation-era voices that are presented throughout the course of the series but in the many particular fields for which their respective lives and ministries are relevant. The Reformation is consequential for historical studies, both church as well as secular history. Biblical and theological studies, to say nothing of pastoral and spiritual studies, also stand to benefit and progress immensely from renewed engagement today, as mediated through the RCS, with the reformers of yesteryear.

Perspectives

In setting forth the perspectives and parameters of the RCS, the following considerations have proved helpful.

---

[5]John Foxe, *The Acts and Monuments of John Foxe: A New and Complete Edition*, 8 vols., ed. Stephen Reed Cattley (London: R. B. Seeley & W. Burnside, 1837), 4:635; quoting Ps 51:8; cited in A. G. Dickens, *The English Reformation*, 2nd ed. (University Park, PA: The Pennsylvannia State University Press, 1991), 102.

[6]WA 49:176-77, quoted in Roland Bainton, "The Bible in the Reformation," in *CHB*, 3:23.

Chronology. When did the Reformation begin, and how long did it last? In some traditional accounts, the answer was clear: the Reformation began with the posting of Luther's Ninety-five Theses at Wittenberg in 1517 and ended with the death of Calvin in Geneva in 1564. Apart from reducing the Reformation to a largely German event with a side trip to Switzerland, this perspective fails to do justice to the important events that led up to Luther's break with Rome and its many reverberations throughout Europe and beyond. In choosing commentary selections for the RCS, we have adopted the concept of the long sixteenth century, say, from the late 1400s to the mid-seventeenth century. Thus we have included commentary selections from early or pre-Reformation writers such as John Colet and Jacques Lefèvre d'Étaples to seventeenth-century figures such as Henry Ainsworth and Johann Gerhard.

Confession. The RCS concentrates primarily, though not exclusively, on the exegetical writings of the Protestant reformers. While the ACCS provided a compendium of key consensual exegetes of the early Christian centuries, the Catholic/Protestant confessional divide in the sixteenth century tested the very idea of consensus, especially with reference to ecclesiology and soteriology. While many able and worthy exegetes faithful to the Roman Catholic Church were active during this period, this project has chosen to include primarily those figures that represent perspectives within the Protestant Reformation. For this reason we have not included comments on the apocryphal or deuterocanonical writings.

We recognize that "Protestant" and "Catholic" as contradistinctive labels are anachronistic terms for the early decades of the sixteenth century before the hardening of confessional identities surrounding the Council of Trent (1545–1563). Protestant figures such as Philipp Melanchthon, Johannes Oecolampadius and John Calvin were all products of the revival of sacred letters known as biblical humanism. They shared an approach to biblical interpretation that owed much to Desiderius Erasmus and other scholars who remained loyal to the Church of Rome. Careful comparative studies of Protestant and Catholic exegesis in the sixteenth century have shown surprising areas of agreement when the focus was the study of a particular biblical text rather than the standard confessional debates.

At the same time, exegetical differences among the various Protestant groups could become strident and church-dividing. The most famous example of this is the interpretive impasse between Luther and Zwingli over the meaning of "This is my body" (Mt 26:26) in the words of institution. Their disagreement at the Colloquy of Marburg in 1529 had important christological and pastoral implications, as well as social and political consequences. Luther refused fellowship with Zwingli and his party at the end of the colloquy; in no small measure this bitter division led to the separate trajectories pursued by Lutheran and Reformed Protestantism to this day. In Elizabethan England, Puritans and Anglicans agreed that "Holy Scripture containeth all things necessary to salvation: so that whatsoever is not read therein, nor may be proved thereby, is not to be required of any man" (article 6 of the Thirty-nine Articles of Religion), yet on the basis of their differing interpretations of the Bible they fought bitterly over the structures of the church, the clothing of the clergy and the ways of worship. On the matter of infant baptism, Catholics and

Protestants alike agreed on its propriety, though there were various theories as to how a practice not mentioned in the Bible could be justified biblically. The Anabaptists were outliers on this subject. They rejected infant baptism altogether. They appealed to the example of the baptism of Jesus and to his final words as recorded in the Gospel of Matthew (Mt 28:19-20), "Go therefore, and make disciples of all nations, baptizing them in the name of the Father, and of the Son, and of the Holy Spirit, teaching them to observe all that I have commanded you." New Testament Christians, they argued, are to follow not only the commands of Jesus in the Great Commission, but also the exact order in which they were given: evangelize, baptize, catechize.

These and many other differences of interpretation among the various Protestant groups are reflected in their many sermons, commentaries and public disputations. In the RCS, the volume editor's introduction to each volume is intended to help the reader understand the nature and significance of doctrinal conversations and disputes that resulted in particular, and frequently clashing, interpretations. Footnotes throughout the text will be provided to explain obscure references, unusual expressions and other matters that require special comment. Volume editors have chosen comments on the Bible across a wide range of sixteenth-century confessions and schools of interpretation: biblical humanists, Lutheran, Reformed, Anglican, Puritan and Anabaptist. We have not pursued passages from post-Tridentine Catholic authors or from radical spiritualists and antitrinitarian writers, though sufficient material is available from these sources to justify another series.

Format. The design of the RCS is intended to offer reader-friendly access to these classic texts. The availability of digital resources has given access to a huge residual database of sixteenth-century exegetical comment hitherto available only in major research universities and rare book collections. The RCS has benefited greatly from online databases such as Alexander Street Press's Digital Library of Classical Protestant Texts (DLCPT) as well as freely accessible databases like the Post-Reformation Digital Library (prdl.org). Through the help of RCS editorial advisor Herman Selderhuis, we have also had access to the special Reformation collections of the Johannes a Lasco Bibliothek in Emden, Germany. In addition, modern critical editions and translations of Reformation sources have been published over the past generation. Original translations of Reformation sources are given unless an acceptable translation already exists.

Each volume in the RCS will include an introduction by the volume editor placing that portion of the canon within the historical context of the Protestant Reformation and presenting a summary of the theological themes, interpretive issues and reception of the particular book(s). The commentary itself consists of particular pericopes identified by a pericope heading; the biblical text in the English Standard Version (ESV), with significant textual variants registered in the footnotes; an overview of the pericope in which principal exegetical and theological concerns of the Reformation writers are succinctly noted; and excerpts from the Reformation writers identified by name according to the conventions of the *Oxford Encyclopedia of the Reformation*. Each volume will also include a bibliography of sources cited, as well as an appendix of authors and source works.

The Reformation era was a time of verbal as well as physical violence, and this fact has presented a challenge for this project. Without unduly sanitizing the texts, where they contain anti-Semitic, sexist or inordinately polemical rhetoric, we have not felt obliged to parade such comments either. We have noted the abridgement of texts with ellipses and an explanatory footnote. While this procedure would not be valid in the critical edition of such a text, we have deemed it appropriate in a series whose primary purpose is pastoral and devotional. When translating *homo* or similar terms that refer to the human race as a whole or to individual persons without reference to gender, we have used alternative English expressions to the word *man* (or derivative constructions that formerly were used generically to signify humanity at large), whenever such substitutions can be made without producing an awkward or artificial construction.

As is true in the ACCS, we have made a special effort where possible to include the voices of women, though we acknowledge the difficulty of doing so for the early modern period when for a variety of social and cultural reasons few theological and biblical works were published by women. However, recent scholarship has focused on a number of female leaders whose literary remains show us how they understood and interpreted the Bible. Women who made significant contributions to the Reformation include Marguerite d'Angoulême, sister of King Francis I, who supported French reformist evangelicals including Calvin and who published a religious poem influenced by Luther's theology, *The Mirror of the Sinful Soul*; Argula von Grumbach, a Bavarian noblewoman who defended the teachings of Luther and Melanchthon before the theologians of the University of Ingolstadt; Katharina Schütz Zell, the wife of a former priest, Matthias Zell, and a remarkable reformer in her own right—she conducted funerals, compiled hymnbooks, defended the downtrodden and published a defense of clerical marriage as well as composing works of consolation on divine comfort and pleas for the toleration of Anabaptists and Catholics alike; and Anne Askew, a Protestant martyr put to death in 1546 after demonstrating remarkable biblical prowess in her examinations by church officials. Other echoes of faithful women in the age of the Reformation are found in their letters, translations, poems, hymns, court depositions and martyr records.

Lay culture, learned culture. In recent decades, much attention has been given to what is called "reforming from below," that is, the expressions of religious beliefs and churchly life that characterized the popular culture of the majority of the population in the era of the Reformation. Social historians have taught us to examine the diverse pieties of townspeople and city folk, of rural religion and village life, the emergence of lay theologies and the experiences of women in the religious tumults of Reformation Europe.[7] Formal commentaries by their nature are artifacts of learned culture. Almost all of them were written in Latin, the lingua franca of learned discourse well past the age of the Reformation. Biblical commentaries were certainly not the primary means by which the Protestant Reformation spread so rapidly across wide sectors of sixteenth-century society. Small pamphlets and broadsheets, later called *Flugschriften* ("flying writings"), with their graphic woodcuts and cartoon-like depictions of Reformation personalities and events, became the means of choice for mass communication in the early age of printing. Sermons and works of

---

[7]See Peter Matheson, ed., *Reformation Christianity* (Minneapolis: Fortress, 2007).

devotion were also printed with appealing visual aids. Luther's early writings were often accompanied by drawings and sketches from Lucas Cranach and other artists. This was done "above all for the sake of children and simple folk," as Luther put it, "who are more easily moved by pictures and images to recall divine history than through mere words or doctrines."[8]

We should be cautious, however, in drawing too sharp a distinction between learned and lay culture in this period. The phenomenon of preaching was a kind of verbal bridge between scholars at their desks and the thousands of illiterate or semi-literate listeners whose views were shaped by the results of Reformation exegesis. According to contemporary witness, more than one thousand people were crowding into Geneva to hear Calvin expound the Scriptures every day.[9] An example of how learned theological works by Reformation scholars were received across divisions of class and social status comes from Lazare Drilhon, an apothecary of Toulon. He was accused of heresy in May 1545 when a cache of prohibited books was found hidden in his garden shed. In addition to devotional works, the French New Testament and a copy of Calvin's Genevan liturgy, there was found a series of biblical commentaries, translated from the Latin into French: Martin Bucer's on Matthew, François Lambert's on the Apocalypse and one by Oecolampadius on 1 John.[10] Biblical exegesis in the sixteenth century was not limited to the kind of full-length commentaries found in Drilhon's shed. Citations from the Bible and expositions of its meaning permeate the extant literature of sermons, letters, court depositions, doctrinal treatises, records of public disputations and even last wills and testaments. While most of the selections in the RCS will be drawn from formal commentary literature, other sources of biblical reflection will also be considered.

Historical Context

The medieval legacy. On October 18, 1512, the degree *Doctor in Biblia* was conferred on Martin Luther, and he began his career as a professor in the University of Wittenberg. As is well known, Luther was also a monk who had taken solemn vows in the Augustinian Order of Hermits at Erfurt. These two settings—the university and the monastery—both deeply rooted in the Middle Ages, form the background not only for Luther's personal vocation as a reformer but also for the history of the biblical commentary in the age of the Reformation. Since the time of the Venerable Bede (d. 735), sometimes called "the last of the Fathers," serious study of the Bible had taken place primarily in the context of cloistered monasteries. The Rule of St. Benedict brought together *lectio* and *meditatio*, the knowledge of letters and the life of prayer. The liturgy was the medium through which the daily reading of the Bible, especially the Psalms, and the sayings of the church fathers came together in the spiritual formation of the monks.[11] Essential to this understanding

---

[8]Martin Luther, "Personal Prayer Book," LW 43:42-43* (WA 10, 2:458); quoted in R. W. Scribner, *For the Sake of Simple Folk: Popular Propaganda for the German Reformation* (Cambridge: Cambridge University Press, 1981), xi.

[9]Letter of De Beaulieu to Guillaume Farel (1561) in J. W. Baum, ed., *Theodor Beza nach handschriftlichen und anderen gleichzeitigen Quellen* (Leipzig: Weidmann, 1851) 2:92.

[10]Francis Higman, "A Heretic's Library: The Drilhon Inventory" (1545), in Francis Higman, *Lire et Découvire: la circulation des idées au temps de la Réforme* (Geneva: Droz, 1998), 65-85.

[11]See the classic study by Jean Leclercq, *The Love of Learning and the Desire for God* (New York: Fordham University Press, 1961).

was a belief in the unity of the people of God throughout time as well as space, and an awareness that life in this world was a preparation for the beatific vision in the next.

The source of theology was the study of the sacred page (*sacra pagina*); its object was the accumulation of knowledge not for its own sake but for the obtaining of eternal life. For these monks, the Bible had God for its author, salvation for its end and unadulterated truth for its matter, though they would not have expressed it in such an Aristotelian way. The medieval method of interpreting the Bible owed much to Augustine's *On Christian Doctrine*. In addition to setting forth a series of rules (drawn from an earlier work by Tyconius), Augustine stressed the importance of distinguishing the literal and spiritual or allegorical senses of Scripture. While the literal sense was not disparaged, the allegorical was valued because it enabled the believer to obtain spiritual benefit from the obscure places in the Bible, especially in the Old Testament. For Augustine, as for the monks who followed him, the goal of scriptural exegesis was freighted with eschatological meaning; its purpose was to induce faith, hope and love and so to advance in one's pilgrimage toward that city with foundations (see Heb 11:10).

Building on the work of Augustine and other church fathers going back to Origen, medieval exegetes came to understand Scripture as possessed of four possible meanings, the famous *quadriga*. The literal meaning was retained, of course, but the spiritual meaning was now subdivided into three senses: the allegorical, the moral and the anagogical. Medieval exegetes often referred to the four meanings of Scripture in a popular rhyme:

> The letter shows us what God and our fathers did;
> The allegory shows us where our faith is hid;
> The moral meaning gives us rules of daily life;
> The anagogy shows us where we end our strife.[12]

In this schema, the three spiritual meanings of the text correspond to the three theological virtues: faith (allegory), hope (anagogy) and love (the moral meaning). It should be noted that this way of approaching the Bible assumed a high doctrine of scriptural inspiration: the multiple meanings inherent in the text had been placed there by the Holy Spirit for the benefit of the people of God. The biblical justification for this method went back to the apostle Paul, who had used the words *allegory* and *type* when applying Old Testament events to believers in Christ (Gal 4:21-31; 1 Cor 10:1-11). The problem with this approach was knowing how to relate each of the four senses to one another and how to prevent Scripture from becoming a nose of wax turned this way and that by various interpreters. As G. R. Evans explains, "Any interpretation which could be put upon the text and was in keeping with the faith and edifying, had the warrant of God himself, for no human reader had the ingenuity to find more than God had put there."[13]

With the rise of the universities in the eleventh century, theology and the study of Scripture moved from the cloister into the classroom. Scripture and the Fathers were still important, but they came to function more as footnotes to the theological questions debated in the schools and

---

[12]Robert M. Grant, *A Short History of the Interpretation of the Bible* (New York: Macmillan, 1963), 119. A translation of the well-known Latin quatrain: *Littera gesta docet/Quid credas allegoria/Moralis quid agas/Quo tendas anagogia*.
[13]G. R. Evans, *The Language and Logic of the Bible: The Road to Reformation* (Cambridge: Cambridge University Press, 1985), 42.

brought together in an impressive systematic way in works such as Peter Lombard's *Books of Sentences* (the standard theology textbook of the Middle Ages) and the great scholastic *summae* of the thirteenth century. Indispensible to the study of the Bible in the later Middle Ages was the *Glossa ordinaria*, a collection of exegetical opinions by the church fathers and other commentators. Heiko Oberman summarized the transition from devotion to dialectic this way: "When, due to the scientific revolution of the twelfth century, Scripture became the *object* of study rather than the *subject* through which God speaks to the student, the difference between the two modes of speaking was investigated in terms of the texts themselves rather than in their relation to the recipients."[14] It was possible, of course, to be both a scholastic theologian and a master of the spiritual life. Meister Eckhart, for example, wrote commentaries on the Old Testament in Latin and works of mystical theology in German, reflecting what had come to be seen as a division of labor between the two.

An increasing focus on the text of Scripture led to a revival of interest in its literal sense. The two key figures in this development were Thomas Aquinas (d. 1274) and Nicholas of Lyra (d. 1340). Thomas is best remembered for his *Summa Theologiae*, but he was also a prolific commentator on the Bible. Thomas did not abandon the multiple senses of Scripture but declared that all the senses were founded on one—the literal—and this sense eclipsed allegory as the basis of sacred doctrine. Nicholas of Lyra was a Franciscan scholar who made use of the Hebrew text of the Old Testament and quoted liberally from works of Jewish scholars, especially the learned French rabbi Salomon Rashi (d. 1105). After Aquinas, Lyra was the strongest defender of the literal, historical meaning of Scripture as the primary basis of theological disputation. His *Postilla*, as his notes were called—the abbreviated form of *post illa verba textus* meaning "after these words from Scripture"—were widely circulated in the late Middle Ages and became the first biblical commentary to be printed in the fifteenth century. More than any other commentator from the period of high scholasticism, Lyra and his work were greatly valued by the early reformers. According to an old Latin pun, *Nisi Lyra lyrasset, Lutherus non saltasset*, "If Lyra had not played his lyre, Luther would not have danced."[15] While Luther was never an uncritical disciple of any teacher, he did praise Lyra as a good Hebraist and quoted him more than one hundred times in his lectures on Genesis, where he declared, "I prefer him to almost all other interpreters of Scripture."[16]

Sacred philology. The sixteenth century has been called a golden age of biblical interpretation, and it is a fact that the age of the Reformation witnessed an explosion of commentary writing unparalleled in the history of the Christian church. Kenneth Hagen has cataloged forty-five commentaries on Hebrews between 1516 (Erasmus) and 1598 (Beza).[17] During the sixteenth century, more than seventy new commentaries on Romans were published, five of them by Melanchthon alone, and nearly one hundred commentaries on the Bible's prayer book, the Psalms.[18] There were

---

[14]Heiko Oberman, *Forerunners of the Reformation* (Philadelphia: Fortress, 1966), 284.

[15]Nicholas of Lyra, *The Postilla of Nicolas of Lyra on the Song of Songs*, trans. and ed. James George Kiecker (Milwaukee: Marquette University Press, 1998), 19.

[16]LW 2:164 (WA 42:377).

[17]Kenneth Hagen, *Hebrews Commenting from Erasmus to Bèze, 1516-1598* (Tübingen: Mohr, 1981).

[18]R. Gerald Hobbs, "Biblical Commentaries," *OER* 1:167-71. See in general David C. Steinmetz, ed., *The Bible in the Sixteenth Century* (Durham: Duke University Press, 1990).

two developments in the fifteenth century that presaged this development and without which it could not have taken place: the invention of printing and the rediscovery of a vast store of ancient learning hitherto unknown or unavailable to scholars in the West.

It is now commonplace to say that what the computer has become in our generation, the printing press was to the world of Erasmus, Luther and other leaders of the Reformation. Johannes Gutenberg, a goldsmith by trade, developed a metal alloy suitable for type and a machine that would allow printed characters to be cast with relative ease, placed in even lines of composition and then manipulated again and again making possible the mass production of an unbelievable number of texts. In 1455, the Gutenberg Bible, the masterpiece of the typographical revolution, was published at Mainz in double columns in gothic type. Forty-seven copies of the beautiful Gutenberg Bible are still extant, each consisting of more than one thousand colorfully illuminated and impeccably printed pages. What began at Gutenberg's print shop in Mainz on the Rhine River soon spread, like McDonald's or Starbucks in our day, into every nook and cranny of the known world. Printing presses sprang up in Rome (1464), Venice (1469), Paris (1470), the Netherlands (1471), Switzerland (1472), Spain (1474), England (1476), Sweden (1483) and Constantinople (1490). By 1500, these and other presses across Europe had published some twenty-seven thousand titles, most of them in Latin. Erasmus once compared himself with an obscure preacher whose sermons were heard by only a few people in one or two churches while his books were read in every country in the world. Erasmus was not known for his humility, but in this case he was simply telling the truth.[19]

The Italian humanist Lorenzo Valla (d. 1457) died in the early dawn of the age of printing, but his critical and philological studies would be taken up by others who believed that genuine reform in church and society could come about only by returning to the wellsprings of ancient learning and wisdom—*ad fontes*, "back to the sources!" Valla is best remembered for undermining a major claim made by defenders of the papacy when he proved by philological research that the so-called Donation of Constantine, which had bolstered papal assertions of temporal sovereignty, was a forgery. But it was Valla's *Collatio Novi Testamenti* of 1444 that would have such a great effect on the renewal of biblical studies in the next century. Erasmus discovered the manuscript of this work while rummaging through an old library in Belgium and published it at Paris in 1505. In the preface to his edition of Valla, Erasmus gave the rationale that would guide his own labors in textual criticism. Just as Jerome had translated the Latin Vulgate from older versions and copies of the Scriptures in his day, so now Jerome's own text must be subjected to careful scrutiny and correction. Erasmus would be *Hieronymus redivivus*, a new Jerome come back to life to advance the cause of sacred philology. The restoration of the Scriptures and the writings of the church fathers would usher in what Erasmus believed would be a golden age of peace and learning. In 1516, the Basel publisher Froben brought out Erasmus's *Novum Instrumentum*, the first published edition of the Greek New Testament. Eras-

---

[19]E. Harris Harbison, *The Christian Scholar in the Age of the Reformation* (New York: Charles Scribner's Sons, 1956), 80.

mus's Greek New Testament would go through five editions in his lifetime, each one with new emendations to the text and a growing section of annotations that expanded to include not only technical notes about the text but also theological comment. The influence of Erasmus's Greek New Testament was enormous. It formed the basis for Robert Estienne's *Novum Testamentum Graece* of 1550, which in turn was used to establish the Greek *Textus Receptus* for a number of late Reformation translations including the King James Version of 1611.

For all his expertise in Greek, Erasmus was a poor student of Hebrew and only published commentaries on several of the psalms. However, the renaissance of Hebrew letters was part of the wider program of biblical humanism as reflected in the establishment of trilingual colleges devoted to the study of Hebrew, Greek and Latin (the three languages written on the *titulus* of Jesus' cross [Jn 19:20]) at Alcalá in Spain, Wittenberg in Germany, Louvain in Belgium and Paris in France. While it is true that some medieval commentators, especially Nicholas of Lyra, had been informed by the study of Hebrew and rabbinics in their biblical work, it was the publication of Johannes Reuchlin's *De rudimentis hebraicis* (1506), a combined grammar and dictionary, that led to the recovery of *veritas Hebraica*, as Jerome had referred to the true voice of the Hebrew Scriptures. The pursuit of Hebrew studies was carried forward in the Reformation by two great scholars, Konrad Pellikan and Sebastian Münster. Pellikan was a former Franciscan friar who embraced the Protestant cause and played a major role in the Zurich reformation. He had published a Hebrew grammar even prior to Reuchlin and produced a commentary on nearly the entire Bible that appeared in seven volumes between 1532 and 1539. Münster was Pellikan's student and taught Hebrew at the University of Heidelberg before taking up a similar position in Basel. Like his mentor, Münster was a great collector of Hebraica and published a series of excellent grammars, dictionaries and rabbinic texts. Münster did for the Hebrew Old Testament what Erasmus had done for the Greek New Testament. His *Hebraica Biblia* offered a fresh Latin translation of the Old Testament with annotations from medieval rabbinic exegesis.

Luther first learned Hebrew with Reuchlin's grammar in hand but took advantage of other published resources, such as the four-volume Hebrew Bible published at Venice by Daniel Bomberg in 1516 to 1517. He also gathered his own circle of Hebrew experts, his *sanhedrin* he called it, who helped him with his German translation of the Old Testament. We do not know where William Tyndale learned Hebrew, though perhaps it was in Worms, where there was a thriving rabbinical school during his stay there. In any event, he had sufficiently mastered the language to bring out a freshly translated Pentateuch that was published at Antwerp in 1530. By the time the English separatist scholar Henry Ainsworth published his prolix commentaries on the Pentateuch in 1616, the knowledge of Hebrew, as well as Greek, was taken for granted by every serious scholar of the Bible. In the preface to his commentary on Genesis, Ainsworth explained that "the literal sense of Moses's Hebrew (which is the tongue wherein he wrote the law), is the ground of all interpretation, and that language hath figures and properties of speech, different from ours: These therefore in the first place are to be opened that the natural meaning of the Scripture, being known, the mysteries of godliness therein implied, may be better discerned."[20]

The restoration of the biblical text in the original languages made possible the revival of scriptural exposition reflected in the floodtide of sermon literature and commentary work. Of even more far-reaching import was the steady stream of vernacular Bibles in the sixteenth century. In the introduction to his 1516 edition of the New Testament, Erasmus had expressed his desire that the Scriptures be translated into all languages so that "the lowliest women" could read the Gospels and the Pauline epistles and "the farmer sing some portion of them at the plow, the weaver hum some parts of them to the movement of his shuttle, the traveler lighten the weariness of the journey with stories of this kind."[21] Like Erasmus, Tyndale wanted the Bible to be available in the language of the common people. He once said to a learned divine that if God spared his life he would cause the boy who drives the plow to know more of the Scriptures than he did![22] The project of allowing the Bible to speak in the language of the mother in the house, the children in the street and the cheesemonger in the marketplace was met with stiff opposition by certain Catholic polemists such as Johann Eck, Luther's antagonist at the Leipzig Debate of 1519. In his *Enchiridion* (1525), Eck derided the "inky theologians" whose translations paraded the Bible before "the untutored crowd" and subjected it to the judgment of "laymen and crazy old women."[23] In fact, some fourteen German Bibles had already been published prior to Luther's September Testament of 1522, which he translated from Erasmus's Greek New Testament in less than three months' time while sequestered in the Wartburg. Luther's German New Testament became the first bestseller in the world, appearing in forty-three distinct editions between 1522 and 1525 with upwards of one hundred thousand copies issued in these three years. It is estimated that five percent of the German population may have been literate at this time, but this rate increased as the century wore on due in no small part to the unmitigated success of vernacular Bibles.[24]

Luther's German Bible (inclusive of the Old Testament from 1534) was the most successful venture of its kind, but it was not alone in the field. Hans Denck and Ludwig Hätzer, leaders in the early Anabaptist movement, translated the prophetic books of the Old Testament from Hebrew into German in 1527. This work influenced the Swiss-German Bible of 1531 published by Leo Jud and other pastors in Zurich. Tyndale's influence on the English language rivaled that of Luther on German. At a time when English was regarded as "that obscure and remote dialect of German spoken in an off-shore island," Tyndale, with his remarkable linguistic ability (he was fluent in eight languages), "made a language for England," as his modern editor David Daniell has put it.[25]

---

[20]Henry Ainsworth, *Annotations Upon the First Book of Moses Called Genesis* (Amsterdam, 1616), preface (unpaginated).

[21]John C. Olin, *Christian Humanism and the Reformation* (New York: Fordham University Press, 1987), 101.

[22]This famous statement of Tyndale was quoted by John Foxe in his *Acts and Monuments of Matters Happening in the Church* (London, 1563). See Henry Wansbrough, "Tyndale," in Richard Griffith, ed., *The Bible in the Renaissance* (Aldershot, UK: Ashgate, 2001), 124.

[23]John Eck, *Enchiridion of Commonplaces*, trans. Ford Lewis Battles (Grand Rapids: Baker, 1979), 47-49.

[24]The effect of printing on the spread of the Reformation has been much debated. See the classic study by Elizabeth L. Eisenstein, *The Printing Press as an Agent of Change* (Cambridge: Cambridge University Press, 1979). More recent studies include Mark U. Edwards Jr., *Printing, Propaganda and Martin Luther* (Minneapolis: Fortress, 1994), and Andrew Pettegree and Matthew Hall, "The Reformation and the Book: A Reconsideration," *Historical Journal* 47 (2004): 1-24.

[25]David Daniell, *William Tyndale: A Biography* (New Haven: Yale University Press, 1994), 3.

Tyndale was imprisoned and executed near Brussels in 1536, but the influence of his biblical work among the common people of England was already being felt. There is no reason to doubt the authenticity of John Foxe's recollection of how Tyndale's New Testament was received in England during the 1520s and 1530s:

> The fervent zeal of those Christian days seemed much superior to these our days and times; as manifestly may appear by their sitting up all night in reading and hearing; also by their expenses and charges in buying of books in English, of whom some gave five marks, some more, some less, for a book: some gave a load of hay for a few chapters of St. James, or of St. Paul in English.[26]

Calvin helped to revise and contributed three prefaces to the French Bible translated by his cousin Pierre Robert Olivétan and originally published at Neuchâtel in 1535. Clément Marot and Beza provided a fresh translation of the Psalms with each psalm rendered in poetic form and accompanied by monophonic musical settings for congregational singing. The Bay Psalter, the first book printed in America, was an English adaptation of this work. Geneva also provided the provenance of the most influential Italian Bible published by Giovanni Diodati in 1607. The flowering of biblical humanism in vernacular Bibles resulted in new translations in all of the major language groups of Europe: Spanish (1569), Portuguese (1681), Dutch (New Testament, 1523; Old Testament, 1527), Danish (1550), Czech (1579–1593/94), Hungarian (New Testament, 1541; complete Bible, 1590), Polish (1563), Swedish (1541) and even Arabic (1591).[27]

Patterns of Reformation

Once the text of the Bible had been placed in the hands of the people, in cheap and easily available editions, what further need was there of published expositions such as commentaries? Given the Protestant doctrine of the priesthood of all believers, was there any longer a need for learned clergy and their bookish religion? Some radical reformers thought not. Sebastian Franck searched for the true church of the Spirit "scattered among the heathen and the weeds" but could not find it in any of the institutional structures of his time. *Veritas non potest scribi, aut exprimi*, he said, "truth can neither be spoken nor written."[28] Kaspar von Schwenckfeld so emphasized religious inwardness that he suspended external observance of the Lord's Supper and downplayed the readable, audible Scriptures in favor of the word within. This trajectory would lead to the rise of the Quakers in the next century, but it was pursued neither by the mainline reformers nor by most of the Anabaptists. Article 7 of the Augsburg Confession (1530) declared the one holy Christian church to be "the assembly of all believers among whom the Gospel is purely preached and the holy sacraments are administered according to the Gospel."[29]

Historians of the nineteenth century referred to the material and formal principles of the

---

[26]Foxe, *Acts and Monuments*, 4:218.

[27]On vernacular translations of the Bible, see *CHB* 3:94-140 and Jaroslav Pelikan, *The Reformation of the Bible/The Bible of the Reformation* (New Haven: Yale University Press, 1996), 41-62.

[28]Sebastian Franck, *280 Paradoxes or Wondrous Sayings*, trans. E. J. Furcha (Lewiston, NY: Edwin Mellen Press, 1986), 10, 212.

[29]BoC 42 (BSLK 61).

Reformation. In this construal, the matter at stake was the meaning of the Christian gospel: the liberating insight that helpless sinners are graciously justified by the gift of faith alone, apart from any works or merits of their own, entirely on the basis of Christ's atoning work on the cross. For Luther especially, justification by faith alone became the criterion by which all other doctrines and practices of the church were to be judged. The cross proves everything, he said at the Heidelberg disputation in 1518. The distinction between law and gospel thus became the primary hermeneutical key that unlocked the true meaning of Scripture.

The formal principle of the Reformation, *sola Scriptura*, was closely bound up with proper distinctions between Scripture and tradition. "Scripture alone," said Luther, "is the true lord and master of all writings and doctrine on earth. If that is not granted, what is Scripture good for? The more we reject it, the more we become satisfied with human books and human teachers."[30] On the basis of this principle, the reformers challenged the structures and institutions of the medieval Catholic Church. Even a simple layperson, they asserted, armed with Scripture should be believed above a pope or a council without it. But, however boldly asserted, the doctrine of the primacy of Scripture did not absolve the reformers from dealing with a host of hermeneutical issues that became matters of contention both between Rome and the Reformation and within each of these two communities: the extent of the biblical canon, the validity of critical study of the Bible, the perspicuity of Scripture and its relation to preaching and the retention of devotional and liturgical practices such as holy days, incense, the burning of candles, the sprinkling of holy water, church art and musical instruments. Zwingli, the Puritans and the radicals dismissed such things as a rubbish heap of ceremonials that amounted to nothing but tomfoolery, while Lutherans and Anglicans retained most of them as consonant with Scripture and valuable aids to worship.

It is important to note that while the mainline reformers differed among themselves on many matters, overwhelmingly they saw themselves as part of the ongoing Catholic tradition, indeed as the legitimate bearers of it. This was seen in numerous ways including their sense of continuity with the church of the preceding centuries; their embrace of the ecumenical orthodoxy of the early church; and their desire to read the Bible in dialogue with the exegetical tradition of the church.

In their biblical commentaries, the reformers of the sixteenth century revealed a close familiarity with the preceding exegetical tradition, and they used it respectfully as well as critically in their own expositions of the sacred text. For them, *sola Scriptura* was not *nuda Scriptura*. Rather, the Scriptures were seen as the book given to the church, gathered and guided by the Holy Spirit. In his restatement of the Vincentian canon, Calvin defined the church as "a society of all the saints, a society which, spread over the whole world, and existing in all ages, and bound together by the one doctrine and the one spirit of Christ, cultivates and observes unity of faith and brotherly concord. With this church we deny that we have any disagreement. Nay, rather, as we revere her as our mother, so we desire to remain in her bosom." Defined thus, the church has a real, albeit relative and circumscribed, authority since, as Calvin admits, "We cannot fly without

---

[30]LW 32:11-12* (WA 7:317).

wings."[31] While the reformers could not agree with the Council of Trent (though some recent Catholic theologians have challenged this interpretation) that Scripture and tradition were two separate and equable sources of divine revelation, they did believe in the coinherence of Scripture and tradition. This conviction shaped the way they read and interpreted the Bible.[32]

Schools of Exegesis

The reformers were passionate about biblical exegesis, but they showed little concern for hermeneutics as a separate field of inquiry. Niels Hemmingsen, a Lutheran theologian in Denmark, did write a treatise, *De methodis* (1555), in which he offered a philosophical and theological framework for the interpretation of Scripture. This was followed by the *Clavis Scripturae Sacrae* (1567) of Matthias Flacius Illyricus, which contains some fifty rules for studying the Bible drawn from Scripture itself.[33] However, hermeneutics as we know it came of age only in the Enlightenment and should not be backloaded into the Reformation. It is also true that the word *commentary* did not mean in the sixteenth century what it means for us today. Erasmus provided both annotations and paraphrases on the New Testament, the former a series of critical notes on the text but also containing points of doctrinal substance, the latter a theological overview and brief exposition. Most of Calvin's commentaries began as sermons or lectures presented in the course of his pastoral ministry. In the dedication to his 1519 study of Galatians, Luther declared that his work was "not so much a commentary as a testimony of my faith in Christ."[34] The exegetical work of the reformers was embodied in a wide variety of forms and genres, and the RCS has worked with this broader concept in setting the guidelines for this compendium.

The Protestant reformers shared in common a number of key interpretive principles such as the priority of the grammatical-historical sense of Scripture and the christological centeredness of the entire Bible, but they also developed a number of distinct approaches and schools of exegesis.[35] For the purposes of the RCS, we note the following key figures and families of interpretation in this period.

Biblical humanism. The key figure is Erasmus, whose importance is hard to exaggerate for Catholic and Protestant exegetes alike. His annotated Greek New Testament and fresh Latin translation challenged the hegemony of the Vulgate tradition and was doubtless a factor in the decision of the Council of Trent to establish the Vulgate edition as authentic and normative. Erasmus believed that the wide distribution of the Scriptures would contribute to personal spiritual renewal and the reform of society. In 1547, the English translation of Erasmus's *Paraphrases*

---

[31]John C. Olin, ed., *John Calvin and Jacopo Sadoleto: A Reformation Debate* (New York: Harper Torchbooks, 1966), 61-62, 77.

[32]See Timothy George, "An Evangelical Reflection on Scripture and Tradition," *Pro Ecclesia* 9 (2000): 184-207.

[33]See Kenneth G. Hagen, "'*De Exegetica Methodo*': Niels Hemmingsen's *De Methodis* (1555)," in *The Bible in the Sixteenth Century*, ed. David C. Steinmetz (Durham: Duke University Press, 1990), 181-96.

[34]LW 27:159 (WA 2:449). See Kenneth Hagen, "What Did the Term *Commentarius* Mean to Sixteenth-Century Theologians?" in Irena Backus and Francis M. Higman, eds., *Théorie et pratique de l'exégèse* (Geneva: Droz, 1990), 13-38.

[35]I follow here the sketch of Irena Backus, "Biblical Hermeneutics and Exegesis," *OER* 1:152-58. In this work, Backus confines herself to Continental developments, whereas we have noted the exegetical contribution of the English Reformation as well. For more comprehensive listings of sixteenth-century commentators, see Gerald Bray, *Biblical Interpretation* (Downers Grove, IL: InterVarsity Press, 1996), 165-212; and Richard A. Muller, "Biblical Interpretation in the Sixteenth and Seventeenth Centuries," *DMBI* 22-44.

was ordered to be placed in every parish church in England. John Colet first encouraged Erasmus to learn Greek, though he never took up the language himself. Colet's lectures on Paul's epistles at Oxford are reflected in his commentaries on Romans and 1 Corinthians.

Jacques Lefèvre d'Étaples has been called the "French Erasmus" because of his great learning and support for early reform movements in his native land. He published a major edition of the Psalter, as well as commentaries on the Pauline Epistles (1512), the Gospels (1522) and the General Epistles (1527). Guillaume Farel, the early reformer of Geneva, was a disciple of Lefèvre, and the young Calvin also came within his sphere of influence.

Among pre-Tridentine Catholic reformers, special attention should be given to Thomas de Vio, better known as Cajetan. He is best remembered for confronting Martin Luther on behalf of the pope in 1518, but his biblical commentaries (on nearly every book of the Bible) are virtually free of polemic. Like Erasmus, he dared to criticize the Vulgate on linguistic grounds. His commentary on Romans supported the doctrine of justification by grace applied by faith based on the "alien righteousness" of God in Christ. Jared Wicks sums up Cajetan's significance in this way: "Cajetan's combination of passion for pristine biblical meaning with his fully developed theological horizon of understanding indicates, in an intriguing manner, something of the breadth of possibilities open to Roman Catholics before a more restrictive settlement came to exercise its hold on many Catholic interpreters in the wake of the Council of Trent."[36] Girolamo Seripando, like Cajetan, was a cardinal in the Catholic Church, though he belonged to the Augustinian rather than the Dominican order. He was an outstanding classical scholar and published commentaries on Romans and Galatians. Also important is Jacopo Sadoleto, another cardinal, best known for his 1539 letter to the people of Geneva beseeching them to return to the church of Rome, to which Calvin replied with a manifesto of his own. Sadoleto published a commentary on Romans in 1535. Bucer once commended Sadoleto's teaching on justification as approximating that of the reformers, while others saw him tilting away from the Augustinian tradition toward Pelagianism.[37]

Luther and the Wittenberg School. It was in the name of the Word of God, and specifically as a doctor of Scripture, that Luther challenged the church of his day and inaugurated the Reformation. Though Luther renounced his monastic vows, he never lost that sense of intimacy with *sacra pagina* he first acquired as a young monk. Luther provided three rules for reading the Bible: prayer, meditation and struggle (*tentatio*). His exegetical output was enormous. In the American edition of Luther's works, thirty out of the fifty-five volumes are devoted to his biblical studies, and additional translations are planned. Many of his commentaries originated as sermons or lecture notes presented to his students at the university and to his parishioners at Wittenberg's parish church of St. Mary. Luther referred to Galatians as his bride: "The Epistle to the Galatians is my dear epistle. I have betrothed myself to it. It is my Käthe von Bora."[38] He considered his

---

[36]Jared Wicks, "Tommaso de Vio Cajetan (1469-1534)," *DMBI* 283-87, here 286.

[37]See the discussion by Bernard Roussel, "Martin Bucer et Jacques Sadolet: la concorde possible," *Bulletin de la Société de l'histoire de protestantisme français* (1976): 525-50, and T. H. L. Parker, *Commentaries on the Epistle to the Romans, 1532-1542* (Edinburgh: T&T Clark, 1986), 25-34.

[38]WATR 1:69 #146; cf. LW 54:20 #146. I have followed Rörer's variant on Dietrich's notes.

1535 commentary on Galatians his greatest exegetical work, although his massive commentary on Genesis (eight volumes in LW), which he worked on for ten years (1535–1545), must be considered his crowning work. Luther's principles of biblical interpretation are found in his *Open Letter on Translating* and in the prefaces he wrote to all the books of the Bible.

Philipp Melanchthon was brought to Wittenberg to teach Greek in 1518 and proved to be an able associate to Luther in the reform of the church. A set of his lecture notes on Romans was published without his knowledge in 1522. This was revised and expanded many times until his large commentary of 1556. Melanchthon also commented on other New Testament books including Matthew, John, Galatians and the Petrine Epistles, as well as Proverbs, Daniel and Ecclesiastes. Though he was well trained in the humanist disciplines, Melanchthon devoted little attention to critical and textual matters in his commentaries. Rather, he followed the primary argument of the biblical writer and gathered from this exposition a series of doctrinal topics for special consideration. This method lay behind Melanchthon's *Loci communes* (1521), the first Protestant theology textbook to be published. Another Wittenberger was Johannes Bugenhagen of Pomerania, a prolific commentator on both the Old and New Testaments. His commentary on the Psalms (1524), translated into German by Bucer, applied Luther's teaching on justification to the Psalter. He also wrote a commentary on Job and annotations on many of the books in the Bible. The Lutheran exegetical tradition was shaped by many other scholar-reformers including Andreas Osiander, Johannes Brenz, Caspar Cruciger, Erasmus Sarcerius, Georg Maior, Jacob Andreae, Nikolaus Selnecker and Johann Gerhard.

The Strasbourg-Basel tradition. Bucer, the son of a shoemaker in Alsace, became the leader of the Reformation in Strasbourg. A former Dominican, he was early on influenced by Erasmus and continued to share his passion for Christian unity. Bucer was the most ecumenical of the Protestant reformers seeking rapprochement with Catholics on justification and an armistice between Luther and Zwingli in their strife over the Lord's Supper. Bucer also had a decisive influence on Calvin, though the latter characterized his biblical commentaries as longwinded and repetitious.[39] In his exegetical work, Bucer made ample use of patristic and medieval sources, though he criticized the abuse and overuse of allegory as "the most blatant insult to the Holy Spirit."[40] He declared that the purpose of his commentaries was "to help inexperienced brethren [perhaps like the apothecary Drilhon, who owned a French translation of Bucer's *Commentary on Matthew*] to understand each of the words and actions of Christ, and in their proper order as far as possible, and to retain an explanation of them in their natural meaning, so that they will not distort God's Word through age-old aberrations or by inept interpretation, but rather with a faithful comprehension of everything as written by the Spirit of God, they may expound to all the churches in their firm upbuilding in faith and love."[41] In addition to writing commentaries on all four Gospels, Bucer published

---

[39]CNTC 8:3 (CO 10:404).

[40]DMBI 249; P. Scherding and F. Wendel, eds., "Un Traité d'exégèse pratique de Bucer," *Revue d'histoire et de philosophie religieuses* 26 (1946): 32-75, here 56.

[41]Martin Bucer, *Enarrationes perpetuae in sacra quatuor evangelia*, 2nd. ed. (Strasbourg: Georg Ulrich Andlanus, 1530), 10r; quoted in D. F. Wright, "Martin Bucer," *DMBI* 290.

commentaries on Judges, the Psalms, Zephaniah, Romans and Ephesians. In the early years of the Reformation, there was a great deal of back and forth between Strasbourg and Basel, and both were centers of a lively publishing trade. Wolfgang Capito, Bucer's associate at Strasbourg, was a notable Hebraist and composed commentaries on Hosea (1529) and Habakkuk (1527).

At Basel, the great Sebastian Münster defended the use of Jewish sources in the Christian study of the Old Testament and published, in addition to his famous Hebrew grammar, an annotated version of the Gospel of Matthew translated from Greek into Hebrew. Oecolampadius, Basel's chief reformer, had been a proofreader in Froben's publishing house and worked with Erasmus on his Greek New Testament and his critical edition of Jerome. From 1523 he was both a preacher and professor of Holy Scripture at Basel. He defended Zwingli's eucharistic theology at the Colloquy of Marburg and published commentaries on 1 John (1524), Romans (1525) and Haggai-Malachi (1525). Oecolampadius was succeeded by Simon Grynaeus, a classical scholar who taught Greek and supported Bucer's efforts to bring Lutherans and Zwinglians together. More in line with Erasmus was Sebastian Castellio, who came to Basel after his expulsion from Geneva in 1545. He is best remembered for questioning the canonicity of the Song of Songs and for his annotations and French translation of the Bible.

The Zurich group. Biblical exegesis in Zurich was centered on the distinctive institution of the *Prophezei*, which began on June 19, 1525. On five days a week, at seven o'clock in the morning, all of the ministers and theological students in Zurich gathered into the choir of the Grossmünster to engage in a period of intense exegesis and interpretation of Scripture. After Zwingli had opened the meeting with prayer, the text of the day was read in Latin, Greek and Hebrew, followed by appropriate textual or exegetical comments. One of the ministers then delivered a sermon on the passage in German that was heard by many of Zurich's citizens who stopped by the cathedral on their way to work. This institute for advanced biblical studies had an enormous influence as a model for Reformed academies and seminaries throughout Europe. It was also the seedbed for sermon series in Zurich's churches and the extensive exegetical publications of Zwingli, Leo Jud, Konrad Pellikan, Heinrich Bullinger, Oswald Myconius and Rudolf Gwalther. Zwingli had memorized in Greek all of the Pauline epistles, and this bore fruit in his powerful expository preaching and biblical exegesis. He took seriously the role of grammar, rhetoric and historical research in explaining the biblical text. For example, he disagreed with Bucer on the value of the Septuagint, regarding it as a trustworthy witness to a proto-Hebrew version earlier than the Masoretic text.

Zwingli's work was carried forward by his successor Bullinger, one of the most formidable scholars and networkers among the reformers. He composed commentaries on Daniel (1565), the Gospels (1542–1546), the Epistles (1537), Acts (1533) and Revelation (1557). He collaborated with Calvin to produce the *Consensus Tigurinus* (1549), a Reformed accord on the nature of the Lord's Supper, and produced a series of fifty sermons on Christian doctrine, known as *Decades*, which became required reading in Elizabethan England. As the *Antistes* ("overseer") of the Zurich church for forty-four years, Bullinger faced opposition from nascent Anabaptism on the one hand and resurgent Catholicism on the other. The need for a well-trained clergy and scholarly resources, including Scripture commentaries, arose from the fact that the Bible was "difficult or obscure to the unlearned, unskillful, unexercised, and malicious or corrupted wills." While forswearing papal claims to infallibility, Bullinger and other leaders of the magisterial Reformation saw the need for a kind of Protestant magisterium as a check against the tendency to read the Bible in "such sense as everyone shall be persuaded in himself to be most convenient."[42]

Two other commentators can be treated in connection with the Zurich group, though each of them had a wide-ranging ministry across the Reformation fronts. A former Benedictine monk, Wolfgang Musculus, embraced the Reformation in the 1520s and served briefly as the secretary to Bucer in Strasbourg. He shared Bucer's desire for Protestant unity and served for seventeen years (1531–1548) as a pastor and reformer in Augsburg. After a brief time in Zurich, where he came under the influence of Bullinger, Musculus was called to Bern, where he taught the Scriptures and published commentaries on the Psalms, the Decalogue, Genesis, Romans, Isaiah, 1 and 2 Corinthians, Galatians and Ephesians, Philippians, Colossians, 1 and 2 Thessalonians and 1 Timothy. Drawing on his exegetical writings, Musculus also produced a compendium of Protestant theology that was translated into English in 1563 as *Commonplaces of Christian Religion*.

Peter Martyr Vermigli was a Florentine-born scholar and Augustinian friar who embraced the Reformation and fled to Switzerland in 1542. Over the next twenty years, he would gain an international reputation as a prolific scholar and leading theologian within the Reformed community. He lectured on the Old Testament at Strasbourg, was made regius professor at Oxford, corresponded with the Italian refugee church in Geneva and spent the last years of his life as professor of Hebrew at Zurich. Vermigli published commentaries on 1 Corinthians, Romans and Judges during his lifetime. His biblical lectures on Genesis, Lamentations, 1 and 2 Samuel and 1 and 2 Kings were published posthumously. The most influential of his writings was the *Loci communes* (*Commonplaces*), a theological compendium drawn from his exegetical writings.

The Genevan Reformers. What Zwingli and Bullinger were to Zurich, Calvin and Beza were to Geneva. Calvin has been called "the father of modern biblical scholarship," and his exegetical work is without parallel in the Reformation. Because of the success of his *Institutes of the Christian Religion* Calvin has sometimes been thought of as a man of one book, but he always intended the *Institutes*, which went through eight editions in Latin and five in French during his lifetime, to serve as a guide to the study of the Bible, to show the reader "what he ought especially to seek in Scripture and to what end he ought to relate its contents." Jacob Arminius, who modified several principles of Calvin's theology, recommended his commentaries next to the Bible, for, as he said, Calvin "is incomparable in the interpretation of Scripture."[43] Drawing on his superb knowledge of Greek and Hebrew and his thorough training in humanist rhetoric, Calvin produced commentaries on all of the New Testament books except 2 and 3 John and Revelation. Calvin's Old Testament

---

[42]Euan Cameron, *The European Reformation* (Oxford: Oxford University Press, 1991), 120.

[43]Letter to Sebastian Egbert (May 3, 1607), in *Praestantium ac eruditorum virorum epistolae ecclesiasticae et theologicae varii argumenti*, ed. Christiaan Hartsoeker (Amsterdam: Henricus Dendrinus, 1660), 236-37. Quoted in A. M. Hunter, *The Teaching of Calvin* (London: James Clarke, 1950), 20.

---

commentaries originated as sermon and lecture series and include Genesis, Psalms, Hosea, Isaiah, minor prophets, Daniel, Jeremiah and Lamentations, a harmony of the last four books of Moses, Ezekiel 1–20 and Joshua. Calvin sought for brevity and clarity in all of his exegetical work. He emphasized the illumination of the Holy Spirit as essential to a proper understanding of the text. Calvin underscored the continuity between the two Testaments (one covenant in two dispensations) and sought to apply the plain or natural sense of the text to the church of his day. In the preface to his own influential commentary on Romans, Karl Barth described how Calvin worked to recover the mind of Paul and make the apostle's message relevant to his day:

> How energetically Calvin goes to work, first scientifically establishing the text ('what stands there?'), then following along the footsteps of its thought; that is to say, he conducts a discussion with it until the wall between the first and the sixteenth centuries becomes transparent, and until there in the first century Paul speaks and here the man of the sixteenth century hears, until indeed the conversation between document and reader becomes concentrated upon the substance (which must be the same now as then).[44]

Beza was elected moderator of Geneva's Company of Pastors after Calvin's death in 1564 and guided the Genevan Reformation over the next four decades. His annotated Latin translation of the Greek New Testament (1556) and his further revisions of the Greek text established his reputation as the leading textual critic of the sixteenth century after Erasmus. Beza completed the translation of Marot's metrical Psalter, which became a centerpiece of Huguenot piety and Reformed church life. Though known for his polemical writings on grace, free will and predestination, Beza's work is marked by a strong pastoral orientation and concern for a Scripture-based spirituality.

Robert Estienne (Stephanus) was a printer-scholar who had served the royal household in Paris. After his conversion to Protestantism, in 1550 he moved to Geneva, where he published a series of notable editions and translations of the Bible. He also produced sermons and commentaries on Job, Ecclesiastes, the Song of Songs, Romans and Hebrews, as well as dictionaries, concordances and a thesaurus of biblical terms. He also published the first editions of the Bible with chapters divided into verses, an innovation that quickly became universally accepted.

The British Reformation. Commentary writing in England and Scotland lagged behind the continental Reformation for several reasons. In 1500, there were only three publishing houses in England compared with more than two hundred on the Continent. A 1408 statute against publishing or reading the Bible in English, stemming from the days of Lollardy, stifled the free flow of ideas, as was seen in the fate of Tyndale. Moreover, the nature of the English Reformation from Henry through Elizabeth provided little stability for the flourishing of biblical scholarship. In the sixteenth century, many "hot-gospel" Protestants in England were edified by the English translations of commentaries and theological writings by the Continental reformers.

---

[44]Karl Barth, *Die Römerbrief* (Zurich: TVZ, 1940), ii, translated by T. H. L. Parker as the epigraph to *Calvin's New Testament Commentaries*, 2nd ed. (Louisville, KY: Westminster John Knox, 1993).

The influence of Calvin and Beza was felt especially in the Geneva Bible with its "Protestant glosses" of theological notes and references.

During the later Elizabethan and Stuart church, however, the indigenous English commentary came into its own. Both Anglicans and Puritans contributed to this outpouring of biblical studies. The sermons of Lancelot Andrewes and John Donne are replete with exegetical insights based on a close study of the Greek and Hebrew texts. Among the Reformed authors in England, none was more influential than William Perkins, the greatest of the early Puritan theologians, who published commentaries on Galatians, Jude, Revelation and the Sermon on the Mount (Mt 5–7). John Cotton, one of his students, wrote commentaries on the Song of Songs, Ecclesiastes and Revelation before departing for New England in 1633. The separatist pastor Henry Ainsworth was an outstanding scholar of Hebrew and wrote major commentaries on the Pentateuch, the Psalms and the Song of Songs. In Scotland, Robert Rollock, the first principal of Edinburgh University (1585), wrote numerous commentaries including those on the Psalms, Ephesians, Daniel, Romans, 1 and 2 Thessalonians, John, Colossians and Hebrews. Joseph Mede and Thomas Brightman were leading authorities on Revelation and contributed to the apocalyptic thought of the seventeenth century. Mention should also be made of Archbishop James Ussher, whose *Annals of the Old Testament* was published in 1650. Ussher developed a keen interest in biblical chronology and calculated that the creation of the world had taken place on October 26, 4004 B.C. As late as 1945, the Scofield Reference Bible still retained this date next to Genesis 1:1, but later editions omitted it because of the lack of evidence on which to fix such dates.[45]

Anabaptism. Irena Backus has noted that there was no school of "dissident" exegesis during the Reformation, and the reasons are not hard to find. The radical Reformation was an ill-defined movement that existed on the margins of official church life in the sixteenth century. The denial of infant baptism and the refusal to swear an oath marked radicals as a seditious element in society, and they were persecuted by Protestants and Catholics alike. However, in the RCS we have made an attempt to include some voices of the radical Reformation, especially among the Anabaptists. While the Anabaptists published few commentaries in the sixteenth century, they were avid readers and quoters of the Bible. Numerous exegetical gems can be found in their letters, treatises, martyr acts (especially *The Martyrs' Mirror*), hymns and histories. They placed a strong emphasis on the memorizing of Scripture and quoted liberally from vernacular translations of the Bible. George H. Williams has noted that "many an Anabaptist theological tract was really a beautiful mosaic of Scripture texts."[46] In general, most Anabaptists accepted the apocryphal books as canonical, contrasted outer word and inner spirit with relative degrees of strictness and saw the New Testament as normative for church life and social ethics (witness their pacifism, nonswearing, emphasis on believers' baptism and congregational discipline).

We have noted the Old Testament translation of Ludwig Hätzer, who became an antitrinitarian, and Hans Denck that they published at Worms in 1527. Denck also wrote a notable commentary

---

[45] *The New Scofield Reference Bible* (New York: Oxford University Press, 1967), vi.

[46] George H. Williams, *The Radical Reformation*, 3rd ed. (Kirksville, MO: Sixteenth Century Journal Publishers, 1992), 1247.

on Micah. Conrad Grebel belonged to a Greek reading circle in Zurich and came to his Anabaptist convictions while poring over the text of Erasmus's New Testament. The only Anabaptist leader with university credentials was Balthasar Hubmaier, who was made a doctor of theology (Ingolstadt, 1512) in the same year as Luther. His reflections on the Bible are found in his numerous writings, which include the first catechism of the Reformation (1526), a two-part treatise on the freedom of the will and a major work (*On the Sword*) setting forth positive attitudes toward the role of government and the Christian's place in society. Melchior Hoffman was an apocalyptic seer who wrote commentaries on Romans, Revelation and Daniel 12. He predicted that Christ would return in 1533. More temperate was Pilgram Marpeck, a mining engineer who embraced Anabaptism and traveled widely throughout Switzerland and south Germany, from Strasbourg to Augsburg. His "Admonition of 1542" is the longest published defense of Anabaptist views on baptism and the Lord's Supper. He also wrote many letters that functioned as theological tracts for the congregations he had founded dealing with topics such as the fruits of repentance, the lowliness of Christ and the unity of the church. Menno Simons, a former Catholic priest, became the most outstanding leader of the Dutch Anabaptist movement. His masterpiece was the *Foundation of Christian Doctrine* published in 1540. His other writings include *Meditation on the Twenty-fifth Psalm* (1537); *A Personal Exegesis of Psalm Twenty-five* modeled on the style of Augustine's *Confessions*; *Confession of the Triune God* (1550), directed against Adam Pastor, a former disciple of Menno who came to doubt the divinity of Christ; *Meditations and Prayers for Mealtime* (1557); and the *Cross of the Saints* (1554), an exhortation to faithfulness in the face of persecution. Like many other Anabaptists, Menno emphasized the centrality of discipleship (*Nachfolge*) as a deliberate repudiation of the old life and a radical commitment to follow Jesus as Lord.

Reading Scripture with the Reformers

In 1947, Gerhard Ebeling set forth his thesis that the history of the Christian church is the history of the interpretation of Scripture. Since that time, the place of the Bible in the story of the church has been investigated from many angles. A better understanding of the history of exegesis has been aided by new critical editions and scholarly discussions of the primary sources. The *Cambridge History of the Bible*, published in three volumes (1963–1970), remains a standard reference work in the field. The ACCS built on, and itself contributed to, the recovery of patristic biblical wisdom of both East and West. Beryl Smalley's *The Study of the Bible in the Middle Ages* (1940) and Henri de Lubac's *Medieval Exegesis: The Four Senses of Scripture* (1959) are essential reading for understanding the monastic and scholastic settings of commentary work between Augustine and Luther. The Reformation took place during what has been called "le grand siècle de la Bible."[47] Aided by the tools of Renaissance humanism and the dynamic impetus of Reformation theology (including permutations and reactions against it), the sixteenth century produced an unprecedented number of commentaries on every book in the Bible. Drawing from this vast storehouse of exegetical treasures, the RCS allows us to read

---

[47]J-R. Aarmogathe, ed., *Bible de tous les temps*, 8 vols.; vol. 6, *Le grand siècle de la Bible* (Paris: Beauchesne, 1989).

Scripture along with the reformers. In doing so, it serves as a practical homiletic and devotional guide to some of the greatest masters of biblical interpretation in the history of the church.

The RCS gladly acknowledges its affinity with and dependence on recent scholarly investigations of Reformation-era exegesis. Between 1976 and 1990, three international colloquia on the history of biblical exegesis in the sixteenth century took place in Geneva and in Durham, North Carolina.[48] Among those participating in these three gatherings were a number of scholars who have produced groundbreaking works in the study of biblical interpretation in the Reformation. These include Elsie McKee, Irena Backus, Kenneth Hagen, Scott H. Hendrix, Richard A. Muller, Guy Bedouelle, Gerald Hobbs, John B. Payne, Bernard Roussel, Pierre Fraenkel and David C. Steinmetz. Among other scholars whose works are indispensible for the study of this field are Heinrich Bornkamm, Jaroslav Pelikan, Heiko A. Oberman, James S. Preus, T. H. L. Parker, David F. Wright, Tony Lane, John L. Thompson, Frank A. James and Timothy J. Wengert.[49] Among these scholars no one has had a greater influence on the study of Reformation exegesis than David C. Steinmetz. A student of Oberman, he has emphasized the importance of understanding the Reformation in medieval perspective. In addition to important studies on Luther and Staupitz, he has pioneered the method of comparative exegesis showing both continuity and discontinuity between major Reformation figures and the preceding exegetical traditions (see his *Luther in Context* and *Calvin in Context*). From his base at Duke University, he has spawned what might be called a Steinmetz school, a cadre of students and scholars whose work on the Bible in the Reformation era continues to shape the field. Steinmetz serves on the RCS Board of Editorial Advisors, and a number of our volume editors have pursued doctoral studies under his supervision.

In 1980, Steinmetz published "The Superiority of Pre-critical Exegesis," a seminal essay that not only placed Reformation exegesis in the context of the preceding fifteen centuries of the church's study of the Bible but also challenged certain assumptions underlying the hegemony of historical-critical exegesis of the post-Enlightenment academy.[50] Steinmetz helps us to approach the reformers and other precritical interpreters of the Bible on their own terms as faithful witnesses to the church's apostolic tradition. For them, a specific book or pericope had to be understood within the scope of the consensus of the canon. Thus the reformers, no less than the Fathers and the schoolmen, interpreted the hymn of the Johannine prologue about the preexistent Christ in consonance with the creation narrative of Genesis 1. In the same way, Psalm 22, Isaiah 53 and Daniel 7 are seen as part of an overarching storyline that finds ultimate fulfillment in Jesus

---

[48]Olivier Fatio and Pierre Fraenkel, eds., *Histoire de l'exégèse au XVIe siècle: texts du colloque international tenu à Genève en 1976* (Geneva: Droz, 1978); David C. Steinmetz, ed., *The Bible in the Sixteenth Century* [Second International Colloquy on the History of Biblical Exegesis in the Sixteenth Century] (Durham: Duke University Press, 1990); Irena Backus and Francis M. Higman, eds., *Théorie et pratique de l'exégèse. Actes du troisième colloque international sur l'histoire de l'exégèse biblique au XVIe siècle, Genève, 31 août-2 septembre 1988* (Geneva: Droz, 1990); see also Guy Bedouelle and Bernard Roussel, eds., *Bible de tous les temps*, 8 vols.; vol. 5, *Le temps des Réformes et la Bible* (Paris: Beauchesne, 1989).

[49]For bibliographical references and evaluation of these and other contributors to the scholarly study of Reformation-era exegesis, see Richard A. Muller, "Biblical Interpretation in the Era of the Reformation: The View From the Middle Ages," in *Biblical Interpretation in the Era of the Reformation: Essays Presented to David C. Steinmetz in Honor of His Sixtieth Birthday*, ed. Richard A. Muller and John L. Thompson (Grand Rapids: Eerdmans, 1996), 3-22.

[50]David C. Steinmetz, "The Superiority of Pre-Critical Exegesis," *Theology Today* 37 (1980): 27-38.

Christ. Reading the Bible with the resources of the new learning, the reformers challenged the exegetical conclusions of their medieval predecessors at many points. However, unlike Alexander Campbell in the nineteenth century, their aim was not to "open the New Testament as if mortal man had never seen it before."[51] Rather, they wanted to do their biblical work as part of an interpretive conversation within the family of the people of God. In the reformers' emphatic turn to the literal sense, which prompted their many blasts against the unrestrained use of allegory, their work was an extension of a similar impulse made by Thomas Aquinas and Nicholas of Lyra.

This is not to discount the radically new insights gained by the reformers in their dynamic engagement with the text of Scripture; nor should we dismiss in a reactionary way the light shed on the meaning of the Bible by the scholarly accomplishments of the past two centuries. However, it is to acknowledge that the church's exegetical tradition is an indispensible aid for the proper interpretation of Scripture. And this means, as Richard Muller has said, that "while it is often appropriate to recognize that traditionary readings of the text are erroneous on the grounds offered by the historical-critical method, we ought also to recognize that the conclusions offered by historical-critical exegesis may themselves be quite erroneous on the grounds provided by the exegesis of the patristic, medieval, and reformation periods."[52] The RCS wishes to commend the exegetical work of the Reformation era as a program of retrieval for the sake of renewal—spiritual réssourcement for believers committed to the life of faith today.

George Herbert was an English pastor and poet who reaped the benefits of the renewal of biblical studies in the age of the Reformation. He referred to the Scriptures as a book of infinite sweetness, "a mass of strange delights," a book with secrets to make the life of anyone good. In describing the various means pastors require to be fully furnished in the work of their calling, Herbert provided a rationale for the history of exegesis and for the Reformation Commentary on Scripture:

> The fourth means are commenters and Fathers, who have handled the places controverted, which the parson by no means refuseth. As he doth not so study others as to neglect the grace of God in himself and what the Holy Spirit teacheth him, so doth he assure himself that God in all ages hath had his servants to whom he hath revealed his Truth, as well as to him; and that as one country doth not bear all things that there may be a commerce, so neither hath God opened or will open all to one, that there may be a traffic in knowledge between the servants of God for the planting both of love and humility. Wherefore he hath one comment[ary] at least upon every book of Scripture, and ploughing with this, and his own meditations, he enters into the secrets of God treasured in the holy Scripture.[53]

Timothy George
General Editor

---

[51]Alexander Campbell, *Memoirs of Alexander Campbell*, ed. Robert Richardson (Cincinnati: Standard Publishing Company, 1872), 97.
[52]Richard A. Muller and John L. Thompson, "The Significance of Precritical Exegesis: Retrospect and Prospect," in *Biblical Interpretation in the Era of the Reformation: Essays Presented to David C. Steinmetz in Honor of His Sixtieth Birthday*, ed. Richard A. Muller and John L. Thompson (Grand Rapids: Eerdmans, 1996), 342.
[53]George Herbert, *The Complete English Poems* (London: Penguin, 1991), 205.

INTRODUCTION TO ACTS

"Actors on This Same Stage"

Just before their arduous journey across the Atlantic to the New World in 1622, John Donne exhorted and encouraged the members of the Virginia Company in a sermon on Acts 1:8: "But you will receive power when the Holy Spirit has come upon you, and you will be my witnesses in Jerusalem and in all Judea and Samaria, and to the end of the earth."

> The Acts of the Apostles were to convey that name of Christ Jesus, and to propagate his Gospel throughout the whole world. Beloved, you too are actors on this same stage. The end of the earth is your scene. Act out the acts of the apostles. Be a light to the Gentiles who sit in darkness. Be content to carry him over these seas, who dried up one red sea for his first people, and who has poured out another red sea—his own blood—for them and for us.[1]

For Donne, the book of Acts is not merely about what *has* happened, it is about what *is* happening, what *continues* to happen and what *will* happen. This first-century narrative written by a Hellenistic Jew about Jesus' exodus—his Red Sea passage through the cross—is, for that reason, also about sixteenth-century barflies and seventeenth-century sailors. The discovery and rediscovery of what Scripture says not only refines but also reforms the church's mission. Such self-critique asks both "What are we doing that we should not?" and "Are we doing what we should?" Most, if not all, early modern Christian interpreters of Scripture would have agreed with Donne. Acts is God's own prescribed model of the church's ministry and its life together, the script that narrates the drama of the body of Christ across all times and places.

There are various shades of opinion among these commentators; nonetheless, the emphasis of Donne—"You too are actors on this same stage"—seen in Reformation commentary generally is in key respects at odds with a great deal of contemporary biblical scholarship. Many in this audience do not see themselves as standing on the stage and taking direction, building on the successes (or learning from the failures) of past performances. We today much prefer to parse and interpret every nuance of the debut performance; our early modern commentators, however, understand themselves as building on the reception of this original performance, and consequently recognized their own contributions as part of the broader Christian tradition of interpretation.

---

[1] John Donne, *The Works of John Donne*, 6 vols., ed. Henry Alford (London: John Parker, 1839), 6:225.

Script(ure) and Tradition

To direct and perform a classic play is no easy task. How does one preserve the character of the work without making it a wooden repetition that reduces its original genius? How does one alter the performance enough to make it fresh, but not so much that the integrity of the author's intent is compromised? A tragedy like *Romeo and Juliet* has been acted and reenacted countless times since its first performance. Today, around four hundred years after its initial release, its conversation, context and culture can be difficult to grasp. How might a modern director make this tragedy more accessible—without compromising its message—to a modern audience? Swords might become guns; feuding families could be competing business moguls. However, the genre, characters and themes can be tempered but not transformed; chiefly, the star-crossed lovers must remain the same: a boy and girl who love each other passionately despite everything conspiring against them—and they both must die.[2] In such cases the play's typical reception has been recast or reinterpreted, but the play has not been *rewritten*. This relationship between text and interpretation in dramatic performances bears on our present purpose: what is the character of the relationship between Scripture and tradition for our commentators, approaching and unfolding the drama of Acts?

For many Protestants, Luther and Calvin are exegetical and theological iconoclasts, smashing the husks of tradition against the Scriptural rock. However, upon closer inspection, the reformers appear to have been quite fond of a particular sort of tradition and quite cool toward another sort. Luther changed relatively little of the Latin Mass's medieval liturgy when he translated it into German. Calvin appealed to the church fathers to counter accusations of innovation, depicting the Reformed church as a restored and faithful heir of the early church.[3] Balthasar Hubmaier assured his accusers that he too knelt in prayer and still rang bells for worship.[4] These men along with the majority of their colleagues continued to affirm the perpetual virginity of Mary.[5] Of course, the Protestant reformers in unison rejected papal and even conciliar decisions as de facto authoritatively binding. They discarded the somewhat younger tradition of transubstantiation (declared as dogma by Lateran IV in 1215), and—most famously—they desired to cast purgatory, indulgences and the treasury of merit headlong into the abyss. Were they inconsistent?

Anthony Lane reminds us that "the essence of the *sola Scriptura* principle ... is not that Scripture

---

[2]We are thinking of Baz Luhrmann's *Romeo + Juliet* (1996); there are numerous other remakes to contemplate, e.g., *West Side Story*.
[3]Anthony N. S. Lane, *John Calvin: Student of the Church Fathers* (Grand Rapids: Baker Books, 1999), 52-54; Esther Chung-Kim, *Inventing Authority: The Use of the Church Fathers in Reformation Debates over the Eucharist* (Waco, TX: Baylor University Press, 2011). See also Lane's theses on Calvin's patristic appropriation, 1-13. He notes that Calvin used the fathers "primarily [as] a polemical appeal to authorities," and that he was often critical of particular exegetical decisions in his own commentaries while generally approving their theology (3-4).
[4]CRR 5:544-45 (QGT 9:476).
[5]Interestingly enough, Cardinal Cajetan was less sure of Mary's immaculate conception and ascension than many first- and second-generation reformers. See Patrick Preston, "Cardinal Cajetan and Fra Ambrosius Catharinus in the Controversy over the Immaculate Conception of the Virgin in Italy, 1515-51," in *The Church and Mary: Papers Read at the 2001 Summer Meeting and the 2002 Winter Meeting of the Ecclesiastical History Society*, ed. R. N. Swanson (Suffolk, UK: The Boydell Press, 2004), 185. For more on Reformation views of Mary, see Beth Kreitzer, *Reforming Mary: Changing Images of the Virgin Mary in Lutheran Sermons of the Sixteenth Century* (Oxford: Oxford University Press, 2004); David F. Wright, "Mary in the Reformers," in *Chosen by God: Mary in Evangelical Perspective*, ed. David F. Wright (London: Marshall Pickering, 1989), 161-83; and other chapters in Swanson, *The Church and Mary*.

is the sole resource, the sole source or the sole authority."[6] It is not the total rejection of all tradition. It is not *nuda Scriptura*, bare Scripture.[7] The reformers were deeply indebted to other resources and sources: Greek and Hebrew lexicons, rabbinic interpretation, the writings of the church fathers, critical editions of the biblical text. "What then is the essence of the *sola Scriptura* principle? It is that Scripture is the *final* authority or norm for Christian belief."[8] So then, for the reformers it was not inconsistent to wield the creeds confidently or to cite the fathers or even to affirm Mary's perpetual virginity.[9] These and other resources were to be investigated in the court of Scripture.

For the reformers the "tradition" that governed all others is Jesus Christ, his person and work (of course Christian proclamation and the sacraments were implicated in this conviction). Luther is so bold as to apply this touchstone to the Bible itself: "In sum, Christ is Lord not servant; he is Lord of the Sabbath, the law and everything. Scripture is to be understood not against, but for Christ. Therefore it must either refer to him or not be considered true Scripture."[10] Jesus is Lord of Scripture.[11] All other traditions must be viewed in this context and through this lens: Does an aspect of traditional faith and practice obscure or distort the gospel of Christ? Protestants from Geneva to Moravia, Strasbourg to Wittenberg, Canterbury to Zurich would have agreed that every teaching that alters who Jesus is (the only-begotten Son of the Father, fully God, and the last Adam, fully man), or what he has done for us (redeemed us fully to the Holy Trinity through his death and resurrection) must be discarded. Text, time and place are unified in Jesus Christ.

Acts of *the Apostles?*

But what about that title "The Acts of the Apostles"? Actually the reformers questioned whether it was the best title for this book (it has, after all, no distinct title in the Greek original). The

---

[6]Anthony N. S. Lane, "*Sola Scriptura?* Making Sense of a Post-Reformation Slogan," in *A Pathway into the Holy Scripture*, ed. Philip E. Satterthwaite and David F. Wright (Grand Rapids: Eerdmans, 1994), 297-327, here 323; for a briefer but nuanced examination of *sola Scriptura*, see Timothy George, *The Theology of the Reformers* (Nashville: B & H, 1988), 79-86.

[7]George, *Theology of the Reformers*, 81. J. Todd Billings restates this approach succinctly in *The Word of God for the People of God: An Entryway to the Theological Interpretation of Scripture* (Grand Rapids: Eerdmans, 2010), esp. 44-54. Instead of the individualistic slant on *sola Scriptura* more common in the modern era, Kevin Vanhoozer describes an interpretative quadrangle for relating Scripture and tradition: the Holy Spirit's direction, apostolic tradition, the church as interpreter, and the canon of Scripture. Kevin J. Vanhoozer, *The Drama of Doctrine: A Canonical-Linguistic Approach to Christian Theology* (Louisville, KY: Westminster John Knox, 2005), 117-20. See also Timothy George's discussion of this above in the general introduction, xl-xlii.

[8]Lane, "*Sola Scriptura?*" 323, our emphasis.

[9]After all Ezekiel 44:2—"And the Lord said to me, 'This gate shall remain shut; it shall not be opened, and no one shall enter by it, for the Lord, the God of Israel, has entered by it. Therefore it shall remain shut.'"—would have been a compelling proof-text to readers with such a christocentric mindset as the reformers. See Carl L. Beckwith, ed., *Ezekiel, Daniel*, Reformation Commentary on Scripture Old Testament 12 (Downers Grove, IL: IVP Academic, 2012), 215-16.

[10]WA 39,1:47; alluding to Mt 12:8; cf. Ewald Plass, ed., *What Luther Says: An Anthology*, 3 vols. (St. Louis: Concordia, 1959), 1:98. David C. Steinmetz, "Luther, Martin (1483–1546)," in *Dictionary of Biblical Interpretation*, 2 vols., ed. John H. Hayes (Nashville: Abingdon Press, 1999), 1:96-98, here 98. "[Luther's] emphasis on the christological center of Scripture and on the teaching of justification by faith alone led him to reopen briefly the question of canon. . . . While he soon gave up any thought of revising the canon, he always retained the notion that the biblical books are of unequal value, that the Bible should be interpreted from its christological center, and that sacred Scripture is its own best interpreter and critic." For a helpful discussion of this christocentric hermeneutic in the early church, see Donald Fairbairn, *Life in the Trinity: An Introduction to Theology with the Help of the Church Fathers* (Downers Grove, IL: InterVarsity Press, 2009), 109-16.

[11]Timothy George has noted that for the reformers indeed "Christ ever remains the Lord of Scripture, which is a means to faith but not an object of faith." George, *Theology of the Reformers*, 84.

Lutheran catechist Johann Spangenberg notes that such a title seems to imply that the story is about the apostles, though it is actually about their deeds in the power of Jesus by the Spirit: "It should rightly be titled not merely 'the Acts of the Apostles' but even better 'the Acts of Christ.' . . . In this book . . . the resurrected and glorified Christ is described."[12] So then the Acts of the Apostles—or the Acts of the Risen Christ—is not primarily a narrative about the earliest history of the Christian community, but the continuation of the powerful work of the ascended Jesus by his Spirit through those he commissioned to bear his gospel ministry.

Further, a title like "The Acts of the Risen Christ" would better reflect that the amazing events and unexpected achievements of the apostolic church were in fact the outflow of Christ's victory over sin and death and the fruits of his ongoing work of reconciliation in the world, good news to be embraced by faith. Early modern exegetes phrase this in different ways. Luther and Spangenberg state bluntly that justification by faith is the purpose of the book, while Calvin implies as much, saying that Luke teaches his readers that the gospel, not the law, is to govern the church whom Christ has gathered.[13] This is the primary purpose of the apostles' preaching and their actions, and, as Donne reminds us, we too participate in this preaching and acting. What implications do this preaching and acting, especially as viewed through the unifying lens of the good news of justification by faith in the risen Christ, have for our commentators and their communities? There are four particularly prominent themes in Reformation comment on this apostolic history: the office of the Word, the sacrament of baptism, the community of goods, and suffering.

The Office of the Word. The premier gospel office for the reformers was preaching. Yes, the sacraments carried great importance and were cherished, but without the preached Word of Christ's gospel promise, these signs would be empty shells. The inscripturated and incarnate Word can be distinguished but not separated. The content of the inscripturated Word reflects the work of the incarnate Word. Thus, Scripture is *necessarily* effective. God's Word will never return empty (Is 55:11). It convicts. It consoles. It kills and brings life. Christ by his Word and through his Spirit is quietly but mightily present with his people. An important aspect of this is that the Lord in his providence has called human beings to the office of mediating this eternal Word through their very mortal lips. The new covenant requires a "living voice" unlike "the law and old covenant [which] is a dead writing, composed in books."[14]

Emphasizing the eminence of the pastoral office in this way, the reformers endeavored to craft a robust teaching and practice of the office of the Word. They nevertheless acknowledged the world's inverted view of the ministry's eminence—after all, as Theodore Beza groused, it is "the most despised

---

[12]Johann Spangenberg, *Der Apostel Geschichte: Kurtze auslegung Fur die jungen Christen inn Frage verfasset* (Wittenberg: Georg Rhau, 1545), IV. Contemporary biblical studies has also noted this; see, e.g., Alan J. Thompson, *The Acts of the Risen Lord Jesus: Luke's Account of God's Unfolding Plan* (Nottingham: Apollos; and Downers Grove, IL: InterVarsity Press, 2011), esp. 48-54. Others emphasize the Word as the main character of Acts, who vanquishes as he travels; see David W. Pao, *Acts and the Isaianic New Exodus* (Tübingen: Mohr Siebeck, 2000), 147-80.

[13]See prefatory remarks below from Luther and Calvin; LW 35:363-64 (WADB 6:415-17); and CNTC 6:2-3* (CO 18:156-57). Spangenberg agrees almost verbatim with Luther's prefatory remarks; see Spangenberg, *Der Apostel Geschichte*, A2v-A3r.

[14]WA 10,1.2:204 (Postil for the Gospel of the Fourth Sunday in Advent, John 1:19-28).

vocation today."[15] So preachers should not be deceived: this strength and power is totally unlike human or worldly strength and power. Its strength is through weakness. What we naturally think is shameful the Word often lauds as honorable; what we naturally think is honorable the Word often puts to open shame.[16] Yes, to be a faithful minister a person must reject worldly notions of success and praise, and patiently trust God to accomplish his purposes. Luther put it bluntly: "I simply taught, preached and wrote God's Word; otherwise I did nothing. And while I slept, or drank Wittenberg beer with my friends Philip and Amsdorf, the Word so greatly weakened the papacy that no prince or emperor ever inflicted such losses upon it. I did nothing; the Word did everything."[17]

Acts provided Reformation preachers and teachers an especially tantalizing opportunity to dicuss the office of the Word. According to John Donne's count there are twenty-two apostolic sermons in this book—plenty of illustrious examples of the theory and practice of preaching![18] Early modern commentators found in the preaching of the apostles models for how to distinguish and apply law (for conviction and exhortation) and gospel (for encouragement and strengthening in faith and love); how to meet the audience where they are; how to speak to the perennial concerns of life and the pressing needs of the moment. Our commentators, from their various confessions and vantage points, disagreed to varying degrees about titles and marks for the office of bishop, elder and deacon; however, they all agreed that the primary role of the preacher is *to proclaim the pure gospel of Christ by the Spirit's inspiration*. There was also bitter debate about the nature of the relationship between the roles of the human preacher and the Spirit—the magisterial reformers generally advocated careful study and preparation, while the Radicals tended toward a less mediated approach, emphasizing the Spirit's impromptu personal guidance. All the same, there was consensus that in this office through a sinful human being the congregation hears the very Word of God.[19]

The Sacrament of Baptism. In his *Babylonian Captivity of the Church* (1520), Luther had the audacity to accept only three—later, two—sacraments of the church, not seven.[20] This challenge began the almost ceaseless sixteenth-century feuding over the sacraments. The quarrels over the Eucharist and the mode of Christ's presence are still notorious, and they indeed succeeded in snuffing out any hope for Christian unity between Rome, Wittenberg, Zurich and Geneva.[21]

---

[15]Theodore Beza, *Sur l'histoire de la passion et sepulture de nostre seigneur Iesus Christ* (Geneva: Jean le Preux, 1592), 784; quoted in Scott M. Manetsch, "'The Most Despised Vocation Today': Theodore Beza's Theology of Pastoral Ministry," in *Théodore de Bèze (1519–1605): Actes du colloque de Gèneve, Septembre 2005*, ed. Irena Backus (Geneva: Droz, 2007), 244.

[16]WA 10,1.1:6-7.

[17]LW 51:77 (WA 10,3:18-19).

[18]Donne, *Works*, 6:225.

[19]Anne T. Thayer, "Preaching and Worship," in *T & T Clark Companion to Reformation Theology*, ed. David M. Whitford (London: T & T Clark, 2012), 161-63.

[20]At first Luther includes penance as a sacrament (LW 36:18; WA 6:501), but then in his concluding remarks he changes his mind because it "lacks the divinely instituted visible sign" (LW 36:124; WA 6:572).

[21]Through the Consensus Tigurinus (1549), Zurich and Geneva came to agreement over the Eucharist—although Calvin forfeited a great deal in the interest of this unity. For a concise summary of this event, see Bruce Gordon, *Calvin* (New Haven, CT: Yale University Press, 2009), 179-80. For a detailed and contextualized treatment, see Paul Rorem, "Calvin and Bullinger on the Lord's Supper, Part II: The Agreement," *Lutheran Quarterly* 2, no. 3 (1988): 357-89. Gordon understands Calvin to have forfeited the negotiations to Bullinger, allowing him "to dictate the terms" (179). Rorem is more nuanced, but agrees that Calvin deftly achieved a unity of appearances by omitting his teaching on the sacraments as a means of grace (379, 383).

However, the debates over baptism are much more pronounced in their Acts commentaries. The divergence concerning the sacrament of baptism, particularly as administered to infants, was often seen as far more insidious than the variety in opinions on the Eucharist. So much so, in fact, that in 1526 the city of Zurich made mere association with this denial—just being present at such a sermon!—punishable by death. They made good on their promise within the year.[22]

Baptism had always been understood as the doorway into the church (and, in most of European history, the entrance into legitimate society). The medieval church, following long-established tradition, taught that it was fitting and right to administer baptism to infants of believers.[23] Faith was intimately connected with the grace conveyed at baptism.[24] So much so, in fact, that "It would be against all reason," Johann Eck argued, "that the grace of God dwells in the child but not faith! For since faith is the substance and foundation of spiritual edification, how can grace and love exist without the foundation of faith?"[25] In order for the faith signified and granted in baptism to blossom, however, instruction in the church's faith and participation in its life are absolutely necessary.[26] The *Glossa ordinaria*, for example—the premier biblical commentary at the time—adds this disclaimer to 1 Peter 3:21 ("baptism now saves you"): "It is insufficient for a baptized person [merely] to have a good conscience if, under examination by the church, he does not demonstrate his faith."[27]

Luther, arguably the most conservative reformer, largely agreed with medieval baptismal theology. He complained rather that the medieval church had neglected to instruct believers about this sacrament.[28] After the first Saxon church visitations in 1528, Luther realized that the ignorance of pastors and parishioners was worse than he had previously thought, motivating him to write the *Small* and *Large Catechisms*.[29] In his catechisms, Luther makes clear that in baptism water and Word are brought together, visibly granting the promise of divine salvation in Jesus Christ.[30] Of course, the baptismal promise would not benefit the believer if the promise were not believed. "Unless faith is present or is conferred in baptism, baptism will profit us nothing. . . .

---

[22]George H. Williams, *The Radical Reformation*, 3rd ed. (Kirksville, MO: Sixteenth Century Journal Publishers, 1992), 241-42. Luther lamented the reports of Anabaptist execution, saying that false faith should be confronted with Scripture, not fire (LW 40:230; WA 26:145-46). Calvin advocated a more nuanced stance toward the Anabaptists. Against the political leaders of the Swiss Confederation in Bern, he promoted dialogue before punishment, hoping to win back the Anabaptists to Genevan orthodoxy. Still, he was not unopposed to punishment, particularly against insolent and stubborn individuals. See Willem Balke, *Calvin and the Anabaptist Radicals*, trans. William J. Heynen (Grand Rapids: Eerdmans, 1981), esp. 171-83 and 196-97.

[23]For the relationship between baptism and salvation, see *The Catechism of the Council of Trent*, trans. J. Donovan (Baltimore: F. Lucas, 1829), 107, 123, 132-33; for the other effects of baptism see 126-33.

[24]For the distinguishable but inseparable nature of baptism and faith, see *The Catechism of the Council of Trent*, 19-20, 124, 126.

[25]Johann Eck, *Christenliche Predigten*, 5 vols. (Ingolstadt: Apian, 1530–1539), 4:21r. In fact, to begin the baptismal ritual the priest would ask what the individual wanted from the church, and the godparents, on behalf of the child, would respond "faith." Susan C. Karant-Nunn, *The Reformation of Ritual: An Interpretation of Early Modern Germany* (London and New York: Routledge, 1997), 43-50, here 44.

[26]*Catechism of the Council of Trent*, 124-25.

[27]*Bibliorum Sacrorum cum Glossa Ordinaria*, 6 vols. (Venice: Iuntus, 1603), 6:1333-34.

[28]BoC 456 (WA 30,1:212).

[29]For example, during this tour Philipp Melanchthon asked a pastor how teaching the Ten Commandments was going. His answer: "I don't have that book yet." See Susan C. Karant-Nunn, *Luther's Pastors: The Reformation in the Ernestine Countryside* (Philadelphia: American Philosophical Society, 1979), 17.

[30]BoC 359-60, 456-62 (WA 30,1:309-15, 212-18).

No sin can condemn someone save unbelief alone."[31] In any case, the Word of God is efficacious: "it is not the treasure that is lacking; rather, what is lacking is that it should be grasped and held firmly."[32] Luther turned to the reality promised in baptism throughout his life, almost at every step. He encouraged people to wake up in the morning and, before anything else, cross themselves, thus remembering their baptism.[33] Throughout his career he appealed to this promise and held it out to others. So for Luther the Anabaptist rejection of paedobaptism was a rejection not of ceremony but of assurance—that God is indeed good and loving, faithful to the promises he makes in baptism.

For many soon-to-be Anabaptists the concepts presented in Zwingli's sacramental teachings were likely fundamental to their approval of the discontinuity between believers' baptism and traditional views. In 1525, Zwingli wrote a tract that he hoped would settle once and for all what the biblical doctrine of baptism is, in which he admitted that it had been quite some time since the church had properly understood this sacrament: "In baptism—may everyone forgive me!—I am unable to conclude anything other than that every teacher since the time of the apostles has erred quite significantly."[34] In Zwingli's opinion, the church had long improperly comingled the sign and the thing signified. The sign is only a representation, a reminder; it has no power but to represent, like military insignia on a uniform.

> Now before we begin to talk about baptism, we must indicate what this word *sacrament* means. We Germans imagine, that when we hear this word *sacrament*, it means a thing that removes sin from us or makes us holy. This, however, is a grievous error. Nothing is able to remove sin or to make us Christians holy other than Christ Jesus alone, not some external thing! . . . *Sacramentum*, as it is used here, means a sign of duty. As when someone sews a white cross on his [clothes], he indicates that he is Swiss [*Eydgnoß*]. . . . Now whoever enters himself into baptism wants to listen to what God says to him, to learn [God's] commands and to direct his life accordingly.[35]

Here we seem to have in germ the assumptions that inform the Radical approach to baptism. In contrast to Luther's emphasis on what God does in baptism, for Zwingli, the function of baptism is more about *our* witnessing to *others* about God's promises.[36] Still, for Zwingli, baptism is a communal event akin to circumcision and thus can be applied to infants, but it does not grant faith, nor even remove sins.[37]

Calvin tried to find a way to hold together the teachings of Luther and Zwingli on baptism,

---

[31]LW 36:59, 60* (WA 6:527, 529).

[32]BoC 461 (WA 30,1:217).

[33]BoC 362 (WA 30,1:318-21); cf. the story of a brave doctor who remembered his baptism and tore out of the wall a goat horn with which the devil meant to torment him, LW 22:356-58 (WA 47:81-83).

[34]ZSW 4:216; cf. LCC 24:130.

[35]ZSW 4:217-28; cf. LCC 24:131. Bryan Spinks argues that Zwingli's idiosyncratic understanding of *sacramentum* is a result of his emphasis on constraining the meaning of that vast and ambiguous Latin word to a military oath. See Bryan Spinks, "The Sacraments," in *T & T Clark Companion to Reformation Theology*, 126.

[36]George, *The Theology of the Reformers*, 140.

[37]Ibid., 140-42.

asserting it is "first, to serve our faith before [God]; second, to serve our confession before others."[38] Baptism is indeed a sign, but it is not an empty sign. Thus,

> they who regarded baptism as nothing but a token and mark by which we confess our religion before humans, as soldiers bear the insignia of their commander as a mark of the profession, have not weighed what was the chief point of baptism. It is to receive baptism with this promise: "Whoever believes and is baptized will be saved."[39]

The water in and of itself does not do this, but Christ's blood; the water is the means through which the Spirit applies the promises of God to all and seals Christ's benefits to the elect. United with Christ in baptism, sustained by the Word through his Spirit, Christians are daily to contemplate the cleansing blood of Christ and to participate in the new life granted through this fellowship.[40] Calvin did not deny that infants might have faith, but he also built a case for paedobaptism by connecting circumcision, the sacrament of initiation in the old covenant, to baptism. Surely baptism and its benefits must be *at least* as good as circumcision![41] Theologically and pastorally, paedobaptists approached baptism primarily as a merciful and mysterious condescension of the Holy Trinity, the Father incorporating his children into Christ by the Spirit through faith.

Radicals based their rejection of infant baptism on a more strictly literal scriptural hermeneutic, especially as applied to the New Testament.[42] For example, Michael Sattler, followed by other Radicals, combed the Scriptures for a specific baptismal blueprint applicable to every occurrence of baptism in the New Testament.[43] They were attentive to the text itself, not wanting to cloud the clear and pure Word with human traditions and teachings. This baptismal blueprint followed the order of *first* instruction, *then* belief and *lastly* baptism.[44] This sequential formula became, like paedobaptism for their opponents, a basic commitment that was argued from more often than argued to.[45]

---

[38]LCC 21:1304* (CO 2:962); *Institutes* 4.15.1. Spinks, "The Sacraments," 131. Anthony Lane makes a similar observation about how Calvin tried (un)successfully to strike a balance between Luther and Zwingli on the Eucharist. Lane's interesting conclusion is that Calvin was torn between his heart, which was "more Lutheran," and his head, which was "more Zwinglian . . . than he wished or was prepared to admit" (41). See Anthony N. S. Lane, "Was Calvin a Crypto-Zwinglian?" in *Adaptations of Calvinism in Reformation Europe: Essays in Honour of Brian G. Armstrong*, ed. Mack P. Holt (Aldershot, UK: Ashgate, 2007), 21-41.

[39]LCC 21:1304* (CO 2:962); *Institutes* 4.15.1; alluding to Mk 16:16.

[40]LCC 21:1307-8; 1325 (CO 2:965, 977); *Institutes* 4.15.6; 4.16.2.

[41]LCC 21:1327 (CO 2:978-79); *Institutes* 4.16.4. For a succinct and helpful treatment of Calvin and baptism, see Wim Janse, "The Sacraments," in *The Calvin Handbook*, ed. Herman J. Selderhuis (Grand Rapids: Eerdmans, 2009), 344-55, esp. 348-50. See further Karen E. Spierling, *Infant Baptism in Reformation Geneva: The Shaping of a Community, 1536–1564* (Aldershot, UK: Ashgate, 2005; reprint, Louisville, KY: Westminster John Knox, 2009).

[42]George, *Theology of the Reformers*, 274; Williams, *Radical Reformation*, 1255-60.

[43]See, for example, Michael Sattler, "How Scripture Should Be Discerningly Exposited," in CRR 1:150-77. Grammatically, Anabaptists always assumed the conjunction *and* (Gk., *kai*) to be sequential in the New Testament. Their magisterial counterparts understood this conjunction in a more complex fashion depending on the grammatical habitat: sometimes *and* is indeed sequential; however, in the texts concerning baptism paedobaptists tend to exegete *and* as a hendiadys, that is, as a whole rather than divisible and separable parts. For paedobaptists, preaching, faith and baptism are *distinguishable but inseparable*. For this phrase, see J. Todd Billings, *Calvin, Participation, and the Gift: The Activity of Believers in Union with Christ* (Oxford: Oxford University Press, 2007), e.g., 15. Billings applies this "inseparable but distinguishable" language to Calvin's teaching on the *duplex gratia* of justification and sanctification.

[44]See above, general introduction, xxii-xxiii.

[45]For example, Leonhard Schiemer interprets Matthew 28:19 in this way: "Christ sends his disciples, first to teach, second to bring to faith, and third—thereafter—to baptize." He goes on to say that anyone who acts otherwise is like a person who shoots blindly

---

Anabaptists were frequently incensed by what they considered to be moral laxity among the magisterial Protestants. They argued from the epistle of James (Jas 2:14-26) that works necessarily affirm and testify to saving faith; without the evidence of love Anabaptists were unwilling to allow someone to assert through baptism that they were Spirit-filled. Of course, this too comes back to what baptism *is*. Luther asserted that baptism as God's word of promise requires no human aid to be effective. Faith adds nothing to baptism (or the Eucharist for that matter!); faith *receives* the abundance and blessing of the sacrament. In contrast to paedobaptists, Anabaptists thought of baptism primarily as a believer's faithful, Spirit-enabled response to the good news offered by the Triune God and embraced by faith.

Thus Anabaptists were often motivated by somewhat different soteriological concerns—since baptism is primarily an expression of personal faith and commitment, an authentic baptism needs to *follow* a clear, personal experience of saving faith.[46] Because believers must choose to accept God's grace through faith and repentance, without faith baptism is invalid, not merely unfulfilled. Describing the quite typical Radical exposition of Menno Simons along these lines, Timothy George remarks that he "tried to strike a balance between the 'works righteousness' of medieval Catholic soteriology and the theological determinism of the mainline Protestants."[47] Grace indeed, but by "my own choice."[48]

The Community of Goods. Due to technological advances in various sectors, Europe's economy began to flourish in many locales during the late Middle Ages.[49] New markets were carved out; old markets were revitalized and expanded. In particular the increased ease and efficiency of silver mining propelled early modern European society to a more homogeneous currency market. As the barter economy dwindled, economic transactions had the potential to become more and more about making money rather than supporting families or communities. Brad Gregory summarizes the danger pointedly: "An absent maker or merchant did not have to look a buyer in the eyes—only a seller did."[50] In this atmosphere, profiteering blossomed, resulting in new opportunities for wealth and new forms of poverty.[51] In a European cultural context where the baptized membership of the institutional church was more or less coextensive with the broader civil society, ministers had to learn to deal with these new opportunities and challenges as well.

The medieval church had taught that "lowliness—not cleanliness—was next to godliness."[52]

---

and then turns to their neighbor to inquire where the target is. See CRR 12:259 (QGT 17:336), and Walpot's comment, QGT 12:65.

[46]George, *Theology of the Reformers*, 265.

[47]Ibid., 271.

[48]Ibid., 271-72. The irony of this cleavage is that in *The Babylonian Captivity*, Luther praised and thanked God that he had "preserved in his church this sacrament, untouched and untainted by human ordinances" (LW 36:57*; WA 6:526). He was nonetheless unsurprised when attacks against infant baptism surfaced. In response to a request for advice on how to respond to Radicals, Luther wrote: "I have been waiting for Satan to attack this sensitive spot—but he decided not to make use of the papists. Now he is making efforts in and among us Evangelicals to produce the worst conceivable schism. May Christ quickly trample him under his feet" (LW 48:371-72; WABr 2:427); quoted in Heiko A. Oberman, *Luther: Man Between God and the Devil*, trans. Eileen Walliser-Schwarzbart (New Haven, CT: Yale University Press, 2006), 229-30.

[49]This paragraph is reliant on Carter Lindberg, *The European Reformations*, 2nd ed. (Malden, MA: Wiley-Blackwell, 2010), 36-40.

[50]Brad S. Gregory, *The Unintended Reformation* (Cambridge, MA: Belknap Press, 2012), 244-53, here 250.

[51]Lindberg, *European Reformations*, 38.

[52]Ibid., 108-29, here 108.

This emphasis on care for the poor, ironically, often worsened their situation. The traditional approach to almsgiving was not geared toward lifting the poor out of their squalor—after all Jesus seemed to intimate that poverty is intractable (Mt 26:11)—instead it was a sacrificial act before God that focused on the almsgiver's own salvation. The burgeoning ranks of mendicant monks further deprived needed alms from those not sworn to poverty by choice; and people were often more likely to give alms to the religious because of the meritorious implications.[53] Stories in Acts of early believers sharing their possessions served as a way to offer both commentary on the biblical text but also on the state of social welfare and poor relief in early modern Europe. As Timothy Fehler has stated, "the organization of poor relief is a point of convergence for the interests of early modern politics, religion and society," since both civil and religious leaders were concerned for the threatening problems of poverty and vagrancy.[54]

On the foundation of his theology and biblical interpretation, Luther sought to recast early modern poor relief and social welfare. Not only did he renounce the medieval glorification of poverty as a religious virtue, he "also provided a theological rationale for social welfare that was translated into legislation."[55] Seeing an organic relationship between holy worship and common welfare, Luther lobbied for expansive civic reform in Wittenberg as well as other surrounding Saxon communities. Alms-begging was banned, and a community fund was founded to support impoverished families to finance their businesses, to educate their children and even to pay for dowries.[56] Monetary distribution was governed by a committee of nobility, city council members, commoners and peasants. The seed fund was provided by discontinued church endowments and was to be maintained by free donation and graduated taxation.[57]

Calvin, too, assiduously interceded for the poor. Under his guidance deacons were recast in the mold of the Lukan exemplar (Acts 6:1-6). The medieval diaconate had undergone a metamorphosis from caring for the poor and infirm to reading the Gospel and epistle texts for Mass, and occasionally preaching and distributing the host—almost a priestly apprenticeship.[58] Under Calvin's direction, deacons were now charged with taking care of the sick, exiles, widows and orphans; they purchased necessities, kept records and found employment. The *bourse Française*—a fund

---

[53]Carter Lindberg, "Sanctification, Works, and Social Justice," in *T & T Clark Companion to Reformation Theology*, 113-14.

[54]Timothy G. Fehler, *Poor Relief and Protestantism* (Aldershot, UK: Ashgate, 1999), 4.

[55]Lindberg, *European Reformations*, 109.

[56]Ibid., 115. The community was encouraged to help those specifically who were in need due to involuntary circumstance. "No men or women beggars shall be tolerated in our parish . . . since anyone not incapacitated by reason of age or illness shall work. . . . But those among us who are impoverished by force of circumstances, or are unable to work because of old age or illness, shall be supported in suitable fashion by the ten officials out of our common chest." See "Ordinance of a Common Chest," LW 45:169-94, here 186 (WA 12:11-30, here 123).

[57]Lindberg, *European Reformations*, 115-17.

[58]Karant-Nunn, *Luther's Pastors*, 7. The deacon was apparently not ordained for administering baptism or presiding over a marriage. Peter Dykema has noted that few priests attended university; they were mentored by experienced clergy. Peter A. Dykema, "Handbook for Pastors: Late Medieval Manuals for Parish Priests and Conrad Porta's *Pastorale Lutheri* (1582)," in *Continuity and Change: The Harvest of Late Medieval and Reformation History: Essays Presented to Heiko A. Oberman on His 70th Birthday*, ed. Robert J. Bast and Andrew C. Gow (Leiden: Brill, 2000), 151. Deacons also were expected to uphold clerical celibacy, though some questioned their status as clergy, leaving them in a sort of ministerial limbo between laity and clergy. See LW 36:15n18 (WA 6:499); LW 45:28 (WA 10,2:285).

pooled together from wealthy French donors—provided assistance and services for immigrants and refugees, such as those whom Geneva's *Hôpital générale* wold not be able (or obliged) to handle.[59] Geneva's Company of Pastors preached against business fraud, usury and the abuse of the poor—not to mention numerous other public sins. Not only this, but through the Consistory Calvin's clergy were able to punish such behavior. Due to their perceived deleterious effects on Geneva's social and moral fabric, price gouging, usury and other unscrupulous economic practices required public confession before the congregation as part of restitution to return to good standing in the community.[60]

While the magisterial reformers attempted to rectify the social welfare system, their attempts at "social engineering" were not nearly so drastic as those of the Radicals. Equally disappointed with the rampant abuse of the old medieval system as with the poor actualization of Protestant faith failing to work itself out in love sufficiently, Radicals strove to establish a new community life based directly on Jesus' teaching and the example of the church in Acts, so that socioeconomic injustice would be extinguished.[61] For the Anabaptists, "salvation was inseparable from economic realities"; how a person spends, earns and shares wealth reveals their faith in and relationship with Jesus Christ.[62] Still, across the various strands of Anabaptism, there was great variance in what this new society should look like. Pilgram Marpeck and his followers emphasized union with Christ first and foremost; flowing out of this relationship, believers will freely give to and care for those in need.[63] Menno Simons conceded that honest merchants and retailers could be found, though he believed they faced the persistent and dangerous prospect of sinking, often unavoidably, into greed.[64] For the Hutterites personal property is an impediment to union with Christ; no one is able to serve two masters. Instead believers must reflect the relationship of the Father and Son, sharing all property and goods, neither buying nor selling.[65] For Peter Walpot and other Hutterites, where there is individual ownership of property there can be no true church.[66]

The most extreme experiment in social revolution and enforced community of goods is found in the ill-fated kingdom of Münster (1534–1535). After Jan Matthijs (d. 1534) took control of the city, believers' baptism became a sign of allegiance to this "New Jerusalem"; those who were unwilling to submit to rebaptism—and who had not already fled—were given until March 2,

---

[59]Gordon, *Calvin*, 200-202; see further, Jeannine Olson, *Calvin and Social Welfare* (Selinsgrove, PA: Susquehanna University Press, 1989).

[60]Scott Manetsch, *Calvin's Company of Pastors: Pastoral Care and the Emerging Reformed Church, 1536-1609* (Oxford: Oxford University Press, 2012), 193-95. Calvin, in solidarity with the Genevan city magistrates, did allow for interest up to five percent. See W. Fred Graham, *The Constructive Revolutionary: John Calvin and His Socio-Economic Impact* (Richmond, VA: John Knox Press, 1971), 116-27.

[61]Arnold Snyder, "Anabaptist Spirituality and Economics," in *Anabaptist/Mennonite Faith and Economics*, ed. Calvin Redekop, Victor Krahn and Samuel Steiner (Lanham, MD: University Press of America, 1994), 3-18.

[62]Gregory, *Unintended Reformation*, 264.

[63]John D. Rempel, "Introduction," in *Jörg Maler's Kunstbuch: Writings of the Pilgram Marpeck Circle*, ed. John D. Rempel, Classics of the Radical Reformation 12 (Kitchener, ON: Pandora Press, 2010), 11-12.

[64]Snyder, "Anabaptist Spirituality and Economics," 8.

[65]Thomas N. Finger, *A Contemporary Anabaptist Theology: Biblical, Historical, Constructive* (Downers Grove, IL: InterVarsity Press, 2004), 237-39; Snyder, "Anabaptist Spirituality and Economics," 7.

[66]QGT 12:184. See further Finger, *Contemporary Anabaptist Theology*, 235-43.

1534, to leave, after which they were to be either forcibly rebaptized or slaughtered.[67] Matthijs destroyed church towers in the city, rebranding the churches "stone pits." He razed the library (sparing only the Bible) and instituted a militaristic-communal civil society. Meals were shared among these "Israelites" in public squares. Families were still allowed to keep their homes, but, since these buildings were now common property, the doors had to be open at all times.[68] Jan Beukels (d. 1536) anointed himself as prophet-king of Münster after Matthijs's death. Beukels intensified Matthijs's program, instituting polygamy and punishing sin (of all sorts) with capital punishment.[69] In June 1535, a coalition of Catholic and Protestant forces defeated Beukels, slaying almost every citizen left in Münster. Beukels and his chief lieutenants were publicly tortured with red-hot tongs and suspended in iron cages from the cathedral tower.[70] This quite anomalous fiasco nonetheless deeply tinted the magisterial reformers' conception of Anabaptism.

The magisterial reformers resisted such social revolution, even when it was much less extreme and even nonviolent by conviction. To legislate charity would be to coerce believers into generosity; this, for reformers like Luther and Calvin, is a contradiction that actually extinguishes love. Faith must be active in love, but neither faith nor love can be compelled. Unfortunately the arguments on either side were not always tactful. Philipp Melanchthon, for example, suggested that the "rebaptizers" were simply too lazy to work. "[Enforced community of goods] attracts that lazy rabble who do not like work and who know much better how to guzzle what they have than to earn it honestly. But that such teaching establishes pure thievery and chaos every person can understand easily."[71] Walpot on behalf of the Radicals denied this, of course, but argued in response that Melanchthon and those like him are "unchristian" to want to own goods and property or to make a profit from God's creation.[72] This exchange is especially fierce in expositions of Acts chapters 2, 4 and 11.

Suffering. Acts never strays far from the theme of suffering, but it becomes especially poignant as Paul travels toward Rome to his eventual martyrdom. Some of the suffering is caused by human anger and jealousy—false imprisonment, assault, murder—some caused by nonhuman agents—sickness, famine, shipwreck. Is God the ultimate agent behind all this suffering? If he is, why and in what sense can he be good? These questions and similar ones often come to mind as we read Luke's account of the struggling early church; Reformation commentators were also interested in such questions.

The Reformation caused a revolution in the Christian theology of suffering.[73] Late medieval piety tended to connect suffering and salvation. The Christian's "sweet" suffering to a degree pre-

---

[67]Williams, *Radical Reformation*, 564; Lindberg, *European Reformations*, 208.

[68]Williams, *Radical Reformation*, 566.

[69]After one of his many wives questioned his authority, he beheaded her and "trampled on her body while the rest of his harem looked on" (Williams, *Radical Reformation*, 581-82).

[70]For a lively historical account, see Williams, *Radical Reformation*, 561-82.

[71]Philip Melanchthon, *Verlegung etlicher unchristlicher Artikel: Welcher die Widerteuffer furbegen* (Wittenberg: Georg Rhau, 1543), C3r.

[72]QGT 12:231-32.

[73]Ronald K. Rittgers, *The Reformation of Suffering: Pastoral Theology and Lay Piety in Late Medieval and Early Modern Germany* (Oxford: Oxford University Press, 2012).

paid on future discipline in purgatory (connected to penance) and brought the believer into closer union with Christ, the Suffering Servant.[74] Like the exaltation of poverty discussed earlier, rather than ameliorating Christians' experience of suffering, this exaltation of common Christian misery could often exacerbate it. Some might well worry they were not suffering enough; others might feel God to be distant or hateful.[75] Luther saw this as the sure result of considering the reality of suffering through reason instead of revelation.[76] Suffering and persecution were not abstract ideas for the reformers (any more so than their medieval forebears). They and their communities were intimately connected to suffering in both mind and body, whether chronic illnesses, insufficient remedies, stillbirths or torture. They believed that human beings are the *objects* of medicine; God alone is the *subject*; he ultimately chooses to allow affliction or to bring healing.

Luther and his counterparts strove instead not to present suffering itself as sweet, but the truly sweet promises of Christ to those mired in suffering—whether sick or sinful. Luther counseled that Christians should run to the Eucharist; confess their sins and receive the soothing salve of the words of absolution; enjoy fellowship with friends and preach the gospel to one another (and perhaps buy one another beer).[77] Through the means of grace and by faith the Christian is united with Christ and conformed to his image. Suffering is an opportunity for God to strengthen faith.

Some of the Radicals found Luther's new twist on Christian suffering still too "honey-sweet."[78] Surely the magisterial reformers were not helping but further harming their parishioners by telling them what they wanted to hear. The "bitter" Christ must be preached as well, since believers must experience suffering in order to have true faith. So while Luther claimed that Christ is both gift and example but must first be gift (otherwise he is no better than human saints), Thomas Müntzer argued that Christ must first be an example with whom to suffer before a Christian may taste the "sweet" Christ by faith. "Whoever is not willing to have the bitter Christ will eat himself to death with honey. . . . For whoever does not die with Christ is not able to rise again with him."[79]

As Paul makes his way slowly toward Rome through shipwreck and floggings, the apostle himself and our commentators begin to wonder whether the Lord will be faithful to his promises. Paul's encounters with local and imperial authorities (e.g., Festus and Agrippa, Acts 25–26) become an opportunity for Reformation commentators to scrutinize and discuss the proper behavior of subjects toward magistrates, and vice versa, especially in circumstances where those in authority and those under it do not claim to share the same ultimate allegiance. God himself has appointed these offices and grants "civic wisdom, tactfulness and friendliness" to those who oc-

---

[74]Ibid., 24-32, 81-82.

[75]Ibid., 118.

[76]Ibid., 118.

[77]Ibid., 121-24.

[78]Ibid., 155-61, here 157.

[79]Thomas Müntzer, "Von dem getichten glawben," in *Schriften und Briefe: Kritische Gesamtausgabe*, ed. Paul Kirn and Günther Franz (Gütersloh: Gütersloher Verlagshaus Gerd Mohn, 1968), 217-24, here 222-23. In contrast, see "A Brief Instruction on What to Look For and Expect in the Gospels," LW 35:119-21 (WA 10,1.1:10-14); for analysis, see Rittgers, *Reformation of Suffering*, 158-59.

cupy them.[80] Nevertheless, pastors are reminded that political power should not intimidate them, preventing them from fulfilling the vocation given to them by God. "Whoever is in the preaching office is commanded by God to discipline all estates, spiritual and worldly, poor and rich."[81] Certainly they should preach the good news of Christ without partiality!

At times our commentators' explication of suffering may seem too accepting of it as an unfortunate fact of life rather than actively resisting or addressing the causes of that suffering. Yet there is a constant recognition that God, in Christ, suffers with them *and* he is sovereign over that suffering.[82] "There is no cross so great, so grisly, so horrible," Johann Spangenberg asserted, "that very little good is brought with it."[83] The inverted nature of the gospel kingdom means that unintentionally or unexpectedly the persecution and destruction of Christians causes the church to thrive.[84] Rudolf Gwalther urges that trials and temptations are an opportunity for God to show his love and faithfulness to his people.[85]

The Company of Commentators

Incorporating recent developments in Reformation studies, this volume reflects the expanding boundaries of what is considered Reformation exegesis and theology to include reform-minded Catholics and Radicals as well as magisterial Protestants.[86] The **Lutheran** commentators in this volume consistently apply a strongly christological hermeneutic in their exegesis of Acts. These pastors and theologians affirm that Scripture is factual and historical and treat it as such, but emphasize its existential import as the living and active Word that by the Spirit creates and strengthens faith, dispels sin and doubt, justifies the ungodly and fosters holy love. Two authors are especially prominent: Johann Spangenberg and Martin Luther.

For thirty years Johann Spangenberg served as pastor and catechist in several Saxon congregations. He had a deep interest in parish preaching and biblical literacy, especially among children and commoners. Among numerous works, his postils were particularly popular—only Luther's surpassed his in number of editions—so much so that a Franciscan purged overt anti-Catholic statements, and published these postils under his own name, Johannes Craendonch.[87] The postil

---

[80]Spangenberg, *Der Apostel Geschichte*, 178v-179r.

[81]Ibid., 209v.

[82]Rittgers, *Reformation of Suffering*, 257-63, here 260-61.

[83]Spangenberg, *Der Apostel Geschichte*, 99v. Donne similarly reminds his hearers that the Lord's ways are not our ways, and he is indeed capable of striking with a bruised reed: "that all their spitting should but macerate him, and dissolve him into a better mould, a better plaster; that all their beatings should but knead him and press him into a better form. All their scoffing and insolence should be prophecies. 'Behold your King' and 'This is the king of the Jews,' these words—those who spoke them thought to be lies—in their own mouths should become truths. He truly is the king, not only of the Jews but of all nations, too. Their nailing him on the cross should be a settling of him on an everlasting throne" (Donne, *Works*, 1:315).

[84]Our Reformation commentators wholeheartedly agreed with Tertullian's famous phase: "Christian blood is the seed of the church" (Tertullian, *Apology*, ANF 3:55).

[85]Gwalther, *Homelyes or Sermons upon the Actes*, 832* (In Acta Apostolorum, 258r).

[86]David Bagchi and David Steinmetz, "Introduction: The Scope of Reformation Theology," in *The Cambridge Companion to Reformation Theology*, ed. David Bagchi and David C. Steinmetz (Cambridge University Press, 2004), 1-4, here 2.

[87]Very little is known about Craendonch; see John M. Frymire, *The Primacy of the Postils: Catholics, Protestants, and the Dissemination of Ideas in Early Modern Germany* (Leiden: Brill, 2010), 277n78, 478.

is an amorphous genre. It could be a collection of actual sermons to be preached by inexperienced and untrained pastors, or an accessible running commentary on the lectionary readings for the church year.[88] Spangenberg's fit well in the latter category.[89] In the dedication for his first volume of the *Postilla Teütsch*, he states:

> I have taken the Sunday Gospel readings, from Advent to Easter, out of the postils of our dear father, Dr. Martin, and others, like [Johannes] Brenz, [Antonius] Corvinus, etc., setting these readings in question-answer form for the daily edification of young Christians, both boys and girls.[90]

In this way Spangenberg's postils function as a digest of leading Lutheran exegesis and pastoral application. His postil on Acts was published in 1545.

Luther is known best for his revolutionary commentaries and sharp polemics. However, in a typical week, Luther was just as likely to be heard behind the pulpit at St. Mary's (or a church he was visiting) as behind the lectern at Wittenberg. There are extant notes or transcriptions of over two thousand sermons, not to mention the nine volumes of postils (probably the reason so few Luther scholars have focused on this genre!). We have included excerpts from both his own self-edited postils and postils consisting of revised sermon transcripts edited by Luther's colleagues, which he either disparaged (Stephan Roth's), or praised highly (Caspar Cruciger's).[91] Cruciger's editing is certainly true to Luther's theology, though the reformer's language has been "improved and augmented."[92] While such redactions cause headaches for some forms of scholarship, it matters less for the goals of the Reformation Commentary on Scripture.[93] We have also included transcriptions of Luther's sermons. Because of his comingling of theology, polemics, exegesis and exhortation, it is difficult to generalize about the "typical" Luther sermon.[94] Certainly

---

[88]For the medieval lectionary appended to the Luther Bible, see WADB 7:536-44. Johann Eck's postils are an example of the former; Luther's self-edited postils are an example of the latter. The Gospel selections from his Christmas postil can be found in English translation in LW 52. Concordia Publishing House will augment its expansion of *Luther's Works* with eight volumes of Luther's postils: five volumes (LW 75-79) for Luther's self-edited *Christmas, Advent* and *Lenten Postils* (WA 10,1.1; 10,1.2:1-208; 17,2:1-247) and the *Summer Postil*, edited by Caspar Cruciger (WA 21:195-551; 22), and three volumes (LW 80-82) for the *House Postil*, edited by Veit Dietrich (WA 52). Luther penned one Lenten postil in Latin in 1521, which will not be included in the LW; see WA 7:463-537. For an excellent study of postils in early modern Germany, see Frymire, *Primacy of the Postils*.

[89]Johann Spangenberg, *Postilla Teütsch: Für die iungen Christen Knaben und Meidlein in Fragstuck verfasset Vom Aduendt biß auff Ostern* (Augsburg: Valentein Othmar, 1543); *Postilla Teütsch: Für die jungen Christen Knaben und Meidlein in Fragstuck verfasset Von Ostern biß auff das Aduendt* (Augsburg: Valentein Othmar, 1543); *Postilla Teütsch: Für die jungen Christen Knaben und Meidlin in Fragstuck verfasset Von den fürnemsten Festen durch das gantze Jar* (Augsburg: Valentein Othmar, 1544); [*Postilla Teütsch:*] *Auslegung der Episteln, so auff die Sonntage vom Advent biß auff Ostern in der Kirchen gelesen werden* (Magdeburg: Michael Lotter, 1544); [*Postilla Teütsch:*] *Auslegung der Episteln, so auff die Sonntage von Ostern biß auff das Advent in der Kirchen gelesen werden* (Augsburg: Valentein Othmar, 1545); and [*Postilla Teütsch:*] *Auslegung der Episteln, so auff die fürnemeste Feste in der Kirchen gelesen werden* (Nürnberg: Hans Daubmann, 1550).

[90]Johann Spangenberg, *Postilla Teütsch für die jungen Christen Knaben und Meidlein in Fragstuck verfasset Vom Aduendt biß auff Ostern* (Augsburg: Valentein Othmar, 1543), iii-v.

[91]"You have a much higher opinion (*honorificentius sentis*) of [Roth's] postil than I. For I want that entire book torn to shreds (*extinctum*). And I am setting this in motion by charging Dr. Caspar Cruciger with bringing the entire [book] into a new and better form, which the whole church everywhere can use." WABr 7:328-29. For Roth's postils, see WA 10,1.2:209-441; 17,2:249-516; WA 21:1-193; for Cruciger's, see above note 88.

[92]WA 21:201; cf. WATR 5:41, no. 5275.

[93]For the four goals of the RCS, see above xix-xxi.

[94]Eberhard Winkler, "Luther als Seelsorger und Prediger," in *Leben und Werk Martin Luthers von 1526 bis 1546: Festgabe zu seinem 500. Geburtstag*, ed. Helmar Junghans (Göttingen: Vandenhoeck & Ruprecht, 1983), 236-37. See also Fred W. Meuser, "Luther as

---

the main point of all his sermons is the same: Christ as gift and example. Appealing to Song of Songs 1:13—"My Lord is like a bushel of myrrh that hangs between my breasts"—he warned that preachers "should always carry this bushel of myrrh, that is they should preach Christ, how he suffered. For the myrrh means the passion of Christ. Those preachers who do not preach Christ or do not carry Christ with them in their office, are not the breasts of this bride."[95]

Among *Pre-Tridentine Catholic* commentators we have made use of the erudite but fragile Desiderius Erasmus, the philologically focused Cardinal Cajetan, and Luther's nemesis at the Leipzig Disputation (1519), Johann Eck.[96] These three authors represent a cross-section of sixteenth-century biblical comment: paraphrase, commentary and sermon. Inspired by Lorenzo Valla, Erasmus published a paraphrase of the New Testament (minus John's Apocalypse). Erasmus began this project in 1517 with the Pauline Epistles, hoping to instill a profound love and appreciation for Scripture, while also clarifying the sometimes enigmatic meaning of the text. Erasmus was pleased with the acclaim his paraphrase received, even wondering if perhaps he had not chosen the wrong path by pursuing his controversial and oft-maligned critical edition of the New Testament.[97] Though Erasmus generally does not stray far from the original text in his paraphrases, they are quietly insightful, and at times he does allow himself an aside, opinion, comment or gospel bit of doxology.

In contrast to Erasmus's pastoral paraphrases, Cajetan's commentaries reflect a rigorous, almost historical-critical hermeneutic.[98] It may shock some readers that the Cardinal who pressed Luther in 1518 to recant his professedly biblical views should be so "literal" in his approach to the Bible, even more so than many Protestant commentators. Cajetan wrote commentaries in this fashion on every book in the canon, avoiding only Song of Songs and Revelation—he was uncomfortable interpreting them because they are so thoroughly allegorical or metaphoric in character. Cajetan may have brushed too closely to Protestant views on justification, resulting in the censorship of his works by the Sorbonne and later by the Council of Trent. He urged Pope Clement VII (1478–1534) to allow communion in both kinds and clerical marriage.

Probably the most surprising inclusion in this Reformation commentary is Johann Eck. Unfortunately this man has been typecast merely as Luther's vindictive opponent at Leipzig, who devoted the rest of his career to hounding Luther.[99] It can come as quite a surprise to learn that Eck was a pastor from 1519 until his death in 1543. Indeed, this adversary of the Reformation *loved*

Preacher of the Word of God," in *The Cambridge Companion to Martin Luther*, ed. Donald K. McKim (Cambridge: Cambridge University Press, 2003), 136-48; and Beth Kreitzer, "The Lutheran Sermon," in *Preachers and People in the Reformations and Early Modern Period*, ed. Larissa Taylor (Leiden: Brill, 2001), 35-63. Kreitzer asserts Luther preached verse-by-verse (43); Meuser disparages this idea (142). Perhaps the monograph that best treats Luther as preacher is Ulrich Asendorf, *Die Theologie Martin Luthers nach seinen Predigten* (Göttingen: Vandenhoeck & Ruprecht, 1988).

[95]WA 9:649-50. The verse cited is Luther's own paraphrase.

[96]Cardinal Cajetan, *Evangelia cum Commentariis* (Venice: Luccantonii, 1530); Desiderius Erasmus, *In Acta Apostolorum Paraphrasis* (Basel: J. Froben, 1524); Erasmus, *Paraphrase on the Acts of the Apostles*, ed. John J. Bateman, trans. Robert D. Sider, Collected Works of Erasmus 50 (Toronto: University of Toronto Press, 1995); and Johann Eck, *Christenliche Predigen*, 5 vols. (Ingolstadt: Apian, 1530–1539).

[97]CWE 42:xiv-xv.

[98]This paragraph is generally reliant on Jared Wicks, "Cajetan," in OER 1:233-34.

[99]For more on Eck, see Erwin Iserloh, *Johannes Eck (1486–1543): Scholastiker, Humanist, Kontroverstheologe* (Münster: Aschendorff, 1981), esp. 71-74. Also see Frymire, *Primacy of the Postils*, esp. 4-7.

to preach; he preferred it to adminstering the sacraments.[100] Eck considered both the Mass and sermon essential to the Christian life, but saw the sermon as more important since it delivers God's Word, which teaches faith.[101] Our selections, translated into English for the first time, come from Eck's five-volume postil published during the 1530s in order to supply Catholic pulpits with solid *Catholic* sermon material. Luther's postils were so popular among Catholic priests who would read them from the pulpit that Eck felt compelled to supply a homegrown alternative.[102]

While Christians of all stripes in the early modern period desired to drink deeply from the living water stored up in the Bible's ancient cisterns, the **Continental Reformed** clung perhaps most tenaciously to *sola Scriptura*. The Reformed in Geneva, for example, jettisoned all forms for worship not explicitly prescribed in the biblical witness, abandoning organ music, hymns and stained glass.[103] Along these lines, it is unsurprising that many in the Continental Reformed movement had a keen interest in the Acts of the Apostles, the clearest and most direct biblical testimony to the life, ministry, worship and witness of the very earliest churches. Among the Reformed commentators and confessions we have excerpted in this volume, two are especially prominent: that famous Frenchman, John Calvin, and the lesser-known *antistes* of Zurich, Rudolf Gwalther.

Calvin's commentary on Acts was the offspring of a sermon series he began in 1549 at the Temple of St. Gervais. Committed to the literary ideal of "lucid brevity," Calvin was somewhat embarrassed by his two thick volumes on Acts.[104] In the dedication to the second edition (1560), Calvin held up the Acts of the Apostles as a firm and steady consolation to the people of God through the sweet music of the gospel:

> If, when the heat of battle was at its greatest and fiercest, the harmonious music of pipes had so much influence on the Spartans, that it calmed the ferocity innate in that warlike people, and tempered the violence, which, on that occasion, runs riot and gets out of hand, even in people who are otherwise gentle by nature, how much better and more effectively will the Kingdom of Christ bring this about by the heavenly music of the Holy Spirit? And I say this because it not only tames savage beasts, but makes lambs out of wolves, lions and bears, because it turns spears into pruning-hooks, and makes swords into ploughshares.[105]

Despite all appearances, trials and suffering, the gospel by the Word and through the Spirit will bear the fruit of blessing and peace. For Calvin, an exile for virtually his entire career, this promise was life-sustaining.

---

[100]Iserloh, *Johannes Eck*, 73.

[101]"Know that it is far better to guide a child to the sermon than to the Mass—although you should do both. Now there is one child who hears Mass again and again until he turns fourteen years old, but he hears no sermon, and then there is another child who hears fourteen years of sermons, but no Mass; which will be a better Christian? Without a doubt the one who listens to preaching! For he knows more about faith. Faith comes from hearing, Saint Paul tells us and the Lord through Isaiah: 'My Word that goes out from my mouth will not return empty.'" Eck, *Christenliche Predigen*, 5:32r-v.; alluding to Rom 10:17; quoting Is 55:11.

[102]Frymire, *Primacy of the Postils*, 6, 54-57.

[103]See Manetsch, *Calvin's Company of Pastors*, 31-37.

[104]See T. H. L. Parker, *Calvin's New Testament Commentaries* (Grand Rapids: Eerdmans, 1971), 23-25; and Raymond Blacketer's article in *The Calvin Handbook*, ed. Herman J. Selderhuis (Grand Rapids: Eerdmans, 2009), 181-92, here 187.

[105]CNTC 6:3 (CO 18:157).

It will prove helpful to recall Calvin's theological program, as we read his biblical comment: his *Institutes* and commentaries were meant to dovetail in such a way that the written Word was clearly understood by pastors. The *Institutes* focus on theological loci, providing the necessary foundation to read Scripture *theologically*, while the commentaries, free from doctrinal asides and digressions, were to focus on the textual and historical contexts of specific passages.[106] For Calvin, to leave out either theology or the linguistic-historical context is to risk the entire exegetical enterprise.[107] In this volume, then, Calvin is an important source for the context and background of the text, while offering a somewhat more streamlined theological interpretation than can be found in his *Institutes*.

Rudolph Gwalther's numerous homilies on Acts are a regular feature throughout this volume. Gwalther, as Zurich's third Reformed *antistes* (akin to the president of the synod), dedicated his volume to the city council, emphasizing that Luke's record of the very first churches is the pristine example of the life and ministry of the body of Christ. He reminded the council that Acts is about both the Lord's providence and human responsibility, noting that they should take good stock of the patterns of Christian repentance, faith and sacramental participation through which the church is "knit together in love" (Col 2:2). In his relatively short expositions, Gwalther is attentive to the relationship between such temporal rulers and the Lord of lords. He is most often concerned, however, to bring hope in the daily spiritual and physical suffering that his congregation experiences.

Commentary on the book of Acts from the early **English Reformers** did not usually shine as brightly as that of their Continental peers. A great deal of it tended to comingle the biblical text with current issues in the complex interactions of English politics—the Spanish Match, the wisdom or folly of being ruled by a female monarch, and so on. Thus such famous examples of biblical comment as the works of Thomas Cranmer or the *Book of Homilies* are not especially relevant for a volume synthesizing Reformation comment on Acts.[108] Other English writers, like John Mayer and John Lightfoot, were more concerned with explaining or harmonizing perceived errors or contradictions in the biblical text than in elucidating the content.[109] However, we found three sources particularly fruitful: the *English Annotations* (sanctioned by the Westminster Assembly), John Donne's remarkable sermons and poetry, and the Book of Common Prayer (1549).[110]

John Downame and other unnamed colleagues edited *The English Annotations*, which collate

---

[106]Cf. LCC 20:4-5 (CO 1:255-56); and CNTC 8:1-4 (CO 10:402-6).

[107]For a helpful treatment of Calvin's exegetical method, see Randall C. Zachman, *John Calvin as Teacher, Pastor, and Theologian: The Shape of His Writings and Thoughts* (Grand Rapids: Baker Academic, 2006), 103-30. Bruce Gordon also has a good summary and synthesis of Calvin's approach to commentary-writing as seen through his dedication to the Romans commentary; see Gordon, *Calvin*, 103-20.

[108]A fair amount of John Trapp's commentary was also excluded for this local political emphasis.

[109]John Mayer, *A Commentary upon the New Testament* (London: John Bellamie, 1631), and *A Treasury of Ecclesiasticall Expositions, upon the Difficult and Doubtful Places of the Scriptures, Collected out of the Best Esteemed Interpreters, Both Anncient and Moderne, Together with the Authors Judgement, and Various Observations* (London: John Bellamie, 1622); and John Lightfoot, *A Commentary upon the Acts of the Apostles: Chronicall and Criticall* (London: Andrew Crooke, 1645).

[110]John Downame, ed., *Annotations upon all the Books of the Old and New Testament* (London: Evan Tyler, 1657); John Donne, *The Works of John Donne*, 6 vols., ed. Henry Alford (London: John Parker, 1839); Donne, *The Poems of John Donne*, ed. Herbert J. C. Grierson (Oxford: The Clarendon Press, 1912); and The Book of Common Prayer (1549), in *The Two Liturgies, AD 1549 and AD 1552*, ed. Joseph Ketley (Cambridge: Cambridge University Press, 1844), 9-158.

and make more accessible rich biblical resources such as Calvin's commentaries, Theodore Beza's technical *Annotationes majores*, and Giovanni Diodati's *Annotations*. *The English Annotations* are meant to guide the reader to understand what is written, not simply to recognize the words on the page. In the eyes of Downame and his associates, the difference can be quite serious:

> It is conceived (by some of eminent note) that if Origen had met with a sound Comment or Marginal Note upon Matth. 19.12. it might have prevented his Castration of himself, whereto he was induced, by taking (and thereby mistaking) the words in the extreamest rigour of the litteral sense.[111]

John Donne is typically remembered for his erotic poetry; however, Donne's textual corpus is an interesting amalgam of erotic *and* divine verse—in fact at times the two intersect in a provocative manner, particularly in "Batter My Heart."[112] His published works also include a great many sermons, accumulated from his regular preaching as the dean of St. Paul's Cathedral in London. They are strongly evangelical.[113] Donne tended to focus on one verse, leading his audience to dwell on the significance of the text through wordplay, quasi-poetic repetition and vivid imagery.

Finally, the collects for Sundays or feast days with Acts as an epistle reading have been included from the Book of Common Prayer. The collect is the opening prayer to "the service of the word," which consists of two scriptural readings from an Old Testament or usually a New Testament epistle and a Gospel prior to the sermon. This opening prayer is meant to make explicit the crimson thread running through the two passages, helping the congregation to concentrate on the shared theme of the texts. Sometimes these prayers connect more strongly to the namesake of the particular liturgical feast (e.g., St. Stephen's Feast).[114]

Reformation-era ***Radicals and Anabaptists*** wrote very few formal commentaries[115], and since they in large measure abandoned the lectionary as "papal dross" they also did not contribute substantively to the popular early-modern postil genre.[116] In fact, very few of the Radical reformers' works were published—instead many of them were hand-copied and circulated within small communities. There are nevertheless two kinds of Radical writings that are particularly apro-

---

[111]Downame, ed., "Preface," in *Annotations*, unpaginated. The editors' marginal notes refer the reader to the work of Eusebius (*Church History* 6.8) and Jerome (Letter [84] to Pammachius, NPNF² 6:176-81). Eusebius describes Origen's self-castration as indicative of "an immature and youthful mind" (see NPNF² 1:254-55); while Jerome sees this act as "out of a zeal for God but yet not one according to knowledge" (NPNF² 6:179).

[112]Donne, *The Poems of John Donne*, 328.

[113]For example, before setting out on a voyage with several English emissaries to Germany, he admonished his congregation to remember Christ, so that "Christ Jesus remember us all in his kingdom, to which, though we must sail through a sea, it is the sea of his blood, where no soul suffers shipwreck." Donne, *Works*, 6:32. For the context of this sermon and a comparison to "Hymne to Christ," see R. C. Bald, *John Donne: A Life* (Oxford: Oxford University Press, 1970), 7-9.

[114]These collects stand in strong continuity with the medieval Catholic tradition. Like Luther, Cranmer and the later editors of the Book of Common Prayer basically translated the collects from the Latin Mass into the vernacular, elliding any invocations to the saints or to the Blessed Virgin. Also, Acts was not nearly as prominent in the medieval lectionary as it is in the Revised Common Lectionary, which substitutes Acts for Old Testament readings during the Easter Season.

[115]There are, of course, exceptions; see above, general introduction, xxxix-xl.

[116]Surprisingly, there were some Radicals who still interacted with the lectionary, likely, as John Frymire postulates, because they were in Lutheran or Catholic lands where the lectionary still held great importance. See Frymire, *Primacy of the Postils*, 513n4, 514n6.

pos for this volume: so-called article books and confessions of faith. Both genres are focused on catechizing the faithful in the tenets of the community's shared beliefs, and both are generally ordered around theological loci. Article books tend to be organized around the sacraments, the community of goods, the use of the sword, and divorce, while the confessions (like their counterparts among other confessional traditions) tend to follow the order of the Apostles' Creed.

The majority of the Radical selections are from Dirk Philips's *Enchiridion*, Peter Walpot's *Great Article Book*, and Peter Riedemann's *Confession of Faith*, each crafted to help Christians wade through the sticky process of applying Scripture to real life by making crystal clear the chief tenets of the faith. There are also numerous passages from the *Kunstbuch*—rediscovered in 1956—a devotional work punctuated by interludes of praise and prayer centered on the theme of the church as Christ incarnate.

Before we continue on to the commentary proper, two caveats need to be offered. First, the Greek text of the Acts of the Apostles has an uncommonly high rate of textual variants.[117] This stems from differences in the two branches of Acts's textual family tree: the "Alexandrian" and "Western" text-types.[118] Reformation exegetes, by and large, were working with Erasmus's *Novum Instrumentum* and the Latin Vulgate. Both of these resources privilege the Western text-type (in large part because it was all that was available).[119] The most important differences between these two branches is that the Western text is longer and more polished—generally it is assumed that the copyists over the years attempted to clear up ambiguities in language or meaning. Most English translations in current use, however—except the KJV and NKJV—are based more on the Alexandrian witnesses. For our purposes, this means that the reformers are often working with a text that is slightly different than ours. In general we have pointed out these discrepancies in the notes, particularly when it is as noticeable as the presence of commentary on an entire verse missing from many modern Bibles (e.g., Acts 8:37).

Second, because early modern exegetes largely considered the sermons of Acts to be intelligible on their own terms, their comment begins to thin out as the chapters go on, especially after the Jerusalem Council (Acts 15). Aside from Calvin—who kept a steady pace from beginning to end—very few of our commentators give the same amount of attention to the latter half of Acts that they give to earlier chapters.

---

[117]Most modern commentators address this "base text" issue in their prolegomena; see especially Richard I. Pervo, *Acts* (Minneapolis: Fortress, 2009), 1-5, and Jaroslav Pelikan, *Acts* (Grand Rapids: Brazos, 2003), 32-34. Pelikan privileges the Western witness, calling it the "text accepted by [the] church fathers" (33). While sympathetic with Pelikan's motive, C. Kavin Rowe and Richard B. Hays criticize this choice as a "rejection of the consensus findings of New Testament textual criticism" (C. Kavin Rowe and Richard B. Hays, "What Is a Theological Commentary?" *Pro Ecclesia* 16, no. 1 [2007]: 26-32, here 28). Of course, this may have partially motivated Pelikan's decision.

[118]For a description of the various text-types, see Bruce M. Metzger, *The Text of the New Testament: Its Transmission, Corruption, and Restoration*, 3rd ed. (Oxford: Oxford University Press, 1992), 213-16. There is quibbling over the names for text-types; the adjective *so-called* occurs often in contemporary discussions.

[119]Erasmus worked on his critical edition of the New Testament from 1516, when it was first published, until the end of his life. In the four editions after 1516, he altered the title to *Novum Testamentum* (1519, 1522, 1527, 1535).

❖   ❖   ❖

In the contemporary world, historic Christian centers in Western Europe and North America dwindle, while those in Africa, Latin and South America, and Asia swell. In this globalization of the church, we are more aware than ever of the seemingly impossible demands of the Vincentian Canon: "Now in the Catholic Church itself we take the greatest care to hold *that which has been believed everywhere, always and by all.*"[120] For preachers, teachers and researchers who have tried to present the temporally and spatially expansive character of Christianity, the simple question of where to begin is already problematic. The earliest disciples? The waves of persecution and subsequent martyrdoms? The ecumenical councils? Often our current situations—whether in a culture hostile to Christian faith or in one quite familiar with Christian mores (though not necessarily faith)—will dictate different starting points.

Still, the Acts of the Apostles makes for a compelling beginning. Through Jesus' death, resurrection and ascension, God is now present with his people in a revolutionary new way through his indwelling Spirit (though presaged by the prophets, Acts 2:16-33). In the power of this Spirit believers are to preach the word of the risen Lord in Jerusalem, Judea, Samaria and to the ends of the earth (Acts 1:8). And as is so often the case, the Triune God proves too controversial for his people: he couldn't have really meant to include Gentiles, right? Much of Acts—like the history of Christianity—is a case study in how the people of God accept or reject the radical inclusivity of the Lord's purposes—his radically good news for *all* sinners—through the *one* person, Jesus of Nazareth.

Esther Chung-Kim
Todd R. Hains

---

[120]Henry Bettenson and Chris Maunder, eds., *Documents of the Christian Church*, 3rd ed. (Oxford: Oxford University Press, 1999), 91-93, here 92, emphasis original.

WEST.

44
43
42
41
40
39
38
37
36
35
34
33
32
31
30

Illyria, or Sclauonia.

The sea.

THE SEA ADRIATIKE.

Macedonia.

ITALIE

ROMA

PVTEOL

PHILIPPI　NEAPOLIS

AMPHIPOLIS

APOLLONIA

THESSALS　SAMO

THRAC

BEROE

TROAS

ASOS

MYS

RHEG

LESBOS

ANT

ASIA

Sicilia.

CHIOS

EPHES

GRECIA

MILET

SIRAGVSE

ATHENE

SAMOS

MYRA

CENCHREA

HAVEN

COOS

LI

CIA

PA

ACHAIA

CORINT

GNID

RHODES

HAVEN

PHENIX

FAIRE

HAVENS

MALTA

CLAVDA

CRETA

THE SEA MEDITERRAN.

The great gulffe.

Part of Affrica
toward Cyrene.

EGY

Pontike.

The sea Hircan.

onteus Bythinia.

Galatia.

Cappadocia.

rygia.

Armenia.

Euphrates riuer.

Tigris riuer.

Media.

PISIDIA

LYCAONIA

ICONIA

ADERBE

IPHILIA

APERGA

ANTIO
CH

CHARRAM

CILICIA TARSVS

ATALIA

Mesopota-
mia.

BABYLÕ

The way toward
the Parthians.

PAPHOS
SALAM

SELVCIA

CYPRES

LAODICEA

SYRIA

PHENICE

Sidon.

Tyre.

DAMAS-

CALDEA

Elamis, or Perſis.

Prolemais

eſarea.

oppe.

ada.

SICHEM

SAMARI

Arabia the deſerte.

IERVSAL.

IVDEA

SINAI

Arabia the ſtonie.

TE

THE RED SEA

The ſea Perſike.

EAST.

44
43
42
41
40
39
38
37
36
35
34
33
32
31
30

COMMENTARY ON ACTS

OVERVIEW: Despite many reformers' preference for the more theological or explicitly doctrinal books of the Bible, such as Romans, they nevertheless emphasize the usefulness of Acts for teaching important Christian doctrine, especially justification by faith alone. These commentators believed that the lessons learned from the early church were beneficial to the developing Reformation communities, not only because they served as good examples but also because many of the reformers saw their churches as aligning with the ancient church. In their interpretations of Acts, Reformation commentators begin with the premise that God works in and through history. They make a concerted effort to uphold both God's sovereignty in historical events and the faithfulness of human agents who serve God's purposes. In discussing Christ's acts mediated through human beings by his Spirit and Word, the reformers reiterate the presence of the kingdom of God through preaching and miraculous deeds. Such an emphasis on the power of God's Spirit prompts the reformers to urge believers to embrace the gospel with a steadfast faith despite feeling opposition and persecution. In the midst of suffering, when it *feels* like the Lord is not staying true to his promises, still he is faithful and near. This consolation is built on the trustworthiness of Christ. Thus, the reformers do not want to be mere narrators; they want to be participants, and they want their audience to be coparticipants with them. This story is historical, but it is not merely historical, because it is a story for the church to read as its story.

Prolegomena: the Acts of the Risen Christ

THE SIGNIFICANCE OF ACTS. THEODORE BEZA: "Acts," *Praxeis*. Not a few people translate it as Acts; some translate it as Deeds and others as Actions. This includes not only more recent translators but also older ones. For the Latins call Acts records of things done publicly, composed for the sake of public memory. Therefore, I admit that the meaning of *praxeis* is wider among the Greeks than is the meaning of Acts among the Latins, but because this book embraces (as it were) distinguished public records and annals, it was right to arrange the beginning and now to recall the administration of the whole Christian church. I at least would prefer to call it Acts than to call it by any other name you might like. ANNOTATIONS ON THE TITLE OF ACTS.[1]

WHY IS THIS BOOK CALLED THE ACTS OF THE APOSTLES? JOHANN SPANGENBERG: For this reason: in this book the stories of the apostles are described, not what they have done from their own power but what they have done in the power of our Lord Jesus Christ. It should rightly be titled not merely "the Acts of the Apostles" but even better "the Acts of Christ." For in other books the humiliated, despised and condemned Christ is described; in this book, however, the resurrected and glorified Christ is described—how he ascended into heaven and sits at the right hand of the Father. Prolegomena.[2]

---

[1]Beza, *Annotationes Majores*, 1:447.
[2]Spangenberg, *Der Apostel Geschichte*, 1r-v.

A BOOK FILLED WITH PREACHING. JOHANN SPANGENBERG: This book is filled with the beautiful preaching of the holy apostles—Peter, Stephen, Philip, Paul and James—which, if accepted in faith, guides people out of the grisy darkness of unbelief to the shining light of faith, out of the most extreme unrighteous to the most extreme righteousness, out of deep grief to blessed joy, out of this world to the kingdom of heaven, out of death to eternal life. What are the miracles and mighty works recorded in this book other than testimony given from heaven confirming the preaching of the oral word? For in order that the gospel of Christ could be preached throughout the entire world, the Holy Spirit was sent to the holy apostles on Pentecost. PREFATORY EPISTLE TO PRINCE JOACHIM OF ANHALT.[3]

MAKE THESE ACTS YOURS. JOHN DONNE: There are reckoned in this book twenty-two sermons of the apostles. And yet this book is not called the Preaching but the Practice, not the Word but the Acts of the Apostles. Now the Acts of the Apostles were to convey that name of Christ Jesus and to propagate his gospel throughout the whole world. Beloved, you too are actors on this same stage. The end of the earth is your scene. Act out the acts of the apostles! Be a light to the Gentiles who sit in darkness! Be content to carry over these seas him who dried up one red sea for his first people and who has poured out another red sea— his own blood—for them and for us. A SERMON ON ACTS 1:8.[4]

LUKE'S PURPOSE IN WRITING THIS STORY. THE ENGLISH ANNOTATIONS: The penman of this Scripture was Luke the Evangelist ... for the most part an eyewitness to the events he records, since he was a co-laborer with Paul. His purpose in writing this story was, as he intimates in his first preface, that the church might have the sure knowledge of Christ, his gospel and kingdom, so that our faith might not be built on the unsure reposts of pretenders to truth. Also he wanted to show how God fulfilled his promise in calling the Gentiles, and how the apostles fulfilled their charge and office by preaching the gospel to all nations. He wanted to forearm all the faithful by revealing the rage and malice of Satan, who persecutes the true ministers and promulgators of the gospel, even since its very first announcement. And [he wanted to illustrate] the gracious providence of God, by which he preserves and increases his church in the midst of all its troubles, giving us an evident assurance of the truth of the gospel, not only in that the powers of hell, all the machinations of Satan and the malice of the wicked could never prevail against it, but also that God's providence by these oppositions confirmed the gospel in the heart of Christians through the constancy of those who suffered persecution for it. ANNOTATIONS ON ACTS, THE ARGUMENT.[5]

ACTS DEPICTS THE BEGINNING OF CHRIST'S REIGN AND THE WORLD'S RENEWAL. JOHN CALVIN: The things that Luke sets down here for our instruction are great things and of extraordinary benefit. At the beginning when he reports that the Holy Spirit was sent to the apostles, he not only confirms that Christ was true to the promise he made, but he teaches that he also remembers his own and is the perpetual Governor of his church, because the Holy Spirit has descended for that purpose. From that we learn that spatial distance does not prevent Christ from being always present with his own, as he promised. The beginning of the reign of Christ and, as it were, the renewal of the world is being depicted here. For even if the Son of God had already gathered some of the church by his preaching before his departure from the world, yet in fact the Christian church began to exist in its proper form only when the apostles were endowed with new power and preached that that one and only Shepherd had both died and been raised from the dead, so that by his guidance all who had previ-

---

[3]Spangenberg, *Der Apostel Geschichte*, A4v-A6v.
[4]Donne, *Works*, 6:225*.
[5]Downame, ed., *Annotations*, GGG1r*; alluding to Lk 1:1-4.

ously been wandering and scattered might come together into the one sheepfold. Therefore both the origin and the progress of the church, from the ascension of Christ, by which he was declared the supreme King of heaven and earth, are reviewed here for us. THE ARGUMENT OF THE ACTS OF THE APOSTLES.[6]

ACTS DISPLAYS THE TRUTH OF JUSTIFICATION BY FAITH ALONE. MARTIN LUTHER: Contrary to what has sometimes been the practice, this book should not be read or regarded as though Saint Luke had written about the personal work or history of the apostles simply as an example of good works or good life. Even Saint Augustine and many others have looked on the fact that the apostles had all things in common with Christians as the best example which the book contains. Yet this practice did not last long and in time had to stop. Rather, it should be noted that by this book Saint Luke teaches the whole of Christendom, even to the end of the world, that the true and chief article of Christian doctrine is this: We must all be justified alone by faith in Jesus Christ, without any contribution from the law or help from our works.

This doctrine is the chief intention of the book and the author's principal reason for writing it. Therefore he emphasizes so powerfully not only the preaching of the apostles about faith in Christ, how both Gentiles and Jews must thereby be justified without any merits or works, but also the examples and the instances of this teaching, how the Gentiles as well as Jews were justified through the gospel alone, without the law. . . . Thus in this book Saint Luke puts side by side both the teaching of faith and the example of faith.

Therefore this book might well be called a commentary on the epistles of Saint Paul. For what Paul teaches and insists on with words and passages of Scripture, Saint Luke here points out and proves with examples and instances to show that it has happened and must happen in the way Saint Paul teaches, namely, that no law, no work justifies people, but only faith in Christ. PREFACE TO THE ACTS OF THE APOSTLES (1533).[7]

ACTS A LIVING PICTURE OF THE KINGDOM OF CHRIST. JOHN CALVIN: As often as things in the world seem to be turned upside down, no more suitable or firmer support can be found for strengthening consciences than, when, placing the kingdom of Christ before our eyes as we now see it, we consider what the pattern and nature of it was, and what sort of state and condition it had, in the beginning. When we talk about the kingdom of Christ, we must take note of two things in particular, first, the teaching of the gospel by which Christ gathers the church to himself and by which he governs it when it has been gathered; second, the actual fellowship of the godly, who, having been united among themselves by the sincere faith of the gospel, are truly regarded as the people of Christ.

It is better to become thoroughly acquainted with the living picture of both these things, which Luke clearly draws in the Acts of the Apostles, by reading the whole book, than to believe either my account of it or that of anyone else. For although the Son of God has always reigned from the very beginning of the world, yet it was after his revelation in the flesh and the publication of his gospel that he began to set up a judgment seat plainer to see than ever before, as a result of which he now too appears in the highest degree conspicuous. If we turn our eyes to this book we shall feast them not on an empty picture (as Virgil says about his Aeneas) but on the sound knowledge of those things from which we must seek life. . . . This is the best refuge for consciences, where, amid those tumults and commotions by which the world is shaken, they may rest at peace. DEDICATORY EPISTLE TO THE COMMENTARY ON THE ACTS OF THE APOSTLES.[8]

---

[6]CNTC 6:17-18* (CO 48:vii); alluding to Jn 10:16.

[7]LW 35:363-64* (WADB 6:415-17); alluding to Acts 2:44-45; 4:32-37.
[8]CNTC 6:2-3* (CO 18:156-57).

1:1-11 THE PROMISE OF
THE SPIRIT AND THE ASCENSION

In the first book, O Theophilus, I have dealt with all that Jesus began to do and teach, [2]*until the day when he was taken up, after he had given commands through the Holy Spirit to the apostles whom he had chosen.* [3]*He presented himself alive to them after his suffering by many proofs, appearing to them during forty days and speaking about the kingdom of God.*

[4]*And while staying*[a] *with them he ordered them not to depart from Jerusalem, but to wait for the promise of the Father, which, he said, "you heard from me;* [5]*for John baptized with water, but you will be baptized with*[b] *the Holy Spirit not many days from now."*

[6]*So when they had come together, they asked him, "Lord, will you at this time restore the kingdom to Israel?"* [7]*He said to them, "It is not for you to know times or seasons that the Father has fixed by his own authority.* [8]*But you will receive power when the Holy Spirit has come upon you, and you will be my witnesses in Jerusalem and in all Judea and Samaria, and to the end of the earth."* [9]*And when he had said these things, as they were looking on, he was lifted up, and a cloud took him out of their sight.* [10]*And while they were gazing into heaven as he went, behold, two men stood by them in white robes,* [11]*and said, "Men of Galilee, why do you stand looking into heaven? This Jesus, who was taken up from you into heaven, will come in the same way as you saw him go into heaven."*

a Or eating   b Or in

OVERVIEW: A recurring concern for exegetes of Acts is to explain how Christ continues his work among believers. Therefore, the beginning of Acts establishes that Christ will be present in a new way, namely through the Holy Spirit. This new mode of Christ's presence also addresses the initial misunderstanding about the restoration of the kingdom. Rather than an earthly political reign, exegetes understand Acts as a record of God's indwelling work in the church and world, sometimes through human obedience and other times despite human disobedience. The meaning of the divine acts consists of recognizing Christ's Spirit as an agent in establishing God's spiritual kingdom, in which believers stand as witnesses to and coparticipants in Christ's life and work. At the same time, exegetes seek to offer guidance for how to demonstrate faith and trust in a risen Lord. This then leads to the dual emphasis by the Reformation commentators on God's activity and human works, which are not mutually exclusive but are held in tension. Believers are empowered to witness, proclaim and share, yet the source of their confidence is Christ's power.

1:1-3 Dedication to Theophilus

WHO WAS THEOPHILUS? JOHANN SPANGEN-BERG: Whether the evangelist Luke had a good friend by this name or whether he understood by this little word Theophilus—which translated means "God's friend"—every lover and friend of God should not worry us. This is certain, that Luke in this book intended to instruct not just one person but every lover and friend of God in the highest things that are beneficial and necessary for salvation. BRIEF EXEGESIS OF ACTS 1:1.[1]

THE UNITY OF LUKE-ACTS. DESIDERIUS ERAS-MUS: Clearly I wanted to join this book of Luke together with the earlier one. Whereas [Luke] embraced evangelical history in two volumes, of

---

[1]Spangenberg, *Der Apostel Geschichte,* 2r.

which he wrote both to the same Theophilus, and beginning the later book, he makes mention of the earlier, as if to say "I was afraid of the rest, that Acts might seem to distract from the Gospels." Although this history is something other than a part of the Gospel, still, in my judgment, it is not insignificant. If in fact in that matter the church is described as a grain of wheat, planted alone, this book describes its being born, opening its own leaves little by little and bringing forth fruit. Which unless we had known this by Luke, in what ways Christ will have left the earth, where, in what place, by what ways would that promised Spirit have come, by what beginnings would the church have started, by what things would it have been polluted, for what reasons would the church have grown, if we had not known a good part of the gospel? And would that holy Luke would have continued this narrative longer, just as he had commenced it, and likewise, would that he had touched on not a few of the deeds of the rest of the apostles! ANNOTATIONS ON ACTS 1:1.[2]

CHRIST'S PERSON AND WORK ARE THE SUM OF THE GOSPEL. JOHN CALVIN: Now we see that the sum of the gospel comprises these two parts—the teaching of Christ and his acts—in that he not only brought people the comission committed to him by the Father but also accomplished in deed all that could be required of the Messiah. He inaugurated his kingdom, he reconciled God by his sacrifice, he expiated the sins of people by his own blood, he subdued death and the devil, he restored us to true liberty, he won for us justice and life. But that all that he did and said might be ratified, he attested himself by his miracles to be the Son of God. So the words "to do" extend also to the miracles, but they must not be restricted to these only. From this we must note that those who simply know the bare history do not have the gospel, unless there is added to it a knowledge of the teaching, which reveals the fruit of the acts of Christ. For this is a holy knot, which may not be

dissolved. Therefore whenever mention is made of the teaching of Christ, let us learn to join to it the works as seals by which its truth is established and its effects shown forth. But, in order that the death and resurrection of Christ may be profitable for us, and that his miracles may have their value, let us be equally attentive to the words that he speaks. For this is the true rule of Christianity. COMMENTARY ON ACTS 1:1.[3]

THOUGH NOT VISIBLE, CHRIST IS PRESENT IN HIS CHURCH. JOHN CALVIN: By these words Luke reminds us that Christ though he departed from the world did not thereby abandon his concern for us. For in establishing a perpetual government in the church, he gave proof of his will to provide for our salvation. Indeed he has given assurance of his intention to be present in power and succor to his own people even to the end—even as in truth he is present by his ministers. Luke means therefore that Jesus did not depart without first having provided for the government of the church whereby we recognize his concern for our salvation. COMMENTARY ON ACTS 1:2.[4]

WHAT WERE THE "MANY PROOFS"? JOHANN ECK: During this forty-day delay all that was necessary for Christ to prove the truth about his resurrection took place, for on this article of faith everything is founded. . . . From Easter day, when he first appeared, to the ascension, when he last appeared, forty days elapsed in which he appeared to many, as is now narrated; and Saint Paul indicates even more appearances [than just these recorded in Acts], for he appeared to Saint James and then five hundred brothers. Now the arguments and testimonies of his resurrection are documented in the gospel. He ate with them, he showed them the wounds in his hands, his feet and his side, he showed them his flesh and bone. "For a spirit," he says, "does not have flesh and bone as you see that I have." Yes, Saint Thomas even placed his finger in the wound of the

---

[2]LB 6:433.

[3]CNTC 6:21-22* (CO 48:1-2).
[4]CNTC 6:23 (CO 48:3); alluding to Mt 28:20.

Lord. He also ate fish and honey[5] with them. All of these things were arguments, testimonies and proofs of his resurrection. First Sermon on the Feast of Christ's Ascension (1531).[6]

The Apostles Experienced the Risen Christ with Absolute Certainty. Moïse Amyraut: Since they saw him several times with their own eyes during the span of forty days, they conversed with him so familiarly that they took their meals together, they examined the scars from his wounds, they heard him speaking things concerning the gospel and the kingdom of God for which reason he had come. All the senses that can give people the certainty of something, and there were none that did not fully testify to the truth of this. Paraphrase sur les Actes des Saints Apostres 1:3.[7]

Jesus Prepares His Disciples Thoroughly. Desiderius Erasmus: The chief point of these deeds was that everyone be persuaded that Jesus had truly died and had truly come to life again on the third day, not in what merely appeared to be a body but in that same mortal body—now immortal—which he bore on earth and which had been buried lifeless in the tomb. Accordingly, he did not think it enough to present himself alive again to his disciples merely once; he appeared to them frequently, and not as ghosts usually do, but showing with various clear proofs that he had assumed again a living body. For this reason, he remained on earth for forty days, during which, however, he wanted to be visible to no one except his own.

Not only did he present himself to them to be seen with their eyes, to be heard with their ears, to be touched with their hands, but he lived with them in close association and took food with them; and no other sign of a living body is more certain than this. Meanwhile, he often spoke with them about

the kingdom of God, calling to mind what he had done and taught before his death so that they might eventually recognize that everything had happened as he had predicted. At the same time he warned them what they were either to do or to expect in the future. Paraphrase of Acts 1:3.[8]

1:4-5 *"Wait for the Promise"*

"They Should Not Depart but Wait." Rudolf Gwalther: Now Saint Luke sets forth very diligently [Christ's] last conversation and actions with his apostles, partly so that we might perceive the endeavor and good will of Christ toward us and partly to declare what things are chiefly necessary for the ministers of his Word. First of all, he proves the truthfulness of his resurrection by many arguments, for six weeks. Because this is the ground of our salvation, whoever does not understand and know it will not prevail in preaching the gospel. Second, he expounds and opens the mysteries of the kingdom of God, both because he would put out of their mind the opinion conceived by common error of a merely earthly kingdom of Christ and because they should perceive the right ways in which they ought to handle the business of our faith and salvation through preaching the gospel. To these two he adds a third point, that is, the promise of the Holy Spirit, which he repeats and confirms by grave testimony. Homily 3, Acts 1:4-5.[9]

"He Will Baptize You with Fire." Martin Luther: How is this said in German? [Can it mean,] "I will baptize you with water"? How? Especially since being burned by fire blackens and does not clean us. In contrast water washes and makes us clean. Exactly! [This] fire should not blacken or burn but rather baptize and wash white, so it must be a fire above all other kinds of fire, since [usually fire] blackens where it has been and everything smells and is charred. . . . But Christ

---

[5]𝔐 includes the variant και απο μελισσιου κηριου ("and of honeycomb"); Lk 24:42.
[6]Eck, *Christenliche Predigen*, 3:119v*; alluding to 1 Cor 15:5-7; Lk 24:39; Jn 20:27.
[7]Amyraut, *Paraphrase sur les Actes des Saints Apostres*, 1:4.

[8]CWE 50:6 (LB 7:661).
[9]Gwalther, *Homelyes or Sermons upon the Actes*, 16* (*In Acta Apostolorum*, 5v).

[said], "I will send fire of such a kind in which they were baptized as in water. It will not consume them but will give them life and strength. It will not blacken but whiten." Therefore, this fire of Christ's is of a different nature, etc. The text is clear: "You will receive the power of the Holy Spirit." . . . In this passage he also calls the Holy Spirit an excellent fire, because it makes what is blackened and dead white and alive. Therefore he calls it baptism, because it is abundant with the Spirit, as Paul says. [This baptism] is not performed with little droplets, as when something is dipped in water, but instead we are plunged into this baptism, as if someone wanted to drown us. So, the Holy Spirit does not flutter down in a flickering flame but [rushes down] in fire! By this fire you all are plunged and overwhelmed so that it seems as if there is nothing in you other than fire. As a fish in water, so are you in fire. . . . Through the abundant outpouring of the Holy Spirit [Christ] wants to subsume Christianity, so that those drifting and living in the midst of this heavenly fire will not be consumed and charred, but will be made bold, brave, excellent, perfect, bright and pure. "In this way, my Holy Spirit will baptize my people." SERMON ON THE EVENING OF PENTECOST (1535).[10]

THE DIFFERENCE IN CHRIST'S BAPTISM IS THE HOLY SPIRIT. CARDINAL CAJETAN: Jesus declares that the difference between his own baptism and the baptism of John does not rest with the elements (because either one uses the element of water) but rests with this: "John baptized in water alone; you, however, will be baptized in the Holy Spirit." And indeed, all who are baptized in Christ are baptized in the Holy Spirit. Christ speaks to the true literal sense about the baptism of disciples by the visible sign of the Holy Spirit, and he clearly places the baptism of the apostles out of the region of the baptism of John. And if he had spoken more openly, he would have said that John gathered the people together by a perceptible baptism of water; you, however, will father the

world by a perceptible baptism of the Holy Spirit. From this, nothing relates to this new baptism by a perceptible sign of the Holy Spirit, or the apostles would have formerly been baptized by the baptism of Christ. COMMENTARY ON ACTS 1:5.[11]

TWO KINDS OF BAPTISM. JOHANN SPANGENBERG: There are two kinds of baptism: by water and by fire. John, and after him the apostles, used water baptism; Christendom still uses it. This baptism delivers the foundational gifts of the Holy Spirit, such as faith and trust in God, solace and joy of conscience during trials, the death of the old Adam and new life. But Christ used fire baptism, when on Pentecost he sent the Holy Spirit to the apostles, so that people visibly witnessed on them cloven tongues as if on fire. These [fiery tongues] brought wonderful and unusual gifts, such as speaking in tongues, performing mighty signs and preaching the gospel unafraid and undaunted, publicly, before the entire world, recognizing the name of Christ. . . . Between the baptism of John and Christ there is no other difference than that John is merely a servant and aid but Christ is the Master, Lord and true Foreman. . . . Now this word of John must also be understood, when he says, "I baptize you with water, but after me is coming a mightier person, who will baptize you with the Holy Spirit and fire." As if he wanted to say, "I am only a slave and servant through whom you have come to faith, but he who is coming after me, Jesus Christ, he is the true Foreman, who gives the true substance, so that you increase in faith and persist in it until the very end." BRIEF EXEGESIS OF ACTS 1:5.[12]

CHRIST HIMSELF IS THE ONE WHO BAPTIZES. JOHN CALVIN: Christ did not baptize with the Holy Spirit only at the time when he sent him under the form of tongues of fire. He had before this conferred this baptism on the apostles, and he baptizes all the elect thus daily. Because the sending

---

[10]WA 41:242-44; alluding to Acts 1:8 (cf. Lk 24:49); Tit 3:6 .

[11]Cajetan, *In Acta Apostolorum*, 213v.
[12]Spangenberg, *Der Apostel Geschichte*, 4v-5v; alluding to 1 Cor 3:5-7; Lk 3:16; Col 2:17.

of the Holy Spirit in so spectacular a manner was a symbol of the hidden grace wherewith the Lord continuously inspires his elect, it is appropriate that he should apply to it the testimony of John. Besides the fact that the apostles did not receive the Spirit for themselves alone but for the benefit of all the faithful, there was also mirrored forth the universal grace of Christ toward his church, while he poured forth the gifts of his Spirit in full measure. . . .

Today ministers ought to speak of themselves only in such a way as to acknowledge Christ as the Giver of all which they set forth in baptism and leave nothing to themselves except only the outward administration. For when baptism is entitled the laver of regeneration, a washing from sin, participation in the death and burial of Christ and ingrafting into his body, there is no declaration thereby of what the person is doing who administers the external sign, but rather what Christ is doing, who alone makes the sign effectual. We must always make this distinction lest by adorning people we rob Christ's glory. COMMENTARY ON ACTS 1:5.[13]

1:6-8 The Promise of the Holy Spirit

CHRIST'S IS NOT AN EARTHLY KINGDOM. JOHN CALVIN: They ask him concerning the kingdom, but they dream of an earthly kingdom, dependent on wealth, luxury, outward peace and blessings of this nature. And while they assign the present as the time for restoring this kingdom, they desire to enjoy the triumph before fighting the battle. Before setting hands to the work for which they are ordained they desire their wages; they also are mistaken in this, that they confine the kingdom of Christ to fleshly Israel, which is to be extended to the farthest parts of the world. The whole question is at fault in this, that they desire to know things which are not right for them to know. No doubt they were well aware of what the prophets had said about the restoration of the kingdom of David, for they had often heard Christ speaking of this, and it was a common saying that in the depths of the cap-

tivity of the people everyone's spirit was revived by the hope of the kingdom to come. They hoped that this restoration would take place at the coming of the Messiah, and so the apostles, when they saw Christ raised from the dead, at once turned their thoughts to this. But in so doing they betrayed what poor progress they had made under so good a Master. Therefore Christ in his short reply briefly reprimands their errors one by one, as I shall presently include. "To restore" in this passage means to set up again that which was broken down and disfigured by many ruins. For "out of the dry stock of Jesse should spring a branch, and the tabernacle of David, which was miserably laid waste, should rise again." COMMENTARY ON ACTS 1:6.[14]

"IT IS NOT FOR YOU TO KNOW." CARDINAL CAJETAN: Because the apostles were asking in good faith (whoever understands less must ask), the Lord responds directly to their asking by explaining what the question was, imparting knowledge to them. And if those men did not know the time of this matter, undoubtedly we ought to believe that this knowledge was communicated to no other man of this sort. Nor does Christ say that it is not yours to know times or moments (because many times and many moments are known to us in the future), but he limits their knowledge with respect to those things which the Father had placed in his very own power. COMMENTARY ON ACTS 1:7.[15]

"BUT YOU WILL RECEIVE POWER." JUSTUS JONAS: Now by these words he indicates what the nature of his kingdom will be. It is as if he were saying, "You will receive the Holy Spirit, who will teach you what reason does not grasp, indeed, that through my death I inaugurated my kingdom. Also I am now going to the Father, and I will indeed rule with power on earth, just as the Scriptures foretold, not a fleshly kingdom but rather a spiritual one. I will fulfill all things." Therefore, Christ has died and [Christ] has risen, so that he might fulfill

---

[13]CNTC 6:27-28* (CO 48:6-7); alluding to Tit 3:5; Rom 6:4.

[14]CNTC 6:29* (CO 48:8).
[15]Cajetan, *In Acta Apostolorum*, 213v.

all things and so that he might truly reign in the hearts of every believer, justifying them and rendering them, through faith in the gospel, invincible against the world, Satan, sin, death and all creation. . . . "Therefore you will be witnesses of this kingdom. This kingdom you will proclaim to every nation to the end of the earth. In this way I will have dominion from sea to sea, just as the prophets said." ANNOTATIONS ON ACTS 1:8.[16]

THE APOSTLES MUST RELY ON THE STRENGTH OF THE SPIRIT. RUDOLF GWALTHER: [Jesus says] "You are appointed to the setting forth of my kingdom among the Gentiles. For this thing will not be accomplished by human strength, which I perceive in you to be very small and little regarded. Here one needs a heavenly and divine strength from above, which I have often promised you shall not lack, and now again I promise you the same. For the Holy Spirit shall come upon you, which shall give you courage and strength that shall make you able to fulfill your office." . . .

He expressly teaches what the apostles have to do in their office in this kingdom: "you shall be my witness. This shall be your kingdom, your office, your dignity to bear witness of my doctrine, life, miracles, passion, death, burial, resurrection from death and ascension into heaven and—briefly—of all the things which I have done and suffered for human salvation. Neither shall you expound the history of things done by me only, but declare the end and use of them, that all nations may acknowledge me [as] their only Teacher, Savior and Redeemer." HOMILY 4, ACTS 1:6-8.[17]

CHRIST EVEN COMMANDS THEM TO GO TO THE HERETICS. CARDINAL CAJETAN: He mentioned Samaria because the Samaritans were almost like heretics or excommunicates among the Jews, and in an earlier circumstance, Jesus prohibited his own disciples from going to the Samaritans.

And if he had spoken more openly, the distinction between Jews and Samaritans would not have been fuller, but "I send you to all people. . . ." Likewise, he had prohibited them earlier, "Lest you depart into the way of the nations." After these things, he simply declares that they should go to the whole world. COMMENTARY ON ACTS 1:8.[18]

THE HUMILITY OF THE HOLY SPIRIT. JOHN DONNE: The Holy Spirit has fallen on everyone who has been compelled in themselves to propagate the gospel of Christ Jesus. The Son of God did not abhor the Virgin's womb when he was made man. When he was made man, he did not disdain to ride on an ass into Jerusalem. The third person of the Trinity, the Holy Spirit, is as humble as the second. He refuses no vehicle, no door of entrance into you. Whether the example and precedent of other good people, or a probable imagination of future profit or a willingness to concur to the vexation of the enemy, whatever collateral drew you in, if now you are in, the main cause is the glory of God. That occasion, whatever it was, was the vehicle of the Holy Spirit. That was the petard that broke open your iron gate. That was the chariot by which he entered into you. Now he is fallen on you.

If you do not *depose* (lay aside all consideration of profit forever, never to look for return), no not *sepose* (leave out the consideration of profit for a time), . . . but if you do but *post-pose* the consideration of temporal gain and study first the advancement of the gospel of Christ Jesus, the Holy Spirit has fallen on you. And by this you receive power. SERMON ON ACTS 1:8.[19]

1:9-11 *Christ's Ascension, Reign and Return*

CHRIST'S ASCENSION AND RETURN ARE FOUNDATIONAL ARTICLES OF FAITH. RUDOLF GWALTHER: Now at length follows Christ's depar-

---

[16]Jonas, *Annotationes in Acta*, A7r-v; alluding to Eph 1:22-23; Rom 8:38-39; Ps 72:8.

[17]Gwalther, *Homelyes or Sermons upon the Actes*, 30* (*In Acta Apostolorum*, 10r, 10v).

[18]Cajetan, *In Acta Apostolorum*, 213v.

[19]Donne, *Works*, 6:233-34*.

ture from earth into heaven, which Luke describes with great diligence, and we ought to consider the same with as much earnestness; because in the description thereof, two notable articles of our Christian faith are comprehended, in the which, the chief hope of all Christians is grounded. That is to say, Christ's ascension into heaven, and his return, which shall be at the end of the world when he will come in the clouds to judge both the living and the dead. HOMILY 5, ACTS 1:9-11.[20]

THE APOSTLES MUST NOW LOOK TO CHRIST WITH THE EYES OF FAITH. DESIDERIUS ERASMUS: The time had come for them to stop depending on the visual presence of the body, so that they might rather begin to be spiritual and might look on Jesus now with no other eyes than those of faith. . . . Weak as they still were, they simply could not be torn away from the one they singularly loved. PARAPHRASE ON ACTS 1:8.[21]

THE FEAST OF THE ASCENSION AFFIRMS THE SECOND ARTICLE OF THE CREED. MARTIN LUTHER: In this feast we celebrate the consoling article of Christian faith, which we confess and state as, "I believe in Jesus Christ, God's only Son our Lord, who ascended to heaven, is seated at the right hand of God, from there he will come to judge the living and the dead." I have often said that it is excellent that the articles of the Christian faith are assigned to particular feasts throughout the year and are arranged in Christendom in such a way that at a particular time we celebrate them and preach about them, so that not only we elderly continue to know and believe them, but also young people, thus growing year by year in this confession, being instructed in it, so that they grasp this knowledge and mature and thrive in it. For it is knowledge which cannot be learned and comprehended enough. SERMON ON THE FEAST OF THE ASCENSION (1531).[22]

CHRIST'S LIKENESS AFTER THE ASCENSION. CARDINAL CAJETAN: We perceive Christ's likeness in heaven in that [galaxy] which is called the Milky Way. COMMENTARY ON ACTS 1:9.[23]

THE GLORY OF THE ASCENSION. JOHN DONNE:
Salute the last and everlasting day,
Joy at the uprising of this Sun and Son,
Ye whose just tears, or tribulation
Have purely washed,
     or burnt your drowsy clay;
Behold the Highest, parting hence away,
Lightens the dark clouds,
     which he treads upon,
Nor doth he by ascending, show alone,
But first he, and he first enters the way.
O strong Ram, which hast batter'd
     heaven for me,
Mild Lamb, which with thy blood,
     hast mark'd the path;
Bright Torch, which shin'st,
     that I the way may see,
Oh with thy own blood quench
     thy own just wrath,
And if thy holy Spirit, my Muse did raise,
Deign at my hands this crown
     of prayer and praise.

LA CORONA.[24]

THE ASCENSION IS A SALVE. JUSTUS JONAS: Nothing is more effective for consoling afflicted consciences than the ascension. The account of Christ is of absolutely no benefit to you unless you know Christ's accomplishments, that is, his death, resurrection and ascension. He died for our sins. He rose again for our justification. When he ascended he took captive captivity, that is, sin, death, hell and the kingdom of the devil. ANNOTATIONS ON ACTS 1:9.[25]

DO NOT NEGLECT THE ASCENDED CHRIST'S BLESSINGS. MARTIN LUTHER: We are called to

---

[20]Gwalther, *Homelyes or Sermons upon the Actes*, 33* (*In Acta Apostolorum*, 11r).
[21]CWE 50:8* (LB 7:662-63).
[22]WA 34, 1:401.8-19.

[23]Cajetan, *In Acta Apostolorum*, 213v.
[24]Donne, *Poems of John Donne*, 321.
[25]Jonas, *Annotationes in Acta*, A8r; alluding to Eph 4:8.

the kingdom, sealed, registered through baptism, the gospel, the Sacrament, the forgiveness of sin. And how do we receive it? How are we so lazy? Not taken aback by the apostles' laziness, we go on, worrying as if this life here and now were all there is and we must die of hunger! So, however, here we are warned. We are lazy and drowsy, go begrudgingly to the Sacrament and sermon. If baptism were locked away in the altar, almost none of you would be baptized![26] . . . But you should act in this way, when you are on the street and stare up to heaven, you should think: "There sits my Lord, who ascended there, and I too will ascend there; he doesn't need me, but accomplished it for my benefit." Instead we go around, caring for our belly like a pig loves its slop. . . .

Our Lord gives it to us at no cost. When you are baptized, the pastor gives you not even a penny, nothing temporal is given then. Instead eternal life, ascension, eternal status as God's children in eternal joy and glory without worry and sorrow, that is what is given at baptism. To this the world responds, "Did I ask for that? I must eat and drink. I need money, clothes; preach what you want." Should we, however, not respond in this way? "I am registered, I have the ascension before me. I belong there, it is promised to me and accomplished for my benefit." If someone gives you a hundred florin, you can't thank them enough. But what do you do, now that God has given you the kingdom of heaven at no cost? . . .

He will not leave us standing naked; rather, he will give us every need we require. So then do not shove your snout into the pile of hay, or your eyes into the pig trough! Look at yourselves! You are not created for the pig trough. Instead, lift your eyes up, look to heaven, the sun and the stars, which cattle cannot see, for they are not created for that. You are children of the ascension; "You also belong where I am ascending." This journey continues without interruption and will be brought to completion on the Last Day when the body will also ascend. However, to believe this is difficult. For the devil,

flesh and blood continually pull us down: "What? Let heaven be heaven, look! here you have plenty." Indeed, for that you are not created. Heaven calls: "Here, up here, here is where you belong!" But if you deny heaven, then on the Last Day it will deny you and be locked to you. "Bah! Get lost! You have let me appear to you and cry out to you, saying that you belong up here, to the ascension, and that you are an heir of the kingdom of heaven! This you have made me cry in vain. Now, therefore, I will also not listen to you." So, heaven, sun and moon will stand against us as witnesses. SERMON ON THE FEAST OF THE ASCENSION (1544).[27]

THE ANGELS PROVE TO US THAT CHRIST'S PRESENCE IN THE BREAD IS A LIE. PETER WALPOT: Thus, God through two angelic witnesses made clear that we should not think or believe that [Jesus] enters into the bread in another form; rather, he enters into the clouds of heaven openly and visibly. Therefore, the words of these angels and our own Christian faith should be trusted more than a giant heap of all the priests and false prophets. THE GREAT ARTICLE BOOK: ON EUCHARIST.[28]

CHRIST IS TRULY PRESENT WITH BELIEVERS IN THE EUCHARIST. FORMULA OF CONCORD: We believe, teach and confess that in the Holy Supper the body and blood of Christ are truly and essentially present, truly distributed and received with the bread and wine. We believe, teach and confess that the words of the covenant of Christ are not to be understood in any other way than in their literal sense, that is, not that the bread symbolizes the absent body and the wine the absent blood of Christ, but that they are truly the true body and blood of Christ because of the sacramental union. . . . [This is true] "because the right hand of God is everywhere."[29] Christ, really and truly placed at this right hand of God according to his human nature, rules presently and has in his hands and under his

---

[26]Luther refers to the fact that host is stored in a church tabernacle, an ornate container, or an aumbry, a cabinet set into the church wall or altar itself.

[27]WA 49:419-22; alluding to Mt 26:40.
[28]QGT 12:142-43.
[29]Confession Concerning Christ's Supper (1528); LW 37:214 (WA 26:326.32).

feet everything in heaven and on earth. No other human being, no angel, but only Mary's Son, is so placed at the right hand of God, and on this basis he is able to do these things. ARTICLE 7, THE LORD'S SUPPER.[30]

CHRIST UNITES US TO THE FATHER BY HIS SPIRIT. THE GALLIC CONFESSION: Now, as it is certain and beyond all doubt that Jesus Christ has not enjoined to us the use of his sacraments in vain, so he works in us all that he represents to us by these holy signs, though the manner surpasses our understanding and cannot be comprehended by us, as the operations of the Holy Spirit are hidden and incomprehensible. In the meantime we do not err when we say that what is eaten and drunk by us is the proper and natural body and the proper blood of Christ. But the manner of our partaking of the same is not by the mouth, but by the Spirit through faith. Thus, then, though Christ always sits at the right hand of his Father in the heavens, yet he does not, therefore, cease to make us partakers of himself by faith. This feast is a spiritual table, at which Christ communicates himself with all his benefits to us and gives us there to enjoy both himself and the merits of his sufferings and death, nourishing, strengthening and comforting our poor comfortless souls, by the eating of his flesh, quickening and refreshing them by the drinking of his blood. ARTICLE 35, OF THE HOLY SUPPER OF OUR LORD JESUS CHRIST.[31]

THROUGH YOUR SPIRIT, DRAW US NEAR TO YOU. BOOK OF COMMON PRAYER (1549): O God, the King of glory, who has exalted your only Son Jesus Christ with great triumph into your kingdom in heaven; we beseech you not to leave us comfortless, but send us your Holy Spirit to comfort us and exalt us to the same place where our Savior Christ has already gone, who lives and reigns [with you in the same Spirit one God, world without end]. THE COLLECT FOR THE SUNDAY AFTER THE ASCENSION.[32]

CHRIST'S SECOND ADVENT. THE SECOND HELVETIC CONFESSION: We believe that our Lord Jesus Christ, in the same flesh, did ascend above all the visible heavens into the very highest heaven, that is to say, the seat of God and of the blessed spirits, unto the right hand of God the Father. Although it does signify an equal participation of glory and majesty, yet it is also taken for a certain place; of which the Lord, speaking in the Gospel, says that "He will go and prepare a place for his" (Jn 14:2). Also the apostle Peter says, "The heavens must contain Christ until the time of restoring all things" (Acts 3:21).

And out of heaven the same Christ will return unto judgment, even then when wickedness shall chiefly reign in the world, and when Antichrist, having corrupted true religion, shall fill all things with superstition and impiety and shall most cruelly waste the church with fire and bloodshed. Now Christ shall return to redeem his, and to abolish Antichrist by his coming and to judge the living and the dead (Acts 17:31). For the dead shall arise, and those who shall be found alive in that day (which is unknown unto all creatures) "shall be changed in the twinkling of an eye" (1 Cor 15:51-52). And all the faithful shall be taken up to meet Christ in the air (1 Thess 4:17), that thenceforth they may enter with him into heaven, there to live forever (2 Tim 2:11); but the unbelievers, or ungodly, shall descend with the devils into hell, there to burn forever, and never to be delivered out of torments (Mt 25:41).

We therefore condemn all those who deny the true resurrection of the flesh, and those who think amiss of the glorified bodies, as did John of Jerusalem,[33] against whom Jerome wrote. We also condemn those who have thought that both the devils and all the wicked shall at length be saved and have an end of their torments; for the Lord himself has absolutely set it down that "Their worm does not die, and the fire is not quenched" (Mk 9:48). CHAPTER 11, OF JESUS CHRIST.[34]

---

[30]BoC 505* (BSLK 797-99).
[31]*Creeds*, 3:429-30*.
[32]BCP 1549, 58*.

[33]See "To Pammachius Against John of Jerusalem," in NPNF² 6:424-47.
[34]*Creeds*, 3:852-53* (Latin, 256-67).

1:12-26 MATTHIAS CHOSEN TO REPLACE JUDAS

¹²Then they returned to Jerusalem from the mount called Olivet, which is near Jerusalem, a Sabbath day's journey away. ¹³And when they had entered, they went up to the upper room, where they were staying, Peter and John and James and Andrew, Philip and Thomas, Bartholomew and Matthew, James the son of Alphaeus and Simon the Zealot and Judas the son of James. ¹⁴All these with one accord were devoting themselves to prayer, together with the women and Mary the mother of Jesus, and his brothers.ᵃ

¹⁵In those days Peter stood up among the brothers (the company of persons was in all about 120) and said, ¹⁶"Brothers, the Scripture had to be fulfilled, which the Holy Spirit spoke beforehand by the mouth of David concerning Judas, who became a guide to those who arrested Jesus. ¹⁷For he was numbered among us and was allotted his share in this ministry." ¹⁸(Now this man acquired a field with the reward of his wickedness, and falling headlongᵇ he burst open in the middle and all his bowels gushed out. ¹⁹And it became known to all the inhabitants of Jerusalem,

so that the field was called in their own language Akeldama, that is, Field of Blood.) ²⁰"For it is written in the Book of Psalms,

"'May his camp become desolate,
and let there be no one to dwell in it';
and
"'Let another take his office.'

²¹So one of the men who have accompanied us during all the time that the Lord Jesus went in and out among us, ²²beginning from the baptism of John until the day when he was taken up from us—one of these men must become with us a witness to his resurrection." ²³And they put forward two, Joseph called Barsabbas, who was also called Justus, and Matthias. ²⁴And they prayed and said, "You, Lord, who know the hearts of all, show which one of these two you have chosen ²⁵to take the place in this ministry and apostleship from which Judas turned aside to go to his own place." ²⁶And they cast lots for them, and the lot fell on Matthias, and he was numbered with the eleven apostles.

a Or brothers and sisters. The plural Greek word adelphoi (translated "brothers") refers to siblings in a family. In New Testament usage, depending on the context, adelphoi may refer either to men or to both men and women who are siblings (brothers and sisters) in God's family, the church; also verse 15   b Or swelling up

OVERVIEW: Three interrelated themes emerge concerning the early apostles: the ignominious demise of Judas, the inclusion of certain women in the earliest company of disciples, and, most notably, the selection of a replacement apostle. The fall of Judas is linked not only with the loss of his apostleship, but to his stubborn wickedness and unrelenting despair. Commentators also briefly discuss the meaning of Luke's reference to women as a reference most likely to the apostles' wives who were among the company of the apostles, although it is not clear in what capacity they served. Because the Protestant reformers espoused clerical marriage as an acceptable and even noble calling of

ministers, some interpret the presence of women who were apostles' wives as an indictment of clerical celibacy.

Based on the early formation of the believing community, the issue of leadership selection serves as a springboard for elaboration on righteous and pious leaders who can be chosen either by God or the congregation. Specific criteria for choosing the next disciple include: (1) a firm belief in God's sovereign choice, (2) a trust in those who have the Spirit of God and (3) the community's prayerful consideration of worthy candidates. Once chosen, those who are called by God must be guided by the Word of God.

1:12-14 *In the Upper Room*

Jerusalem and the Upper Room Symbolize Spirit-Filled Believers. Desiderius Erasmus: Consider now with me for a little while the first beginnings of the nascent church. The city of Jerusalem, which in Hebrew means "vision of peace," pleases them. Those whose native land is this world do not inhabit Jerusalem. The Holy Spirit does not dwell in the heart of such people. The upper room . . . was also agreeable. For the lower parts of a house are usually occupied either by shops or workplaces. But whoever prepares himself as a dwelling for the Holy Spirit must be far removed from sordid cares. This is that holy congregation which the Lord Jesus had chosen out of all. This upper room was the first abode of the church of the gospel. Paraphrase of Acts 1:13.[1]

The Disciples Were United by Prayer and Praise. Moïse Amyraut: But the affection that they had for one another, and the common expectation that they shared of what had to happen, did not allow them to be separated, nor did their condition and the state of their affairs allow them to be scattered, because they were greatly counting on one another. Thus, they would go up to this room and there they would meditate on all these things. . . . It is necessary to mention here that [God's] goodness had joined them together. Thus, all of them not only remained in the same dwelling but also spent time together in common affection, with a singular diligence, and with great perseverance in the practice of prayer and praise, asking God to grant the blessings that Jesus had promised them and to deliver them from wicked people and the persecution with which they were threatened by their enemies. Paraphrase of the Acts of the Apostles 1:13.[2]

"The Women" Were the Apostles' Wives. Rudolf Gwalther: Luke writes that there were also women in the company of the apostles, which some think were only there when Christ came out for the last time from Galilee to Jerusalem. I will not deny this, but some of the number might abide with the apostles, so I think these women would be very well understood as the apostles' wives. For the Gospel plainly expresses that Peter had a wife. And if we affirm the same of Matthew, we do it not in vain, seeing it plainly appears that he both had his own dwelling and kept a family and household. And Paul manifestly testifies that the apostles led their wives when they preached the gospel.

Although I am not ignorant of how the maintainers of unchaste singleness expound that place of certain faithful women who followed the apostles, but the peevish people perceive not what injury they do to the apostles with what they say. For what excuse is left for the apostles, if they leave their own wives and care about other men's wives? God defends therefore that we should not think such absurdity, peevishness and dishonesty in the most holy legates and ambassadors of Jesus Christ. I surely believe that the apostles' wives came from Galilee with their husbands the apostles, for whom it was not lawful to depart from the city, until this present day. For where they were ordained to take part with the apostles of all their travels and dangers, it was requisite that they should be prepared and strengthened with some special gift of the Holy Spirit. Those who contend that the single life is of necessity to be enjoined of ecclesiastical persons are more foolish than those whom we need much to confute, in so great light of the gospel, considering that it is plain to all: that wedlock is honorable in all persons, and the bed undefiled. Homily 6, Acts 1:12-14.[3]

The Virgin Mary. Rudolf Gwalther: Among these women was also the holy Virgin, the mother of Jesus Christ, and certain brothers of Christ, whom according to the custom of the Hebrew tongue we

---

[1]CWE 50:10* (LB 7:663-64).
[2]Amyraut, *Paraphrase sur les Actes des Saints Apostres*, 1:24-26.

[3]Gwalther, *Homelyes or Sermons upon the Actes*, 45-46* (*In Acta Apostolorum*, 15r-v); alluding to 1 Cor 9:5; Heb 13:4.

understand to have been his kinsmen.[4] Christ just before his death had committed the daily needs of her to John the beloved disciple, who took care of her and most faithfully kept her. And here is the last place that the Scriptures make any more mention of her. What happened to her after this, the Holy Spirit wanted to have buried in oblivion, lest it be an occasion for superstition, which he knew would arise from the worship of her. Certainly it is surprising that God kept the actions of Mary in silence, while he wanted the actions and teaching of the apostles to be written with such careful diligence. But by this we are admonished that we should not be overtaken by the superstitious worship of human beings, but rather the teaching of the apostles. HOMILY 6, ACTS 1:12-14.[5]

1:15-26 Peter Speaks and Matthias Is Chosen

MUST THERE BE TWELVE APOSTLES? JOHANN SPANGENBERG: Just as according to the Roman custom, in important things there must be seven witnesses, so by the Jews twelve witnesses were required, for example, the twelve tribes of Israel or other such instances. This is why Moses sent out twelve spies to inspect the land of Canaan and why the children of Israel discovered twelve springs and seventy palm trees in Elim. Joshua had twelve stones taken from the midst of the Jordan and erected on land as an eternal remembrance that the children of Israel with dry feet crossed through the Jordan into the land of Canaan. So then, since there is no more important thing in the entire world than the gospel of Christ, Christ also wanted to have twelve apostles who publicly before all people testified to his death and resurrection. BRIEF EXEGESIS OF ACTS 1:15-26.[6]

THE CHURCH IS THE NEW ISRAEL. DIRK PHILIPS: From Jacob were born twelve patriarchs from whom came the twelve tribes of Israel. These twelve patriarchs represent to us the twelve apostles who were born again out of the Spirit and endowed with power from above. These are the spiritual fathers who through the gospel and through faith in Jesus Christ have brought forth the Israel of God. Such believing Christians are the true Israelites and the seed of Abraham, and those whom they have won to Christ through God's Word, these are the fathers, as the apostles themselves testify; . . . All this is from God, who is named the true Father over all that is in heaven and on earth. THE ENCHIRIDION: CONCERNING SPIRITUAL RESTITUTION.[7]

LIKE JUDAS, THE TEMPLE WILL BE DESTROYED. DESIDERIUS ERASMUS: The unfortunate Judas lost his place in the apostolic ministry; in the same way the temple will also one day be destroyed, as well as the priesthood and the authority of the scribes and Pharisees, together with Jerusalem itself. The impious Jews will be driven out and the true Jews will follow in their place—those who, circumcised in mind but not in body, acknowledge the Messiah whom the former crucified. PARAPHRASE OF ACTS 1:18-19.[8]

AN ALLEGORY ON JUDAS. MARTIN LUTHER: "When Judas had hanged himself, his insides spilled out." This is an example and figure of how those who betray Christ perish. It is signified in their

---

[4]In order to preserve the doctrine of Mary's perpetual virginity, commentators understood the brothers of Jesus to mean his cousins, not other children born of Mary. Few, if any, of the reformers challenged Mary's status as ever-virgin. Not only did Bullinger, Calvin, Luther and Zwingli hold to this, but even Hubmaier. See CRR 5:299 (QGT 9:273). For more on Mary and the Reformation, see Beth Kreitzer, *Reforming Mary: Changing Images of the Virgin Mary in Lutheran Sermons of the Sixteenth Century* (Oxford: Oxford University Press, 2004); and David F. Wright, "Mary in the Reformers," in *Chosen by God: Mary in Evangelical Perspective*, ed. David F. Wright (London: Marshall Pickering, 1989), 161-83. [5]Gwalther, *Homelyes or Sermons upon the Actes*, 46* (*In Acta Apostolorum*, 15v); alluding to Jn 19:26-27.

[6]Spangenberg, *Der Apostel Geschichte*, 10v-11r; alluding to Num 13; Ex 15:27; Josh 4. Spangenberg is here dependent on Luther's remarks recorded in WATR 1:317 no. 630. [7]CRR 6:327* (BRN 10:352-53); alluding to Lk 24:47; Acts 1:13; 1 Cor 3:5; Gal 2:8; 4:19; 6:13; Rom 4:12; 2 Cor 3:6; Eph 3:7; 1 Jn 2:1; Eph 3:14-16.). [8]CWE 50:11 (LB 7:664-65).

leader that the Jews will be destroyed in the same way. Now there is a mystery or allegory in the word *stomach* and also in the particular word *bowels*. The stomach is itself an entire kingdom that will pass away—nothing will remain there. The bowels are spilled out, by which he wants to indicate that even their sons and their posterity will perish. Another [interpretation] is that it means: Wherever the Word goes, there people only become more irritated and more stubborn. This example and spectacle was shown to those in Judea, so that they might repent and come to their senses. But totally unmoved they persisted in their wickedness, until they themselves perished. The sun melts wax, but it hardens mud. So it is, if the impious are not moved by those miracles and examples, which God displays to them for their correction. A third interpretation is that it is taught by this example that, despite seeing his miracles, the impious do not stop persecuting Christ and his Word, until they lie on the ground [dead]; like Sodom, Pharaoh, Babylon, Jerusalem. TABLE TALK, NIKOLAUS MEDLER.[9]

"THERE'S NO SHAME IN FALLING, BUT THERE'S SHAME IN REMAINING DOWN AND NOT WANTING TO STAND BACK UP." JOHANN AGRICOLA: Since we all are broken, we must fall often. This proverb excuses the fall as something we are unable to escape—instead it accuses remaining down. The holy Scriptures say, "The righteous falls every day seven times," that is, often, "and nevertheless always rises again." This is an excellent metaphor for us to apply to spiritual things: Whoever falls and sins but remains down must despair.

So, Judas and Cain fell. They allowed their sins to weigh them down, so that they thought their sins were greater than God's lovingkindness. For a person who wallows in distress affirms nothing good, focusing more and more on what he has done against God. In addition he thinks that God wants to punish him and deal wickedly with him. But against this remaining still and evil thinking God commands that in every distress we scream to him for help. And we

can do God no greater honor or service than in our distress to ascribe much good to him. Likewise, he is more willing to give than we to ask. God has always punished and will still punish murderers, adulterers and thieves, but much more will he punish those who do not call out to him in their distress.

Saint John says, "Whenever our heart condemns us, God is greater than our heart." Greater, that is, his mercy is greater. Thus, no one should despair of God's mercy. So, if someone has fallen, then cry out to God for mercy, and stand up again, just as Saint Peter and David did. Therefore, to fall is not sin, to sin out of weakness is not a sin that condemns, but not to be willing to call to God for his lovingkindness, this is a sin that leads to death and to condemnation. SEVEN HUNDRED FIFTY GERMAN PROVERBS.[10]

THE VOCATION OF PREACHERS. MENNO SIMONS: According to the Scriptures the mission and vocation of Christian preachers takes place in two ways. Some are called by God alone, without any human agent, as was the case with the prophets and apostles. Others are called by means of the pious. . . . Therefore, we your willing servants, companions and fellow mortals humbly admonish each of you in the office and service and rank to which you are called, in all love to consider the salvation of your immortal souls and to ponder carefully the vocation or mission, the doctrine and conduct of the bishops, pastors and preachers of your churches. Examine them by the Spirit of the Lord and the doctrines and customs of the apostles, seeing you persecute and destroy so many pious God-fearing Christians because of the idol temples of the ungodly or the blood clamor of the learned ones. We do not doubt that if you do this with a sincere heart you will soon perceive that we miserable humans do nothing more in this matter than the Word of God teaches and commands. FOUNDATION OF CHRISTIAN DOCTRINE (1539).[11]

---

[9]WATR 1:317 no. 670*.

[10]Agricola, *Die Sprichwörtersammlungen*, 1:552; alluding to Prov 24:16; Mt 7:11; Rom 8:32; Eph 3:20; 1 Jn 3:20; 5:16.
[11]Simons, *Complete Writings*, 159-61*.

THE ELECTION OF MINISTERS. RUDOLF GWAL-THER: As the church has great need of ministers of the Word, by whom it may be instructed and confirmed in the knowledge of God and mysteries of the true faith, so it is fitting that the same be duly and truly chosen and ordained so that all may perceive them to be chosen and appointed by God.... The first thing to be observed is that Saint Peter referred the whole matter to the congregation, to be discussed by their whole consent and counsel. We are taught that nothing ought to be appointed or decreed in the church by any one's private authority. For where the church is, as Paul says, [there is] God's building and God's husbandry, yes the household and family of God. None must take on themselves so much authority as to think they have power to prescribe anything from their own head. And although the rashness of some goes so far, yet they will profit little among the true sheep of Christ, which follow the voice of Christ only. Let the ministers be chosen openly, before the congregation. HOMILY 9, ACTS 1:23-26.[12]

IS CASTING LOTS SINFUL? JUSTUS JONAS: Many writers discuss whether today it is lawful to cast lots, and they say it should not be allowed—not even by Jonah's example nor the apostles'—because it is often carried out with trickery and deceit, as can happen in voting. As well, when we trust in lots, it may become idolatry and thus be contrary to the divine will. However, I think that we are able to use lots piously—in the election of bishops, etc.—so that if six or ten erudite men, who have the Spirit of God, are ordained and cast lots among themselves, then whoever's lot is chosen can be trusted to be called. For whoever casts lots in faith places the entire matter in the hand of God who determines the lots. Because here the matter is committed to lots, it is committed to the will of God. ANNOTATIONS ON ACTS 1:26.[13]

MATTHIAS CHOSEN AS A DISCIPLE. JOHN CALVIN: For there was this difference between the apostles and pastors, that whereas the pastors were chosen simply by the church, the apostles must be called by God. Thus Paul in the preface of his epistle to the Galatians declares himself to be an apostle "neither of men nor made by man." Therefore as the distinction of this office was so great, it was fitting that in the election of Matthias, however well people had done their duty, the final decision should be left to God. Christ had appointed the others with his own voice; if Matthias had been adopted into their ranks by the choice of people alone, his authority would have been less than theirs. COMMENTARY ON ACTS 1:23.[14]

CALLED BY GOD, MINISTERS MUST WALK DILIGENTLY. MENNO SIMONS: These teachers did not go about peddling their services ... but they were called and urged of God, as were Aaron, Jeremiah, Isaiah, Zechariah, Paul and others. Others, born of the blameless church of Christ, were chosen by lot as was Matthias. Being called, they were constrained by the Spirit to teach, to admonish, to console, to reprove, to serve and defend their poor brothers and sisters according to God's holy Word with all their strength. When they were thus called, and felt in them an urging of the Spirit, and moved by love as was said above, they reasonably worked at their trade with all solicitude and diligence, watching day and night for the eternal salvation of their sheep. BRIEF AND CLEAR CONFESSION (1544).[15]

---

[12]Gwalther, *Homelyes or Sermons upon the Actes*, 66* (*In Acta Apostolorum*, 22r); alluding to 1 Cor 3:5-15; Jn 10:27
[13]Jonas, *Annotationes in Acta*, B2v-B3r; alluding to Jon 1:7.
[14]CNTC 6:45* (CO 48:22-23); quoting Gal 1:1.
[15]Simons, *Complete Writings*, 442-43.

2:1-13 THE OUTPOURING OF THE HOLY SPIRIT

When the day of Pentecost arrived, they were all together in one place. ²And suddenly there came from heaven a sound like a mighty rushing wind, and it filled the entire house where they were sitting. ³And divided tongues as of fire appeared to them and rested*a* on each one of them. ⁴And they were all filled with the Holy Spirit and began to speak in other tongues as the Spirit gave them utterance.

⁵Now there were dwelling in Jerusalem Jews, devout men from every nation under heaven. ⁶And at this sound the multitude came together, and they were bewildered, because each one was hearing them speak in his own language. ⁷And they were amazed and astonished, saying, "Are not all these who are speaking Galileans? ⁸And how is it that we hear, each of us in his own native language? ⁹Parthians and Medes and Elamites and residents of Mesopotamia, Judea and Cappadocia, Pontus and Asia,¹⁰Phrygia and Pamphylia, Egypt and the parts of Libya belonging to Cyrene, and visitors from Rome,¹¹both Jews and proselytes, Cretans and Arabians—we hear them telling in our own tongues the mighty works of God." ¹²And all were amazed and perplexed, saying to one another, "What does this mean?"¹³But others mocking said, "They are filled with new wine."

a Or And tongues as of fire appeared to them, distributed among them, and rested

---

Overview: In the first part of Acts 2, Reformation exegetes display a robust pneumatology as they recognize the day of Pentecost to be an unequivocal demonstration of the Holy Spirit's activity in the world. This recognition of the Spirit's powerful work—"not designed to be ostentatious, but purposeful" (Gwalther)—sets the foundation for the narratives in Acts. In order to gain a deeper understanding of these stories, the commentators stress the role of preachers in elucidating divine mysteries; Word and Spirit are not to be divorced. The reformers connect the new and old covenants through the event of Pentecost, showing the distinguishable yet inseparable character of law and gospel. In a jaw-dropping display of power, Jesus indwells his people through his Spirit. Now these fallible and weak human beings are fleshly temples of God, transformed by the power, love and unity of the Holy Spirit. The preaching of the Word is intimately interconnected with the Spirit, but still the office of the Spirit is not just to entertain or expand intellectual horizons, but to share fellowship with others in love and conversation, drawing them into the divine life.

2:1-4 The Day of Pentecost

WHY IS THIS FESTIVAL CALLED PENTECOST? JOHANN SPANGENBERG: Because it is the fiftieth day after Easter. On Easter the children of Israel departed from Egypt through the Red Sea into the wilderness. Now on the fiftieth day after their departure they received the law through Moses on Mount Sinai. . . . But what is Pentecost? A revelation, both of the law and the gospel: Of the law in the old covenant on Mount Sinai, and of the gospel in the new covenant on Mount Zion, as Isaiah says, "The law will go out from Zion, and God's Word from Jerusalem." And just as in the old covenant among the Jews the fiftieth year is called a Jubilee or a "free year," in which everyone must be given their freedom and all goods must be returned to their true, natural heir, so also among Christians on the fiftieth day after the resurrection of Christ, the Holy Spirit was given, who renders every believing heart and conscience free, empty and clear of every sin and guides them to Christ as their true Lord. BRIEF EXEGESIS OF ACTS 2:1.[1]

---

[1]Spangenberg, *Der Apostel Geschichte*, 12v, 13r-v; quoting Is 2:3.

THE FESTIVAL OF *PFINGSTEN*. MARTIN LU-THER: This festival, which we call *Pfingsten*, has its origin from the following. When God led the children of Israel out of Egypt, he had them hold the Easter festival that same night and commanded them to celebrate it yearly at the same time in remembrance of their redemption and departure from Egypt. From that very day they proceeded into the wilderness for fifty days until Mount Sinai. At that very place the law of God was given to them through Moses, and it was commanded to them to keep [a feast of] remembrance of this event every year, fifty days after Easter. From this the feast gets its name, which we call *Pfingsten*. For the little word *Pfingstag* comes from the Greek *Pentecoste*, which means the fiftieth day, which our Saxon language states somewhat closer to the Greek as *Pfingsten*. Thus, Luke says here, when the same fifty days after the Easter festival were over, and they had begun to tell the story of how God had given his people the law on Mount Sinai, then the Holy Spirit came—just as Christ had promised them!—and gave them a new law. So, we celebrate this feast not for the sake of the old but rather the new story, namely, on account of the sending of the Holy Spirit. POSTIL FOR PENTE-COST, CRUCIGER'S SUMMER POSTIL (1544).[2]

WAS THIS THE BEGINNING OF THE DAY OR THE END? CARDINAL CAJETAN: If you should marvel that it is said, "And when the day was completed" (when what should have been said there was, "And when the day began," for the thing mentioned was done in the morning of that day), let it be known that among the Hebrews the day begins from the first hour of the night. By this thing done early in the morning, the third hour is correctly described as that which completes the day. Because the day was divided among the Hebrews into two parts (that is, from evening until morn-ing and from morning until evening), part of the second day was already spent at the third hour. By this, that day was not then beginning but was be-ing completed. COMMENTARY ON ACTS 2:1.[3]

THE BETTER PENTECOST OF THE NEW COV-ENANT. MARTIN LUTHER: Now in the Old Testa-ment stories we see, as Paul says, what happened to the Jews was a foreshadowing of certain events which should take place in the New Testament, in the time of grace. Thus, just as we in the New Cov-enant have a different and better Easter lamb to eat, so also we have in the New Covenant a different and better Pentecost than they had in the Old Covenant. For there in Egypt the blood of the dear lamb with which they smeared the doorposts only protected them, so that the angel, the destroyer, could not harm the body and kill the fruit of the firstborn, in contrast our dear Easter lamb's blood, Christ Jesus' blood serves to redeem us from the true Egypt, namely, from the devil's tyranny, from sin and eternal death. HOUSE POSTIL FOR PENTECOST (1544).[4]

I HEARD THE WIND BLOWING. DAVID JORIS:

> I heard the wind blowing,
> the Spirit breathed in my senses;
>
> And I stopped sowing
> my grain, to my loss;
> I did not produce any fruit
> or blessings.
> I must seek them in love,
> for they are always gathered for my good.
>
> I grasp in my hands the understanding
> which must come from God.
> It is love, as you know,
> which comes to the pious people.
> Esteem love above all,
> and do what you will.
> Do no other work than this,
> And be at peace in it.
>
> All that you do on earth,
> protect the ciborium of God.

---

[2]WA 21:438. As a result of his belief that the church has existed since Adam and Eve, Luther regularly referred to Israelite feasts and festivals by their "Christian" names.

[3]Cajetan, *In Acta Apostolorum*, 214v.
[4]WA 52:314; alluding to 1 Cor 10:6.

Highly esteem God's temple,
do all to the glory of God.
Seek the profit of the many,
of one another, but not of yourself.
Heal your brothers' wound,
Just as love commands.

Protect the simple as well as the sick,
Do not let them perish.
Give offense neither to
the Jews nor the Greeks.
Neither injure God's people,
as the Scriptures testify.
For there is no salvation in such action,
For God values such people.

For the nuts are produced in love,
and they will be unmeasured.
It is all concluded
in the Law and Prophets.
It will all be provided for me
without any harvesting.
Store up love to the last measure,
Otherwise it is not preserved.

I HEARD THE WIND BLOWING (1534).[5]

THE IRRESISTIBLE WORK OF THE HOLY SPIRIT.
HEINRICH BULLINGER: As the law was received on
Mt. Sinai, so the Spirit was sent as a gift on Mt. Zion.
Thus, indeed, the prophets had predicted that the law
would proceed from Zion, and the Word of the Lord
from Jerusalem. Those on Mt. Sinai heard the blasts
of trumpets, the crash of thunder, and they witnessed
the terrifying flames of lightning—just one of these
things was able to shatter human minds (*mentes*).
Indeed all these things signified God's power and
vengeance (I do not know of anything else that the
terror of the law could refer to), without a doubt
provided for those who would despise God's law....
We truly hear the noise as if it were the violent blowing of a coming assault. Through this the Holy Spirit
indicated that his teaching will expand throughout
the entire world by this extraordinary event and by
this remarkable blessing. Nor is there anyone who is

capable of resisting his assault. Thus, we see a wind
with extraordinary speed and which no one is able to
oppose, blowing through the whole world. COM-
MENTARY ON ACTS 2:2.[6]

THE HOLY SPIRIT ARRIVED WITH A POWER-
FUL YET SWEET WIND. JOHANN SPANGENBERG:
How did the Holy Spirit come? With a powerful
but indeed sweet wind, in order to show that the
word of the gospel is a far more friendly word than
the terrifying word of the law was.

Was this also a natural wind? This wind was not
natural; otherwise it would have roared through all
of Jerusalem, yes, the entire Jewish land! Rather, a
gust of wind was ordained by God to be a herald
and forerunner of the Holy Spirit. For kings and
princes let their arrival be promulgated through
the blast of trumpets, bugles and rifles, so that we
assume them to be even more magnificent. How
much more should the high Majesty of God do
this and promulgate the arrival of the Holy Spirit
through powerful signs! And as the law of Moses is
given on Mount Sinai in the midst of a storm, dark
clouds, fiery smoke, steam, thunder and lightning,
in savage tumult and the trumpet blasts of God, so
also the Holy Spirit is given in Jerusalem in a great
flurry and gust of wind by which God demonstrates the power of the law and the gospel....

From where did the Holy Spirit come? From
heaven, not secretly but publicly in a mighty gust
of wind. Just as a mighty torrential downpour,
suspended for a time in the air, is finally released
in free fall, so also the Holy Spirit rushes out with
such violence as if he wanted to drown everything,
filling with his flood every valley, grave and pit until
they overflow. In this way the Holy Spirit works.
Whenever he arrives, he arrives with such fullness
that he drenches every humble heart so richly with
his grace and gifts that they overflow immediately,
unable to contain themselves, they must break out
and proclaim to all the world the wonders God has
worked in them. BRIEF EXEGESIS OF ACTS 2:2.[7]

---

[5]CRR 7:105-6.

[6]Bullinger, *In Acta Apostolorum*, 20v, alluding to Is 2:3; Mic 4:2.
[7]Spangenberg, *Der Apostel Geschichte*, 13v-15r.

2:5-13 *The Signs of the Holy Spirit*

RECEIVE THE INVISIBLE MARK OF THE HOLY SPIRIT AS IF IT WERE VISIBLE. JOHANN ECK: I hope to God that there are many pious hearts among you, who have invisibly received the Holy Spirit on this wedding day in his grace and gifts and have specially prepared themselves in a God-fearing manner with contemplation, confession and the reception of the Sacrament, just as the holy apostles and other faithful among them received him visibly. This is a powerful confirmation of our holy faith. This was a confirmation of the apostles who earlier were fearful and fled from the Lord, even denied him, but now they confess and proclaim the name of Jesus undaunted. Now we would like to speak further about the visible sending of the Holy Spirit, so that we may act fruitfully, pleading for his mercy with our heart and mouth, singing with joy, "Come Holy Spirit, Lord God" . . . .

But why does this visible appearance of the Holy Spirit no longer happen in the church? Pious Christian, you should not imagine that the Holy Spirit is not present in baptism or in confirmation. He is indeed just as present now as during the time of the apostles, but not visibly, for in the beginning this happened for the benefit of the church. However, since through the teaching of the apostles, through their miracles and the martyrs' miracles, the church is now well-founded and confirmed, it is no longer necessary for the Holy Spirit to appear in a miraculous fashion. . . . Yes, the holy teachers state that at the end time, when the Antichrist has almost arrived, the miraculous signs will completely cease, so that the patience of the saints and the conversion of the wicked are displayed. Now this has clearly happened today among the New Christians,[8] who so humiliate and disgrace the dear saints. THE SECOND SERMON ON PENTECOST.[9]

WHY DOES THE HOLY SPIRIT REVEAL HIMSELF THROUGH TONGUES OF FIRE? JOHANN SPANGENBERG: The tongue is an obliging organ for the Holy Spirit. For through the tongue God's word is preached, conveying the gospel into the human heart like through a canal or conduit. Why cloven tongues? In order to show that the gospel should be preached throughout the entire world in every language and tongue. For just as God in the Old Testament through many languages and tongues scattered throughout the world the construction workers of the Tower of Babel, so the Holy Spirit in the New Testament gathers the construction workers of Christendom from many languages and tongues into the unity of faith from every part of the world. Why fiery tongues? The most distinguished work of the Holy Spirit is that he kindles human hearts, ignites them in faith and love and strengthens them in the Word of God, both through hearing and preaching, as the two disciples traveling to Emmaus confessed. BRIEF EXEGESIS OF ACTS 2:3-4.[10]

A PRAYER TO THE HOLY SPIRIT. JOHN DONNE:

> O Holy Ghost, whose temple I
> Am, but of mudde walls, and condensed dust,
>   And being sacrilegiously
> Half wasted with youth's fires, of pride and lust,
>   Must with new storms be weatherbeat;
>   Double in my heart thy flame,
> Which let devout sad tears intend; and let
> (Though this glass lantern, flesh,
>   do suffer maime)
> Fire, Sacrifice, Priest, Altar be the same.

THE HOLY GHOST.[11]

CHRIST THE TRUE SOLOMON BUILDS HIS SPIRITUAL TEMPLE. DIRK PHILIPS: Christ has stepped forward as the peaceful Solomon, our peace and hope before God the Father. Through his apostles who were clothed with power from

---

[8]This is Eck's preferred phrase for the self-described evangelical parties of the Reformation.
[9]Eck, *Christenliche Predigen* 3:135r-v.

[10]Spangenberg, *Der Apostel Geschichte*, 15r-v; alluding to Lk 24:32.
[11]Donne, *Poems of John Donne*, 338-39.

on high on the day of Pentecost, he has built the temple in Jerusalem, that is, the Christian congregation, and has adorned it with manifold spiritual gifts, as is clearly demonstrated in the apostolic congregation.... The promise of Solomon was applied to Christ by the apostles. For that God had promised David that the fruit of his loins should sit on his throne, this was fulfilled according to the letter when Solomon became king over Israel in his father's place. But according to the Spirit it is to be understood as the true Solomon, Jesus Christ, who has a throne which abides throughout eternity, and he is King over his congregation, over all of spiritual Israel. THE ENCHIRIDION: CONCERNING SPIRITUAL RESTITUTION.[12]

SPEAKING MANY LANGUAGES A WONDERFUL MIRACLE. RUDOLF GWALTHER: Beginning with the apostles, [Luke] attributes two things to them, which they received by the operation of the Holy Spirit. The first is that by and by, after they had received the Holy Spirit, they began to speak with strange and diverse tongues. This is so great and wonderful a miracle, as I know not whether ever there happened a greater among people. For who is ignorant how much labor and industry is required even from our childhood to learn diverse tongues? We see that people grown in years are scarcely able to learn any one tongue, and the perfect use thereof. But the apostles, unlearned men of mature age, who had spent their childhood and youth not in the study of learning but in handy occupations, even in a moment became notable and excellent in the knowledge and use not of one tongue, or two, but of all tongues at once. Who here acknowledges not the evident work of God? Who reverences not the operation of the Holy Spirit? For what could the industry or dexterity of a person's wit have done in so short a time? Neither was this miracle superfluous, as serving only for bare and vain ostentation (as the things done by jugglers are), but very profitable and necessary for the apostles in

discharging their duty and office. For where Jesus Christ had appointed them to be teachers of all the world, that through their ministry the doctrine of the gospel might be published among all nations, it was necessary they should be understood by all nations. HOMILY II, ACTS 2:4-13.[13]

THE HOLY SPIRIT DOES NOT WRITE ON PAPER BUT ON HUMAN HEARTS. MARTIN LUTHER: In this passage you hear that the Holy Spirit came from above and filled the disciples who earlier wallowed in sorrow and fear, rendering their tongues fiery and cloven, igniting them so that they are bold and preach Christ freely and do not fear for themselves. Thus, you clearly see that his office is not to write books or to make laws. Rather, he is such a Spirit who writes on the heart and creates a new courage, so that this person can be joyful before God and grow in love for him and finally serve others with joyous courage. POSTIL FOR PENTECOST, CRUCIGER'S SUMMER POSTIL (1544).[14]

THE NEW WINE TORE THE OLD WINESKINS. DESIDERIUS ERASMUS: Of course, extreme intoxication is very much like madness.... But no madness enables all to understand what you say. [Some in the crowd], indeed, said this in derision, but nothing forbids the truth sometimes to be spoken even in jest. They were completely filled with the new wine which the Lord did not want entrusted to old skins. The old wine of the Mosaic law failed at the wedding of the church, and the cold and tasteless sense of the Law was changed into new wine through Christ. Whatever is carnal is tasteless and weak; whatever is spiritual is lively, effective and appealing to the taste. PARAPHRASE OF ACTS 2:13.[15]

GRANT US, O GOD, THE SAME HOLY SPIRIT. BOOK OF COMMON PRAYER (1549): God, who

---

[12]CRR 6:327* (BRN 10:363); alluding to Ps 132:11-12; 1 Kings 8:20; Heb 1:8.

[13]Gwalther, *Homelyes or Sermons upon the Actes*, 82* (*In Acta Apostolorum*, 27r).

[14]WA 21:440.

[15]CWE 50:16* (LB 7:668).

on this day [Pentecost] taught the hearts of your faithful people by sending to them the light of your Holy Spirit. Grant us by the same Spirit to have a right judgment in all things and always to rejoice in his holy comfort, through the merits of Christ Jesus, our Savior, who lives and reigns with you in the unity of the same Spirit, one God world without end. THE COLLECT FOR PENTECOST.[16]

[16]BCP 1549, 58*.

2:14-36 PETER'S PENTECOST SERMON

[14]*But Peter, standing with the eleven, lifted up his voice and addressed them: "Men of Judea and all who dwell in Jerusalem, let this be known to you, and give ear to my words.* [15]*For these people are not drunk, as you suppose, since it is only the third hour of the day.*[a] [16]*But this is what was uttered through the prophet Joel:*

[17]*"'And in the last days it shall be, God declares,*
that I will pour out my Spirit on all flesh,
and your sons and your daughters shall prophesy,
and your young men shall see visions,
and your old men shall dream dreams;
[18]*even on my male servants and female servants*[b]
in those days I will pour out my Spirit, and
they shall prophesy.
[19]*And I will show wonders in the heavens above*
and signs on the earth below,
blood, and fire, and vapor of smoke;
[20]*the sun shall be turned to darkness*
and the moon to blood,
before the day of the Lord comes, the great
and magnificent day.
[21]*And it shall come to pass that* c*everyone*
who calls upon the name of the Lord
shall be saved.'

[22]*"Men of Israel, hear these words: Jesus of Nazareth, a man attested to you by God with mighty works and wonders and signs that God did through him in your midst, as you yourselves know—*[23]*this Jesus,*[c] *delivered up according to the definite plan and foreknowledge of God, you crucified and killed by the hands of lawless men.* [24]*God raised him up, loosing the pangs of death, because it was not possible for him to be held by it.* [25]*For David says concerning him,*

"'I saw the Lord always before me,
for he is at my right hand that I may not be
shaken;
[26]*therefore my heart was glad, and my tongue*
rejoiced;
my flesh also will dwell in hope.
[27]*For you will not abandon my soul to Hades,*
or let your Holy One see corruption.
[28]*You have made known to me the paths of life;*
you will make me full of gladness with your
presence.'

[29]*"Brothers, I may say to you with confidence about the patriarch David that he both died and was buried, and his tomb is with us to this day.* [30]*Being therefore a prophet, and knowing that God had sworn with an oath to him that he would set one of his descendants on his throne,* [31]*he foresaw and spoke about the resurrection of the Christ, that he was not abandoned to Hades, nor did his flesh see corruption.* [32]*This Jesus God raised up, and of that we all are witnesses.* [33]*Being therefore exalted at the right hand of God, and having received from the Father the promise of the Holy Spirit, he has poured out this that you yourselves are seeing and hearing.* [34]*For David did not ascend into the heavens, but he himself says,*

"'The Lord said to my Lord,
"Sit at my right hand,
[35]*until I make your enemies your footstool."'*

[36]*Let all the house of Israel therefore know for certain that God has made him both Lord and Christ, this Jesus whom you crucified."*

a That is, 9 a.m.   b Greek *bondservants*; twice in this verse   c Greek *this one*

OVERVIEW: Our commentators celebrate the recitation of Joel's prophecy as evidence of the Holy Spirit's distribution of gifts, and read passages from the Psalms as indications of God's promise and fulfillment. Peter's sermon is a clear example of christological interpretation in which the prophetic texts are understood to hold a kernel of the gospel when seen through the lens of Christ. Peter's address also demonstrates the Holy Spirit's effectiveness and how the Spirit works. The main work of the Spirit is to renew the hearts of individuals and incorporate them into Christ. Therefore, the radical change in Peter himself and the growth of the believing community stand as the most palpable examples of the Spirit's transformative work.

Related to the issue of God's sovereignty and human agency, the problem of suffering and evil comes up such that God is not responsible for evil (evildoers are culpable for their actions), yet God has ordained all things and turns even these evil actions to ultimate good.

GOD TRANSFORMS THOSE WHO CAN BARELY SPEAK THEIR MOTHER TONGUE INTO POLYGLOTS.

MARTIN LUTHER: The Holy Spirit arrives, fills the entire house, but this was not frightening. For he immediately entered into their hearts, not as gilded flames but living, fiery flames! The Holy Spirit revealed himself in the wind in order to make them strong, steadfast and courageous, who were earlier hiding themselves. And so in this way he rested on each and every person, how precisely we do not know, but there must have been something that they could see and feel—perhaps it was fiery tongues; the wind is an external thing just like fiery flames are external. Thus the Holy Spirit allowed himself to be seen as also he—indeed, the holy Trinity—came to us humans in the form of a dove. Now they were suddenly transformed. They were poor people from Galilee, they couldn't read or write, someone had to read them the Scriptures. Peter did not have a fiery tongue, but here he receives the understanding of the Scriptures and of every language. Peter, who can barely speak his mother tongue, is so suddenly transformed that he is able to speak every language under the sun! This is a powerful sign, about which everyone must have been puzzled. The rule that the sign must be tested by its work should be applied here. Yes, this is even greater, that he opens the holy Scriptures! Peter and women became doctors and

prophets greater than all the prophets, speaking of Christ as it stands written in all the prophets. Such an unlearned man so suddenly receives such a complete understanding that no one else is able to understand skillfully. The [temple] rulers in Jerusalem were complete fools compared with this ability, that is, that they could speak with other tongues that they had never learned or even heard. SERMON ON PENTECOST MONDAY IN THE AFTERNOON (1545).[1]

A SIMPLE FISHERMAN TRANSFORMED BY THE MIGHTY GIFTING OF THE HOLY SPIRIT.

JOHANN SPANGENBERG: But what was Peter for a man? A simple, uneducated person: a fisherman. And what became of him? A learned preacher, an exegete of Scripture, an apostle of Christ. Before he could not stand up to the high priest Caiaphas's servant girl; now he stands up to the entire world. Before a woman's shadow petrified him, so that he denied Christ; now he freely confesses Christ before all people, Jews and Gentiles. Before he struck Malchus with the physical sword; now he strikes the entire world with the spiritual sword, with God's word. Is this not the work of God and the power of the Holy Spirit? What human power, wisdom and cleverness could have been able to transform Peter's disposition so quickly? BRIEF EXEGESIS OF ACTS 2:14-36.[2]

JOEL'S PROPHECY.

JUSTUS JONAS: The beginning of Peter's sermon focuses on interpreting this miracle. For whenever a new Word is revealed, God adds a miracle in order to confirm the Word. Consequently the apostles through the miracle bring about faith in the Word, and with the same miracle they also bring about faith through Scripture. So then Peter summarizes, first, "See! This sort of miracle the prophets foretold, testifying to the kingdom of the Messiah or the Christ, now you see, our sons are prophesying, they are speaking various languages. The other signs you saw [fulfilled] in

---

[1]WA 49:748-49.
[2]Spangenberg, *Der Apostel Geschichte*, 19v-20r.

the passion, as they were foretold in Psalm 18, 'The earth reeled and rocked.'"

Second, that passage in Joel describes the kingdom of Christ that will exist spiritually, "I will pour out my Spirit," etc. Third, "all who call upon the name of the Lord will be saved"—that is justification by faith, as if Peter were saying, "This will be the kingdom of the Messiah, because faith in him justifies sinners and snatches them out of the kingdom of darkness or of Satan." (This passage is also cited in Romans 10.) Now by whom salvation is [accomplished] and how Christ now rules in Spirit, he says more clearly below. "Exalted at the right hand of God," as if he were saying, "Here the Mediator is now clearly revealed, who was formerly promised, through whom we are able to pray to the Father and on account of whom we are heard. He has even given us the Holy Spirit." So you see how strongly by this sermon Peter urges knowledge of Christ and his kingdom, which exists spiritually. ANNOTATIONS ON ACTS 2:16-21.[3]

A New Priesthood Without Distinctions Is Established. MARTIN LUTHER: "Flesh," that is every kind of person. "There will be no distinction, I will pour out the Holy Spirit from heaven, so that all people will prophesy." Therefore the Levitical priesthood will be revoked and a new priesthood will be established, as he indicates by "your sons, daughters, my servants." This means "every kind of flesh" or person. I will accept women, young girls, and I will teach them all how they should prophesy. Slaves will enter [the prophetic] office, just like Anna and young girls. Therefore the [old] priestly courses are abolished. Against this the Jews cannot assert that we abolish [the priesthood altogether]. For our preaching office must be correct, and it is not hampered just because it is not from the tribe of Aaron. Peter was not from the priestly estate, nor were any of the apostles, nor was Christ. This new office is not started by priests but by others from the other tribes. . . . Here Joel

says every kind of person can be bishop, priest, pope and cardinal. This is a powerful text that throws down the priesthood. . . .

Now it happens that priests are ordained from every tribe. Today there are rural boys who become priests, who are suitable and have the grace to preach, whom we can use in that office. Thus, "I will pour out," and so on. "I am unwilling to make distinctions between city dweller and farmer." So, this text establishes a new priesthood that has no distinction of persons. . . . Here a person is devout as anyone else, nun, monk, father. This passage affirms that a man is not a man, a saint not a saint, a sinner not a sinner. As Paul says, "In Christ there is neither Greek nor priest." This is an irritating word, that over Caiaphas the powerful, excellent man a tax collector should come first. A Carthusian[4] who has been in the order for forty years should be no better than a maid who carries grass to the cows. SERMON FOR PENTECOST MONDAY (1531).[5]

God Is Not the Author of Evil, but He Is Sovereign over It. JOHN CALVIN: Peter would seem to suggest that the wicked obeyed God, from which one of two absurdities would follow: either that God is the author of evil or that humans do not sin whatever evil they might commit. Concerning the second, I would reply that the wicked are very far from obeying God, in whatever way they execute what God in his own counsels has appointed. For obedience springs from a voluntary affection, and we know that something far different is true of the wicked. Again, no one obeys God except the person who knows his will. Obedience therefore depends on the knowledge of the will of God. Furthermore, God has revealed his will to us in the law. Therefore only those who obey God do what is agreeable to the law of God; again, they submit themselves willingly to his government. . . .

---

[3]Jonas, *Annotationes in Acta*, B6r-v; alluding to Ex 4:1-16; Col 1:13; Rom 10:13; quoting Ps 18:7; Joel 2:28, 32; Acts 2:33.

[4]The Carthusians were known for their strict ascetic monastic rules: they were only allowed to eat one meal a day except during high festivals of the church, and their diet consisted chiefly of vegetables, bread and water.

[5]WA 34, 1:482-83, 484-85; alluding to Lk 2:36-38; Acts 21:9; quoting Gal 3:28.

As for the other point, I deny that God is the author of evil because this expression carries certain implications. For a wicked deed is judged according to the end at which it is aimed. When people commit theft or murder, they sin in being thieves or murderers; in theft and murder there is a criminal intention. But God who uses their wickedness stands on a different level. His object is far different, for he wishes to chastise the one and exercise the patience of the other. But in this he never declines from his own nature, that is, from perfect righteousness. COMMENTARY ON ACTS 2:23.[6]

THE LORD INVERTS HUMAN ACTIONS. JOHN DONNE: If we could have been in paradise and seen God take a clod of red earth and make that wretched clod of contemptible earth such a body as should be fit to receive his breath, an immortal soul, fit to be the house of the second person of the Trinity, for God the Son to dwell in bodily; fit to be the temple for the third person, for the Holy Spirit, should we not have wondered more than at the production of all other creatures? It is more that the same Jesus whom they had crucified is exalted thus, to sit in that despised flesh at the right hand of our glorious God. All their spitting should but macerate him and dissolve him into a better mold, a better plaster. All their beatings should but knead him and press him into a better form. All their scoffing and insolence should be prophecies. "Behold your King" and "This is the King of the Jews," these words—those who spoke them thought to be lies—in their own mouths should become truths. He truly is the king, not only of the Jews but of all nations, too. Their nailing him on the cross should be a settling of him on an everlasting throne. Their lifting him up on the cross, awaiting on him, so far on his way to heaven, that this Jesus, whom they had thus evacuated, thus crucified, should be thus exalted, was a subject of infinite admiration but mixed with infinite confusion, too. SERMON AT SAINT PAUL'S, EASTER EVENING (1623).[7]

THE FORMER PROMISES ARE ALL FULFILLED IN CHRIST. BALTHASAR HUBMAIER: These promises comforted and preserved the confessing sinner, that he would not despair in his sins, for a Messiah will come to atone for the sins, to release the debtors from prison and to lead them with him into the promised fatherland. It is as if one directed the sick person to a good physician who will surely make him well, but he is not yet well. The gospel, however, completely calms the person, helps him to rest in his conscience and makes him completely well, for it shows that the Law is now fulfilled in Christ, who has paid the debt of sin for us and has already vanquished death, devil and hell. Thus the patriarchs of old had the benefit of the promises of God as in Abraham's bosom, where they were preserved until the time of Christ's descent into hell. When the gospel was proclaimed to them there by the Spirit of Christ, only then did they really live in the Christ who had been given them and obtain redemption and eternal joy through the joyful message that he has vanquished sin, death, devil and hell. Only then were the holy fathers freed of their pains in hell which they (but not the soul of Christ) had suffered there for a long time. A CHRISTIAN CATECHISM (1526).[8]

THROUGH THE HOLY SPIRIT WE PARTICIPATE IN THE TREASURES OF OUR LORD. MARTIN LUTHER: Now believing the gospel belongs with preaching the gospel. For this purpose, God sends the Holy Spirit, who imprints this good news on the heart, so that it clings to and lives in the heart. It is indeed certainly true that Christ accomplished all this, totally removing our sins and conquering everything, so that through him we can be lords over all things. But if the treasure lies in a heap, then it cannot be distributed everywhere, nor can it be used. So then, if we are to have [this treasure], the Holy Spirit must come and place it in our heart, so that we believe and confess, "I too am one of those who will have this benefit." Through the gospel each person who hears it is offered and

[6]CNTC 6:66* (CO 48:40).
[7]Donne, *Works* 1:314-15*.

[8]CRR 5:347-48* (QGT 9:312).

called to this grace, as [Jesus] says: "Come to me all you who are heavy laden." POSTIL FOR PENTECOST, CRUCIGER'S SUMMER POSTIL (1544).[9]

THE KNOWLEDGE OF THE TRUE MESSIAH IS THE FOUNDATION OF THE HOUSE OF ISRAEL. JOHN DONNE: For this knowledge that is proclaimed here, which is the knowledge that the true Messiah has come and that there is no other to be expected, is such a knowledge that even the house of Israel itself is without a foundation, if it is with-

out this knowledge. Is there any house that needs no reparations? Is there a house of Israel? (Let it be the library, the depository of the oracles of God, a true church, that has the true Word of the true God, let it be the house fed with manna that has the true administration of the sacraments of Christ Jesus.) Is there any such house, that needs no further knowledge? There are always thieves about the house that would rob us of that Word and of those sacraments. SERMON AT SAINT PAUL'S, EASTER EVENING (1623).[10]

---

[9]WA 21:441; quoting Mt 11:28.

[10]Donne, *Works*, 1:311-12*.

2:37-41 REPENTANCE, BAPTISM AND THE HOLY SPIRIT

[37]Now when they heard this they were cut to the heart, and said to Peter and the rest of the apostles, "Brothers, what shall we do?" [38]And Peter said to them, "Repent and be baptized every one of you in the name of Jesus Christ for the forgiveness of your sins, and you will receive the gift of the Holy Spirit. [39]For the promise is for you and for your children and for all who are far off, everyone whom the Lord our God calls to himself." [40]And with many other words he bore witness and continued to exhort them, saying, "Save yourselves from this crooked generation." [41]So those who received his word were baptized, and there were added that day about three thousand souls.

OVERVIEW: Peter's pastoral exhortation to the Pentecost crowd to repent and baptize instigates the first of many fierce baptismal debates among the Reformation commentators in their exegesis of Acts. Lutheran, Reformed and Catholic reformers uphold infant baptism because of the ultimate reliance on God's preeminent grace as the primary act above any human act. Radicals challenge that infant baptism has no clear Scriptural basis; for them, baptism is primarily a human response of faith, an external badge witnessing to their experience of grace in Christ.

THE HEALING OF THE SPIRIT GROWS STRONGER THROUGH THE WORD. MARTIN LUTHER:
They both—the Holy Spirit *and* our sin and imperfection—must always be intermingled, so that we feel them both. Our condition is like that of a sick person who is under the care of the doctor's hands and will indeed get better because of the doctor. Thus, no one should think, "This person has the Holy Spirit! Therefore he should be absolutely strong, should do only precious works and should have no brokenness [in him]." No! This is not so. For it cannot be this way while we live on earth in our flesh, that we should be without every weakness and brokenness. Even the holy apostles themselves often lamented their temptations and sorrows. And the Holy Spirit himself was hidden under these feelings, despite which he strengthened

and sustained them through Word and faith.

For this reason the Holy Spirit is given to no one other than to those who stand in sorrow and fear. There the gospel bears fruit and profit. For this gift is too great and noble for God to cast it before dogs and pigs, who once they come across it—that is, hear it preached—devour it without knowing what they are devouring. This gift must be given to such hearts that feel and see their misery and are unable to free themselves from it. The heart must writhe, if the Holy Spirit is to come and help. No one should imagine that this happens any other way. POSTIL FOR PENTECOST, CRUCIGER'S SUMMER POSTIL (1544).[1]

PETER IS A GENTLE PASTOR. DESIDERIUS
ERASMUS: Here Peter presents the image of a gentle shepherd. What does he do? He does not rage at them with harsh reproaches, he does not magnify their sin, he does not thrust them away and put them off, he does not prescribe sacrifices and burnt offerings but shows the remedy prepared for the conscience-stricken, making no distinction between those who had crucified Jesus and those who had not agreed to the impious deed, for no one was free from sin. PARAPHRASE OF ACTS 2:38.[2]

CHRISTIAN BAPTISM IS ONE. CARDINAL

---

[1]WA 21:443; alluding to Mt 7:6.
[2]CWE 50:22* (LB 7:672).

CAJETAN: From this it appears that it is the same thing to be baptized in the name of Christ and to be baptized in the name of the Father and of the Son and of the Holy Spirit. If in fact the apostles had a command from Christ to baptize in the name of the Father and of the Son and of the Holy Spirit, it would not have changed the substantial form of baptism (so that they would teach something else and do something else), if this form and that form had been different. For it is permitted that there be diversity with respect to the words [by which it is done], but nevertheless the words are the same with respect to the signification. COMMENTARY ON ACTS 2:38.[3]

JESUS CANNOT BE SEPARATED FROM THE FATHER AND THE HOLY SPIRIT.

MARTIN LUTHER: We should learn to understand baptism and cherish it, because it contains the name of the Father, the Son and the Holy Spirit—or even just the name of Christ, as reported in Acts. It is sufficient to be baptized in the name of Christ, because the Father and the Holy Spirit are there also. So do not separate the water from the Word, but say, "The water is ordained by God to make us pure for Christ's sake, for the sake of the Father and the Holy Spirit. They are there in the water to purify us from sin and death." Whoever is in sin, plunge them into baptism, and their sin will be extinguished. Whoever is in death, plunge them into baptism, and death will be gobbled up. For baptism has divine power, the power to break sin and death. That's why we are baptized. If later we fall into error or sin, we have not demolished our baptism; but we return to it, saying, "God has baptized me, plunged me into the baptism of his Son, of the Father and the Holy Spirit. There I return, and I trust that my baptism will take away my sin—not for my sake, but for the sake of the man Christ, who instituted it." SERMON ON EPIPHANY (1534).[4]

WHY SHOULD THE THREE PERSONS OF THE DIVINITY BE CALLED ON EQUALLY?

PHILIPP MELANCHTHON: This is because we should acknowledge God's being and will as he himself has revealed this. And this revelation is often expressed in Scripture, especially in the baptism of Christ where the three persons are displayed distinctly. Also, in the word of our baptism: "You will baptize them in the name of the Father, Son and Holy Spirit." Again in the Symbols.[5]

We should listen and learn what is understood by this word *person*. Namely, this is not some tormented and dead concept; it is also not a random, changing thing that clings to some other being. It is not a piecemeal or separable thing, but rather is something material, living, not in many, but distinct, unified and rational. It is not supported and sustained by some other attached being. You are a person, but your body is not alone a person. For it is supported by a more noble nature, namely, by the soul. Thus if the soul departs, then the body decays and festers. EXAMINATION OF CANDIDATES FOR ORDINATION (1552).[6]

FOLLOW THE ORDER OF CHRIST.

BALTHASAR HUBMAIER: On the one hand [proponents of infant baptism] see the serious baptismal command of Christ, but on the other they fear the stigma of rebaptism, since there are none in their own circle of acquaintances. So that they may be helped out of this confusion, I have brought together in writing for the praise of God and the use of all people the ground and reasons, so that it be thereby indisputably proven that every believing person who has available water and a baptizer is responsible for [the sake of] his soul to have himself also baptized in water according to the order of Christ, regardless of his having been bathed in water in his childhood. . . .

---

[3]Cajetan, *In Acta Apostolorum*, 216r.
[4]Frederick J. Gaiser, trans., "'This Is My Son, the Beloved': Sermon on the Baptism of Jesus, The Epiphany of Our Lord (January 6, 1534)," *Word & World* 16, no. 1 (1996), 10* (WA 37:253).

[5]By "symbols" Melanchthon means the three most important creeds for the life and worship of the church: the Apostles' Creed, the Nicene Creed and the Athanasian Creed. See also the note on Johann Eck's comment on Acts 15 (p. 213), where he cites Jerome, who describes the creeds as "watchwords" of the Christian faith.
[6]MWA 6:178-79; quoting Mt 28:19.

You have until now so diligently grasped the pleasing verse of Paul where he says, "Because of harlotry each man should have his own wife and each woman her own husband," and this verse you have often called out with high voice and loudly for the justification of priestly marriage. When Paul says, "each man," no one is excluded. Why then do you not give the same weight to the words, "each one, each one" in this verse of Peter, where he says with the same authority, let "each one" of you be baptized in the name of Jesus Christ for the forgiveness of sins? I warn you by the righteous judgment of God that you do not push away the earnest word of Peter, which serves souls for the forgiveness of sins. Therefore let the Scriptures of both Peter and Paul remain in equal weight teaching, truth, power and effect. GROUND AND REASON (1527).[7]

IF WE FOLLOW THE GREEK LETTERS, WE (PAEDOBAPTISTS) WIN. HULDRYCH ZWINGLI: We have previously shown that if we insist on the very letters [of Scripture], we will certainly win. For only after baptizing, not before, does it say, "Teach them to hold all the things which I have commanded you." So then, before baptizing it simply says "teach," and it is not clearly expressed what they should teach. And if the baptism deniers would say, "What follows is an explanation of what comes first, namely, what they should teach," then I answer, "You insist on the order of the words. Therefore, you must let the words stand still for me. This is not the only passage where 'to baptize' comes before 'to teach,' as will soon be shown. But if you do not insist on the order of the very letters, with what will you then overthrow infant baptism, since you no longer have this passage?" So then, either you must leave the order of the letters or they are for us and not for you. For we too discover that in the very first use of baptism, that baptism precedes teaching. Thus, saying to the wicked, slanderous, contentious devil, "I deny you," you will then understand the meaning of this simple truth. When Christ says here, "Going forth,

teach all people, baptizing them in the name," the Greek has no "and," so that it says "teach and baptize," but rather, "teach, baptizing them." By this manner of speech we clearly observe that here Christ did not speak the order of the words with emphasis. For this phrase "baptizing them" is not closely connected but rather floats freely, so that according to the very letters, it may be taken before or after the word *teach*, as we can demonstrate even more clearly from Mark 16. There we read, "Whoever has believed and is baptized will be saved." See, whether or not here "is baptized" floats freely, although it is connected with the conjunction "and." Not that I mean that John administered or poured out water baptism before he had begun to teach. For in the beginning we must indeed teach why we baptize; otherwise, today no one could bring his child to baptism before he himself was taught. But after we are taught, then we bring our children also to baptism (as we see with the ancients). More on this later. And therefore, this is the meaning of Christ's words, "Go forth, teach all people," then [they know that] I am their complete salvation, and so they believe. So, go forth and lead them to me. "Baptize them"—this is unconnected, so that it means "baptizing them," as is shown above—"in the name of the Father and the Son and the Holy Spirit." ON BAPTISM, ON REBAPTISM AND INFANT BAPTISM.[8]

"AND" PROVES TEMPORAL SEQUENCE IN CHRIST'S COMMAND. BALTHASAR HUBMAIER: Ah, what a childish counterargument [from Zwingli]. I learned the same arguments in Latin school.... If you want to hear this mandate still more explicitly, you will find it...: "Repent and be baptized."... I think that you have the little word *and* here explicitly so that the sequence is testified as teaching, believing and after that baptizing. Baptism does not hang free as you force from Scripture. DIALOGUE WITH ZWINGLI'S BAPTISM BOOK.[9]

---

[7]CRR 5:367-69* (QGT 9:328-29, 330-31); alluding to Mt 28:19; Mk 16:15; Acts 2; quoting 1 Cor 7:2.

[8]ZSW 4:234-35 (cf. LCC 24:143-44); quoting Mt 28:18-20; Mk 16:16.
[9]CRR 5:200* (QGT 9:190).

BELIEVER'S BAPTISM IS BIBLICAL. MENNO SI-
MONS: They say that children should be baptized
in order that they might be better trained in the
Word of God and his commandments. We reply
that we desire to know where this is expressed and
written in the holy Scriptures.... For however
industriously we may search day and night, we find
but one baptism in water, pleasing to God, which
is expressed and contained in his Word, namely,
baptism on the confession of faith, commanded
by Christ Jesus, taught and administered by his
holy apostles; a baptism administered and received
for the forgiveness and remission of sins in such a
manner as we have fully proved above by the words
of Peter. But this other baptism, that is, infant
baptism, we do not find.

Because this infant baptism is nowhere commanded or implied in the divine Word, therefore we
testify before you and all the world that we have no
regard for it, but believe and proclaim it to be idolatrous, useless and empty, and we do this not only
with words but also at the cost of our lives, as has
been proved by events in many Germanic lands. The
reason is this. It is administered without the Word
and commandment of God; righteousness is sought
therein; and because of this infant baptism the true
baptism of Jesus Christ—that is, believer's baptism—
is so lamentably rejected and trampled on by all as a
heretical baptism. CHRISTIAN BAPTISM (1539).[10]

GOD'S PEOPLE NEED A SIGN OF HIS FAVOR.
JOHANN ECK: Why is it that the rebaptizers will
not allow children entry to the Christian congregation through baptism? For indeed the prophet in
the Old Testament explicitly demonstrates that
they belong to the assembly of the synagogue. For
Joel says: "Sing along with trumpets in Zion, consecrate the fast, call the assembly, gather the people,
consecrate the congregation, gather together the
old, gather the little children and those nursing
at the breast," etc. Why then do these miserable
Christians exclude young children and deny them
the Christian covenant?

I conclude that even though in the book of the
Acts of the Apostles their names are not explicitly
mentioned, nevertheless infants were baptized
too. Yes, it can indeed be assumed. For on Pentecost when three thousand were baptized, who
will claim that it was only men as if no women
were thought of? And after this the five thousand
mentioned were only men, no women or children!
Then, for that reason should no woman at all be
baptized? Not a single child? Without a doubt
men were themselves baptized along with their
wives and children.

So if you want to say that children were not
baptized because "it does not stand written," then
I will say that women were not baptized, for in
these same passages "it also does not stand written." Certainly the baptized adult Jews would have
grumbled if their children were not baptized. They
would have said, "We have the circumcision of
infants from God. Now if you do not want to keep
circumcision, then give our children a different
covenant sign!" The apostles would have had no
other sign that could have replaced circumcision
other than baptism, as Saint Paul indicates in his
letter to the Colossians, as well as in other passages.
Now how could they have denied the adults when
they sought baptism for their children? Surely they
would not have accepted that their children should
not have God's covenant. They would have allowed
this before circumcision. Saint Paul says to the
Galatians: "You are all God's children through faith
in Jesus Christ. For however many of you were
baptized have put on Christ." Why then would
they not also want their children to put on Christ?
SECOND SERMON ON THE FEAST OF CHRIST'S
ASCENSION (1531).[11]

**INDEED! THUS, CIRCUMCISION CANNOT BE
A TYPE FOR BAPTISM.** MICHAEL SATTLER:
Circumcision cannot be an analogy to baptism. If
it were we would have to observe exactly the eight
days, and God would have to coerce us too with

---

[10]Simons, *Complete Writings*, 249, 253-54*.

[11]Eck, *Christenliche Predigen*, 3:123r-v; quoting Joel 2:15-16; Gal
3:26-27, alluding to Acts 2:41; 4:4; Col 2:11-12.

threatening. And Christ would have had to have himself baptized in his infancy, for he must have known well what baptism is and means, something other children cannot know. And one should not baptize the little girls, for they were not circumcised; the law does not apply to them as to boys. And the rule would need to remain after the translation. Whenever an infant boy is not baptized on the eighth day, his soul shall be rooted out, or damned. The child baptizers press circumcision hard and how baptism is supposed to be instituted in its place, but they have not so much as a dot in all Scripture; as little as they have for godparenthood, or that it were said: "baptize the infants as soon as they leave the mother's womb." Thus, baptizing little children, godparenthood, exorcism, chrysm, oils, salt, mud are all together vain, notions of humans, without command of Christ or apostolic usage. Therefore let us be on guard against them! HOLY SCRIPTURE SHOULD BE DISCERNINGLY EXPOSITED.[12]

TO BAPTIZE INFANTS IS TO SEAL AN EMPTY LETTER. PETER WALPOT: Thus, the apostles always taught first; then they baptized the believers but not the children. But whoever baptizes [first] and then teaches fires off his rifle, and then finally asks where the target is that he should shoot at, sealing an empty letter in which nothing has been written yet. For you believers are a letter of Christ, Paul says, prepared through our ministry. Nursing children are not able to be prepared through the ministry of the Word! Once the letter is written, then we are asked to come and, not before then, to apply the seal to it. THE GREAT ARTICLE BOOK: ON BAPTISM.[13]

INFANT BAPTISM IS INDEED EFFICACIOUS. APOLOGY OF THE AUGSBURG CONFESSION: We confess that baptism is necessary for salvation, that children are to be baptized and that the baptism of children is not ineffective but is necessary and efficacious for salvation. Since the gospel is purely and carefully taught among us, we have received, by God's favor, this additional fruit from it: that no Anabaptists have arisen in our churches, because the people have been fortified by God's Word against the ungodly and seditious factions of these crooks. Among the many other errors of the Anabaptists we also condemn their assertion that the baptism of little children is useless. For it is most certain that the promise of salvation also pertains to little children. But it does not pertain to those who are outside the church of Christ, where there is neither Word nor sacrament, because Christ regenerates through Word and sacrament. Therefore it is necessary to baptize little children in order that the promise of salvation might be applied to them according to Christ's mandate, "Baptize all nations" (Mt 28:19). Just as salvation is offered to all in that passage, so baptism is also offered to all—men, women, children and infants. Therefore it clearly follows that infants are to be baptized because salvation is offered with baptism.

Second, it is evident that God approves the baptism of little children. The Anabaptists who condemn the baptism of little children teach wickedly. That God approves the baptism of little children is shown by the fact that God gives the Holy Spirit to those so baptized. For if this baptism had been ineffectual, the Holy Spirit would have been given to no one, none would have been saved, and ultimately there would be no church. Even taken by itself, this point can sufficiently strengthen good and godly minds against the godless and fanatical opinions of the Anabaptists. ARTICLE 9, BAPTISM.[14]

"THOSE WHO ARE FAR AWAY." JOHN CALVIN: Last of all are mentioned the Gentiles, who were formerly strangers. Those who refer it to the Jews who were driven into distant countries

---

[12]CRR 1:169-70*. Sattler is referring to the medieval ceremony of baptism, which involved exorcising, anointing and salting the infant. For an excellent description, see Karant-Nunn, *Reformation of Ritual*, 43-71.
[13]QGT 12:65; aluding to 2 Cor 3:3 .

[14]BoC 183-84 (BSLK 246-47; cf. MO 27:533-34).

are completely in error. Peter is not speaking of distance in terms of place but of the distinction between Jews and Gentiles; for the Jews were the first to be joined to God because of the covenant and so became part of his family and household, but the Gentiles were banished from his kingdom. Paul uses the same terms when he says that the Gentiles who were strangers to the promise are now brought near to God through Jesus Christ. For Christ has broken down the dividing wall and has reconciled both Jews and Gentiles to the Father, and by his coming has preached peace to those who were near and to those who were far off. COMMENTARY ON ACTS 2:39.[15]

"CROOKED GENERATION." HEINRICH BULLINGER: Now Peter is an example of the instructor who exhorts candidates of the Christian religion to guard themselves from this crooked generation. ... For *skolios* means spiteful, treacherous, ruthless and tortuous. Truly this name is fitting for these blabbermouths whom Paul elsewhere calls "dogs," enemies of the cross of Christ, "liars, evil beasts and lazy gluttons." These same people John the Baptist and Christ call "a brood of vipers." ... Therefore, guard yourself from the company of the wicked! Indeed, "a little yeast corrupts the whole lump." As the proverb goes, "whoever lives with a cripple soon himself learns to limp." COMMENTARY ON ACTS 2:40.[16]

---

[15]CNTC 6:83* (CO 48:55); alluding to Eph 2:11.

[16]Bullinger, *In Acta Apostolarum*, 32v; quoting Phil 3:2; Tit 1:12; Mt 3:7; 12:34; 23:33; 1 Cor 5:6; Gal 5:9; alluding to Phil 3:18.

2:42-47 THE FELLOWSHIP OF THE BELIEVERS

[42] And they devoted themselves to the apostles' teaching and the fellowship, to the breaking of bread and the prayers. [43] And awe[a] came upon every soul, and many wonders and signs were being done through the apostles. [44] And all who believed were together and had all things in common. [45] And they were selling their possessions and belongings and distributing the proceeds to all, as any had need. [46] And day by day, attending the temple together and breaking bread in their homes, they received their food with glad and generous hearts, [47] praising God and having favor with all the people. And the Lord added to their number day by day those who were being saved.

a Or *fear*

OVERVIEW: The example of the early Christian community prompts Reformation commentators to uphold the fellowship of believers as a model for Christian relationships. Some—especially the Hutterites—believe that the example set forth is meant to be prescriptive for Christian communities, while others reject such interpretations that seek to turn the Jerusalem church's use of property and possessions into a universal standard for all Christian communities. Nonetheless, there appears to be general agreement that the sharing and selling of possessions to provide for those in need within the community is praiseworthy and ideal, demonstrating unity in Christ through the Holy Spirit, while such practices are not meant to become new, compulsory laws for believers.

WHAT IS "FELLOWSHIP" IN CHRIST'S CHURCH? JOHN CALVIN:

With regard to the apostles' teaching and to prayer, the meaning is clear. Fellowship and the breaking of bread may be understood in different ways. Some think that breaking of bread means the Lord's Supper, others that it refers to alms, others again that the faithful had their meals together in common. Some think that "fellowship" (κοινωνία) is the celebration of the Holy Supper; I hold rather with those who believe that this is meant by the breaking of bread. For "fellowship" (κοινωνία), without addition, is never found in this sense. I therefore refer it to mutual association, alms and other duties of brotherly fellowship. The reason why I would rather have breaking of bread to be understood here of the Lord's Supper is because Luke is recording those things which constitute the form of the church visible to the public eye. Indeed, he defines four marks by which the true and genuine appearance of the church may be distinguished. Do we seek the true church of Christ? Here for us it is depicted as a living portrait. Luke begins with doctrine, which is the soul of the church. He does not name doctrine of any kind, but that of the apostles which the Son of God had delivered by their hands. Therefore, wherever the pure voice of the gospel sounds forth, where people continue in the profession of it, where they apply themselves to the regular hearing of it, so that they may profit from it, there beyond all doubt is the church. COMMENTARY ON ACTS 2:42.[1]

BREAKING BREAD REFERS TO THE EUCHARIST. MARTIN LUTHER:

I think that Luke signifies participation in the Sacrament by the breaking of bread, because truly they broke bread in their homes. The reason is that in those days the disciples or Christians would not have had public temples in which they would have been permitted to gather together. TABLE TALK, NIKOLAUS MEDLER.[2]

---

[1]CNTC 6:85* (CO 48:57).
[2]WATR 1:315 no. 667.

Christ Dwells in the Believer Through Faith, Not Food. Peter Walpot: Christ dwells in our hearts through faith, not through the physical eating of the mouth. From this it follows that there is no physical eating of Christ, but only a spiritual eating, which is nothing other than faith. The faithful are the temple of God and a temple of the Holy Spirit. Thus, it is not necessary first to eat Christ in the bread. Through physical eating he cannot enter into the temple of the heart. The Great Article Book: On the Eucharist.[3]

The Spirit Produced a Supernatural Unity. Desiderius Erasmus: Above all, however, that heavenly Spirit produced mutual benevolence and concord in all he inspired. Certainly Jesus had bidden his disciples to be recognized by this special sign, that love for one another held them together. For all who had believed the gospel frequently gathered together in one place and exhorted and comforted themselves by mutual discourse. There were many, and all were admitted without respect to persons: young, old, women, men, slaves, free, poor, rich. Indeed, the love of Christ implanted in their hearts joined together such disparate people with so much oneness of heart that they regarded all things as common among themselves, which is something rare even among genuine brothers. Paraphrase of Acts 2:42-47.[4]

Should Christian Churches Still Worship Like This? Johann Spangenberg: Indeed! First, in the Christian congregation a beneficial sermon should be given, then after the sermon a sincere prayer, after this feed the hungry and give the thirsty something to drink. Then, since some also hunger or thirst spiritually, share the most precious sacrament of the body and blood of Christ. Finally, also, so that we may practice the fruits of the Sacrament, praise and thank God, we should give food and drink to our neighbor, that is, help, serve and advise him in word and deed.

Wherever these things take place, there certainly the Holy Spirit cannot long be excluded, but rather he will soon arrive with all his goods, mercies and gifts, temporal and eternal. So help us God! Amen. Brief Exegesis of Acts 2:42-47.[5]

This Example Is For Us, Not Just Jerusalem. Peter Riedemann: The more a person is attached to property and claims ownership of things, the further away he is from the fellowship of Christ and from being in the image of God. For this reason, when the church came into being, the Holy Spirit reestablished such community in a wonderful way. "No one said any of the things they possessed were their own, but they had all things in common." This admonition by the Spirit is true for us even today. . . . Where this is not the case, it is a blemish on the church that should truly be corrected. Someone may say that this only applies to what took place in Jerusalem and therefore does not apply today. In reply, we say that even if it did only happen in Jerusalem, it does not follow that it should not happen now. The apostles and the churches were not at fault, but the opportunity, the right means and the right time were lacking.

This, therefore, should never be a reason for us to hesitate. Instead, it should move us to greater and better effort, for the Lord now gives us both the time and the occasion. It was not the fault of either the apostles or the churches, as is shown by the ardent efforts of both. The apostles directed people to the church with great diligence and spared no pains to teach them true surrender, as all their epistles still prove today. . . .

On the basis of this, we can recognize that the churches favorably inclined their hearts to practice community and were willing and ready to do so, not only in spiritual but also in material things. They wished to follow Christ their Master, become like him and be one of mind with him. He went before us in this way and commanded us to follow him. Confession of Faith.[6]

---

[3]QGT 12:151.
[4]CWE 50:25* (LB 7:675).

[5]Spangenberg, *Der Apostel Geschichte*, 23v-24r.
[6]CRR 9:121-22*; alluding to Phil 2:2-4.

COMMUNITY OF GOODS MUST BE PROPERLY UNDERSTOOD. JOHN CALVIN: So Luke proceeds in the proper order, in that beginning with what they thought, he goes on to their liberality which was the fruit of that. He therefore lets us see that they were truly united among themselves with brotherly love, and gave evidence of this, in that the rich sold their goods to help the poor. Now this is a striking example of love, and Luke records it so that we may learn that we are to relieve the poverty of our brothers out of our abundance.

A sound exposition of this passage is necessary, on account of fanatical spirits who devise a "fellowship" (κοινωνία) of goods whereby all civil order is overturned. In our own day the Anabaptists have clamored for this, because they thought there was no church unless everyone's possessions are heaped into a great pile from which everyone can take indiscriminately. We must beware of two extremes. For many on a pretext of civil order conceal what they possess and defraud the poor, thinking that they are doubly righteous so long as they do not seize another person's goods. Others are carried away to the opposite error, desiring to have everything mingled together.

But what does Luke say? Surely he notes a different system when he says that selection was made in the distribution. To the objection that no one had anything of his own since all things were common, there is a simple answer that common sharing of this kind must be held in check in the interest of what is stated next, namely, that the poor should be relieved according to each person's need. We have the old proverb: "All things are common among friends." When the Pythagoreans spoke thus, they did not mean that a man was not to govern his own house privately or that they intended wives to be held in common. So this community of goods of which Luke speaks does not do away with household government. This will be more clearly seen in Acts 4, where Luke names two people alone who sold possessions worth so many thousands. Thus we may gather even as I have just said, they brought forth their goods and held them in common only with the object of relieving immediate necessity.

The impudence of the monks who profess to abide by the apostles' rule is grotesque, because they call nothing their own, and yet they sell nothing, show no concern if anyone is in need, but stuff their idle bellies with the blood of the poor and have no other interest in the community of goods than seeing that they are fully and luxuriously provided for, even if the whole world should starve. COMMENTARY ON ACTS 2:44.[7]

PERSONAL PROPERTY IS UNNATURAL. PETER WALPOT: Community is and can mean nothing other than out of love for neighbor to share everything equally or in common and not to have anything of one's own. This cannot happen any more nobly, better or perfectly than for each person to present himself and to place himself and his things in common use, as here they desire to suffer both the bad and the good, even the lovely and the terrible. Wherever someone strives to be a debtor, member and advocate for his neighbor, that is where the Christian church and community of the saints is, which does not act tyrannically or unnaturally, nor is this impossible, where love dwells. If fleshly fathers, who live somewhat wickedly, willingly deprive themselves of food so that they can support and help their children, and also if a mother forcibly removes something from her own starving stomach and regurgitates it for her own dear child [as a mother bird does with her chicks], should not believers be able to hold their temporal goods together and in common with each other? Any other way would be unchristian! We are supposed to love our neighbors and members [in faith] as ourselves, sharing with them in abundance, in need, in sorrow, present with them through thick and thin. Anything different is no community, no unity, no membership or common purpose; [instead] his own house, his own field and goods, his own kitchen, his own cupboard and own table, just as they say.

Therefore, personal property does not belong in

---

[7]CNTC 6:87-88* (CO 48:59-60).

the Christian church, but rather personal property is in the world, it belongs to paganism, it belongs to those who do not share the divine love, it belongs to those who are plagued with weeds, yes, to those who live for themselves. For if there were no individual desire there would be no personal property. But the true community of goods belongs to believers, for by divine law all things should be common and no one should be without what is God's, which includes nothing less than air, rain, snow or water, as well as the sun and elements. As these things cannot be divided, so also the temporal goods—which God gives in equal proportion and measure for common use—should not and may not be made one's own. According to divine and Christian law this cannot be. For what is one's own and personal property is against nature and the very character of his creation, which should be and is free to all. Whoever separates and possesses creation acts against the One who has made and created it free, and is in sin, as the *Theologia Germanica* states.[8] However, through the inherent wickedness of humans, out of jealousy, through miserliness, each person shoves everything into his own bag for himself, and says, "This is mine!" Another says, "This is mine!" Thus among human beings a great rupture has happened, yes, a great inequality has occurred in this life. In fact, unfortunately it has come to this: that they want to possess the sun and moon, as well as the elements, they make them their own and sell them for money. THE GREAT ARTICLE BOOK: ON PEACE AND JOINT PROPERTY.[9]

LUKE DOES NOT REJECT BUT ENDORSES PRIVATE OWNERSHIP. RUDOLF GWALTHER:

We will easily prove it was not in the apostle's mind or intention that all things should be common without any property belonging to anyone. . . . [Our] Lord never used anyone's goods against the will of the owner. For he took the donkey on which he rode into the city by request and entreaty, and the house where he kept his last Passover he obtained by the permission of the good man of the house. What injustice would it be for some people to charge more interest in another's goods than Christ's example? . . . And even in this book, there are examples of various persons whose faith is singularly commended and who neither sold their houses nor made their goods common. Of which number are Tabitha, Lydia, Mary the mother of Mark, Simon the tanner, Cornelius the centurion, Philip and many others. What shall we say of Caius, the host of the whole congregation? What of Philemon, who had a servant bought with his own money, which Paul so little reproved that he sent back again his servant who ran away from him?

But what need have we of examples set from other passages when this present passage evidently proves a property and possession of goods? . . . Furthermore, Luke makes mention here of distribution, whereby goods were given to every person according to need. It was not lawful for every person to take as much as one pleased. Besides that, no one was compelled to sell what one had, or to give it, but all this distribution depended on each person's goodwill. HOMILY 19, ACTS 2:44-47.[10]

ON CHRISTIANS' GOODS. THE ARTICLES OF RELIGION: The riches and goods of Christians are not common, as touching the right, title and possession of the same, as certain Anabaptists do falsely boast. Notwithstanding every person ought, of such things as he possesses, generously to give alms to the poor, according to his ability. ARTICLE 38.[11]

---

[8]See *Theologia Germanica: The Book of the Perfect Life*, trans. David Blamires (Walnut Creek, CA: AltaMira, 2003), 89-93, esp. 92. Luther discovered this anonymous work in 1516, publishing it two years later with an effusive preface, placing it on par with Scripture and Augustine; see *Eyn deutsch Theologia: das ist Eyn edles Buchleyn von rechtem vorstand was Adam und Christus sey und wie Adam yn uns sterben und Christus ersteen sall*, ed. Martin Luther (Wittenberg: Johann Grünenberg, 1518), I3r-KIv, esp. KIr. Luther's preface can be found in LW 31:75-76; WA 1:378-79.
[9]QGT 12:231-32; alluding to Phil 2:2-4.

[10]Gwalther, *Homelyes or Sermons upon the Actes*, 144* (*In Acta Apostolorum*, 46v).
[11]*Creeds*, 3:513.*

"THE LORD ADDED TO THEIR NUMBER DAILY."
DESIDERIUS ERASMUS: You will note here, Theophilus, that the rise of the church happily took its beginnings from concord and joy. There must be concord where the Spirit is, the one who makes peace for all; there must be joy where the conscience is pure and confidence in the promises of the gospel is sure. Further, though in putting Jesus to death priests, Pharisees, scribes, the foremost of the people everywhere present, here in the felicitous beginnings of the nascent church there is no mention of them. No one came to this association under compulsion; no force kept them in compact. Those who were added continued of their own accord, and day by day the Lord drew in first some, then others, whom he had destined for salvation. The grain of mustard was slowly emerging, soon to spread its branches over the whole world. PARAPHRASE OF ACTS 2:42-47.[12]

---

[12]CWE 50:26* (LB 7:675).

3:1-10 PETER AND JOHN HEAL A LAME BEGGAR

Now Peter and John were going up to the temple at the hour of prayer, the ninth hour.[a] *²And a man lame from birth was being carried, whom they laid daily at the gate of the temple that is called the Beautiful Gate to ask alms of those entering the temple. ³Seeing Peter and John about to go into the temple, he asked to receive alms. ⁴And Peter directed his gaze at him, as did John, and said, "Look at us." ⁵And he fixed his attention on them, expecting to receive something from them. ⁶But Peter said, "I have no silver and gold, but what I do have I give to you. In the name of Jesus Christ of Nazareth, rise up and walk!" ⁷And he took him by the right hand and raised him up, and immediately his feet and ankles were made strong. ⁸And leaping up he stood and began to walk, and entered the temple with them, walking and leaping and praising God. ⁹And all the people saw him walking and praising God, ¹⁰and recognized him as the one who sat at the Beautiful Gate of the temple, asking for alms. And they were filled with wonder and amazement at what had happened to him.*

a That is, 3 p.m.

OVERVIEW: Peter and John encounter a man who, because of his physical limitations, was relegated to an unfortunate and oppressive situation. Many commentators focus on the cycle of injustice suffered by the man as an indictment of personal and social greed and exploitation. Warning their readers about the consequences of greed, the reformers exhort believers to love others as Christ loves them. The Spirit works through willing human vessels, who by faith confirm the deeds and Word of Christ. Peter merely speaks words in faith and believes those words to be true and powerful.

WHY DO PETER AND JOHN GO TO PRAY AT THE NINTH HOUR? JOHANN SPANGENBERG:
What does Luke mean by "the ninth hour"? The Jews had appointed two hours for prayer, one in the morning and one in the evening. During morning prayer they sacrificed the burnt offering; during evening prayer the evening offering. Now since by the ancients the day was divided into just twelve hours, this ninth hour is around evening, when we Christians hold vespers. This is when Peter and John entered the temple to pray, but the worldly hearts around this time, and even earlier, go to open a tab and begin drinking and carousing rather than going to church.

Why do they enter the temple to pray? Couldn't they have prayed at home? Or is prayer in the church better than at home? They went to the temple to pray for this reason, that they proclaimed God's Word and the gospel concerning Christ's resurrection to the people who gathered there. They made known the name of Christ to the entire world. For this purpose God created an excellent opportunity, namely, this lame man who sat and begged in front of the temple. BRIEF EXEGESIS OF ACTS 3:1-2.[1]

THIS BEGGAR WAS EXPLOITED FOR PROFIT.
DESIDERIUS ERASMUS: At the entrance to the temple sat a certain beggar, well known to the people, lame from his mother's womb. So great was the deformity of his body that he was carried by porters. His misfortune, as it happens, provided support for many, since it was for gain that they set him out at the gate of the temple which the people call "Beautiful" to ask alms from those entering (for this gate was most crowded). Mendacity has

---

[1]Spangenberg, *Der Apostel Geschichte*, 24v-25r; alluding to Ex 29:38-46.

its own talent; it knows that those who go into a temple are so disposed that they give alms quite freely, or wish to seem so disposed. PARAPHRASE OF ACTS 3:2.[2]

SHOULD THE POOR AMONG CHRISTIANS ALSO BEG? JOHANN SPANGENBERG: From the beginning the tithe was appointed for the poor, the widows, the orphans and ministers of the church—the same is true of hospital donations and alms. But here the rule . . . is that whoever can snatch this money has it. Additionally we are far more quick to give a *groschen* to the bar or theater than a penny to God's offertory. What will follow as a punishment, in the end we will receive internally. BRIEF EXEGESIS OF ACTS 3:3.[3]

THE NAME OF JESUS IS THE SOURCE OF HEALING. THE ENGLISH ANNOTATIONS: They want him diligently to mark by what power he should be healed; they being well assured of the certain event, by the Spirit of God, would have him mark by whose name he should be healed and to whom he should ascribe the honor and praise for so great a mercy received. It is as if they said, "Believe that you will receive something from us; look at us, but believe in Christ Jesus." ANNOTATIONS ON ACTS 3:4.[4]

TWO IMPORTANT CHARACTERISTICS OF PETER. RUDOLF GWALTHER: Peter professes two things very profitable to be marked. The first is poverty and that he has neither silver nor gold. For he was one of that company that had left all they had and followed Christ. Therefore, he could not have the riches of the world. Shall we, therefore, think him unhappy and in misery? God forbid! Let no one, therefore, measure felicity by the goods and riches of this world. For he who possesses Christ cannot be miserable, even if he were bereft of all his goods. Peter had neither silver nor gold. If Peter lacked these goods, how did Peter's succes-

sors come by so great an abundance? How is it that Peter's patrimony is such that nowadays the church has not only the greatest revenues of gold and silver but also whole countries and kingdoms? Surely we have nothing in the Scriptures written about it; neither do credible histories make any mention of it. Only of Judas is there mention, who sought gold and silver by unlawful means, which was the cause of his desperation and destruction. And of the Antichrist, there is a prophecy that he will possess the treasures of the earth. . . .

Second, Peter professes a promptness and readiness of goodwill to benefit and to do good when he says, "What I do have I give to you," which is as much as if he should say, "if I had money I would give it to you also. However, I will give you what I have." These words show an example of a willing mind, which we also ought to have in the exercise of benevolence. There are those who profess an earnest good will, but they say they know not what, nor how much they should give to the poor. The law of love and good will answer these questions, commanding us to love our neighbor as our self. Thus, those who do not inquire how much they should give but seek what their neighbor needs, and if they find that they have it, give it to their neighbor generously. Therefore, if they have money, they help the needy with money. If they have plenty of food, they distribute it out among the hungry. If they have clothing, they clothe those who they see go naked. And if they have none of these, at least they give their heart to their poor brothers and sisters, the goodwill by which they declare with friendly words, with counsel and comfort, by which they support and cheer up the poor body that is afflicted. So, following the example of Peter, they give whatever they have. Therefore, we gather that those who ask what and how much they should give to the poor are void of charity and have no affection for doing good. HOMILY 20, ACTS 3:1-8.[5]

---

[2] CWE 50:26 (LB 7:675).
[3] Spangenberg, *Der Apostel Geschichte*, 25v-26r.
[4] Downame, ed., *Annotations*, GGG3r*.

[5] Gwalther, *Homelyes or Sermons upon the Actes*, 153-55* (*In Acta Apostolorum*, 49v-50r); cf. Dan 11:43.

THE BEGGAR'S HEALING IS A FIGURE OF OUR SPIRITUAL RESTORATION. JOHN CALVIN: We see how God works through his Word, both by giving success to the preaching of it so that it pierces human hearts. . . . Moreover, he does not allow faith to be in vain, but it truly gains possession of all the blessings which it looks for and which are offered to it through the Word. We must remember what I have already said, that in this history we have a universal type of our spiritual restoration; namely, that as the Word, laid hold of by faith restored the cripple to health, so the Lord by his Word pierces our souls, so that he may restore them too. First of all, he speaks by the mouth of a human being and urges us to the obedience of faith. Then he moves our hearts inwardly by his Spirit, so that the Word may take living root within us. Finally, he stretches forth his hand, and by every means completes his work in us. COMMENTARY ON ACTS 3:1-7.[6]

DIVINE HEALING TRANSCENDS HUMAN HEALING. THE ENGLISH ANNOTATIONS: This demonstrates a perfect cure and proclaims the truth and excellence of the miracle performed in the name of Jesus Christ. Here there was no residue of the old malady, which so commonly is seen in the best cures of human art. Now having at once received perfect soundness and vigor of his limbs, he leaps up, and walks with the apostles into the temple. ANNOTATIONS ON ACTS 3:8.[7]

FAITH HEALS THE BEGGAR. MARTIN LUTHER: It certainly is not our merit or power [that accomplishes such], but faith granted them this power. This man lay very long, forty years, there before the temple. This indeed was acknowledged by those who knew him. He goes about and leaps like a deer; he gives praise and is so joyous in his heart. This cannot be witchcraft. They would be crazy and foolish [to say] "money and gold I do not have, but faith I do have, with this I will help you." The beggar does not believe, but Peter believes. "In the name [of Jesus] stand up," for I believe. He stands up, leaps and is joyous. Peter must have had powerful courage, and a completely different courage than he had on Good Friday. SERMON ON PENTECOST TUESDAY (1544).[8]

---

[6]CNTC 6:94* (CO 48:65).

[7]Downame, ed., *Annotations*, GGG3r*.
[8]WA 49:459.

3:11-26 PETER'S SPEECH IN SOLOMON'S PORTICO

[11]*While he clung to Peter and John, all the people, utterly astounded, ran together to them in the portico called Solomon's.* [12]*And when Peter saw it he addressed the people: "Men of Israel, why do you wonder at this, or why do you stare at us, as though by our own power or piety we have made him walk?* [13]*The God of Abraham, the God of Isaac, and the God of Jacob, the God of our fathers, glorified his servant[a] Jesus, whom you delivered over and denied in the presence of Pilate, when he had decided to release him.* [14]*But you denied the Holy and Righteous One, and asked for a murderer to be granted to you,* [15]*and you killed the Author of life, whom God raised from the dead. To this we are witnesses.* [16]*And his name—by faith in his name—has made this man strong whom you see and know, and the faith that is through Jesus[b] has given the man this perfect health in the presence of you all.*

[17]*"And now, brothers, I know that you acted in ignorance, as did also your rulers.* [18]*But what God foretold by the mouth of all the prophets, that his Christ would suffer, he thus fulfilled.* [19]*Repent therefore, and turn back, that your sins may be blotted out,* [20]*that times of refreshing may come from the presence of the Lord, and that he may send the Christ appointed for you, Jesus,* [21]*whom heaven must receive until the time for restoring all the things about which God spoke by the mouth of his holy prophets long ago.* [22]*Moses said, 'The Lord God will raise up for you a prophet like me from your brothers. You shall listen to him in whatever he tells you.* [23]*And it shall be that every soul who does not listen to that prophet shall be destroyed from the people.'* [24]*And all the prophets who have spoken, from Samuel and those who came after him, also proclaimed these days.* [25]*You are the sons of the prophets and of the covenant that God made with your fathers, saying to Abraham, 'And in your offspring shall all the families of the earth be blessed.'* [26]*God, having raised up his servant, sent him to you first, to bless you by turning every one of you from your wickedness."*

a Or *child*; also verse 26   b Greek *him*

OVERVIEW: Reflecting on what they praise as a clear and powerful sermon, commentators note that the kingdom of Christ did not begin from worldly fame and fortune, as many people were expecting, but from the ignominious death of their leader. Nevertheless Jesus' death and subsequent resurrection life are placed within the unity and continuity of God's plan, since the prophets foretold this and the earliest disciples are witnesses to it. The prominent theme in this passage is the promise, continuity and fulfillment of salvation for those who put their faith in Christ. The reformers demonstrate a very practical interest in the preaching office for propagating this message. Preaching must revolve around the law and the gospel, exposing human pride and rebellion while proclaiming the forgiveness of sins and the promise of resurrection. For the reformers, Peter models well how to guide others to the true Physician and Prophet.

The commentators also make eschatological observations about Christ's second coming, which will inaugurate a time of full restitution. Despite popular assumptions, here the reformers underscore the *joy* of Judgment Day, when the kingdom of heaven will be fully visible and universal peace will reign.

THIS IS THE RIGHT WAY TO PREACH. RUDOLF GWALTHER: Before we enter into Peter's words, we have an example from him that teaches us the right way to preach the gospel. It consists in making all people understand how the promises of the gospel appertain to them. Unless they are assured of this, they can neither make great account of them nor surely trust in them. This is the reason that Paul is so diligent in proving the calling of the Gentiles. For the gospel would have been preached to them in vain had they already known that the salvation purchased by Christ had belonged to them as well as to the Jews. For this reason, the promises of the gospel are universal and may be applied to all who will embrace them with true faith. . . .

And Paul often ignores any partiality in the business of salvation and testifies that all who believe in Christ have salvation given to them from God. Ministers must so mind and remember these things that they bar none from the universal promises of God, but they must so devise and order the word of the gospel that no one may doubt the certainty of their salvation but may understand that the merit of Christ belongs to them all without partiality. HOMILY 25, ACTS 3:25-26.[1]

THE SIMPLICITY OF PENTECOST PREACHING.

MARTIN LUTHER: Here we see that the apostles on Pentecost, in fact throughout the entire year, had nothing else in their mouth than the forgiveness of sin and the extermination of sin, the resurrection of the dead. These things, they say, are not only so now but have been testified through the mouths of all the prophets, even Moses himself. By this the apostles negate their opponents, because all the prophets have pointed to these days and said, "such and such will happen." So then, we Christians are sure in our faith; we have not only the apostles but all the prophets. The sum of their preaching is, they are Christ killers, traitors and villains, and there is no other man through whom they will be saved. That is their sermon. On this they stand. Here you do not hear Peter say, "You should wear hats [and] do works," but the apostles do not neglect [works]. For in his epistle, he writes diligently about good works. But on Pentecost they could not wait, they had to promulgate what Daniel said

about the seven weeks, that they should preach powerfully concerning the [Lord's] covenant. These seven years, as the book also demonstrates, they did this courageously, speaking with all kinds of languages and healing. That is Pentecost preaching. That is a sermon about the covenant that God made with Abraham. SERMON ON PENTECOST TUESDAY (1544).[2]

GOD GRACIOUSLY TAKES THE NAME OF HIS PEOPLE. RUDOLF GWALTHER: [Peter] calls him

the God of Abraham, Isaac and Jacob, and for short, the God of the fathers, a title or style God himself uses often in the Old Testament. This is a great token of God's love by which he declares to us his goodness. The princes of this world give themselves names of the people and nations that they have vanquished and overrun, and they think it is a great glory to be called Parthians, Gothics, Germans, Africans and Numidians. But what do these people learn by these styles, except that [such princes] have destroyed these people and spoiled their countries with fire and sword? God deals far differently. HOMILY 22, ACTS 3:13-16.[3]

JOSEPH A TYPE OF CHRIST. DIRK PHILIPS:

The figure of Joseph is spiritually fulfilled in Christ Jesus. For Joseph was sent out to his brothers by his father, Jacob, but they out of great jealousy sold him. He thus came into Egypt and because of his piety and innocence was thrown into prison, and by God's providence because of his wisdom was again delievered out of it, placed before King Pharaoh and, after the interpretation of the dreams, installed and exalted to be a lord over all of Egypt. So also it happened to Christ according to the Spirit. He was sent by God his heavenly Father into this world to his brothers. . . . But they did not want to accept him or permit him to be their Lord. Yes, they hated, persecuted, betrayed, sold, hanged, crucified and killed him.

---

[1]Gwalther, *Homelyes or Sermons upon the Actes*, 184* (*In Acta Apostolorum*, 58v); alluding to Rom 10:12; Gal 3:28; Col 3:11.

[2]WA 49:456-57; alluding to 1 Pet 3:1-7; Dan 9:24.
[3]Gwalther, *Homelyes or Sermons upon the Actes*, 163* (*In Acta Apostolorum*, 52v).

Nevertheless, he, the Lord Jesus Christ, is exalted through the right hand of God above all principalities, powers, thrones and dominions, and above every name which may be named in this future world. THE ENCHIRIDION: CONCERNING SPIRITUAL RESTITUTION.[4]

A SIMPLE FISHERMAN KNOCKS OVER THE FOUR PILLARS OF JUDAISM. MARTIN LUTHER: Peter says, "We do nothing out of our own power, although we in fact have a high calling, others will do this, too—like Stephen, also Philip the deacon performs great miracles—but out of the power of the crucified Jesus." Is this not preached beautifully? He casts himself aside so purely, he preaches so purely the mercy and faith, which this mercy contains, so that the Jews see and hear such while remaining obdurate. The people chase after him, they stare. But the apostles do not want themselves to be stared at; instead, they point to the Redeemer. It did not help that among the Jews, they had four pillars on which they built: the place (or the city), the law, the people, the temple. These were the four institutions on which they built.

The city is God's eternal city forever and ever. This is written through and through in the prophets. "Thus says the Lord, whose fire is in Zion and whose furnace is in Jerusalem." He will be the master of the house there, he will dwell there, there they stand now. God grant, someone perform a miracle there, as God wills. The second institution is God's people. Additionally, third, they had the temple. God had founded the worship of God; who then would suffer this sermon preached against the temple and the worship of God? They died for all four institutions. These institutions they brandished against Stephen, who stormed against the four institutions, as we also have four institutions in our administration: pillars, walls, ramparts, rifles. May we pray that our enemies receive our ideas; then we will quickly subdue them. But if they have different ideas than we, we have lost. Peter here offers another idea. He breathes out

a small breath against them: "Whoever wants to be saved, redeemed from death, should believe that the crucified Christ is a Lord over death and life." This is but a breath from a poor fisherman. By it he blows over their four institutions.

On what does he stand? "God has long warned you; Moses, your prophet, wrote concerning and against himself: God will raise up a prophet like me from your flesh and blood, to him you must listen." They all well understood this to be about the Messiah. "Unknot your ears . . . listen to the prophets! Otherwise the four institutions will fall to rubble—the temple, the law, the people and the city. Now, if you do not want to accept the prophets, then it all will be taken away from you, for I gave all this to you until the prophet comes who will preach not only to you in Jerusalem but even farther. Listen to him. If you will not listen to him, then all this is for nothing. I only meant it to point to him until he came, so that you would listen to him." SERMON ON PENTECOST TUESDAY (1544).[5]

PETER TEMPERS HIS WORDS TO GIVE ROOM FOR PARDON. JOHN CALVIN: Our sermons must be so tempered as to profit the hearers. For unless there be some hope of pardon left, dread of punishment hardens human hearts in obstinacy. The words of David are true, that we fear the Lord when we feel that he is favorable to us and able to be appeased. In this way Peter extenuates the sins of his people because of their ignorance. For they could not have supported the awareness of this if they had knowingly and deliberately denied the Son of God and delivered him to be slain. . . . Peter's meaning is therefore that they did it rather

---

[4]CRR 6:327* (BRN 10:353); alluding to Phil 2:9; Eph 1:20-21.

[5]WA 49:459-61; quoting Is 31:9; Deut 18:15. These four pillars of Judaism are strikingly similar to James D. G. Dunn's four pillars: monotheism, election, torah and temple. See James D. G. Dunn, *The Parting of the Ways: Between Judaism and Christianity and Their Significance for the Character of Christianity* (London: SCM Press, 1991). Richard Bauckham believes the Christian spiritualization of the temple—that is, assembled believers are the temple—is the chief cause for the separation of Jews and Christians. See Richard Bauckham, "The Parting of the Ways: What Happened and Why," *Studia Theologica* 47 (1993): 135-51.

through error and blind zeal than through deliberate wickedness. Commentary on Acts 3:17.[6]

Refreshing and Restitution on Judgment Day. Rudolf Gwalther: Here we have to consider the state of the coming day, which Peter expresses in two words. First, he calls it "a day of refreshing" by synecdoche.[7] This pertains only to the godly, who then shall feel refreshed and be delivered from all grief and sorrow.... The sight of Christ our judge cannot be terrible to the godly, because they understand that he is their Savior and Advocate. This is the great benefit that we have by faith, and not otherwise. For faith only makes us bold and sure of salvation at the coming of Christ. Then they shall find no help in riches, in honors or in friendships of the world, which while they lived on earth despised this faith in Christ. Therefore, it behooves us to be armed with this hope, against all the temptations of this world when we are in adversity, and so shall we never be removed from the way of salvation.

Then he calls it a day of restitution, because there shall be a restitution of all things and a perfect and immutable state of creatures, which many look for in vain as long as they live in this world. For this world is full of confusion and breeds new troubles every day, and the kingdom of Christ has been assaulted for some time, as though it might seem to have utterly given in. But in the latter days this kingdom shall be so set up as the prophets have prophesied. When all the power of our adversaries shall be brought under Christ's feet, there will be nothing more to trouble the faithful, and then there will be that joyful and peaceable state of all things of which the prophets mention many times. On that day bodies will be restored again, regardless of how they have perished. For the sea shall give up its dead, as will death and hell. A joyful and blessed condition will be restored to the world. Homily 23, Acts 3:17-21.[8]

Judgment Stimulates the Heart to Joy in Christ. John Calvin: The faithful have a twofold stimulus to encourage them when they hear the word about the last judgment. For in this world the advantages of faith are not evident; indeed, it is those who despise God who seem rather to prosper while the lives of the godly are full of countless miseries. Therefore our hearts would often be dismayed if we did not recall that the day of rest will come, which will cool the fever of our troubles and bring an end to our miseries. The other stimulus that I mentioned is that the fearful judgment of God shakes us out of our pleasures and sloth. So Peter in this passage combines threats and promises partly to win the Jews to Christ, partly to prick them with fear. This is a common practice in the Scriptures, since it speaks both to the reprobate and to the elect, representing the Day of the Lord at one time as dreadful and fearful and at another time as pleasant and desirable. Therefore, Peter, who spurs on the Jews to hope of pardon, rightly presents the Day of Christ to them as a day of joy, so that they would long for it. Commentary on Acts 3:20.[9]

A Prophet Like Moses, but Better. Justus Jonas: Moses said to the fathers in Deuteronomy 18, "[The Lord] will raise up a prophet," etc. And in the final chapter of Deuteronomy it is said, "A prophet like Moses has not arisen since in Israel." Therefore, it is necessary for there still to be promised a certain great prophet who will be like Moses. Now God promised concerning this eminent prophet, that he would bring teaching that they need to hear. It is certain that it is not the teaching of the law that is promised. For clearly Moses delivered that sufficiently. So then, it must be some new and far more excellent teaching. It is the gospel that now you see being confirmed by the miracle of tongues and so many revealing signs. That prophet is Jesus; you are not able to prove that it was some eminent person from Moses' lifetime. Annotations on Acts 3:22.[10]

---

[6]CNTC 6:99-100* (CO 48:69-70); alluding to Ps 130:4.
[7]Synecdoche is a figure of speech in which a part is taken to represent the whole, or vice versa.
[8]Gwalther, *Homelyes or Sermons upon the Actes*, 174-75* (*In Acta Apostolorum*, 56r); alluding to Ps 110:1; Rev 20:13.

[9]CNTC 6:101-2* (CO 48:71-72).
[10]Jonas, *Annotationes in Acta*, C8r; quoting Deut 18:15; 34:10.

CHRIST OUR PROPHET. RUDOLF GWALTHER: [Peter] declares the office of Christ, calling him a prophet. However, Moses was not ignorant of the fact that Christ should be both the King and the Redeemer of humankind and does not deny it in this place but makes mention of his office, which for his purpose and the matter at hand was chiefly required. Prophets, whether they show things to come or by the Word of God admonish people for present things, are the interpreters and openers of God's will. But because Christ should be a priest in the church of God forever, he must not abstain from teaching, which is the chief point required in a priest. HOMILY 24, ACTS 3:22-24.[11]

WHY DOES PETER NOT NAME ANY PROPHETS BEFORE SAMUEL? MARTIN LUTHER: Samuel follows Moses the closest; he correctly established the kingdom. For before the time of the judges the kingdom was a tattered thing. The ark was first here, then soon somewhere else, and so our Lord God wandered and never rested until the time of Samuel, when he said, "I have chosen this place for myself."[12] From Samuel, therefore, the kingdom of Israel begins to be established as if from a kingdom of prophets. TABLE TALK, NIKOLAUS MEDLER.[13]

CLING TO THIS PROPHET, JESUS CHRIST. DIRK PHILIPS: This prophet is Jesus Christ, as both Peter and Stephen testify. Whoever now hears this prophet Jesus Christ, the Son of the most high God, believes in him and keeps his Word, shall be saved. But whoever despises him and does not accept his Word is already judged. "The Word that I have spoken," Christ said, "will judge them on the Last Day." Therefore, beloved brothers and sisters, and fellow heirs of faith, I appeal to you through the mercy of God that you hold fast to Christ and

know and confess him just as the holy Scripture teaches. . . . Remain steadfast in his teaching, keep his commandments in true faith, and follow in his footsteps. Serve him with your whole heart, love him with your whole soul in order that at his appearing we may receive the crown of eternal glory. The grace of the Lord Jesus Christ be with you all. Amen. THE ENCHIRIDION: CONCERNING THE TRUE KNOWLEDGE OF JESUS CHRIST.[14]

GOD'S EVERLASTING COVENANT. PIETER RIEDEMANN: God's covenant is an everlasting covenant, existing from the beginning and continuing into eternity. It shows that it is his will to be our God and Father, that we should be his people and beloved children. Through the covenant, God desires continually to pour into us through Christ every divine blessing and all good things.

That such a covenant of God existed from the beginning is shown in that God created people in his own likeness. All was well with them, and there was no corrupting poison in them. Even when people were deceived and robbed of this likeness by the counsel of the serpent, God's purpose nevertheless endured. The covenant which he had previously made expresses this clearly, namely, that he should be our God and we his people. Out of this comes a promise to take away the devil's power through the woman's offspring. This makes it clear that it was God's intention to redeem us from the devil's power and restore us as his children.

Thus, God made his covenant first with Adam, and then more clearly with Abraham and his descendents. Now he has made this covenant with us through Christ and has established and confirmed it through Christ's death. Just as a will is not valid until the death of the one making the will, in the same way God gave his Son up to death, so that we would be redeemed from death through him and be the children of his covenant forever. CONFESSION OF FAITH.[15]

---

[11]Gwalther, *Homelyes or Sermons upon the Actes*, 178-79* (*In Acta Apostolorum*, 57r).

[12]2 Chron 7:12. Luther seems to have conflated this passage from 2 Chronicles with 2 Samuel 7, where David, during the time of Samuel, vows to build the Lord a dwelling place, but the Lord promises that David's offspring will build a house for the name of the Lord.

[13]WATR 1:319 no. 671.

[14]CRR 6:172* (BRN 10:177-78); alluding to Acts 3:22; 7:37; Rom 1:21; 1 Pet 2:21; quoting Jn 12:48.

[15]CRR 9:98*; alluding to Heb 6:17-20; 2 Cor 6:16.

4:1-22 PETER AND JOHN ARRESTED AND RELEASED

And as they were speaking to the people, the priests and the captain of the temple and the Sadducees came upon them, ²greatly annoyed because they were teaching the people and proclaiming in Jesus the resurrection from the dead. ³And they arrested them and put them in custody until the next day, for it was already evening. ⁴But many of those who had heard the word believed, and the number of the men came to about five thousand.

⁵On the next day their rulers and elders and scribes gathered together in Jerusalem, ⁶with Annas the high priest and Caiaphas and John and Alexander, and all who were of the high-priestly family.⁷And when they had set them in the midst, they inquired, "By what power or by what name did you do this?" ⁸Then Peter, filled with the Holy Spirit, said to them, "Rulers of the people and elders, ⁹if we are being examined today concerning a good deed done to a crippled man, by what means this man has been healed, ¹⁰let it be known to all of you and to all the people of Israel that by the name of Jesus Christ of Nazareth, whom you crucified, whom God raised from the dead—by him this man is standing before you well. ¹¹This Jesusᵃ is the stone that was rejected by you, the builders, which has become the cornerstone.ᵇ ¹²And there is salvation in no one else, for there is no other name under heaven given among menᶜ by which we must be saved."

¹³Now when they saw the boldness of Peter and John, and perceived that they were uneducated, common men, they were astonished. And they recognized that they had been with Jesus. ¹⁴But seeing the man who was healed standing beside them, they had nothing to say in opposition. ¹⁵But when they had commanded them to leave the council, they conferred with one another, ¹⁶saying, "What shall we do with these men? For that a notable sign has been performed through them is evident to all the inhabitants of Jerusalem, and we cannot deny it. ¹⁷But in order that it may spread no further among the people, let us warn them to speak no more to anyone in this name." ¹⁸So they called them and charged them not to speak or teach at all in the name of Jesus. ¹⁹But Peter and John answered them, "Whether it is right in the sight of God to listen to you rather than to God, you must judge, ²⁰for we cannot but speak of what we have seen and heard." ²¹And when they had further threatened them, they let them go, finding no way to punish them, because of the people, for all were praising God for what had happened. ²²For the man on whom this sign of healing was performed was more than forty years old.

a Greek *This one*   b Greek *the head of the corner*   c The Greek word *anthropoi* refers here to both men and women

OVERVIEW: The reformers see God's providence on full display here. The temple rulers' attempt to quash the message of Jesus by arresting Peter and John merely provides another platform to promulgate the good news. The commentators repeatedly stress the particularity of Christ as the Savior of the world and emphasize that faith in Christ, in contrast to works of the law, leads to justification and adoption as children of God. Peter's insight into the Scriptures and his unabashed bravery again underscore the transformative power of the Holy Spirit. Is this not the ignorant fisherman who denied Christ three times? Our commentators observe that God often chooses the lowly or the unlikely in order to demonstrate his power and purpose most clearly.

THE FLICKERING BUT UNDYING LIGHT OF THE GOSPEL. JOHN CALVIN: Three things are to be chiefly noted in this narration. First, that as soon as the truth of the gospel comes to light, Satan sets himself in opposition to it by every means in his power and uses every endeavor to crush it in its earliest beginnings. Second, that God furnishes his children with unconquerable fortitude, that they may stand firm and unmoved against all the devices of Satan and may not yield to the violence of the wicked. Finally, we must note the outcome, that however completely the Enemy may appear to be dominant and in control of events, leaving no stone unturned to blot out the name of Christ, and however much on the other hand the ministers of sound doctrine be as sheep in the mouths of wolves, God nonetheless spreads abroad the kingdom of his Son, keeps alive the light of his gospel and looks to the safety of his children. COMMENTARY ON ACTS 4.[1]

THE METHOD OF SATAN'S PERSECUTION OF THE CHURCH. JOHANN SPANGENBERG: From the beginning Satan has been God's bitter enemy. For that reason he has always raged against the kingdom of Christ. Between them is an eternal hatred, an eternal feud and irreconcilable war. The devil is a destroyer; Christ is a Savior. Satan is a liar; Christ is truthful. Satan thrusts [us] into sin; Christ helps [us] out of sin. Satan blinds people; Christ illuminates them. Satan is a prince of death; Christ is a prince of life. Satan leads to hell; Christ leads to heaven. Satan ushered Adam to the Fall, roused Pharaoh against Israel, Saul against David, the godless Jews against the prophets, the Philistines and other pagans against Judah, the high priests against Christ. So, here too, he rouses the priests and Sadducees against Peter and John.

Does he do this openly? No, instead under [false] appearances; for Satan is able to disguise himself masterfully as an angel of light. To Eve he did not say, "You will die," but instead, "You will be like God." . . . Here the priests and Sadducees are deeply irritated by unlearned people, fishermen and tax collectors, who taught the people and blamed them for Christ's death. It is as if an ignorant person stood up in a land or city and filed a complaint against the judges and councils, that they had

unjustly condemned a poor person and sentenced him to death. This person would certainly be in no little danger. So it is here with Peter and John, too.

Is the gospel then finished? Does the name of Christ lay despised? Are the people terrified on account of Peter and John's imprisonment? Absolutely not! Rather, the gospel goes forth even more magnificently. As they cast the disciples into prison, five thousand men convert to Christ. Here behold the wonder of God! Satan intended through the imprisonment of the disciples to terrify the audience away from the Word of God, to exterminate faith, to make the name of Jesus nothing. But, look, the gospel adds five thousand believers. BRIEF EXEGESIS OF ACTS 4:1-4.[2]

PETER AND JOHN EXPERIENCE JESUS' TRIALS. DESIDERIUS ERASMUS: Here again recognize, I ask you, an example of the kind of trial by which Jesus was condemned. He was convicted through interrogation; they too, then, are questioned about the lame man who had been healed: "By what power or in what name do you do this?" They could have searched this out in the temple before they led them to prison; they could have learned it as the people themselves had, since Peter had given a clear account of this deed. But they preferred to begin with insults. Nor was that followed by any investigation of the truth; rather, they seized the opportunity for injury. This was an indication that the priesthood would soon come to an end, since, full of vices as they were, they had no way to protect their authority except by conspiratorial councils, imprisonment and death. PARAPHRASE OF ACTS 4:5-7.[3]

THE IGNORANCE OF PETER AND JOHN'S OPPONENTS. THE ENGLISH ANNOTATIONS: Here, as in many other places, appears their stupid or intentional ignorance, that they would question the authority of an act which no one other than God could do! They did not ask with any intent to

---

[1]CNTC 6:111* (CO 48:79).

[2]Spangenberg, *Der Apostel Geschichte*, 30v-32r; quoting Gen 3:4-5.
[3]CWE 50:32 (LB 7:679).

believe in Christ but so that they might scare and terrify the apostles under their jurisdiction and authority over all things in and around the temple, especially concerning preaching, lest any new and erroneous doctrine should mislead the people, or any without their ordination should presume to teach them. ANNOTATIONS ON ACTS 4:7.[4]

THE PETER WHO DENIED CHRIST IS GONE.
DESIDERIUS ERASMUS: What ordinary person would not be dumbfounded when he looked on the packed ranks of so grand a council? In great pride the pontiffs and priests sat there, the princes of religion; then the officers, as well as the elders of the people; no authority was absent. . . . At this point what does Peter do, the man who thrice denied the Lord at the threats of a maidservant, a mere woman? Does he become terrified? Does he swoon and lose his wits? Does his voice stick in his throat? None of this! Why so? Doubtless, he had become another person. At that time he had been led by the human spirit: he made great promises, and soon rashly forgetting his promises, fled and broke his oath. Now, however, he was filled with the Holy Spirit: he pleaded his case from first to last bravely and extemporaneously, moderating his speech with admirable prudence so that freedom should not end in abuse, or softness smack of adulation or fear, but that the eloquence of the entire speech should have only one object—it is through Jesus that salvation comes to all. PARAPHRASE OF ACTS 4:8.[5]

CHRIST THE CORNERSTONE. JUSTUS JONAS: Peter calls them builders, as if he were saying, "You are the ones who are teaching the people the external observation of the law. But your building—that is, righteousness of the law which you teach against the judgment of God—will not stand. And you are making nothing other than counterfeit saints and hypocrites. Therefore, when Christ and the gospel came, condemning this righteousness

of the law and all your 'holiness,' immediately you were offended. You rejected Christ, claiming his teaching is Satan's. Now this Christ is the sole foundation of righteousness—a spiritual building. It is astonishing to fleshly and rational eyes. For hypocrisy and the flesh shamefully boast of their good works, but their righteousness is condemned." It is certainly not understood that righteousness is through Christ alone and all our works are nothing unless through the Spirit. The human beast does not have a sense of what is God's. ANNOTATIONS ON ACTS 4:11.[6]

MINISTERS SHOULD BE FAITHFUL BUILDERS. RUDOLF GWALTHER: [A builder] lays a sure foundation on which he sets his whole frame, and his whole care is to have its workmanship finished. The ministers of the church, whom the Lord has called to labor and care, must observe these things. For they are builders of the house of God, which is the congregation, as Paul says. Let them bring all that they are able to the building up of this house, remembering that they have received power to build and not to destroy. Let them lay no new foundation but build on that which the Lord has already laid, which Paul calls the foundation of the prophets and apostles, which is Jesus Christ. HOMILY 27, ACTS 4:5-12.[7]

SALVATION IN CHRIST ALONE. HANS DENCK: From the very beginning Jesus has been one with God in the Spirit, though he was born in time, according to the flesh, and has been subject to all human frailty, except for sin. For this reason it is written and said that everyone who will be saved must be saved through this Jesus, if he is to see the perfection of the Spirit which is the only goal toward which all who seek to be saved must look. The less a person looks to this, the more he will fall short of salvation; the more closely one comes to this goal, the more one escapes

---

[4]Downame, ed., *Annotations*, GGG4r*.
[5]CWE 50:32* (LB 7:679-80).
[6]Jonas, *Annotationes in Acta*, D1v; alluding to 1 Cor 2:6-16.
[7]Gwalther, *Homelyes or Sermons upon the Actes*, 201* (*In Acta Apostolorum*, 64r).

condemnation. Whatever this love has done and taught is truly honorable and good; apart from this, nothing is honorable and good. CONCERNING GENUINE LOVE.[8]

WE ARE CHILDREN OF GOD ONLY THROUGH HIS SON.

KATARINA SCHÜTZ ZELL: Christ has power to save us from sins, death and hell and to give us eternal life. In him is all salvation and in no other creature or work in heaven and earth, for no one comes to God or dares to think of coming to God the Father except through this living Son of God who should be honored as the Father is. . . . He is the Savior of all flesh that believes in him, and there is no other name by which one may be saved, but all who believe in him have the power to become children of God. LAMENT AND EXHORTATION OF KATHARINA ZELL TO THE PEOPLE AT THE GRAVE OF MASTER MATTHIAS ZELL.[9]

THE RELIGIOUS LEADERS WERE ASTONISHED.

JUSTUS JONAS: For, as Paul says, "Those who are foolish according to the world God chose to shame the wise." And, "We have this treasure in clay jars." That is, we apostles are despised, because our excellence is from the power of God and not from us. Through such people, despised before the world, God always causes his Word to be preached, so that it is understood that *he* rules his people. It is the power of God, not of human beings. ANNOTATIONS ON ACTS 4:13.[10]

THE APOSTLES WERE TRAINED IN THE SCHOOL OF CHRIST.

THE ENGLISH ANNOTATIONS: [These were] illiterate men, men without letters, not brought up in the schools of the scribes and Pharisees but in a school incomparably better—that is, in the school of Christ. Therefore this is not said absolutely (for they had spent some time in the study of the holy Scriptures and were all taught by God) but in relation to ordinary

means of attaining learning. ANNOTATIONS ON ACTS 4:13.[11]

CHRIST CHOSE THE FOOLISH TO SHAME THE WISE.

RUDOLF GWALTHER: First, they are filled with admiration and amazement and did not know what way to go, insomuch as they did not know what to say against it. Lest anyone might think they were fools or were at their wit's end for fear, Luke shows the reason they were so perplexed and in doubt. First was the confidence and boldness of speech in the apostles, which they perceived as surpassing their expectation. They knew they were simple and unlearned men, not brought up in faculties or arts beside their mother tongue. They knew they were taken from fishermen's work to be the apostles of Christ. Even still, that old opinion bewitched their minds and caused them to think that none of the scribes or Pharisees sided with Christ; it was only the accursed and rascals, who were ignorant in the law and Scriptures. Therefore, presupposing they should have easily overcome the apostles, they could not but be amazed when they saw them answer their question with such discretion, reprove their injustice so boldly and defend Christ's cause with such wisdom and constancy. They are compelled to acknowledge some power of God in them and perceive that they are led with a far different wisdom than the wisdom of the flesh.

This was the chief reason why Christ would choose ignorant and unlearned apostles. The doctrine of the gospel might be acknowledged to be set forth by the power of God and not through human wisdom, eloquence or authority, and that all the praise and glory for it might return to God alone. The other cause of their amazement was the evident truth of the miracle wrought by the apostles, which they are neither able to call into doubt nor to charge with any suspicion of magic or enchantment. For they see the man standing before them on whom the apostles had bestowed this benefit of health. (I do not know whether he was called by them or joined them of his own accord to see the

---

[8]Denck, *Selected Writings of Hans Denck*, 272*.

[9]Zell, *Church Mother*, 107-8.

[10]Jonas, *Annotationes in Acta*, D2r; quoting 1 Cor 1:27; 2 Cor 4:7.

[11]Downame, ed., *Annotations*, GGG4r*.

end and success of the matter.) Therefore, they are perplexed and do not have one word to answer. So those who thought they had overcome and caught the apostles in some trap by demanding one question are shamefully vanquished and confounded. Homily 28, Acts 4:13-18.[12]

Only the Lawful Government of the Church Is to Be Obeyed. John Calvin: Let us remember to whom they make this answer. For this council did undoubtedly represent the church, yet because they abuse their authority the apostles say they are not to be obeyed. And as it often happens when there is no doubt about the case, they use the verdict to reprove their adversaries. Furthermore, it is worth noting that they set against their decrees the authority of God—which would be inappropriate were it not that those who in other respects were ordinary pastors of the church were at the same time enemies of God. The apostles further make clear that obedience offered to evil and unfaithful pastors even though they exercise lawful authority in the church is contrary to God....

Lest they should think in their usual manner that their authority is being minimized because God is being exalted above them, Peter turns them aside from such complacent thoughts by warning them that this matter must be settled at the judgment seat of God. He says plainly *in the presence of God*, for however people may be blinded, God will never suffer anyone to be preferred before him. And surely the Spirit put this answer into the mouth of the apostles not only to repress the savagery of their enemies but that he might also teach us where our duty lies whenever people become so proud that they shake off the yoke of God and desire to lay their own yoke on us. At such times let us recall the sacred authority of God, which blows away the vain smoke of all human excellency. Commentary on Acts 4:19.[13]

Why Didn't Jesus Himself Heal This Man? The English Annotations: It may seem strange that being so old, and daily laid at the gate of the temple, into which Jesus so often entered (considering that it seems that he never denied to heal or cure anyone who asked), he did not receive help from Jesus all this time, but it is certain that he was reserved for this time. By means of this healing, through the all-disposing providence of God, the apostles were further confirmed, but more importantly so was the gospel. Annotations on Acts 4:22.[14]

---

[12]Gwalther, *Homelyes or Sermons upon the Actes*, 203-4* (*In Acta Apostolorum*, 64v-65r).

[13]CNTC 6:120, 121* (CO 48:87-88).
[14]Downame, ed., *Annotations*, GGG4r*.

4:23-37 THE COURAGE AND UNITY OF THE CHURCH

²³*When they were released, they went to their friends and reported what the chief priests and the elders had said to them.* ²⁴*And when they heard it, they lifted their voices together to God and said, "Sovereign Lord, who made the heaven and the earth and the sea and everything in them,* ²⁵*who through the mouth of our father David, your servant,ᵃ said by the Holy Spirit,*

"'Why did the Gentiles rage,
and the peoples plot in vain?
²⁶*The kings of the earth set themselves,*
and the rulers were gathered together,
against the Lord and against his Anointed'ᵇ—

²⁷*for truly in this city there were gathered together against your holy servant Jesus, whom you anointed, both Herod and Pontius Pilate, along with the Gentiles and the peoples of Israel,* ²⁸*to do whatever your hand and your plan had predestined to take place.* ²⁹*And now, Lord, look upon their threats and grant to your servantsᶜ to continue to speak your word with all boldness,* ³⁰*while you stretch out your hand to heal,* and signs and wonders are performed through the name of your holy servant Jesus."* ³¹*And when they had prayed, the place in which they were gathered together was shaken, and they were all filled with the Holy Spirit and continued to speak the word of God with boldness.*

³²*Now the full number of those who believed were of one heart and soul, and no one said that any of the things that belonged to him was his own, but they had everything in common.* ³³*And with great power the apostles were giving their testimony to the resurrection of the Lord Jesus, and great grace was upon them all.* ³⁴*There was not a needy person among them, for as many as were owners of lands or houses sold them and brought the proceeds of what was sold* ³⁵*and laid it at the apostles' feet, and it was distributed to each as any had need.* ³⁶*Thus Joseph, who was also called by the apostles Barnabas (which means son of encouragement), a Levite, a native of Cyprus,* ³⁷*sold a field that belonged to him and brought the money and laid it at the apostles' feet.*

a Or *child*; also verses 27, 30 **b** Or *Christ* **c** Greek *bondservants*

OVERVIEW: The apostles' release, the reformers assert, confirms the power and efficacy of prayer; just as importantly, this miraculous deliverance empowers the believers to speak more confidently about their faith than before. However, the commentators spend more time reflecting on a proper understanding of the unity of the early church in having "everything in common." Although some Radicals hold that the community of goods was a necessary mark of the true church, most commentators agree that holding possessions in common is (and should be) both voluntary and exemplary. The magisterial reformers emphasize the importance of a *freely* generous heart, while warning that Christian charity should not foster or enable lazi- ness and manipulation. They seek to banish any notions of minimal social responsibility, however, with the warning that a persistent desire for riches is a harmful addiction.

4:23-31 *The Believers Pray for Boldness*

SEEK GOD'S HELP THROUGH PRAYER. RUDOLF GWALTHER: [Luke] tells of how the church sought the support and help of God only by prayer. They were not careless, nor did they make light of the dangers approaching. They did not flee to human wisdom, help or counsel but sought all manner of aid and support by prayers. This is the sure sanctuary of the church, because God promises everywhere to be the defender of those who seek help from him. Homily 30, Acts 4:24-31.[1]

God Establishes and Upholds His Kingdom. John Calvin: After David was chosen by God to be king and was anointed by Samuel, he had the greatest difficulty in taking possession of his kingdom because of the opposition of enemies in every quarter. We know how the rulers and the people conspired together with Saul and his family and how afterwards the Philistines and other foes from without were so contemptuous of the new king that they vied with one another in making war on him. It is not without cause that David complains that the kings rage and take counsel together and the people make their various plans. Yet, because he knows that God is the supporter of his kingdom, he mocks their foolish enterprises and affirms their vanity. Because his kingdom was established to be an image of the kingdom of Christ, David does not remain in the shadow but grasps the solid form. Indeed, the Holy Spirit, as the apostles here remind us, reproves the absurd folly of the world which dares to invade the kingdom of Christ, which God had established as much in the person of David as of Christ himself. Commentary on Acts 4:25.[2]

The Spirit Answers Their Prayers with Signs. Justus Jonas: These signs are presented to us as happening after the prayer, stirring up faith through gratitude so that believers would have assurance and certainly trust that God is never more present with them than during trials or tribulations. As he says in the psalm, "Call upon me in the day of tribulation, I will deliver you and you will honor me." Now believers are taught in tribulations and through tribulations, and if they persevere in faith, the Spirit is magnified. Thus, Romans 5, "We rejoice over our afflictions." Annotations on Acts 4:31.[3]

The Power of the Church's Prayers. Desiderius Erasmus: By this sign the Lord showed that their prayers were heard and their hopes would be fulfilled. Nothing is so effective as the supplication of a church in harmony, for it has to be a mighty force to shake the immovable earth. This was no empty sign: the power of the Holy Spirit was renewed and increased in all, then and there, so that not only did they not conceal the evangelical doctrine because of the threats of the nobles, but they proclaimed the name of the Lord Jesus more freely and more courageously, and even more of their number did so than before. Such is the nature of evangelical progress that, just as saffron and some other things are more productive through injury, so it rises up and forces its way out against a world that is bearing down on it: already, within a few days the number of those professing the name of Jesus had grown large. Paraphrase of Acts 4:31.[4]

4:32-37 The Church Held Everything in Common

To Serve Christ Is to Abandon Mammon. Peter Walpot: "You cannot serve both God and mammon," namely, temporal wealth, personal property. For like a castle, so the love and concern of money possesses your hearts. Therefore you do not want to speak of abundance and to lead [others] to it. Christ once said it is impossible to cherish and cling to both. Thus, you cannot admit that it is possible. For one Lord commands you, "You should deny yourself," but the other, "You should devotedly focus on yourself or make all things yours." One, "You should be in community"; the other, "You should be self-interested and your own individual." How can it be possible to reconcile these contradictory things with one another? Therefore, whoever is a servant of mammon certainly cannot be a servant of Christ. We must dismiss one; the other then we are able to satisfy.

No one can go two ways at once. No one can

---

[1] Gwalther, *Homelyes or Sermons upon the Actes*, 215* (*In Acta Apostolorum*, 68v).
[2] CNTC 6:124* (CO 48:91); alluding to Col 2:17.
[3] Jonas, *Annotationes in Acta*, D3v; quoting Ps 50:15; Rom 5:3.

[4] CWE 50:37 (LB 7:683).

place a foot in more than one place. No vine can be attached to two trunks. No one can cook two porridges in one pan. No one who is sick may be healed with water *and* fire; one must be done away with. Whoever wants to have one must let go of the other. No one has more than just one heart. Thus, no one can love and serve God at the same time as temporal wealth, personal property, money and goods, which he here calls one lord, as Paul calls their stomach a god. All the while, like God himself, they trust and serve money day and night, at home and in the field, on land and water. And they do this with most attentive diligence, with the greatest care, with the noblest seriousness, so that they do not have even a tenth of diligence, care and seriousness left over for God and his worship. By Christ, however, we are redeemed. Therefore, we should not worship and cling to money and gold but rather should forfeit it to God's poor. This does not permit us to be hurled to where the rich man was flung and tormented. The Great Article Book: On Peace and Joint Property.[5]

The Abundance of the Early Church. John Calvin: In those days the believers gave abundantly of what was their own; we in our day are content not only jealously to retain what we possess but also callously to rob others. They set forth their own possessions with simplicity and faithfulness; we devise a thousand cunning devices whereby we may acquire everything for ourselves by hook or by crook. They laid down [money] at the apostles' feet; we do not fear with sacrilegious boldness to convert to our own use what was offered to God. They sold their own possessions in those days; in our day it is the lust to purchase that reigns supreme. At that time love made each person's own possessions common property for those in need; in our day such is the inhumanity of many that they begrudge to the poor a common dwelling on earth or the common use of water, air and sky.

These things then are written for our shame and reproach. Yet even the poor themselves are to

blame for some part of this evil. For since there cannot be such common holding of possessions unless there is godly agreement under the direction of a single heart and spirit, in many people there is such pride or ingratitude, such sloth or greed or such hypocrisy that the desire to do well and the ability to do well are alike hindered and extinguished. We must remember the admonition of Paul that we be not weary in well-doing. The drivelings of the Anabaptists and fanatics, who in our own day have made much ado on the basis of this passage, as if there ought to be no personal right to possession among Christians, I refuted earlier in writing.[6] For Luke does not here prescribe a law for all people which they must of necessity follow in relating the actions of people in whom the Spirit of God was manifest with singular efficacy and power, nor does he speak so generally of all people without exception as to lead us to suppose that no one was regarded as a Christian who did not sell all his possessions. Commentary on Acts 4:32-37.[7]

The Rebaptizers Are Wrong to Impose What Scripture Does Not. Martin Luther: [The rebaptizers] do not want to recognize as Christians those who retain something of their own and do not hold all things in common. However, first of all Scripture itself disproves them: out of such examples no one should make a command or force the people to follow it. For even at that time, this principle was in force. Peter the apostle said to Ananias, "You certainly could have kept your field while you had it, and once it was sold, it was still in your control." Surely, this clearly proves that no one was forced to sell such and to share the proceeds. But whoever personally and unprompted wanted to do this, so that he would aid poor

---

[5]QGT 12:181-82; quoting Mt 6:24; alluding to Phil 3:19; Lk 16:19-31.

[6]See John Calvin, *Treatises Against the Anabaptists and Against the Libertines*, trans. Benjamin W. Farley (Grand Rapids: Baker, 1982); *Briefve instruction … contre les erreurs de la secte commune des Anabaptistes* (1544), CO 7:45-142, and *Contre la secte phantastique et furieuse des Libertins* (1545), CO 7:145-252. For analysis, see Balke, *Calvin and the Anabaptist Radicals*, esp. 270-75.
[7]CNTC 6:130-31* (CO 48:96-97); alluding to Gal 6:9; Acts 2:42-47.

people in this way, no one refused him this. This is truly a good work, and at that time they would have gladly accepted it, because the disciples were still few and had all received the Holy Spirit, so that no one may obtain anything deceptively. Now today everything is completely jumbled, and the majority tend to prefer receiving their nourishment from other people, rather than wanting to work themselves and creating something honest with their own hands. Today such "community" would cause total misery among the godless, wicked people, who without this are already unable to bring themselves to work and turn instead to dishonest panhandling. HOUSE POSTIL FOR THE FEAST OF SAINT STEPHEN (1544).[8]

THE MEANING OF TRUE COMMUNITY. PETER RIEDEMANN: All believers have fellowship in holy things, that is, in God. He has given them all things in his Son, Christ Jesus. Just as Christ has nothing for himself, since all he has is for us, so too, no member of Christ's body should possess any gift for themselves or for their own sake. Instead, all should be consecrated for the whole body, for all the members. This is so because Christ also did not bring his gifts for one individual or the other, but for everyone, for the whole body.

Community of goods applies to both spiritual and material gifts. All of God's gifts, not only the spiritual but also the temporal, have been given so that they not be kept but be shared with each other. Therefore, the fellowship of believers should be visible not only in spiritual but also in temporal things. . . . [Paul shows this] by pointing to the law about manna. According to that rule, the one who gathered much had nothing extra, and the one who gathered little had no lack, since each was given the amount needed.

Furthermore, the creation still testifies today that at the beginning God ordained that people should own nothing individually but should have all things in common with each other. However, by taking what they should have left and by leaving what they should have taken, people have gained possession of things and have become more accustomed to accumulating things and hardened in doing so. Through such appropriating and collecting of created things, people have been led so far from God that they have forgotten the Creator. CONFESSION OF FAITH.[9]

BENEVOLENCE TOWARD THE POOR. RUDOLF GWALTHER: Luke mentions benevolence and helping the poor, the exercise of which those whose minds agree together in Christ cannot omit. This passage is most worthy to be considered both because of the Anabaptists, who (as we declared before in the second chapter) go about by this passage to establish Plato and his communion of all things, and because of false evangelists, who suspend all exercises of Christian contribution. Therefore, for an easier understanding of this discussion, we will first consider the sum of the matter, then the trade and order that the faithful observed in this case and last of all what the fruit and effect of it was.

Luke comprehends the sum of this in a few words, where he says, "No one ought to say that the things that he possessed were his own, but they had all things in common." Here the property of things is not denied, because there is express mention of possession, but he expresses the affection of mind that the faithful had. Although they possessed houses, farms and other such property, no one was so wedded to them that he thought they were given to him alone, but would have them to serve the use and necessity of others also. Therefore, we gather that all things were common among them by will but not by law. . . . In this place the true fountain of Christian benevolence and contribution is declared, that is to say, a mind that is not addicted and tied to the desire of riches but judges correctly concerning riches and the use of them. For according to Paul's saying, the use of riches in this world consists only in food and drink and clothing, and one must also understand that

---

[8]WA 52:588-89; quoting Acts 5:4.

[9]CRR 9:119; alluding to 2 Cor 8:7-15; Ex 16:16-18.

inasmuch as we are born naked into this world, neither shall we carry anything out of it with us. But where the faithful person understands that human nature is sufficed with few things, he cannot be drowned in the abundant desire of heaping riches together, and he does not judge his treasure to consist in riches. Although he sees that they multiply and increase, he does not set his whole heart on them. Rather, he understands that he is but a steward of them. . . .

This consideration makes the goods of the faithful common to each other, even though they keep the right of property to themselves. The manner and order of distribution is observed as follows. . . . First, he says houses and lands were sold, though not everyone did so, nor did those who did sell, sell all, reserving nothing for themselves. For there are various examples of many who had houses of their own and kept families, which Paul not only permitted but also, as we may read, directly commanded them to do. Therefore, they sold as much as seemed requisite for the present necessity of the church, and it was according to everyone's disposition either to keep or sell, as will presently appear in Peter's words to Ananias. Further, they did not lay money down for all to take but brought it to the apostles, whom they thought would handle the distribution well, until deacons were ordained by public consent of the congregation to take that office on themselves. The apostles did not publish the amount of money brought to them, so that each one might take what one listed, but distribution was made to everyone according to need.

Therefore, there was no disorderly communion of goods, no confusion of things, no violent usurping of other people's goods, such as the frenetic and seditious imagine. If we consider all the circumstances well, it will easily appear that this contribution was ordained, so that the church might have some public treasure to help to serve the poor so that they are not compelled through poverty to shrink from the faith of Christ and the body of the congregation. And those who either had goods of their own or were able by some hon-

est labor to get their living had no part of these goods. HOMILY 31, ACTS 4:32-37.[10]

THIS PASSAGE IS SIMPLE. PETER WALPOT: It does not say that each and every person took to themselves whatever they wanted. So it should still be. God permitted and was pleased [to command] this passage, so that we would hold in common all things that serve to the praise of God. Whoever does not do this despises and deserts the footsteps of the first apostolic church. THE GREAT ARTICLE BOOK: ON PEACE AND JOINT PROPERTY.[11]

THE GOSPEL COMPELS US TO SHARE BUT NOT TO NEGLECT OUR FAMILIES. MARTIN LUTHER: It is a great error among the rebaptizers that they require and command such community, that everyone must act accordingly. However, the gospel is not such a teaching that alters anything in government or the household. It leaves both estates alone and teaches how we may come to the forgiveness of sins and eternal life, and it will uproot neither the household nor the government through such teaching.[12] Now it is before our eyes that the uprooting of these estates must follow whenever we want to make everything common. Christians, however, have a different community, in which we should let it remain as it is and not require anything more. John preaches, "Whoever has two coats should give one to the one who has none, and whoever has food should do likewise." And Christ says, "Give to each one who asks you."

For according to this a Christian is required to help wherever he is able, yes, so that Paul's rule remains: not that others have ease and we have burdens, but rather our abundance should serve others' need, that is, wherever there is true need and not laziness or haphazard house management, and you without harm [to your own affairs] are able to help in such need, then you are respon-

---

[10]Gwalther, *Homelyes or Sermons upon the Acts*, 224-25* (*In Acta Apostolorum*, 71r-v); alluding to 1 Tim 6:8.

[11]QGT 12:200.

[12]For Luther, as for most of his contemporaries, change implied disorder and chaos. See above on Münster Rebellion, liii-liv.

sible to help. For some love to give, so they have nothing. Others are able to nourish themselves well, so they either do not work or let themselves take life easy. Such people we should not help. By helping we only make things worse and endorse their begging.

So, this text does not mean that we should make such an example of the first church required and force Christians into such community. We leave it at this, that a Christian should help his neighbor, whenever he is able to do so without harm. For our Lord God does not want this to happen: that you help a beggar and thus make you yourself and your children beggars. HOUSE POSTIL FOR THE FEAST OF SAINT STEPHEN (1544).[13]

---

[13]WA 52:589-90; quoting Lk 6:30; Mt 5:42; alluding to 2 Cor 8:13.

5:1-11 ANANIAS AND SAPPHIRA

But a man named Ananias, with his wife Sapphira, sold a piece of property, ²and with his wife's knowledge he kept back for himself some of the proceeds and brought only a part of it and laid it at the apostles' feet. ³But Peter said, "Ananias, why has Satan filled your heart to lie to the Holy Spirit and to keep back for yourself part of the proceeds of the land? ⁴While it remained unsold, did it not remain your own? And after it was sold, was it not at your disposal? Why is it that you have contrived this deed in your heart? You have not lied to man but to God." ⁵When Ananias heard these words, he fell down and breathed his last. And great fear came upon all who heard of it. ⁶The young men rose and wrapped him up and carried him out and buried him.

⁷After an interval of about three hours his wife came in, not knowing what had happened. ⁸And Peter said to her, "Tell me whether you[a] sold the land for so much." And she said, "Yes, for so much."⁹But Peter said to her, "How is it that you have agreed together to test the Spirit of the Lord? Behold, the feet of those who have buried your husband are at the door, and they will carry you out."¹⁰Immediately she fell down at his feet and breathed her last. When the young men came in they found her dead, and they carried her out and buried her beside her husband. ¹¹And great fear came upon the whole church and upon all who heard of these things.

a The Greek for *you* is plural here

OVERVIEW: The story of Ananias and Sapphira is paired with the worthy example of Joseph from the previous pericope. The reformers remark that Joseph's charity is commendable because his heart and conscience are pure, while Ananias and Sapphira hypocritically seek to be praised for their humility and charity. The commentators see their deaths as a warning that God does not merely want our performance and material gifts; he wants our whole selves. He desires the sacrifice of a contrite spirit (Ps 51:16-17). Peter's words of condemnation to this husband and wife are interpreted either as a warning to those who in the future would be tempted by the sin of Ananias and Sapphira, or as a (missed) opportunity for their repentance. This story warns not only against the allure of money, but also of anything that competes with an undivided allegiance to God.

AN EXAMPLE TO ENCOURAGE, AN EXAMPLE TO DISCOURAGE. DESIDERIUS ERASMUS: Just as the straightforward candor of Barnabas stirred many to emulate his generosity, so an example was provided to discourage anyone from mixing deliberate deceit with spiritual work. For the Spirit loves simplicity of heart and hates every pretense and disguise. Thus among the twelve apostles the example of Judas was provided so that no one should rely on himself but persevere in his duty with all diligence. Now there was in this company a certain man named Ananias, who corresponded all too little to his name because he himself responded all too little to the grace of God. PARAPHRASE OF ACTS 5:1.[1]

THE ALLURE OF AMBITION AND FAME. JOHANNES BRENZ: The believers saw that among the faithful, many were needy. Hence, in order that they might help the poor from their own abundant blessings, they were offering the money fetched from the sale of their possessions to the apostles so that it could be distributed. They did this because they knew that the Lord had commanded that relief be given to the hardship of the poor, and they

---

[1]CWE 50:38 (LB 7:684). Ananias means "the Lord has been gracious."

still remembered what Christ had said: "Whoever, for my name's sake, will leave behind (and to give to the poor is also to "leave behind" for Christ's sake) his field or home will receive back one hundredfold." Therefore, from faith in Christ and charity toward neighbor, they were bringing together their possessions to the common good.

But Ananias and Sapphira had their eyes set on something far different. They noticed that among Christians the act of bringing one's goods into the common good brought with it praise, glory and celebrity, as they saw with Joseph.... Likewise they themselves craved honor and praise and desired to be considered no less important or generous than others. Therefore, they sold their possessions, and they brought and offered up part of the price they had received to the apostles, so that they themselves might receive some nickname from the apostles as a monument to their beneficence, as well as recognition and fame among other Christians. But what else is this than the foulest ambition and the most sordid lust for human glory?

Do you mean, you say, that we should live in an unseemly and disgraceful way so as to avoid human glory? Far from it. Christ says, "Let your light shine before human beings, so that they might see your good works and glorify your father, who is in heaven." And Paul states, "Whatever things are true, whatever good, whatever just, whatever pure, whatever right, whatever is of a good name, if there is anything virtuous and worthy of praise, think about these things, do these things, and the God of peace will be with you." You see that good works should be done before people and that those things that produce praise and good reputation should be pursued. But these must not be done out of ambition or human appetite for glory but from faith in God and for an appetite to give the obedience that is owed to God. Thus, the result will be that this person voluntarily will not chase after the desired human glory. HOMILIES 22, ACTS 5:1-11.[2]

APPEARANCES CAN BE DECEIVING. JOHN TRAPP: Sapphira signifies "beautiful" or "attractive." She might be so on the outside—as those apples of Sodom, the Egyptian temples or Jewish sepulchers[3]—but her heart was rotten and not right with God. Hypocrites are called vipers, which are outwardly attractive, inwardly poisonous. The swan is white in feathers but of black skin and was therefore reputed unclean and unfit for sacrifice. COMMENTARY ON ACTS 5:1.[4]

THE DEVIL MAY CREEP IN THROUGH ANY OPENING. OTTO BRUNFELS: Where a perverse disposition of the will begins to hold sway, there the door is open to the devil. He is constantly circling around, looking for a crack through which he can creep in. And this is what is meant when we say he enters, fills and possesses: during moments of joy or sadness he takes measure of our mind, and once it has been fully discerned and understood, he stirs it up and agitates it and drives it to evil, fueling the flames. ANNOTATIONS ON ACTS 5:3.[5]

ANANIAS IS GUILTY OF MULTIPLE KINDS OF DECEIT. JOHN CALVIN: Luke condemns Ananias for only one crime: his wishing to deceive God and the church with a false offering. But there were many evils lying hidden behind this deceit: contempt of God, of whom he does not stand in awe although God knows of his crookedness; sacrilegious fraudulence, because by stealth he holds on to a part of what was acknowledged to be set apart for God; perverse vanity and ambition, because without a thought for the judgment of God he ingratiates himself with people; infidelity, because he would not have set foot on this forbidden way had he not lacked faith in God; the spoiling of a godly and holy plan; and furthermore the actual hypocrisy was a great evil in itself. And to this there had to be added his deliberate and audacious

---

[2]Brenz, *Acta Apostolica Homiliae*, 46v-47r; quoting Mt 19:29; 5:16; Phil 4:8.

[3]According to medieval mythology "the apples of Sodom" were apples that crumbled to ash once they were picked. For whited sepulchers, see Mt 23:27-28.
[4]Trapp, *Commentary or Exposition*, 127-28*.
[5]Brunfels, *Annotationes*, 207r.

lying. Even if Ananias had given away half of his land, his deed was a splendid and noteworthy one to all appearances. And there is indeed great virtue in a rich person dividing his goods fairly with the poor, but "the sacrifices of the wicked are abominations to God"; and where honesty of heart is absent nothing can be pleasing to him. COMMENTARY ON ACTS 5:3-4.[6]

HYPOCRITES ARE NOT MADE HOLY AUTOMATICALLY THROUGH THE SACRAMENTS. BOHEMIAN CONFESSION OF 1535: [The Scriptures] teach that the sacraments through themselves, or as is sometimes said *ex opere operato*, do not bestow on those who are not first provided with a good intention and have been brought to life within by the Holy Spirit, any grace or justifying faith which makes the human mind in all things yielding, trusting and compliant to God. Indeed, faith must come first (we are talking about adults here), and this makes a person alive through the Holy Spirit and injects good intentions into the heart. Indeed, without faith there is no salvation or justification, nor do the sacraments do any good. Clear testimonies of this fact stand open to us in the Scriptures, especially in the case of Judas Iscariot, who received the sacraments from Christ himself yet took the part of the priests and those who cried out against Christ. We find the same in Ananias and Sapphira his wife, who were bathed with the washing of baptism by the apostles and, as may be legitimately believed, partook of the Lord's Supper as well. Nevertheless they remained in the bonds of malice and evil and lied to the Holy Spirit, and the sacraments did not remove this evil from them or give them the faith which makes alive, the faith which gives a secure and tranquil conscience, and a heart which listens to God. Similarly, circumcision and the sacrifices of the Law did not confer that faith which both justifies and makes alive. ARTICLE II, THE SACRAMENTS.[7]

"AFTER IT WAS SOLD, WAS IT NOT AT YOUR DISPOSAL?" KONRAD PELLIKAN: This clearly enough indicates that Christians are not under compulsion to bring together their property in common but can retain it in their own control, provided that they retain it without lies and deception and faithfully administer it to the needy according to the office of charity and Christian brotherhood. COMMENTARY ON ACTS 5:4.[8]

ALMS ARE PRECIOUS BEFORE GOD. JOHN CALVIN: It was God's purpose to strike the rest with fear by the punishment of one person, so that they might conscientiously abstain from all deceit. . . . For God wished to give a general warning to all generations at that particular time, that all may learn to be sincere in their dealings with him. However, the punishment of this wretch ought to have encouraged the godly to be more liberal afterwards in setting apart their goods for God and the poor, because they could gather how precious alms were in the sight of God, when the profaning of them had been punished so severely. COMMENTARY ON ACTS 5:5.[9]

NOTE THE DILIGENCE OF THE YOUNG. OTTO BRUNFELS: Pay attention to the good manners and voluntary service of the youths. For it is an old state of affairs, not new in the least, that in the congregation of Christians the youth surpass the elders in performing service. ANNOTATIONS ON ACTS 5:6.[10]

LEARN FROM THIS EXAMPLE OF JUDGMENT AND REPENT. THE ENGLISH ANNOTATIONS: Those in the same faults must expect similar punishments or worse (except in the case of timely repentance) which being prolonged are ever greatened. How good a thing it would be if the sacrilegious of today would be timely warned by these examples and remember that it is the same God of unchangeable justice now looking on this sin, who severely punished it in these two. Retaining what-

---

[6]CNTC 6:132-33* (CO 48:97-98); quoting Prov 15:8.
[7]Boh 1535, 22-23.

[8]Pellikan, *In Acta Apostolorum*, 53.
[9]CNTC 6:136* (CO 48:100).
[10]Brunfels, *Annotationes*, 207v.

ever they have received from other unjust people is to consent with them in the same crime, and that, except in the case of restitution and true repentance, they must once suffer grievous punishment, because God is impartially just. Nor will it benefit the hypocrite that he feels pangs of conscience for some sin, or sins, if he willingly ignores them. ANNOTATIONS ON ACTS 5:10.[11]

THE CHURCH MUST SEPARATE THE BELIEVING FROM THE UNBELIEVING. PETER RIEDEMANN: The land of the Israelites, their glory, rule and later the kingdom—these all prefigure and point to Christ the King and his future kingdom; all this had been promised beforehand and was later established. Since that is so, the driving out means separating believers from unbelievers, for unbelievers have no place in the church of God. God desires to have a holy bride without wrinkle, spot or blemish, holy as he is holy. The Lord, the almighty God, was not pleased when Israel allowed the heathen to dwell in the land instead of driving them out. . . .

God would be even more displeased if one were to set up a church together with the world or take the world into the church of the saints. David says the sinner has no place in the congregation of the righteous. . . . The prophets acted rightly and not foolishly in not cutting themselves off from Israel, in spite of the evil the people had done. This is true because at that time to be an heir and to be a servant were not distinguished from one another. Although the prophets were truly heirs and the others were slaves, yet they were kept under outward rules until Christ came. Now that the time appointed by the Father has come, however, heirs and slaves are separated, so that the heirs can receive their inheritance and their freedom. Now through faith in Christ, there are no more slaves but heirs. CONFESSION OF FAITH.[12]

GOD BRINGS GOOD FROM THIS EVIL SITUATION. KONRAD PELLIKAN: Now see the good

fruit from the unfortunate event. From the just death of the two in regard to their body (for the salvation of the souls of either one of them there should not be speculation either way, and even less so about their eternal damnation), a huge fear arose throughout the whole church of believers, but also the fear of this example seized those who did not yet believe. The good were summoned to greater piety by this punishment, but the wicked were being made afraid in their own sins and were being admonished to repentance. So by the punishment of a few, let us all recognize an opportunity for being more holy and prudent. COMMENTARY ON ACTS 5:11.[13]

GOD INSTRUCTS THE WISE THROUGH FEAR. OTTO BRUNFELS: As Solomon says, the wise person is made wiser when the scorner receives a blow. Thus in various ways God strengthens and proves the faith of those who fear him, including by striking down the impious, which in this case is a benefit, because along with it he promises the abundance and goods of the earth, and peace, if we fear him. ANNOTATIONS ON ACTS 5:11.[14]

EXCOMMUNICATION IS AN EXPRESS COMMAND. DIRK PHILIPS: Ananias and Sapphira fell dead at the feet of the apostle Peter for having lied a single time. The Scripture is full of such examples. As these demonstrate, none must despise the commandments of God, well imprinted in his heart. This is confirmed by the apostle, saying, "Who fails at one point is guilty of all." From this it follows thus that excommunication with its effect comprised in the evangelical and apostolic doctrine must be observed as an express commandment of the Lord (as this was said above) in all diligence and Christian discretion, according to the pure understanding of the holy Scripture and the gospel's intention. That is, [excommunication is to be observed] according to the nature of God, the affection of Jesus Christ and the interpretation

---

[11]Downame, ed., *Annotations*, HHH1r*.
[12]CRR 9:165-66*; alluding to Lev 19:2; Ps 1:4-6; Gal 4:21-31.

[13]Pellikan, *In Acta Apostolorum*, 55.
[14]Brunfels, *Annotationes*, 207r-v; alluding to Prov 19:25.

of Jesus Christ in true love, in such patience as is worthy in the gospel and conformed to the faith. EVANGELICAL EXCOMMUNICATION.[15]

WHY IS PETER'S REBUKE SO HARSH? DESIDERIUS ERASMUS: Here perhaps it will occur to someone to wonder at Peter's harshness toward Ananias, when a little while ago he had with so much gentleness held out the promise of pardon to those who had crucified Jesus, attributing their deed to ignorance and offering eternal salvation to those who repented. Here, because a little bit of money was withheld in an otherwise generous act, a fierce rebuke and not a hope of pardon is extended. Doubtless the Lord Jesus, who had commanded that everyone be invited to salvation through baptism and the forgiveness of all their sins, wished to show by the destruction of a few how much more serious it is to fall back into sin after the grace and light of the gospel have been received—not now through thoughtlessness and ignorance but by deliberate pretense.

Peter knew that the chief danger to evangelical sincerity would spring from hypocrisy and avarice, and for this reason, a striking example was produced immediately, at the very beginning of the nascent church. Through this example all might be warned that no one who imitated Ananias would escape divine vengeance, even if punishment did not immediately fall on the guilty person. The issue here was not the loss of money but the absence of confidence in God and the mockery of the Holy Spirit. Moreover, Peter did not inflict the punishment but poured on Ananias the acrimony of rebuke to heal him. But because Ananias did not burst into tears, did not utter a word of repentance, he was smitten that many might be saved. An example of justice was set forth in the one who perished; the gift of mercy was poured out abundantly on the many who by his example took care not to sin. PARAPHRASE OF ACTS 5:1-11.[16]

THESE HARSH PUNISHMENTS SHOULD LEAD US TO REPENTANCE. KONRAD PELLIKAN: An insignificant lie, as it seems, perpetrated without the involvement of an oath, is punished with such a dreadful penalty, so that we may learn what great penalties perjury deserves, along with murder, thievery and other horrific crimes of this nature. The fact that these two lying spouses fell dead on the spot does not mean that everyone who lies or commits a crime will likewise perish in sudden death by an ordained punishment. It happened so that the rest would be summoned to repentance. Or if they do not repent, they might know that the more severely a punishment hangs over them, the later it comes, and that the slowness of the punishment will be balanced by its severity. COMMENTARY ON ACTS 5:10.[17]

DISCIPLINE MUST FIT THE CIRCUMSTANCES. SECOND HELVETIC CONFESSION: And seeing that there must be discipline in the church, and that, among the ancient fathers, excommunication was in use, and there were ecclesiastical judgments among the people of God, wherein this discipline was exercised by godly people, it belongs also to the minister's duty, for the edifying of the church, to moderate this discipline, according to the condition of the time and public estate, and according to necessity. Wherein this rule is always to be held, that "all things ought to be done to edification, decently, and in order" (1 Cor 14:40), without any oppression or tumult. For the apostle witnesses, that "power was given to him by God, to edify and not to destroy" (2 Cor 10:8). And the Lord himself forbade the tares to be plucked up in the Lord's field, because there would be danger lest the wheat also be plucked up with it (Mt 13:29). CHAPTER 18, OF THE MINISTERS OF THE CHURCH, THEIR INSTITUTION AND OFFICE.[18]

---

[15]CRR 6:597*; quoting Jas 2:10; alluding to Mt 18:18.
[16]CWE 50:39-40* (LB 7:684-85).

[17]Pellikan, *In Acta Apostolorum*, 55.
[18]*Creeds*, 3:883 (Latin, 284).

5:12-42 THE APOSTLES ON TRIAL
BEFORE THE SANHEDRIN

¹²Now many signs and wonders were regularly done among the people by the hands of the apostles. And they were all together in Solomon's Portico. ¹³None of the rest dared join them, but the people held them in high esteem. ¹⁴And more than ever believers were added to the Lord, multitudes of both men and women, ¹⁵so that they even carried out the sick into the streets and laid them on cots and mats, that as Peter came by at least his shadow might fall on some of them. ¹⁶The people also gathered from the towns around Jerusalem, bringing the sick and those afflicted with unclean spirits, and they were all healed.

¹⁷But the high priest rose up, and all who were with him (that is, the party of the Sadducees), and filled with jealousy ¹⁸they arrested the apostles and put them in the public prison. ¹⁹But during the night an angel of the Lord opened the prison doors and brought them out, and said, ²⁰"Go and stand in the temple and speak to the people all the words of this Life." ²¹And when they heard this, they entered the temple at daybreak and began to teach.

Now when the high priest came, and those who were with him, they called together the council, all the senate of the people of Israel, and sent to the prison to have them brought. ²²But when the officers came, they did not find them in the prison, so they returned and reported, ²³"We found the prison securely locked and the guards standing at the doors, but when we opened them we found no one inside." ²⁴Now when the captain of the temple and the chief priests heard these words, they were greatly perplexed about them, wondering what this would come to. ²⁵And someone came and told them, "Look! The men whom you put in prison are standing in the temple and teaching the people." ²⁶Then the captain with the officers went and brought them, but not by force, for they were afraid of being stoned by the people.

²⁷And when they had brought them, they set them before the council. And the high priest questioned them, ²⁸saying, "We strictly charged you not to teach in this name, yet here you have filled Jerusalem with your teaching, and you intend to bring this man's blood upon us." ²⁹But Peter and the apostles answered, "We must obey God rather than men. ³⁰The God of our fathers raised Jesus, whom you killed by hanging him on a tree. ³¹God exalted him at his right hand as Leader and Savior, to give repentance to Israel and forgiveness of sins. ³²And we are witnesses to these things, and so is the Holy Spirit, whom God has given to those who obey him."

³³When they heard this, they were enraged and wanted to kill them. ³⁴But a Pharisee in the council named Gamaliel, a teacher of the law held in honor by all the people, stood up and gave orders to put the men outside for a little while. ³⁵And he said to them, "Men of Israel, take care what you are about to do with these men. ³⁶For before these days Theudas rose up, claiming to be somebody, and a number of men, about four hundred, joined him. He was killed, and all who followed him were dispersed and came to nothing. ³⁷After him Judas the Galilean rose up in the days of the census and drew away some of the people after him. He too perished, and all who followed him were scattered. ³⁸So in the present case I tell you, keep away from these men and let them alone, for if this plan or this undertaking is of man, it will fail; ³⁹but if it is of God, you will not be able to overthrow them. You might even be found opposing God!" So they took his advice, ⁴⁰and when they had called in the apostles, they beat them and charged them not to speak in the name of Jesus, and let them go. ⁴¹Then they left the presence of the council, rejoicing that they were counted worthy to suffer dishonor for the name. ⁴²And every day, in the temple and from house to house, they did not cease teaching and preaching that the Christ is Jesus.

OVERVIEW: In this passage, Reformation commentators illustrate two distinct emphases. First they highlight the relationship between faith and the evidence of faith. On the one hand, faith brings about miracles, signs and wonders. On the other, believers ought not to put too much trust in the signs themselves. The faithful deeds of the apostles are the fruit of complete trust in the truth of God, and testify to his trustworthiness. Consequently, faith is the crucial basis for understanding all of God's work. In other words, signs and wonders by Jesus and the apostles confirm their teaching, but watching and waiting for miracles is unnecessary because the kingdom of God now consists of faith and the ministry of the Word. The second emphasis is the importance of obedience to God, because his Word is clear and powerful. Therefore the Christian life is one of proclamation and faith in action.

5:12-16 The Apostles Perform Signs and Wonders

THE MINISTRY OF THE WORD BRINGS LIFE. JOHANN SPANGENBERG: So that no one would think that the apostolic office is an office of death, since merely through the words of Peter, Ananias and Sapphira fell and died, Luke narrates what miracles and signs the apostles performed among the sick. By this he proves that the preaching office is not an office of death and destruction but rather one of life, healing and salvation. Thus he says, "Now through the hands of the apostles many signs and miracles happened among the people." BRIEF EXEGESIS OF ACTS 5:12-16.[1]

WE SHOULD NOT SEEK SIGNS TODAY. OTTO BRUNFELS: Even the teaching of the old law was confirmed by signs. But nowadays, it is useless to seek after signs. . . . For this reason we should be suspicious of any additional signs that come up in the future. For the kingdom of God consists not in signs but in faith and the Word. And elsewhere he bids us to boast in this, not that we do miracles,

but because our names are written in the heavens. Nor can you make a counterargument based on the last chapter of Mark, where it says, "signs will follow them," and so on. This was most certainly fulfilled through the apostles, as we read here in Acts. If we do not perform miracles, that does not make us inferior. Yet, if we understand it in a spiritual sense, sometimes to this day these signs also happen. ANNOTATIONS ON ACTS 5:12.[2]

ONCE WEEDED, THE GARDEN OF THE LORD FLOURISHED. THE ENGLISH ANNOTATIONS: The example of Ananias and Sapphira was so far from discouraging people from Christianity that it grew the church all the more. After these evil branches were cut off, the Lord's vine—the church—flourished the better. ANNOTATIONS ON ACTS 5:14.[3]

ATTRACT OTHERS TO CHRIST BY WORD AND DEED. OTTO BRUNFELS: So long as we pursue a lifestyle of integrity and sincerity—so that people may see our good works—and we preach the Word diligently, the number of believers always grows. The reason is that even though the Father is able to draw people to himself without us, still he has ordained things in this way. Because what he himself accomplished in his Son—who announced to us what had previously been unknown, then offered his life as an example of innocence for us—so we too are to draw our neighbors to Christ by the instruction of salvation and by our good examples. Therefore it is of great importance what is said here: "A multitude of believers was being added to the Lord." Therefore, however many do not believe in the Lord, misguided by the example of our life steeped in wickedness or, on account of us, are deterred from the truth, for every such soul we are held responsible before God. "Whoever offends one of these little ones." ANNOTATIONS ON ACTS 5:14.[4]

---

[2]Brunfels, *Annotationes*, 207v; alluding to Ex 7; Mt 24:4-13; Mk 16:17-18.
[3]Downame, ed., *Annotations*, HHH1r*.
[4]Brunfels, *Annotationes*, 207v; quoting Mt 18:6.

---

[1]Spangenberg, *Der Apostel Geschichte*, 41v-42r.

THE ETERNAL LIGHT IN PETER'S SHADOW.
RICHARD CRASHAW:

> Under thy shadow may I lurk awhile,
> Death's busy search I'll easily beguile:
> Thy shadow, Peter, must show me the sun,
> My light's thy shadow's shadow, or 'tis done.

STEPS TO THE TEMPLE.[5]

DID PETER'S SHADOW REALLY HEAL PEOPLE?
JOHANN SPANGENBERG: His shadow did not do
this, but rather the apostolic office did. We read
that several people wanted to bury a man; seeing
Moabite warriors charge into the land, they threw
the man into the prophet Elijah's grave. And as he
entered the grave and touched the bones of Elijah,
the dead man came back to life and stood on his
feet. Who here resurrected the dead? Not the
bones of Elijah, but God himself, who wanted with
this sign to confirm that Elijah was a true prophet
of God. BRIEF EXEGESIS OF ACTS 5:15.[6]

5:17-42 The Apostles Arrested, Tried and Freed

**THE TEMPLE RULERS COULD NOT BEAR BEING
EMBARASSED BY NOBODIES.** JOHANN SPAN-
GENBERG: The temple rulers knew well that the
apostles were fishermen, tax collectors and uneducated people, and they were being humiliated by
them. This they could not bear; they were after all
the heads and pillars of Judaism. In addition, the
apostles preached the crucified Jesus of Nazareth,
and they dared to say publicly that he was unjustly
crucified and killed by them, resurrected from the
dead and alive eternally. This accusation the temple
rulers were even less able to bear. So they had to
do something. After briefly discussing the matter,
they arose and seized the apostles and cast them
into prison with the plan that in the morning they
would indict them. BRIEF EXEGESIS OF ACTS 5:17.[7]

**THE APOSTLES ARE ALWAYS IN THE LORD'S
HAND.** JOHN CALVIN: The Lord brought the
apostles out of prison, not because he wished to
deliver them from the hand of their enemies forever,
for later on he allowed them to be brought back
again and be beaten with rods. But by this miracle
he meant to demonstrate that they were in his hand
and care for the defense of faith in his gospel, partly
in order that the church might find fresh encouragement from the event and partly to leave the ungodly without any excuse. For that reason we must
not always hope, not even are we to desire, that God
may deliver us from death; but the proper thing for
us is to be content that our life is protected by his
hand, as needs be. COMMENTARY ON ACTS 5:19.[8]

**WHAT IS THE POINT OF THIS MIRACULOUS
ESCAPE?** JOHANN SPANGENBERG: First, it terrified
the enemies of the gospel. In it they see that all
their resistance and opposition is futile, that they
must give up and grant God room and latitutde.
Second, the poor Christians who suffer persecution are consoled and strengthened through this
miracle, because they see that no one is able to oppose or resist God's Word and work, even if every
gate of hell stands in opposition. BRIEF EXEGESIS
OF ACTS 5:19-20.[9]

**THE TEMPLE RULERS WITNESS AGAINST
THEMSELVES.** THE ENGLISH ANNOTATIONS: So
easily God can, whenever he pleases, frustrate the
plans and expectations of his enemies. These very
servants were witnesses that they fought against
God, by whose divine power they must know the
apostles were delivered from prison, which was so
tightly guarded that they could not otherwise have
escaped. But those who willingly shut their eyes
cannot see what is in the clearest light. ANNOTA-
TIONS ON ACTS 5:22.[10]

**THE LIMITS OF OBEDIENCE TO SECULAR
POWER.** BOHEMIAN CONFESSION OF 1535: [The

---

[5]Crashaw, *Complete Works of Richard Crashaw*, 17.
[6]Spangenberg, *Der Apostel Geschichte*, 42v-43r; alluding to 2 Kings 13:20-22.
[7]Spangenberg, *Der Apostel Geschichte*, 44r-v.

[8]CNTC 6:142-43* (CO 48:106).
[9]Spangenberg, *Der Apostel Geschichte*, 45r-v; alluding to Mt 16:18.
[10]Downame, ed., *Annotations*, HHH1r*.

Scriptures] also teach that it is commanded by the word of God that all people are to be subject to the higher powers in all things; that is, in all things which are not contrary to God and his Word: first, indeed, to your Royal Majesty, and then to those others who are constituted in eminence and office, whether they be good or unworthy and evil. And they are to show honor and respect to all who are put into high positions by rank and office, and fulfill all obligations to which they are bound by census or taxes.

But regarding those things which concern souls and faith and salvation, they teach that only God and his ministers are to be heard, as Christ himself says: "Render to Caesar the things that are Caesar's, and to God the things that are God's" (Mt 22:21). If, however, anyone wishes to force them to do those things which fight against and oppose God and his Word, which remain eternally, they teach that they should make use of the example of the apostles who answered the rulers in Jerusalem: "We must obey God rather than humans." ARTICLE 16, SECULAR POWER.[11]

THE THREE CHARGES AGAINST THE APOSTLES. THE ENGLISH ANNOTATIONS: The enraged high priest charges them with three made-up crimes: first contumacy against their authority. . . . The second charge was schism and heresy, which according to their law was a capital crime. . . . Their third charge [was to make the high priests appear to be guilty of Christ's death]: it seemed to be an intolerable disgrace and dishonor to the chief priests and elders to be accused openly of injustice and shedding innocent blood. ANNOTATIONS ON ACTS 5:28.[12]

ULTIMATE ALLEGIANCE IS DUE TO THE PRINCE OF HEAVEN. JUSTUS JONAS: The apostles were certainly called by God and preached at God's command. On this basis Paul often boasts of his calling. On this basis they also respond: "It is neces-sary instead to obey God, etc. Clearly he is the one who sent us." Pay attention to the word that Luke uses here, *peitharchein*, which literally means to obey a prince. By this expression Luke demonstrates the disposition of the apostles. For here they powerfully and freely responded, and absolutely no doubt in their heart had weakened them, as their voices indicate. It is as if they were saying, "You certainly are the magistrates and princes; but we have Christ the prince of heaven, and it is more necessary to obey him than to obey you." ANNOTATIONS ON ACTS 5:29.[13]

EVERYTHING MUST BE FILTERED THROUGH THE WORD. THE GALLIC CONFESSION: We believe that the Word contained in these books [of the Bible] has proceeded from God, and receives its authority from him alone, and not from human beings. And inasmuch as it is the rule of all truth, containing all that is necessary for the service of God and for our salvation, it is not lawful for human beings, nor even for angels, to add to it, to take away from it, or to change it. Whence it follows that no authority, whether of antiquity, or custom, or numbers, or human wisdom, or judgments, or proclamations, or edicts, or decrees, or councils, or visions, or miracles, should be opposed to these Holy Scriptures, but, on the contrary, all things should be examined, regulated, and reformed according to them. ARTICLE 5.[14]

NO CHRISTIAN SHOULD EVER ACT AGAINST GOD AND FAITH. PETER WALPOT: This God forbids us: that we abandon his law and accept the king's constitution [instead]. In our faith we want to step aside neither to the right nor to the left. Such the ancients did, such Peter did, yes, no Christian would *ever* allow himself to be forced to act against God and faith. For this reason from the very beginning on Christians have been martyred, tortured and killed by so many kings and authorities. Thus, [we must do] whatever is right and

---

[11]Boh 1535, 32.
[12]Downame, ed., *Annotations*, HHHiv*; alluding to Deut 13:1-5.
[13]Jonas, *Annotationes in Acta*, D6r.
[14]*Creeds*, 3:362.

Christian, so long as we also demonstrate obedience in all things. To teach anything further never even came into the apostles' heads. THE GREAT ARTICLE BOOK: ON THE SWORD.[15]

THE SUM OF THE GOSPEL: JESUS IS KING AND SAVIOR.

THE ENGLISH ANNOTATIONS: God with his mighty power has established Jesus to be a Prince and Savior. This is the sum of the apostles' teaching, the ground on which the anchor of the souls of those who shall be saved is moored. The office of Christ is described by two things. First in that he is a Prince to govern his kingdom, to beat down the rebellious and to protect his servants and subjects. Second in that he is also a Savior, as his name Jesus intimates and as the angel interprets it. Here Peter reveals the impiety of those who would strive against their Prince and Savior. They are mad who persecute him whom God exalts by his mighty power. ANNOTATIONS ON ACTS 5:31.[16]

REPENTANCE BEGINS AND CONTINUES BY GOD'S GRACE.

JOHN CALVIN: Repentance is indeed a voluntary conversion, but what is the source of this willingness except that God changes our heart, making a heart of flesh out of a heart of stone, one that is pliable out of one that is hard and stiff, and, finally, one that is upright out of one that is crooked? And this happens when Christ regenerates us by his Spirit. Of course, this is not the gift of a single moment but one that must be increased daily all through life until at last we draw near to God completely; and that will take place only when we have put off our flesh. It is certainly the beginning of repentance when a person who was previously alienated from God renounces himself and the world and begins a new life. But because we have only started out on the way and are far from the goal, we must constantly press on. We obtain both these things by the help of Christ. For as he begins repentance

in us, so he also gives us perseverance. COMMENTARY ON ACTS 5:31.[17]

THE BENEFITS OF CHRIST ARE REPENTANCE AND FORGIVENESS.

RUDOLF GWALTHER: Although a person is converted to God, our salvation is still not perfect and full. When we are sinners, we still have need of forgiveness and satisfaction, since nothing else will satisfy God's justice. But as we have said even now that we could not convert to God unless we were regenerated by Christ, much less can we satisfy for our sins. And Christ teaches us that our sins are such a debt that we are not able to pay. Therefore, just as in the first part, Christ supported our infirmity, so in this also he helps us. By the merit of his death he both purges the debt of our sin and makes us just in the sight of God, while he bestows his righteousness on us who believe in him. Therefore, he became sin for us, that we by his means should be that righteousness which is acceptable before God. Both these things without which no one can be saved come as benefits of Christ alone. . . . This is the reason that [Peter], comprehending the sum of the gospel in few words, teaches that repentance and forgiveness of sins must be preached in his name. HOMILY 37, ACTS 5:27-32.[18]

THE RABID RESPONSE OF THE RULERS.

DESIDERIUS ERASMUS: This truly apostolic speech, which should either have terrified them with the fear of punishment or allured them with the hope of ready salvation, exasperated them even more, so that they were bursting with anger and took counsel together to kill them. The priests had already become accustomed to homicide, and from slaughtering beasts in the temple they had derived this one advantage, that they more easily cut the throats of human beings also. No talk here of divine Scripture, no instruction, no reasoning; only, "So we order, so we wish, either obey or die!" PARAPHRASE OF ACTS 5:29-33.[19]

---

[15]QGT 12:268-69.
[16]Downame, ed., *Annotations*, HHHiv*; alluding to Mt 1:21; Ps 2:4-6; Phil 2:9. In Hebrew "Jesus" is *Yeshua* (late form of Joshua), meaning "Yahweh saves."
[17]CNTC 6:149* (CO 48:111); alluding to Ezek 11:19.
[18]Gwalther, *Homelyes or Sermons upon the Actes*, 260* (*In Acta Apostolorum*, 81r-v).
[19]CWE 50:44 (LB 7:688).

THE RULERS WERE ENRAGED. THE ENGLISH ANNOTATIONS: This word, διαπρίω, literally means "to cut with a saw." Here it indicates a bitter perturbation of anger, taken from those who saw or grind their teeth in anger.... Why are they so angry? The apostles spoke no impolite or provoking words to them. It must be the influence of Satan, who hates all truth. Therefore they—like our modern heretics and schismatics—do not regard the clearest proofs from Scripture but burn with a devilish and vengeful malice against the apostles. ANNOTATIONS ON ACTS 5:33.[20]

GAMALIEL'S EXCELLENT SYLLOGISM. JOHANN AGRICOLA: Gamaliel concludes that we should leave the teaching of the apostles be and wait on the outcome. He constructs such a syllogism, that we should fear God and not be quick to judge what God is doing, because we still do not know whether or not it is from God:

Everything that is from God, humans are incapable of thwarting;
If this preaching of the fishermen is from God,
Then you will be incapable of thwarting it.

Or again:

Everything that is not from God has no foundation;
If this fishermen's teaching is not from God,
Then it too has no foundation.

The major premise holds true. FIVE HUNDRED-COMMON NEW GERMAN PROVERBS.[21]

GAMALIEL'S FALSE CONCLUSION. JOHN CALVIN: Gamaliel draws the wrong conclusion from correct premises, because he wrongly adapts what ought to apply to faith only, to outward function and method of acting. Let this be our logic, on the other hand. What is "of God" is bound to stand, even if the whole world is against him. Therefore, faith, which is sustained by the eternal truth of

God, ought to remain unshaken against any assaults whatever of Satan and people. Even if heaven falls, our salvation is secure, for God is its author and protector. Because God guards the kingdom of Christ, no force will ever be able to overthrow it. Because the teaching of the gospel has its foundation in God, no matter how people may fight against it or shake it, still it will remain secure.

Again, no matter how active the ungodly may be, leaving no stone unturned to bring the church into ruins, no matter how they wage furious war against Christ and his church, still they will not prevail, because it is God's property to blast the purposes of people; and in this way he brings punishment on their temerity. We see that both statements are properly applied to faith. But nevertheless it is not the case that the servants of Christ ought to be less diligent in defending the truth; there is no reason why they should allow the church to fall in ruins because of their sloth; there is no cause why they should sit back and connive at the wickedness of those who try to turn everything upside down. COMMENTARY ON ACTS 5:35.[22]

GAMALIEL IS PERCEPTIVE. RUDOLF GWALTHER: Let us mark Gamaliel's counsel, full of wisdom indeed, even though a person may perceive various things he may not yet fully be instructed in the truth. Yet it pleased the Lord to use his help, and it is to be thought that afterward he grew to more godliness. Homily 38, Acts 5:33-39a.[23]

WHO WAS THEUDAS? JOHANN SPANGENBERG: Theudas, as Josephus writes, was a magician but presented himself as a prophet. With his false teaching he seduced many people. Bringing about four hundred men to the Jordan, he promised them that they would cross through it with dry feet according to the examples of Moses and Joshua. However, the procurator Cuspius Fadus assaulted them with knights and foot soldiers, killing

[20]Downame, ed., *Annotations*, HHHiv*.
[21]Agricola, *Die Sprichwörtersammlungen*, 2:156-57.

[22]CNTC 6:152-53* (CO 48:114).
[23]Gwalther, *Homelyes or Sermons upon the Actes*, 264* (*In Acta Apostolorum*, 82v).

many, capturing some as well, but Theudas he had decapitated, bringing his head to Jerusalem as an eternal memorial. Brief Exegesis of Acts 5:36.[24]

Who Was Judas the Galilean? Johann Spangenberg: This Judas lived during the time of Emperor Augustus and taught that it was unfitting that God's people—the Jews, who dedicate the tithe and offer numerous sacrifices to God—should also give tribute to a temporal king. This man perished, too, along with all his followers. Brief Exegesis of Acts 5:37.[25]

On What Grounds Did They Beat the Innocent Disciples? Johann Spangenberg: It stands written, "If a person deserves to be beaten, then before the judge, forty strokes should be given to him, and no more." This law God gave for the godless, so here the Jews invert it and pummel the true preachers of the divine Word. Everything is upside down with them. This same thing our own high priests and tyrants do, persecuting acutely upright preachers of the gospel. But the false teachers and preachers of dreams who teach pure devil's doctrine, human spittle, lies and errors are exalted on a pedestal, giving them whatever their heart desires, land and people, gold and goods, loans and benefices. But God will speak the same curse over them as over the magician Simon. Brief Exegesis of Acts 5:40.[26]

The Apostles' Joy Was Not Naïve. John Calvin: It must not be thought that the apostles were so stolid as not to feel ashamed, and even to suffer from a sense that they had been wronged, for they had not discarded nature completely. But when they thought over the cause, joy got the upper hand. So the faithful ought to be affected in a twofold way, as often as they suffer persecution for the sake of the gospel; although they are certainly afflicted by the bitterness of their punishment, yet they may rise above this sadness with spiritual joy. . . . Let us therefore learn that we must wrestle with affliction and anxiety, in order that we may gladly continue to encounter the cross and carry it when it is laid on us. Commentary on Acts 5:41.[27]

The Temple Rulers' Judgment Is Like Wind Against Fire. The English Annotations: Constancy accompanies their joy. The disciples are not deterred by their enemies' threats but preach the Word freely, in season and out of season. The opposition of the truth is like the confrontation of wind against fire: it inflames it even more. Such is the admirable work of God's Spirit, who gives confidence in Christ and assurance of victory in him. Annotations on Acts 5:42.[28]

Imitate the Constancy of the Apostles and Our Lord. Rudolf Gwalther: Let every person in his calling follow the constancy of the apostles, but particulary those to whom the Lord has committed the governing and ordering of his church and Word. Let them not distrust his aid who for so long has taken great care of his flock. Whoever can give a just account of their ministry to Christ shall be partakers of his kingdom. To him be blessing, honor, glory and power forever. Amen. Homily 39, Acts 5:39b-42.[29]

---

[24]Spangenberg, *Der Apostel Geschichte*, 48r-v. See Josephus, *Antiquities*, 20. 5.

[25]Spangenberg, *Der Apostel Geschichte*, 48v. See Josephus, *Antiquities*, 18.1-10.

[26]Spangenberg, *Der Apostel Geschichte*, 49v-50r; quoting Deut 25:1-3; alluding to Acts 8:20-21.

[27]CNTC 6:155 (CO 48:116).

[28]Downame, ed., *Annotations*, HHHiv*; alluding to 1 Tim 4:2.

[29]Gwalther, *Homelyes or Sermons upon the Actes*, 272-73* (*In Acta Apostolorum*, 85r).

6:1-6 THE APPOINTMENT OF DEACONS

Now in these days when the disciples were increasing in number, a complaint by the Hellenists[a] arose against the Hebrews because their widows were being neglected in the daily distribution.[2] And the twelve summoned the full number of the disciples and said, "It is not right that we should give up preaching the word of God to serve tables. [3] Therefore, brothers,[b] pick out from among you seven men of good repute, full of the Spirit and of wisdom, whom we will appoint to this duty. [4] But we will devote ourselves to prayer and to the ministry of the word." [5] And what they said pleased the whole gathering, and they chose Stephen, a man full of faith and of the Holy Spirit, and Philip, and Prochorus, and Nicanor, and Timon, and Parmenas, and Nicolaus, a proselyte of Antioch. [6] These they set before the apostles, and they prayed and laid their hands on them.

a That is, Greek-speaking Jews   b Or *brothers and sisters*

OVERVIEW: With the notable growth of the early Christian movement, a reorganization of its leadership shows how the first deacons were elected and what their tasks were. Erasmus asserts that when the deacons completed their tasks early, the remaining time would be spent in preaching the gospel, because deacons were next in rank after the apostles. Yet, some commentators make the distinction between apostles as overseers who provide spiritual sustenance and deacons as brothers who provide bodily sustenance. As a result of his innovative doctrine of the internal word, the enigmatic Kaspar von Schwenckfeld concluded that ordination—along with all other external symbols, rites and ceremonies—was unnecessary. Condemnations of his teaching erupted from across the sixteenth-century confessional landscape. In the group dialog below, rooted in the primitive election of deacons, we hear strong affirmations of the divine mandate for ordination. This affirmation is tempered with the prerequisites of a godly life and a strong knowledge of God's revelation in Scripture. Here we see our commentators cutting a *via media* between the views of the Schwenckfeldians and the serial abuse of ordination in many parts of the late medieval church.

The office of deacon addresses practical matters that had arisen within the community, including managing donations, organizing funds and feeding the poor. Although most of the Reformation commentators give priority to the work of prayer and preaching (which is referred to as the administration of the church), they recognize that deacons share in the work of earthly ministry (also called the service of the church). These deacons are ordained by the apostles to share their ministerial status and their work. Many commentators see this passage as a template for proper ordination of officeholders in the church. The rite of ordination includes three things. First, those who are appointed are considered worthy of the office, known to be persons of integrity and probity. Second, the officeholders have the approval of the people from their community. Third, the apostles offer prayers and lay hands on the appointed people in the same manner that Jesus laid hands on those he blessed.

THE PROGRESS OF THE EARLY CHURCH CONTINUES. RUDOLF GWALTHER: The Evangelist Luke thus far has set forth the beginning, proceeding, increase and order of the primitive church, in which we have seen all things very wisely administered according to the Word of God, even among the horrible persecutions and cruel attempts of their enemies, with most prosperous success. However, because such things are treated somewhat generally, now at length the godly writer descends to matters more special, declaring how certain persons employed their great effort to promote and advance Christ's kingdom. Among whom, there is Stephen, who was the first deacon, of whom no mention has been made before. [Luke] conveniently begins his history with the institution of the deacons, and in this present place teaches when the order of deacons was appointed, and shows after what order and manner those first deacons were elected and ordained by the apostles. HOMILY 40, ACTS 6:1-4.[1]

THE HELLENISTS. THEODORE BEZA: They freely call those men Grecians, just as Cato called salt which was for sale at Rome Roman, and Gellius called a little bench Grecian, not because it was made in Greece but because of its likeness to the Greeks. Therefore, the Hellenists differ from those people whom Paul is accustomed to call "Greeks" in contrast to the Jews, and whom the Hebrews indicate by the name of "Gentiles." For Greeks are selected from one nation of Greeks by a general designation. By this general term, "Greeks," taken from the nation of the Greeks, all the uncircumcised were referred to, including even those who— as long as the law had validity—although they were not circumcised, still abhorred idolatry and were instilled with the knowledge of the true God. Luke is accustomed to call them God-fearers in these books. Such was Cornelius, and another was that centurion whose faith Christ praised so greatly. Finally, Hellenists ought to be mentioned. In this passage, Luke calls certain profane people by this name who had joined the people of the Jews by circumcision and afterwards called proselytes. They are deceived who think that the Jews who were scattered among the nations were called Hellenists. The Jerusalem church, however, would scarcely have been able to stand to turn uncircumcised people into Jewish people with themselves; even after much time, the church was gravely offended that Peter went to Cornelius. Paul, although he was truly from Tarsus, calls himself a Hebrew.

Therefore, just as with respect to religion the Greeks are the opposite of the Jews, so also because of a distinction of race, the Hellenists are opposed to the Hebrews. ANNOTATIONS ON ACTS 6:1.[2]

GENTILES WERE NOT YET PART OF THE CHURCH. RUDOLF GWALTHER: The community of believers was the cause of this newly devised order in the church, by reason of a quarrel and grudge grown among the Greeks against the Hebrews. He calls them Greeks, or proselytes, either because they returned from their Gentility to Judaism or because they were born of parents who were Jews and scattered among diverse nations. For it is evident that at this time the Gentiles were not as yet received into the fellowship of the church. We know this because Peter was rebuked for having preached the gospel to Cornelius and his family, men who were not circumcised. The cause of this grudge was that the Greek widows were neglected in the daily administration, that is to say, in the distribution of the resources shared every day among the believers. For it had been previously declared how many had gathered their money and put it at the disposal of the apostles in order to give as anyone should have need.

In this case, it happened either that the apostles, overburdened with a multitude of business, overlooked some among them, or else [the Gentile believers] deemed they were being despised and bitterly complained about it. This situation was why the accustomed order and manner of administration of the money now had to be altered. HOMILY 40, ACTS 6:1-4.[3]

THE GREEK WOMEN WANTED TO SERVE THE APOSTLES. DESIDERIUS ERASMUS: The cause of the grumbling arose from piety. For since the apostles took with them some women who ministered to them, the Greeks were grieved that their widows did not receive the same honor, namely, that they

---

[1]Gwalther, *Homelyes or Sermons upon the Actes*, 40:273-75.

[2]Beza, *Annotationes Majores*, 1:476-77; alluding to Jn 12:20; 2 Cor 11:22.

[3]Gwalther, *Homelyes or Sermons upon the Actes*, 274* (*In Acta Apostolorum*, 85v).

be permitted to attend to the apostles and disciples in the daily ministry, for they understood this to be a position of respect. PARAPHRASE OF ACTS 6:1.[4]

EXHORTATIONS TO THOSE WHO SERVE THE NEEDY. RUDOLF GWALTHER: [It] is to be observed that this grudge arose when the number of Christians increased, when they ought most to have acknowledged God's grace and to have embraced unity. But this is always seen where there is a multitude; there is also murmuring and confusion, because it is impossible in such diversity and desires of minds to satisfy all people's wishes. . . . Let those rather who have the charge and oversight of the poor beware that they give no just occasion for murmuring and complaint, while either they unwillingly distribute such things as they have need of or else wickedly pocket what is given for the poor. For it is no small or trifling fault that they commit here, because they contaminate themselves with great sacrilege and lie to the Holy Spirit, and cause no small offense to the poor in that they give them cause to be angry, who otherwise had need to be comforted.

Let it weigh with them how the primitive church was troubled with no other encumbrances than such as sprang either of unjust or negligent administration of ecclesiastical goods. . . . And in this place the Greeks take no other occasion of their seditious murmuring than for that they thought their widows were neglected in the public distribution of the church goods. HOMILY 40, ACTS 6:1-4.[5]

WHAT SORT OF GRUMBLING WAS THIS? JOHANN SPANGENBERG: No little grumbling, but rather a poisonous rage, a barbed cursing and berating against the dear apostles. There is no doubt this would not have been, had God punished such grumblers as he punished the children of Israel with fiery and poisonous snakes in the wilderness,

or as he punished the agitators, Dathan and Abiram, whom the earth devoured alive, or as Ananias and Sapphira died a sudden death. But God now prefers to use his lovingkindness rather than his wrath. BRIEF EXEGESIS OF ACTS 6:1.[6]

GOD DEMONSTRATES THE NECESSITY OF DEACONS. JOHN CALVIN: Luke is telling us here about the creation of deacons, dealing first with the occasion, second with the deliberation involved and finally with the rite used. Nevertheless he does say that this was the remedy adopted to silence the grumbling that had arisen among the disciples; as the common proverb says, "Bad customs give rise to good laws." But it could appear an extraordinary thing, since this is such an honorable and necessary office in the church, why it never entered the heads of the apostles from the beginning to appoint deacons on their own responsibility, and why the Spirit had not given them advice along these lines, when they now accept it as if under pressure. But in fact what did happen was a better way at that time and is more beneficial to us today as an example. If the apostles had spoken about the electing of deacons before any necessity demanded it, they would have found the people less disposed to it; they themselves would have given the appearance of avoiding irksome labor; many would not have been so generous in handing gifts over to others. It was therefore necessary for the faithful to be convinced by experience, learning that they could not do without deacons, and this really because of their own fault, so that they would be glad to choose them. COMMENTARY ON ACTS 6:1-6.[7]

THE DEVOLUTION OF THE DIACONATE. OTTO BRUNFELS: There came about an increase of disciples, with the result that the sharing of possessions in the church was not able to be passed on to those who came later. . . . But the responsibility for ministering was something that was still kept intact

---

[4]CWE 50:46 (LB 7:689).
[5]Gwalther, *Homelyes or Sermons upon the Actes*, 273-75* (*In Acta Apostolorum*, 86r).

[6]Spangenberg, *Der Apostel Geschichte*, 51v; alluding to Num 21:5-9; Num 16, esp. Num 16:21-25 (cf. Ps 106:17); Acts 5:1-11.
[7]CNTC 6:157* (CO 48:117).

even during the period of the apostles, as you see here. The ministerial responsibilities consisted of this: that among the widows certain ones were put in charge of giving support. Likewise there were deacons, who were giving support to the community. At a later period Saint Lawrence took his turn at being a deacon, as well as many other good men. But then treacherous servants obtained the office, workers of iniquity, who falsified the accounts and converted into their own profit that which was supposed to be dispensed as aid for the poor. Even among the best people emotions sometimes take over, and honest people come to ruin by thinking too highly of individuals. . . . We should not give any credit to human perfection. ANNOTATIONS ON ACTS 6:1.[8]

OUR PRELATES HAVE REVERSED THE APOSTOLIC COMMAND. JOHANN ECK: Notice . . . how a cleric should act, if he is unable to govern temporal and worldly things [as well as eternal and spiritual things]. He should focus on the ministry of the Word of God and entrust the worldly things to the deacons, [city] servants and local government, as the apostles did in this passage. Now, however, our own prelates turn the matter upside down. Whatever spiritual matters there are is too much for them. In episcopal offices they add the auxiliary bishops, while they have their vicars in spiritual matters. In legal transactions they have the magistrates. If they are supposed to preach, then they shove forward some monk. If they are supposed to absolve a distressed sinner, then there is the confessor. However, whatever concerns gold, money and interest, *that* we must bring to "my most merciful lord." It is true indeed, as Saint Ambrose said, that the spiritual children cannot exist long without the temporal, but to let the spiritual be abandoned and concentrate only on the worldly is neither praiseworthy nor right. SECOND POSTIL FOR THE FEAST OF SAINT STEPHEN.[9]

DECISIONS SHOULD BE MADE BY CONGREGATIONAL VOTE. OTTO BRUNFELS: This is the first council of the apostles, in which the Caiaphases and Pilates are not called, but instead the multitude of disciples. To this group the business is laid out, and then it is decided by a majority vote. Therefore, whatever difficult matter must be taken care of in the church, or if someone is about to take the office of minister, it should be handled by the judgment of the multitude, obviously so that the people might look about within their own number for the very ones they judge worthy of the office. Furthermore, if any disturbance or quarrel arises, it should be referred to the multitude or to the bishops together with the multitude. ANNOTATIONS ON ACTS 6:1-2.[10]

THE PAPACY ABUSES THE INSTITUTION OF THE DIACONATE. MARTIN LUTHER: Now today, as you know, in the papacy we have created epistle-readers and Gospel-readers out of deacons. And if we now ordain a bishop, we ordain him not so that he should preach—for he already has the priestly office, just like any other lowly priest—rather only for this: that we set him on a war horse and say, "most merciful prince!" In the same way we do not elect deacons to the office which they served during the time of the apostles; instead, [we elect them] to stand by the altar and read aloud whatever epistle or Gospel reading—and that is sufficient. In this way everything has fallen into abuse. What used to belong to preaching and praying, now we call Mass. What used to belong to caring for people, now we call epistle-readers and Gospel-readers—although the hospital superintendents, the prioresses and advocates for the poor still retain a sliver or image [of this office].

So, whenever we want to establish a congregational fund, we must know what kind of offices will oversee the congregation. "Bishop" means an official of God, who should distribute divine and spiritual goods, preach the gospel and care for the people with the Word of God. He must have

---

[8]Brunfels, *Annotationes*, 209v. Saint Lawrence was a Roman deacon who was martyred during the Valerian persecution (258). He was highly revered as having a deep concern for the poor.
[9]Eck, *Christenliche Predigen*, 3:35r.

[10]Brunfels, *Annotationes*, 209v.

servants, that is, "deacons," who should care for the congregation in this way: that they maintain a register of the poor, care for their every need from the congregation's fund, visit the sick and diligently oversee these goods everywhere. POSTIL FOR THE FEAST OF STEPHAN THE HOLY MARTYR, ROTH'S FESTPOSTILLE (1527).[11]

BE DISCERNING IN THE CHOICE OF DEACONS. OTTO BRUNFELS: Preaching is greater than all the responsibilities in the church. For this reason also the apostle said, "The Lord did not send me to baptize but to preach." At one time the apostles were overseers of the community, and they were providing for not only spiritual things but also bodily things. . . . Our bishops are money-changers, serving only their bellies. They do not distribute alms to the poor, nor do they carry out their ministry by preaching to the people. And for this reason they have continued on as bishops in name only but not in reality. . . . The words are clear: From their congregation should be chosen those who would be put in charge, from those who are called "brothers," not those whom today the pope pushes on us from among the courtiers and constables. They are neither from among us, nor do they know our language. ANNOTATIONS ON ACTS 6:2.[12]

WHAT TRAITS SHOULD CHARACTERIZE DEACONS? JOHANN SPANGENBERG: They should be devout people who have a good name and reputation among the congregation. They should not be greedy, hostile and envious, but rather humble, gracious and kind. Additionally they should be filled with the Holy Spirit and divine wisdom. They should cherish God's Word and cling to the true worship of God. They should be truthful, tolerating no false teacher and seducer of souls. Thus, they are daily in the hospitals and infirmaries, praying, listening to and acting in accordance with God's Word. In ages past they [held] the [Sacrament of the] altar before the eyes [of the sick] and

constructed beds—whoever did not want to do this was dismissed or separated from the devout, as the shepherd separates the goats from the sheep. BRIEF EXEGESIS OF ACTS 6:3-6.[13]

AFTER THE MINISTRY OF THE WORD, NO WORK IS MORE IMPORTANT THAN DIACONAL MINISTRY. MARTIN LUTHER: Now once the apostles found such people, who are honest, God-fearing and competent for such responsibility, they come before the congregation and are presented before the apostles. The apostles then pray and lay their hands on them. This is certainly a very important part. For we have experienced that human wisdom and ability are incapable of completing this task. It must receive God's blessing, and he must provide the growth; otherwise, it will certainly happen that the most capable will conduct themselves most incapably and cause the greatest trouble.

That the dear apostles apply so much diligence in appointing this office—praying so devotedly and laying hands on the elected—all this is an indication that this management of the common church goods or the alms is no common task. Why else should they take so much care and devotion with selecting such people? Of course, it is true that the preaching office is far higher and more important, for through it God nourishes not merely the body with eating and drinking for this temporal life, but rather he nourishes the soul against sin and eternal death. However, after the preaching office there is no higher office in the church than this responsibility that we manage justly and honestly the church's goods, through which poor Christians who are unable to earn and win their nourishment themselves are sustained, so that they do not suffer poverty. HOUSE POSTIL FOR THE FEAST OF SAINT STEPHEN (1544).[14]

CARING FOR THE POOR IS A HOLY COMMISSION. LEUPOLD SCHARNSCHLAGER: When you are assembled . . . a leader (or, if none is present, an elder

---

[11]WA 17, 2:335-36.
[12]Brunfels, *In Acta Apostolorum*, 209v; quoting 1 Cor 1:17.
[13]Spangenberg, *Der Apostel Geschichte*, 53v-54r.
[14]WA 52:590-91; alluding to 1 Cor 3:5-9.

brother) shall remember the poor members for the sake of the Lord with words that are wise, sincere, gentle, transparent, uncoercive, and yet earnest, emphatic words. Thereby hearts may be moved to a voluntary expression of compassion and grow into the nature and power of love that is genuine and pleasing in the sight of God. Above all, a brother known to all the members of the church should always be present with a purse of money. Then each member may know where to place a freewill offering and his gift of blessing, either in the meeting or after, when the Lord admonishes him to, so that at all times when the need arises the poor may be assisted according to the amount available at the time. Then the brother who cares for the funds shall distribute it with a good conscience and in the fear of God, paying diligent heed, whether they are needy or not, whether greedy or not, not as the world deals with the poor, without testing and inquiring about their manner of life and walk. For this is a holy commission. KUNSTBUCH: ARTICLE 3, CONGREGATIONAL ORDER FOR CHRIST'S MEMBERS.[15]

ONLY CHRIST RULES INWARDLY. PETER WALPOT: They may say: Governors are rulers [in the church] and also in the external government. . . . And they say that this is true of civil magistrates, too. But this is not so. For the Scriptures would have given further testimony that at the time of the apostles there was also such worldly, external administration in their churches. But this is not so; rather, the entire Scriptures contradict this. Christ did not entrust external administration to his church, but internal administration, which should be ruled with the Word of truth. So then, for whatever system of state pertains to the administration of external trade, work and essentials, appoint people—overseers and household managers in the congregation of Christ—who will manage and administer such needs. But there should be no administration with the sword. THE GREAT ARTICLE BOOK: ON THE SWORD.[16]

DEACONS ARE FELLOW WORKERS WITH THE APOSTLES. DESIDERIUS ERASMUS: If anyone asks what need there was of these rites for appointing ministers to be in charge of the table, let him know that handling money is indeed a secular and extremely common service, but one that requires an incorruptible fidelity. Judas is a witness—his mind, corrupted by avarice, drove him to betray his Lord. At that time, moreover, since they were not like those of the common herd, but whenever they took food they did so with great religious devotion. For them, all bread when it was broken represented the body of the Lord, all wine pointed to the Lord's blood. Lastly, both the Lord's body and the blood of the Lord were administered to the multitude by the deacons; and if sometimes they were free in the course of their ministry, these also preached the evangelical Word, since they were second in authority to the apostles. PARAPHRASE OF ACTS 6:6.[17]

DO NOT ORDAIN ANYONE HASTILY. ANDREAS VON KARLSTADT: A Christian congregation or individual persons, be they high or low, must be prudent in the laying on of hands. What is this other than that you must know people above all else and inquire about the inner call and the secret will of God and discern God's grace in the one on whom you would lay your hands? The ability to recognize God's grace in another person is not strange to anyone other than the one who does not know God's Spirit or Scripture, for a pharaoh recognized God's grace in Abraham and another in Joseph, Nebuchadnezzar in Daniel and, to mentioin one of the saints, too, Jacob in Ephraim. . . .

A Christian congregation is not to proceed with too much haste and should not trust in its own will and intention but should first know the persons and discern and understand God's inner call, along with his divine will, before choosing a shepherd or pastor. . . . One must rigorously and seriously enquire about the divine secret calling with great diligence and serious prayer and sincere sighs. Then God will inform his people inwardly and

---

[15]CRR 12:407-8* (QGT 17:443).
[16]QGT 12:286.

[17]CWE 50:47* (LB 7:690).

outwardly to know whom he has given to them and sent into his harvest. Only then are they to lay on their hands to indicate thereby that the one on whom their hands have been placed has divine wisdom and good will in sufficient measure and is prepared and graced by God to lead God's sheep faithfully. REASONS WHY ANDREAS KARLSTADT REMAINED SILENT FOR A TIME.[18]

ORDAINED FOR SERVICE TO PEOPLE. MARTIN LUTHER: In this passage you hear that we bishops—that is, preachers and pastors—are called not to watch over geese or cows but over the congregation God purchased with his own blood. We should feed them with the pure Word of God and be on guard lest wolves and sects burst in among the poor sheep. This is why he calls it a good work. ORDINATION OF MINISTERS OF THE WORD.[19]

BY ABADONING ORDINATION, THE RADICALS INTRODUCE CONFUSION INTO CHRIST'S CHURCH. THE ENGLISH ANNOTATIONS: By this imposition of hands the primitive church signified a consecration of a man to God in some office or mission. This rite the Hebrews used in their solemn sacrifices and in their prayers and private blessings; this same rite the Christian church used in the ordination of ministers . . . to avoid intrusion into that sacred office and to signify the approval of the church, declaring them fit and authorized for ministry, as if by a public seal. . . . Now this is discarded and despised by schismatics, bringing so much confusion and misery over the church: every vain babbler—without any ordination by imposition of the hands of those whom God entrusted with that power—intrudes at his pleasure into the office of the ministry. ANNOTATIONS ON ACTS 6:6.[20]

THE METHOD OF ORDINATION. PETER RIEDEMANN: If the church needs one or more ministers,

the members must not elect to please themselves but must wait on the Lord to see whom he chooses and indicates. The believers should pray earnestly, asking God to care for them, to answer their need and to show them whom he has chosen for his ministry. After members continue earnestly in prayer, those recognized through God's counsel to be suitable are presented to the church. If there are many, we wait to see by the use of the lot whom the Lord has chosen. If, however, there is only one or just as many as are needed, we need no lot, for the Lord has shown him or them to us. Therefore, we accept him or them in the fear of God, as a gift from him. Appointment to the service is later confirmed before the church through the laying on of the elders' hands. However, no one is confirmed in his service unless he has first been tested and revealed to the church. He must have the reputation of leading a good life, so that he cannot become a victim of slanderers. CONFESSION OF FAITH.[21]

THE EFFICACY OF CEREMONIES DEPENDS ON THE HOLY SPIRIT. JOHN CALVIN: The laying on of hands was a solemn symbol of consecration under the law. The apostles now place their hands on the deacons for this purpose, that they may know that they are being dedicated to God. Because the ceremony was empty in itself, however, there is added at the same time a prayer, in which the faithful commend to God the ministers whom they are presenting to him. This is certainly ascribed to the apostles, for the whole of the people did not lay their hands on the deacons, but when the apostles said prayers on behalf of the church the others added theirs. We gather from this that the laying on of hands is a rite consistent with order and dignity, seeing that it was used by the apostles; not of course that it has any efficacy or virtue in itself, but its power and effect depend solely on the Spirit of God. That must be the general opinion about all ceremonies. COMMENTARY ON ACTS 6:6.[22]

---

[18]CRR 8:177-78 (Hertzsch, ed. *Karlstadts Schriften aus den Jahren 1523-25*, 10-11); alluding to 1 Tim 5:22.
[19]LW 53:125* (WA 38:427).
[20]Downame, ed., *Annotations*, HHHiv*; alluding to Acts 13:3; Gen 48:14; Mt 19:13.

[21]CRR 9:112.
[22]CNTC 6:163 (CO 48:122).

6:7-15 STEPHEN BROUGHT
BEFORE THE SANHEDRIN

[7]And the word of God continued to increase, and the number of the disciples multiplied greatly in Jerusalem, and a great many of the priests became obedient to the faith.

[8]And Stephen, full of grace and power, was doing great wonders and signs among the people.[9]Then some of those who belonged to the synagogue of the Freedmen (as it was called), and of the Cyrenians, and of the Alexandrians, and of those from Cilicia and Asia, rose up and disputed with Stephen. [10]But they could not withstand the wisdom and the Spirit with which he was speaking.[11]Then they secretly instigated men who said, "We have heard him speak blasphemous words against Moses and God." [12]And they stirred up the people and the elders and the scribes, and they came upon him and seized him and brought him before the council, [13]and they set up false witnesses who said, "This man never ceases to speak words against this holy place and the law, [14]for we have heard him say that this Jesus of Nazareth will destroy this place and will change the customs that Moses delivered to us." [15]And gazing at him, all who sat in the council saw that his face was like the face of an angel.

OVERVIEW: The growth of the church included both an increase in new disciples and the internal progress believers made on the road of discipleship. As in the Reformation, the advancement of a new understanding of biblical faith led to heated debates with others who claimed the same Scriptures. Here Reformation commentators identify Stephen as a model deacon, pastor and martyr who faced overwhelming opposition with steadfastness. This passage also demonstrates the broader role that deacons took in addition to service, namely preaching and teaching. Our exegetes comment on the need for modern-day Stephens who could boldly face opposition to the faith in their own time.

"THE WORD OF GOD CONTINUED TO IN-CREASE." JOHN CALVIN: Luke again tells about increases to the church, the better to illustrate the grace and power of God in its continual advancement. Certainly the sudden raising up of the church, in a moment as it were, was already a remarkable work of God. But just as much admiration should deservedly be given to this, that he furthers the work begun by him in spite of so many obstacles and that the number is increased by the very people whom the world works so hard to cut down, even to the point of destroying the whole stock. When he says that "the Word of God grew," the meaning is that it was propagated further. The Word of God is said to grow in a twofold way, either when new disciples are added to its obedience or in proportion as each one of us makes progress in it. Luke is dealing here with the former kind of growth, for he explains himself immediately after by speaking of "the number of the disciples." Nevertheless he confines this increase of faith to a single city. For even if it is credible that disciples were scattered in other places also, still the only place where there was a definite body was Jerusalem. COMMENTARY ON ACTS 6:7.[1]

MANY JEWS BELIEVED, NOT JUST PRIESTS. THE ENGLISH ANNOTATIONS: The sense is that now many of the Levitical priests—who before were the most ruthless enemies to Christ and the most active adversaries of the gospel—were converted to the faith and truth of the gospel. It is quite probable that this phrase (πολύς τε ὄχλος, a

---

[1]CNTC 6:164* (CO 48:123).

"great multitude" or "company") refers to the Jews in general, not just the priests in particular. ANNOTATIONS ON ACTS 6:7.[2]

STEPHEN "FULL OF GRACE" IN A WAY DIFFERENT FROM JESUS OR MARY. JOHANN ECK: Luke says, "Stephen, full of grace and strength, performed miracles and great signs among the people." This is to say Christ is full of grace in a different way than Mary and Saint Stephen. For Christ is so filled with grace that it overflows in abundance, as Saint John says: "From his fullness we all have received." Mary is surpassingly full, but Saint Stephen sufficiently full. SECOND POSTIL FOR THE FEAST OF SAINT STEPHEN.[3]

EVERY VILLAGE NEEDS MANY STEPHENS. MARTIN LUTHER: The bothersome devil sees quite well how this will end. Therefore it is of great importance that in large principalities and cities, yes, even in each and every village, there be many Stephens, who assume such service with seriousness and manage justly churches' goods, who rather than concentrating on their own needs and desires minister to those who are truly in need, such as those who, first, serve the church in the ministry of the Word and on account of this ministry are unable to gather their own [physical] necessities; second, those poor Christians who because of sickness or some other situation are unable to gain their own nourishment; and third, excellent, capable young boys who study daily and who otherwise would have no provision. HOUSE POSTIL FOR THE FEAST OF SAINT STEPHEN (1544).[4]

THE MIGHTY WORKS OF STEPHEN. JOHANN SPANGENBERG: When Stephen, as a steward and table waiter, went to the market and encountered the people, he began to preach about Christ. He performed great miracles and signs; condemned the sin, crime and unrighteousness of the Jews, especially their unbelief and unthankfulness that they

did not acknowledge the time of their visitation from God; urged and exhorted them to repentance; and revealed to them the condemnation that was present over Jerusalem and the entire Jewish land. BRIEF EXEGESIS OF ACTS 6:8.[5]

DEACONS IN ANCIENT TIMES ALSO PREACHED. RUDOLF GWALTHER: We may note here that the deacons in the primitive church were not wholly debarred from the ministry of the Word. Although they were chiefly occupied with the distribution of the church goods, yet they bestowed their labor as far as they were able in other services of the church, that by this means, as Paul says, "they might gain a good standing for themselves." HOMILY 42, ACTS 6:8-15.[6]

WHAT WERE THE JEWS DISPUTING WITH STEPHEN? JOHANN SPANGENBERG: The Messiah, circumcision, the law and the temple.... How did Stephen answer? He powerfully demonstrated with the Scriptures that Jesus of Nazareth, the Son of Mary, is the true Messiah and Savior of the world—starting with Adam in paradise after the Fall, to the patriarchs, to the promise to the Jews in the law. Further, he argued that both circumcision and the law were accomplished through Christ. Also, the city and temple will be destroyed. And in sum, he said that every human deed, word, work, being and life apart from faith is pure sin. We are unable to capture God in wood and stone, in gold and silver, nor is it the true worship of God to build wood and stone temples. Instead, the hearts of believers are the true temple and dwelling place of God. He proved this sermon from the prophet Isaiah, where he says, "Thus says the LORD, heaven is my throne and the earth is my stool, what then for a house would you build me or where is the place I should rest? My hand made everything, whatever exists, declares the LORD." BRIEF EXEGESIS OF ACTS 6:8-10.[7]

---

[2]Downame, ed., *Annotations*, HHH1v-HHH2r*.
[3]Eck, *Christenliche Predigen* 3:35v; quoting Jn 1:16.
[4]WA 52:591.

[5]Spangenberg, *Der Apostel Geschichte*, 55r.
[6]Gwalther, *Homelyes or Sermons upon the Actes*, 286* (*In Acta Apostolorum*, 89r); quoting 1 Tim 3:13.
[7]Spangenberg, *Der Apostel Geschichte*, 56r-v; quoting Is 66:1.

THE SYNAGOGE OF THE FREEDMEN. THEODORE BEZA: It is an established fact that those who were freed and were formerly slaves are called freedmen (*libertinos*) in Latin, because their condition seems more vile among free men (*ingenuos*) and those born from free men (*ingenuis*).... Evidently during the reign of Tiberius, a good part of the city some distance across the Tiber was held by the Jews, of whom there were many freedmen (*libertini*), who had been led away as captives (from war) by their masters. They had been given their freedom, and nothing compelled them to abandon the customs of their fathers. Although he knew them to have their own places of prayer, in which they principally came together on the Sabbath, their places of prayer were truly also called synagogues, among which also that synagogue at Rome was synonymous with the freedmen (*libertinis*), whence it is probable that this place of prayer had also originally come from Jerusalem. ANNOTATIONS ON ACTS 6:9.[8]

THE FREEDMEN WERE PROSELYTES. PHILIPP MELANCHTHON: There were at Jerusalem many colleges, and more schools, in which young men were being educated out of other nations and out of other provinces sent there to learn, just as in many academies there are colleges of particular nations, such as the Germanic nation has its own college at Prague; the Spanish their own, the Polish and Bohemians likewise their own. Thus Jerusalem was adorned with many colleges and schools, which were called synagogues. In one place, the young men of Cyrene were being instructed; in another place, the sons of their own Jews, who were at Alexandria; and in another place, freedmen.

I think that the freedmen (*libertini*) were proselytes, whose parents came into slavery, who were afterwards manumitted or redeemed by a price and had been given their liberty. Those freedmen (*libertini*) were segregated from others, because other free men (*ingenui*) wished to be more noble. Perhaps it had been founded by special almsgiving,

set aside for captives and slaves, and set up the sons of these men in school. How do a free man (*liber*) and a freedman (*libertus*) differ? He who is not and who has not been a slave is a free man (*liber*). He is a freedman (*libertus*) who has been manumitted and freed from slavery. So also the free men (*ingenui*) and the freedmen (*libertini*) differ. The free men (*ingenui*) have been born of free (*liber*) parents. Freedmen (*libertini*) are born of freed (*libertus*) parents. A slave is called so from being protected. Because he was protected in war and came later into someone's power, by him he is enslaved. POSTIL FOR THE FEAST OF STEPHEN.[9]

WE LEARN THREE THINGS FROM STEPHEN'S EXCHANGE WITH THE TEMPLE RULERS. JOHANN ECK: Notice, first of all, a pious Christian should not let himself be moved; even if he hears that the New Christians[10] somehow, be it with booklets or sermons, oppose his own Christian preacher, he should not turn aside. The wicked stood against Saint Peter, Saint Paul, Saint Stephen, yes, even against Christ's own preaching! ...

Second, notice that Saint Stephen debated with them. This is against some who believe we should absolutely not debate with the New Christians and with the heretics, as it is forbidden in imperial law,[11] and as Saint Paul says to Timothy, "You should not battle with words, for it is of no use" other than to convert those listening. That we, however, for the solace of the good-hearted and pious Christians, should not freely debate with the heretics, who otherwise would howl out from behind the oven, cannot be wrong, since Saint Stephen did it here! ...

---

[9]MO 24:90.

[10]This is Eck's preferred phrase for the self-described "evangelical" parties of the Reformation.

[11]It seems that Eck is alluding to the Edict of Worms (May 25, 1521), which condemned Luther and stated flatly that such an "open heretic" should not be given a hearing or further questioned, since they are stuck in their wicked obstinancy. See *Der Römischen Kaiserlichen Maiestate Edict wider Martin Luther Bücher un d lere seyne anhenger, Enthalter, und nachvolger unnd Etlich annder schmeliche schrifften* (Worms, 1521); accessible via www.gateway-bayern.de.

---

[8]Beza, *Annotationes Majores*, 1:478.

Notice also the divine assistance, because the Jews did not want to stand against the Wisdom and the Spirit who spoke in Saint Stephen. So then, learn that everyone who debates victoriously against the New Christians should not grant honor to himself but rather should give God the honor, as well as the Spirit who speaks through him. Whoever in good hope, divine truth and aid sets himself against the soul-murdering teachers, to him God will grant mercy as he promised his disciples. "So, you will stand before kings and governors; you should not worry what you will say, for it will be given to you in the precise hour what you should say. For you are not the ones speaking, but rather the Spirit of your Father speaks in you." SECOND POSTIL FOR THE FEAST OF SAINT STEPHEN.[12]

THE WICKED TREAT THE DISCIPLE NO DIFFERENTLY THAN THE MASTER. DESIDERIUS ERASMUS: Recognize at this point the way of the wicked. When they come away from a disputation, inferior in the truth on their side, they take refuge in lies, and overcome by the wisdom of the Spirit, they turn to diabolical deception. For they secretly induced certain men to say that they had heard Stephen uttering blasphemous words against Moses and God. Now among the Jews there is no [greater] capital charge than blasphemy, and none more terrible in the eyes of the people. Recognize here, reader, the same machinations against the servant as there were against the Lord: talebearers are suborned so that those offended should not appear to wish to avenge their own vexation because they had left the disputation defeated. A terrible charge is sought, and religious zeal is a cloak for malice. PARAPHRASE OF ACTS 6:11.[13]

TRUE WORSHIP OF GOD CENTERS ON JESUS CHRIST. JOHANN AGRICOLA: Here we must stand still and contemplate what is the true worship of God and how the "schoolteachers" have desecrated this same true worship of God, making pure idolatry out of it. [We must consider] as well what moved them to flee from Christ and God's truth, following lies and their own ideas instead. The true worship of God, and the piety through which people are made righteous before God, is founded in trust in God's goodness and lovingkindness and in despair in ourselves (we are all children of wrath, because we are born from Adam). Our efforts stifle the life-giving concepts of God's law and Word, . . . and no work or any creature on earth can help us, unless we are conquered by God. Our soul is a spirit and lasts forever; work and every creature are temporary. Therefore, our soul is unable to find rest in any creature on earth, and precisely for that reason God promised Adam that the seed of a woman would crush the head of the snake which had orchestrated the wicked Fall.

We became slaves of sin and would have perished, because God should eternally condemn and kill us. And we must die eternally if we do not believe and confess that God has bestowed everything on us out of his grace and wants to grant and pardon us, the same sinners, on account of the blessed seed. If we believe in him alone and despair of ourselves, so that we confess that we are capable of nothing on our own, but through him we are able to do all things. Thus, salvation is not founded in our reason or our holy works and virtuous life. . . . All the patriarchs and righteous ones from Adam on, until the end of the world, have been saved and will be saved because they believed and hoped in this same seed, that he would come. SEVEN HUNDRED FIFTY GERMAN PROVERBS.[14]

THE SUBSTANCE OF THE LAW BELONGS TO CHRIST. JOHN CALVIN: They speak of Christ with contempt in this way, as if the memory of him was detestable. At the same time it can be inferred from their calumnies that in abrogating the law Stephen set the body[15] (*corpus*) over

---

[12]Eck, *Christenliche Predigen* 3:35v; quoting 2 Tim 2:14; Mt 10:18-20.
[13]CWE 50:48* (LB 7:691).

[14]Agricola, *Die Sprichwörtersammlungen*, 1:251-52; alluding to Eph 2:3; Gen 3:14-15.
[15]Cf. Col 2:17. The ESV and most modern English translations render this verse more idiomatically than Calvin and his contempo-

against the shadows, and the substance over against the forms. For if ceremonies are abolished by Christ, their true nature is spiritual. The Jews were wishing them to last forever and thought that they consisted of nothing but what was solid, carnal, earthly and plain to see. In a word, if the ceremonies had been continually in use, they would be fleeting and vanishing, because they would have nothing except an outward appearance, so nothing substantial would underlie them. Therefore their true perpetuity consists in their being abrogated by the coming of Christ, because from then on it follows that their virtue and purpose are established in Christ. COMMENTARY ON ACTS 6:14.[16]

STEPHEN'S SPEECH AND FACE WERE BRILLIANTLY CLEAR. JOHANN ECK: Notice the clarity of Saint Stephen's face that God the Lord gave him, not just wisdom to speak, as he promised in Luke: "I will give you a mouth and wisdom which none of your adversaries will be able to stand against and contradict," but he also gave him a shining face, like an angel of God. This gift he had as a testimony from God concerning his sanctity and innocence; that should have immediately turned the raving Jews away from their evil conduct. But as the wise man says, "Their wickedness has blinded them, they have not hoped for the reward of righteousness, they have not shown the

honor of the saints." SECOND POSTIL FOR THE FEAST OF SAINT STEPHEN.[17]

CONFIDENCE IN GOD'S JUDGMENT. JUSTUS JONAS: Look, here again we are warned so that in tribulation we would learn to trust and believe that at that very moment the Lord is indeed present by our side. For here they see heavenly glory in the face of Stephen. His face is like the face of an angel, even as they drag him off to the council and condemn him as a blasphemer and a heretic. Truly the judgment of the world does not agree with the judgment of God. ANNOTATIONS ON ACTS 6:15.[18]

GOD GRANTS COMFORT IN TRIALS. RUDOLF GWALTHER: And without all doubt, Stephen in the meanwhile had some incredible comfort of God's Spirit, risen in his mind. Furthermore, God gave him here a token or taste of the glory to come, through the hope that those who shall happen to be in danger for the testimony of his name may overcome all adversity. We have many examples in the histories of the martyrs.... This is a great glory of our faith, that even then it most comforts and cheers our hearts when all things seem most horrible and fearful. Let us therefore labor to keep this faith with all diligence, that having passed the race of this life and gulf of persecutions with merry minds and cheerful conscience, we may attain to the joy of the glory in heaven, promised us in Christ Jesus. HOMILY 42, ACTS 6:8-15.[19]

raries. Calvin has preserved the Greek reference to "body" (*sōma*), while the ESV has rendered the same word as "substance." For further clarification see Calvin's comment on this passage, RCS NT 11:200-201; CTS 192-93 (CO 52:110-11).
[16]CNTC 6:169-70* (CO 48:127).

[17]Eck, *Christenliche Predigen*, 3:36r; quoting Lk 21:15; Wis 2:21-22.
[18]Jonas, *Annotationes in Acta*, E1r.
[19]Gwalther, *Homelyes or Sermons upon the Actes*, 290* (*In Acta Apostolorum*, 90v).

7:1-53 STEPHEN'S DEFENSE

And the high priest said, "Are these things so?" ²And Stephen said:

"Brothers and fathers, hear me. The God of glory appeared to our father Abraham when he was in Mesopotamia, before he lived in Haran, ³and said to him, 'Go out from your land and from your kindred and go into the land that I will show you.' ⁴Then he went out from the land of the Chaldeans and lived in Haran. And after his father died, God removed him from there into this land in which you are now living. ⁵Yet he gave him no inheritance in it, not even a foot's length, but promised to give it to him as a possession and to his offspring after him, though he had no child. ⁶And God spoke to this effect—that his offspring would be sojourners in a land belonging to others, who would enslave them and afflict them four hundred years. ⁷'But I will judge the nation that they serve,' said God, 'and after that they shall come out and worship me in this place.' ⁸And he gave him the covenant of circumcision. And so Abraham became the father of Isaac, and circumcised him on the eighth day, and Isaac became the father of Jacob, and Jacob of the twelve patriarchs.

⁹"And the patriarchs, jealous of Joseph, sold him into Egypt; but God was with him ¹⁰and rescued him out of all his afflictions and gave him favor and wisdom before Pharaoh, king of Egypt, who made him ruler over Egypt and over all his household. ¹¹Now there came a famine throughout all Egypt and Canaan, and great affliction, and our fathers could find no food. ¹²But when Jacob heard that there was grain in Egypt, he sent out our fathers on their first visit. ¹³And on the second visit Joseph made himself known to his brothers, and Joseph's family became known to Pharaoh. ¹⁴And Joseph sent and summoned Jacob his father and all his kindred, seventy-five persons in all. ¹⁵And Jacob went down into Egypt, and he died, he and our fathers, ¹⁶and they were carried back to Shechem and laid in the tomb that Abraham had bought for a sum of silver from the sons of Hamor in Shechem.

¹⁷"But as the time of the promise drew near, which God had granted to Abraham, the people increased and multiplied in Egypt ¹⁸until there arose over Egypt another king who did not know Joseph. ¹⁹He dealt shrewdly with our race and forced our fathers to expose their infants, so that they would not be kept alive. ²⁰At this time Moses was born; and he was beautiful in God's sight. And he was brought up for three months in his father's house, ²¹and when he was exposed, Pharaoh's daughter adopted him and brought him up as her own son. ²²And Moses was instructed in all the wisdom of the Egyptians, and he was mighty in his words and deeds.

²³"When he was forty years old, it came into his heart to visit his brothers, the children of Israel. ²⁴And seeing one of them being wronged, he defended the oppressed man and avenged him by striking down the Egyptian. ²⁵He supposed that his brothers would understand that God was giving them salvation by his hand, but they did not understand. ²⁶And on the following day he appeared to them as they were quarreling and tried to reconcile them, saying, 'Men, you are brothers. Why do you wrong each other?' ²⁷But the man who was wronging his neighbor thrust him aside, saying, 'Who made you a ruler and a judge over us? ²⁸Do you want to kill me as you killed the Egyptian yesterday?' ²⁹At this retort Moses fled and became an exile in the land of Midian, where he became the father of two sons.

³⁰"Now when forty years had passed, an angel appeared to him in the wilderness of Mount Sinai, in a flame of fire in a bush. ³¹When Moses saw it, he was amazed at the sight, and as he drew near to look, there came the voice of the Lord: ³²'I am the God of your fathers, the God of Abraham and of Isaac and of Jacob.' And Moses trembled and did not dare to look. ³³Then the Lord said to him, 'Take off the sandals from your feet, for the place where you are standing is holy ground. ³⁴I have surely seen the affliction of my people who are in Egypt, and have heard their groaning, and I have come down to deliver them. And now come, I will send you to Egypt.'

[35]"This Moses, whom they rejected, saying, 'Who made you a ruler and a judge?'—this man God sent as both ruler and redeemer by the hand of the angel who appeared to him in the bush. [36]This man led them out, performing wonders and signs in Egypt and at the Red Sea and in the wilderness for forty years. [37]This is the Moses who said to the Israelites, 'God will raise up for you a prophet like me from your brothers.' [38]This is the one who was in the congregation in the wilderness with the angel who spoke to him at Mount Sinai, and with our fathers. He received living oracles to give to us. [39]Our fathers refused to obey him, but thrust him aside, and in their hearts they turned to Egypt, [40]saying to Aaron, 'Make for us gods who will go before us. As for this Moses who led us out from the land of Egypt, we do not know what has become of him.' [41]And they made a calf in those days, and offered a sacrifice to the idol and were rejoicing in the works of their hands. [42]But God turned away and gave them over to worship the host of heaven, as it is written in the book of the prophets:

"'Did you bring to me slain beasts and sacrifices,
    during the forty years in the wilderness, O
        house of Israel?
[43]You took up the tent of Moloch
    and the star of your god Rephan,

a Some manuscripts *for the house of Jacob*

the images that you made to worship;
    and I will send you into exile beyond Babylon.'

[44]"Our fathers had the tent of witness in the wilderness, just as he who spoke to Moses directed him to make it, according to the pattern that he had seen. [45]Our fathers in turn brought it in with Joshua when they dispossessed the nations that God drove out before our fathers. So it was until the days of David, [46]who found favor in the sight of God and asked to find a dwelling place for the God of Jacob.[a] [47]But it was Solomon who built a house for him. [48]Yet the Most High does not dwell in houses made by hands, as the prophet says,

[49]"'Heaven is my throne,
    and the earth is my footstool.
What kind of house will you build for me, says
        the Lord,
    or what is the place of my rest?
[50]Did not my hand make all these things?'

[51]"You stiff-necked people, uncircumcised in heart and ears, you always resist the Holy Spirit. As your fathers did, so do you. [52]Which of the prophets did your fathers not persecute? And they killed those who announced beforehand the coming of the Righteous One, whom you have now betrayed and murdered, [53]you who received the law as delivered by angels and did not keep it."

OVERVIEW: The focal point of Stephen's sermon or speech, according to Reformation commentators, is that on account of human weakness and sin God has accommodated himself to us through signs (e.g., circumcision and the temple) and other sinful people (e.g., Abraham, Joseph, Moses), but that his gracious condescension is to our condemnation if we miss God's clearest and most obvious accommodation: entering human flesh to redeem us in and through it. Some of our commentators find Stephen's words so self-evident and manifest that they need not comment on the text. Others worry that readers will become uninterested or confused during this lengthy narrative, and thus try to con-

dense the main point into the briefest and simplest words possible.

All our exegetes emphasize that God is faithful to his promises, no matter how things may appear. Consider Abraham, who lost home, friends and wife; or Joseph, who was rejected by his family; or Moses, a lifelong exile. None of them saw the fulfillment of the promise given to them, and still they believed.

Despite agreement about God's loving-kindness, commentators disagree about the nature and significance of the signs he has given to his church as expressions of that love. The Radicals accuse the magisterial reformers and Catholics of, in effect, clinging to creation instead of looking to the Creator; by baptizing infants and asserting Jesus' real presence in the Eucharist, they are in danger of worshiping idols made with human hands. The magisterial reformers and Catholics counter that these external signs point to and seal internal realities through God's agency. Believers must cling to the signs *God* has given, neither rejecting them nor inventing new ones—*that* would be idolatry. All the same, everyone agrees that this sermon demonstrates the true key to unlocking the Old Testament and the various ceremonies of both ancient Jews and contemporary Christians: Jesus Christ.

This Pericope Is So Clear There Is No Need to Explain It. Martin Luther: Now this epistle reading is simple. It gives us in St. Stephen an example of faith in Christ. So, this passage needs very little exegesis, and we can run through it quickly. Postil for the Epistle on the Feast of Saint Stephen, Weihnachtenpostil (1522).[1]

The Trial Is Rigged from the Start. John Calvin: Up to now some semblance of fairness is apparent in the high priest and the council, and yet there is the most unfair prejudice in his words. For he does not ask what grounds Stephen had for teaching in this way and does not admit him to the defense that the law provides, although the defense was the chief thing, but he briefly inquires whether Stephen used those words, whatever they may mean. Commentary on Acts 7:1.[2]

Stephen's Defense Consists of Two Arguments. Philipp Melanchthon: Then Stephen answers quite seriously and learnedly, retracing their history from the time of Abraham until the recent times of this nation. Out of this long narrative, the main concern or the scope is that it is neither blasphemy nor sedition to teach against ceremonial forms of worship and to preach the [ultimate] purpose of this system: the Messiah. These are the two main arguments of the entire passage.

The First Argument:
This worship, which was not among the fathers, is not the original form of worship.
Such worship in external ceremonies was not among the fathers.
Therefore it is not the original form of worship.

The Second Argument:
A promise was made to the fathers.
The fathers did not accept this system.
Therefore this system is not principally what was promised, but there is something else greater.

The major premise in each argument is itself obvious. For it is necessary for there to be one and the same worship of God in all times. When God spoke with the fathers themselves, he gave them a promise which first and foremost grants blessing—also to them. Stephen proves the minor premise through this historical narrative. Because it is so long, many readers do not consider what it pertains to or what [ultimate] purpose it refers to. They think it is improper and unsuitable for court, against custom itself. Therefore the scope of this narrative needs to be impressed into their minds. Stephen retold the highlights of the Old Testament from the call of Abraham to the arrival of the Messiah. Postil for the Feast of Stephen.[3]

7:1-8 God's Promise to Abraham

The Temple Rulers Were Still Leaders of God's People. The English Annotations: Stephen quiets them in this way, because, although they were professed enemies of the gospel, still they were governors of the church of Israel, which God had not yet rejected, and thus he sought to gain their attention for his sermon, hoping that some of them would be convinced. He prayed for this, and indeed it happened. Annotations on Acts 7:2.[4]

---

[1] WA 10, 1.1:251.
[2] CNTC 6:171* (CO 48:128).
[3] MO 24:91-92.
[4] Downame, ed., *Annotations*, HHH2r*. In saying "it happened," Downame is likely referring to Saul's conversion (Acts 9).

THE FULFILLMENT OF THE PROMISES HAS BEEN GIVEN TO THE FAITHFUL. DESIDERIUS ERASMUS: It is not blasphemy to set forth to the best of our ability what Moses sketched out in figures; what the prophets, inspired by the Spirit of God, predicted; what the Son of God, sent to earth on this account, both began and entrusted to his followers to complete; what the Holy Spirit now continues for the salvation of all races through those who believe the gospel. But it is impiety, it is blasphemy, to struggle so obstinately against the will of God, a will so manifest, so benign. This, indeed, is what this race began not in recent times to do, but what it already long ago set out to do and has never ceased doing. Thus it should seem neither strange nor unjust, if it turns out as Jesus predicted it would, namely, that this temple in which you glory, this state in which you rule, the priesthood, the Law, which you misuse for your gain and glory, should be taken away from you; and that this glory should be transferred to those who through evangelical faith worship God in a pure way, and keep the spiritual law, and offer themselves a living and holy temple for the Holy Spirit. It was to this that God in so many ways summoned our ancestors; yet he has always been spurned by this rebellious and obstinate people. PARAPHRASE OF ACTS 7:2.[5]

WE TOO MUST FOLLOW ABRAHAM'S EXAMPLE. JOHN CALVIN: But even if it was Abraham's particular situation to be ordered to depart from his native land and travel to a distant country, and to be led around in all directions by God, there is yet a figurative description of the calling of all of us in these same words. We are not all plainly ordered to leave our native land, but we are ordered to deny ourselves; we are not ordered to go forth from our father's house, but we are ordered to bid farewell to our own will and to the desires of our flesh. Finally, if father and mother, wife and children, keep us back from following God, they must all be given up. Abraham is given the simple commandment to

move, but we are enjoined to do the same thing in certain conditions. For if we may not be allowed to serve God in any particular place, then we must choose exile rather than remain dispirited and inactive in a nest. Therefore let the example of Abraham always be before our eyes. He is the father of the faithful and was tried in every way. . . . And the chief exercise of faith is certainly trusting in God, even when we see nothing. Indeed, God will often show us a land in which he grants us our abode, but yet, because we are strangers in the world, we have no fixed and permanent settlement anywhere. COMMENTARY ON ACTS 7:2-3.[6]

ABRAHAM'S RIGHTEOUSNESS. LUCAS LOSSIUS: This is an example of justification by faith. That is, God considers people just, he forgives (*remittit*) them their sins, he adopts them as sons, he makes them heirs of eternal life, by grace (*gratis*) through faith because of the Mediator, his Son, who was promised to Abraham and who has now been revealed, crucified for us, and raised again, apart from the works of the law—as Saint Paul demonstrates (from Genesis 15 as quoted in Romans 4) by the example of Abraham who was justified by grace (*gratis*) through faith, saying, "Abraham believed in God, and it was imputed to him as righteousness." But to those who strive to do works, the reward is not imputed according to grace but according to debt. Again, to those who do not strive to do works but believe in him who justifies the impious, their faith is imputed to them as righteousness. There is, therefore, the following consequence: Abraham was justified by grace (*gratis*) through faith, or through the reliance in the promise of mercy. Therefore, everyone else is considered just by grace (*gratis*) through faith. ANNOTATIONS ON ACTS 7:3.[7]

THE PERSEVERING FAITH OF ABRAHAM. RUDOLF GWALTHER: These words contain three things that are important for understanding the

---

[5]CWE 50:49.

[6]CNTC 6:174* (CO 48:131); alluding to Mt 16:24-25; 10:37; Rom 4:16-17.
[7]Lossius, *Annotationum in Novum Testamentum*, 3:282; quoting Rom 4:3; Gen 15:6.

setting forth of Abraham's faith. First, when he came into the Promised Land, and [God] guided him through many labors and perils, he found it was not empty but inhabited and possessed by the Canaanites, a very fierce people. And he was so far from possessing it, that he could not say there was one foot of ground there that was his. Every day he felt more misfortunes than the last, for he had barely set up his tents when he was constrained through famine to fly into Egypt. [Second], returning again from there, he broke company with his nephew Lot, who was his only comfort among such hostile people, by reason of their herdsmen and shepherds' contention and falling out. And not long after he was wrapped in perilous wars against the kings of the East. And many other things had happened so that when Sarah his wife died he was expected to buy from Ephron the Hittite a place to bury her. Might he not therefore think he was deceived of his hope? This done, he explains what stayed and comforted Abraham in all these adversities and troubles, namely, the promise of the land that God had made him. But how uncomfortable a thing it is to trust a bare promise, without any further assurance or confirmation, daily experience teaches, especially if things are not successful when compared with the promise as we said a while before this matter came to pass.

But a third thing is yet more grievous than all the rest, which is that God's promise, to human wisdom, might seem ridiculous. For God promised this land to Abraham's seed or posterity, whereas he had no child, and by reason of his age was unlikely to have any, being a hundred years old, and Sarah his wife being barren and past the age for bearing children. Who couldn't see how many ways and how strongly Abraham's faith was shaken and assaulted, and how many occasions he had to distrust God's promises? But none of all these things could vanquish or scare that godly heart. For "he believed in hope beyond all hope and did not regard his own body which was now dead, nor how his wife Sarah was past child bearing: he did not stagger at the promise of God through unbelief but became strong in faith and gave God the praise,

being fully certified that he who had promised the same, was able also to make it good." And this is that faith which Moses says was imputed to him for righteousness. HOMILY 44, ACTS 7:5-8.[8]

GOD ONLY APPEARS TO CONTRADICT HIMSELF. JOHN CALVIN: Immediately after, we read that that seed will be taken away to another place to serve foreigners. And for how long? For four hundred years. Does he not seem in this way to be withdrawing his hand, so that he may not carry out what he has promised? Let us realize that this has not been done on one occasion only, for God often deals with us like that, so that he may appear to be contradicting himself. He even speaks in such a way that he may appear to be retracting what he had promised. It is therefore not unlikely that the flesh will conclude that he is self-contradictory, but faith knows that the words of God agree very well with each other and with his works. And it is God's purpose to show his promises from far off, as if a great space intervened, in order to extend farther the view of our faith. Therefore it is our duty to press on and strive toward the salvation held out to us, through innumerable digressions, through various obstacles, through a great distance, through the midst of abysses and finally through death itself. Moreover, when we observe that the people chosen by God were slaves to the Egyptians and were inhumanly ill-treated, we ought not to be discouraged if the same condition befalls us today. COMMENTARY ON ACTS 7:6.[9]

INFANT BAPTISM IS NOT ANALOGOUS TO CIRCUMCISION. PETER WALPOT: Circumcision is in no way a foreshadowing of infant baptism, but of the circumcision of the heart, which happens in the Spirit, so that we are never uncircumcised in heart and ears. . . . If circumcision were a figure for infant baptism, then we must only baptize little boys and not little girls. This would satisfy the

---

[8]Gwalther, *Homelyes or Sermons upon the Actes*, 44:297* (*In Acta Apostolorum*, 92v); quoting from Rom 4:19-21, and alluding to Gen 15:6.
[9]CNTC 6:177* (CO 48:134).

figure, since little girls were never circumcised. . . . Circumcision must take place on the eighth day, but baptism is not bound to a certain time or day. And if circumcision were a type for baptism, then we must baptize all eight-day olds. . . . Circumcision is a covenant of servitude, to which people were forced and ordered, even if they did not want it or had any desire for it. But the baptism of Christ is a covenant of love and free will, to which no one is forced, nor are they in some other way dragged to it, nor should they be ordered to it. . . .

Therefore, it is not analogous, and they abuse the figure as they want. Rather, just as impossible as it is for a little boy to want to be circumcised before birth, so also is it impossible for a person to be baptized in the correct manner and mode without first hearing a sermon and confessing their faith. Whoever wants to "improve" and conform Christ to Moses and not Moses to Christ displays that he is more a Jew than a Christian. He wants to drop Christ with the cross, so that he can be with Moses without the cross. THE GREAT ARTICLE BOOK: ON BAPTISM.[10]

INFANT BAPTISM IS THE TRUE FULFILLMENT OF THE HOLY SPIRIT'S COMMAND TO CIRCUMCISE. BELGIC CONFESSION: We believe and confess that Jesus Christ, who is the end of the law, has made an end, by the shedding of his blood, of all other sheddings of blood which humans could or would make as a propitiation or satisfaction for sin; and that he, having abolished circumcision, which was done with blood, has instituted in its place the sacrament of baptism, by which we are received into the church of God, and separated from all other people and strange religions, so that we may wholly belong to him whose insignia and banner we bear, and which serves as a testimony to us that he will forever be our gracious God and Father.

. . . We believe that everyone who is earnestly studious of obtaining eternal life ought to be but once baptized with this only baptism, without ever repeating the same, since we can not be born twice.

Neither does this baptism only avail us at the time when the water is poured over us and received by us, but also through the whole course of our life. Therefore we detest the error of the Anabaptists, who are not content with the one and only baptism they have once received, and moreover condemn the baptism of the infants of believers, who, we believe, ought to be baptized and sealed with the sign of the covenant, as the children in Israel formerly were circumcised upon the same promises which are made to our children. And, indeed, Christ shed his blood no less for the washing of the children of the faithful than for adults; and, therefore, they ought to receive the sign and sacrament of what Christ has done for them; as the Lord commanded in the law, that they should be made partakers of the sacrament of Christ's suffering and death shortly after they were born, by offering for them a lamb, which was a sacrament of Jesus Christ. Moreover, what circumcision was to the Jews, baptism is to our children. And for this reason Paul calls baptism "the Circumcision of Christ" (Col 2:11). ARTICLE 34, OF HOLY BAPTISM.[11]

7:9-16 *The Israelites in Egypt*

JOSEPH IS A TYPE FOR JESUS. DESIDERIUS ERASMUS: Among the patriarchs were some who were unmindful of the divine covenant and, moved by envy, they devised against their brother Joseph what their descendants devised against Jesus of Nazareth: they cast him into a cistern, then sold him to merchants who took him to Egypt. But just as God raised Jesus when he had been slain and lifted him up when he had been cast down, so at that time he delivered Joseph from all his sufferings, and he caused him, through his character and his skill in divining, to find favor with Pharaoh the king of Egypt, so that he set him over all of Egypt and over his own house. PARAPHRASE OF ACTS 7:9-10.[12]

---

[10]QGT 12:82-83.

[11]*Creeds*, 3:425-28*.
[12]CWE 50:50 (LB 7:692-93).

GOD'S PRESENCE IS ALWAYS EFFECTIVE FOR GOOD.

THE ENGLISH ANNOTATIONS: This was the effect of God's presence, never ineffective for the good of his servants. He did eventually deliver Joseph from the slavery and calamity into which his brothers sold him; from the malice and calumny of his lewd mistress [Potiphar's wife]; and from prison. If God is with you, do not fear! The soul cannot be in the body without some evidence and effects of life, much less can the Spirit of God be with the elect in vain. ANNOTATIONS ON ACTS 7:10.[13]

THREE QUESTIONS RAISED BY THIS TEXT.

CARDINAL CAJETAN: Many questions come up here, which Jerome's "Letter to Pammachius" leaves unsolved.[14] The first is concerning the tomb purchased by Abraham. It is known that that tomb was in Hebron, and not in Shechem. This question, however, is easy to solve by saying that these refer to different places. Thus, the clause "They were brought across into Shechem" refers to Joseph and his brothers, as Jerome says. The clause "And they were placed in the tomb which Abraham bought" then refers to Jacob and, as Josephus says, to the patriarch's sons.

Another unsolved question among worthy [interpreters] arises concerning those who sold the tomb, since here it is said, "from the sons of Emor," but it was said in Genesis that Abraham bought it from Ephron the son of Zohar. Nor do I see a neat solution unless that Ephron or his father Zohar would have also been named Emor. . . .

The third question is forced and strongly departs from the text. It interprets that passage, "They were brought across into Shechem by the sons of Emor," but this seems so deformed that I would not think of pursuing it. Then, this universal literal meaning would be able to be otherwise construed in such an order: "And they were brought across into Shechem," that is, our

sons of Jacob, "and they were placed by the sons of Shechem, the sons of Emor, in the tomb which Abraham bought with the price of silver"—so that we may understand that the Shechemites, mindful of the destruction which the sons of Jacob carried on against them, did not allow their bodies to remain honorably in Shechem, and afterwards placed them in Hebron. Even if this interpretation should agree with the deed that was done, the literal meaning of the text would not support such narrow interpretations. This passage, at any rate, alludes to what Josephus said, that the sons of the patriarch Jacob were buried in Hebron. COMMENTARY ON ACTS 7:13-16.[15]

LUKE DOES NOT REPORT THE CORRECT BURIAL LOCATION.

JOHN CALVIN: It is observed that the bones of Joseph were buried, but no mention is made of the others. A few make the reply that Moses names only Joseph for the sake of honor, seeing that he had given express instructions about his bones; and we do not read of that being done by the others. And in writing about the travels of Paula, Jerome certainly says that when she journeyed through Shechem she saw there the sepulchers of the twelve patriarchs, but in another place he mentions only Joseph's grave.[16] And it is possible that cenotaphs were erected for the others. I have no definite statement to make, except that either there is synecdoche here, or Luke has reported this not so much from Moses as from ancient tradition, as the Jews long ago used to have many things handed down, as it were, from their ancestors. But when he goes on to say that they were buried in the sepulcher which Abraham had bought from the sons of Hamor, it is obvious that an error has been made in the name Abraham. For Abraham bought a double cave, to bury his wife, from Ephraim the Hittite, but Joseph was buried elsewhere, namely, in the field which his father Jacob had bought from the sons of Hamor for a

---

[13]Downame, ed., *Annotations*, HHH2v*.

[14]Jerome, Letter 57, "To Pammachius on the Best Method of Translating," NPNF[2] 6:117.

[15]Cajetan, *In Acta Apostolorum*, 219v.

[16]Jerome, Letter 108, "To Eustochium," NPNF[2] 6:201; Josephus, *Antiquities*, 2.8.

hundred lambs. This verse must be amended accordingly. COMMENTARY ON ACTS 7:16.[17]

7:17-43 The Ministry of Moses

GOD SHOWS HIS POWER IN HIS PEOPLE'S WEAKNESS. JOHN CALVIN: It is not for nothing that Stephen notes the circumstances of the time. Moses was born when the king had ordered all the male children to be exposed to death. Therefore the agent of redemption appears to be dead before his birth. But when there is no human help or advice available then it is that God has the greatest opportunity for doing something. And it is also perfectly plain how God makes his power perfect in people's weakness. Moses is preserved for three months, but out of regard for their own lives, his parents are forced to cast him out on the river. Only they put him into a small chest so that he might not perish quickly. When Pharaoh's daughter takes him out, he escapes death, it is true, but only to go over to an alien nation and be cut off from the children of Israel. And what is more, he was going to be a most troublesome enemy to his people one day, if God had not kept a hold on his mind. Forty years go by before he shows any sign of brotherly friendliness. COMMENTARY ON ACTS 7:20.[18]

MOSES "VISITS" HIS PEOPLE. THE ENGLISH ANNOTATIONS: This word indicates to visit for help and comfort, as physicians visit their patients. . . . Now that Moses, after being raised in Pharaoh's court for forty years, should all of a sudden desire to look into the condition of his afflicted brothers the Isrealites, this appears to be the inspiration and movement of God's Spirit to do what neither they nor Moses thought to do before. ANNOTATIONS ON ACTS 7:23.[19]

MOSES BECOMES A SHEPHERD. JOHN CALVIN: It was a hard exchange to be driven out from the pleasures of a palace and a life of splendor to take up the humble and wearisome task of keeping sheep. And in particular, since all the time he was banished in the wilderness Moses was aware that a long period of time was slipping away, what other conclusion could he come to, indeed, but that God's promise to him was an empty mockery? Since he was already eighty years old when he was engaged in looking after his father-in-law's flock, when would he have hoped that his services would be used in liberating the people? It is beneficial to keep thinking about these struggles of godly men, until they are thoroughly imprinted in our memory, so that our spirits may not fail, if at any time the Lord keeps us in a state of suspense longer than we should wish. Again, Moses gives a remarkable example of restraint, for in all the intervening time he causes no trouble, he stirs up no tumults and does not push himself in any way to seize a position of preeminence, as troublemakers are in the habit of doing. But he devotes himself to his shepherd's task as if he had never been called to any greater office. But while he waits quietly like this, the Lord appears to him in due time. COMMENTARY ON ACTS 7:30.[20]

THE BURNING BUSH WAS A FITTING SIGN FOR MOSES. JOHN CALVIN: It is a commonplace that God accommodates signs to realities by some sort of analogy, and this is quite a common procedure with the sacraments. Moreover nothing more suitable could have been shown to Moses for strengthening his faith in the present undertaking. He was well aware of the state in which he had left his own people. For even though their numbers were enormous, yet they were not unlike a bush. For the denser a bush is, and the thicker it is with masses of branches, the more liable it is to catch fire, with the flames raging all over it. Similarly, the Israelite nation was a weak company, exposed to injuries of all kinds, and the multitude, unfit for war though

---

[17]CNTC 6:182* (CO 48:138); alluding to Josh 24:32; Gen 23:9; cf. LXX Gen 33:19. A cenotaph is a monument erected in honor of the dead, e.g., the Lincoln Memorial in Washington, DC.
[18]CNTC 6:184-85* (CO 48:140); alluding to 2 Cor 12:9.
[19]Downame, ed., *Annotations*, HHH2v*.

[20]CNTC 6:189-90* (CO 48:144).

it was, and crippled by its own bulk as it were, had inflamed the ferocity of Pharaoh merely by the success and prosperity of increasing. Therefore the people who are oppressed by a fearful tyranny are like so much firewood that is completely smothered in flames, with nothing to prevent it being reduced to ashes, unless the Lord is established in the midst of it. But although an unaccustomed fire of persecution was blazing at that time, yet because the church of God in the world is never entirely immune and free from afflictions, its perennial condition is depicted here to a certain degree. For what else are we but fuel for the flames? It is true that innumerable firebrands of Satan are constantly hovering about, to set fire to our souls as well as our bodies, but with wonderful and extraordinary kindness the Lord delivers and protects us from being consumed. It is therefore necessary for the fire to blaze, that it may burn us in this life. But because the Lord dwells in our midst he will see to it that no afflictions will cause us harm. COMMENTARY ON ACTS 7:30.[21]

TRUE FAITH SEES WHAT IS INVISIBLE. PETER RIEDEMANN: Faith is not an empty illusion, as it would seem from those people who only speak of faith and know nothing more about it. They think that Christianity consists of words only. Therefore, they look on all who confess Christ with their lips as Christians, no matter how they live. True and well-founded faith, however, is not a human attribute. It is a gift from God, given only to those who fear God. That is why Paul says that not every person has faith. Such faith is the assurance of what is not seen. It grasps the invisible, one and only, mighty God, making us close to God and at one with him, and able to partake of his nature and character. It dispels all wavering and doubt and makes our heart hold steadfastly and firmly to God through all distresses.

God, therefore, gives us assurance and confirms all his promises as definitely as, for example, a man holding an object in his hands is certain that he has

it. In the same way faith grasps the promise of God, which is invisible, and clings to it as though it were visible. CONFESSION OF FAITH.[22]

WHEN GOD CALLS, WE MUST ANSWER. RUDOLF GWALTHER: Moses' example teaches us our duty, that when God stirs and draws us, we must yield to him and show ourselves to be obedient. For God's calling is of such force with the faithful that it cannot fail to have an effect, for as Christ says, this is the property of his sheep, to hear his voice and to follow it. Which they used to do, with such fervency and zeal that they despise all things that might hinder their calling as noisome and like dung, and again think nothing intolerable or too hard that is joined with God's calling. Both these things we see in the example of Moses. For as soon as he hears the Word of God speaking in his heart, without any delay he refuses the delicacies of the court, the pomp of the realm, the dignities of public authority, the friendship of great men, riches, ease, and whatsoever else like that which is to be had in the court. Instead of these, he chooses travails, poverty, shame and infinite dangers, where he saw the people of God every day vexed under most cruel enemies. And that which we see that Moses did, the same we see the apostles doing, who although they did not forsake so great riches, yet that little they had, they forsook, with as earnest an affection and zeal as he did. . . .

With their example, if we compare our own sluggish slothfulness, who thinks it unreasonable, to lose or suffer anything for Christ's sake, it shall plainly appear how far we yet are from Christian perfection. For forsaking and denying of themselves is what Christ requires of his disciples. This is that obedience of faith that Paul urges everywhere, and without which the profession of a Christian name is unprofitable. HOMILY 47, ACTS 7:17-22.[23]

---

[21]CNTC 6:190-91* (CO 48:145); alluding to Ps 46:5.

[22]CRR 9:84*; alluding to 2 Thess 3:1-2.
[23]Gwalther, *Homelyes or Sermons upon the Actes*, 320-21* (*In Acta Apostolorum*, 99r-v).

Moses, Too, Is a Type for Jesus. Desiderius Erasmus: Notice how clearly Jesus of Nazareth has been represented in Moses. The people of Israel refused Moses, who was still unknown, saying, "Who made you a ruler and a judge over us?" In the same way, Jesus heard from our people, "By whose authority do you do this, and who gave you this authority?" They did not yet know that God at that time through pity for our race sent the leader and prince of liberty, and the author of eternal life. And, indeed, God exalted Moses, though despised by his own, and made him leader, ruler and liberator of his people, and the power of the angel who appeared to him in the burning bush was present to assist him. By Moses' help God led his people out of Egypt, working many miracles and wonders in the land of Egypt, next to the Red Sea, finally, in the wilderness also throughout the forty years. What Moses was to one people, this, truly, Jesus of Nazareth is to all who are willing to follow his leading. Paraphrase of Acts 7:35-37.[24]

Moses Is Subject to Christ. John Calvin: Moses is called "redeemer" in no other sense than that he was a minister of God, and in this way the glory of the whole undertaking remains entirely in the hands of God alone. Let us therefore learn that as often as people are honored with God's titles, God is not stripped of his own honor; but because the work is carried out by their agency, they are commended in this way. What Stephen is saying amounts to this, that this responsibility was entrusted to Moses at the hand of the angel. For in this way Moses is made subject to Christ, so that under his guidance and auspices he may show his obedience to God. Commentary on Acts 7:36.[25]

The Holy Spirit Now Writes His Laws Directly on Our Hearts. Pilgram Marpeck: Without this copier of the law of Christ, I mean the Holy Spirit, the apostles could neither understand nor bear the teaching of their master.

He repeated in them again what Christ had said, taught and commanded. He is the true pledge of our salvation and the true witness to our faith; he is the true repeater, teacher and reminder of our perfect law, no longer written on stone tablets but in the hearts of the faithful. The Holy Spirit no longer takes [the law] from the appearance or the mediation of angels, nor does he take it through fire, clouds or darkness, as Moses received it and took it from God. He takes it from the Father and the Son and gives it to the hearts of all the faithful. In them the laws and new commandments of Christ the Lord are written by the finger of God. Kunstbuch: Concerning the Lowliness of Christ.[26]

Jewish Idolatry Was Learned from the Egyptians. Philipp Melanchthon: [Stephen] makes mention of manifold idolatries in his account of the history of the Israelites in the desert. He says [here] that they had made a calf. This idolatry was without a doubt born out of the superstition of the Egyptians, with which many of the Jews had become familiar. In [his history], Herodotus tells that among the Egyptians, the Apis, a certain strange or peculiar bull or calf, was worshiped like a deity. Postil for the Feast of Stephen.[27]

Why Did Aaron Make the Calf? John Calvin: God certainly does accommodate himself to our ignorance to this extent, that he allows us to see himself after a fashion under figures. For under the Law there were very many symbols to testify to his presence; and today he comes down to us by means of baptism, and the Supper and even in the external preaching of the Word. But people sin

---

[24]CWE 50:52*; quoting Mt 21:23.
[25]CNTC 6:195* (CO 48:149).

[26]CRR 12:606-7* (QGT 17:582); alluding to Jn 6:60; 2 Cor 3:3; Ezek 36:26; Heb 8:10.
[27]MO 24:95; alluding to Ex 32. Herodotus describes this "Apis" as a large black calf with a square of white on its forehead, the figure of an eagle on its back, and a beetle on its tongue. It is the offspring of an infertile cow impregnated by a lightning flash from the sky. See Herodotus, *The Histories of Herodotus*, trans. Henry Clay (New York: D. Appleton & Company, 1904), 142, 163-64; accessible via books.google.com.

here in a double way. First, not content with the means appointed by God, they boldly seek new things for themselves. At present it is no small fault that people, knowing no limit, are always itching for new inventions, and so they do not hesitate to jump over the bounds that God has set. But there can be no true image of God except such as he himself has ordained. Therefore whatever things are contrived contrary to his words by the will of people are false and counterfeit.

Second, there follows another fault, just as intolerable; as the human mind conceives nothing about God except what is solid and earthly, so it transfers all signs of the divine presence into the same materialism. Not only does a person so mistakenly find pleasure in idols made by himself, but also he corrupts and spoils whatever God has instituted, twisting it to serve a contrary purpose. God does indeed come down to us, as I have said, but for this purpose, that he might lift us up into heaven. But we who are attached to the earth wish to have him similarly on the earth. COMMENTARY ON ACTS 7:40.[28]

7:44-53 The Tabernacle and the Temple

THE TEMPLE IS A TYPE FOR THE CHURCH. DE-SIDERIUS ERASMUS: And yet, in truth, this temple is only a figure for the true spiritual temple, the church, which is now being built by Jesus of Naza-reth, your King, of whom Solomon was the type. . . . If God rests, he does not rest in buildings made by human hands, since, in any case, the sky is his seat and the earth his footstool; but he delights to rest in hearts that are quiet and obedient to the Holy Spirit. Accordingly, it is the one who gives trouble to those who obey the Holy Spirit who violates the temple of the Lord. Now just as one does not injure Moses by putting Jesus before him, and does not violate the Law which he conveyed by putting the gospel before it, so he does not violate this temple by giving precedence to the spiritual temple in which God has greater delight. It is right that

shadows yield to the truth, which is now thrusting itself forward into the light. PARAPHRASE OF ACTS 7:47-50.[29]

"NOT MADE WITH HANDS." BALTHASAR HUB-MAIER: In this passage you clearly hear that we can-not make wooden, stone, silver or golden houses for Christ. Therefore it is all in vain, the expenses that until now have been invested in such costly monastaries and monstrances.[30] However they are well called monastaries and monstrances, [derived] from [the root] "monstrosity." . . . How can some wretched monster . . . be crafted and shown to us, and then we see and worship an earthly thing for a heavenly good, a perishable thing for an eternal thing, a creature for the Creator and for God him-self in monastaries and monstrances! A SIMPLE INSTRUCTION.[31]

GOD IS SAID TO DWELL IN HEAVEN. JOHN CALVIN: The scriptural teaching concerning God's immense and spiritual essence ought to be enough, not only to banish popular delusions, but also to refute the subtleties of secular philosophy. One of the ancients seems aptly to have remarked, "What-ever we see, and whatever we do not see, is God." According to this, he fancied that divinity was poured out into the various parts of the world. But even if God to keep us sober speaks sparingly of his essence, yet by those two titles that I have used he both banishes stupid imaginings and restrains the boldness of the human mind. Surely, his im-mensity ought to make us afraid to try to measure him by our own senses. Indeed, his spiritual nature forbids our imagining anything earthly or carnal of him. For the same reason, he quite often assigns to himself a dwelling place in heaven. And yet as he is incomprehensible he also fills the earth itself. But because he sees that our slow minds sink down upon the earth, and rightly, in order to shake off our sluggishness and inertia he raises us

---

[28]CNTC 6:201* (CO 48:153).

[29]CWE 50:54.
[30]A monstrance is a vessel, used primarily in the Roman Catholic tradition, to display the consecrated Eucharist.
[31]CRR 5:335* (QGT 9:302).

above the world. . . . Who even of slight intelligence does not understand that, as nurses commonly do with infants, God is wont in a measure to "lisp" in speaking to us? Thus such forms of speaking do not so much express clearly what God is like as accommodate the knowledge of him to our slight capacity. To do this he must descend far beneath his loftiness. INSTITUTES 1.13.1.[32]

TODAY SOME TRY TO PLACE GOD IN BREAD. PETER RIEDEMANN: This is what the children of Israel did in misusing their silver and gold for making a calf, to their own great dishonor and shame. These ornaments had been given them for their use, adornment and honor. But they said, "These are our gods that have led us out of Egypt." In that way they stole the honor from God and gave it to a graven image made with their own hands. People today do the same with bread. They reject the usage as instituted by Christ, in which the meal becomes a comfort. They make something idolatrous out of it, which is an abomination to our God. It is idolatry to honor as God that which is not God, and to look for him where he is not. "God does not live in temples made by human hands." These words are proof that he is not in the bread, because bread is always made by human hands. Therefore, God is not in the bread. CONFESSION OF FAITH.[33]

THE HOLY SPIRIT WORKS THROUGH THE WORD AND SACRAMENTS. MARTIN LUTHER: Now, all the same, prayer alone is actually not enough. For if you are in a corner, and you pray for the Holy Spirit but are not willing to cling tenaciously to the Word and holy sacraments, then your prayer will bear fruit sluggishly. The reason: the Holy Spirit does his work only through the Word and holy sacraments. Whoever then evades the same will never again be visited by the Holy Spirit. Therefore we allow ourselves to be baptized, we attend the Lord's Supper, we listen to God's

Word, we covet absolution. For we know that all of these things are instruments through which the Holy Spirit orchestrates his work in us. . . .

Thus, if you desire the gifts of the Holy Spirit to come to you, then above all other things you must ask the Father in the name of Jesus for such gifts and then clutch tightly to his Word, remember with diligence your baptism—what God promised to you then and how he has made a covenant with you through baptism—and attend often the Lord's Supper, seek absolution, and so on. For through the Word and sacraments the Holy Spirit desires to kindle our hearts with the new light of faith, so that we do not merely hear the Word . . . but in fact we understand it and through it become new people and receive new hearts. HOUSE POSTIL FOR PENTECOST (1544).[34]

BELIEVERS ARE THE TEMPLE. DIRK PHILIPS: The congregation also needs no external temple, which is made with hands and counts as nothing with God. Therefore none is found in the congregation, but the tabernacle of God is with it, and the dwelling of the Most High is in its midst. And, once again, thus the congregation is itself the temple of the living God, just as it is written: "I will live in them and walk in them, and they shall be my people, and I will be their God, says the Lord Almighty." THE ENCHIRIDION: THE CONGREGATION OF GOD.[35]

THE TWO "HERESIES" OF STEPHEN'S SERMON. MARTIN LUTHER: Here dissonance arose between the Jews and Stephen over the part of Saint Stephen's sermon in which he proclaimed the Christian faith. This you hear immediately from the words of this verse. They accused him, saying that he had spoken and preached against the holy temple and the law of Moses. This he refuted, saying, "I know well that Solomon built the temple—David wanted to build it, too, so also

---

[32]LCC 20:120-21 (CO 2:89-90), quoting Seneca, *Natural Questions*, prologue, 1.13.
[33]CRR 9:114; alluding to Ex 32:1-6.

[34]WA 52:319.
[35]CRR 6:380* (BRN 10:412); alluding to Ps 48:9; Rev 21:22; quoting 1 Cor 3:16; 2 Cor 6:16.

the patriarchs had the tabernacle; but God does not live in temples." This was the first heresy. The second one that he preached was that they could not be saved through their works. Moreover, that they could never uphold the law. If they wanted to be saved, then they must pursue another way, they must have Christ. To this they said, "Hey! This man also blasphemes Moses! He says we must have some person from Nazareth who altered the law."

These two heresies have been castigated since the beginning of the world, and will continue to be until the end, as we now see. While they accused him, he was silent; he could have shoved it down their throat, demonstrating reasons and principles, so that they would have had to understand. He gives the following reason from Isaiah: "Heaven is my throne, the earth my footstool, what then for a house would you build me, in which I could dwell?" Look, this passage is so strong and clear that it cannot be contradicted; all their cleverness crumbles to the earth, knocked to the ground. He lays down so strong a justification, who can strive against it? Because God says, "heaven is my throne, the earth my bench," how then can he dwell in the temple? "It is surely far beneath me, what then will you build for me? Look up to heaven, compare heaven with your temple!" When they heard this they could not let this prophet stand, so they rushed to him and dragged him away with force, shouting, "He said we should not build temples and we should not keep the law."

Unbelief is an evil weed. As soon as it "pops up,"[36] it stinks. It will not yield; the more it is trampled, the more bitter it will become. Therefore you should not imagine that you will convert the unbelieving, even if you have such a clear passage that they themselves feel that it is so obvious that they are unable to contradict it. Nevertheless they still find a way out, so that they might excuse their unbelief and evade Christ's teaching. SERMON ON THE FEAST OF SAINT STEPHEN (1523).[37]

THE STUBBORNESS OF THE UNCIRCUMCISED HEART. DIRK PHILIPS: Christ Jesus, the true Isaac, has reopened the clogged-up fountains of the holy Scripture and brought the darkened Word of God again to the light of day. He has allowed the pure clear gospel to be preached everywhere through his servants and apostles. But the uncircumcised Philistines, the scribes and the Pharisees, the uncircumcised at heart, the antichrists and the false teachers set themselves against it and quarrel with the servants of Isaac, the ministers of Jesus Christ, on account of the fountains of living waters which they regard and reckon as their own. For they alone wish to be interpreters of the Scripture and say boldly, "Our tongue shall have the upper hand; to us alone belongs the right to speak. Who is our master?" THE ENCHIRIDION: CONCERNING SPIRITUAL RESTITUTION.[38]

THE LEADERS HAVE THICK EARS. JOHANN AGRICOLA: Whoever is slow to listen and does not want to hear has thick ears, which are impenetrable. Thin ears are those which listen and understand easily. Listening serves most of all for learning and understanding. Thus, thick ears reveal an ignorant person. For what we do not hear, we do not understand either. Saint Stephen in the Acts of the Apostles said to the Jews that they had uncircumcised ears and hearts for listening to and accepting what God had done with their ancestors, and that because of their thick ears and ignorance they strangled all the prophets and opposed the Holy Spirit. The eyes see, the ears hear; the heart understands, instructed by these two. But what the eyes do not see, the ears do not hear, this too the heart does not understand. So Saint Paul says, "What no eye has seen, no ear has heard, this has also not ascended to the human heart, what

---

[36]Luther here slurs together the Saxon equivalent of *bis auf*, so that it sounds like he is saying *bischoff*, "bishop." This seems to be an implicit barb against his contemporary bishops, as if he were saying, "As soon as a priest becomes a bishop, his faith is done with." See also his passage above on Acts 6:1-6.

[37]WA 12:694; quoting Is 66:1.
[38]CRR 6:325-26* (BRN 10:351).

God has prepared for those who love him." SEVEN HUNDRED FIFTY GERMAN PROVERBS.[39]

STEPHEN EXPOSES THE PROUD. MARTIN LUTHER: Ah, dear God, this treasure of the holy Scriptures belongs only to a contrite heart and a humble and God-fearing spirit. The ungodly must be exposed and their boasting put down. This is what Stephen did when he spoke against the place of Jerusalem, against the law, against the prosperous people, against a demanding God. Truly it was an excellent and sharp sermon! TABLE TALK, ANTON LAUTERBACH (1539).[40]

---

[39] Agricola, *Die Sprichwörtersammlungen*, 1:128; quoting 1 Cor 2:9; see also Is 64:4.

[40] LW 54:344 no. 4470* (WATR 4:328-29).

7:54-60 THE STONING OF STEPHEN

54Now when they heard these things they were enraged, and they ground their teeth at him. 55But he, full of the Holy Spirit, gazed into heaven and saw the glory of God, and Jesus standing at the right hand of God. 56And he said, "Behold, I see the heavens opened, and the Son of Man standing at the right hand of God." 57But they cried out with a loud voice and stopped their ears and rushed together aat him. 58Then they cast him out of the city and stoned him. And the witnesses laid down their garments at the feet of a young man named Saul. 59And as they were stoning Stephen, he called out, "Lord Jesus, receive my spirit." 60And falling to his knees he cried out with a loud voice, "Lord, do not hold this sin against them." And when he had said this, he fell asleep.

a Or *rushed with one mind*

OVERVIEW: Our commentators are deeply impressed by Stephen's martyrdom. A condemned man does not curse his wrongful accusers, does not fight back, but prays for them! Stephen models how Christians are to accept Christ as both gift and example. Knowing that he has true life in Christ, Stephen is unafraid to abandon everything, including his own temporal life, for Jesus' sake. This, the reformers emphasize, is what it is to have true faith, which issues in fervent love for God and neighbor.

Martyrdom was not an abstract concept for the reformers. Luther was certain that after the Diet of Worms he would die. The French Reformed parishioners constantly faced the threat of death—famously realized for many of them during the St. Bartholomew's Day Massacre in 1572. Almost the entire first generation of Radical reformers were martyred through a state-administered "final baptism" by drowning or burning: Conrad Grebel, Felix Manz, Michael Sattler, Georg Blaurock and Hans Hut. The English Reformation was particularly brutal; after Thomas More's death numerous theologians were publicly executed—some, like Paul Fagius, were even disinterred to be ceremoniously executed again under Queen Mary I ("bloody Mary"). Not all the reformers persevered in persecution, either; Thomas Cranmer and Balthasar Hubmaier recanted, although in the end both suffered martyrdom willingly.

Stephen's condemnation before this human court makes clear these people's own condemnation before God. Nevertheless, our commentators urge that these mistaken murderers are not beyond the pale of the Lord's mercy and salvation. They exhort their audience to have compassion on those around them, even their enemies, and to pray for them. Prayer is effective, because God has promised to listen (especially obvious, they point out, in the fact that Stephen's prayer was answered through the conversion of Saul).

THE BLESSING OF MARTYRDOM. JOHN DONNE:

> And since thou so desirously
> Did'st long to die, that long before thou could'st,
>   And long since thou no more couldst die,
> Thou in thy scatter'd mystic body wouldst
>   In Abel die, and ever since
>   In thine; let their blood come
> To beg for us, a discrete patience
> Of death, or of worse life: for Oh, to some
> Not to be Martyrs, is a martydom.

THE MARTYRS.[1]

THE TEMPLE RULERS COULD NOT BEAR THEIR GLORY BEING DIMINISHED. DESIDERIUS ERASMUS: It is worth the effort here to consider the pattern of this judgment. Charges had been put forward; an answer was given to everything.

---

[1]Donne, *Poems of John Donne*, 341.

A young man brought forth the testimonies of the Law and the prophets; the case was won with solid arguments. Nothing was said about God that was not pious, nothing about Moses that was not honorable, nothing about the Law that was not according to the intent of the Law; nothing was spoken with disdain about the temple. And yet these people are bursting with anger and grind their teeth like madmen. So little do they tolerate having their own glory diminished and the glory of him proclaimed whose glory alone God wants proclaimed among all.

If he had exalted Moses or Abraham, they would have borne it; that Jesus was alive, that Jesus was standing at the right hand of God according to the prophecy of David, this they cannot bear, but turning to frenzy straightaway, they stop up their ears against a discourse so salubrious, and with frantic cries they all rush on Stephen with a common purpose. . . . And so Stephen, corresponding to his name,[2] was the first of all to win the martyr's crown and to offer the Lord the firstfruits of the evangelical sacrifice. PARAPHRASE OF ACTS 7:54.[3]

STEPHEN'S EXAMPLE. RUDOLF GWALTHER: When Stephen was put to this cruel death, we learn three things about him. First he called on the Lord, something we believe he continually used to do. His entire sermon is summarized [here]: "Lord Jesus, receive my spirit." These words have in them the confession of a true faith and token of a great and strong belief. Surrounded by imminent death, still he acknowledges and confesses that Christ is his Savior, following the example of the thief crucified with Christ. Further, he believes that the souls do not die with the body in death but pass to the state of a better life, for he knows that even in death through faith in Christ, believers find life. . . .

Second, Stephen models love, which cannot be separated from faith. For following the example and commandment of Christ, he prays for his enemies, that God would not punish them for their

sin, as they deserved. . . . Let us learn to extend our charity, even to the ungrateful, and with godly prayers commend to God those who most grievously offend against us. . . .

Last of all Stephen, having thus spoken, fell asleep. . . . The Scripture often uses this word *sleep* speaking of the death of the godly. For so is the condition and property of death set forth. Death is the resolution or dissolution of a human being, consisting of soul and body. In this death the soul neither dies nor sleeps but passes into life everlasting, as Christ says. So death has aptly been called a passing into heaven. The body is said to sleep because it is laid in the earth as it were to sleep, out of which in the end of days it shall be raised up by Christ, that it may also enjoy the bliss of heavenly life. . . .

Let us place Stephen before us as an example, so that when we depart this life our souls cross over into that home of blessing [heaven], and in the end our bodies are also gloriously resurrected, so that we may enjoy the inheritance of heaven through Christ Jesus our Lord. Homily 55, Acts 7:55-60.[4]

STEPHEN IS AN EXAMPLE OF HOW THE CHRIST CHILD TRANSFORMS US. MARTIN LUTHER: We want to say a little more again about the birth of Christ, how we should apply it. The example of Stephen points us to this: Whomever this child's birth should benefit, he must, as I have said, forfeit absolutely everything else. He must abandon everything, all the things that he holds dear, not only carnal desire, but also every human virtue and all honor that we had before must be set aside—body, life, wealth and honor. He must surrender himself with joyous courage to humiliation and dishonor, to poverty and to death, in order to receive the child worthily. The old skin must be stripped away, and the old self with all its desires must be killed. Then the child comes and creates in us a new person. SERMON ON THE FEAST OF SAINT STEPHEN (1520).[5]

---

[2]In Greek, Stephen (Στέφανος) means "crown."
[3]CWE 50:55-56* (LB 7:696-97).

[4]Gwalther, *Homelyes or Sermons upon the Actes*, 355-56* (*In Acta Apostolorum*, 109v-110r); alluding to Jn 5.
[5]WA 9:526. The Feast of St. Stephen is December 26.

JUDGE AND KING. JOHANN ECK: It is true—as the passages of Scripture mentioned before indicate—that the Lord Jesus sits and stands. For standing belongs to those who help someone else, as we say in German, "He stood by him." Therefore, the Lord Christ helped Saint Stephen in his battle; he said calmly that he saw him standing. But when we speak of Christ's rule or of his judgment, then we are talking about him sitting. For a king sits on his throne, a judge on his bench. SECOND POSTIL FOR THE FEAST OF SAINT STEPHEN.[6]

THROUGH WORD AND SPIRIT, GOD IS PRESENT WHEREVER HE WISHES. MARTIN LUTHER: This glimpse Stephen saw with his physical eyes. We today do not see this physically, but in the Word we, too—praise God!—see this. . . . As Christ promised that his Spirit will be with us, comforting and strengthening us, so that we will have complete joy and solace in him, and he will bring our cause to the light of day, so that we must sense that it is not we but the Spirit of God who is speaking. As we hear from Stephen in this passage, he gives such an excellent response to the false charges of the Jews and confirms that the temple in Jerusalem is not God's house, that he is not constrained to it, and it will be destroyed on account of their sins. He demonstrates how God was among his people and needed no such house. HOUSE POSTIL FOR THE FEAST OF SAINT STEPHEN (1544).[7]

RAVENOUS WOLVES DEVOUR THIS MEEK LAMB. JOHANN ECK: The Jews assaulted Saint Stephen, who was still possessed by no blasphemy, whose face they had seen as the face of an angel; they could not turn away from him. They were bloodhounds and ravenous wolves, as the Lord said to his disciples: "See, I am sending you out like little sheep in the midst of wolves." They were unable rationally to discard the words of Stephen. After this out of their jealousy they had to do

something, and they stoned him as a blasphemer of God. THIRD POSTIL FOR THE FEAST OF SAINT STEPHEN.[8]

A CHRISTIAN'S DEATH IS BUT A SLEEP BECAUSE OF CHRIST. JOHANN SPANGENBERG: After he had prayed, he fell asleep. The Christian's death is not a death but a sleep, as Christ said about the deceased Lazarus. . . . Such mercy Christ has gained for us with his death, so that we die peacefully and death will not approach us bitterly, as he says: "Truly I say to you, that whoever keeps my Word will never see death." As if he wanted to say, "The Word will snatch this person up and slay him, so that he falls asleep in God's peace and dies gently. The Word, I say, will bring you past the devil, death and hell without any harm into eternal life." BRIEF EXEGESIS OF ACTS 7:60.[9]

CHRIST PROTECTS US EVEN IN DEATH. JOHN CALVIN: It is an inestimable comfort to know that when our souls leave our bodies, they do not wander about haphazardly but are taken into Christ's safe protection, if only we place them in his hands. This confidence ought to teach us to face death calmly; yes! and what is more, everyone who commits his soul to Christ with a serious attitude of trust must, at the same time, necessarily resign himself to a total obedience to his will.

Finally, this verse clearly testifies that the soul of a person is not a vanishing breath, according to the ravings of some madmen, but that it is an essential spirit and survives this life. Moreover, we are taught from this that it is right and proper for us to call on Christ, because all power has been given to him by the Father, so that all people may give themselves into his protection (*fidem*). COMMENTARY ON ACTS 7:59.[10]

---

[6]Eck, *Christenliche Predigen*, 3:36v; alluding to Mk 16:19; Col 3:1; Rev 4:1-6; 5:7.
[7]WA 52:594; alluding to Mk 13:11.

[8]Eck, *Christenliche Predigen*, 3:37r; quoting Mt 10:16.
[9]Spangenberg, *Der Apostel Geschichte*, 65v-66r; quoting Jn 11:11 (cf. 1 Thess 4:13); alluding to Jn 8:51. On Luther's views of death as sleep, see Philip J. Secker, "Martin Luther's Views on the State of the Dead," *Concordia Theological Monthly* 38, no. 7 (1967): 422-35.
[10]CNTC 6:222* (CO 48:171).

WHY DOES LUKE NARRATE STEPHEN'S LIFE AND DEATH? JOHANN SPANGENBERG: Not so that he may receive human praise, but rather so that Christendom would have an example, from which they learn that not only riches, honor, power, health and life are gifts of God, but also temptation, adversity, persecution, misery, sickness, cross, suffering and death. For on whomever God places cross, suffering and death for the sake of righteousness, to this person he also grants his Spirit, so that he is able to remain faithful in cross and death, and finally, as it happened with Saint Stephen, to enter eternal life. To this may God help us, Amen. BRIEF EXEGESIS OF ACTS 7:60.[11]

SUFFERING IS NOT SILENCE. KATARINA SCHÜTZ ZELL: As is proper for a Christian, I would suffer such insults and lies with patience, as Christ teaches, but along with that, for the sake of the simple, I would declare my innocence of such lies.... Christ also did this when Ananias's servant hit him in the face. He did not strike back; he did not flee; he did not resist the evil at all, as he had previously taught his disciples. However, he did not keep silent about it as if the servant acted rightly, but he said, "If I have spoken evil, give proof of it, but if not, why do you strike me?" For it is sufficient that we Christians suffer injustice; we should not say that injustice is justice. To keep silence is not patience; to suffer is patience. I should tell my innocence to the one who lies about me, and after that if he will not turn back from what he is doing, then I should suffer his injustice. Otherwise by keeping silence I give him grounds to continue in his trumped-up lies, and that, in my judgment, is against brotherly love. For I would be unwilling to be left in error and lies without instruction; why should I not also in turn correct the error and lies that my neighbor believes? APOLOGIA FOR MASTER MATTHIAS ZELL.[12]

PRAY TO THE VERY END LIKE JESUS AND STEPHEN. JOHANN ECK: Through this we learn

first that we should pray to the death, as also the Lord Jesus did on the cross. And if the sick person is already so weak that he himself cannot pray, then others should surround him and pray something aloud to him or read something devotional, like the suffering of the Lord or about something else like the final judgment or God's lovingkindness. Second, we should learn how we should commend our spirit, our nature and soul to God the Lord at the time of our death; indeed, daily we should do this, as we said more in depth above in the passion.[13] For the Lord Jesus left us this word last of all. THIRD POSTIL FOR THE FEAST OF SAINT STEPHEN.[14]

THE POWER OF STEPHEN'S PRAYER. MARTIN LUTHER: When [Martin Luther] was asked whether somebody else's faith will secure salvation for a person, [he said], "By all means! In fact, the faith of one person may obtain another's whole conversion. Accordingly it is said that Paul was converted and saved by Stephen's prayer. However, Paul was not accepted on account of Stephen's faith, but Stephen's faith obtained faith for Paul from God, and by this faith he was saved in God's sight. Many people have been preserved by prayer, as we prayed Philip back to life.[15] Ah, prayer accomplishes much."

Somebody else asked, "But, Doctor, wasn't Paul converted long after the death of Stephen?" The doctor responded, "Not at all! He

---

[13]See Eck, *Christenliche Predigen*, 1:158r-v. During the late medieval and early modern period *ars moriendi* manuals were wildly popular. For, as Susan Karant-Nunn puts it, "the true *ars moriendi* was the *ars vivendi*" (Karant-Nunn, *The Reformation of Ritual: An Interpretation of Early Modern Germany* [New York: Routledge, 1997], 149).

[14]Eck, *Christenliche Predigen* 3:37r. In the early modern period it was incredibly important how someone died: their death indicated God's judgment—a holy person should die as peacefully as a candle smolders out. The dying person was to pray constantly until they could no longer do so, then clerics would take over during the Sacrament of Extreme Unction. For an excellent and detailed treatment of the evolution of the Sacrament of Extreme Unction during the sixteenth century, see Karant-Nunn, *Reformation of Ritual*, 138-45, esp. 138-39.

[15]In 1540 Melanchthon recovered from sickness; Luther believed his own prayers had effected this healing. See WABr 9:170-71.

---

[11]Spangenberg, *Der Apostel Geschichte*, 66r-v.

[12]Zell, *Church Mother*, 65-66*; alluding to Mt 5:39-40; quoting Jn 18:22-23.

was converted that same year. He was still a fine, young man and was learned. He adhered to the righteousness of the law: 'By doing these things a man shall live.' He thought he was pleasing God in this way. It is impossible that God should not hear a prayer of faith. Whether he always does is another matter. God does not give according to the prescribed measure, but he presses it down and shakes it together, as he said. . . . So James said well, 'Pray for one another,' for 'the prayer of a righteous person has great power in its effects.' This is one of the best verses in that epistle. Prayer is a powerful thing, if only one believes in it, for God has attached and bound himself to it [by his promises]." TABLE TALK, CASPAR HEYDENREICH (1543).[16]

CHRISTIANS MUST NOT TAKE VENGEANCE.
MENNO SIMONS: True Christians do not know vengeance, no matter how they are mistreated. In patience they possess their souls. And they do not break their peace, even if they should be tempted by bondage, torture, poverty, and besides by the sword and fire. They do not cry, "Vengeance, vengeance", as the world does; but with Christ they supplicate and pray: "Father, forgive them; for they know not what they do." REPLY TO FALSE ACCUSATIONS.[17]

SAINT STEPHEN EXEMPLIFIES HOW WE ARE TO LOVE OTHERS. MARTIN LUTHER: Here both true faith and true love come together, as they both must be together. For a Christian should accept his neighbor as himself, not only with temporal aid but much more with spiritual aid—much more is dependent on such aid. Thus, it goes straight to this holy man's heart that the devil has so snared these poor sinners' hearts and blinded them so that they still despise and persecute their very own salvation, even if they should lose body and life and everything else.

This, too, we should learn from the holy

Stephen, rather than—as the world is accustomed to do—fuming whenever other people treat us badly. Indeed, it causes pain, but think like Stephen: "They, however, cannot do anything more than harm my property and, if they do their worst, my body." Then again, it is certain, the more harm they do to your body and property, the more harm they do to their own souls. Now what do you want to do with such poor, miserable people? Do you want to rage against them and harm them? Are you able to do so much? They have already done a thousand times more harm to themselves, and you will ruin your case before the Lord God through such impatience and vindictiveness. If you patiently suffer it, God will take up your case himself and will abundantly reward and heal such harm done to you. Thus, there is nothing better than, with Stephen, to abandon all wrath and hostility and to take to heart the great harm these poor people do to their souls and to pray to God for them, that he would forgive them, accept them into his grace and mercifully protect them from the death and condemnation into which the devil has thrown them.

In addition to such teaching we also have this solace here, that we should not doubt: God will grant such a prayer and will be merciful to sinners. Otherwise Stephen would not have prayed this, if such a request were contrary to the Lord Christ. Because he prays for such great sinners who were unwilling to hear or see the Son of God and who persecuted and killed his saints, such is a proof that no sinner should despair but through Christ should hope for grace and the forgiveness of his sins. As Luke assiduously reports, Paul took pleasure in Stephen's death and at the time held onto the witnesses' clothes, as they stoned Stephen. But, as Paul himself said, it is without a doubt through this prayer he experienced grace, so that Christ exhibited every patience in him, for the benefit of those who believe in Christ to eternal life.

Thus, dearly beloved, you have the story of holy Saint Stephen, what he did, how he confessed Christ and how, in the end, on account

---

[16]LW 54:453-54 no. 5565* (WATR 5:244-45); alluding to Acts 7:59-60; Lev 18:5; Rom 10:5; Lk 6:38; quoting Jas 5:16.
[17]Simons, *Complete Writings*, 555; alluding to Lk 21:18; quoting Lk 23:34; Acts 7:60.

of such a confession sacrificed his life. Christ with his Spirit comforted him and through the hope of eternal life strengthened him, so that he gladly placed his temporal life in danger for the sake of Christ. May our dear God in heaven, for the sake of Christ through his Holy Spirit enlighten our hearts so powerfully and save us. Amen. House Postil for the Feast of Saint Stephen (1544).[18]

God Grant That We Too Would Live Like Stephen. Book of Common Prayer (1549): Grant us, O Lord, to learn to love our enemies by the example of your martyr Saint Stephen, who prayed to you for his persecutors, who lives and reigns with your dearly beloved Son and the Holy Spirit, one true and everlasting God, world without end. Amen. The Collect for the Feast of Saint Stephen.[19]

---

[18]WA 52:597-98; alluding to Gal 1:15-16.

[19]BCP 1549, 44*.

8:1-25 SAUL'S PERSECUTION, PHILIP'S PREACHING AND SIMON'S SORCERY

And Saul approved of his execution.

And there arose on that day a great persecution against the church in Jerusalem, and they were all scattered throughout the regions of Judea and Samaria, except the apostles. ²*Devout men buried Stephen and made great lamentation over him.* ³*But Saul was ravaging the church, and entering house after house, he dragged off men and women and committed them to prison.*

⁴*Now those who were scattered went about preaching the word.* ⁵*Philip went down to the city*ᵃ *of Samaria and proclaimed to them the Christ.* ⁶*And the crowds with one accord paid attention to what was being said by Philip when they heard him and saw the signs that he did.* ⁷*For unclean spirits, crying out with a loud voice, came out of many who had them, and many who were paralyzed or lame were healed.* ⁸*So there was much joy in that city.*

⁹*But there was a man named Simon, who had previously practiced magic in the city and amazed the people of Samaria, saying that he himself was somebody great.* ¹⁰*They all paid attention to him, from the least to the greatest, saying, "This man is the power of God that is called Great."* ¹¹*And they paid attention to him because for a long time he had amazed them with his magic.* ¹²*But when they believed Philip as he preached good news about the kingdom of God and the name of Jesus Christ, they were baptized, both men and women.* ¹³*Even Simon himself believed, and after being baptized he continued with Philip. And seeing signs and great miracles*ᵇ *performed, he was amazed.*

¹⁴*Now when the apostles at Jerusalem heard that Samaria had received the word of God, they sent to them Peter and John,* ¹⁵*who came down and prayed for them that they might receive the Holy Spirit,* ¹⁶*for he had not yet fallen on any of them, but they had only been baptized in the name of the Lord Jesus.* ¹⁷*Then they laid their hands on them and they received the Holy Spirit.* ¹⁸*Now when Simon saw that the Spirit was given through the laying on of the apostles' hands, he offered them money,* ¹⁹*saying, "Give me this power also, so that anyone on whom I lay my hands may receive the Holy Spirit."* ²⁰*But Peter said to him, "May your silver perish with you, because you thought you could obtain the gift of God with money!* ²¹*You have neither part nor lot in this matter, for your heart is not right before God.* ²²*Repent, therefore, of this wickedness of yours, and pray to the Lord that, if possible, the intent of your heart may be forgiven you.* ²³*For I see that you are in the gall*ᶜ *of bitterness and in the bond of iniquity."* ²⁴*And Simon answered, "Pray for me to the Lord, that nothing of what you have said may come upon me."*

²⁵*Now when they had testified and spoken the word of the Lord, they returned to Jerusalem, preaching the gospel to many villages of the Samaritans.*

a Some manuscripts *a city*   b Greek *works of power*   c That is, a bitter fluid secreted by the liver; bile

OVERVIEW: After Stephen's death a full-scale persecution of the Jerusalem church began, initiating the latter stages of Jesus' programmatic commission in Acts 1:8 ("You will be my witnesses in Jerusalem and in all Judea and Samaria, and to the end of the earth"). Several of the reformers here continue their contemplation of Christian suffering. Believers ought not to be surprised by affliction; indeed, faithful servants of the Word should expect it. The reformers do not pause very long to lament the deaths of the persecuted. They remind their audience that the grave is only a temporary holding place, with no real power over the elect, who will rise again in triumph. To modern ears this likely sounds dispassionate—as Ronald Rittgers reminds us—though it is perhaps unfortunate that our Christian forebears were less fluent in lament, they still teach us that in Christ God does not merely suffer with us but he also is in control.[1] Nor do the reformers idolize martyrdom: it is not something to be chased after but faithfully accepted.

Some of the firstfruits of the scattered and persecuted gospel community are harvested in Samaria. But there is little time to celebrate; Simon Magus, impressed by the deeds and power of the apostles, longs to have this ability for himself. This episode causes the reformers to meditate on the contemporary abuse of the bishop's office, the nature of the church and the proper use of the keys (church discipline). At the time of the Reformation the office of bishop was often quite lucrative. For this reason, some would take out large loans at high interest to purchase a bishopric; it was not uncommon for a bishop to hold several bishoprics, harvesting tithes from distant palaces. Catholics and Protestants alike acknowledge that this practice desperately needed to be reformed: the care of souls should not be a temporal bargaining chip for personal wealth.

Concerning the nature of the church's unity and purity, there is less agreement among the commentators. The Radicals insist that the church must be kept pure and that hypocrites like Simon have not truly received baptism because they do not express sorrow for their sin, demonstrate faith or seek to amend their ways. Magisterial reformers like Melanchthon counter that the purpose of baptism is not *if-then* (if you live as a faithful child of God, then your baptism will be valid), but *because-therefore* (because you are truly baptized into Christ, you will live as becomes a child of God).[2]

Finally, there is extended reflection on excommunication, which our commentators generally agree is a loving punishment intended to exhort Christians to repentance and holiness.

8:1-3 *Saul Pursues the Christians*

SOME INVOLVED IN STEPHEN'S STONING ACTED FROM IGNORANT ZEAL. DESIDERIUS ERASMUS: There were in that crowd some who were not yet persuaded that Jesus was the Son of God. This error to some extent alleviated the dreadful character of the crime, though it did not excuse them from homicide, since, blinded by their own desires, they preferred to punish rather than to learn the truth. Nevertheless, no one was less able to be excused than the priests, scribes and Pharisees. Again, there were some who erred from honest motives, believing they were offering a sacrifice pleasing to God because they were executing those who were trying to overturn the Law handed down by God. But evangelical charity excuses even things that cannot be excused. Among those who erred without malice was Saul of Tarsus, a young man zealous for the Mosaic law, who, from being a wolf became a sheep, and from being a ruthlessly fierce persecutor became a brilliantly keen advocate of evangelical liberty. He himself indeed at that time threw no stones at Stephen, but he assented to those who had condemned and stoned him, and his intention in protecting their clothes was to be one with those who were throwing stones. PARAPHRASE OF ACTS 8:1-3.[3]

THE TEMPLE RULERS BECAME BOLDER AFTER STEPHEN'S EXECUTION. JOHANN SPANGENBERG: Because God did not deliver Stephen out of the hands of the Jews as he delivered the apostles out of prison, [the temple rulers] gained courage and began to rage and scream against the new Christians: "Where is your God? Your Help and Savior in whom [Stephen] placed his confidence and trust? Why didn't he stand by him? Why didn't he protect him? It is finished with this Jesus of Nazareth. His help has an end." They did this in the same way that the high priests and scribes

---

[1]Ronald K. Rittgers, *The Reformation of Suffering: Pastoral Theology and Lay Piety in Late Medieval and Early Modern Germany* (Oxford: Oxford University Press, 2012), 257-63, esp. 260-61.
[2]Cf. Carter Lindberg, "Sanctification, Works and Social Justice," in *T & T Clark Companion to Reformation Theology*, ed. David M. Whitford (London: T & T Clark, 2012), 107.

[3]CWE 50:56 (LB 7:697).

mocked and taunted Christ on the cross. BRIEF EXEGESIS OF ACTS 8:1.[4]

THE WINDS OF PERSECUTION CARRIED THE GOSPEL ABROAD. DESIDERIUS ERASMUS: Jewish malice could do nothing against the apostles, nor for that matter could it do anything against the others except by the permission of the Lord Jesus. The Lord Jesus had permitted this so that under pressure of persecution they would flee from city to city. This was not so much a matter of terror on the part of the disciples as of divine dispensation, that as the seed was broadly spread, an abundant harvest of evangelical confession would quickly appear. PARAPHRASE OF ACTS 8:1.[5]

BELIEVERS ARE JUST IN FLEEING FAITHFULLY. JUSTUS JONAS: It is permitted to flee death and persecution when enemies seek nothing other than death, if I am able to do so without offense to the gospel, if I have a sound conscience and it is possible to do without sacrificing the teaching office and the church. Thus Paul, in a passage below, could be lowered down in a basket. Death should not be openly sought after, but when God sends it, it must be endured with joy and faith. ANNOTATIONS ON ACTS 8:1.[6]

SHOULD BELIEVERS REMAIN OR TAKE FLIGHT? JOHN CALVIN: He does not include the apostles in this number, not because they were beyond common danger but because it is the duty of the good pastor to intercept raiding wolves for the safety of the flock.... To sum up, Luke mentions it as a praiseworthy thing that they did not follow the others into voluntary exile in order to avoid persecution. But yet he does not condemn the flight of those who did not have the same responsibility. For the apostles were reflecting on what was peculiar to their calling, that is, to stick to their post when wolves were attacking the sheepfold. Tertullian and those like him were far too severe in making no exception to their denial of the right to flee from

fear of persecution. Augustine is better, in permitting flight so long as churches are not surrendered to their enemies because of the desertion of their pastors.[7] That is certainly a very good compromise, because he is neither being too indulgent to the timidity of the flesh nor rashly rushing to their death those who have a chance of saving their lives. COMMENTARY ON ACTS 8:1.[8]

REJOICE FOR THE MARTYR, MOURN FOR THE MURDERER. DESIDERIUS ERASMUS: Among Christians the death of those who perish for the sake of the glory of Christ is worthy of applause and triumphal celebration. If there are some tears there, they are not shed for the one who has died, but either for the murderers who invoke hell upon themselves, or for the flock deprived of its needed shepherd. PARAPHRASE OF ACTS 8:2.[9]

THE TOMB IS THE WAITING CHAMBER OF RESURRECTION. JOHN CALVIN: For they could not truly live to Christ if they were not prepared to be included in the fellowship of death along with Stephen. Therefore their zeal in burying the martyr was practice for them in the invincible steadfastness that comes from openly professing their faith. So they were not busy with something that was useless, in order to provoke their opponents with unconsidered zeal. Nevertheless, there is little doubt that the general reason, which ought to be valid among the godly always and everywhere, also carried weight with them. For the rite of burial looks to the resurrection hope, because God ordained it for this purpose from the beginning of the world. Accordingly it was always regarded as a monstrous barbarity to leave bodies unburied deliberately. Unenlightened people did not know why they should consider the rite of burial to be such a sacred thing, but to us the purpose is certainly not unknown: that those still living may know that bodies are committed to the earth as to a prison,

---

[4]Spangenberg, *Der Apostel Geschichte*, 68r*.
[5]CWE 50:57 (LB 7:697-98).
[6]Jonas, *Annotationes in Acta*, E5r; alluding to Acts 9:25.

[7]Tertullian, *De fuga in persecutiones*, ANF 4:116-25, and see Augustine to Honoratus, Letter 228, NPNF 1:577-81.
[8]CNTC 6:225, 226* (CO 48:173, 174).
[9]CWE 50:57 (LB 7:698).

until they are raised up from it. It is evident from that, that this ceremony is of value to the living rather than to the dead. And yet it is also part of our human nature to bestow due honor on the bodies, to which we know blessed immortality has been promised. COMMENTARY ON ACTS 8:2.[10]

8:4-8 Philip Preaches in Samaria

THE FURTHER THE GOSPEL GOES, THE GREATER ITS HARVEST. DESIDERIUS ERASMUS: The further the gospel seed moves away from Jerusalem and the closer it comes to the Gentiles, the richer is its harvest. See how much the savagery of the Jews has helped. From being a deacon Philip has become an apostle, and instead of a few Jerusalemites, whole cities embrace the teaching of the gospel. PARAPHRASE OF ACTS 8:4-8.[11]

MAY WE BE COUNTED AMONG SUCH BRAVE DISCIPLES. JOHN CALVIN: The voice of the gospel, which was being heard only in one place, is now resounding everywhere. At the same time we are warned by this example that we must not give in to persecutions but that we must rather discipline ourselves to bravery. For when the faithful flee from Jerusalem they are not broken by exile and the distresses of the moment, or by any fear of the future, so that they degenerate into cowardice or inactivity, but they are just as keen to proclaim Christ as if they had never gone through any trouble. Yes, and Luke seems to indicate that they led a wandering life, with frequent changes of lodgings. Therefore if we wish to be counted as brothers of these people, let us eagerly urge ourselves on, so that no bitterness of the cross or fear may discourage us from continuing to make open confession of our faith, and so that we may never grow weary of promoting the teaching of Christ. For it is absurd that exile and flights, which are the first things to experience in martyrdom, should make us dumb and lifeless. COMMENTARY ON ACTS 8:4.[12]

PHILIP'S NET CATCHES GOOD AND BAD FISH. JOHANN SPANGENBERG: This Philip—one of the seven chosen [deacons]—enters into Samaria and casts out the net of the gospel and catches, as Christ says, both good and bad fish. For not only did Samaritans believe and let themselves be baptized, but also Simon [Magus] believed and allowed himself to be baptized. He followed Philip, and as he witnessed his great deeds and signs, he was amazed. BRIEF EXEGESIS OF ACTS 8:4-8.[13]

GREAT JOY IN SAMARIA. THE ENGLISH ANNOTATIONS: This was the effect of faith, the hope of reconciliation to God and the future salvation—the effect of God's kingdom. Such disparate effects the one and the same preached word produces: devils and the wicked are vexed and cut to the heart with it, but the elect who have interest in Christ are glad and rejoice in it. In this one example observe what confidence concerning religion and sanctity may be reposed either in places or human councils and societies. The gospel was blasted, blasphemed and persecuted at Jerusalem, the once holy city, by the scribes, Pharisees, high priests, elders and their great councils, and the same is joyfully received in the despised Samaria. ANNOTATIONS ON ACTS 8:8.[14]

8:9-13 Simon the Magician Believes

HYPOCRITES INSIDE THE CHURCH ARE WORSE THAN ENEMIES OUTSIDE. DESIDERIUS ERASMUS: Now a more noxious bane comes to the church from those who join it with insincere hearts than from those who openly persecute the church. An example of this has been given to us that we might the more beware of wolves in sheep's clothing. PARAPHRASE OF ACTS 8:9.[15]

MANY PURSUE RELIGION FOR PROFIT AND GAIN. RUDOLF GWALTHER: After the common manner of the Scriptures, [Luke] does not only

---

[10]CNTC 6:227* (CO 48:175).
[11]CWE 50:58 (LB 7:698).
[12]CNTC 6:228-29* (CO 48:176).

[13]Spangenberg, Der Apostel Geschichte, 70r-v; alluding to Mt 13:47-50.
[14]Downame, ed., Annotations, HHH4r*; alluding to Rom 14:17; Acts 7:54.
[15]CWE 50:58 (LB 7:698).

describe the prosperous success of the primitive church and the notable examples of the faithful, but also he shows the manners of the false Christians and hypocrites and the vices that they brought with them into the church. So before this, he declared the history of Ananias [and Sapphira], and the grudge and quarrel that began in the church. And likewise now he declares the horrible example of Simon, who contaminated the profession of faith with sacrilegious ambition and covetousness. The use of these examples is that we are able to understand that there will always be hypocrites in the church, who will be authors of grievous offenses. Still believers must not be offended by this, thinking that every offender must be condemned or else they must forsake the church, as we have seen the Anabaptists do. HOMILY 59, ACTS 8:18-24.[16]

WHOM DOES SIMON REPRESENT? JOHANN SPANGENBERG: Simon the Magician is a figure for those who treat God's work with trickery and false motives. He has left many [heirs] behind, namely, those folks who almost pride themselves as evangelical, not because they put much importance in the gospel but rather because they receive their pleasure and earnings from it. . . . If these people do not lead a different and better life than still exists in the papacy and turn themselves back to God and repent, then certainly what happens to them will be no different from what Simon the Magician experienced. BRIEF EXEGESIS OF ACTS 8:9.[17]

"SIMONS" ARE UBIQUITOUS. OTTO BRUNFELS: They are Simons who with their astrological nonsense bewitch the simple, ignorantly priding themselves as those who possess the secrets of God. For this reason they also try to reveal mysteries, to scrutinize treasures, to make claims through trickery, and so on. . . . This also is the foundation of the papist religion, which is obeyed for no other

reason than that it has been in power for so long. For this reason they also shout: "Tradition, tradition, tradition! The fathers, the fathers, the fathers!" ANNOTATIONS ON ACTS 8:9.[18]

THE SIN OF SIMONY. CARDINAL CAJETAN: The reason given why the vice of simony is named from this Simon is that he subjected the free gift of God alone to buying and selling. Under this name, then, comes not only the consecrations which depend on God alone but also the care of souls by divine gift. For this gift [the care of souls] is from God alone and surpasses all consecrations. All consecrations are ordered toward the salvation of souls; they are on account of the salvation of souls and not the reverse. So the office of the care of souls is the chief and most spiritual gift of God. Because of these things, to buy and sell that office is the very nature of simony, and not because it is prohibited by the church. Wherefore, if any consecrated bishop of the church should buy the papacy, without doubt he would not buy [anything] except the care of souls, because that bishop was already consecrated. The purchase of this office would designate him as a simoniac. Likewise, if any cardinal of the holy Roman church should then buy the papacy, he would buy a spiritual office. For a cardinal of the Roman church is received into the responsibility of that anxiety which no doubt is the spiritual care of the universal church. Accordingly its very nature is the entirety [of this] care, and part of this care then is the office of the care of the universal church (which office belongs entirely to the highest pontifex), it is known to be a spiritual office. By this, its resposibilities which the cardinals receive ought to be understood to be spiritual. Also, the type of office has a regard for the choosing of a spiritual shepherd. Therefore, when cardinals are chosen for the choosing of the highest shepherd, their office is known to be spiritual in every way.

. . . I should have spoken these things plainly, lest anyone be deceived by hearing that you are permit-

---

[16]Gwalther, *Homelyes or Sermons upon the Actes*, 369-70* (*In Acta Apostolorum*, 114r-v).

[17]Spangenberg, *Der Apostel Geschichte*, 72v-73r.

[18]Brunfels, *Annotationes*, 214r.

ted to sell these offices, so that he may know how to distinguish and understand the one who asserts that this office is not spiritual. Buying or selling the spiritual office of the care of souls (whether in whole or in part) is simony by its very nature. For by it the gift of God, which truly God alone communicates to men, is sold, with the result that that man shares in what belongs to God alone, namely, [the giving of] the office of the care of souls. COMMENTARY ON ACTS 8:9-13.[19]

AUTHENTIC BAPTISM IS SPIRITUAL. DIRK PHILIPS: We believe and confess that there is a Christian baptism which must take place internally and externally, internally with the Holy Spirit and with fire, but externally with water in the name of the Father and the Son and the Holy Spirit. The baptism of the Spirit is administereed by Jesus Christ himself to the penitent and beliving. . . . The external baptism with water is a witness to spiritual baptism, a proof of true sorrow and a sign of faith in Jesus Christ. [This baptism] is given on the command of the almighty Father, his Son Jesus Christ and his Holy Spirit, and in the name of the same only God is administered by a messenger and servant of the Lord in the office and power of the Spirit. [It is administered] to those who have sorrow for their sins, seek improvement [in their life], believe the gospel, confess their faith and desire to be baptized upon it. These dedicate themselves willingly to God as a service of righteousness, yes, to servanthood of God in fellowship with Jesus Christ and all the saints. THE ENCHIRIDION: THE BAPTISM OF OUR LORD JESUS CHRIST.[20]

THROUGH BAPTISM WE ARE CLEANSED AND PLACED IN CHRIST. PHILIPP MELANCHTHON: What does it mean, "I baptize you in the name of the Father, Son and Holy Spirit"? Answer: I, the minister says, baptize you and call out for you to

the true God, who is the eternal Father of our Lord Jesus Christ and his eternal Son and eternal Holy Spirit. I testify that this true God accepts you and forgives you your sins for the sake of his Son Jesus Christ, and he washes you with this baptism, meaning that your sins are blotted out with his blood and that he will sanctify you with his Holy Spirit to new and eternal righteousness and blessedness.

All of this is graciously promised to you in baptism. And so this promise states that you should confess, call on and praise this true God and separate yourself from all idolatry. This understanding of baptism we should often extend and explain to people, so that they may constantly take consolation from their baptism. EXAMINATION OF CANDIDATES FOR ORDINATION (1552).[21]

WE DO NOT ADVOCATE REBAPTISM BUT REAL BAPTISM. DIRK PHILIPS: We have introduced no rebaptizing but we show and practice with it the true and only Christian baptism, which is valid before God, which takes place in spirit and in truth, which is practiced according to Scripture and is received on the confession of faith and whose praise is not from people but from God.

Whenever . . . Scripture will be fulfilled and the righteous judgment of God shall come on the world, then the world shall comprehend that we are no rebaptizers and that we have not been rightly baptized more than once on the confession of our own faith, according to the institution of our Lord Jesus Christ and according to the example of the teaching which we have received from the apostles. THE ENCHIRIDION: AN APOLOGY OR REPLY.[22]

NO REBAPTISM INDEED! PHILIPP MELANCHTHON: We should baptize little infants. For this is quite sure, that the promise of grace, the Holy Spirit and salvation also belongs to dear infants. As the Lord says, "To such belongs the kingdom

---

[19]Cajetan, *In Acta Apostolorum*, 221r.
[20]CRR 6:72 (BRN 10:68-70); alluding to Acts 2:38, 41; Mt 28:19; Mk 16:15-16; 11:30; Acts 8:12; 16:33.
[21]MWA 6:201.
[22]CRR 6:176-177* (BRN 10:183-84); alluding to Mt 28:19; Mk 16:16.

of heaven." Again, "It is not the Father's will that even one of these infants should be lost." Now it is certain that this is spoken only concerning these infants who are part of the body of the church and who are brought to the Lord Christ. Outside the church there is no salvation. From this it follows that we should baptize infants and bring them to the Lord Christ and make them members of the church. This solace of infant baptism, people should mark well, so that they know, and thank God, that their baptized infants are members of the true church and are under God's grace and protection.

This, however, is what the devilish rebaptizers scream: "Infants understand absolutely nothing and have no faith. Therefore their baptism is a void, useless ceremony." Against this you should hold firmly these words of the Lord Christ, "Let the infants come to me, for to such belongs the kingdom of heaven." It is indeed very true that no one is an heir of the kingdom of heaven except through the Lord Christ and through the Holy Spirit. And the kingdom of heaven in this passage means the forgiveness of sins, righteousness, the Holy Spirit and the inheritance of eternal salvation. So it is certain that the Lord Christ grants to infants in baptism the Holy Spirit, who works in them according to their measure. EXAMINATION OF CANDIDATES FOR ORDINATION (1552).[23]

A PERSON'S HEART IS FOR GOD ALONE TO DISCERN. OTTO BRUNFELS: But in what sense did Simon really believe, since his intention was corrupt (as follows in a few verses)? I reply: No one can ever be excluded from the church and from baptism who promises to be a believer—even if he seems to be a wicked person. Instead he must be commended to God. For even if someone deceives himself, he can never deceive God. . . . When such people join themselves to us, they must not be despised, but instructed. If they are pretenders, this will be made clear. ANNOTATIONS ON ACTS 8:13.[24]

8:14-25 Simon the Magician Rebuked

LAYING ON OF HANDS IS FOR CONFIRMATION. PETER WALPOT: The laying on of hands is rather a sign of confirmation or a further commendation in the congregation. Or, if a baptized person in the congregation sins—so that he is separated from the congregation—and he repents, then through the laying on of hands he is confirmed and accepted back into the congregation. Therefore, infant baptism is not to be derived out of Christ's laying his hands on infants; rather, Christ here only displays his friendliness and affection for the infants, as also his holding and kissing them shows. THE GREAT ARTICLE BOOK: ON BAPTISM.[25]

THE NATURE OF SIMON'S SINS. RUDOLF GWALTHER: It was declared before how Simon believed, and that he wondered about the strange miracles and was baptized with others. But he was one of the people who will not forsake the desires of the flesh. . . . And these people for a while cloak the corruption of their mind, but they cannot hide it forever. And so Simon betrays himself and sins in two ways.

First, by being puffed up with ambition, he desires to be like the apostles in dignity of ministry and so claims to himself godly honor, and he covets to have such power given to him, that he might after his own will give the Holy Spirit to others. Now greed, [second,] is a companion with ambition. Being blinded [by greed], he makes religion a matter of gain and lucre and thinks he may make merchandise of the gifts of the Holy Spirit. For therefore he would buy this power with money, with the intent afterward to make a greater gain of the same. [Such was] an unholy consideration of God and his gifts, and farthest off from the meaning of Christ, who when he endowed the apostles with these gifts, said, freely you have received, give freely. This example of Simon teaches us that pride is the cause of all evil, and, as the wise man says, the beginning of sin. HOMILY 59, ACTS 8:18-24.[26]

---

[23]MWA 6:201-2; quoting Mt 19:14; 18:14; alluding to Jn 3:5, 26.
[24]Brunfels, *Annotationes*, 214r-v.

[25]QGT 12:79-80; alluding to Mt 19:14; Mk 10:16.
[26]Gwalther, *Homelyes or Sermons upon the Actes*, 370* (*In Acta*

THOSE WHO WORSHIP GREED ARE SURE TO BE CONDEMNED. OTTO BRUNFELS: So, we have said that they ought to be condemned, who equate the gifts of God with money, whose god and highest good is their belly, honor and greed. Indeed bishops must rebuke those who are like this and excommunicate them from the church—unless they themselves are diseased by the same vice. The gifts of God are not comparable to money. Otherwise, through power of these gifts they would be the strongest who have the most influence through their wealth. Nor can the gifts of God be compared with gold, silver or any other precious item. And what good are riches for a fool, when he cannot buy wisdom? ANNOTATIONS ON ACTS 8:20-23.[27]

SIMON AND HIS MONEY ARE CONDEMNED. RUDOLF GWALTHER: Moreover, it is worthy to note how Peter by a grave sentence condemns not only Simon but also Simon's money. Therefore whatever serves the wicked against the glory of God is accursed as well as they are. . . . What need do we have to speak of the goods and revenues of monasteries, when a great part (as appears) was gathered together by simoniacal sleights of such persons used to sell all things in religion. For it is as clear as day that these goods are so unhappy that commonly they are a stumbling stone to them whom the gospel has shined on while they are more earnestly busied in getting them into their hands, than in setting forth Christ's glory. So unhappy and unprosperous is this mischievous simony. HOMILY 59, ACTS 8:18-24.[28]

"THE GALL OF BITTERNESS." JUSTUS JONAS: Peter alludes to the words of Moses, "Lest there be among you a root sprouting forth poison and bitterness." . . . You are willing to provoke the wrath of God toward you, asking him to inflict on you the bitterness of conscience. Indeed, as you struggle, so to speak, with snares and knots, you will bind

yourself, so that perversion will seize you. Or because of that intolerable burden you may bind to yourself, your conscience will burn and destroy. ANNOTATIONS ON ACTS 8:23.[29]

THE STATE OF THOSE EXCOMMUNICATED. THE ARTICLES OF RELIGION: That person who by open denuciation of the church is rightly cut off from the unity of the church and excommunicated ought to be considered by the whole multitude of the faithful as a heathen and publican, until he is openly reconciled through penance and received into the church by a judge who has such authority. ARTICLE 33.[30]

CHRIST SHARES NOTHING WITH BELIAL. THE SCHLEITHEIM ARTICLES: Since all who have not entered into the obedience of faith and have not united themselves with God so that they will to do his will are a great abomination before God, therefore nothing else can or really will grow or spring forth from them than abominable things. Now there is nothing else in the world and all creation than good or evil, believing and unbelieving, darkness and light, the world and those who have come out of the world, God's temples and idols, Christ and Belial, and none will have part with the other.

To us, then, the commandment of the Lord is also obvious, whereby he orders us to be and to become separated from the evil one, and thus he will be our God and we shall be his sons and daughters (2 Cor 6:17). Further, he admonishes us therefore to go out from Babylon and from the earthly Egypt, that we may not be partakers in their torment and suffering, which the Lord will bring on them.

From all this we should learn that everything which has not been united with our God in Christ is nothing but an abomination which we should shun. By this are meant all . . . things of the kind which the world regards highly, and yet which are carnal or flatly counter to the command of God, after the pattern of all the iniquity which is in the world. From all this we shall be separated and have no part with such,

---

Apostolorum, 114v); alluding to Mt 10:8; Sir 10:13.
[27]Brunfels, Annotationes, 214v.
[28]Gwalther, Homelyes or Sermons upon the Actes, 372* (In Acta Apostolorum, 115r).

[29]Jonas, Annotationes in Acta, E6r; quoting Deut 29:18.
[30]Creeds, 3:508*.

for they are nothing but abominations, which cause us to be hated before our Christ Jesus, who has freed us from the servitude of the flesh and fitted us for the service of God and the Spirit whom he has given us. ARTICLE 4, SEPARATION.[31]

EXCOMMUNICATE THE AVARICIOUS. MARTIN LUTHER: Avarice cares nothing about heaven but takes gold [as its god]—[gold] must hold the honor and name of our Lord God. The [true] honor given to the Lord is that my heart clings to him; whoever trusts [him] honors God and calls on [him] aright, so that we say, "Merciful God, you are my God in poverty, wealth, death, need; in poverty and misery I place my confidence in you." The honor that belongs to God—to rely entirely on God to satisfy in times of need—this the avaricious person gives to the impotent *gulden*, because he trusts that so long as he has a sack full of *gulden*, all will be well. And when the sack is not entirely full, he supposes, "If [only] I had enough money"—then he would be happy.

Thus, in the presence of God, the church of Christ and of the angels, every greedy person is called an idolater, who robs honor from God and gives it to money. In so doing, he is insolent and merry, but that is absolutely nothing at all, because his god is nothing at all. But is this not a disgraceful title? They are baptized and supposed to be Christians, and yet are openly avaricious. If I knew of someone like this in particular, he should not come to me for the Sacrament, as they [are accustomed to] do. When death came, I would not give him the Sacrament, but say, "Let your own god help you, who is mighty and strong; call on [your] land full of grain! If you die, I will give you to the ravens; let your sack full of *gulden* come to your aid! I deny you the grace of God." And if we do not do so—if we are aware but instead keep silent and do not excommunicate him—then I become a participant in a sin that I myself did not commit.

I should not be avaricious myself but should contend in the Spirit, and I should not conspire with your avarice and thus go to hell on your account. You should not come to the Sacrament, and prayer will be of no avail to you. THE FOURTEENTH SUNDAY AFTER TRINITY (1545).[32]

EXCOMMUNICATION IS FOR THE CHURCH, THE SWORD IS FOR THE WORLD. PETER WALPOT: This power [of the keys] Christ gave to his apostles and his congregation, but the power of the sword he never commended to any apostle or disciple or anyone in his congregation. You will search yourself to death if you think you can find it in his covenant! Now, the ban, as used in the church of Christ, and the sword, as used in the world, are so completely different as evening and morning, they are such incompatible things as death and life. For that reason they may not be mixed together.

The power of the keys, the ban of Christians, through separation purges from the congregation what is evil. The sword of the world purges from the very face of the earth. The Christians' punishment is loving, yes, a brotherly punishment; the sword's punishment is merciless and filled with wrath. After the Christians' ban we can seek and perform repentance again; after the sword or worldly judgment repentance and reformation are eternally abbreviated. The ministers of the keys are vessels of lovingkindness; the ministers of the worldly sword are vessels of wrath. The power of the keys is wielded and held for the benefit of the Christian community, banning greed and personal property. The power of the sword is held for the benefit of greed and personal property, making individual property and individual people. Thus, the power of the sword in past ages under many different names is called "the worldly authority." That is the reason why this office cannot be joined with the unblemished church. For both follow different paths that go opposite ways and never meet. THE GREAT ARTICLE BOOK: ON THE SWORD.[33]

THE PROPER USE OF EXCOMMUNICATION. THE BOHEMIAN CONFESSION OF 1535: [The Scrip-

---

[31]CRR 1:38*.

[32]LW 58:290-91* (WA 51:55).
[33]QGT 12:253.

tures] teach that those who are manifestly impious, impenitent and obstinate, that is, those who will not hear the admonition of the church, should be corrected by the censure and punishment which is generally called anathema or excommunication. And this should be administered without partiality to all whose impiety is publicly known and who, being addicted to the grossest sins, still persist in them even though they have often been admonished about this.

And these conspicuous and open sinners who refuse to repent, of whatever status or condition, ecclesiastical or secular, should be excluded from the fellowship of the church, not by human force but by the word and interdiction of the Lord who ordered this to be done. Matthew 18[:15-17]: "If a member of the church sins against you, go and point out the fault when the two of you are alone. If this member will not hear you, then take with you one or two others; and if this person still will not hear, then tell the church; and if this person will not hear even the church, then such a person is to be to you as a Gentile and a tax-collector." . . .

In addition to this they teach that there have always been, and will be to the Last Day, hypocrites and impious persons in the church who do evil in secret and cannot easily be accused or excommunicated. Concerning these the Lord says that in the Last Day "the angels will separate them out of the midst of the just and send them into a furnace of fire, where there will be weeping and gnashing of teeth" (Mt 13:41-42). Article 8, The Holy Catholic Church.[34]

There Is Still Hope for the Excommunicated. John Calvin: When he curses a sacrilegious person like this, he is not looking so much to the person as to what he has done. For we ought to be incensed against people's offenses in such a way that we reach after the people themselves with mercy. The sentences of God are like that, for they appoint to destruction adulterers, thieves, drunkards and rogues. Indeed, in so far as they are people,

they do not cut off hope of salvation, but they are made to apply only to their present state, and they declare what kind of end awaits them if they stubbornly persist. Commentary on Acts 8:20.[35]

"Pray to the Lord for Me." The English Annotations: At least for fear of God's judgment, he commends himself to the prayers of the church. Whether he truly converted or not, since the Scripture is silent, we cannot determine. Annotations on Acts 8:24.[36]

Simon Likely Repented After Being Rebuked. John Calvin: We gather from this that he did not so much take Peter's threat to heart, as that he came to realize that his salvation was being sought. And even though Peter was the only one who had spoken, he attributed the speech to them all without distinction, because of their general consent. Now, the question is raised, what are we to suppose happened to Simon? Scripture takes us no further than conjecture. He yields to reproof, is touched by a sense of sin, fears the judgment of God, and then turns to the mercy of God and commends himself to the prayers of the church. Since these are certainly not the minimum signs of repentance, we are therefore entitled to conjecture that he did repent. And yet the fathers unanimously record that later on he was a serious adversary to Peter and argued with him for three days at Rome. . . . Accordingly the safest course is to have nothing to do with uncertain opinions imposed on us and simply to embrace what is recorded in Scripture. What we read about Simon elsewhere can rightly be regarded with suspicion for many reasons. Commentary on Acts 8:24.[37]

---

[35]CNTC 6:239* (CO 48:185); alluding to1 Cor 6:9-10; Eph 5:5. For a complete treatment of Calvin's views on excommunication see *Institutes* 4.12.1-10 (LCC 21:1229-38); see also Scott M. Manetsch, *Calvin's Company of Pastors: Pastoral Care and the Emerging Reformed Church, 1536–1609* (Oxford: Oxford University Press, 2012), 182-220. For Justin Martyr and Irenaeus's speculation on Simon, see ANF 1:171-72, 347-48.
[36]Downame, ed., *Annotations*, HHH4v*.
[37]CNTC 6:242* (CO 48:187-88).

[34]Boh 1535, 17-18*.

8:26-40 PHILIP AND THE ETHIOPIAN EUNUCH

[26]Now an angel of the Lord said to Philip, "Rise and go toward the south[a] to the road that goes down from Jerusalem to Gaza." This is a desert place. [27]And he rose and went. And there was an Ethiopian, a eunuch, a court official of Candace, queen of the Ethiopians, who was in charge of all her treasure. He had come to Jerusalem to worship [28]and was returning, seated in his chariot, and he was reading the prophet Isaiah. [29]And the Spirit said to Philip, "Go over and join this chariot." [30]So Philip ran to him and heard him reading Isaiah the prophet and asked, "Do you understand what you are reading?" [31]And he said, "How can I, unless someone guides me?" And he invited Philip to come up and sit with him. [32]Now the passage of the Scripture that he was reading was this:

"Like a sheep he was led to the slaughter
and like a lamb before its shearer is silent,
so he opens not his mouth.

[33]In his humiliation justice was denied him.

Who can describe his generation?
For his life is taken away from the earth."

[34]And the eunuch said to Philip, "About whom, I ask you, does the prophet say this, about himself or about someone else?" [35]Then Philip opened his mouth, and beginning with this Scripture he told him the good news about Jesus. [36]And as they were going along the road they came to some water, and the eunuch said, "See, here is water! What prevents me from being baptized?"[b] [[37]And Philip said, "If you believe with all your heart, you may." And he replied, "I believe that Jesus Christ is the Son of God."] [38]And he commanded the chariot to stop, and they both went down into the water, Philip and the eunuch, and he baptized him. [39]And when they came up out of the water, the Spirit of the Lord carried Philip away, and the eunuch saw him no more, and went on his way rejoicing. [40]But Philip found himself at Azotus, and as he passed through he preached the gospel to all the towns until he came to Caesarea.

a Or go at about noon   b Some manuscripts add all or most of verse 37

OVERVIEW: This unexpected encounter between Philip and the eunuch incites the reformers to wrestle with the mystery that God sovereignly accomplishes the purposes of his Word through human agency. In their comments we can see the complexity of *sola Scriptura*. The eunuch's inquiry into the meaning of the text shows that believers must seek Christ in the Scriptures, although sometimes he is veiled underneath it. Of course, the history of the Old Testament is meaningful, but the eunuch teaches that it is insufficient to stop there, for the Holy Spirit has penned a coextensive—if at times somewhat hidden—narrative. Calvin reminds us that the Lord has granted us numerous aids for understanding the good news, among them commentaries, teachers and ministers of the Word. It is therefore important to have a teachable spirit willing to ask others for help. Without such humility it will be difficult indeed to find the true meaning of the Bible. At the same time, Gwalther cautions that we must place our trust in Christ and not the means by which we receive him.

The most disputed verse in this pericope among Reformation commentators is actually omitted from the majority of modern translations of Acts (the KJV and NKJV excepted): "And Philip said, 'If you believe with all your heart, you may.' And he replied, 'I believe that Jesus Christ is the Son of God'" (Acts 8:37). The manuscript tradition that affirms the inclusion of verse 37 is rather dubious.[1]

---

[1]A single uncial from the sixth century (E) preserves this verse;

Nevertheless all the commentators excerpted here agreed that it is authentic; this leads to some serious interpretive wrangling over the order of baptism. The Radicals triumphantly highlight this pericope as sure evidence that profession of faith must be prior to baptism, claiming that the eunuch himself will one day testify against the idolatrous infant baptizers. The magisterial reformers try to fend off this argument, which they find inconclusive. In this particular case, the magisterial reformers recognize that the Ethiopian eunuch is clearly seeking greater understanding of the sacred text. They also assume that this eunuch receives baptism because he has heard and accepted the good news, but they do not take this story to be a prescription for all future baptisms.

Philip Is an Example of Abrahamic Obedience. Johann Spangenberg:
Here you witness the obedience of Philip. He does not ask, "What am I supposed to do in the wilderness? Should I preach to birds or thieves or murderers?" Instead, according to the example of Abraham, he is obedient to God. Brief Exegesis of Acts 8:26-27.[2]

The Eunuch with a Godly Mind. Desiderius Erasmus:
This eunuch had set out for Jerusalem for the sake of religion; so great was the renown of the temple that even Gentiles came there from afar and brought gifts with them. Hence the anger of the priests against those who

said that someday this temple was to be destroyed. The eunuch had a godly mind, but he was in error, seeking in the temple of the Jews the religion that was about to depart from there to the Gentiles. And so, when he was returning home, sitting in his chariot, he did not give his time to reading stories or to sleep, but out of love of religion was reading the prophet Isaiah. He showed us where Jesus must be sought: he does not hide in temple but in sacred books. Paraphrase of Acts 8:27-28.[3]

The Ethiopian an Example of True Conversion. Rudolf Gwalther:
The Evangelist Luke diligently describes the history of the Ethiopian who converted to Christ, for many reasons, including that it contains an example of true conversion, whereby we are taught how God deals with us when he receives us into the society of salvation. First Luke shows how God is the efficient cause of this conversion who of his mere favor sent Philip, through whose ministry the eunuch of Ethiopia should be converted. The same God, who chose us all before the foundations of the world were laid, without any respect to our good works: so by his grace he ministers to us. . . .

Next, Philip is an instrument of this conversion, and God uses his help here, according to his custom. For while our infirmity is not able to abide the majesty of God, he ordains that we shall be taught and led by the ministry of people, which is a special argument of God's goodness toward us and therefore is everywhere accounted first among the benefits of God. The instrument that Philip uses is the Word of God, not such an indescribable and imaginary word—as some "angelic" and fanatic theologians dream—but the very same word that is contained in the Scriptures. For out of these must come all sermons, and the whole doctrine of salvation is taken, neither must we look for any new kind of doctrine unheard of until this day. Homily 61, Acts 8:32-35.[4]

---

the rest of the Greek witnesses are from the tenth century or later (mss. 36, 323, 453, 945, 1739, 1891). However, this verse is included in several ancient translation traditions. The weightiest voices for including this verse come from Irenaeus and Cyprian. Cottrel Carson argues that this verse is wrongly excluded from modern editions of Acts. He cites a papyrus witness ($\mathfrak{P}^{50}$) as proof of its antiquity. He alleges as well that verse 37 was likely removed under Constantine, making the first Gentile convert Cornelius, a Roman (Acts 10), perhaps legitimizing Christianity in the Empire. His latter point is highly speculative, and is also based on the assumption that the Eunuch's baptism would not have rendered him "converted" to fourth-century Christians. See Cottrel R. Carson, "Acts 8:37—A Textual Reexamination," *Union Seminary Quarterly Review* 51, vols. 1-2 (1997): 57-78. Also see ACCS NT 5:101. Chrysostom seems to exclude 8:37, while Bede comments directly on it.
[2]Spangenberg, *Der Apostel Geschichte*, 73v.

[3]CWE 50:61 (LB 7:700-701).
[4]Gwalther, *Homelyes or Sermons upon the Actes*, 379* (*In Acta Apostolorum*, 117r-v).

This Man Understands the Meaning of Prophecy. DESIDERIUS ERASMUS: Observe the eunuch, willing to be taught.... He was aware that in the nature of prophecy what seemed to be said about this or that person according to the historical sense often referred to another according to the more hidden sense. One who asks questions in this way is willing to be taught! PARAPHRASE OF ACTS 8:32-34.[5]

God Chooses to Disciple Us Through Preachers and Teachers. JOHN CALVIN: Now if any of us is diffident about himself but shows that he is teachable, angels will come down from heaven to teach us, rather than that the Lord allow us to labor in vain. However, following the example of the eunuch, we must make use of all the aids which the Lord sets before us for the understanding of Scripture. Fanatics seek inspirations (ἐνθουσιασμούς) from heaven, and at the same time despise the minister of God, by whose hand they ought to have been ruled. Others, relying on their own penetrating insight, do not deign to hear anybody or to read any commentaries. But God does not wish the aids, which he appoints for us, to be despised, and does not allow contempt of them to go unpunished. And we must keep in mind here that not only is Scripture given to us, but interpreters and teachers are also added to help us. That is why the Lord chose Philip for the eunuch rather than an angel. For what was the purpose of this roundabout process, where God summons Philip by the voice of an angel and does not send the angel himself direct, except that he wished us to become accustomed to hearing people? It is certainly no ordinary recommendation of outward preaching that the voice of God sounds on the lips of people, while the angels keep silence. COMMENTARY ON ACTS 8:31.[6]

Philip Teaches the Mystery of the Second Article of Faith. DESIDERIUS ERASMUS: This was the Son of God through whom God had determined (and through his prophets had promised) to give salvation to all who put their trust in him; for this reason he wanted him to assume a human body and be born, now from Mary, a virgin. Moreover, both nativities are ineffable: the one by which he is always being born from the Father, outside of time, and the one by which he was born of a virgin through the activity of the Holy Spirit without the work of a man—assuming a human nature in such a way that he did not lose his divine nature....

Further, here was that true paschal lamb by whose death the Father had destined to free from the bondage of sins and from eternal death not only the Israelites but all races. On this account he gave him over into the hands of the priests, the scribes, the Pharisees and the leaders of the people, through whom he was led to Pilate, the governor, that he might be crucified by him. Since he was willing to die for our salvation, he made in Pilate's presence no reply that would set him free, but like a sheep offered himself to all their insults and torments; for on that occasion he concealed his majesty and for the sake of humanity cast himself down to the lowest humiliation. The Jews, thinking he was only what he seemed, condemned him and sent him to death.... An innocent man was condemned, a man who will one day return lofty and exalted and will judge the living and the dead.

But God called his Son back to life on the third day. Thereafter for forty days he remained on earth with a body that could be seen and touched, and he repeatedly showed himself to his disciples. Lastly, he was taken away up into heaven while they were looking on. Then on the tenth day after the ascension, he sent the Holy Spirit from heaven, who breathed on the minds and tongues of the apostles so that they might fearlessly preach Jesus of Nazareth, prince of salvation and life, to all the nations of the entire world, a salvation and life not attained through the law of Moses but through faith and baptism. There is not one of these things that has not been denoted by figures in the law of Moses, has not been predicted by the prophets, has not been handed down and promised by Jesus himself. PARAPHRASE OF ACTS 8:35.[7]

---

[5]CWE 50:61-62 (LB 7:701).
[6]CNTC 6:247-48* (CO 48:192).

[7]CWE 50:62* (LB 7:701-2).

TEACH US, O LORD. THE BOOK OF COMMON PRAYER (1549): Almighty God, to know you truly is everlasting life: Grant us perfectly to know your Son Jesus Christ to be the way, the truth and the life, as you have taught Saint Philip and the other apostles; through Jesus Christ our Lord. Amen. THE COLLECT FOR THE FEAST OF SAINTS PHILIP AND JAMES.[8]

THE ETHIOPIAN BELIEVES BEFORE HE IS BAPTIZED. MENNO SIMONS: They baptized all who accepted this gospel by faith and none others, as is shown in many Scriptures' treatment of the Acts of the Apostles. . . .

When Philip was led by the angel of the Lord to the chariot of the eunuch who came from Ethiopia and was reading the gospel of Jesus Christ from Isaiah the prophet, they came to a certain water and the eunuch said, "See, here is water; what hinders me from being baptized?" And Philip said, "If you believe with all your heart, you may be." And he answered and said, "I believe that Jesus Christ is the Son of God." . . .

If all the earth were full of learned speakers and highly renowned doctors and these were exalted as high as heaven by sharp subtlety and human philosophy; yet by the grace of God the word will never be snatched from us, because where there is no faith, no baptism should be administered according to the Word of God. Or else we must first admit that the commandment of Christ Jesus is wrong. Or that the holy apostles have taught erroneously. Or that the holy Philip asked a wrong question here. Or that more was required of the eunuch than of all the rest of people. . . . Philip, the true servant of God who preached and taught with the same spirit [as Peter and Paul with all the pious witnesses of Christ], would not baptize until the illustrious and famous man had sincerely confessed his faith. CHRISTIAN BAPTISM (1539).[9]

THE EXAMPLE OF THE ETHIOPIAN CANNOT BE APPLIED TO CHILDREN. JOHANNES BRENZ:

But why does he want to receive baptism? Is it not enough for him that he believed? He also wants to be sealed and confirmed through the external sign. For Christ said, "Whoever believes and is baptized will be saved." Accordingly baptism is precisely the correct sign through which our faith is confirmed, so that we might be certain that every benefit, which we believe is conferred on us by Christ, is our own and belongs to us. So, baptism is called a bath of purification, rebirth and renewal by the Holy Spirit, since it seals and confirms that we have received purification, rebirth and renewal through the Word of faith.

It should also be diligently observed that Philip did not baptize the treasurer before he indicated how and what he believed. For we should baptize no one who believes anything other than that baptism is a seal and affirmation of those goods which we receive and possess with faith. From this the irrational rebaptizers think their abomination and error is confirmed, asserting that we should definitely not baptize children but instead wait until they reach a reasonable age, so that they know how to give an account of their faith—for they pretend that children are unable to have faith—like this treasurer who was first baptized at a mature age, whose example is supposed to show that not children but only grown-ups should be baptized. . . . It is ridiculous that the rebaptizers think from this example their abomination and error can be pressed out. For examples are not rules and commands that we must do or avoid; instead, the Word of God alone is a certain, unfalsifiable rule in all things. THE ACTS OF THE APOSTLES 8:37.[10]

BAPTISM COMES LAST IN THE ETHIOPIAN'S CONVERSION. BALTHASAR HUBMAIER: The treasurer of Queen Candace of Egypt will say . . . , "Philip instructed me in faith in the chariot. After that I desired water baptism according to the order of Christ. But Philip did not want to baptize me before I had publicly affirmed my faith with my mouth. As soon as I did that and

---

[8]BCP 1549, 70*.
[9]Simons, *Complete Writings*, 275*.

[10]Brenz, *Das Buch der Apostelgeschicht*, AA5r-v; quoting Mk 16:16.

confessed that Jesus is Christ, Son of the living God, only then did Philip command the chariot to stop and baptize me in water." See, if we had no other Scriptures than these, they would be enough to prove that baptism should be given to believers and not to young children—until they also have been instructed in the Word of God and faith, confessing and expressing the same with their mouths. OLD AND NEW TEACHERS ON BELIEVER'S BAPTISM (1526).[11]

ACTS 8:37 IS MISSING IN SOME MANUSCRIPTS.

THEODORE BEZA: I discovered that this whole verse is missing in five codices, and even in the Complutensian edition, as well as in the Syriac and Arabic translation. Although this verse is missing, I think it has been expunged. For it contains a clear summary of the formula of confession which was required from baptized adults, truly used in apostolic times, and it openly declares what it is to be baptized in the name of Christ. ANNOTATIONS ON ACTS 8:37.[12]

BAPTISM FOLLOWS FAITH, BUT THIS DOES NOT TOPPLE INFANT BAPTISM. JOHN CALVIN:

A general rule is to be adopted from the fact that the eunuch is not admitted to baptism without professing his faith, that is, that those who have previously been outsiders should not be received into the church before they have testified that they believe in Christ. For baptism is, so to speak, the appendix of faith and therefore subsequent in order. Second, if it is given without faith, of which it is the seal, it is an impious and extremely gross profanation. But fanatics stupidly and wrongly attack infant baptism on this pretext. Why was faith bound to precede baptism in the case of the eunuch? It is because those who are to be baptized must be engrafted into the church, because Christ distinguishes only the members of the family of the church with this sign. But as it is certain that adults are engrafted by faith, so I say that the chil-

dren of the godly are born children of the church and are numbered among the members of Christ from birth, because God adopts us on the principle that he is also the Father of our children. Therefore even if faith is required in the case of adults, it is wrong to carry this over to children, since the pattern for them is quite different.

Again, certain great men have made wrong use of this evidence when they wish to prove that faith has no confirmation from baptism. For they used to argue in this way: the eunuch is ordered to bring complete faith to baptism; therefore, nothing could be added. But Scripture often takes "the whole heart" to mean "sincere" and "not false." So there is no reason for us to imagine that those who believe "with all their heart" believe completely, since it will be possible for faith that is weak and thin to exist in a person whose mind will yet be sound and free of all pretense. That is the proper way to explain David's statement that he loves the Lord with his whole heart. Philip had indeed baptized the Samaritans before, and yet he knew that they were still far from the goal. Therefore the faith of the whole heart is that which has living roots in the heart and yet desires to increase every day. COMMENTARY ON ACTS 8:37.[13]

PHILIP'S SUDDEN REMOVAL A CONFIRMATION OF GOD'S SENDING. THE ENGLISH ANNOTATIONS: Philip was suddenly taken away and transported by the Spirit of God. This was done so that the eunuch might know that Philip was sent to him by God. ANNOTATIONS ON ACTS 8:39.[14]

CLING TO THE SPIRIT, NOT YOUR PASTOR.

RUDOLF GWALTHER: He did not complain of Philip's so sudden departure, nor did he carefully ask about him, much less did he detest him as if he had been some crafty trickster. From this no evidence of any inconstant or kind mind can be gathered. Now he imbued with faith and

---

[11]CRR 5:262* (QGT 9:238-39).
[12]Beza, *Annotationes Majores*, 1:491.

[13]CNTC 6:252-53* (CO 48:196-97).
[14]Downame, ed., *Annotations*, HHH4v*; alluding to 1 Kings 18:12; Ezek 3:12, 14.

instructed by the Holy Spirit, who according to Christ's promise brought all knowledge and by his testimony confirmed the doctrine of faith which Philip had taught him. Therefore he could easily settle his mind.

By this example we learn that we must not so cling to our ministers that once they are gone, we must despair in matters of faith and religion. Let us acknowledge them as God's coworkers and stewards of the mysteries of God by whom he gives us faith. Again, let us understand that the Spirit of Christ truly fulfills the tasks of a teacher and that Christ will not fail us, although sometimes he takes away those to whom we know we are very attached. For God's Spirit cannot be bound to persons or places but blows wherever he likes. HOMILY 62, ACTS 8:36-40 .[15]

---

[15]Gwalther, *Homelyes or Sermons upon the Actes*, 387* (*In Acta Apostolorum*, 120r); alluding to 1 Cor 3–4; Jn 3:5-8.

9:1-19A SAUL'S CONVERSION

But Saul, still breathing threats and murder against the disciples of the Lord, went to the high priest [2]and asked him for letters to the synagogues at Damascus, so that if he found any belonging to the Way, men or women, he might bring them bound to Jerusalem. [3]Now as he went on his way, he approached Damascus, and suddenly a light from heaven shone around him. [4]And falling to the ground he heard a voice saying to him, "Saul, Saul, why are you persecuting me?" [5]And he said, "Who are you, Lord?" And he said, "I am Jesus, whom you are persecuting. [6]But rise and enter the city, and you will be told what you are to do." [7]The men who were traveling with him stood speechless, hearing the voice but seeing no one. [8]Saul rose from the ground, and although his eyes were opened, he saw nothing. So they led him by the hand and brought him into Damascus. [9]And for three days he was without sight, and neither ate nor drank.

[10]Now there was a disciple at Damascus named Ananias. The Lord said to him in a vision, "Ananias." And he said, "Here I am, Lord." [11]And the Lord said to him, "Rise and go to the street called Straight, and at the house of Judas look for a man of Tarsus named Saul, for behold, he is praying,[12]and he has seen in a vision a man named Ananias come in and lay his hands on him so that he might regain his sight." [13]But Ananias answered, "Lord, I have heard from many about this man, how much evil he has done to your saints at Jerusalem. [14]And here he has authority from the chief priests to bind all who call on your name." [15]But the Lord said to him, "Go, for he is a chosen instrument of mine to carry my name before the Gentiles and kings and the children of Israel. [16]For I will show him how much he must suffer for the sake of my name." [17]So Ananias departed and entered the house. And laying his hands on him he said, "Brother Saul, the Lord Jesus who appeared to you on the road by which you came has sent me so that you may regain your sight and be filled with the Holy Spirit." [18]And immediately something like scales fell from his eyes, and he regained his sight. Then he rose and was baptized; [19]and taking food, he was strengthened.

OVERVIEW: Here with the first of three accounts of Saul's conversion (cf. Acts 22:6-16; 26:12-17), our commentators rejoice in this unexpected twist: Saul the persecutor, a murderer and blasphemer, becomes Paul the apostle, a coheir with Christ! In commenting on this passage, the reformers speculate about the content of Christ's sermon to Paul, and they reflect on the high privilege of the office of the Word. Christ removes the veil from Paul's eyes by blinding him, revealing that the entirety of the Scriptures teaches and points to him. This truth, for the reformers, is the foundation of the preaching office: if pastors are blind to the reality that all of Scripture is about Jesus, how will they be able to share the light of the gospel with anyone else? These exegetes are quick to add that gospel ministry is counterintuitive, even foolish to the

world; preachers do not proclaim their own words, but instead through frail and sinful human lips and lives the Triune God himself proclaims the very Word of God, the Son of God.

9:1-9 Jesus Commissions Paul

TEACH US TO LISTEN, O LORD. THE BOOK OF COMMON PRAYER (1549): God, who has taught all the world through the preaching of your blessed apostle Saint Paul, grant, we beseech you, that we who remember his wonderful conversion may follow and fulfill the holy doctrine that he taught; through Jesus Christ our Lord. Amen. THE COLLECT FOR THE FEAST OF THE CONVERSION OF SAINT PAUL.[1]

---

[1]BCP 1549, 68-69*.

THE RESULT MAKES EVERYTHING ELSE GOOD.
JOHANN AGRICOLA:

Our Lord guides what each should;
He alone will make the end good.
Now Saint Paul first lifted up the wicked,
But then was a holy man against them pitted.
While Judas before he God betrayed
Did miracles as the twelve, amazed,
And yet could not keep hold of grace—
Unbelief and folly instead set his pace.

FIVE HUNDRED COMMON NEW GERMAN PROVERBS.[2]

THE IMPORTANCE OF PAUL'S CONVERSION. RU-
DOLF GWALTHER: Although we ought diligently to consider the conversions and callings of all apostles, yet Paul's conversion of all others deserves to be particularly noted: partly because it contains in it a rare example of God's mercy toward sinners, and partly because Paul labored more than all the apostles, nor is there any other whose writings are more often cited, either of the old writers or new, in matters of faith and religion. It is therefore necessary that we know who he was, how God called him and converted him, that we may have his doctrine with more authority, which is the cause of why Luke writes his history so diligently. HOMILY 65, ACTS 9:10-16.[3]

PAUL IS GUILTY OF MURDER AND BLASPHEMY.
MARTIN LUTHER: Here Luke describes the sins of Saint Paul, two in particular. First, that he was a murderer and has shed blood. Threats, such [as Paul had made], were in and of themselves great sins against the fifth commandment, just as when someone assaults his neighbor and murders him. But it is a much greater sin yet to murder Christians and to spill the blood of saints, as Paul has done here. In truth it is an exceedingly great, terrible and damnable sin. But Paul's second sin is far higher and greater than murder and bloodshed:

namely, that he also abused and blasphemed the name of the Lord. And that was not only for himself and his person. He was not satisfied with his own sins committed against God and his Word; rather, he provoked and compelled other people to take part so that they had to blaspheme and abuse God along with him. And whoever refused to do it and instead held fast to the Word, he recorded in a register, both men and women, and submitting the register to the court, he formally indicted them and urgently pressed to have them sentenced and killed. He breathed [threats] and was utterly furious with rage against the Christians. He said that Christ was a criminal who had taught seditiously against God's ordinance, and accordingly he was rightly and justly sentenced and condemned by the proper authorities to be nailed to the cross. Thus [Paul] with his blasphemous words deterred all kinds of people from believing in the crucified Christ or regarding him as the true Messiah. SERMON ON THE CONVERSION OF SAINT PAUL (1546).[4]

JACOB'S PROPHECY OF BENJAMIN IS FULFILLED
IN PAUL. JOHANN SPANGENBERG: From which tribe of Israel was this Paul? From the tribe of Benjamin, for it stands written, Since Jacob was sick and lay on his deathbed, he called his sons and said, "Gather yourselves together, so that I can proclaim to you what will happen to you in the last days." And then he blessed each one with a special blessing. When he came to Benjamin, he said, "Benjamin is a ravenous wolf, in the morning he will devour the spoils, but in the evening he will divide the spoils." This prophecy is fulfilled in Paul. For just as it is the wolf's manner whenever it enters a sheepfold and is hungry and has time, it does not stop strangling the sheep until each one lies before it dead, so also Saul did this, as Luke writes here. "Paul still growled out threats and murder against the disciples of the Lord." That is, he was exceedingly fierce and vindictive toward Christians, he stormed and railed violently [against them], he rushed here and there in houses, in cities and

---

[2]Agricola, *Die Sprichwörtersammlungen*, 2:246.
[3]Gwalther, *Homelyes or Sermons upon the Actes*, 399* (*In Acta Apostolorum*, 123v).

[4]LW 58:376* (WA 51:140-41).

villages, wrenching Christians out with violence, sparing no one, neither man nor woman, sacrificing them on the chopping block. Yes, because he was experienced in the Law and the Prophets, he knew how to have them condemned easily. "So he went to the high priest and requested letters to the synagogues in Damascus, so that if he found any belonging to the Way, both men and women, he could lead them bound to Jerusalem." Here you see the ravenous wolf and persecutor of Christ's disciples. BRIEF EXEGESIS OF ACTS 9:1.[5]

SAUL TYPIFIES ALL TYRANTS WHO RAGE AGAINST CHRIST. RUDOLF GWALTHER: Paul's mind therefore was inflamed and incensed against the church, a sign that he had given before at the stoning of Stephen and when he caused havoc in the church at Jerusalem. . . . Yet now seeing that his efforts prevail him nothing, but that the church spreads every day further and further, he conceives such a fury and rage in his mind that he can do nothing now but breathe out and dream of cruel threats, bloody slaughters and destructions. For as we said before, such is the nature of tyrants and the enemies of the church, that after they have once tasted the blood of the godly, the more they rage, and like beasts they have cast from them all sense of humanity and are not able to put away that rage of mind that they have conceived, unless they are tamed by the mighty hand of God. Examples of this cruelty can be seen everywhere in history. Contemplating about them serves a purpose for us, to make us understand what to hope for with the tyrants of these days, whom we see now so used to blood that they thirst after it more cruelly than any tigers. HOMILY 63, ACTS 9:1-5.[6]

THOUGH LEARNED, SAUL DID NOT RIGHTLY UNDERSTAND SCRIPTURE. MARTIN LUTHER: Paul was a learned man, thoroughly acquainted

with Scripture—not crass, unlearned and inept like our pope and cardinals, along with those coarse asses, the monks. Nevertheless, he did not possess the [right] understanding of holy Scripture [to know] that one must search for Christ, the true Savior and Messiah, in Moses and the Prophets. He neither thought nor believed that Christ was hidden there. The Scripture and the understanding of Scripture were closed to him; he did not pay attention to what Moses spoke clearly: "The Lord your God will raise up for you a prophet like me from among you and your brothers—him you shall obey." For Moses was not such a blockheaded teacher that he—such a great and eminent prophet—would teach nothing of Christ. No, on the contrary, he taught and said, "You are to wait for another master who will come after me. When he comes and takes up his office, I shall cease. See to it, then, that you diligently listen to him." Thus Moses points to the coming Messiah, Christ Jesus, the Son of God the heavenly Father. SERMON ON THE CONVERSION OF SAINT PAUL (1546).[7]

UNLESS MINISTERS ARE CALLED BY GOD, ALL THEY DO IS VAIN. MENNO SIMONS: All those who are not so sent by God or by an unblamable Christian church after the regulations of Christ and the apostles, . . . those who are not called by the Holy Spirit, by the pure, unfeigned love of God and their brothers and with the true and genuine confession and zeal for the divine Word, but seeking people's favor, praise, money and profit, a soft and easy life: these will never gather fruit in the vineyard of the Lord, no matter how eloquent they may be, how esteemed and equipped. All that they attempt is wasted effort. They will rise too early or go out too late; their harangue is without power; their service is vain, their labor without fruit, yes, it is nothing but sowing by the seashore and reaping the wind. For no one can serve in this high and holy office conformable to God's will, except the one whom the Lord of the vineyard has made

---

[5]Spangenberg, *Der Apostel Geschichte*, 76r-77r; quoting Gen 49:1, 27.
[6]Gwalther, *Homelyes or Sermons upon the Actes*, 390* (*In Acta Apostolorum*, 120v).

[7]LW 58:378-79* (WA 51:143); quoting Deut 18:15.

capable by the Spirit of his grace. FOUNDATION OF CHRISTIAN DOCTRINE (1539).[8]

THE LORD'S MERCIFUL HUMBLING OF THOSE WITH A SINCERE HEART. DESIDERIUS ERASMUS: Saul was undertaking this from a sincere heart; according to the saying of the Lord, he thought he was doing a service pleasing to God. For this reason, God did not allow him to be polluted with the blood of the innocent but called him back at the midpoint of his savage course.... The Lord smites in such a way that he heals, casts down in such a way that he raises up, takes away sight so that he illuminates. PARAPHRASE OF ACTS 9:3.[9]

CHRIST'S SERMON TO PAUL. MARTIN LUTHER: "Listen, Saul, you do not know what you are doing. You do not understand Moses correctly, [and] that is why you do not know me and you persecute me. But listen to me, I will explain Moses to you properly so that you understand him."... Here Jesus Christ the Lord built a beautiful church and school, extending from the earth into heaven. In this church and school, there is none but the greatest and only doctor and teacher, Christ Jesus, the eternal Son of God, who preaches and teaches from heaven, saying, "Rise," and so on. Likewise there is no other disciple and student here except for Paul, who listens to the greatest schoolmaster, Christ. Here our dear Lord, Christ Jesus, calls him to be an apostle and preacher, ordains him and confirms him as a preacher of the Word, to be a witness of Jesus Christ together with the other apostles....

The school and church where this sermon was delivered and heard, as well as accepted and believed, is a small one. But the Master here is great, and he produces a great student, Paul, the only one who heard this and thereafter became our teacher, who still teaches us today. For Christ here is saying, "Did you hear that, Paul? The whole world is wavering in darkness and error and does not know me. But you are to call them and lead them

from darkness into light, from the devil's kingdom into the kingdom of God, from death to life." "Yes, [but] how?" [Paul asks.] "By what means am I to accomplish this?" "through the Word, which you, Paul, have now heard from me in this sermon, namely, that you should preach repentance and the forgiveness of sins in my name." SERMON ON THE CONVERSION OF SAINT PAUL (1546).[10]

IN THE EUCHARIST, OUR FLESH AND BLOOD BECOME CHRIST'S FLESH AND BLOOD THROUGH FAITH. HANS SCHLAFFER AND LEONHARD FRICK: Thus, if we eat the flesh of Christ and drink his blood, then in death we offer our body—that is, the flesh—and shed our blood for the sake of his name, Word and command (in the small matters as well as in the big ones). For once again it is no longer our flesh or body, nor is it our blood, but Christ's. For that reason he said to Paul, "Saul, Saul, why do you persecute me?" It is as though he said, "Why do you kill my flesh and why do you shed my blood?" For to put it simply, eating the flesh of Christ and drinking his blood happens through no other means than faith, which is an act and gift from God, that is in us. We want in every sense to become embodied, participating, conforming—one entity with Christ in his life, suffering and death according to the flesh—becoming members and heirs of the resurrection and glory of his kingdom. I can understand it in no other manner without making all of Scripture false, which is not allowable. KUNSTBUCH: A SIMPLE PRAYER.[11]

LATER SCRIBES HARMONIZED THIS ACCOUNT OF PAUL'S CONVERSION WITH ACTS 26:14. THEODORE BEZA: All of the rest are lacking these words, until "to himself," first in the Syriac and then in the Arabic translation, and completely [missing] in all the old codices which we examined. It seems that these words were added from those which are recorded below at Acts 22:10 and Acts 26:14. In those passages, then, the text reads thus:

---

[8]Simons, *Complete Writings*, 161-62*.
[9]CWE 50:63, 64 (LB 7:702, 703).
[10]LW 58:380-81* (WA 51:144-45).
[11]CRR 12:293-94* (QGT 17:364-65).

ὃν σὺ διώκεις· ἀλλὰ ἀνάστηθι, "whom you persecuted, but go, get up," and so on. Next, it must also be observed that in the same place both translations have "it is hard for you" lying under the fourth verse, not under the fifth verse, as we read in the Greek codices. ANNOTATIONS ON ACTS 9:5.[12]

THE IMPORTANCE OF A PROPER VOCATION TO MINISTRY. RUDOLF GWALTHER: Moreover we are taught how expedient it is that all things be done rightly and duly in the outward ministry of the Word. For unless the ministers be duly called and well assured of their calling, and the hearers well prepared to receive their sayings, there can follow no worthy fruit and purpose of their actions. "For how shall they preach, except they be sent?" With what arguments shall they be emboldened against the threats and enterprises of the wicked, which craftily have usurped and intruded upon the office of teaching? Again, if the hearers do not come prepared to hear the Word of the Lord, then shall they receive that wholesome seed, either into the road, or into the stony places or among the thorns, and there shall be many impediments that shall cause them to bring forth no worthy fruits. Whereas Christ requires honest minds which will hold fast the seed that they have once received, and being armed against all suggestions of Satan, the world and the flesh, bring forth worthy fruits with patience. HOMILY 65, ACTS 9:10-16.[13]

THE CONFUSION OF PAUL'S COMPANIONS. GIOVANNI DIODATI: Now in Acts 22:9, it is said that they saw the light but did not hear the voice. Therefore, we must conclude that they heard Saul's voice but not Christ's—or some other confused sound, or perhaps the sound of the Hebrew words the Lord spoke but not the

meaning, as in Matthew 27:47.[14] ANNOTATION ON ACTS 9:7.[15]

YOU MUST HAVE A FORETASTE OF ETERNAL LIFE BEFORE YOU CAN EMBRACE IT. LEONHARD SCHIEMER: No one may firmly believe in eternal life, and no one die for it, unless they have first tasted it. Christ calls this foretaste the comfort of the Holy Spirit. For those who truly receive his communion and taste it, for them it is no longer possible to taste worldly joy; rather, they despise the world with its lust, love, riches, life and honor. That is the little bottle of which people speak.[16] If you are sincere, you will know it. Whoever drinks from this little bottle or cup of the Lord sells what he has and seeks this treasure. This comfort cannot be given to anyone unless he is first placed in utter comfortlessness, robbed of all comfort in creation, even as light cannot enter us until darkness disappears. KUNSTBUCH: THE TWELVE ARTICLES OF THE CHRISTIAN FAITH.[17]

WHAT HAPPENED TO PAUL IN DAMASCUS DURING THESE THREE DAYS? JOHANN SPANGENBERG: Saul had to become externally blind so that he could be internally enlightened. For during the time he could not see with his external and physical eyes, he saw with his internal and spiritual eyes the Creator of all things. . . . It was then that he obviously learned the gospel. BRIEF EXEGESIS OF ACTS 9:9.[18]

THREE DAYS OF ANXIOUS PRAYER AND FASTING. JOHN CALVIN: "For behold, he is praying." Luke shows that during those three days Paul was intent on prayer, and perhaps this is one of the reasons why he fasted, although it is certain, as we

---

[12]Beza, *Annotationes Majores*, 1:492. All modern English translations—except the KJV and NKJV, which are based on the Majority Text—agree with Beza that σκληρον σοι προς κεντροα λακτιζειν ("it is hard for you to kick against the goads") is not an authentic variant.
[13]Gwalther, *Homelyes or Sermons upon the Actes*, 400*; (*In Acta Apostolorum*, 123v-124r); alluding to Rom 10:14-16; Mt 13:1-9, 18-23.

[14]The bystanders of the crucifixion misunderstood Jesus' Aramaic recitation of Ps 22:1, thinking *Eloi* referred to Elijah, not "my God."
[15]Diodati, *Pious Annotations*, AA4r* (*I Commenti alla Sacra Biblia*, 1100).
[16]Apparently this is Schiemer's pet phrase for God's grace; see CRR 12:206-34 (QGT 17:245-97).
[17]CRR 12:255-56 (QGT 17:330); alluding to Rev 3:20.
[18]Spangenberg, *Der Apostel Geschichte*, 79v; alluding to 2 Cor 12:1-4; Gal 1:11-12.

have already said, that he was suffering hunger for so long, because, so to speak, he had been deprived of sensation, as usually happens to people in an ecstasy. Christ is certainly not speaking about a brief momentary prayer here but rather indicates that Paul was persisting in this kind of exercise until a quiet and thoroughly composed mind might be granted to him. For apart from other causes of terror, that voice could still have been ringing in his ears, "Saul, Saul, why are you persecuting me?" And there is no doubt that the anxious anticipation of a full revelation strangely tormented his mind, and the reason why the Lord kept him waiting for three days was that he might fan his ardor for prayer into stronger flames. COMMENTARY ON ACTS 9:11.[19]

9:10-19a Ananias Sent to Paul

FAITH COMES THROUGH HEARING, NOT HALLUCINATING. JUSTUS JONAS: Although God could directly reveal his Word within the heart and through an internal word [per internum auditum] could kindle faith, and could impart his Spirit, still through human beings he desires to preach the gospel to other human beings, to demonstrate that the church and Christ are one body. Through a special miracle he could impart his Spirit without the external ministers of the Word, as also he is able to produce grain without farmers, but still the usual method of justification, established by God, is first the external Word is heard, and the external voice of the gospel, as Paul says in Romans, "How will they believe what they have not heard?" So, here [the Lord] sends Ananias to Paul; so also below, after a vision he sends Cornelius to Peter. Still Paul does not receive the gospel from Ananias. That is, [it is] truth [certitudinem] because it is the Word of God. Paul receives the knowledge of Christ not from a human being, but through the Spirit and revelation of Jesus Christ. ANNOTATIONS ON ACTS 9:10-12.[20]

ANANIAS'S HIGH AND HUMBLE OFFICE. JOHN CALVIN: With these words Christ appoints Ananias to act for him, as far as the office of teaching is concerned, not because he transfers his own authority to him but because he will be a faithful and sincere minister of the gospel. Therefore this guiding principle must always be preserved, that God alone is heard in Christ, and only Christ himself, but speaking through his ministers. But we must be on our guard against these two errors: that ministers are not proud on the pretext of such a valuable function or that their humble circumstances detract from the heavenly wisdom. COMMENTARY ON ACTS 9:6.[21]

CHRIST CALLS BOTH ANANIAS AND PAUL. RUDOLF GWALTHER: First the Lord calls Ananias, that Paul may take orders by his ministry. And of Ananias Luke speaks only a little but Paul quite a bit; he commends him for his godliness and says he deserved among the Jews the testimony of a good and innocent man. The Lord certifies him by his will, by a vision, and likewise prepares Paul in his prayers, by another vision, worthily to receive Ananias. Here our Savior Christ is well to be marked, who instructs them both by evident visions. For this passage indicates the ardent desire that Christ has for the salvation of all humankind, revealed and proclaimed to all—especially in seeking the lost sheep, as he testifies elsewhere. This brings us consolation intertwined with instruction, that we should work rather to save sinners than to destroy them, and not follow those who, when glorying in their fervent zeal of God's glory, rashly reject and condemn all those whom they see once to have swerved from the way of truth. HOMILY 65, ACTS 9:10-16.[22]

THROUGH CHRIST THE WOLF HAS BEEN MADE A LAMB. JOHANN SPANGENBERG: It is as if he wanted to say, "Dear Ananias, be at peace! Do

---

[19]CNTC 6:264* (CO 48:205-6).
[20]Jonas, Annotationes in Acta, E8v; quoting Rom 10:14.
[21]CNTC 6:262* (CO 48:204).
[22]Gwalther, Homelyes or Sermons upon the Actes, 399-400* (In Acta Apostolorum, 123v).

not fear, do not worry! Do you believe that I want to send you to a wolf or a murderer? No, Ananias. 'Are there not twelve hours in a day?' Do not fear, I will make everything right. It is true that he has been a wolf, but I have made a lamb out of a wolf, a preacher to the Gentiles out of a persecutor of Christians—out of a Pharisee, an apostle and witness who will carry my name before the entire world." BRIEF EXEGESIS OF ACTS 9:15-16.[23]

BY GOD'S CHOICE EVEN OUR VOICE IS HIS.
JUSTUS JONAS: God alone chose the vessel of his Word. We have seen that this is the case with many preachers [concionatores]. But [some preachers] have not proclaimed the name of the Lord, but only works-righteousness and human trifles. Who does this? Those who were not vessels chosen by God. True ministers of the Word know and are certain that it is not they themselves who speak, but the Spirit of the Father. They are nothing more than a vessel or instrument through whom God speaks. "We are engaged as ambassadors of Christ as if God himself appeals to you through us." That is, our voice is not our own, but it is Christ's. Thus what John the Baptist said—he is a voice crying out—can also be applied to [our ministry]. ANNOTATIONS ON ACTS 9:15.[24]

PAUL IS ANOTHER EXAMPLE OF BELIEVER'S BAPTISM. BALTHASAR HUBMAIER: Paul will stand up and testify powerfully against us with his example, teaching and practice of baptism. "See, you know well and cannot deny that the Word of God was first preached to me by Ananias; second, the old scales fell from my eyes; third, I received eyesight in faith; fourth, I arose and let myself be baptized.[25] So has my most dear co-worker in the gospel, Luke, whose praise is great in the church, written to you faithfully how I first preached to Lydia the seller of purple and the jailer, the Corinthians and the twelve men at Ephesus. Then they accepted the Word and believed and not until then were they baptized."

. . . Thus, let us go forth to Christ, first of all with a true heart in perfection of faith; second, purified in our heart of an evil conscience, which is with internal baptism; and third, after that, the body washed with pure water. The outward baptism comes then only, for without the internal baptism it is only hypocrisy. OLD AND NEW TEACHERS ON BELIEVER'S BAPTISM (1526).[26]

THE LITTLE DOCTOR ANANIAS. MARTIN LUTHER: Ananias was not even one finger tall before Paul—he was like a candle before the sun. Still, Paul in this way received light from this little matchstick, from this little doctor Ananias. We should look and listen carefully: He recovers his sight, then, through the minister, acquires an understanding of who Christ is and what baptism is, and he stands up and is a different man. As much blood that he shed, indeed a thousand times more, he [later] made Christians. I say, is this not a miracle, that *this* man preaches? He rouses them much more than they roused him. It is a beautiful legend, which shows to us our Lord God's consoling miracle, so that we thank him that we got Master Paul! SERMON ON SAINT PAUL'S CONVERSION (1534).[27]

---

[23]Spangenberg, *Der Apostel Geschichte*, 81r-v.
[24]Jonas, *Annotationes in Acta*, F1v; alluding to Mt 10:20; quoting 2 Cor 5:20; Mt 3:3 (cf. Mk 1:3; Lk 3:4; Jn 1:23; Is 40:3).
[25]David Steinmetz has noted the vital connection between the Anabaptist theology of baptism and the freedom of the human will. As he puts it: "Since free human decision is essential as preparation for regeneration, and regeneration is essential as a precondition for the reception of baptism, it follows that baptism cannot be administered to infants." Hubmaier was one of the few, in Steinmetz's estimation, who saw this clearly. See David C. Steinmetz, "Luther and Hubmaier on the Freedom of the Human Will," in *Luther in Context*, 2nd ed. (Grand Rapids: Baker Academic, 1995), 59-71, here 70.
[26]CRR 5:262* (QGT 9:239); alluding to Acts 9:1-19; 22:1-21; 16:14-15, 23; 18:5; 19:1-7.
[27]WA 37:269-70.

9:19B-31 SAUL PREACHES IN DAMASCUS AND JERUSALEM

For some days he was with the disciples at Damascus. [20]*And immediately he proclaimed Jesus in the synagogues, saying, "He is the Son of God."* [21]*And all who heard him were amazed and said, "Is not this the man who made havoc in Jerusalem of those who called upon this name? And has he not come here for this purpose, to bring them bound before the chief priests?"* [22]*But Saul increased all the more in strength, and confounded the Jews who lived in Damascus by proving that Jesus was the Christ.*

[23]*When many days had passed, the Jews[a] plotted to kill him,* [24]*but their plot became known to Saul. They were watching the gates day and night in order to kill him,* [25]*but his disciples took him by night and let him down through an opening in the wall,[b] lowering him in a basket.*

[26]*And when he had come to Jerusalem, he at-tempted to join the disciples. And they were all afraid of him, for they did not believe that he was a disciple.* [27]*But Barnabas took him and brought him to the apostles and declared to them how on the road he had seen the Lord, who spoke to him, and how at Damascus he had preached boldly in the name of Jesus.* [28]*So he went in and out among them at Jerusalem, preaching boldly in the name of the Lord.* [29]*And he spoke and disputed against the Hellenists.[c] But they were seeking to kill him.* [30]*And when the brothers learned this, they brought him down to Caesarea and sent him off to Tarsus.*

[31]*So the church throughout all Judea and Galilee and Samaria had peace and was being built up. And walking in the fear of the Lord and in the comfort of the Holy Spirit, it multiplied.*

a The Greek word *Ioudaioi* refers specifically here to Jewish religious leaders, and others under their influence, who opposed the Christian faith in that time
b Greek *through the wall*   c That is, Greek-speaking Jews

OVERVIEW: Despite the persecution against Christians continuing from the previous chapter, the Christian faith is spreading beyond its headquarters in Jerusalem. Since suffering is not to be sought out intentionally, many disciples are choosing exile, escape and migration. In all circumstances, the reformers urge believers to find sufficient consolation in the Spirit. Briefly examining this passage, they focus most intently on the last few verses concerning the respite that the church experienced. They highlight the surprising ways of God's grace: he transforms the greatest enemy of the gospel into its greatest advocate; he uses the harsh winter of persecution to produce abundant fruit, the continued multiplication of the church. Perhaps, Calvin reasons, this is because especially in times of persecution believers are driven to the solace of the gospel by the Spirit, apart from whom nothing can flourish.

SAUL REFUTES TWO ERRORS ABOUT JESUS. THE ENGLISH ANNOTATIONS: Saul declares Jesus to be the Son of God and Savior of the elect. Without a doubt he delivered this with clarity through the largeness of heart that the Holy Spirit gave him, beating down that double error of the Jews who thought (1) that this Jesus the Son of Mary was not Christ and (2) that the Messiah was to be a mere man, a victorious and glorious secular prince. ANNOTATIONS ON ACTS 9:20.[1]

IS IT LAWFUL THAT THE DISCIPLES HELPED SAUL ESCAPE? JOHANN SPANGENBERG: If we are able to rescue an innocent person, then civic law must yield to God's law, which says, "Love your neighbor as yourself." Thus, here the disciples

---

[1]Downame, ed., *Annotations*, JJJ1r*.

demonstrate true brotherly and Christian love to Paul, as Christ teaches. BRIEF EXEGESIS OF ACTS 9:23-25.[2]

PAUL'S THREE YEARS IN ARABIA. THE ENGLISH ANNOTATIONS: Between his conversion and coming again to Jerusalem three years expired. During that time he preached in some regions of Arabia and then returned to Damascus. During this time the unbelieving Jews conspired against him. But he escaped and came to Jerusalem, wanting to unite in external communion with the disciples since he was now included in the faith of Christ. But remembering his former rage against them, they suspected his pretense was a great trial against them. ANNOTATIONS ON ACTS 9:26.[3]

ARE DEEDS OF CHARITY NECESSARY? RUDOLF GWALTHER: Barnabas is to be examined, who because of his generosity relieved the needy of the whole church and therefore was called "the son of encouragement," so now by his testimony he maintains Paul's good name while he is in danger and is not ashamed of him who he knew everybody suspected. This deed of charity is singular and very necessary, because there is scarcely anything among people more common than sinister and wrong suspicion. For when we are blinded with self-love, we flatter ourselves: so we diligently note other people's manners and seek every little occasion to backbite their good name. Therefore it is a great offense when they aggravate the faults of those wrongfully suspected, when they ought to care for and defend their good name and reputation. HOMILY 67, ACTS 9:23-30.[4]

PAUL DISPUTED THE HELLENISTS. THEODORE BEZA: We explained above [cf. Acts 6:1] who these Hellenists are. It is not surprising that Paul, as he was able in Tarsus, disputed with them separately and individually. There in fact [he disputed] more eagerly because when controversy had been stirred up by these same people against Stephen, no one in their ranks was more zealous than this very Paul. The Jews also accused Paul falsely, as Epiphanius says somewhere, saying that because Paul could not marry the daughter of the chief priest, he was offended and therefore embraced Christianity.[5] The murderer of spirits even to this very day continues to contrive many such fables today against the faithful servants of God, whether living or dead. ANNOTATIONS ON ACTS 9:29.[6]

THE COLDER THE WINTER, THE BETTER THE SUMMER. JOHANN SPANGENBERG: From where did such sudden peace come? From God's goodness. This happens for two reasons. First, to show that God can create peace in his congregation whenever he wants without any concern for the raging or looming threats of tyrants. Second, to show that God, soon after profound affliction, is accustomed to comforting us.

Here is an example. "A woman," Christ says, "when she is giving birth has sorrow, because her hour has come, but when she has delivered the child, she no longer thinks of the anguish for the sake of her joy that a person has been born into the world." Consider winter and summer. If someone had never before seen winter and suddenly sees everything blanketed with snow and frozen with ice, he would lose all hope in the world's survival. So, there is a proverb: a good winter, that is, a cold winter, also brings a good summer. The harsher and colder the winter is, that much more fruitful the following summer will be. Thus, it follows that after a Christian experiences profound affliction, then comes eternal joy. BRIEF EXEGESIS OF ACTS 9:31.[7]

---

[2]Spangenberg, *Der Apostel Geschichte*, 83v; quoting Mt 19:19; Lev 19:18; alluding to Jn 13:34.

[3]Downame, ed., *Annotations*, JJJiv*; alluding to Gal 1:17-18.

[4]Gwalther, *Homelyes or Sermons upon the Actes*, 412-13* (*In Acta Apostolorum*, 128r).

[5]This is likely a reference to the *Panarion* (Medicine Chest, also *Adversus Haereses* [377]) by Bishop Epiphanius of Salamis (d. 403); see BNP 4:1119-20.

[6]Beza, *Annotationes Majores*, 1:494-95.

[7]Spangenberg, *Der Apostel Geschichte*, 84v-85v; quoting Jn 16:21; alluding to Jn 16:22-24.

The Church's Peace Was All Too Brief.
John Calvin: Let us realize that the peace, which, Luke says, existed in the churches, was not in fact perpetual but simply that the Lord granted some relief to his servants for a short time. For he makes allowance for our weakness in this way when he quiets or lessens the whirlwinds and tempests of persecutions, so that by their persistent pressure they may not push us beyond our limits. And this blessing, of the churches at peace, is no ordinary blessing and is not to be despised. But Luke adds other things which are more valuable, that is, that the churches were being edified, that they were walking in the fear of the Lord and that they were filled with the comfort of the Spirit. For as we are accustomed in peacetime to abandon ourselves to a riot of luxury, the churches are for the most part more blessed in the midst of the tumults of war than if they are enjoying the quietest and most pleasant time they could desire. But if the holy conversation and the consolation of the Spirit, by which their situation thrives, are taken away, not only do they lose their happiness, but they are reduced to nothing.

Therefore let us learn not to abuse external peace by being involved in pleasures and idleness, but, the more rest that is given us by our enemies, to make up our minds to make diligent progress in piety, when we get the chance. But if God ever gives free rein to the ungodly to trouble us, let the consolation of the Spirit within be sufficient for us. Finally, both in peace and in war let us always strive with eagerness toward the One who supervises our course. Commentary on Acts 9:31.[8]

The Church Is a Living Building. The English Annotations: The church continued to increase in the number of the faithful, and they grew in knowledge, faith, love and holiness. This word οἰκοδομουμέναι,[9] "edified," is a metaphorical expression taken from building. Spiritually the church is the house of God, because every faithful servant of Christ is a temple of the Holy Spirit. We are all living materials, prepared and fitted here by the word preached, which is compared with a hammer that breaks the rock, so that in the finishing and the establishment in heaven there will be no noise, as in the building of Solomon's temple, neither hammer nor ax was heard. Annotations on Acts 9:31.[10]

---

[8]CNTC 6:274-75* (CO 48:214-15).
[9]𝔐 gives this as a plural participle.
[10]Downame, ed., *Annotations*, JJJ1v*; alluding to 1 Tim 3:15; 1 Cor 3:16; 6:19; 1 Pet 2:5; Jer 23:29; 1 Kings 6:7.

9:32-43 PETER HEALS IN LYDDA AND JOPPA

³²Now as Peter went here and there among them all, he came down also to the saints who lived at Lydda. ³³There he found a man named Aeneas, bedridden for eight years, who was paralyzed. ³⁴And Peter said to him, "Aeneas, Jesus Christ heals you; rise and make your bed." And immediately he rose.³⁵And all the residents of Lydda and Sharon saw him, and they turned to the Lord.

³⁶Now there was in Joppa a disciple named Tabitha, which, translated, means Dorcas.ᵃ She was full of good works and acts of charity. ³⁷In those days she became ill and died, and when they had washed her, they laid her in an upper room. ³⁸Since Lydda was near Joppa, the disciples, hearing that Peter was there, sent two men to him, urging him, "Please come to us without delay." ³⁹So Peter rose and went with them. And when he arrived, they took him to the upper room. All the widows stood beside him weeping and showing tunicsᵇ and other garments that Dorcas made while she was with them. ⁴⁰But Peter put them all outside, and knelt down and prayed; and turning to the body he said, "Tabitha, arise." And she opened her eyes, and when she saw Peter she sat up. ⁴¹And he gave her his hand and raised her up. Then calling the saints and widows, he presented her alive. ⁴²And it became known throughout all Joppa, and many believed in the Lord. ⁴³And he stayed in Joppa for many days with one Simon, a tanner.

a The Aramaic name *Tabitha* and the Greek name *Dorcas* both mean *gazelle*   b Greek *chiton*, a long garment worn under the cloak next to the skin

---

OVERVIEW: In the previous pericope our commentators focused on the power of God's Word; in this passage they comment on the powerful deeds performed by the disciples through faith in God's Word. First they warn that we should not assume that those who are sick or afflicted are being punished for their own sin—indeed, God often transforms such misery into occasions for displaying his glory and grace. All Christians, therefore, should take comfort concerning God's good purposes in their own suffering as well. Second the reformers focus on good works and their connection to faith. While they affirm justification by faith alone, this does not inhibit them in proclaiming the importance of faith working through love. Faith justifies, but it does not stop there; it enables the believer to turn toward God and neighbor in faithfulness.

CHRIST'S CHURCH IS BUILT WITH WORDS, NOT STONES. JOHANNES BRENZ: Do you see here, how and into what form the congregations through the apostles are built? Clearly, not with stones but with the preaching of the gospel of Jesus Christ and with miraculous deeds in his name. These two are brought together so that many people believed in Jesus Christ, and these believers truly are called the church or congregation of Christ. THE ACTS OF THE APOSTLES 9:32-43.[1]

THE DIFFERENCE THE SPIRIT MAKES IN PETER. THE ENGLISH ANNOTATIONS: Peter [spoke to Aeneas] being assured of the will of God in this matter, demonstrating that he was merely a servant to the power of Christ who actually wrought the cure. Here appears the excellent faith of Peter, assured of the truth of Christ's promises. See the marvelous difference between a man left to his own pathetic strength (as he was when he denied Christ) and the same confirmed by the power of the Holy Spirit, as Peter now was when he confidently told Aeneas, "Jesus Christ heals you," and in full confidence of a cure beyond all human ability or creaturely power asks him to rise and make his bed. ANNOTATIONS ON ACTS 9:34.[2]

---

[1]Brenz, *Das Buch der Apostelgeschicht*, DD4r.
[2]Downame, ed., *Annotations*, JJJ1v*; alluding to Mt 26:70-75.

ILLNESS DOES NOT INDICATE ETERNAL CONDEMNATION. JOHANNES BRENZ: Because Luke writes that Peter healed this paralytic in the name of Christ, it should not be thought that this means that in the name of Christ all paralytics must be healed physically or that those who are not physically healed in the name of Christ are godless. For in Elijah's time there were many poor widows and among them there were without any doubt several who were pious, but he was sent to none of them, as Christ says: "Elijah was sent only to Zarephath in Sidon, to a widow. And there were many lepers in Israel in the prophet Elisha's time, and none of them were cleansed, but only Naaman from Syria." . . .

So then by this all who are sick are encouraged through the example of one sick person or several to be of good, trusting hope that God will certainly not let their sickness destroy them, not that they long only to be healed, but rather that they are confident that their sickness does not damn them. "For we know," Paul says, "that for those who love God all things serve for the best, for those called according to his purpose." Therefore we, who have been called through the preaching of the gospel, so that we could become his people, should rest in the highest hope in all afflictions and in strong confidence that all our afflictions will aid and help us to attain true salvation through Jesus Christ who [lives and reigns] with [God the Father and the Holy Spirit, one God, forever and ever.] Amen. THE ACTS OF THE APOSTLES 9:32-35.[3]

DO NOT JUDGE THOSE WHO SUFFER. RUDOLF GWALTHER: The elect are not free from common calamities which human beings are used to suffering. For they are punished with sickness, suffer hunger, feel the pangs of banishment and experience many other adversities. But as Paul testifies, "all things work together for good." For in this way God's glory is declared and believers' faith is tested and tried. Always in these trials clear evidence of God's goodness appears. This the example of the blind man teaches us, who, Christ says, was born blind so that the works of God might be showed in him. And when he heard that Lazarus was sick, he said, "This illness does not lead to death. It is for the glory of God, so that the Son of God may be glorified through it."

And the joyful and prosperous success of that matter declares that the example of Dorcas should grant the same result. She is restored to life, and by this many are won to Christ. These things teach us that we neither should be offended at the adversities that befall us nor that we should too hastily judge those who fall into adversity and misery. Often they are excellent vessels of God's mercy and grace that, because of continual adversity, seem to be vessels of wrath according to the world's judgment. HOMILY 69, ACTS 9:36-43.[4]

TABITHA'S FAITH AND WORKS. JOHN CALVIN: But Luke first commends Tabitha, on whom the miracle was performed, and does so in a twofold description, that is, that she was a disciple of Christ and gave proof of her faith in good works and alms. Several times already he has used the word *disciple* for a Christian man, and in case we might think that it is suitable for men only, he applies the same word to a woman. But this title warns us that Christianity does not exist without teaching, and that the learning prescribed is of such a kind that the same Christ may be the only Teacher for all. This is the highest commendation, this is the basis of a holy life, this is the root of all virtues, to have learned from the Son of God what is the way to live and what true life is. The fruits of good works afterwards spring forth from faith. Now I take good works to mean the voluntary acts of love by which our neighbors are helped, and Luke instances a particular example of this, in almsgiving. Well-doing is highly commended, because, according to the witness of the Holy Spirit, it contains in itself the whole of a godly and perfect life. COMMENTARY ON ACTS 9:36.[5]

---

[3]Brenz, *Das Buch der Apostelgeschicht*, DD4r-v; quoting Lk 4:26-27; Rom 8:28.

[4]Gwalther, *Homelyes or Sermons upon the Actes*, 420-21* (*In Acta Apostolorum*, 130v); quoting Rom 8:28; Jn 11:4; alluding to Jn 9:3. [5]CNTC 6:278* (CO 48:217).

The Nature of Truly Good Works. Rudolf Gwalther: This example teaches us what are indeed good works. For we have heard she was a disciple of Christ, and now works of charity are attributed to her. Therefore they are good works, which the Christians do through faith, according to the rule of charity. For where we are not able to think well of ourselves, whatever we do without faith, it must be sin, as Paul says. Furthermore, it cannot be called good that serves for the benefit of none, because God himself is for this cause called good, because he most liberally pours his treasures of grace on all his creatures. Therefore Christ has taught us that the law is fulfilled by love or charity, and in the prophets he exacts love of them who were puffed up in confidence of the ceremonies of the law, thought that people were saved by the observing of those ceremonies. Indeed, he teaches us that charity or love is the cognizance whereby his people and servants may be known, and he says that in the day of judgment he will have most respect for it. Homily 69, Acts 9:36-43.[6]

The Relationship Between Faith and Love. Martin Luther: As we have often said, we must distinguish faith and love in this way: faith is directed to the person, and love to works. Faith eradicates sin and makes a person pleasing and righteous [before God]. Now once the person has become pleasing and righteous, then the Holy Spirit and his love is given to him, so that he might do good joyously. The way of the law is that it seizes the person and demands such good works from him, and it will not quit until it gets them. Thus, the person is unable to do such works without the Spirit and love. In this way through the law they are forced to admit what they lack. . . . This is said for this reason, so that we would recognize the true nature and characteristics of the law, faith and love, and then each person will correctly and appropriately understand the nature and sayings of Scripture. Namely, that faith makes righteous but still does not fulfill the law; love does not make righteous, but indeed does fulfill the law. Lent Postil (1525), Fourth Sunday After Epiphany.[7]

Adopt Peter's Attitude Toward the Weak. Desiderius Erasmus: In this way, the weak must be raised up toward godliness. First, there must be prayers to God that he will have mercy on them. Then they must be addressed with teaching, rebuke and exhortation. Finally, we must with hand extended assist them toward the more perfect things. Paraphrase of Acts 9:40-41.[8]

Peter's Exemplary Modesty. Rudolf Gwalther: Luke adds a few things to prepare for what follows. For he says that Peter remained in Joppa for several days in the house of one Simon, a tanner. . . . Here let us observe of what kind of people the primitive church was comprised, seeing Peter had no other host but one who got his living by hard labor, and not fine labor at that. Paul teaches us that we should rejoice in the Lord alone. Further, Peter's modesty is displayed here. He did not disdain such a resting place, while today kings' palaces are scarcely good enough for his counterfeit successor. Let us immitate the modesty of the apostle, believing in and serving Jesus Christ. Homily 69, Acts 9:36-43.[9]

---

[6]Gwalther, *Homelyes or Sermons upon the Actes*, 420* (*In Acta Apostolorum*, 130v); alluding to Rom 14.

[7]WA 17,2:97-98.
[8]CWE 50:69* (LB 7:706).
[9]Gwalther, *Homelyes or Sermons upon the Actes*, 423* (*In Acta Apostolorum*, 131r-v); alluding to 1 Cor 1:31; Phil 3:1.

10:1-33 CORNELIUS,
THE EARLY GENTILE CONVERT

At Caesarea there was a man named Cornelius, a centurion of what was known as the Italian Cohort, ²a devout man who feared God with all his household, gave alms generously to the people, and prayed continually to God. ³About the ninth hour of the day[a] he saw clearly in a vision an angel of God come in and say to him, "Cornelius." ⁴And he stared at him in terror and said, "What is it, Lord?" And he said to him, "Your prayers and your alms have ascended as a memorial before God.⁵And now send men to Joppa and bring one Simon who is called Peter. ⁶He is lodging with one Simon, a tanner, whose house is by the sea." ⁷When the angel who spoke to him had departed, he called two of his servants and a devout soldier from among those who attended him, ⁸and having related everything to them, he sent them to Joppa.

⁹The next day, as they were on their journey and approaching the city, Peter went up on the housetop about the sixth hour[b] to pray. ¹⁰And he became hungry and wanted something to eat, but while they were preparing it, he fell into a trance ¹¹and saw the heavens opened and something like a great sheet descending, being let down by its four corners upon the earth. ¹²In it were all kinds of animals and reptiles and birds of the air. ¹³And there came a voice to him: "Rise, Peter; kill and eat."¹⁴But Peter said, "By no means, Lord; for I have never eaten anything that is common or unclean."¹⁵And the voice came to him again a second time, "What God has made clean, do not call common."¹⁶This happened three times, and the thing was taken up at once to heaven.

¹⁷Now while Peter was inwardly perplexed as to what the vision that he had seen might mean, behold, the men who were sent by Cornelius, having made inquiry for Simon's house, stood at the gate¹⁸and called out to ask whether Simon who was called Peter was lodging there. ¹⁹And while Peter was pondering the vision, the Spirit said to him, "Behold, three men are looking for you. ²⁰Rise and go down and accompany them without hesitation,[c] for I have sent them." ²¹And Peter went down to the men and said, "I am the one you are looking for. What is the reason for your coming?" ²²And they said, "Cornelius, a centurion, an upright and God-fearing man, who is well spoken of by the whole Jewish nation, was directed by a holy angel to send for you to come to his house and to hear what you have to say." ²³So he invited them in to be his guests.

The next day he rose and went away with them, and some of the brothers from Joppa accompanied him. ²⁴And on the following day they entered Caesarea. Cornelius was expecting them and had called together his relatives and close friends. ²⁵When Peter entered, Cornelius met him and fell down at his feet and worshiped him. ²⁶But Peter lifted him up, saying, "Stand up; I too am a man." ²⁷And as he talked with him, he went in and found many persons gathered. ²⁸And he said to them, "You yourselves know how unlawful it is for a Jew to associate with or to visit anyone of another nation, but God has shown me that I should not call any person common or unclean. ²⁹So when I was sent for, I came without objection. I ask then why you sent for me."

³⁰And Cornelius said, "Four days ago, about this hour, I was praying in my house at the ninth hour,[d] and behold, a man stood before me in bright clothing ³¹and said, 'Cornelius, your prayer has been heard and your alms have been remembered before God. ³²Send therefore to Joppa and ask for Simon who is called Peter. He is lodging in the house of Simon, a tanner, by the sea.' ³³So I sent for you at once, and you have been kind enough to come. Now therefore we are all here in the presence of God to hear all that you have been commanded by the Lord."

a That is, 3 p.m. b That is, noon c Or *accompany them, making no distinction* d That is, 3 p.m.

OVERVIEW: As Luke sets the stage for the major event of this chapter (the coparticipation of the Gentiles in the people of God through the Spirit), the reformers again address the preaching office. Some of the Radicals tend to overemphasize the Spirit's operation, seeming—at least in the magisterial reformers' view—to sever the connection between Word and Spirit. This passage serves as confirmation for such Radicals that God continues to reveal himself in extraordinary ways, and therefore the church should be open and willing to hear visions from godly people. The magisterial reformers emphasize the interrelatedness of God's Word and Spirit, which cannot be in dissonance; so then, how should this obvious discontinuity with the Old Testament (the abolition of food purity laws) be understood? They argue that God uses Peter's doubts about the meaning of his vision to affirm that the Lord desires the salvation of all people, both Jew and Gentile. Again the commentators reveal their amazement that, although able to plant the gospel in Cornelius's mind or to send an angel in magnificent splendor, God instead delights in human mediation of his salvific message, choosing to accommodate himself to human weakness. While acknowledging that ministers deserve deep respect, all the reformers here cited agree that reverent homage and invocation is due to the Lord alone. They lament the medieval church's confusion on this issue, urging that the true way to honor our brothers and sisters who have gone on in the faith before us is to follow their example (rather than pray to them).

10:1-8 *Cornelius Sends for Peter*

NO MISSION TO THE GENTILES YET. DESIDERIUS ERASMUS: None of the apostles had as yet turned aside to the Gentiles—it was a favorable opportunity that drew in the Ethiopian eunuch. Nevertheless, for some of the heathen it was a help to have been in the neighborhood of the apostles. PARAPHRASE OF ACTS 10:1.[1]

WHO WAS CORNELIUS? JOHANN SPANGENBERG: According to the flesh he was a Gentile, an uncircumcised person. According to his office, a centurion of the cohort of Italian and Roman troops. For since the Romans had brought Syria and Judea under their power, they stationed centurions with their cohorts in every large city and district, so that the Jews could not rise up and riot against the emperor, as they were accustomed to do. According to his life he was devout and God-fearing, along with his entire household. As the father of the house was, so also the entire household: devout, honorable, chaste, truthful and God-fearing, gentle and kind to the poor, diligent and meditative in prayer. BRIEF EXEGESIS OF ACTS 10:1-2.[2]

CORNELIUS'S EXAMPLE DOES NOT CONFIRM INFANT BAPTISM. MENNO SIMONS: Behold, brothers, if now they say that we rob the children of the promise and of the grace of God, you will observe that they contradict us out of hatred and envy and do not tell the truth. Tell me, who has the strongest ground and hope for the salvation of his children? Is it he who places his hopes on an outward sign, or is it he who bases his hopes on the promises of grace, given and promised by Christ Jesus? . . .

Paedobaptists object quite foolishly, saying that the apostles baptized whole households, as the household of Cornelius . . . included in it they say it may be presumed that there were also small children. From this argument, beloved brothers, they show unwittingly that they cannot produce Scriptures to prove that infants should be baptized. For wherever mere presumption is followed, there evidently no proof is available.

To this objection I would reply in plain language thus: . . . If [Cornelius and his entire household] served and feared God, as Luke writes, then they were not baptized without faith, as is plainly shown in the same chapter; for Peter commanded that those should be baptized who had received the Holy Spirit, who spoke with tongues

---

[1]CWE 50:69 (LB 7:707).

[2]Spangenberg, *Der Apostel Geschichte*, 87v-88r.

and glorified God, which are all fruits of faith, as every intelligent person will admit. CHRISTIAN BAPTISM (1539).[3]

CORNELIUS IS FRESH WATER AMID BRINE.

JOHANN SPANGENBERG: Isn't it strange that a Gentile, a soldier, is God-fearing, gentle and prayerful? It's true! Our troops who claim to be Christians have little fear of God, preferring to steal the lion's share rather than being gentle and kind or doing good to the poor. Yes, in an entire week they "pray" a great deal, but not a single Our Father from the heart, dumbfounded that they should meditate in prayer; instead, they prefer to curse and swear by God's agony and wounds, so that sun and moon, indeed all the elements, shake and tremble. BRIEF EXEGESIS OF ACTS 10:1-2.[4]

CORNELIUS SOUGHT PETER BY THE LEADING OF GOD. HANS DENCK: Cornelius was a spiritual

and God-fearing person long before he came to know Christ. Paul had a righteous and divine zeal for the law of God before the revelation of Christ. The disciples of Christ left house and home, wife and children at once for the sake of Christ without yet knowing who he was. All the elect seek something and rejoice in it and do not themselves know what they look for and why they rejoice. All this is no detriment to the gospel of Christ. For such work did not emanate from human beings but from God, from whom comes all which can truthfully be called "something," as the gospel testifies. Therefore, no one may boast of his works of his faith before God as if these were out of himself. For anyone who boasts in himself is self-satisfied and is one of those rich persons whom God leaves empty and unsatisfied. WHETHER GOD IS THE CAUSE OF EVIL.[5]

WHY DIDN'T THE ANGEL PROCLAIM THE GOSPEL TO CORNELIUS? JOHANN SPANGENBERG:

Here God wants to confirm the preaching office and the spoken word contrary to the "heavenly prophets,"[6] who assert that we must sit open-mouthed in silence and gawk into heaven, trying to hear what the Spirit is saying. [However,] God wants us to preach the Word orally, and through this he will grant faith and the Holy Spirit, as Saint Paul says. So then, Christ also sent the apostles into the world to preach the gospel, and he sent Ananias to Paul, and here Peter to Cornelius. BRIEF EXEGESIS OF ACTS 10:4-6.[7]

THE ASCENT OF ALMS AND PRAYERS.

GIOVANNI DIODATI: A kind of speech taken from the ancient sacrifices to signify that these works of piety in Cornelius had, as one should say, kept his memory alive before God, and had as it were excited the Lord to remember him, to confer his full knowledge and grace on him by his gospel, after he had prepared him by those secret and intial operations of his Spirit. ANNOTATION ON ACTS 10:4.[8]

THE PREACHED WORD IS THE VERY WORD OF GOD. THE SECOND HELVETIC CONFESSION:

When this Word of God is now preached in the church by preachers lawfully called, we believe that the very Word of God is preached, and received by the faithful; and that neither any other Word of God is to be feigned nor to be expected from heaven: and that now the Word itself which is preached is to be regarded, not the minister that preaches; who, although he be evil and a sinner, nevertheless the Word of God abides true and good.

---

[6]This is the contemptuous title Luther and his colleagues gave to Andreas Bodenstein von Karlstadt and his followers, who threatened to radicalize the Wittenberg Reformation severely. After hearing reports about Karlstadt's erratic and swift changes to the Mass in the Wittenberg parishes in 1522, Luther returned from his exile at the Wartburg, preaching the famous Invocavit sermons (LW 51:1-64; WA 10,3:1-64) to still the fomented religious strife. See also his "Against the Heavenly Prophets in the Matter of Images and Sacraments (1525)," LW 40:73-223 (WA 18:62-125, 134-214).
[7]Spangenberg, Der Apostel Geschichte, 89v-90r; alluding to Rom 10:14-17; Mk 16:15.
[8]Diodati, Pious Annotations, AA4v* (I Commenti alla Sacra Biblia, 1101-2); alluding to Lev 2:2; 24:7; Ps 141:2.

[3]Simons, Complete Writings, 281*.
[4]Spangenberg, Der Apostel Geschichte, 88r-v.
[5]Denck, Selected Writings of Hans Denck, 208*; alluding to Phil 3:4ff.; Mt 19:27; Eph 2:8-9; Lk 1:53.

Neither do we think that therefore the outward preaching is to be thought as fruitless because the instruction in true religion depends on the inward illumination of the Spirit or because it is written "No person shall teach his neighbor; for all people shall know me" (Jer 31:34), and "Whoever waters or whoever plants is nothing, but God alone causes the growth" (1 Cor 3:7). For albeit "No person can come to Christ, unless he be drawn by the heavenly Father" (Jn 6:44) and be inwardly illuminated by the Holy Spirit, yet we know undoubtedly that it is the will of God that his Word should be preached even outwardly. God could indeed, by his Holy Spirit or by the ministry of an angel, without the ministry of Saint Peter, have taught Cornelius in Acts; but, nevertheless, he refers him to Peter, of whom the angel says, "He will tell you what you must do" (Acts 10:6). CHAPTER I, OF THE HOLY SCRIPTURE BEING THE TRUE WORD OF GOD.[9]

10:9-16 Peter's Vision

CHRISTIANS SHOULD PRIORITIZE PRAYER. JOHN CALVIN: In prayer solitude is a great help, which even Christ did not neglect, since the mind is free of all distractions and concentrates better on God. . . . In those days the sixth hour was noon. And there is no doubt that it was according to custom that Cornelius devoted himself to prayer at that time. For, because almost the whole day we are distracted by a variety of occupations, and we are constantly bustling about unless we hold ourselves in check by applying the bridle, it is useful to have hours set apart for prayer, not because we are tied down to hours but so that prayer may not escape our memory when it ought to take priority over all our concerns. Finally, the same thing must be felt about time as about place, that is, that they are remedies which assist our weakness. COMMENTARY ON ACTS 10:9.[10]

PETER IS CARRIED OFF IN THE SPIRIT. DESIDERIUS ERASMUS: This is granted especially to those who pray and fast; to those who are sated and drowsy the mysteries of God are not unsealed. PARAPHRASE OF ACTS 10:10.[11]

FOUR ASSURANCES THAT THIS WORK IS OF THE SPIRIT. PILGRAM MARPECK: The apostles and their followers were each moved according to the measure of their faith. So also they are moved even today through the Holy Spirit as children and not as servants, who with good and true knowledge know what their Father and Lord has in mind, namely, in such a way that they always know and are assured of the basic reason why they are moved by the Holy Spirit. This assurance and certainty consists principally in four things or reasons.

First is love for God and granting my neighbor what God has granted and given to me, for his praise and the salvation of my soul. Second is to count it as loss and to give up life to the point of death, to suffer for the sake of Christ and the gospel in all patience. Third, to realize when God unlocks or opens a door, that one enters the same with the teaching of the gospel. No one shall open a door that God has not opened, in order that the office of the Holy Spirit remain his own and free. For it is he who opens, and no one closes; it is he who closes, and no one opens, in order that the pearls be not cast before swine or the holy things before the dogs, lest they turn about and mangle them. Fourth, that one be free and sound in teaching and judgments and in truth, in order that none speak unless Christ works through his Holy Spirit. . . .

These four parts are the true proof that the movement is of the Holy Spirit; also that it brings forth fruit at each season. Where Christ does not find this fruit through the Word that is proclaimed, a curse and barrenness soon befall them, as they befell the fig tree. All trees are to have fruit, wherever and whenever Christ arrives, be it in season or out of season. Therefore it behooves us to give diligent heed that we distinguish our own move-

---

[9]*Creeds*, 3:832* (Latin, 237-38).
[10]CNTC 6:292-93* (CO 48:230).

[11]CWE 50:72 (LB 7:708).

ments sharply and diligently from the movements of the Holy Spirit. KUNSTBUCH: CONCERNING THE HUMANITY OF CHRIST.[12]

WHAT DOES THIS VISION MEAN? JOHANN SPANGENBERG: Nothing other than that pagans too should be accepted into the community of faith and the gospel. For what are unclean animals other than the idolatrous pagans? What is butchering unclean animals other than to preach the gospel to pagans, unconcerned about the law, circumcision and the like? No longer is it, "I am sent to no one other than the lost sheep of the house of Israel alone," but now, "Go forth into all the world and preach the gospel to all creatures." BRIEF EXEGESIS OF ACTS 10:9-16.[13]

COMMON OR UNCLEAN. THE ENGLISH ANNO-TATIONS: That is, what the prescription of the law made such. Peter did not yet understand well how this rapture and vision agreed with this law of God. Therefore, lest he should have done anything rashly or with a reluctant conscience, he expresses his scruple—probably so that he might be better informed and satisfied in this matter, lest he should do that which according to the law would render him profane or unclean. ANNOTATIONS ON ACTS 10:14.[14]

VISIONS ARE NECESSARY TO KNOW GOD'S WILL. THOMAS MÜNTZER: Yes, it is a true spirit of the apostles, patriarchs and prophets who waits on visions and receives them with painful tribulation. So, it is no wonder that Brother Fattened-swine or Brother Soft-life rejects visions. If a person has not grasped the clear Word of God in his soul, then he must receive visions. As when Saint Peter, in the Acts of the Apostles, did not understand the law (Leviticus 11), he had doubts about food and about the Gentiles—whether he should

accept them into his company—so God gave him an ecstatic vision.... And what need is there to bring forth the many other witnesses of Scripture? It would never be possible in such momentous and dangerous matters—as those which true preachers, dukes and rulers have—that they guard themselves in all things, acting confidently and blamelessly, if they do not live according to God's revelation, as Aaron heard from Moses and David from Nathan and Gad. For this reason the beloved apostles were completely and totally accustomed to visions, as the text proves. SERMON TO THE PRINCES.[15]

THE PURPOSE OF PETER'S VISION. JOHN CAL-VIN: Before going further we must establish what the aim of the vision was. Some people argue about that more subtly than, in my opinion, this verse demands. Therefore I think that it is shown to Peter, in a general way, that the distinction which God had formerly imposed is now removed. But, just as he had made a division between the animals, so, having chosen one people for himself, he used to regard all the nations as unclean and common. The distinction between the animals having now been removed, he teaches, as a consequence, that people are no longer divided as they used to be and that a Jew is no different from a Greek. From this, Peter is warned not to shrink, afterwards, from the Gentiles as unclean. There is no doubt that God wished to encourage Peter to come to Cornelius without fear. But he had separated one nation to himself from the rest... . Therefore he used to call it his own inheritance and his private property....

Therefore Peter would never have dared to open the gate of heaven to the Gentiles, unless God himself had removed the wall and thrown open a plain way and entrance for all.... But now God has made common to the whole world the

---

[12]CRR 12:363-64* (QGT 17:412-13); alluding to Mt 21:19; Lk 13:6-9.

[13]Spangenberg, *Der Apostel Geschichte*, 90v-91r; quoting Mt 21:19; Mk 16:15.

[14]Downame, ed., *Annotations*, JJJ2r*.

[15]Thomas Müntzer, "Sermon to the Princes," in *The Radical Reformation*, ed. and trans. Michael G. Baylor (Cambridge: Cambridge University Press, 1991), 23, 24* (Thomas Müntzer, *Schriften und Briefe: Kritische Gesamtausgabe*, eds. Paul Kirn and Günther Franz, [Gütersloh: Gerd Mohn, 1968], 254-55); alluding to Job 28:12-13; Acts 10:10-16; Ex 4:15; 2 Chron 29:25.

covenant of life, which he had deposited in one nation as if it were hidden treasure. And from that we conclude that this vision is of no small value for us. For when it teaches that the separation between Jews and Gentiles was only temporary, it is just as if God proclaimed from heaven that he is gathering all the peoples of the world into his grace, so that he may be God of all. COMMENTARY ON ACTS 10:12.[16]

GOD WORKS THROUGH PETER'S DOUBTS.

JOHN DONNE: As no one resolves of anything wisely, firmly, safely, of which they never doubted, never debated, so neither does God withdraw a resolution from anyone who doubts with a humble intent to settle their own faith and not with a wrangling intent to shake another person's faith. God rectifies Peter's doubt immediately, and he recitifies it fully. He presents him a book and a commentary, the text and the exposition: he lets down a sheet from heaven with all kind of beasts and fowl and tells Peter that nothing is unclean. And he tells him by the same Spirit, that there were three men below, asking for him. They were sent by God to apply this visible parable. What God meant by saying nothing is unclean is that the Gentiles generally—in particular this centurion Cornelius—were not incapable of the gospel or unfit for his ministry. SERMON 31, PREACHED ON PENTECOST.[17]

ALL FOOD IS CLEAN.

SWISS BRETHREN CONFESSION OF HESSE (1578): We believe, acknowledge and confess that all creatures which God created in order to nourish humankind are good and not to be disdained by the believers, in as much as they are received and enjoyed without annoyance, with thanksgiving to God. ARTICLE 36, CONCERNING FOOD.[18]

LIVE FREE, BUT CONSIDER THE WEAK.

JOHANN AGRICOLA: At the time when the gospel first began to be preached by the apostles according to Christ's command, they encountered both Jews and Gentiles, with whom Jews were forbidden to eat in the law of Moses. Since, however, the gospel preached a righteousness of the heart that is valid and pleasing before God, the gospel frees all creatures for the use and need of humans without injury to conscience. It also abolishes the false law-worship of God.

The Jews stumbled over this. After Saint Peter in Antioch created a crisis by upholding the law and its dietary rules, Saint Paul heartily chastised him before the entire world. For Saint Peter threw the consciences of the Gentiles into confusion, so that they imagined that without such differentiation among foods they could not be saved—which is clearly false and contrary to the gospel.

Thus, God allows us to eat all that we find at the marketplace, for it stands written, "The earth is the Lord's and all its fullness." This is no less true if someone must eat with the weak, or if something is served that was sacrificed to idols, ox, sheep, lamb or calf. Still, for the sake of the conscience of the weak—who are still ignorant that there are no [real] idols in the world—we should not ask. In this case we should spare the weak and say, "If food makes my brother stumble, then I will never again eat meat, so that I do not cause my brother to stumble." FIVE HUNDRED COMMON NEW GERMAN PROVERBS.[19]

WHY IS THE GREAT SHEET TAKEN BACK TO HEAVEN?

JOHANN SPANGENBERG: For no other reason than that poor sinners justified through faith in Christ are drawn into heaven, as Christ says: "the kingdom of heaven suffers violence [gewalt] and the violent pull it near to them." And, "The tax collectors and prostitutes will enter the kingdom of heaven before you Pharisees and hypocrites." BRIEF EXEGESIS OF ACTS 10:9-16.[20]

---

[16]CNTC 6:293-94* (CO 48:230-31).
[17]Donne, Works, 2:22-23*.
[18]CRR 11:89.

[19]Agricola, Die Sprichwörtersammlungen, 2:49-50; alluding to Gal 2:11-14; quoting 1 Cor 10:26; Ps 24:1; 1 Cor 8:13.
[20]Spangenberg, Der Apostel Geschichte, 91r-v; quoting Mt 11:12; 21:31. The words translated here as violence (gewalt) and "violent" (die gewalt thun) carry a less marked meaning in German here than in English. There is no moral judgment; instead, urgency and longing are emphasized.

10:17-33 *Peter Visits Cornelius*

CORNELIUS'S CHARACTER. THE ENGLISH ANNO-
TATIONS: Since Cornelius was a Gentile and a soldier,
they tell Peter about his character in three excellent
attributes: he was a just man, he feared God, and he
lived in good esteem and reputation of all the Jews
who knew him. This was not said—as meddlesome
sycophants do—to flatter Cornelius but to do him
justice, also to free Peter from such suspicion as might
otherwise make him afraid to come to Cornelius. In
sum, here is a good example for servants honestly to
give their masters their due honor and faithfully to
obey them. ANNOTATIONS ON ACTS 10:22.[21]

THE FIRST INGRAFTING OF THE GENTILES.
DESIDERIUS ERASMUS: This was the beginning
of the association of the Jews with the Gentiles,
who were of their own accord hastening towards
partnership in the gospel. But the hesitation of the
apostles in this matter stemmed from their concern
that it be recognized that the Gentiles' admission
to the grace of the gospel had been undertaken
clearly at God's command, and not rashly. Cornelius invites, but on the admonition of the angel;
Peter goes down and meets the messengers, but
instructed by a vision. On the one side was a
glowing eagerness for the grace of the gospel; on
the other an alacrity and promptitude on the part
of one who thirsted for the salvation of all races.
PARAPHRASE OF ACTS 10:23.[22]

**MINISTERS SHOULD BE RESPECTED, NOT
WORSHIPED.** DESIDERIUS ERASMUS: So we
ought to reverence Christ in his ministers, but in
such a way that the glory of God is not attributed
to a human being. Accordingly, Peter offered an
example of how stewards of Christ ought to be free
from ambition and not claim for themselves any
praise for what they do by the power and and the
name of Christ. PARAPHRASE OF ACTS 10:25-26.[23]

DO NOT PRAY TO MERE HUMANS BEINGS.
THE SECOND HELVETIC CONFESSION: Let all
the prayers of the faithful be poured forth to God
alone, through the mediation of Christ only, out
of a true faith and pure love. As for invocation of
saints, or using them as intercessors to entreat for
us, the priesthood of our Lord Christ and true
religion will not permit us. CHAPTER 23, OF THE
PRAYERS OF THE CHURCH.[24]

**WE DO NOT NEED ENDLESS INTERMEDIAR-
IES TO APPROACH GOD.** JOHN DONNE: This
is a misery, which our time has become well-
acquainted with and has too much experience
with, and which continues to grow among us.
When people have been mellowed with the fear of
God and by heavy corrections and calamities are
brought to a greater tenderness of conscience than
before, in that distemper of melancholy and inordinate sadness they have been too easily seduced
and withdrawn to a superstitious and idolatrous
religion. I say this because from the highest to the
lowest place there are sentinels planted in every
corner to watch all advantages. If a person lose his
preferment at court or lose his child at home or
lose any such thing as affects him much, imprint-
ing a deep sadness for its loss, they work on that
sadness to make him a papist. When people have
long lived apart from God, they never think that
they can come near enough to him unless they
go beyond him. Because they have never tried to
come to him before, now when they want to they
imagine God to be so hard to access that there is
no coming to him unless by the intervention and
intercession of saints. They think that that church
in which they have lived ill cannot be a good
church. Whereas, if they would accustom themselves in the daily performance of Christian duties
to an ordinary presence of God, religion would
not be such a stranger, nor devotion such an illness
to them. SERMON 31, PREACHED ON PENTECOST.[25]

---

[21]Downame, ed., *Annotations*, JJJ2r*.
[22]CWE 50:72 (LB 7:708-9).
[23]CWE 50:72 (LB 7:709).

---

[24]*Creeds*, 3:897 (Latin, 296-97).
[25]Donne, *Works*, 2:31*.

Worship Is Due to God Alone. Bohemian Confession of 1535: [The Scriptures] teach that the honor and worship due to God is not to be transferred to the saints or to their images. As it is written in Isaiah: "I am the Lord; this is my name. I will not give my glory to another, or my praise to idols" (Is 42:8). They teach, however, that the saints are to be honored in this way: that on set and prescribed days and times all gather in one place to hear the Word of God and to offer worship to God, that they might celebrate the memory of the saints, and of the benefits and gifts which God conferred on them, and through them to the church, remembering their faith and life and actions, by which they are stirred to imitate these that they might bear fruit in every good work through the word of God. Article 17, The Worship of the Saints.[26]

Fasting Makes Us Less Likely to See Strange Forms. John Calvin: The brain of a person who is fasting and observing reasonable moderation does not easily admit hallucinations in the shape of apparitions. Cornelius therefore means that an angel did appear to him, when he was giving strict attention to the practice of prayer, with his mind free of all hindrances which usually leave us exposed to phantasms and apparitions. Commentary on Acts 10:30.[27]

Do Not Cast Pearls Before Swine. Desiderius Erasmus: Peter spoke to everyone that he might gain them all, aware that they had assembled together so that they might hear the word of the gospel. How shrewdly Peter plays the role of pastor! He imparts the mystery of the evangelical doctrine only to those who declare their eagerness to learn. Paraphrase of Acts 10:28-29.[28]

Cornelius and His Household Are Ready to Listen to Peter "in the Presence of God." The English Annotations: Cornelius probably said this to assure Peter that he would be a careful and attentive listener of the mysteries of faith, which is a great encouragement to ministers to execute their ministry cheerfully. By contrast, a drowsy or inattentive audience not only disheartens the minister but also intercepts the blessing of God which comes on them through the minister. Thus, the power of the word preached is hindered. Annotations on Acts 10:33.[29]

---

[26]Boh 1535, 34*.

[27]CNTC 6:304* (CO 48:239).
[28]CWE 50:73 (LB 7:709).
[29]Downame, ed., *Annotations*, JJJ2v*.

10:34-48 GENTILES BELIEVE AND RECEIVE THE HOLY SPIRIT

[34] So Peter opened his mouth and said: "Truly I understand that God shows no partiality, [35] but in every nation anyone who fears him and does what is right is acceptable to him. [36] As for the word that he sent to Israel, preaching good news of peace through Jesus Christ (he is Lord of all), [37] you yourselves know what happened throughout all Judea, beginning from Galilee after the baptism that John proclaimed: [38] how God anointed Jesus of Nazareth with the Holy Spirit and with power. He went about doing good and healing all who were oppressed by the devil, for God was with him. [39] And we are witnesses of all that he did both in the country of the Jews and in Jerusalem. They put him to death by hanging him on a tree, [40] but God raised him on the third day and made him to appear, [41] not to all the people but to us who had been chosen by God as witnesses, who ate and drank with him after he rose from the dead. [42] And he commanded us to preach to the people and to testify that he is the one appointed by God to be judge of the living and the dead. [43] To him all the prophets bear witness that everyone who believes in him receives forgiveness of sins through his name."

[44] While Peter was still saying these things, the Holy Spirit fell on all who heard the word. [45] And the believers from among the circumcised who had come with Peter were amazed, because the gift of the Holy Spirit was poured out even on the Gentiles. [46] For they were hearing them speaking in tongues and extolling God. Then Peter declared, [47] "Can anyone withhold water for baptizing these people, who have received the Holy Spirit just as we have?" [48] And he commanded them to be baptized in the name of Jesus Christ. Then they asked him to remain for some days.

OVERVIEW: For our commentators, great preaching is proclamation that persuasively demonstrates the significance of the gospel history, its value and power for the contemporary audience. Our exegetes are especially enamored with the phrase "the good news of peace through Jesus Christ" (v. 36).

The end of the chapter stimulates another baptismal debate. Against Kaspar von Schwenckfeld's thorough spiritualization of baptism, these commentators agree that this passage proves that water is indeed necessary for baptism. The ceremony is a fitting depiction of the meaning of baptism: the baptized person is "buried" and then "raised" again in identity with Christ, sealing in them the promises and benefits of Christ's resurrection. The Anabaptists bristle at the idea that infants can receive this seal. Who sends a blank letter? The magisterial reformers retort that baptism is God's Word and human faith can add nothing to it (which for the Anabaptists makes Philip's words in Acts 8:37 meaningless). Ever-present in the background of this debate is the question: Do the children of believers belong to the kingdom of God?

10:34-43 Cornelius's Household Hears the Good News

PETER PREACHES THE POWER OF THE GOSPEL. MARTIN LUTHER: This is a beautiful sermon and testimony of Christ's resurrection. As the preaching of the apostles and the gospel should be, he does not merely narrate the history but also the power and use of this history. POSTIL FOR EASTER MONDAY, CRUCIGER'S SUMMER POSTIL (1544).[1]

DO NOT BE CONCERNED WITH CITING CHAPTER AND VERSE. JOHN DONNE: Saint Peter took his text here out of Deuteronomy, "Truly I

---

[1] WA 21:216.

understand that God shows no partiality." Where, because the words are not precisely the same in Deuteronomy as they are in this text, we find just occasion to note that neither Christ in his preaching nor the Holy Spirit in penning the Scriptures of the New Testament were so curious as our times in citing chapters and verses or such distinctions. No, not even in citing the words of the exact place. SERMON 31, PREACHED ON PENTECOST.[2]

LUKE DOES NOT RECORD THE WHOLE SERMON. HEINRICH BULLINGER: So then, you see the benefit derived from the obscurity of this passage. Luke, desiring brevity, did not insert the entirety of Peter's sermon, but only the main points of the sermon. Luke is accustomed to writing in a concise and succinct style. Here, therefore, he carefully constructs the gospel history of Christ: who he is, why and how he came, and what benefits he grants. COMMENTARY ON ACTS 10:34-43.[3]

"PERSON"[4] REFERS TO OUTWARD STATE OR APPEARANCE. JOHN CALVIN: By this word ["person"] there ought to be understood the outward state or appearance, as it is commonly called, and whatever there is about a person that procures him favor or deprives him of it. Riches, nobility of birth, dependents, honors make a person highly respected; poverty, low birth, and anything like that make him contemptible. The Lord continually forbids persons to be accepted on this basis, because there cannot possibly be a right judgment, as often as external considerations distract the judge from the cause. In this verse it refers to race, and the meaning is that uncircumcision does not prevent God being pleased with and approving the righteousness in a Gentile. But in this way it will seem that respect of person did influence God for a time. For when he passed over the Gentiles and chose the Jews for his own people, did he not respect

persons? I reply that the reason for this discrimination must not be sought in people, but it depends altogether on the secret purpose of God. But when he adopted Abraham to himself and made his covenant with him rather than with the Egyptians, he was not moved by any external consideration to do so, but the whole reason for it remained in his wonderful purpose. Therefore God was never bound to persons. COMMENTARY ON ACTS 10:34.[5]

THE CLEAR AND SINGULAR MEANING OF PETER'S WORDS. DIRK PHILIPS: These words of Peter have one sense or meaning . . . namely, that whether they are Jews or Gentiles, circumcised or uncircumcised, the important thing is that they fear God, believe in Christ Jesus and do right. Thus they are God's children, well pleasing to him and heirs of his kingdom, according to the promise which he gave to Abraham saying, "In your seed" (which is Christ) "shall all the heathen be blessed." THE ENCHIRIDION: THE NEW BIRTH AND THE NEW CREATURE.[6]

THE MESSIAH IS KING, THE PREACHER OF PEACE. MARTIN LUTHER: That is the sermon, a magnificent sermon it is! The Messiah, the King, is a preacher, what more can he be? He is a Lord over everything! His name is not Doctor Martin or Pomeranius;[7] no, all other preachers, princes and lords are nothing in comparison with him! The preacher should not preach him as silver and gold, but as peace. This is the beautiful, magnificent sermon: that no one else but he himself has established peace between God and us—as well as all creatures! What is all the wisdom, knowledge and power on earth if we are not one with God? If this peace stands, I will not be pestered much by the devil, death, sin and hell. They can be as evil as they want; I have grasped hold of the Word and am at peace with God. But if the devil does not want to leave me in peace, what do I care? For my

---

[2]Donne, *Works*, 2:29*; quoting Deut 10:17; alluding to Heb 4:4.
[3]Bullinger, *In Acta Apostolorum*, 128v.
[4]Calvin's Latin translation of προσωπολήμπτης (*personarum acceptor*) is less idiomatic than the ESV ("partiality") and closer to the KJV ("respecter of persons").

[5]CNTC 6:307* (CO 48:242).
[6]CRR 6:305 (BRN 10:327); quoting Gen 22:18; Gal 3:1.
[7]Johannes Bugenhagen was the pastor at Saint Mary's in Wittenberg, where Luther regularly preached.

heart stands in the true assurance of God's peace. The man named Jesus of Nazareth—Lord over everything—is *my* Lord, so you cannot devour me! I was indeed damned, but now he came and brought me a sermon of peace. "Do not be alarmed," as he says in the Gospel.

This is now Christ's kingdom. So that I can be an heir of the eternal kingdom of heaven, he has given the seal, his blood he has poured over it. He is a Lord over all the world. This sermon has gone out everywhere, as you know, it has traveled around helping everyone. There is nothing able to oppose this peace that he has brought. Now we have it in the Word firm and strong. He has sealed, signed and secured it in our hearts. This sermon the Man delivered about the kingdom of heaven, but what was his thanks? The cross. Ridicule. And murder. For he was not a Messiah who would bring a worldly kingdom, which is what they coveted. "So, they strangled him and gave him his reward. God resurrected him and did not let all the people see him, but only us. The sermon that he brought he entrusted to us to promulgate; he is a judge of the living and the dead. Now I see that God also wants to have the Gentiles [in his kingdom], since I have been sent to Gentiles who must hear the sermon of peace and become kings in the kingdom of heaven." We want this, too. We too hear it. SERMON ON EASTER MONDAY AFTERNOON (1544).[8]

"ANYONE WHO FEARS GOD." THE ENGLISH ANNOTATIONS: That is, whoever is truly religious toward God and just toward humankind. By the fear of God the Hebrews understood the whole worship of God. Peter, intimating that Cornelius feared God in that he believed in him who came into the world to save sinners, shows that the sacraments are seals of adoption in children and faith, of those who are of age. So they are deceived who so tie the Holy Spirit and the effects of him to the reception of the sacrament of baptism, as if no one could fear God or be accepted by him and saved by him who is not baptized. For first, none before

Christ received this seal, as we now do, and second it is the contempt, not the privation, which God condemns here. Here it appears that Cornelius was accepted by God before he had received the external seal of his covenant. ANNOTATIONS ON ACTS 10:35.[9]

FAITH, BEFORE OR AFTER BAPTISM, DEPENDS ON THE WORD. THE SCHMALKALD ARTICLES: Both those who believe prior to baptism and those who become believers in baptism have everything through the external Word that comes first. For example, adults who have reached the age of reason must have previously heard, "The one who believes and is baptized will be saved" (Mk 16:16), even though they were at first without faith and only after ten years received the Spirit and baptism. In Acts 10, Cornelius had long since heard from the Jews about a future Messiah, through whom he would be justified before God. His prayers and alms were acceptable in such faith (so Luke calls him "righteous and God-fearing"). Without such a preceding Word or hearing he could neither believe nor be righteous. However, Saint Peter had to reveal to him that the Messiah now had come. (Up until then he had believed in him as the one who was to come.) His faith in the future Messiah did not hold him captive along with the hardened, unbelieving Jews, but he knew that now he had to be saved by the present Messiah and not, in consort with the Jews, deny or persecute him. PART 3, ARTICLE 8, CONCERNING CONFESSION.[10]

ISRAEL'S COVENANT IS FOR ALL. JOHN CALVIN: Peter shows the purpose for which Christ has been revealed to the world. Moreover, he intentionally begins by reminding them that God has sent his Word to the children of Israel. . . . The fame of the eternal covenant which God had made with the children of Israel was widespread at that time. There was nothing more commonly known among

---

[8]WA 49:363-64; quoting Mk 16:6.

[9]Downame, ed., *Annotations*, JJJ2v*; alluding to Rom 4:11; Acts 10:44; Jn 3:5.
[10]BoC 322-23 (WA 50:245-46).

the Jews than that, to the patriarchs of long ago, there had already been promised a Redeemer, who would restore things that had fallen down into a prosperous and blessed state. All who were on friendly terms with the Jews used to know about this also. Therefore, in order to gain more credence for himself, Peter prefaces his speech by saying that he will not be speaking about something that is unknown or new but about the restoration of the church, which was dependent on the eternal covenant of God and which has now been manifested in no obscure way and publicly proclaimed by the talk of all. Commentary on Acts 10:36.[11]

The Gospel Is a Word of Peace. John Calvin:

I take peace here for the reconciliation of God and people, which nevertheless contains within itself the complete and perfect salvation of the church. For just as horrible confusion, and, one might say, hideous chaos, follows his separation and alienation from us, so as soon as the fatherly favor of God dawns, he gathers his church together out of its dispersion, and true happiness springs up again. Peter therefore means by this that in Christ God showed himself favorable to his people and once again embraced the sons of Abraham, whom he had appeared to have temporarily rejected, so that he might establish a prosperous and flourishing state among them. Now, just as he makes God the source of this peace, so he sets forth Christ openly as its pledge, so that it may be unalterable and holy. Commentary on Acts 10:36.[12]

The Meaning of "Anointed." Giovanni Diodati:

God has endowed Jesus in his human nature with the fullness of the gift of his Spirit and has consecrated his whole person to the office of Mediator—the two things signified by the ancient anointment. Annotation on Acts 10:38.[13]

Jesus Was Seen by Five Hundred

Brothers. The English Annotations: God showed Christ alive from the dead, but not to all the Jews, but to all those who were appointed witnesses of the same. This was not a few people. He was seen alive after his resurrection from the dead by more than five hundred brothers at once. He did not appear to his enemies, because his state of humiliation and suffering by them was finished. It no longer concerned them (whose unrepentance and unbelief he knew and foresaw), other than that they will see him coming again in the clouds to judge them. Annotations on Acts 10:41.[14]

The Forgiveness of Sins Is the Ultimate Peace. Martin Luther:

By this Preacher of Peace—as the prophets call him—it is shown not that he will be a fleshly king but rather that in his name all who believe will receive the forgiveness of sins. This is the main thing. The kingdom of heaven commits no violence, compels no one; instead, it suffers violence. That is, when poor sinners hear "the forgiveness of sins," they press forward to it and will force their way in, so that violence is done to the kingdom of heaven, as violence is done to its doors, because people are forcing their way in. They want to be redeemed from the devil's power and terror so badly that they hurry and scurry when they merely hear that peace and the forgiveness of sins are being proclaimed. Therefore, this and other passages are inscribed with golden letters onto our heart. All the prophets have written that the forgiveness of sins will be received by all those who believe in him.

The gospel is trumpeted, is violent (praise God!) in all of Germany. Now you need only believe and secure it in your heart, saying, "Amen, Amen, this I believe." It is true, if you do this, then you believe that you have the forgiveness of sins in his name. Now this is the good news, that we cannot escape sin and death other than through the Savior. All people who hear this good news and cling to it with their heart will have the forgiveness of sins, that is, peace. For what Peter above calls

---

[11]CNTC 6:309-10* (CO 48:244).
[12]CNTC 6:310* (CO 48:244).
[13]Diodati, *Pious Annotations*, AA4v* (*I Commenti alla Sacra Biblia*, 1102).
[14]Downame, ed., *Annotations*, JJJ2v*; alluding to 1 Cor 15:6; Rev 1:7.

peace, he clarifies here with the word "forgiveness of sins," that is, repentance through which we turn ourselves from sin to the nature of faith and from then on live joyously, as is fitting for Christians. In the Savior's name you gain this, so that you can say, "I believe that not even the most insignificant sin can be forgiven me by a single angel or human being, but rather only in the Name!"

For that reason you should understand correctly what forgiveness means. Not papal penance, but rather that God is unwilling to know about sin. "You are no longer a sinner to me. I will not damn you, or anyone else, because you believe in the Man whom I have appointed." So the forgiveness of sins means that God will not impute or recognize sin—even if there is some still there in the maggot sack,[15] it will soon die. If now sin is gone, then you cannot be called a sinner any more or you cannot be damned, as long as you believe. If you cannot believe, let your heart heave and scream, "O Father, help me! So that I can believe that I can grasp it tightly like I know it is true." If, however, your faith is still weak, stand; just don't fall from it! Whatever it yearns for, whatever it desires, is still alive, whatever does not move, it is dead . . . it is murder. Then, there is no forgiveness of sins nor freedom. Even if your flesh is already pulling you down, do not give up! Do not become sluggish! Instead, plead for a strong faith; then you will be saved, and death will be drowned. Death cannot have you; even if it is already feasting on the maggot sack, still you must not taste death. "Death, shut up, I believe! God knows of a sinner no more. For death will not consume the saints and the innocent, to whom life belongs; death will reign over the damned [and] the devil. You have no power over the saints of God. Leave me untroubled!" SERMON ON EASTER MONDAY AFTERNOON (1544).[16]

LORD, IMPLANT YOUR GRACE WITHIN US. THE BOOK OF COMMON PRAYER (1549): Almighty God, who through your only begotten Son Jesus Christ, has overcome death and opened to us the gate of everlasting life: we humbly beseech you, that as by your special grace, going before us, you place in our minds good desires, so by your continual help we may bring the same to good effect through Jesus Christ our Lord: who lives and reigns [with you in the same Spirit one God, world without end]. Amen. THE COLLECT FOR EASTER MONDAY.[17]

10:44-48 Cornelius's Household Receives the Spirit and Is Baptized

THE HOLY SPIRIT DESCENDS THROUGH THE WORD, NOT LONG SERMONS. JOHN DONNE: Humanly speaking, the Holy Spirit had an extraordinary, an unnatural ambition, to go downwards, to enlarge himself in his working by falling. He fell. And then, he fell so, as a shower of rain falls that does not lie in those round drops in which it falls but diffuses and spreads and enlarges itself. He fell on all. But then, it was because all heard. They came not to see a new action, preaching or preacher (Peter) or to see one another at a sermon. He fell on all who heard. Where also, I think, it will not be impertinent to make this note: that Peter is said to have spoken those words, but they on whom the Holy Spirit fell are said to have heard the Word. It is not many words (long sermons) or good words (witty and eloquent sermons) that induce the Holy Spirit, for all these are words of human beings. Now the whole sermon is the ordinance of God, the whole sermon is not the Word of God, but when all the good gifts of people are modestly employed and humbly received as "vehicles of the Spirit," as Saint Augustine calls them, the chariots of the Holy Spirit as means afforded by God to convey the word of life into

---

[15]"Maggot sack" (*Madensack*) is one of Luther's favorite euphemisms for the human body in its current subjection to frailty and death.
[16]WA 49:365-67; alluding to Mt 11:12. The German words translated in this passage as "violence" (*gewalt*) or "violent" (*gewaltig*) have a more neutral meaning than in English. Luther is emphasizing the urgency and longing that all people have to hear

that Jesus loves them and has given them true peace. See above Spangberg comment on Acts 10:9-16.
[17]BCP 1549, 55*.

us, in *those* words we hear the Word, and there the Word and the Spirit go together. SERMON 31, PREACHED ON PENTECOST.[18]

THE MYSTERY OF THE HOLY TRINITY. JOHN DONNE: As the Trinity is the most mysterious point of our religion and the hardest to comprehend, so in the Trinity, the Holy Spirit is the most mysterious person and the hardest to be expressed. We are called the household of God and the family of the faithful, and therefore out of a contemplation and ordinary acquaintance with the parts of families, we are more likely to conceive any such thing in God himself as we see in a family. We seem not to go so far out of our way of reason to believe a Father and a Son, because father and son are pieces of families; nor in believing Christ and his church, because husband and wife are pieces of families. We go not so far in believing God's working on us either by ministering from above or by his spiritual ministers here on earth, for masters and servants are pieces of families. But does there arise any such thing out of any of these couples—father and son, husband and wife, master and servant—as should come from them and they be no whit before neither? Is there anything in natural or civil families that should assist our understanding to apprehend this, that in heaven there should be a Holy Spirit, so, as that the Father and the Son being all spirit and all holy and all holiness, there should be another Holy Spirit who has all their essential holiness in him and another holiness too? A holiness that makes us holy?

It was hard work for the apostles and their successors at first to draw the Godhead into one, into a unity. . . . But these mysteries are not to be chewed by reason, but to be swallowed by faith. We professed three persons in one God, in the simplicity of our infancy at our baptism. We have sealed that contract in the other sacrament often since. And this is eternal life, to die in that belief. . . . In that testimony we rest—that there is a Holy Spirit—and in the testimony of this text, that this Holy Spirit falls down on all who hear the word of God. SERMON 31, PREACHED ON PENTECOST.[19]

THE SPIRIT POURS OUT HIS GIFTS TO DISPLAY THE UNITY OF JEWS AND GENTILES. DESIDERIUS ERASMUS: The reality itself accompanied the sign they had seen with their eyes. For they began to speak in different tongues to all those who were listening, extolling with their praises the kindness of God. This sign, so clear, was given to the circumcised who were present so that they should not in the future hesitate to call to Christ even the uncircumcised. It was given to the friends of Cornelius as well so that they should have no doubt that through belief they were equal to the Jews without the help of the Law. The normal order, however, as it was under the control of God, was reversed: first baptism is given to the catechumens, then the Holy Spirit through the imposition of hands so that the apostle would not hesitate to add the lesser after God had of his own accord bestowed the greater. PARAPHRASE OF ACTS 10:44-48.[20]

THE HOLY SPIRIT IS A PRINTER. JOHN DONNE: As Christ in his miracles, so the Holy Spirit in his powerful instructions. It is true, there is a growth in knowledge, and we overcome ignorances by degrees and by succession of more and more light. Christ himself grew in knowledge as well as in stature. But this is in the way of experimental knowledge, by study, by conversation, by other acquisitions. But when the Holy Spirit takes a person into his school, he deals with him not as a painter, who makes an eye and an ear and a lip, passing his pencil a hundred times over every muscle and every hair, and so in many sittings makes up one man, but he deals as a printer, so that in one strain he delivers a whole story. SERMON 31, PREACHED ON PENTECOST.[21]

THE SPIRIT'S DESCENT CONFIRMS THE

---

[18]Donne, *Works*, 2:21*.

[19]Donne, *Works*, 2:31-33*.
[20]CWE 50:75 (LB 7:711).
[21]Donne, *Works*, 2:22*.

Gentiles' Ingrafting into God's Covenant. John Calvin: God now confirms by a new miracle that the teaching of his gospel is shared by the Gentiles equally with the Jews. And this is indeed an extraordinary sign of the call of the Gentiles, because the Lord would never have thought the Gentiles deserving of the graces of his Spirit, unless it happened to prove that those very people were also elected into the fellowship of the covenant. Indeed, these gifts mentioned by Luke are different from the grace of regeneration; nevertheless, there is no doubt that in this way God put his seal not only on the teaching of Peter but also on the faith and godliness of those who had heard. He says that they were all endowed with the Spirit, just as we have already seen that they all became animated with the desire to learn and obey.

Now this visible symbol shows us, as if in a picture, how effective the preaching of the gospel is as an instrument of the divine power. For as Peter was speaking God poured out his Spirit to show that he does not send teachers for the purpose of beating the air with the sound of empty words, but so that he might work powerfully through what they say and quicken their words by the power of his Spirit for the salvation of the godly. Commentary on Acts 10:44.[22]

Out of Water All Things Were Made; So Too the Citizens of the Kingdom. Peter Walpot: That the water [of baptism] is profoundly important is quite obvious since before the water, the Holy Spirit came on these people; however, the apostle did not let them rest in this. Instead, in order to show the necessity of the water, he said, "Can anyone withhold the water with which we were baptized to these who have received the Holy Spirit just as we have?" And he commanded them to be baptized. Thus, this is a just connection from God which is fitting for us to fulfill. What then is the importance of the water? Namely, a hidden mystery is revealed to us under it. First, the judgment of God is accomplished in

it: burial, death, resurrection, new life—all these things at once. Second, as people are plunged into the water, they are covered by it; thus, in water baptism it is like a grave, and in it the old self of the one who receives the water on his head is buried. And as someone plunged into water lifts his head up out of the water, so also by the baptized person the new self will be resurrected.... Therefore, we too will experience the resurrection. And these two things we say at once, so, on account of all these things, this is called the second, new, spiritual rebirth or creation from above, because we are created anew.

For just as in the beginning or the creation of the first human being the earth consisted of one element but everything happened through God, so also here in this place in the creation of the new self. Water is the element, but all the action is out of spiritual causation; yes, by the power of the Father, Son and Holy Spirit all things are achieved. Then he created human beings in God's image; now he draws people into friendship with God, yes, [he makes them] into children of God. Then he designated human beings as inhabitants of paradise, now, however, as inhabitants of the kingdom of God into which they enter through this birth, and they enter into this birth through faith. This creation or second birth was secretly foreshadowed from the very beginning through the creation of the first human being and the second human being, namely, that Eve was created from the man's side. God indicated by this that later out of two he would create a new person. The Great Article Book: On the Eucharist.[23]

Baptism Is the Seal of the Benefits of Christ. Rudolf Gwalther: Peter saw now the gift of the Holy Spirit given to those who hear and believe it: he easily acknowledges that the grace of the gospel belongs to the Gentiles also, and to the uncircumcised also, so that if they believe in Christ, they ought to be received into the fellowship of the church, because God does promise to give them

---

[22]CNTC 6:317* (CO 48:250-51).

[23]QGT 12:122-23; alluding to Col 2:12; Rom 6:4; Col 3:4.

his Holy Spirit. For drawing an argument from the thing to its sign, he says, "Can any person forbid water, that these should not be baptized, who have received the Holy Spirit as well as we did?" Which is as much as if he should say: As many as are the members of Christ must be received by baptism into the fellowship of Christ's church. But no one can doubt that these people are the members of Christ, seeing they have received the Spirit of Christ just as we did. Therefore, it is because of this reason that they should be baptized. And immediately he commands them to be baptized in the name of the Lord, that is to say, to be consecrated to Christ the Lord and numbered with his church. . . .

Of these things it is easy to fathom all the meaning of baptism. Peter surely acknowledges baptism to be the first sacrament of God's people and church, whereby outwardly the benefits of regeneration and adoption, and whatever else is given to us in Christ, are sealed to us, and thereby as many as are partakers of them are admonished of their duty. HOMILY 77, ACTS 10:44-48.[24]

A DEFENSE OF THE BAPTISM OF INFANTS.

MARTIN LUTHER: The church has baptized infants for a thousand years, and God has given the Holy Spirit to those who have been baptized as infants. Moreover, this conclusion is valid *a posteriori*, for Peter also infers this: "We have preached Christ among the Gentiles, and God gave his testimony by the Holy Spirit." This is an argument from the act, or *a posteriori*. God gave his blessing to the Gentiles without the law, and therefore they are without the law.

Second, for more than a thousand years the church has baptized infants. Moreover, because the church never existed except among the baptized, and it was necessary that the church always exist, therefore infant baptism is true baptism. So I argue *a priori* that Christ commanded that all nations be taught and baptized, and this included children. Again, it is not the minister as a person who

baptizes, but it is Christ who baptizes. Now, if an infant is baptized by Christ, how can I take this away and say that he is not baptized? . . .

The Anabaptists and Waldensians[25] rest the sacraments on the faith of the person, and therefore they reject the baptism of infants, arguing that one ought first to teach and only afterward to baptize. I respond: There Christ spoke not of the institution but of the effect [of baptism]. If I should hold that the baptism of children is without effect, it does not follow that they should be rebaptized when they grow up and believe, for if some at Mount [Sinai] had not believed in the law (whether or not they believed in God), would it have been necessary to make a law again after they had come to believe? It is one thing to have the effect of a work, and it is another to have the work. Everything depends on distinguishing between the work of God and the work of people. The work of God is unchangeable. TABLE TALK, VEIT DIETRICH (1533).[26]

TEACH, THEN BAPTIZE. LEONHARD SCHIEMER:

In the entire Scripture of the New Testament, I find no other seal of faith than baptism. . . . The water of baptism is a confirmation of the inward covenant with God. It is like writing a letter and preparing it to be sent. Then you want to have it sealed. But no one will give a seal to a letter without knowing what is in it. When you baptize a child, you are sealing an empty letter. Christ sends his disciples, first to teach, second to bring to faith, and third—thereafter—to baptize. Likewise no one waits for a drink unless he knows what is being served. Whoever is willing to teach children may baptize them, to the extent that they accept the teaching. . . . Whoever baptizes first and teaches af-

---

[24]Gwalther, *Homelyes or Sermons upon the Actes*, 462* (*In Acta Apostolorum*, 143v).

[25]The Waldensian movement, named for Peter Waldo (d. 1184), was a medieval lay Catholic reform movement in the south of France that centered on simple living and allowed for lay preaching and administration of the sacraments. On account of this lay involvement, contra the prescribed church hierarchy, the Vatican branded the Waldensians heretics and sought to eliminate them, unsuccessfully; the Waldensian Church still exists.

[26]LW 54:113-14* no. 650 (WATR 1:306-7); alluding to Mt 28:19; Mk 16:16; Ex 19:17–20:17.

terward, shoots first and later asks the whereabouts of the target he was aiming for. Whoever lifts a child out of the baptismal font is like someone who shoots while someone else goes in search of the target. KUNSTBUCH: THE TWELVE ARTICLES OF THE CHRISTIAN FAITH.[27]

BELIEVERS' CHILDREN ARE MEMBERS OF THE KINGDOM FROM THE WOMB. JOHN CALVIN: Peter argues from the reality to the sign. For since baptism is an appendage to the spiritual grace, a person who receives the Spirit is at the same time fit to receive baptism. And this is the proper order, so that a minister admits to the external sign those whom God has testified to be his children by the pledge and proof of his Spirit. So teaching and faith play their parts first. But the inference that ignorant people draw from this, that infants must be debarred from baptism, is absolutely groundless. I admit that those who are outside the church must be instructed before the symbol of adoption is conferred on them, but I maintain that believers' children, who are born within the church, are members of the family of the kingdom of God from the womb. Yes, and what is more, I turn back on them the argument which they absurdly use against us. For since God has adopted the children of believers before they are born, I establish from that, that they must not be cheated of the external sign. COMMENTARY ON ACTS 10:47.[28]

CHILDREN ARE NOT MEMBERS OF THE KINGDOM UNLESS THEY BELIEVE. PETER RIEDEMANN: Infants have not been born of God in the Christian sense, that is, through the proclamation of the Word, through faith and the Holy Spirit. Therefore, they cannot receive true baptism, which is acceptance into the church of Christ. Now, since all who are born of Adam share in his heritage, any who wish to be incorporated into the church of

Christ must be born of Christ in the Christian way. They may then be accepted in the right way, which Christ revealed to his church.

As said above, the birth of Christ took place through the proclamation of the Word. Mary believed the angel and received the Holy Spirit through faith. The Spirit worked together with her faith so that she conceived Christ, and he was born of her. Whoever wishes to be born in the Christian way must first, like Mary, hear the Word and believe it. Thus, when that person's faith is sealed with the Holy Spirit, one may in truth be accepted into the church of Christ. This is how it was done by the apostles.

Nowhere do we find that the apostles baptized children; on the contrary, we find that they obeyed their Master's instructions and teaching. They said, "If you believe, you may indeed be baptized." This implied, "If you do not believe, you may not be baptized." CONFESSION OF FAITH.[29]

IF FAITH IS REQUIRED FOR THE RECEPTION OF BAPTISM, IS IT NOT ALSO REQUIRED FOR THE RECEPTION OF PREACHING? MARTIN LUTHER: You do not baptize infants, as you say, because they do not believe. Then why do you preach the Word to adults who are without faith, but who might over time come to believe? Certainly you do so for this reason alone: that it has been decreed by God. If you baptize me because I am able to say these words "I believe," then you baptize me on the basis of nothing else than me myself and in my name. Now because it is unknown to you whether the person being baptized is believing or unbelieving, such baptizing takes place only because of God's decree or command. Therefore infants should not be excluded from baptism because you administer baptism according to the common rule or decree without distinction to everyone, whether he believes or does not believe.

And it would be horrible if I should be baptized on the basis of my own confession. What would you do if in secret you know that the person who

---

[27]CRR 12:257, 258-59 (QGT 17:332, 335-37); alluding to 1 Pet 3:21; Mt 28:19.
[28]CNTC 6:318-19* (CO 48:252).

[29]CRR 9:102*; alluding to Mt 28:18-20; Mk 16:15-16.

publicly desires baptism or the sacrament is unbelieving? You cannot deny it to him, and yet you know full well that there is no faith present—just like Christ when he offered Judas the sacrament. Therefore we must allow everyone to come to baptism. . . . and we must commend his faith and the salvation of his soul to God. LUTHER'S MARGINALIA ON MARK 10:14.[30]

NEW BELIEVERS SHOULD THIRST FOR THE WORD. RUDOLF GWALTHER: Finally, it is declared how Cornelius behaved himself after all these things. They sought to have Peter (says Luke) to abide with them a few days. And there was no other cause of this desire, but that they were enflamed with the love of the gospel and desired to hear him every day, because they would be more confirmed in the knowledge of true salvation. Furthermore, they could not be so soon satisfied with the presence of their friend, who they perceived had ministered so great a grace to them. And here is truly expressed the property of those that faithfully believe. They do not loathe the teaching of that Word or attribute so much to themselves to think that they shall have hereafter no more need of it. . . .

Moreover, they show themselves thankful and kind toward the ministers of God, by whose diligence they are taught in matters of faith and salvation. For they think it a matter of no great weight to requite them with carnal benefits which give to them spiritual riches. For they understand that their salvation depends chiefly on these spiritual riches. HOMILY 77, ACTS 10:44-48.[31]

---

[30]WA 48:120; cf. Plass, ed., *What Luther Says*, 1:52.

[31]Gwalther, *Homelyes or Sermons upon the Actes*, 464* (*In Acta Apostolorum*, 144r).

11:1-18 PETER'S REPORT TO
THE JERUSALEM CHURCH

Now the apostles and the brothers[a] who were throughout Judea heard that the Gentiles also had received the word of God. ²So when Peter went up to Jerusalem, the circumcision party[b] criticized him, saying, ³"You went to uncircumcised men and ate with them." ⁴But Peter began and explained it to them in order: ⁵"I was in the city of Joppa praying, and in a trance I saw a vision, something like a great sheet descending, being let down from heaven by its four corners, and it came down to me. ⁶Looking at it closely, I observed animals and beasts of prey and reptiles and birds of the air. ⁷And I heard a voice saying to me, 'Rise, Peter; kill and eat.' ⁸But I said, 'By no means, Lord; for nothing common or unclean has ever entered my mouth.' ⁹But the voice answered a second time from heaven, 'What God has made clean, do not call common.' ¹⁰This happened three times, and all was drawn up again into heaven. ¹¹And behold, at that very moment three men arrived at the house in which we were, sent to me from Caesarea. ¹²And the Spirit told me to go with them, making no distinction. These six brothers also accompanied me, and we entered the man's house. ¹³And he told us how he had seen the angel stand in his house and say, 'Send to Joppa and bring Simon who is called Peter; ¹⁴he will declare to you a message by which you will be saved, you and all your household.' ¹⁵As I began to speak, the Holy Spirit fell on them just as on us at the beginning. ¹⁶And I remembered the word of the Lord, how he said, 'John baptized with water, but you will be baptized with the Holy Spirit.' ¹⁷If then God gave the same gift to them as he gave to us when we believed in the Lord Jesus Christ, who was I that I could stand in God's way?" ¹⁸When they heard these things they fell silent. And they glorified God, saying, "Then to the Gentiles also God has granted repentance that leads to life."

a Or brothers and sisters   b Or Jerusalem, those of the circumcision

---

OVERVIEW: Peter's retelling of the events of Acts 10 to the church in Jerusalem does not elicit a great deal of comment from the reformers—for them, Acts 10 is clear enough. They return to a common theme: the ministry of the Word is commissioned and enabled by God. They detail the painstaking efforts Peter took not to offend devout Jews, so that they would understand the inclusion of the Gentiles to be God's work. While it might be surprising that there is so much resistance to the inclusion of the Gentiles—considering Jesus' commission to be witnesses "in Jerusalem and in all Judea and Samaria, and to the end of the earth" (Acts 1:8; cf. Lk 24:47)—Calvin and Beza surmise that these believers understood Jesus' words according to their preconceptions about the new covenant, which still incorporated the old covenant ceremonies. The reformers highlight Peter's calm, kind and humble response to such a churlish group; this is praised as the best way to combat and correct error.

THE STORY IS ALREADY CLEAR. CARDINAL CAJETAN: This chapter is sufficiently clear as history. Therefore, there will only be a few annotations. COMMENTARY ON ACTS 11:1-18.[1]

PETER WAS CAREFUL NOT TO OFFEND JEWISH BELIEVERS. DESIDERIUS ERASMUS: Peter took every precaution so that this could not be censured justly. God also reassured him: so that no scruple should stick in his mind, the vision was presented three times. Further, it was through the Spirit that he learned that a delegation from

---

¹Cajetan, *In Acta Apostolorum*, 223v.

Cornelius was at hand. He does not admit them into his house at once, lest a Jew should seem to be eager for relations with Gentiles, but he greets them in front of the door and asks, with witnesses on hand, why they had come. He makes this inquiry for the sake of the Jews who were present, rather than for himself. Then when he learns that the two visions corresponded, he does not set out there except with some Jews of approved faith in his company, who might be witnesses and give consent to the proceedings, so that later they could turn from witnesses into defenders against critics. Again, when they came to the house of Cornelius, Peter did not enter immediately, as though he were longing for a conversation, but he sent a man to announce that he was there, so that Cornelius might meet him and bring him in—Peter was not unaware how eagerly he would be received.

The centurion fell at his feet and worshiped Peter. This showed to the Jews who were present Cornelius's remarkable readiness of mind. Further, Peter asks in the presence of these Jews why he was summoned, so that the story, heard from Cornelius's mouth, might have more credibility for his Jewish companions. Finally, the Holy Spirit was sent without anyone asking: prayers were not yet poured forth, hands had not been imposed, baptism had not been given. Even so he did not baptize them without addressing the circumcised who were present and showing that it was not right to deny baptism to those on whom God had bestowed his Holy Spirit.

Such, truly, was that evangelical prudence of Peter, the shepherd. He knew the nature of the Jews, how they prided themselves on account of a little bit of cut-off foreskin, how they shunned the uncircumcised. Accordingly, he does everything to avoid the slightest offense. He desired that Gentiles should come into the fellowship of the gospel, but, if possible, without the loss of the Jewish race. PARAPHRASE OF ACTS 11:1.[2]

SOME THOUGHT THE NEW COVENANT STILL INCLUDED SUBMISSION TO THE LAW OF MOSES.

JOHN CALVIN: Luke recounts that the report of this one household's conversion had become common knowledge among the brothers everywhere; [this renown] arose from shock. The Jews regarded it as monstrous that Gentiles be added to them, just as if they had heard that people had been created out of stones.... But since so many predictions of the prophets had foretold that the church must be gathered from all the people after the coming of the Messiah, and Christ had given the commandment to the apostles about preaching the gospel throughout the whole world, how is it possible that the conversion of a few people disturbs some as if it were something unheard of and truly horrifies others as if it were a monstrosity? I reply that all that had been predicted about the calling of the Gentiles had been so interpreted as if the Gentiles would submit to the law of Moses in order to have a place in the church. But the manner of the calling, the beginnings of which they were then seeing, was not only unknown but appeared to be inconsistent with all reason. For they were imagining that, with the ceremonies abolished, it is impossible for the Gentiles to be joined with the sons of Abraham to form one body, without grave injury being done to the sacred covenant of God. COMMENTARY ON ACTS 11:1.[3]

TRUE CHRISTIANS RECEIVE THE WORD OF GOD.

RUDOLF GWALTHER: Here is also to be considered the phrase or manner of speaking, where [Luke] says the Gentiles "received the Word of God," whereas he might have said they received Christendom and were made partakers of Christ and his church. But this way he thought to say something more, and to make a difference between true Christianity and false posturing by some people. For they receive the Word of God who acknowledge it to be the Word of God, and therefore they labor to be transformed into it and to become followers of God. HOMILY 78, ACTS 11:1-17.[4]

---

[3]CNTC 6:320, 321* (CO 48:253-54).
[4]Gwalther, *Homelyes or Sermons upon the Actes*, 466* (*In Acta Apostolorum*, 144v-145r).

[2]CWE 50:76-77* (LB 7:711-12).

The Party of the Circumcision. Theodore Beza: Luke begins to distinguish circumcised believers from uncircumcised believers, just as Paul is accustomed to call the former Jews and the latter Greeks, as Luke will soon also do. Why therefore, you may say, did he not call them Jews here? Assuredly because this would have been too general a name, because then those who were not counted in the church would also thus have been included with these. Nevertheless there was not an exchange with Peter, for then those would be distinguished from these, whom he called brothers; this is evident by the apostles and the presbytery of the church, who were probably not arguing with Peter. Finally, Luke wished to show the origin of the controversy in this way. From this, it becomes evident that those people did not yet know the abolition of circumcision, and they thought that the Law must be joined with the gospel. Because of this, though afterwards they are said to have accepted Peter's words (or at least a good number had come to agree with him), they still judged that Gentiles should be circumcised after baptism. So they stirred up a great commotion in the church. τὸ διεκρίνοντο, I translate this as "to dispute" [*Altercari*], but in other passages as "to doubt" [*Addubitare*]. There are those who, when they are uncertain about something among themselves, discuss the reasoning for both sides. There are also those of whom it is said, obstinately they do not want to be persuaded by another opinion; so they grasp at anything for the sake of disputing. Annotations on Acts 11:2.[5]

The Importance of Being Sent. Peter Riedemann: Christ begins by saying, "Go into all the world." The disciples could not carry out his charge before he had commanded them. Without his command, they would have known nothing of mission, and above all, nothing of going into all the world. The story of the disciples murmuring against Peter for entering a Gentile's house is proof of that. Even Peter testified that it was an unusual thing for a Jew to enter the house of a Gentile, but he did it on account of a revelation from the Lord. What Peter says makes it clear that if he had not had a special revelation, he would not have gone to the Gentiles, in spite of the command Christ had already given him. Even less would he have gone there to preach without being commissioned. . . .

Since they cannot preach without first being sent, it is certain that God, in giving them his command to go out, puts his word in his messengers' mouths. The Lord himself testifies to this. . . . Therefore all who have not been sent have no word from God. They only have what they have stolen from the Scriptures or from one another. That is the main reason God's commission is necessary. Confession of Faith.[6]

Believers Should Be Subject to the Judgment of the Church. The English Annotations: Peter willingly submitted to the judgment of the church, to give them account of what he had had done. By this means he taught us what each of us ought to do and better instructed those who erred. Peter did not pretend to be greater than the church. Annotations on Acts 11:4.[7]

The Holy Spirit Carefully Cultivates His Hearers. John Donne: As a gardener takes every bough of a young tree or of a vine and leads them and places them against a wall where they will have the best advantage and thus produce the most and the best fruit, so the Holy Spirit leads and places the words and sentences of the preacher, one on a usurer, another on an adulterer, another on an ambitious person, another on an active or passive briber, even when the preacher knows of no usurer, no adulterer, no ambitious person, no briber active or passive in the congregation. No, it is not only "while he was still speaking," but, as Saint Peter himself reports the same story, "As I began to speak, the Holy

---

[5]Beza, *Annotationes Majores*, 1:504; alluding to Jude 9.

[6]CRR 9:186-87; alluding to Rom 10:15; Jer 1:9-10.
[7]Downame, ed., *Annotations*, JJJ2r*; alluding to 1 Cor 14:29.

Spirit fell on them." SERMON 31, PREACHED ON PENTECOST.[8]

THE FOUR-FOOTED CREATURES ARE GENTILES. DESIDERIUS ERASMUS: [Peter says:] "Now the events themselves have shown me what was intended by the riddle of the vision I had seen. These [people] were, clearly, those four-footed creatures, creeping things and fowl that we circumcised abhor but that God has decided to make clean through faith. He does not want us to regard anything as unclean which has been sanctified through evangelical faith." PARAPHRASE OF ACTS 11:15-16.[9]

CHRIST HIMSELF CONFIRMS THE SALVATION OF THE GENTILES. JOHN CALVIN: We must also call to mind that Christ uses the word *Spirit* to describe not only the gift of tongues and similar things but also the whole grace of our renewal. But since those gifts are a remarkable proof of the power of Christ, this sentence is very well suited to them. Let me put it more clearly. Since Christ bestowed the visible graces of the Spirit on the apostles he made it plain that the Spirit is in his hands, so in this way he testified that he is the one and only source of purity, righteousness and complete regeneration. Now Peter applies this to his plan of action in this way, that, since Christ led the way, bearing the power of baptism along with him, he himself was bound to follow with the accessory, that is, the outward symbol of water. COMMENTARY ON ACTS 11:16.[10]

WHAT DOES PETER'S RESPONSE TEACH US? JOHANN SPANGENBERG: First, according to Peter's example we are to answer the wrathful and cantankerous winsomely, amicably and reasonably. For Solomon says, "A lenient answer calms wrath, but a harsh word stirs up fury." Second, we should let ourselves be satisfied with a friendly and humble response, especially if the matter is itself divine, useful and salvific—even if it seems quite different to the world. And we should not merely be content with God's grace, but much more we should praise, worship and give thanks in the highest to God for this. BRIEF EXEGESIS OF ACTS 11:1-18.[11]

---

[8]Donne, *Works*, 2:25*.
[9]CWE 50:78 (LB 7:713).
[10]CNTC 6:324-25* (CO 48:257).
[11]Spangenberg, *Der Apostel Geschichte*, 98v-99r; quoting Prov 15:1.

11:19-30 THE CHURCH IN ANTIOCH

[19]Now those who were scattered because of the persecution that arose over Stephen traveled as far as Phoenicia and Cyprus and Antioch, speaking the word to no one except Jews. [20]But there were some of them, men of Cyprus and Cyrene, who on coming to Antioch spoke to the Hellenists[a] also, preaching the Lord Jesus. [21]And the hand of the Lord was with them, and a great number who believed turned to the Lord. [22]The report of this came to the ears of the church in Jerusalem, and they sent Barnabas to Antioch. [23]When he came and saw the grace of God, he was glad, and he exhorted them all to remain faithful to the Lord with steadfast purpose, [24]for he was a good man, full of the Holy Spirit and of faith. And a great many people were added to the Lord. [25]So Barnabas went to Tarsus to look for Saul, [26]and when he had found him, he brought him to Antioch. For a whole year they met with the church and taught a great many people. And in Antioch the disciples were first called Christians.

[27]Now in these days prophets came down from Jerusalem to Antioch. [28]And one of them named Agabus stood up and foretold by the Spirit that there would be a great famine over all the world (this took place in the days of Claudius). [29]So the disciples determined, every one according to his ability, to send relief to the brothers[b] living in Judea. [30]And they did so, sending it to the elders by the hand of Barnabas and Saul.

a Or Greeks (that is, Greek-speaking non-Jews)   b Or brothers and sisters

OVERVIEW: Now that the initial disagreements in Acts over the inclusion of the Gentiles have been settled peaceably, our reformers focus on gospel growth among the believers in Antioch. The Acts 1:8 commission continues to blossom. The dispersion of Jerusalem believers instigated by the persecution after Stephen's death has begun to bear fruit beyond Jerusalem, Judea and Samaria. The reformers emphasize the wisdom of the disciples in sending Barnabas to Antioch to ensure that those new converts have good pastoral care and are united in common faith with believers elsewhere.

Agabus's prophecy of the looming famine prods Reformation commentators to ask again about the purpose of suffering, as well as to consider the church's social responsibility in lean times. Calvin provides an extensive list of the advantages of recognizing God's approaching judgment, since judgment and suffering are God's gracious and merciful methods of offering opportunities for sinners—that is, both good and bad people according to human judgment—to repent and be drawn back into fellowship with him.

Contemplating the church's social responsibility leads to the third and final debate featured in this commentary between the Radical and magisterial reformers over the community of goods. Notice that all the magisterial reformers quoted here advocate for robust Christian charity, lamenting contemporary greed that seeks riches from others' basic human needs. However, they stop short of legislating a community of goods; instead parishioners should give freely and according to their ability. Still, some Anabaptists feel a community free of personal property is essential for a truly biblical church to exist.

11:19-26 The Fruitfulness of the First Christians in Antioch

"CHRISTIAN BLOOD IS THE SEED OF THE CHURCH." JOHANN SPANGENBERG: There is no cross so great, so grisly, so horrible that very little good is brought with it for Christendom. For in the cross and persecution of Christians, faith increases, the gospel is in full force, the hearts of Christians are kindled and prepared to suffer for Christ's sake whatever they must. The more Christians are persecuted and slaughtered, the more Christians are born. For Tertullian writes, "The Christian's blood is the seed out of which Christians grow."[1] And in Christians' blood the devil must be drowned. Brief Exegesis of Acts 11:19-25.[2]

The Dispersed Christians Initially Confined Their Witness to Fellow Jews.

Desiderius Erasmus: True, those who had been scattered by the storm of persecution that arose after the death of Stephen went through the villages and cities all the way to Phoenicia and Cyprus (the island facing it), as well as to Antioch, which separates Phoenicia from Cilicia, proclaiming among all the evangelical word they had received from the apostles. They did not, however, dare to share it with anyone except those of the Jewish race alone—not indeed from invidious motives, but out of regard for religion, thinking it was not allowed to give what was holy to dogs, which the Lord had forbidden. Paraphrase of Acts 11:19.[3]

Grace, an Antidote Against the Devil.

The Book of Common Prayer (1549): Lord, we beseech you, grant your people grace to avoid the infections of the devil, and with pure heart and mind to follow you, the only God. Through Jesus Christ our Lord. Amen. The Collect for the Eighteenth Sunday after Trinity.[4]

God Works Even Through Christian Differences.

Rudolf Gwalther: All were dispersed because of the same faith and doctrine of Christ, even though they did not agree in all points touching the order and ministry of the gospel. Some of them preached to the Jews only, who were ignorant of the things done between Peter and Cornelius; some others, Luke writes, were from Cyprus and Cyrene, came to Antioch and preached to the Greeks, that is, to the Gentiles. So it often times happens that in some things they who are counted the most faithful servants of Jesus Christ disagree, and God so disposes his gifts that his Word may be of the more authority and that its success should not seem to depend on human harmony. . . . Therefore let it offend no one if nowadays they see anything similar going on in the church. Homily 79, Acts 11:18-21.[5]

Barnabas Sent to Affirm the Gentiles.

Desiderius Erasmus: Barnabas, the Levite, a Cypriot by race and a man of apostolic sincerity, was sent [to Antioch] by the apostles, so that by being present he might look carefully into what was going on there; if he found that what had been done was of the will of God, he should confirm it with the authority of the apostles. So great was the caution in admitting the Gentiles to the gospel. Not that the apostles did not greatly desire this, but they feared that if it were rashly done it might later be annulled by the Jews, or that the Gentiles would have little self-confidence, as though they might need support of the Law. Paraphrase of Acts 11:22.[6]

Barnabas and the Beginnings of the Antiochene Church.

The English Annotations: The burden of forming and ordering the church of Christ, appointing and designating pastors and ministers to the several congregations and holding them in holy unity, they now lay on the apostles. Therefore, to confirm those who were converted to the faith they send this son of consolation to Antioch, where a famous church was now beginning to order and establish itself. Annotations on Acts 11:22.[7]

Faith's Beginning and End Belong to God.

Rudolf Gwalther: Luke declares a

---

[1]Tertullian, *Apology*, ANF 3:55.
[2]Spangenberg, *Der Apostel Geschichte*, 99v-100r.
[3]CWE 50:78 (LB 7:713); alluding to MT 7:6; 15:26.
[4]BCP 1549, 65*.

[5]Gwalther, *Homelyes or Sermons upon the Actes*, 473, 474* (*In Acta Apostolorum*, 147r).
[6]CWE 50:79* (LB 7:714).
[7]Downame, ed., *Annotations*, JJJ3r*.

notable success of the gospel. . . . He first declares the efficient cause, lest anyone might ascribe it to merely human ministry. For he says the hand of the Lord was with them. By this we gather that all success of faith and salvation depends on God and that nothing is to be attributed to us other than the outward ministry. . . . And it is good oftentimes to remember this, both because ministers should not grow too proud and so that they whom God has illuminated with true faith might learn to be thankful to him. Also the evangelist expresses the proper end of Christian faith, which is that they who through ignorance, superstition or sin have turned from God might repent and turn again to him. HOMILY 79, ACTS 11:18-21.[8]

THE SIMPLICITY OF GOSPEL PREACHING. HEINRICH BULLINGER: Barnabas introduced no new doctrine to the church in Antioch but, correctly and simply, plants this institution in Christ Jesus, he confirms them and he strengthens them, encouraging them to continue to cling to the Lord with all their heart. COMMENTARY ON ACTS 11:22-24.[9]

WHAT WERE CHRISTIANS CALLED BEFORE THIS TIME? JOHANN SPANGENBERG: Before this they were called brothers and disciples. Here in Antioch they first received this name, so that they were called Christians—from Christ their Master and Savior. This is our gain as Christians—not without danger, but still given to us out of God's providence. BRIEF EXEGESIS OF ACTS 11:26.[10]

THE CHRISTIAN NAME. THE ENGLISH ANNOTATIONS: Before they were called disciples and Nazarenes. . . . Now at Antioch they were first called Christians. This city had so much honor that from there Christ spread, as it were, his banner, so that it

might appear to the world that there was a people who would follow him and glory to be called by his sacred name. ANNOTATIONS ON ACTS 11:26.[11]

IS THE NAME "CHRISTIAN" COMFORTING? JOHANN SPANGENBERG: Certainly in every way. For Messiah in Hebrew means *Christos* in Greek, *Unctus* in Latin, [that is,] an "anointed king" in German. From this, we Christians are called anointed royalty, not like servants of kings but rather friends and brothers of the King of all kings. For we have all things in common with Christ, even his holy and blessed name. Now if a Christian is afflicted by the devil, the world and tyrants, he should remember only his name, that he is God's child, he is Christ's brother and co-heir, then he will certainly overcome, [receiving] consolation and joy in heart and conscience. If he is afraid of sin, death and hell, he should remember his name; then he will be comforted. For in Christ, the devil, death, sin and hell are extinguished and gobbled up like a little spark of fire in an enormous sea—so long as we remain in faith, giving the devil no opportunity nor making a covenant with sin. BRIEF EXEGESIS OF ACTS 11:26.[12]

11:27-30 *Famine Relief for Judea*

GOD'S ECONOMY OF PROSPERITY AND PERSECUTION. RUDOLF GWALTHER: Although our Lord and Savior Jesus Christ is always present with his church, still, as he foretold diversely and in many ways, he allows the church to be troubled, having adversity, as it were, by continual difficulties, yet still in prosperity. The principal cause is partly that he would bridle the lustiness of our flesh and partly because he would teach us that he is as well able to deliver his people in adversity as to maintain them in prosperity. We have heretofore seen certain notable examples of this.

For in the beginning the gospel was being prosperously preached at Jerusalem and brought a great

---

[8]Gwalther, *Homelyes or Sermons upon the Actes*, 475* (*In Acta Apostolorum*, 147v); alluding to 1 Cor 3. An efficient cause is the primary, effective cause of change or movement in any sequence of causes.
[9]Bullinger, *In Acta Apostolorum*, 134v-135r.
[10]Spangenberg, *Der Apostel Geschichte*, 100v.

[11]Downame, ed., *Annotations*, JJJ3r*.
[12]Spangenberg, *Der Apostel Geschichte*, 100v-101v.

number of disciples to Christ. Shortly after rose a tempest of persecution that drove down the flourishing of the church flat to the ground. By and by, when Saul was converted to Christ, suddenly the church was quiet, and the doctrine of Christ was being carried to the Gentiles, with the likelihood of great increase, seeing that at Antioch, the noblest city in all Syria, there was a church of Gentiles assembled together and were there first called that noble name of Christians. But, behold, a great and strange adversity followed, namely, a famine, which as it troubled the whole world, so it most miserably afflicted the faithful, whose goods were spent partly in funding the poor of the church and partly were taken from them in the rage of persecution.

The consideration of this is most profitable for us, for here we may learn to be offended the less if a similar adversity befell us in these days. And of all others, this present place is worthy to be diligently considered, as well for the manifold comfort as for the instruction which the Holy Spirit here sets forth. For he declares the famine that was in the church, and he sets out the fatherly providence of God, having concern for the church, and shows what way and counsel the faithful took, seeing the public calamity which was likely to ensue. HOMILY 81, ACTS 11:27-30.[13]

THE GOOD NEWS OF BAD NEWS. JOHN CALVIN: But yet the prophecy about the famine seems to have been a calamitous and very undesirable one. For what was the point of making people miserable by the prediction of a dismal event before the time for it? I reply that, when the judgments of God and due punishments for sins are threatening, there are many reasons why it is advantageous for people to be warned well beforehand about them. . . . I pass over others which occur all through the prophets; that an opportunity is given for people to come to their senses, so that those who are provoking his wrath against themselves may anticipate the judgment of God; that the faithful are warned

in time so that they may prepare themselves for endurance; that the stubborn ill will of the ungodly is overcome; that good people, just like bad, learn that calamities and misfortunes do not befall them by chance, but that they are punishments by which God takes vengeance on the sins of the world; that, in this way, those who are too self-satisfied, even in their faults are aroused from their torpor. The value of the present prediction is perfectly plain from the context because it was a stimulus to the people of Antioch to give help to the brothers in their distress. COMMENTARY ON ACTS 11:28.[14]

ANCIENT HISTORIANS INFORM US OF THE SEVERITY OF THIS FAMINE. JOHN CALVIN: Suetonius also mentions this famine and narrates that crusts were thrown at Claudius's head in the open forum, and that he was so stricken with fear of stoning that for the whole of his life afterwards he paid particular attention to the food supply.[15] But Josephus in the fifteenth book of the *Antiquities* relates that Judea was afflicted by a serious scarcity because of a succession of droughts. COMMENTARY ON ACTS 11:28.[16]

THIS FAMINE WAS A PUNISHMENT FROM GOD. JOHANN SPANGENBERG: This famine was a punishment and plague sent by God on account of the ingratitude of those who valued so poorly the magnificent, great light of the gospel and who did not turn away from their pagan sins, such as idolatry, witchcraft, fornication and such similar vices. BRIEF EXEGESIS OF ACTS 11:28.[17]

"AS EACH WAS ABLE TO GIVE." JOHN CALVIN: Here we see that the Antioch church adhered to the method which Paul prescribes, whether they did so of their own accord or whether they had been informed about his direction. And it is surely not to be doubted that he was consistent in both

---

[13]Gwalther, *Homelyes or Sermons upon the Actes*, 481* (*In Acta Apostolorum*, 149v).

[14]CNTC 6:333 (CO 48:264).
[15]Suetonius, *The Twelve Caesars*, 5.18; contrary to the CO editors' note, see CO 48:264; cf. CNTC 6:334 n. 1.
[16]CNTC 6:334* (CO 48:264); citing Josephus, *Antiquities*, 15.9.
[17]Spangenberg, *Der Apostel Geschichte*, 102r.

places. Therefore this rule must be followed, that each one consider how much has been given to himself, and kindly share with the brothers, as one who is going to render an account, so the result will be that the poor person has a liberal mind, and a small gift is looked on as a rich and splendid sacrifice. Commentary on Acts 11:29.[18]

The Antiochene Example of Charity. Rudolf Gwalther: After the people of Antioch had believed the prophesying of Agabus, they called to mind the state of their needy brothers, and weighing diligently with themselves what a famine was likely to be like at that time, they prepared themselves to do the deeds of Christian charity and devotion, a thing not common among the children of this world. For when they perceive that a famine is likely to follow, they apply themselves to their gainful devices, they heap up corn and hoard in their storehouses to make from a public calamity their private profit and advantage. Indeed, by these fellows' subtleties it comes to pass that they who are in need are the more distressed with poverty, and the famine holds on longer, because they still greedily gaze after more profit.

But the Christians at Antioch whom Christ allowed to be called after his own name did otherwise. For their chief care was how to support their poor and needy brothers. And in this case they think their brothers the Jews have the most need, partly because they knew their goods were taken from them . . . and partly because they knew they were bound to them, in that they had received from them the wholesome doctrine of the gospel and knowledge of Christ their Savior. For being godly and wise people, they did easily perceive that it was not without the providence of God that they whose goods as yet were not consumed should for this end be admonished by the famine to ensue. Therefore, they thought that God in this public scarcity did on their brothers' behalf require this deed of charity from them. This is a very notable example of Christian gratitude, whereby we are taught

what duty students owe to their teachers, seeing the Antiochians acknowledge themselves to be debtors to all the Jews because they had learned the truth from the Jews. Homily 81, Acts 11:27-30.[19]

Wherever Property Is Not Held in Common, There Is No Church. Peter Walpot: Whoever lives in personal property is a liar in the confession of his faith. For the Christian faith establishes a holy Christian church and community of the saints.[20] Where there is no community of the saints, there is no true, unblemished Christian church. Therefore, they all are lying who say that community is not necessary and is no foundation of [Christian] teaching. It is, however, indeed an article of the faith and an institution of Christ and the Holy Spirit and his teaching. Thus, as it is essential to hold to the teaching of the apostles, to prayer, to the breaking of bread, so also it is essential to hold to the community of goods. For community is not some curiosity that the apostles did for the sake of novelty but is a serious divine command and should be rightly and reasonably practiced in Jerusalem as elsewhere. The Great Article Book: On Peace and Joint Property.[21]

Those Rebaptizers Just Do Not Like to Work! Philipp Melanchthon: This article[22] attracts that lazy rabble who do not like work and who know much better how to guzzle what they have than to earn it honestly. But that such teaching establishes pure thievery and chaos every person can understand easily. So then, in order to warn and instruct the simple, we want to demonstrate briefly from God's Word and command that Christians may have personal property and that it is chaos and contrary to God to command everyone to hold all goods in common. . . .

---

[18]CNTC 6:334* (CO 48:265); alluding to 2 Cor 8:3.

[19]Gwalther, *Homelyes or Sermons upon the Actes*, 484-85* (*In Acta Apostolorum*, 150v).
[20]A reference to the third article of the Apostles' Creed.
[21]QGT 12:184.
[22]"Christians must hold all their goods in common and cannot have personal property." In this pamphlet Melanchthon lists five articles of the Anabaptists and refutes them by listing several prooftexts from Scripture that he briefly expounds.

"Your cistern should flow freely, but you should remain lord over it." Here holy Scripture teaches that each person should remain lord over his own estate, but from these fruits and benefits we should help others. This is what he means when he says, "Your cistern should flow freely." And this truly is a consolation to a reasonable, God-fearing Christian, because he knows that this worldly order pleases God—that we possess goods and seek nourishment and that God therefore will protect his order and wants to help nourish us. But contrary to this, the rebaptizers lift up the apostles' example when the Christians in Jerusalem shared their goods in common. This is not a command. For at the time there were also many Christians who did not hold things in common in this manner, but rather their goods remained in their possession, as we can prove from Paul. There Paul also teaches that we should not be forced to give our goods to anyone but instead should give alms as each has decided.

But since there was a great persecution in Jerusalem and Christians' possessions were taken from them and they were chased away daily, it was beneficial to them that they sell their own goods and pooling together the money, keep it for essentials. Thus, they did this due to persecution and not because such works were a new holiness, as some monks, rebaptizers and other crazy saints understand such confusion and interruption of the natural order and government to be a precious and heavenly existence, not understanding that Christian holiness must be in the heart and that it pleases God that we act in our external life according to normal and orderly government. THE REFUTATION OF SEVERAL UNCHRISTIAN ARTICLES WHICH THE ANABAPTISTS ASSERT.[23]

CARE FOR THOSE IN NEED. SWISS BRETHREN CONFESSION OF HESSE (1578): We believe, acknowledge and confess that the believing, newborn Christians and children of God are responsible to look after the poor members among their fellow believers: the old, the sick, the widows, the orphans; to feed and provide for them and in addition to show common love to others in need. ARTICLE 33, REGARDING THE POOR.[24]

DO WE PREPARE FOR FAMINES IN THE SAME WAY AS THE DISCIPLES DID THEN? JOHANN SPANGENBERG: Yes, backwards like the crab. When the rich usurers and scrooges hear and note that a famine is present, God help us, how they go into a frenzy of purchasing, gathering and storing up! Not because they want to help the poor in need, but only to abuse them and clean them out. How masterfully the prophet Amos describes such people! These Christians did not act in this way; instead, they helped each other in need and made friends with mammon. In the end God accepted them into his abode, into eternal life. Amen. BRIEF EXEGESIS OF ACTS 11:29-30.[25]

---

[23]Melanchthon, *Verlegung etlicher unchristlicher Artikel*, C3r-v, C4r-v; alluding to Prov 5:15; 2 Cor 9:6-14.
[24]CRR 11:86*.
[25]Spangenberg, *Der Apostel Geschichte*, 102v; alluding to Amos 8:4-6; Lk 16:9.

12:1-5 PETER IMPRISONED AND DELIVERED

About that time Herod the king laid violent hands on some who belonged to the church. ²He killed James the brother of John with the sword, ³and when he saw that it pleased the Jews, he proceeded to arrest Peter also. This was during the days of Unleavened Bread. ⁴And when he had seized him, he put him in prison, delivering him over to four squads of soldiers to guard him, intending after the Passover to bring him out to the people. ⁵So Peter was kept in prison, but earnest prayer for him was made to God by the church.

OVERVIEW: Again temporal peace vanishes, compounding the affliction of the famine; Herod seizes Peter and slays James. The reformers acknowledge the often-forceful nature of affliction. Christians ought not to be surprised by persecution and suffering; more importantly, they should meditate daily, especially in times of affliction, on the sufferings of Jesus on their behalf, recalling how they end in glory, peace and life, not only for him but for them.

Calvin's comment on this passage reminds students of the Reformation that it was not only the Anabaptists who were threatened with execution (although they were indeed far more likely to suffer it). French Protestants too faced grisly state-sponsored opposition. The purgation of evangelicals was particularly fierce during the 1540s, when thousands of Waldensians were executed, the Meaux Circle was extinguished and many others died. Although there were nonlethal forms of punishment for heresy in France, the lethal methods were savage: their tongues were torn out, and they were paraded to the pyre, then burned alive.[1] Keeping this and the wars of religion in the Empire (e.g., the Schmalkaldic War) in mind, the discussion of the prayers of the church for Peter and their own contemporary intercession for the persecuted is a grave and important matter for the reformers.

HOW IS IT THAT THERE IS SUDDENLY SUCH VIOLENT PERSECUTION? JOHANN SPANGENBERG: Christianity is like April weather, which is erratic and changes nearly every hour: now it is snowing, soon it begins to rain, now the sun is shining, but then it is cloudy. So it went in the early church: Christ preached in Judea and Galilee in good peace for a season, then came a storm. Christ was imprisoned, crucified and killed. But this storm dissipated quickly, Christ arose from the dead, ascended to heaven, sent his Holy Spirit. Whenever the dear Son shone, the Christians rejoiced, but before they could look around, it thundered and there was lightning again! Stephen was stoned; the other Christians were persecuted and pursued. But this thunder and lightning also had an end; the dear Son broke out again. Samaria accepted God's Word; Saul—the Christians' greatest enemy and persecutor—was converted; Damascus, Lydda, Joppa and many other cities accepted the gospel. Most recently the Gentiles, Cornelius and his entire household company, converted to Christ. And everything continued along quite blissfully. The disciples even received a new name in Antioch: now they were called Christians. BRIEF EXEGESIS OF ACTS 12:1-4.[2]

SATAN'S CONTINUED ATTEMPTS TO THWART THE CHURCH. DESIDERIUS ERASMUS: This was, no doubt, Satan attempting through his instruments what he had attempted before, though he

---

[1] Bruce Gordon, *Calvin* (New Haven, CT: Yale University Press, 2009), 181-97. One very interesting fold in Calvin's discussions of persecution is the Nicodemites—French evangelicals who conformed their external behavior to Catholic standards—whom he condemned firmly.

[2] Spangenberg, *Der Apostel Geschichte*, 103v-104v.

succeeded only in making the name of Jesus more glorious. PARAPHRASE OF ACTS 12:1-2.[3]

AFFLICTIONS SHOULD BE EXPECTED. RUDOLF GWALTHER: And if one would consider and weigh the people of Israel's estate, as well in Egypt as in the wilderness, one shall see continual trials and, as it were, fresh floods of afflictions flowing by course. Now also as the primitive church proves, [afflictions] came in the years following. Neither is there any cause why we should look for any better in these days than the oracles of Christ declared shall be in the last days, where we are taught that the church shall be tested with famine, plague, wars and persecutions in all parts. Therefore it behooves us to prepare ourselves to suffer that when these things come to pass, we may consider how judgment must begin at the house of God and that we be judged by God to the end we should not be condemned with the unrepentant world. HOMILY 82, ACTS 12:1-5.[4]

WHICH HEROD? JOHANN ECK: So that you do not err and think that under the name Herod the same person is meant—not only in holy Scripture but also with the divine teachers, when the material requires it—we will here lay out the genealogy [see figure 1]. SERMON ON THE FEAST OF SAINT JAMES.[5]

PERSECUTION FUELED BY PERSONAL AMBITION. JOHN CALVIN: Therefore we must realize that there are many different causes for the church being assailed from all sides. Indeed, perverse zeal often does drive the ungodly headlong to fight eagerly for their superstitions and to offer a sacrifice to their idols by shedding innocent blood. But the majority are led only by their private concerns. For example, when, long ago, Nero knew that after the burning of the city he was infamous and hateful to the people, he chased after favor by this cunning

means, or at least made an effort to put an end to reproaches and complaints by murdering several thousand believers. In the same way, in order to win over the people who were anything but devoted to him, Herod delivers Christians to death, just as if they were a price for buying back favor. And in our day things are no different. COMMENTARY ON ACTS 12:3.[6]

THE POLITICAL CAUSES OF CHRISTIAN PERSECUTION. RUDOLF GWALTHER: Luke makes mention of the church, which in points of religion had divided themselves from the rest of the Jews. It seems that Agrippa was incensed against them, as authors of schism. For tyrants [cannot tolerate any] likelihood of schisms, however small, among their subjects, not because they delight so much in peace but because they fear their state, which they know stands in great hazard through schism and dissension. [This] is the cause that, although they are void of all religion, they seek to have in their realm a uniform consent in religion. HOMILY 82, ACTS 12:1-5.[7]

FATTENED IN CHRIST'S GOOD PASTURE, THE SHEEP APPROACH THE SLAUGHTERING BENCH WILLINGLY. DIRK PHILIPS: Commit yourself to endurance, and be content [in your] heart with the good will of God, your eternal and merciful Father, who on account of your salvation chastizes [you] and portrays to you the yieldedness of all the saints, prophets, apostles and witnesses to the truth, especially the perseverance and suffering of our Lord Jesus Christ, who was led to the slaughtering bench as an innocent Lamb and was speechless before his shearer, as the prophet said.

And you also are a sheep from the flock of the only Good Shepherd, Jesus Christ; led for a long time on his precious pasture and given to drink the clear water out of the fountain of his grace and truth. Through that your soul is fattened well

---

[3]CWE 50:80 (LB 7:715).
[4]Gwalther, *Homelyes or Sermons upon the Actes*, 487* (*In Acta Apostolorum*, 151v).
[5]Eck, *Christenliche Predigen*, 3:190r. Figure 1 appears on page 162.

[6]CNTC 6:337* (CO 48:267); alluding to Tacitus, *Annals*, 15.44 (cf. Suetonius, *The Twelve Caesars*, 6.16).
[7]Gwalther, *Homelyes or Sermons upon the Actes*, 488* (*In Acta Apostolorum*, 152r).

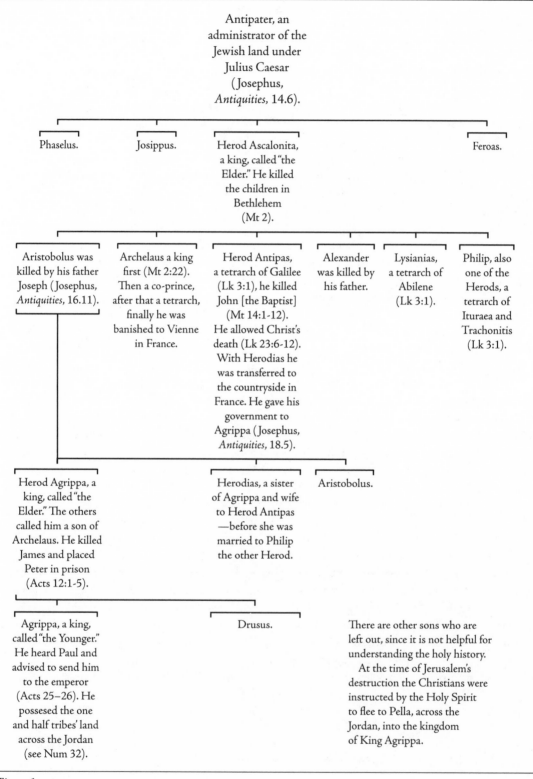

Antipater, an
administrator of the
Jewish land under
Julius Caesar
(Josephus,
Antiquities, 14.6).

Phaselus.

Josippus.

Herod Ascalonita,
a king, called "the
Elder." He killed
the children in
Bethlehem
(Mt 2).

Feroas.

Aristobolus was
killed by his father
Joseph (Josephus,
Antiquities, 16.11).

Archelaus a king
first (Mt 2:22).
Then a co-prince,
after that a tetrarch,
finally he was
banished to Vienne
in France.

Herod Antipas,
a tetrarch of Galilee
(Lk 3:1), he killed
John [the Baptist]
(Mt 14:1-12).
He allowed Christ's
death (Lk 23:6-12).
With Herodias he
was transferred to
the countryside in
France. He gave his
government to
Agrippa (Josephus,
Antiquities, 18.5).

Alexander
was killed by
his father.

Lysianias,
a tetrarch of
Abilene
(Lk 3:1).

Philip, also
one of the
Herods, a
tetrarch of
Ituraea and
Trachonitis
(Lk 3:1).

Herod Agrippa, a
king, called "the
Elder." The others
called him a son of
Archelaus. He killed
James and placed
Peter in prison
(Acts 12:1-5).

Herodias, a sister
of Agrippa and wife
to Herod Antipas
—before she was
married to Philip
the other Herod.

Aristobolus.

Agrippa, a king,
called "the Younger."
He heard Paul and
advised to send him
to the emperor
(Acts 25–26). He
possesed the one
and half tribes' land
across the Jordan
(see Num 32).

Drusus.

There are other sons who are
left out, since it is not helpful for
understanding the holy history.
    At the time of Jerusalem's
destruction the Christians were
instructed by the Holy Spirit
to flee to Pella, across the
Jordan, into the kingdom
of King Agrippa.

Figure 1.

according to my undoubted hope through such spiritual food and drink. Be still, patient and courageous in your suffering, so that you conquer for the sake of righteousness; and if you will be led to the slaughter bench at any time, reflect on your only good, trustworthy Shepherd Jesus Christ, who has gone before you and left you an example that you should follow in his footsteps. For it happens with Christians just as the prophet said: O Lord, we are killed daily for your sake and are counted as sheep for the slaughter, but in all this we conquer, says the apostle, through the one who has loved us. EPISTLE TO THE WIFE OF I. THE S. WHO LAY IMPRISONED AT ANTWERP.[8]

THE DAY OF THE AZYMA[9] PROTECTS PETER.

DESIDERIUS ERASMUS: Herod was, however, prevented from immediately killing Peter too by the day of the *azyma*, which in fact fell just then, an exceedingly holy day among the Jews, the time when the Jews had also feared to kill Jesus. And such is Jewish religion in its observance of feast days: they do not fear to propitiate the people with the blood of an innocent man, but they are afraid to violate a feast day, as though one is innocent of homicide who has already decided to kill! PARAPHRASE OF ACTS 12:3-5.[10]

PRAYER: THE CHRISTIAN'S WEAPON.

JOHANN SPANGENBERG: Now the congregation of Christians was much too weak to stand up against Herod and free Peter from prison through force. Therefore the Christians turned to God and prayed for Peter. The reverent prayer that penetrates through the clouds into heaven before God—that was their weapon, sword and rifle with which they freed Peter. They knew well that God had promised to hear whenever we merely call out to him in

the Spirit and in truth. Now if they could penetrate heaven with their prayer, how much more Herod's prison! BRIEF EXEGESIS OF ACTS 12:5.[11]

BE FERVENT IN PRAYER.

JOHN CALVIN: They testify by their prayers that they are persisting to the utmost of their ability in defending the cause for which Peter was suffering even at the risk of his life. This verse teaches, first of all, how we ought to be affected whenever we see our brothers attacked by the ungodly because of their testimony to the gospel. For if we do nothing and are not made anxious by their dangers, not only do we cheat them of the rightful duty of charity, but we are also treacherously abandoning the confession of our faith. And of course if we have common cause with them, even more if they are fighting for our safety, we are failing not so much them as ourselves and Christ. And the pressing need at present is that all who wish to be counted as Christians undertake prayer with far more eagerness than we can generally see. We see some of our brothers living in exile after they have been reduced to the direst straits, others in fetters, many plunged in stinking, foul pits, many dragged off to the flames, yes, and we even see the frequent devising of new instruments of torment, in which they are tortured for a long time and feel themselves dying. If these incentives do not spur us on at least to a desire to pray, we are worse than stupid. Therefore, as soon as some persecution arises, we ought to have recourse to prayer.

It is also probable that the church was the more concerned about the life of Peter because it would suffer too great a loss by his death. Luke not only says that prayer was made but at the same time adds *earnest* or *continual*. By that he means that the faithful did not pray in indifferent or cursory fashion, but as long as Peter was battling it out, they were bent on helping him, in what way they could, without flagging. COMMENTARY ON ACTS 12:5.[12]

---

[8]CRR 6:621-22* (BRN 10:678-79); alluding to Lk 21:19; 2 Cor 1:3; Heb 12:6; Job 1:21; Mt 23:31; Acts 4:3; 16:23; quoting Is 53:7 (cf. Acts 8:32); Ezek 34:18; Mal 4:3; Rom 12:12; Mt 5:10; 1 Pet 2:21; Rom 8:36.
[9]Erasmus has here transliterated instead of translating the Greek ἄζυμα, which means "unleavened bread."
[10]CWE 50:80 (LB 7:715).

[11]Spangenberg, *Der Apostel Geschichte*, 105v-106r; alluding to Jn 4:24-25 (cf. Ps 145:18).
[12]CNTC 6:338-39* (CO 48:268).

A TRUE CHRISTIAN TRUSTS AND KNOWS GOD'S PROVIDENCE. HANS HAS VON HALL-STATT: When a true Christian is plagued by tyrants, such a Christian will endure all suffering without despair. He is now certain and believes steadfastly that all misfortune must bring about the best for him. Then he will become joyful and defiant in the Spirit, like a joyful warrior against all trials, strong as a rock. He considers it an especially great joy and grace whenever a variety of tribulations come to him.

When tribulation and persecution come to an end, when he has experienced and learned from it that God deals wonderfully and kindly with his own, he would not exchange many goods for the misfortunes he suffered and the friendly grace of God he experienced in them. He becomes intimately aware of how powerful, gracious and merciful God is, that all things are in his hands and that our free will can do nothing in such matters. And when tyrants seriously undertake to deal with Christians doing this and that to them, inflicting this and that sort of martyrdom on them, threatening them hard and fast with the sword and other things, a true Christian knows, however, and is certain that they may not harm a hair on his head, may inflict no harm on him any more than God will allow. No matter how they rage, the look of tyranny in their eyes, we see often enough in the Bible that God's eye is on them and cares for his own. KUNSTBUCH: CONCERNING THE COMFORT OF CHRISTIANS IN PERSECUTION.[13]

MAY WE BE FAITHFUL TO DEATH. THE BOOK OF COMMON PRAYER (1549): Grant, O merciful God, that as your holy apostle James, leaving his father and all that he had, without delay, was obedient to the calling of your Son Jesus Christ and followed him: So we, forsaking all worldly and carnal affections, may be evermore ready to follow your commandments. Through Jesus Christ our Lord. Amen. THE COLLECT FOR THE FEAST OF SAINT JAMES THE APOSTLE.[14]

---

[13]CRR 12:449* (QGT 17:471); alluding to Rom 5:3-5; Lk 12:4-5; Mt 10:30; Lk 21:18.
[14]BCP 1549, 73*; alluding to Mt 4:18-21.

12:6-25 PETER'S APPEARANCE TO THE BELIEVERS AND HEROD'S DEATH

⁶Now when Herod was about to bring him out, on that very night, Peter was sleeping between two soldiers, bound with two chains, and sentries before the door were guarding the prison. ⁷And behold, an angel of the Lord stood next to him, and a light shone in the cell. He struck Peter on the side and woke him, saying, "Get up quickly." And the chains fell off his hands. ⁸And the angel said to him, "Dress yourself and put on your sandals." And he did so. And he said to him, "Wrap your cloak around you and follow me." ⁹And he went out and followed him. He did not know that what was being done by the angel was real, but thought he was seeing a vision. ¹⁰When they had passed the first and the second guard, they came to the iron gate leading into the city. It opened for them of its own accord, and they went out and went along one street, and immediately the angel left him. ¹¹When Peter came to himself, he said, "Now I am sure that the Lord has sent his angel and rescued me from the hand of Herod and from all that the Jewish people were expecting."

¹²When he realized this, he went to the house of Mary, the mother of John whose other name was Mark, where many were gathered together and were praying. ¹³And when he knocked at the door of the gateway, a servant girl named Rhoda came to answer. ¹⁴Recognizing Peter's voice, in her joy she did not open the gate but ran in and reported that Peter was standing at the gate. ¹⁵They said to her, "You are out of your mind." But she kept insisting that it was so, and they kept saying, "It is his angel!"¹⁶But Peter continued knocking, and when they opened, they saw him and were amazed. ¹⁷But motioning to them with his hand to be silent, he described to them how the Lord had brought him out of the prison. And he said, "Tell these things to James and to the brothers."ᵃ Then he departed and went to another place.

¹⁸Now when day came, there was no little disturbance among the soldiers over what had become of Peter. ¹⁹And after Herod searched for him and did not find him, he examined the sentries and ordered that they should be put to death. Then he went down from Judea to Caesarea and spent time there.

²⁰Now Herod was angry with the people of Tyre and Sidon, and they came to him with one accord, and having persuaded Blastus, the king's chamberlain,ᵇ they asked for peace, because their country depended on the king's country for food. ²¹On an appointed day Herod put on his royal robes, took his seat upon the throne, and delivered an oration to them. ²²And the people were shouting, "The voice of a god, and not of a man!" ²³Immediately an angel of the Lord struck him down, because he did not give God the glory, and he was eaten by worms and breathed his last.

²⁴But the word of God increased and multiplied.

²⁵And Barnabas and Saul returned fromᶜ Jerusalem when they had completed their service, bringing with them John, whose other name was Mark.

a Or brothers and sisters   b That is, trusted personal attendant   c Some manuscripts to

OVERVIEW: The themes of prayer and suffering continue in these passages. The juxtaposition of Peter's release against James's death reminds the reformers that it is not always God's will to deliver his children from affliction. They do not offer explanations or exhortations concerning this mystery of the secret counsel of God, however; with Rhoda they rejoice for how the Lord has more than answered their prayers. The surprise of both Peter and the believers in Mary's house reveals that God has "outdone" himself here; these Christians were merely praying that the church might not be snuffed out after their leaders have been executed. Our commentators stress that as comembers in the body of Christ, Christians should participate with their brothers and sisters in both joy and sorrow.

The final verses of Acts 12 recount Herod's unexpected death. The reformers remind their readers that Luke's account is entirely in agreement with the ancient Jewish historian Josephus's account. While it is true that tyrants continue to flourish, still Herod's death is a reminder that the Lord does not let such rebellion go unpunished. The reformers recognize that the Lord sometimes delays in mercy, hoping for the repentance of the wicked. These exegetes intimate that James's death is in some sense vindicated here, but more importantly this passage indicates to them that despite the oppression of the sword, the Word of God, against all opposition, grows and multiplies.

12:6-11 *Peter Escapes from Prison*

GOD WILL TAKE CARE OF HIS PERSECUTED CHURCH. RUDOLF GWALTHER: Luke by suggestion of the Holy Spirit has described in this chapter a most grievous persecution of the church of Christ; by this example we are taught the state of the church here on earth. At the same time, he sets forth a notable example of the goodness and providence of God, who defends the faithful in their distress and most faithfully performs the help which long ago he promised. For, as we saw, the Lord was at hand with Peter the apostle when he seemed destitute of God's help as well as of anyone else's....

[God sent an] angel to loosen the iron chains, he opened the doors in an amazing way, he defeated the watch of the soldiers and brought Peter out of all danger and set him at liberty when the sentence of death was already given against him. And even though all who are imprisoned and in chains for Christ's sake are not delivered in such wonderful ways, yet there are universal promises that all who give themselves to God's service are under his protection. HOMILY 84, ACTS 12:12-19.[1]

IT IS NOT IMPORTANT HOW THE LIGHT SHINED. THE ENGLISH ANNOTATIONS: Light was given to Peter to assure him of assistance from heaven. Whether it shone to Peter only or in the place where he was or went, we do not know. The guards probably were either asleep or so stupified that they could either not perceive or not resist. Nor is it helpful to inquire what the light was? from where or how it shone? whether it were only the reflection of an angelic nature or of some natural cause permitted to the power of angels? If these or similar things had been necessary for salvation, they would have been recorded. ANNOTATIONS ON ACTS 12:7.[2]

PETER WAS BESIDE HIMSELF. THE ENGLISH ANNOTATIONS: Before Peter was like a man in a trance or dream—out of himself, amazed at what was happening to him. But now, after recovering a better understanding, he knew what God had done for him. This manner of speaking the Latins also used, who in great and sudden joy or vehement anger used to say *vix sum apud me*, "I am beside myself!" ANNOTATIONS ON ACTS 12:11.[3]

DO NOT BE DAUNTED. HANS HAS VON HALLSTATT: This and many other examples happened so that we could learn to recognize that it rests in God's might and power alone to rescue his own from these things, regardless of how great and how terrible the enemy and the persecution might be. Even today God moves the hearts, courage and intentions of tyrants to inflict all manner of plagues and misfortunes on his elect, just as he moved the hearts of the Egyptians. As David says, he transforms the hearts of those who are harmful to his people and act maliciously to his servants. Of what good is that blind and miserable people on this earth than that they behave as God's rods and instruments to be used on his Christians, as God ordains them to do, and reveal his glory through them, as noted above?

---

[1]Gwalther, *Homelyes or Sermons upon the Actes*, 497* (*In Acta Apostolorum*, 154v).

[2]Downame, ed., *Annotations*, JJJ3v*.
[3]Downame, ed., *Annotations*, JJJ3v*.

Do not be daunted! If God sends suffering to you, he will also send grace and comfort to you. May you suffer all the adversity with great patience, praying earnestly that his fatherly will might come to pass. He is the Father and knows how to deal with his children in a proper manner. There is no emergency as long as this almighty Father is present and keeps a diligent eye on us. The Scriptures cannot show often enough the great love that God has for his faithful. They often demonstrate that he loves us all as a father loves his children, as one spouse loves the other, yet divine love exceeds all earthly love. KUNSTBUCH: CONCERNING THE COMFORT OF CHRISTIANS IN PERSECUTION.[4]

12:12-19 Peter Meets with the Believers in Secret

DID THEY REALLY PRAY AT NIGHT? JOHANN SPANGENBERG: Certainly. Their need taught them to pray and cry out to God. But look, these new Christians are by each other and pray at night. We, who have been raised in Christendom, hardly even gather to pray together during the day! And if we are by each other at night, it is not so that we can pray, but rather so that we can gorge ourselves and get drunk—whatever our present need may be. BRIEF EXEGESIS OF ACTS 12:12.[5]

PRAYER MEETINGS OF THE EARLY CHURCH. JOHN CALVIN: It is evident that this [Mary] was a woman of exceptional piety, whose house was a kind of temple of God,[6] where meetings of the brothers were in the habit of being held.... For I have no doubt that companies were also gathered together elsewhere, because with many of the multitude of believers praying, one cannot believe that the apostles were not engaged in the same duty, and one house would not have been capable of

holding such a great crowd.... The circumstances of the time must always be kept in mind, that, with their enemies burning with cruelty, the godly were still assembling together. For if this exercise is useful at any time, then it is particularly necessary when sharp conflicts are threatening. COMMENTARY ON ACTS 12:12.[7]

MARY, A DISCIPLE OF GREAT FAITH. RUDOLF GWALTHER: This Mary was the mother of John Mark, which according to many old and later writers is thought to be Mark the Evangelist (this opinion is not altogether certain). It is obvious that this Mary was a woman of rare faith and godliness, even from this one argument: that while Agrippa so cruelly persecuted the disciples of Christ, yet she let them come to her house, as to a public temple, where they met together and exercised themselves in the Word of God and in prayers, which she could not do without apparent and manifest peril. HOMILY 84, ACTS 12:12-19.[8]

HYSTERICAL REJOICING! THE ENGLISH ANNOTATIONS: Sudden joy—like any other extreme affection—disturbs reason, and for a time distorts its faculties (as here, in Rhoda), sometimes to such an extent that some have died from sudden joy! ANNOTATIONS ON ACTS 12:14.[9]

THE LORD OUTDOES THE BELIEVERS' PRAYERS. JOHN CALVIN: When they suppose that the girl, who announces Peter's arrival, is mad, we gather from that that they were not expecting the liberation of Peter. And yet we shall not say that they prayed without faith, because they were looking for other results: that Peter, armed with heavenly power, would be ready to glorify the name of Christ whether by his life or by his death, that the flock might not be scattered in terror at the violent inrush of wolves, that the weak might not give way, that the Lord might disperse

---

[4]CRR 12:450-51* (QGT 17:472); alluding to Ex 4:21; 7:3; Ps 105:25; 1 Cor 1:6.
[5]Spangenberg, *Der Apostel Geschichte*, 108r-v.
[6] Calvin and his compatriots referred to their churches as temples. Thus, Calvin is likely intimating that Mary's home was one of the first churches. See Manetsch, *Calvin's Company of Pastors*, 19.

[7]CNTC 6:342 (CO 48:271).
[8]Gwalther, *Homelyes or Sermons upon the Actes*, 497-98* (*In Acta Apostolorum*, 154v-155r).
[9]Downame, ed., *Annotations*, JJJ3v*.

that hurricane of persecution. But the Lord, with his immeasurable goodness, outdid their prayers, granting them more than they had hoped for. COMMENTARY ON ACTS 12:13.[10]

JEWISH LEGENDS OFTEN DEPICT THE SPIRITS OF THE DEAD. GIOVANNI DIODATI: Among the Jews, as it appears in their histories, there were very frequent apparitions of dead persons, and these phatasmaes (which questionlessly were diabolical) were thought by the common people to be the spirits of the persons whom they represented; and they thought there were some good and some bad, according to the diversity of the persons and the past life. Now here it seems that they were so startled by this unexpected event that they followed popular opinion. Thereby they inferred that Peter's death was inevitable, seeing his spirit did already begin to appear. ANNOTATION ON ACTS 12:15.[11]

WHAT DOES "HIS ANGEL" MEAN? THEODORE BEZA: He appears to the church at that time. From the Word of God the faithful know that they are surrounded by a guard of angels; [the church] also was accustomed to receiving visions in this way. For they speak about the angel of Peter as about a matter neither new nor ambiguous. Some think that these people are dull and simple, because they should say these things, speaking out of common opinion. I fear that those people doubt, with the Sadducees, whether there are angels, or think that no people are more powerful. Also, several people translate the passage thus, "It is a messenger from him," with the result that an angel (ἄγγελος) is not received on behalf of a spirit but on behalf of a person, who is the messenger of Peter. That is, he would have been sent by Peter, or he would have come to announce something about Peter, just as the angel of the Lord says, "I am a messenger sent from the Lord." ANNOTATIONS ON ACTS 12:15.[12]

PETER WANTED THIS MIRACLE TO BE PROCLAIMED FOR GOD'S GLORY AND THE CHURCH'S COMFORT. JOHANNES BRENZ: Peter yearns for this miracle to be proclaimed, not because he wants to create a magnificent name for himself—for he knew very well that his deliverance was not at all due to his own ability or righteousness—rather because through this [he wants] the name of divine grace and power to be promulgated to and praised by everyone, and so that all people should know how near the Lord is to all those who are mired in urgent need and call out to him ardently through his Son Jesus Christ. Additionally, Peter longs for this miracle to be proclaimed to the brothers for this reason, namely, that out of his liberation they would receive consolation in their sorrow which they experienced because of the death of James, the son of Zebedee, and because of Peter's imprisonment. For it is indeed fitting that friends not only share in common difficulties and adversity but also joy and felicity. THE ACTS OF THE APOSTLES 12:17.[13]

WAS GOD UNJUST TO ALLOW THE GUARDS TO BE EXECUTED? JOHANNES BRENZ: But no one should imagine, according to the flesh, that in this matter either God is an unjust judge or the soldiers are innocent. Although the soldiers had no guilt because Peter escaped, nevertheless it was an excessively great concession that the soldiers through their guarding collaborated with the godless king, so that the innocent Peter would be killed. It is fine if a servant suffers his fleshly lord treating *him* somewhat unfairly and unjustly, but he should never allow it to come to doing something godless to please his fleshly lord or helping him to carry out his godlessness or performing and completing such deeds by himself. For suffering unjustly is not wicked; however, acting unjustly is truly wicked. Accordingly it happens out of the just and fair judgment of God that these guards are punished. By Herod they are indeed unjustly beaten, because Peter escaped without their fault

---

[10]CNTC 6:342-43* (CO 48:271-72).

[11]Diodati, *Pious Annotations*, BB1r* (*I Commenti alla Sacra Biblia*, 1104).

[12]Beza, *Annotationes Majores*, 1:506.

[13]Brenz, *Das Buch der Apostelgeschicht*, KK1v.

or help, but before the face of God they are punished completely justly. . . .

What seems to us to be repulsive, the same through God's decree will be entirely transformed for us to pure fortune and blessing, so that we can endure it in faith in Jesus Christ. So, the guards do not remain unpunished before God because they aided this godless king in killing the pious. What then has the king himself as chief instigator and commander of such atrocious murder earned for a punishment? THE ACTS OF THE APOSTLES 12:19.[14]

12:20-23 The Death of Herod

WHY DID HEROD GRUMBLE? JOHANN SPANGENBERG: It is a common plague on earth that neighbors rarely get along. Great lords in particular like to bicker over a foot-width of land or for some other ridiculous reason. Why do [the people of Tyre and Sidon] ask for peace? For the sake of their nourishment and their belly, as the pagans tend to do. We Christians should keep peace not only with our neighbors but also with all people— as much as is possible, and not for the sake of our belly but for the sake of Christ. BRIEF EXEGESIS OF ACTS 12:20.[15]

THE ACCOUNTS OF JOSEPHUS AND LUKE AGREE. JOHN CALVIN: Luke has reported that peace was granted to the people of Tyre and Sidon, because this provided the king with the opportunity of delivering an oration, doubtless in order to make them subject to him afterwards. A similar account is to be found in book 19 of the *Antiquities* of Josephus, except that throughout he uses the name Agrippa, while Luke calls him Herod. It is very likely that Agrippa was his proper name and that he was called nothing else so long as he led a private life, and that, after he in fact gained possession of the kingdom, he sought to obtain royal dignity by using his grandfather's name. Josephus and Luke indeed do agree wonderfully about the

actual incident and all the details. COMMENTARY ON ACTS 12:21.[16]

WHY DID THE ANGEL OF GOD STRIKE HEROD? JOHANN SPANGENBERG: For this reason, that Herod tolerated the people's blasphemy against God, and he did not give God the glory. On account of this he had to suffer such a wretched affliction, that the worms ate him alive and no human could remain near him due to the stench and filth. "O dear friends," he said, "what a pathetic god I am! Look, your god must die!" Then he gave up his spirit and took his reward near him whose servant he was. BRIEF EXEGESIS OF ACTS 12:21-23.[17]

THE SACRILEGE OF NOT HONORING GOD. JOHN CALVIN: Herod is convicted of sacrilege not only because he allowed himself to be called God but because, forgetting himself, he transferred to himself the honor due to God. . . . Accordingly the offense of sacrilege is one that is common to all proud people, because, by arrogating to themselves more than is permissible, they obscure the glory of God, and so in the manner of the giants they try, as hard as they can, to remove God from his own throne. Although they may not usurp the title of God and may not openly make boastful statements that they are gods, yet because they appropriate to themselves what belongs to God, by infringing on his rank they desire to be gods and to be regarded as gods. COMMENTARY ON ACTS 12:23.[18]

SUCH UNDUE PRAISE BIRTHS TYRANTS AND OPPRESSION. DESIDERIUS ERASMUS: Such adulation of the people often contributes to their having tyrants instead of kings, when they attribute divinity to those scarcely worthy of the name of human being. The rulers in turn fawn on the people with shows and obscene plays, and sometimes even with the slaughter of good men, just as earlier Herod had commended himself to the

---

[14]Brenz, *Das Buch der Apostelgeschicht*, KK2r-v.
[15]Spangenberg, *Der Apostel Geschichte*, 109v-110r.
[16]CNTC 6:346* (CO 48 274-75); alluding to Josephus, *Antiquities*, 19.8.
[17]Spangenberg, *Der Apostel Geschichte*, 110v.
[18]CNTC 6:348* (CO 48:276).

people by the slaughter of James. Herod did not refuse or abhor an adulation so blasphemous but was delighted to be regareded as a god though he was but a wretched man, soon to perish. PARAPHRASE OF ACTS 12:22.[19]

THE PERSEVERANCE OF THE CHURCH. RUDOLF GWALTHER: We see the church stand fast and survive all its enemies and all tyrants, for it is born and conserved by the Word of God, which endures forever. This thing the histories of all times and nations teach us. For miserably and filthily died Pharaoh, the Canaanites, Sennecherib, the Babylonians, Antiochus, the three Herods, Nero, Domitian, Trajan, Antony, Severus, the Maximinus, Decius, Valerian, Aurelius, Diocletian, the two Maximinianes, Licivius, Maxentius, Julian, and as many as ever after all these who dared to set on Christ's church. For it flourishes and lives, and shall live forever, under its trusty and most victorious defender, Jesus Christ. HOMILY 85, ACTS 12:20-25.[20]

12:24-25 But the Word of God Increased and Multiplied

LORD, GRANT THE GIFTS OF THE HOLY SPIRIT AND THEIR USE. THE BOOK OF COMMON PRAYER (1549): Lord Almighty, who endowed your holy apostles Barnabas [and Paul] with the singular gifts of your Holy Spirit: let us not be destitute of your manifold gifts, nor of the grace to use them always to your honor and glory: Through Jesus Christ our Lord. Amen. THE COLLECT FOR THE FEAST OF SAINT BARNABAS THE APOSTLE.[21]

THE CHURCH ALWAYS FLOURISHES UNDER OPPRESSION. JOHN TRAPP: The church is invincible. Thus, truth may only be oppressed for a time, but not totally supressed. The Israelites never increased so much as when Pharaoh beat them down. Fish thrive best in salt waters. The ground that is raked up is the most fruitful. . . . All the power of the empire could not prevail against Luther. ANNOTATIONS ON ACTS 12:24.[22]

SAUL AND BARNABAS RETURN WITH JOHN MARK. THE ENGLISH ANNOTATIONS: This is here set down to prepare and transition into the following history. To better understand this, we must consider what we read concerning the disciples' determination to send relief to the Christian brothers in Judea by the hand of Barnabas and Saul. ANNOTATIONS ON ACTS 12:25.[23]

---

[19]CWE 50:83* (LB 7:717).
[20]Gwalther, *Homelyes or Sermons upon the Actes*, 507* (*In Acta Apostolorum*, 157v).

[21]BCP 1549, 71*.
[22]Trapp, *Commentary on Acts*, 152*.
[23]Downame, ed., *Annotations*, JJJ4r*; alluding to Acts 11:29-30.

13:1-12 BARNABAS
AND SAUL SET OFF

*Now there were in the church at Antioch proph-
ets and teachers, Barnabas, Simeon who was called
Niger,ª Lucius of Cyrene, Manaen a lifelong friend
of Herod the tetrarch, and Saul.²While they were
worshiping the Lord and fasting, the Holy Spirit
said, "Set apart for me Barnabas and Saul for the
work to which I have called them." ³Then after fasting and praying they laid their hands on them and
sent them off.*

*⁴So, being sent out by the Holy Spirit, they
went down to Seleucia, and from there they sailed
to Cyprus. ⁵When they arrived at Salamis, they
proclaimed the word of God in the synagogues of
the Jews. And they had John to assist them. ⁶When
they had gone through the whole island as far as
Paphos, they came upon a certain magician, a Jewish false prophet named Bar-Jesus. ⁷He was with
the proconsul, Sergius Paulus, a man of intelligence,
who summoned Barnabas and Saul and sought to
hear the word of God. ⁸But Elymas the magician
(for that is the meaning of his name) opposed them,
seeking to turn the proconsul away from the faith.
⁹But Saul, who was also called Paul, filled with the
Holy Spirit, looked intently at him ¹⁰and said, "You
son of the devil, you enemy of all righteousness, full
of all deceit and villainy, will you not stop making
crooked the straight paths of the Lord? ¹¹And now,
behold, the hand of the Lord is upon you, and you
will be blind and unable to see the sun for a time."
Immediately mist and darkness fell upon him, and
he went about seeking people to lead him by the
hand. ¹²Then the proconsul believed, when he saw
what had occurred, for he was astonished at the
teaching of the Lord.*

a *Niger* is a Latin word meaning *black*, or *dark*

OVERVIEW: After Cornelius and other Gentiles
are reported to have received the Holy Spirit,
the church in Jerusalem agrees to send teachers
to the church in Antioch. Now the church in
Antioch sets up an initiative for a new mission.
In the next two chapters, Barnabas, Saul (who
after Acts 13:9 is called Paul) and their companions go on their first outreach expedition through
Cyprus and into Pamphylia and Pisidia in Asia
Minor (present-day Turkey). Based on this
journey, commentators note that the preaching
of the Word always brings forth new adherents,
but also enemies of the gospel or false prophets,
who—whether out of ill will or ignorance or
both—continue to resist the message. As people
come to faith from various regions and ethnic
groups, commentators recognize the universal
appeal of the gospel.

13:1-3 *The Spirit Commissions Barnabas and Saul*

**THE GOSPEL OF CHRIST IS LIKE A MIGHTY
FLOOD.** JOHANN SPANGENBERG: The gospel of
Christ acts like a mighty flood that has poured
itself out. If we dam up the water in one place
and hold it back, still it breaks out in some other
place, until finally it completely breaks loose, pours
forth and fills up everything. In this same way the
gospel of Christ flowed out of Jerusalem into the
surrounding cities in Judea and Galilee, then out
of Judea into the entire world. BRIEF EXEGESIS OF
ACTS 13 (PROLEGOMENA).[1]

WHO IS MANAEN? THE ENGLISH ANNOTA-
TIONS: [He was] Herod's close friend, that is,

---

[1]Spangenberg, *Der Apostel Geschichte*, IIIv-II2r.

Herod Antipas who killed John the Baptist. This commends Manaen's religion, who in contempt of the world embraced the gospel, as Moses had done, the truth of religion and the worship of the true God. Or at least this shows how among all sorts and degrees of people there are some who fear God. ANNOTATIONS ON ACTS 13:1.[2]

WHY DID THEY FAST? JOHANN SPANGENBERG: Not because they wanted to wash away their sins and attain God's grace through it, but rather because they were eager and inclined to prayer and to the Lord's Supper. For a full stomach does no good, as we see with drunkards. BRIEF EXEGESIS OF ACTS 13:2-3.[3]

THE SERIOUSNESS OF PRAYER AND FASTING. THE ENGLISH ANNOTATIONS: [They ministered] in the public service of God—prayer, preaching, administering the sacraments and other ministerial offices. And here mention is made of fasting, to show how intent and serious they were in their holy duties from which they allowed no distraction by things that at other times were necessary for the maintenance of life and health. ANNOTATIONS ON ACTS 13:2.[4]

ORDINATION IS A FUNCTION OF FIRST DISCERNING THE DIVINE WILL. ANDREAS VON KARLSTADT: Apostolic commissioning followed divine commissioning; and the apostles first recognized God's will before they sent out the above-named two apostles. That they were serious about this is shown by their fasting, prayer and laying on of hands. It must be noted that it is not written that the Spirit spoke through visions in their sleep or through dreams. Rather, without any addition, the Spirit spoke. It is likely, therefore, that the Spirit of God addressed and taught the apostles inwardly that they were to set apart Barnabas and Paul.

It follows clearly that those who appoint or place shepherds and desire to call someone to proclaim God's Word must first know God's pleasure before they choose, lest they choose, contrary to God's will, one whom God has rejected. Those who are carnal cannot understand God's will and grace as do those who are spiritual. Therefore, only those are to choose, call and appoint whom God's Spirit compels to do so and who have the Spirit of Christ, the supreme Shepherd. REASONS WHY ANDREAS KARLSTADT REMAINED SILENT FOR A TIME.[5]

GOD'S WILL BE DONE, NOT YOURS. DIRK PHILIPS: Therefore, everyone may well see to it that he does not run by himself before he is called by the Lord or by his congregation according to these previously described methods. But now no one will be sent by the Lord or correctly chosen by the congregation, except through the Holy Spirit, who must touch his heart, make him fiery with love in order voluntarily to feed, lead and send out the congregation of God. THE ENCHIRIDION: THE SENDING OF PREACHERS.[6]

THOSE CHOSEN BY THE LORD MUST SHARE HIS NATURE. PETER RIEDEMANN: If anyone is to go out for the Lord, he must be chosen by the Lord and endowed with his power; he must feel that power working in him. Above all, he must let the Lord's power rule over him and lead him. What he does must be in keeping with the Lord's nature and character; then he will be conformed to his Master in word and life and give those who follow an example of blessedness. Such a messenger was Paul, who said, "Be imitators of me, as I am of Christ." Everyone who wants to gather with Christ must be of his nature, mind and Spirit. Whoever does not have the Spirit of Christ is not one of his. CONFESSION OF FAITH.[7]

GOD SENDS HIS GOSPEL TO ALL NATIONS. RUDOLF GWALTHER: So that no doubt might remain, the doctrine of salvation is now carried

---

[2]Downame, ed., *Annotations*, JJJ4r*; alluding to Mt 14:1.
[3]Spangenberg, *Der Apostel Geschichte*, 113r.
[4]Downame, ed., *Annotations*, JJJ4r*.
[5]CRR 8:178 (Hertzsch, ed., *Karlstadts Schriften aus den Jahren 1523-25*, 12-13).
[6]CRR 6:203* (BRN 10:212).
[7]CRR 9:184*; quoting 1 Cor 4:16; 11:1.

to diverse nations, and those things are openly accomplished, in the calling of the Gentiles, which the Prophets long before prophesied of. But lest anyone should think that Paul and Barnabas did in this business anything from their own reasoning and presumption, Luke begins this history with their calling and sending.... The kingdom of God and the whole matter of salvation were transferred and brought to the Gentiles, not by human device but by the appointment and commandment of God. HOMILY 86, ACTS 13:1-5.[8]

13:4-12 Barnabas and Saul (Paul) on Cyprus

THE BEGINNING OF PAUL'S FIRST MISSIONARY JOURNEY. JOHANN SPANGENBERG: Here Paul's journeys and pilgrimages begin, as Luke describes them in an orderly fashion. Why does Luke narrate Paul's journeys so precisely? So that he might demonstrate Paul's great diligence and vehemence which he with his companions practiced in the preaching office. Through this Luke wants to remind us that we should attend to our own vocation—however small, however despised it may be—with diligence. BRIEF EXEGESIS OF ACTS 13:4-5.[9]

GOD'S GOOD PLEASURE IN HIS BOUNTEOUS WORD. MARTIN LUTHER:

May God bestow on us his grace
With blessings rich provide us
And may the brightness of his face
To life eternal guide us
That we his saving health may know
His gracious will and pleasure
And also to the nations show
Christ's riches without measure
And unto God convert them.

Thine over all shall be the praise
And thanks of ev'ry nation

And all the world with joy shall raise
The voice of exultation.
For thou shalt judge the earth, O Lord
Nor suffer sin to flourish
Thy people's pasture is thy Word
Their souls to feed and nourish
In righteous paths to keep them.

O let the people praise thy worth
In all good works increasing
The land shall plenteous fruit bring forth
Thy Word is rich in blessing.
May God the Father, God the Son
And God the Spirit bless us!
Let all the world praise him alone
Let solemn awe possess us.
Now let our hearts, say "Amen!"

MAY GOD BESTOW ON US HIS GRACE.[10]

PREACH TO THE GENTILES BUT DO NOT FORGET THE JEWS. THE ENGLISH ANNOTATIONS: Here they preached the Word of God in the synagogues of the Jews. For although they were sent out chiefly for the conversion and confirmation of the Gentiles, still they were to preach the gospel first to the Jews, when and wherever they found opportunity to do so. Again it is something to note that they could hardly find any other places for public assemblies—the pagan temples were furnished with such abominations that the servants of God could not enter. ANNOTATIONS ON ACTS 13:5.[11]

WHAT DID THIS MAGICIAN DO? JOHANN SPANGENBERG: First, he calls himself Bar-Jesus, that is, the Son of God, and Elymas, that is God's king, messiah or anointed one.... This magician is one of whom Christ said, "Many will come in my name and say 'I am the Christ' and will lead many astray." They follow the example of the father of lies, the devil, who often disguises himself as an angel of light, as Saint Paul says.

[8]Gwalther, *Homelyes or Sermons upon the Actes*, 508* (*In Acta Apostolorum* 158r).
[9]Spangenberg, *Der Apostel Geschichte*, 114r.
[10]The Commission on Worship of The Lutheran Church—Missouri Synod, ed., *Lutheran Service Book* (St. Louis: Concordia, 2006), no. 823.
[11]Downame, ed., *Annotations*, JJJ4r*.

Second, he attached himself to the company of the proconsul, Sergius Paulus, by whom he hoped to have protection, as the false prophets often do. The devil's teaching, lies and errors seek protection; God's Word and the truth do not. But the proconsul was an intelligent man; he saw the grace of God in Paul and Barnabas, and thus he summoned them to him and heard God's Word from them. BRIEF EXEGESIS OF ACTS 13:6-8.[12]

SERGIUS, A GODLY MAGISTRATE. RUDOLF GWALTHER: Luke displays in this Sergius the example of a good and godly magistrate. For he is both very desirous to learn the truth and does not hastily condemn the ministers of a doctrine unheard of before, but calling them before him gives them liberty to declare their doctrine. The princes of our days should do well to imitate this man. Many of them condemn the doctrine of truth before they know it and use cruelty to punish them whose faith and religion they are utterly ignorant of. But let them remember, they shall not be excused through ignorance, considering it is their responsibility to do nothing from ignorance but diligently to search out and examine all causes. HOMILY 87, ACTS 13:6-12.[13]

DOES THE APOSTLE HAVE TWO NAMES? GIOVANNI DIODATI: It is uncertain whether he always had these two names—Paul, his Roman name, and Saul, his Hebrew name—or whether he took the Roman name after he was specially appointed apostle to the Gentiles. ANNOTATION ON ACTS 13:9.[14]

LUKE SHIFTS TO PAUL'S ROMAN NAME AS PAUL'S MINISTRY SHIFTS TOWARD ROME. CARDINAL CAJETAN: Thus far Luke has used his Hebrew name (namely, Saul or Saulus), and in this place he first begins to use the Latin name by which the proconsul of Cyprus called him. Afterwards Luke always calls him Paul, implying that this man who from then on was called Paul either began to use his Roman name because he had two names or because his name was changed by the proconsul. Paul, however, gladly assumed this name because it is a name of humility. For it is a diminutive of "little."[15] The diminutive conveyed what the apostle of the Gentiles wished to communicate to the Gentiles in his name, changed at first by a Gentile of great dignity and authority; Paul took the name for himself, whether it was original or changed. COMMENTARY ON ACTS 13:9.[16]

THE SPIRIT FILLS PAUL AND REBUKES ELYMAS. RUDOLF GWALTHER: But let us see how Paul refuted this wicked enchanter. First Luke says he was full of the Holy Spirit, whereby he means that he was moved by the Spirit somewhat above his ordinary wont, which he therefore declares beforehand, that we might think he did nothing of fleshly affection, when we hear his heavy and intolerable weight of words. At the same time we are admonished to fight against the enemies of truth, not with the blind affection of flesh but by the conduct and counsel of the Holy Spirit, whom undoubtedly they shall find to be their enemy, be they never so well guarded with worldly power. Then he goes on in his business, fixing his eyes fast on Elymas, which is an argument of a well-meaning and fearless mind. And verily it becomes us to resist, boldly and constantly, anti-Christians, that they may think people do not fear them. For why should we fear them, seeing he is greater who is on our side? Why also should they be the more encouraged through our cowardliness, who already are in turmoil with the terrors of their evil conscience? HOMILY 87, ACTS 13:6-12.[17]

---

[12]Spangenberg, *Der Apostel Geschichte*, 115r-v; quoting Mt 24:5; alluding to 2 Cor 11:14.

[13]Gwalther, *Homelyes or Sermons upon the Actes*, 514* (*In Acta Apostolorum*, 160r).

[14]Diodati, *Pious Annotations*, BB1v* (*I Commenti alla Sacra Biblia*, 1105).

[15]*Paulus* in Latin is the adjective "little" or "small."

[16]Cajetan, *In Acta Apostolorum*, 224v.

[17]Gwalther, *Homelyes or Sermons upon the Actes*, 515-16* (*In Acta Apostolorum*, 160r-v).

VISION AND BLINDNESS IN CYPRUS. JOHANN SPANGENBERG: The magician becomes blind; the proconsul becomes able to see. Unbelief makes the magician blind. Belief makes the proconsul able to see. For when the proconsul saw this event, he believed and was astonished by the teaching of the Lord. BRIEF EXEGESIS OF ACTS 13:11-12.[18]

WHAT SHOULD WE LEARN FROM PAUL'S CURSE ON ELYMAS? JOHANN SPANGENBERG: Through this Paul wants to show that God's physical punishment is not always eternal but rather temporal, not for destruction but rather for improvement. God says indeed through the prophets, "As surely as I live I do not desire the death of sinners; instead, I long that they would turn to me and live." Thus, Paul handed over to the devil the one who took his father's wife for the destruction of his flesh, so that his spirit would be saved on the day of the Lord Jesus, so that he would identify himself differently and would become a different person. BRIEF EXEGESIS OF ACTS 13:11.[19]

---

[18]Spangenberg, *Der Apostel Geschichte*, 116v.

[19]Spangenberg, *Der Apostel Geschichte*, 116v; quoting Ezek 18:23; alluding to 1 Cor 5:5.

13:13-41 PAUL AND BARNABAS GO TO PISIDIA

[13]Now Paul and his companions set sail from Paphos and came to Perga in Pamphylia. And John left them and returned to Jerusalem, [14]but they went on from Perga and came to Antioch in Pisidia. And on the Sabbath day they went into the synagogue and sat down. [15]After the reading from the Law and the Prophets, the rulers of the synagogue sent a message to them, saying, "Brothers, if you have any word of encouragement for the people, say it." [16]So Paul stood up, and motioning with his hand said:

"Men of Israel and you who fear God, listen. [17]The God of this people Israel chose our fathers and made the people great during their stay in the land of Egypt, and with uplifted arm he led them out of it. [18]And for about forty years he put up with[a] them in the wilderness. [19]And after destroying seven nations in the land of Canaan, he gave them their land as an inheritance. [20]All this took about 450 years. And after that he gave them judges until Samuel the prophet. [21]Then they asked for a king, and God gave them Saul the son of Kish, a man of the tribe of Benjamin, for forty years. [22]And when he had removed him, he raised up David to be their king, of whom he testified and said, 'I have found in David the son of Jesse a man after my heart, who will do all my will.' [23]Of this man's offspring God has brought to Israel a Savior, Jesus, as he promised. [24]Before his coming, John had proclaimed a baptism of repentance to all the people of Israel. [25]And as John was finishing his course, he said, 'What do you suppose that I am? I am not he. No, but behold, after me one is coming, the sandals of whose feet I am not worthy to untie.'

[26]"Brothers, sons of the family of Abraham, and those among you who fear God, to us has been sent the message of this salvation. [27]For those who live in Jerusalem and their rulers, because they did not recognize him nor understand the utterances of the prophets, which are read every Sabbath, fulfilled them by condemning him. [28]And though they found in him no guilt worthy of death, they asked Pilate to have him executed. [29]And when they had carried out all that was written of him, they took him down from the tree and laid him in a tomb. [30]But God raised him from the dead, [31]and for many days he appeared to those who had come up with him from Galilee to Jerusalem, who are now his witnesses to the people. [32]And we bring you the good news that what God promised to the fathers, [33]this he has fulfilled to us their children by raising Jesus, as also it is written in the second Psalm,

'You are my Son,
today I have begotten you.'

[34]And as for the fact that he raised him from the dead, no more to return to corruption, he has spoken in this way,

'I will give you the holy and sure blessings of David.'

[35]Therefore he says also in another psalm,

'You will not let your Holy One see corruption.'

[36]For David, after he had served the purpose of God in his own generation, fell asleep and was laid with his fathers and saw corruption, [37]but he whom God raised up did not see corruption. [38]Let it be known to you therefore, brothers, that through this man forgiveness of sins is proclaimed to you, [39]and by him everyone who believes is freed[b] from everything from which you could not be freed by the law of Moses. [40]Beware, therefore, lest what is said in the Prophets should come about:

[41]'Look, you scoffers,
be astounded and perish;
for I am doing a work in your days,
a work that you will not believe, even if one
tells it to you.'"

a Some manuscripts he carried (compare Deuteronomy 1:31)   b Greek justified; twice in this verse

OVERVIEW: According to Reformation commentators, the essence of this passage is not merely the arc of salvation history but its significance: that through Jesus Christ, the seed promised to David, believers have obtained the forgiveness of sin and are coheirs with the Son of God. God does not forget nor renege on his promises. Some commentators choose to underscore the coexistence and intermingling of Jews and Gentiles, even in the synagogues, so that many Gentiles would have already been accustomed to Jewish preaching and teaching. A larger portion of commentators reiterate the blessings that the Messiah has brought to humanity through redemption from sin.

13:13-15 Paul and Barnabas in the Synagogue

JOHN MARK'S DEPARTURE. JUSTUS JONAS: Here we learn from this man's fear that "whoever stands firm should take heed lest he fall." Below in Acts 15, it is said about this same John: "He did not continue with us," Paul says, "in the work of God." Therefore this John—even though he was a disciple of the same sort as Paul who also believed he was called to the work and way of the gospel—fell away most seriously either because of dread or some other emotion. Thus, 2 Timothy 4, "Demas, in love with this present world, has deserted me." Whether this John repented is not made explicit in this passage. Certainly Paul, in Acts 15 below, refused him. Because of this, enmity arose between Paul and Barnabas. ANNOTATIONS ON ACTS 13:13.[1]

PAUL'S INVITATION TO SPEAK IN THE SYNA-GOGUE. GIOVANNI DIODATI: It was the custom among the Jews that if anyone came to their ecclesiastical meetings who was known to have some gift of understanding the holy Scripture which was read every Sabbath day, they would entreat him to exercise [this gift] in their midst

for their common edification. ANNOTATION ON LUKE 4:16.[2]

GOD'S FOREORDINATION OF THE JEWISH DIASPORA FOR THE DISSEMINATION OF THE GOSPEL.

MARTIN LUTHER: Saint Paul gave this sermon in the school at Antioch in the district of Pisidia, where the Jews and many of the Greeks who had converted to Judaism were gathered. For in whatever cities the Jews were, there they also had their schools in which they taught and preached—many of the Gentiles came there, too, and were turned to God through God's Word out of Scripture. Without a doubt God wonderfully ordained for the Jews to be strewn throughout the entire world among the Gentiles after the first destruction by the Assyrians, so that through them God's Word had to be proliferated. Thus, this people also had to serve for the salvation of the Gentiles and the gospel. Through the apostles the gospel should be preached in all the world, preparing the way. Wherever the apostles came to, there they found these schools of the Jews, so that there they had space to preach as in an orderly gathering, and then their sermon could be proliferated even further because many Gentiles also came to these gatherings. But if the Jews and their schools had not already existed there, then the [inhabitants] would have treated the apostles as strange, foreign people and would not have listened to or allowed them to preach. SERMON ON EASTER TUESDAY IN CRUCIGER'S SUMMER POSTIL (1544).[3]

13:16-25 Paul Recounts Israel's History Fulfilled in Christ

THE THESIS OF PAUL'S SERMON. JUSTUS JONAS: "From this man's seed God [has brought to Israel a Savior]." This is the main proposition and scope of his sermon. For he wants to say that

---

[1]Jonas, *Annotationes in Acta*, G1r; quoting 1 Cor 10:12; Acts 15:38; 2 Tim 4:10.

[2]Diodati, *Pious Annotations*, M3r* (*I Commenti alla Sacra Biblia*, 1018).
[3]WA 22:437.

Jesus is that seed promised to the patriarchs and that now on the throne of David he occupies this kingdom, where he remains for all eternity as had been promised to David. ANNOTATIONS ON ACTS 13:16-41.[4]

WHAT IS PAUL DOING IN THIS SERMON?

JOHANN SPANGENBERG: He runs through the entire Scriptures and demonstrates six points in this sermon. First, he recounts God's goodness, grace and lovingkindness: how he chose the people of Israel as his own and brought them into Egypt during the great famine under Joseph, and, after three hundred years, led them out of Egypt through Moses and drowned all the Egyptians in the Red Sea.

Second, how God endured their disobedience, disbelief, grumbling and reluctance for forty years in the wilderness, but he did not punish their disobedience; instead, he fed them out of his grace for forty years with bread from heaven, and he gave them water to drink from the rock. He led them in battle against their enemies the Amalekites, Moabites and Ammonites. He gave them the law in two stone tablets and established a beautiful worship of God among them in the tabernacle and tent.

Third, how God led them after the forty years through the Jordan and before their eyes exterminated seven people groups of Gentiles, namely, thirty-one kings, and distributed the entire land of Canaan (in their possession) to the eleven[5] tribes of Israel.

Fourth, how God after the prophet Moses gave them judges, namely, Joshua, Judah, Gideon, Samson, and others, who ruled for four hundred years until the prophet Samuel. Then, according to the nations' custom they also wanted their own king, and God gave them Saul from the tribe of Benjamin, who, because he was disobedient to God, had his kingdom taken away from

him and was struck dead in a battle with the Philistines. David was selected by God to become king in his place.

Fifth, how God promised David a seed who will sit eternally on his throne and rule and his kingdom will have no end. Paul interpreted this promise concerning Jesus Christ, the son of Mary who John the Baptist pointed to with his finger and baptized in the Jordan. The high priests, the Pharisees, scribes and the entire crowd of Jews sacrificed him on the cross and killed him. And after he was buried in the earth, on the third day God resurrected him from the dead, and he revealed himself to his [disciples] for forty days, ate with them and finally ascended into heaven and now rules with God the Father eternally.

Sixth, Paul turns to the Jews and exhorts them that they should believe in this Jesus of Nazareth, whom he proclaimed to them. [The apostle] focuses on [the truth] that they, through him, receive righteousness and the forgiveness of sins, which they cannot receive through the law of Moses. For Isaiah says, "Through his knowledge my servant, the righteous one, will make many righteous." That is, what he says here, whoever believes in this Christ is righteous. As also Saint Paul says, "Christ became to us wisdom from God and righteousness and salvation and redemption." This is the basis of the entire Christian teaching which separates Christianity from all other religions and worship of God. BRIEF EXEGESIS OF ACTS 13:16-32.[6]

THE GOSPEL, GRANTED TO JEWS AND GENTILES, IS NOT ALWAYS WELCOMED BY EITHER.

MARTIN LUTHER: There were not only Jews but also Gentiles present at this sermon. . . . In this sermon Paul says, "Dear brothers, you who are of Abraham's family," that is, born Jews, and "those among you who fear God," that is, the Gentiles. And even though it was an irritating and very bad sermon to Jewish ears, still he certainly starts out

---

[4]Jonas, *Annotationes in Acta*, Giv.

[5]Not twelve, because Levites were not alloted a parcel of land but were distributed throughout all the tribes of Israel (see Num 18:20-32; Josh 13:14; 14:3-4).

[6]Spangenberg, *Der Apostel Geschichte*, 120r-122r; quoting Is 53:11; 1 Cor 1:30.

very friendly and pleasantly. He wants them to welcome this sermon, so that they listen quietly and assiduously. He praises them very highly: they are *the* people whom God chose before all other nations, and they are children of the holy patriarchs, as is fitting considering what God promised to their ancestors. But then he ruins it by proclaiming to them nothing other than the crucified and resurrected Messiah. And finally he concludes that their law and government under Moses will not count as anything before God or help them any more than the Gentiles....

That is starting the sermon bluntly and unapologetically! He quickly includes both, Jews and Gentiles, together in one clump. Yes, he clearly tells them that from the beginning until now, the law of Moses has not helped, nor will it help them before God. Instead, only through this good news will they be and are they—and all the Gentiles—saved from sin, death and the devil's power, so that they will become God's children and lords over all things. And this [good news] brings nothing by which such great things—Paul calls them salvation and redemption—can be seen or felt, other than that he preaches about it. I hear the Word and I see Paul, who is a pathetic human being, but this salvation, grace, life and peace, these I do not see. Instead, much more often I must see the opposite, daily seeing and feeling sin, terror, misfortune, suffering and death, so that it seems as if no people are so completely abandoned by God as the Christians. So, they hear this Word.

But that is the high teaching that we must learn and know—if we want to be God's children and to experience his kingdom in us. Neither the Jews from their law nor the Gentiles from their reason [and] wisdom know or experience any of this. Our salvation and redemption stand in the Word. So here Saint Paul promulgates Christ, so that it should be called, and *is*, a Word of salvation and peace. POSTIL ON EASTER TUESDAY, CRUCIGER'S SUMMER POSTIL (1544).[7]

"THE GOD OF THIS PEOPLE ISRAEL." GIOVANNI DIODATI: The purpose is to show that God, after governing his people by many human beings and many kinds of government, has at last established the everlasting kingdom of the Messiah, the Son of David according to the flesh, to whom all God's promises relate and to whom all other governments refer. ANNOTATION ON ACTS 13:17.[8]

GOD BEARS WITH AND NOURISHES HIS PEOPLE. JOHN DONWAME: ἐτροποφόρησεν means to bear with or to endure one's manners or qualities.... The Syriac gives "he nourished them," as if God bore them like a nurse, as Moses says. Indeed he did both! He endured their many rebellions with great mercy and did feed and carry them like a tender nurse, though here the apostle focuses on the former, so that he might show that God's free election of their ancestors was the reason his goodness would not contend with their ungrateful wickedness. Numerous times they provoked him to anger, yet God—though he often corrected them—did not destroy them but with admirable leniency bore their perverse qualities, so that in the fullness of time he might fulfill the promise made to their ancestors. ANNOTATIONS ON ACTS 13:18.[9]

CLING TIGHTLY TO CHRIST'S PROMISES IN ALL CIRCUMSTANCES. MARTIN LUTHER: This word of Christ Paul wants them to hear, as if he wanted to say, "Here you have the Word of peace and salvation! Only in the Word, and nowhere else, can you seek and find such. Keep yourself in this Word; then you will have peace, salvation and redemption. Whatever might happen to you, in cross, suffering, discord, unrest, dying, if you are beheaded, burned, or if you endure pestilence, scourging or whatever God requires from you, then look to me, who is the Word, who promises to you that you will not die, and even though you

---

[7]WA 22:438-39.

[8]Diodati, *Pious Annotations*, BB1v* (*I Commenti alla Sacra Biblia*, 1105).

[9]Downame, ed., *Annotations*, JJJ4v*; alluding to Num 11:12; Deut 32:1; Gal 4:4.

die, your death will merely be a sweet sleep, yes, it will be the doorway to life." . . .

"That is what keeping is for," Christ says, that is, cling tightly to the Word—even contrary to all your feelings and senses—so that you do not doubt it; it is certainly as you heard. For the One who says this is not a [mere] human being, but the One who created heaven and earth and everything in it from nothing, and ever since he rules and sustains it. What were you and I, and everyone else who lives now, a hundred years ago other than pure nothingness? Through what or from what then did everything that was not come to be? "He spoke," it says, "and that which was not came to be; he commanded, and it stood firm."

Therefore, since it is called God's Word it is an entirely different thing—all the same if it is spoken through a human mouth, yes, even through a donkey's mouth—than whatever is called a person's word. So, now let it be or let it come: unrest, terror of sin, death or hell, grave and decay, and [let] whatever may happen to you happen. But you just clasp tightly to the Word in your heart, because Christ sent you a sermon of salvation, that is, redemption and victory over everything, and he wants you to believe it! You will see that he, as your God and Creator, will not leave you oppressed, for what can stand against him? Death? the devil? all creation? POSTIL ON EASTER TUESDAY, CRUCIGER'S SUMMER POSTIL (1544).[10]

JOHN THE BAPTIST WAS LIKE NO OTHER PROPHET. THE ENGLISH ANNOTATIONS: The prophets preached for many generations before Christ's coming, but not like John, who could see him . . . or who was present before the face of Christ. John pointed him out concurrently and preached and administered the sacrament of baptism and the doctrine of repentance—a proper preparation for it. ANNOTATIONS ON ACTS 13:24.[11]

13:26-37 *Paul Testifies to Jesus' Person and Work*

THE "WORD OF SALVATION" IS WORTH MORE THAN ANYTHING ELSE. MARTIN LUTHER: So, the glory of this good news about Christ, which Saint Paul here calls a "Word of salvation," is infinitely greater and higher than all kingdoms, riches and glory of the world, even heaven and earth. For what can all this do for me, if I did not have this Word of salvation and eternal life? For when it comes to sin or death or danger, I must indeed say, "Away with everything that is good and joyous to this world, so that I may have and hear just this good news of salvation, sent from Christ!" This you must know and cling to, that only this Word grants eternal peace and joy, and it must be believed, even if it seems totally contrary to everything. Do not follow yourself or your feelings but cling tightly to the divine, eternal, ineffable truth that he has spoken and promulgated. Postil on Easter Tuesday, CRUCIGER'S SUMMER POSTIL (1544).[12]

DOES PAUL CONTRADICT LUKE'S ACCOUNT OF CHRIST'S BURIAL? JOHN CALVIN: Luke's statement that Christ was buried by the same men as had killed him seems to conflict with the Gospel story, but it may be that Luke took the word for burying in an indefinite way. Even if you wish to apply it to those same men, it will be synecdoche. For he was buried by Pilate's permission, but on the other hand guards were placed at the sepulcher by the decision of the priests. Therefore even if Joseph and Nicodemus committed Christ to the sepulcher, it is incorrect, but still not absurd, to attribute that to the Jews, because Paul's intention here is not to praise the act of kindness but to prove the resurrection of Christ, because God brought him out of the sepulcher in which his enemies had shut him up and on which they kept guard. He is therefore pointing out that the body of Christ was not removed in secret or by stealth but was put in a

---

[10]WA 22:440; alluding to Mt 17:5; Jn 8:51; Ps 33:9 about Gen 1:3; Num 2.
[11]Downame, ed., *Annotations*, JJJ4v*.

[12]WA 22:440-41.

place that was much frequented and known to his enemies, that they even set a guard over it and that, nevertheless, it was not found. The deduction from that is the certainty of the resurrection. COMMENTARY ON ACTS 13:29.[13]

THROUGH GOD'S PROMISES WE ARE HIS CHILDREN.

JOHN CALVIN: It is certain that Paul is speaking about the natural children, who derived their origin from the holy fathers. And we must pay attention to that, because certain fanatics, who make allegories out of everything, imagine that no account is to be taken here of descendants but only of faith. . . . They say that it is faith alone that makes children of Abraham. But I take the opposite view that those who are born children of Abraham according to the flesh are also to be regarded as God's spiritual children, unless they cut themselves off by their own unfaithfulness. For the branches are holy by nature, because they have been produced from a holy root, until they are polluted by their own fault. And it is certainly Paul's intention to draw the Jews to Christ. But for that to happen they must be separated and removed from the common order by privilege. But it does not follow from that, what those scoundrels throw out in a hateful way, that the grace of God is bound to the carnal seed, because, even if the promise of life was an inheritance for the descendants of Abraham, still many lost it because of their unbelief. Therefore it is due to faith that few out of a great multitude are regarded as children. Indeed it is by faith that God separates his own. And that is the twofold election which I have mentioned previously. The one is the common election of the whole nation quite equally, because God's first adoption embraces the whole family of Abraham. The other is the one which is limited according to the purpose of God, and is finally confirmed by faith, to be their sure possession.

Therefore Paul is quite right in maintaining that what God promised to the ancestors was fulfilled for the Jews. For the promise had been made to

them also. . . . Still the worthiness of that nation does not prevent the grace of Christ spreading itself out into the whole world at the same time, because the eldest occupies the chief position of honor in such a way that he still leaves the second place to his brothers. COMMENTARY ON ACTS 13:33.[14]

"YOUR HOLY ONE" IS CHRIST.

RUDOLF GWALTHER: It is made clear that David finished the course of his life according to the manner of other people, and after his life ended, he fell asleep and molded to dust. Therefore David speaks not of himself but of Christ, who he knew should be born of his stock, for before he suffered corruption, he rose again the third day in his glorious body. So Paul in few words comprehends all the mysteries of Christ and shows that it is he of whom the prophets everywhere have spoken. HOMILY 92, ACTS 13:32-37.[15]

DAVID "SAW CORRUPTION."

THE ENGLISH ANNOTATIONS: The meaning is that after David had lived uprightly toward God, in his appointed time he died, and therefore what he foretold in these prophecies related to Christ, who saw no corruption, not David. ANNOTATIONS ON ACTS 13:36.[16]

DEATH IS A NECESSARY STEP IN THE ORDER OF SALVATION.

RUDOLF GWALTHER: For this is the immutable sentence of God, that we who took our beginning from dust should be turned into dust again, and so it is requisite for the order of our salvation. "For this corruptible body must put on incorruptibility and this mortal body must put on immortality, because flesh and blood cannot inherit the kingdom of heaven." Therefore we have a great hope in the corruption of our bodies, which we know is the beginning of our regeneration and resurrection to come. And this was the only hope of the saints. . . . Let us therefore comfort ourselves with the same and not fear death, seeing that we

---

[13]CNTC 6:374* (CO 48:297-98); alluding to Mt 27:57.

[14]CNTC 6:376-77* (CO 48:299-300); alluding to Rom 11:16.
[15]Gwalther, *Homelyes or Sermons upon the Actes*, 541* (*In Acta Apostolorum*, 168r).
[16]Downame, ed., *Annotations*, JJJ4v*.

shall be made like Jesus Christ, the Son of God. HOMILY 92, ACTS 13:32-37.[17]

13:38-41 *Paul Gives Promises and Warnings*

THE FORGIVENESS OF SINS KNOWN ONLY THROUGH REVELATION. JOHN CALVIN: The main point to grasp is what blessings the coming of Christ has brought to us and what one must expect from him. Now although Luke mentions in a single sentence that Paul preached about the benefits of Christ, still there is no reason for anyone to doubt that such great matters were dealt with seriously and splendidly in accordance with their grandeur. . . .

Remission of sins is put in the first place, for by it God reconciles us to himself. . . . We must also note this, that God forgives our sins and is made favorable through the Mediator because, apart from him, just as there is no expiation, so there is no pardon or release from guilt. These are the rudiments of our faith, and they are not learned in the philosophic schools: that the whole human race is condemned and overwhelmed by sins, that we possess no righteousness to reconcile ourselves to God, that the only hope of salvation remains in his mercy, when he acquits us out of his favor, that . . . people remain under condemnation except those who flee to Christ and in his death seek expiation for sins. COMMENTARY ON ACTS 13:38.[18]

THE PURPOSE OF PAST CEREMONIES. PILGRAM MARPECK: [Believers] know Christ according to the Spirit and according to the new creature, his spiritual body planted by faith, for the old fleshly nature has passed away in us, and we are spiritually minded according to the humanity of Christ. For the unbelieving, all of Christ's external works, words, deeds and ceremonies are ordained or directed for their salvation in order that their

reason might be captured and blended into the obedience of faith, and in order that they may see. But for the believer, these works, words, deeds and ceremonies are erected for the freedom of the Spirit, which does not mean that they should not be employed; rather, they should be accepted and observed with a free spirit, driven by the acknowledged truth and will of God. A CLEAR AND USEFUL INSTRUCTION.[19]

THE LAW IS POWERLESS TO JUSTIFY. GIOVANNI DIODATI: Because that ceremonial law is only figurative, it had no power of itself over the soul, and, due to its relation to Christ, had nothing but marks and seals of sin and condemnation. The moral law also is without force in sinful people and therefore could not justify but only discover and condemn sin. ANNOTATION ON ACTS 13:39.[20]

GOD'S UNBELIEVABLE GOOD NEWS. DESIDERIUS ERASMUS: Who to this day has believed that a man would be born of a virgin? Who would have believed that through the death of one person immortality has been won for all peoples? Who would have believed that one killed and buried would within three days come to life again into immortality? As he promised, God has worked this incredible work. . . . Do not be despisers; do not perish through obstinate incredulity, but believe and embrace the salvation freely offered you. PARAPHRASE OF ACTS 13:38-41.[21]

SHOULDN'T PAUL BE PUNISHED FOR HIS INSOLENCE? MARTIN LUTHER: Should we not tear Paul's flesh with glowing hot tongs for being a rebellious, yes, public blasphemer who criticizes not only all government but even God himself in his honor? And he dares to say that the leaders of the people all err, knowing nothing of the Scriptures, indeed, [he asserts that] they are murderers

---

[17]Gwalther, *Homelyes or Sermons upon the Actes*, 541-42* (*In Acta Apostolorum*, 168v); quoting 1 Cor 15:53.
[18]CNTC 6:382* (CO 48:304-5).

[19]CRR 2:99-100*.
[20]Diodati, *Pious Annotations*, BBIv* (*I Commenti alla Sacra Biblia*, 1105-6); alluding to Heb 9:9; 10:1-11; Col 2:14; Rom 8:3; 3:20; 4:15; Gal 3:21-22.
[21]CWE 50:89 (LB 7:721).

of the Son of God! . . . You see that he does not let anything stand, and he teaches everyone that they should not be convinced by the shouting and rumbling of the Jews, who claim that they are high priests, teachers, rulers or that they were appointed by God himself to dominion and government and that the people are subject to them. Preaching against them seems to be the same as preaching against obedience to father and mother and to orderly government; indeed, it seems to be preaching against God himself—which we of course would not tolerate. Still Saint Paul does this without timidity as an apostle of God and out of his instruction. He would have been even harsher against our papal masks, who, without God's Word, boast themselves to be the heads of the church and God's people. And they neither teach nor understand the Scriptures but instead mete out their own refuse in place of God's Word.

Now what justification does he have that he can so insolently condemn such powerful people with this judgment? "Hey! This is it," he says, "there is one called Jesus Christ, of whom all the prophets and the entire Scriptures speak, whom you do not want to recognize. He is higher and greater than the priests, the rulers along with the entire temple and the entire city of Jerusalem. This, too, they themselves knew, that when this one came, they would step down and obey him as their Lord and mightiest Ruler." POSTIL ON EASTER TUESDAY, CRUCIGER'S SUMMER POSTIL (1544).[22]

HABBAKUK'S PROPHECY. RUDOLF GWALTHER: It remains for us to consider his conclusion, which contains in it a grievous and very horrible threat . . . that he perceived in the hearers tokens of obstinacy and unbelief. For it is not credible that such a spirit as the apostle had could be so moved without a cause. For he says, "Beware that that fall not on you which is spoken of in the prophets." Therefore he threatens them with punishment and still leaves a place for hope of pardon, while he warns them to beware. . . .

Habakkuk preached during the reign of Manassah, when both idolatry and all kinds of vice reigned under that wicked and cruel king. For it is reported that Manassah brought Judah into error, and the citizens of Jerusalem, so that they surpassed the Gentiles whom God had destroyed, in wickedness. Besides this, he greatly condemned the Word of God and passing all measure hated the truth, against which he was so inflamed that he filled the whole city with the blood of innocents. And still they who were puffed up in the confidence of God's covenant, of their ancestors, of the temple and ceremonies thought they might without consequence do this, and those who admonished them to do otherwise or threatened them with the judgment of God, they wickedly scoffed at. Therefore Habbakuk then prophesied the coming of the Chaldeans, which he said should overthrow the city and temple and should carry all the people away, a thing which they thought to be impossible.

Here Paul seems to say, "You know what befell your ancestors when they despised the sayings of the prophets." They saw the destruction both of the city and temple, and neither could that proud name of the people of God or trust in their ceremonies deliver them from the punishment at hand. . . . For the kingdom of God shall be taken from you, and you shall be forsaken, and that salvation that was promised to your ancestors shall be conveyed to the Gentiles. HOMILY 93, ACTS 13:38-41.[23]

A POWERFUL AND CLEAR SERMON. MARTIN LUTHER: Paul does not forget the main point, the use of this history and how such good news and testimony of the Scriptures should benefit us or what we get from it and how the power and use of this is entrusted to and shared with us, as Saint Peter also did. And he sets out a beautiful, powerful apostolic word and conclusion, how we attain the forgiveness of sins and are saved. Namely, through this One "the forgiveness of sins is proclaimed to

---

[22]WA 22:442.

[23]Gwalther, *Homelyes or Sermons upon the Acts*, 546* (*In Acta Apostolorum*, 170r).

you, but through all that is proclaimed to you in the law of Moses you cannot be justified. Whoever believes in this One is justified." This is a powerful text, so plain and clear that it requires no gloss or further exegesis, and everywhere it is strongly demonstrated and highlighted by Saint Paul in his epistles. It should be enough for us that we observe and cherish such clear words, strengthening ourselves with them and reinforcing the foundation and main tenet of Christian teaching. We see how the apostles' preaching agrees so evenly and clearly with each other as trustworthy, true, unanimous witnesses to Christ, and from this we can conclude and judge with certainty that whatever does not measure up to this or whatever teaches something else concerning the forgiveness of sins and our salvation is not from the church but rather from the devil's accursed teachers and teaching. Postil on Easter Tuesday, Cruciger's Summer Postil (1544).[24]

---

[24]WA 21:237-38; alluding to Gal 1:8.

13:42-52 PAUL AND BARNABAS
TURN TO THE GENTILES

⁴²As they went out, the people begged that these things might be told them the next Sabbath. ⁴³And after the meeting of the synagogue broke up, many Jews and devout converts to Judaism followed Paul and Barnabas, who, as they spoke with them, urged them to continue in the grace of God.

⁴⁴The next Sabbath almost the whole city gathered to hear the word of the Lord. ⁴⁵But when the Jews saw the crowds, they were filled with jealousy and began to contradict what was spoken by Paul, reviling him. ⁴⁶And Paul and Barnabas spoke out boldly, saying, "It was necessary that the word of God be spoken first to you. Since you thrust it aside and judge yourselves unworthy of eternal life, behold, we are turning to the Gentiles. ⁴⁷For so the Lord has commanded us, saying,

"'I have made you a light for the Gentiles,
   that you may bring salvation to the ends of
   the earth.'"

⁴⁸And when the Gentiles heard this, they began rejoicing and glorifying the word of the Lord, and as many as were appointed to eternal life believed. ⁴⁹And the word of the Lord was spreading throughout the whole region. ⁵⁰But the Jewsᵃ incited the devout women of high standing and the leading men of the city, stirred up persecution against Paul and Barnabas, and drove them out of their district. ⁵¹But they shook off the dust from their feet against them and went to Iconium. ⁵²And the disciples were filled with joy and with the Holy Spirit.

a Greek *Ioudaioi* probably refers here to Jewish religious leaders, and others under their influence, in that time

---

OVERVIEW: Paul and Barnabas proclaim the Word of God at the people's request. In the aftermath of preaching to the people of Pisidian Antioch, they issue a warning against unbelief and praise those who accepted the apostolic teaching with sincere faith. The commentators focus on two things. First, Paul's turning away from the Jews to the Gentiles becomes a launching point for exploration of the mysteries of divine election (reflected in this doctrine's codification in several Reformation confessions). Second, there is a pastoral distinction made between spiritual joy and fleshly joy, such that a believer could have one without the other.

13:42-47 The Mixed Response of the Jews

THE PREEMINENCE OF THE JEWS. JOHN CALVIN: Paul accuses them of ingratitude, because, although they had been chosen from all nations by God, so that Christ might present himself to them, they

are maliciously rejecting so great a blessing. But in the first sentence he reminds them of the level of honor and preeminence into which God had raised them. Afterwards there follows the reproach that they are rejecting so great a favor by their own free will. From that he concludes that it is now the time for the gospel to be transferred to the Gentiles. His statement that it ought to have been first preached to them strictly refers to the time of the kingdom of Christ. For under the Law, before Christ was revealed, the Jews were not only first but were also the only ones. Accordingly Moses called them a kingdom of priests and God's special people.

But at that time the adoption of God remained their possession, and only theirs, with the Gentiles passed over, on condition that with the coming of Christ they still ought to have the preference over the Gentiles. For although Christ reconciled the world to the Father, still those who were already near to God and belonged to his family were first in order. It was therefore the proper order for the apostles to gather the church first from the Jews and then from the Gentiles, as we have seen. ... Thus the association of the Gentiles did not remove the right of the firstborn from the Jews, but they would always be preeminent in the church of God. Following this reasoning Paul says that the righteousness of God is manifested in the gospel first to the Jews and then to the Greeks. COMMENTARY ON ACTS 13:46.[1]

GOD DOES NOT PREDESTINE FOR THE PURPOSE OF DAMNATION. SHORT CONFESSION (1610): The cause or reason of humanity's calamity and damnation is their own free choice of darkness (Jn 3:19; Jas 1:15), their affirming of sins and their willingness to live in them. Destruction comes from human beings, not from the good Creator. God, being perfectly good and love itself (according to the nature of perfect love and goodness; Mt 19:17; 1 Jn 4:8), desired the best for his creatures, namely, healing and salvation. Therefore, he neither predestined, determined nor created anyone for damnation, neither willing nor ordaining their sinful life in order to bring them to destruction.

Rather (since as a good God he had no desire, as surely as he lives that anyone should perish but that all might be saved; Ezek 33:11; 2 Pet 3:9), he created all humankind for salvation (1 Tim 2:4; Gen 1:27). When they fell he restored them, with infinite love, through Christ who has become for all humans a medicine of life (Gen 12:3; 22:18; Rom 2:10; Sirach 1:19-20; 1 Jn 2:2; Heb 2:9; Jn 3:16; 4:14). This Christ was given over to be sacrificed and to die for the reconciliation of all humanity (Eph 5:2), affirming his desire that all creatures and nations should hear and have offered to them through evangelical preaching universal love and compassion (Mt 28:19; Mk 16:15; Eph 1:9). All those who now receive or accept this gracious benefit of God in Christ (who came for the salvation of the world) with penitent and believing hearts and remain in him are and continue to be the elect

whom God has ordained before the foundations of the world that they should share his glory (1 Jn 2:2; Mk 15:16; 16; Jn 1:12; Mt 22:5, 14; 24:13; 25:34; Rev 2:10; Eph 1:4).

Those, however, who despise or reject this grace of God, who love darkness more than light, who remain unrepentant and unbelieving, make themselves unworthy of salvation through their own perversity and are therefore justly rejected by God because of their own evil (Jn 3:19; Acts 13:46; 2 Chron 15:2; 1 Kings 15; 22:30; 2 Thess 2:10-11; 1 Pet 2:8; Mt 22:3; Lk 14:16; 17:24). These will not reach the end for which they were created and for which they were ordained in Christ, neither shall they taste the Supper of the Lord to which they had been invited and called in all eternity. ARTICLE 7, CONCERNING GOD'S PREDESTINATION, ELECTION AND REJECTION.[2]

THE FABLE OF FREE WILL IS REPUGNANT. BELGIC CONFESSION: We reject all that is taught repugnant to this concerning the free will of humanity, since people are but slaves to sin (Is 26:12; Ps 94:11; Jn 8:34; Rom 6:17; 7:5, 17) and have nothing of themselves unless it is given them from heaven (Is 26:12; Jn 3:27). For who may presume to boast that he of himself can do any good, since Christ says, "No one can come to me, unless the Father who sent me draws him" (Jn 3:27; 6:44, 65)? Who will glory in his own will, who understands that to be carnally minded is enmity against God (Rom 8:5)? Who can speak of his knowledge, since the natural person receives not the things of the Spirit of God (1 Cor 2:14; Ps 94:11)? In short, who dare suggest any thought, since he knows that we are not sufficient of ourselves to think anything as of ourselves, but that our sufficiency is from God (2 Cor 3:5)? And therefore what the apostle says ought justly to be held sure and firm, that "it is God who works in you, both to will and to work for his good pleasure" (Phil 2:13). For there is no will or understanding, conformable to the divine will and understanding, but what Christ has wrought in

---

[1]CNTC 6:389-90* (CO 48:310-11); alluding to Ex 19:5-6; Rom 1:16.

[2]CRR 11:141-42*.

human beings: which he teaches us when he says, "Without me you can do nothing" (Jn 10:5). Article 14, On the Creation and Fall of Man.[3]

Whether in Mercy or in Justice, God's Glory Is Magnified. Gallic Confession: We believe that from this corruption and general condemnation in which all persons are plunged, God, according to his eternal and immutable counsel, calls those whom he has chosen by his goodness and mercy alone in our Lord Jesus Christ, without consideration of their works (Rom 3:2; 9:23; 2 Tim 2:10; Tit 3:5-7; Eph 1:4; 2 Tim 1:9), to display in them the riches of his mercy (Ex 9:16; Rom 9:22), leaving the rest in this same corruption and condemnation to show in them his justice. For the ones are no better than the others, until God discerns them according to his immutable purpose which he has determined in Jesus Christ before the creation of the world. Neither can anyone gain such a reward by his own virtue, as by nature we cannot have a single good feeling, affection or thought, unless God has first put it into our hearts (Jer 10:23; Eph 1:4-5). Article 12.[4]

We Are Unable to Do Good. The First Helvetic Confession: We ascribe freedom of choice to humanity because we find in ourselves that we do good and evil knowingly and deliberately. We are able to do evil of ourselves, but we can neither embrace nor fulfill the good unless we are illumined, brought to life and impelled by the grace of Christ. For God is the one who effects in us the willing and the doing, according to his good pleasure. Our salvation is from God, but from ourselves there is nothing but sin and damnation (Jn 15:7; 14:15; Phil 2:15; Acts 17:27-28; Hos 13:2, 9). Article 9, On Free Will.[5]

The Doctrine of Predestination Is Comforting. Formula of Concord: This predestination is not to be probed in the secret counsel of God but rather is to be sought in the Word, where it has also been revealed. However, the Word of God leads us to Christ, who is "the Book of Life" [Phil 4:3; Rev 3:5], in whom are inscribed and chosen all who shall be eternally saved, as it is written, "He chose us in Christ before the foundation of the world" [Eph 1:4].

This Christ calls all sinners to himself and promises them refreshment. He is utterly serious in his desire that all people should come to him and seek help for themselves [cf. Mt 11:28; 1 Tim 2:4]. He offers himself to them in his Word. To this end he promises the power and activity of the Holy Spirit, divine assistance in remaining faithful and attaining eternal salvation....

A Christian should only think about the article of God's eternal election to the extent that it is revealed in God's Word. The Word holds Christ before our eyes as the "Book of Life," which opens and reveals for us the preaching of the holy gospel, as it is written, "Those whom he has chosen, he also called" [Rom 8:30]. In Christ we are to seek the Father's eternal election. He has decreed in his eternal, divine counsel that he will save no one apart from those who acknowledge his Son Christ and truly believe in him. We should set aside other thoughts, for they do not come from God but rather from the imagination of the evil foe. Through such thoughts he approaches us to weaken this glorious comfort for us or to take it away completely. We have a glorious comfort in this salutary teaching, that we know how we have been chosen for eternal life in Christ out of sheer grace, without any merit of our own, and that no one can tear us out of his hand [Jn 10:28-29]. For he has assured us that he has graciously chosen us not only with mere words. He has corroborated this with an oath and sealed it with the holy sacraments. In the midst of our greatest trials we can remind ourselves of them, comfort ourselves with them and thereby quench the fiery darts of the devil....

Accordingly, we believe and maintain that those who present the teaching of God's gracious election to eternal life either in such a way that troubled Christians cannot find comfort in it but are driven

---

[3]*Creeds*, 3:399-400*.
[4]*Creeds*, 3:366-67*.
[5]Cochrane, *Reformed Confessions*, 102* (*Creeds*, 3:214).

to faintheartedness or despair, or in such a way that the impenitent are strengthened in their arrogance, are not preaching this teaching according to the Word and will of God but rather according to their own reason and at the instigation of the accursed devil, because (as the apostle testifies) "whatever was written was written for our instruction, so that by steadfastness and by the comfort of the Scriptures we might have hope" [Rom 5:4]. ARTICLE II, ELECTION.[6]

GOD LONGS FOR THE UNITY OF THE JEWS AND GENTILES. JOHN CALVIN: The calling of the Gentiles seems to be announced there in such a way as not to carry with it the disowning of the ancient people. Indeed God is rather associating foreigners with the Jews, who had previously belonged to his household. He says, "It is not enough for you to be a servant to me in teaching Israel, because I have appointed you as a light to the Gentiles." Certainly God appears to make a beginning with his church from the children of Abraham and afterwards to stretch out his hand to the Gentiles, so that they may both form the same church with complete unanimity of faith. COMMENTARY ON ACTS 13:47.[7]

IT'S NOT ABOUT YOU; AUTHORITY TO PREACH COULD HAVE BEEN GIVEN TO ANIMALS. PILGRAM MARPECK: Christ left, until the end of the world, his external authority and command in the Scriptures to all his disciples, brothers and members who possess his Spirit or mind. This same written authority was accepted by Paul, as a member of Christ, when he refers to the verse (interpreting it to refer to the body of members of Christ in Acts 13): "As the Lord commanded us, I have made you a light for the Gentiles that you might be salvation to the ends of the earth." Let everyone beware lest he abuse such authority, lest he represent only himself rather than Christ, who sends him, and lest he be without the seal of au-

thority in his heart. Let him honorably be Christ's representative throughout the whole world, wherever need exists; then he need not be concerned that he is abusing his authority. Yes, even if a dog or a cat were to proclaim the gospel as a testimony through the unbelieving world and deliver it into repentance and improvement, who could declare it wrong? For everything that leads to godliness is good, and not evil, for all visible creatures are placed in the world as apostles and teachers. If such mute creatures could speak, Christ's sending the apostles to elucidate or preach the gospel would have been unnecessary. A CLEAR REFUTATION.[8]

13:48-52 The Joy of the Believing Gentiles

THE GENTILES REJOICE FOR THEIR SALVATION, NOT THE JEWS' REJECTION. DESIDERIUS ERASMUS: It was not that the Gentiles were glad about destruction for the Jews, but that they gave thanks for the mercy of God who was turning the unbelief of the Jews to their own salvation. The Jews attacked the salvific doctrine with blasphemies; the Gentiles, suddenly changed, embraced it with most eager minds and glorified the Word of the Lord. Not indeed all of the Gentiles believed the Word but as many as the divine mercy had ordained to eternal life, for no one attains to this unless called and chosen by God. PARAPHRASE OF ACTS 13:48.[9]

THE POWER OF THE WORD. MARTIN LUTHER: [We] hear the Word well enough, but life, salvation, peace [we] do not see; instead, we see the opposite. "For if I must die, why is it called the Word of life?" Again, "If Christians must bear the cross, where then is peace, where is grace?" It is indeed the Word of life, salvation, peace and all blessedness, and it accomplishes it, too! God sent this Word. It is not the word of a king; instead, God speaks it, and so amicably and dearly through your brother and sister. It is his Word. God is no liar, so

---

[6]BoC 517-19* (BSLK 817-21). See also the "solid declaration," BoC 640-56 (BSLK 1063-93).
[7]CNTC 6:391* (CO 48:312).

[8]CRR 2:56*; alluding to Job 12.
[9]CWE 50:90 (LB 7:722).

what he says must happen, however fantastical it may sound. He says, "Listen to him! You have the Word. If you think, however, that you are dying, cling tightly to it, look up to me, the Word is mine. You will not die; instead, it will be merely a sleep. For I am not a [mere] human being who says this, but God. Through what have I made heaven and earth, moon and stars, and also you?" Where were we before? Nowhere at all. But then "he spoke." He said, "Come forth, heaven, earth, animals and cattle," and so it was. It is a different thing when something is spoken by God than by people, so that we should think, "I feel it, I know it well, death here, death there, but God will not leave me lying [in the ground]. What can be impossible for God . . . ? Of course it must come to be if he says it. After death, after dying, though the maggots feast on me, he can still easily bring me back." . . . God's Word is that which creates and sustains all creatures. . . . It is still a Word of salvation which is more than when God said, "You have earth, sun and stars." What can those help me if I do not know that I will live? I would rather have a word that saves me than that he gives me the word through which he created heaven and earth. . . . This is a Word of peace, of the eternal kingdom, of life—you should believe in that, even if you see something quite the opposite. My body lies under the earth, but God is truthful and cannot lie; therefore, what he promised will certainly happen. Sermon on Easter Tuesday Afternoon (1544).[10]

The Spiritual Armor of God Protects Against Fleshly Weapons. Dirk Philips: As these mockers of Israel then see that their mocking is ignored and that the work of the Lord, the restoration of the holy city, nevertheless goes forward, then they become furious, they make a covenant with each other against the Lord and his congregation and want to resist this so that Jerusalem will not be rebuilt again. The tyrants with their strong mandates and placards, with water, fire and sword, these learned ones with their philosophy,

guile and sharp-wittedness to twist the Scriptures with writing and preaching and with inciting the civil authority that one should drive away, strangle and kill the builders of the city of Jerusalem so that the work of the Lord might be hindered.

But in opposition to this, the people of the Lord arm themselves not with carnal weapons as (alas) has happened to some through misunderstanding,[11] but with the armor of God, with the weapons of righteousness in the right hand and the left, with the helmet of salvation, with the shield of faith with which they can quench all the fiery darts of Satan, and with the powerful two-edged Word of God, and with Christian patience with which they possess their souls and thus overcome all their foes. Thus, they build the walls of Jerusalem with such battle armor and such an undaunted or manly heart and comfort themselves because the God of heaven is their helper in need and the hand of Christ is with them. Heathens (who nevertheless have no part in the house of the Lord or in the city of Jerusalem) cannot with all their might prevent that both the city and the temple should be rebuilt; for the Lord is with his people and helps his servants faithfully. Amen. The Enchiridion: Concerning Spiritual Restitution.[12]

Peace and Joy in the Midst of Tumult. John Calvin: This sentence, that they were filled with joy and the Spirit, can be explained in two ways. The first is by hypallage[13] in this way, "with the joy of the Spirit," or, what amounts to the same thing, "with spiritual joy," because there is no clearness of conscience, peace or joy except from the Spirit of God. That is why Paul says that the kingdom of God is righteousness, peace and joy in the Spirit. Or, second, it may mean that the word *Spirit* includes in itself other virtues and gifts. Still

---

[10]WA 49:370-72; quoting Mt 17:5.

[11]This is likely an allusion to the infamous Münster Rebellion (1534–1535).
[12]CRR 6:346-47* (BRN 10:373-74); alluding to Neh 4:8.
[13]Hypallage is a technical term meaning interchange or exchange; it is a figure of speech in which there is an interchange of two elements of a proposition, the natural relations of these being reversed.

I prefer it that they were filled with joy, because the grace of the Holy Spirit was ruling within them, and this alone makes us so genuinely and thoroughly joyous that we are exalted high above the whole world. For we must pay attention to what Luke had in mind, that far from being agitated or upset by those serious hindrances, by the ignominy of their teachers, by the disturbance of the city, by alarms and threats, even by the fear of imminent dangers, the faithful, out of the depth of their faith, strongly despised the showiness of their spurious sanctity as well as of their power.

And there is no doubt that if our faith is properly founded on God and strikes its roots deep in his Word, and, finally, if it is made thoroughly secure by the protection of the Spirit, as it ought to be, it will foster peace and spiritual joy in our minds, even with the whole world in an uproar. Commentary on Acts 13:52.[14]

What Should We Learn from This Chapter? Johann Spangenberg: First, they are already written down who will be saved. We must preach the Word; God will provide an audience. Second, wherever God's Word is once repudiated and the devil's teaching and human refuse are accepted again, there it requires toil and labor to be and remain faithful and good Christians. Third, though the shaking of the dust from the feet is certainly ridiculous and is viewed derisively before the world, nevertheless Paul has left a grisly punishment behind him. For Christ says, "In whatever community such happens, it will be worse for them than Sodom and Gomorrah." May God grant us the grace to hold his Word in honor and to be included under those foreordained to salvation and eternal life. Brief Exegesis of Acts 13.[15]

---

[14]CNTC 6:396-97* (CO 48:316-17); alluding to Rom 14:17.

[15]Spangenberg, *Der Apostel Geschichte*, 126r-v; quoting Mt 10:14-15.

14:1-18 PAUL AND BARNABAS AT ICONIUM AND LYSTRA

Now at Iconium they entered together into the Jewish synagogue and spoke in such a way that a great number of both Jews and Greeks believed. [2]But the unbelieving Jews stirred up the Gentiles and poisoned their minds against the brothers.[a] [3]So they remained for a long time, speaking boldly for the Lord, who bore witness to the word of his grace, granting signs and wonders to be done by their hands. [4]But the people of the city were divided; some sided with the Jews and some with the apostles. [5]When an attempt was made by both Gentiles and Jews, with their rulers, to mistreat them and to stone them, [6]they learned of it and fled to Lystra and Derbe, cities of Lycaonia, and to the surrounding country, [7]and there they continued to preach the gospel.

[8]Now at Lystra there was a man sitting who could not use his feet. He was crippled from birth and had never walked. [9]He listened to Paul speaking. And Paul, looking intently at him and seeing that he had faith to be made well,[b] [10]said in a loud voice, "Stand upright on your feet." And he sprang up and began walking.

[11]And when the crowds saw what Paul had done, they lifted up their voices, saying in Lycaonian, "The gods have come down to us in the likeness of men!" [12]Barnabas they called Zeus, and Paul, Hermes, because he was the chief speaker. [13]And the priest of Zeus, whose temple was at the entrance to the city, brought oxen and garlands to the gates and wanted to offer sacrifice with the crowds. [14]But when the apostles Barnabas and Paul heard of it, they tore their garments and rushed out into the crowd, crying out, [15]"Men, why are you doing these things? We also are men, of like nature with you, and we bring you good news, that you should turn from these vain things to a living God, who made the heaven and the earth and the sea and all that is in them. [16]In past generations he allowed all the nations to walk in their own ways. [17]Yet he did not leave himself without witness, for he did good by giving you rains from heaven and fruitful seasons, satisfying your hearts with food and gladness." [18]Even with these words they scarcely restrained the people from offering sacrifice to them.

a Or brothers and sisters   b Or be saved

OVERVIEW: After the commentators note the spread of the Word despite opposition—understanding even persecution as God's providential vessel for the continuous growth of believers—they interact at length with the people of Lystra's reaction to Paul's miracle. The reformers roundly condemn the contemporary cult of saints. The saints, at best, are examples of God's grace and of holy living; but only Christ is the *gift itself* of God's righteousness and mercy, as well as the perfect exemplar for his people.

14:1-7 Paul and Barnabas Preach in Iconium

PERSISTENCE AND PERSEVERANCE DESPITE FAILURE. JOHN CALVIN: In the last chapter Luke declared how Paul and Barnabas set about their mission to the Gentiles. But it might seem to be an unhappy and unfortunate beginning in that they were not only expelled from Antioch but also compelled by the obstinate wickedness of certain people to shake off the dust from their feet. But however harshly they were received in one place they do not give up, for they consider that they had been called by the Lord to exercise their ministry throughout the world and specifically in face of the opposition of Satan. We see therefore that they came not only prepared to teach but also armed for the struggle going on undaunted to proclaim the gospel in the midst of conflict. COMMENTARY ON ACTS 14:1.[1]

---

[1]CNTC 7:1* (CO 48:317).

GOD TRANSFORMS EVIL INTO GOOD. JOHANN SPANGENBERG: Here we see that God is a truly adroit Master, for out of human wickedness he can do much good. Was it not a wicked act to persecute the gospel of Christ? Indeed, what worse could happen? And yet God uses this as a medium to spread God's Word far and wide in other lands. But we human beings are masters of wickedness, for out of good we make pure wickedness. Such a wicked trade we learned from our father Adam, so that we are able to do nothing other than sin, plot, speak and carry out wickedness. We are unfaithful, ungracious, arrogant, greedy, envious and hostile, and we foul up all God's gifts with our sins.

. . . When God was so benevolent to the people of Israel in the wilderness in the land of Canaan, they abused everything, grumbling against God, against Moses and the prophets, eventually killing not only the prophets but also the head of all the prophets, Jesus Christ. Today the world acts in the same way. The blessed great Light that God from his mercy has allowed to rise, many people neither want to see nor hear, crawling instead into a hole and burying themselves in the darkness of their heretical, their fanatical and papist ways, like bats and night owls, vilifying and blaspheming God for his magnanimous, unspeakable goodness and benefits.

And so it goes with all God's gifts, be they physical or spiritual. God gives grain; we are not sure for how great a price we will sell it. He gives good wine; we are not even sure how we will drink it all, and there is absolutely no gratitude to be found by us. What will eventually follow other than God's wrath and punishment? If we want to participate with Christ in his kingdom, then we must set aside our wicked trade and learn a new one from Christ our Foreman. The masterpieces we learned from Adam belong in hell, and there is nothing good in them. The abuse of divine goodness, grace and gifts is too flagrant. BRIEF EXEGESIS OF ACTS 14:1.[2]

ICONIUM A RIOTOUS CITY. RUDOLF GWALTHER: Luke goes forward with his history and declares what they did after they were expelled from the coasts of Pisidia. And this place contains a declaration of the things done at Iconium, which we shall note after we have explained such things of Iconium that will supplement our understanding of this history. Iconium, which is in Lycaonia and contains an open passage out of Pisidia to those who travel eastward, has been a very famous city so called in Greek by reason of an idol or an image which, the poets feigned, was made by Prometheus and Minerva at the commandment of Jupiter. . . . By reason of their riches, they lived riotously; because of the ancient superstition of this image, the citizens were given altogether to idolatry, even like the people of our days. HOMILY 96, ACTS 14:1-7.[3]

DO NOT RUSH HEADLONG INTO DEATH. JOHN CALVIN: Note how long the holy champions of Christ held out. They are not put to flight by the mere opposition of enemies, but when the sedition comes to boiling point and the danger of being stoned is threatening, although many favor their teaching they do not persist any further. But, remembering the saying of Christ in which he warned the faithful to possess their souls in patience, they avoid the fury of the enemy. And although they do flee so as not to plunge rashly into death, still their constancy in preaching the gospel makes it clear that they had no fear of danger. For Luke adds that they preached the gospel in other places also. That is the proper kind of fear when the servants of Christ do not run willingly into the hands of their enemies to be cut down by them and yet do not desist from their duty. Nor does fear prevent them from obeying God when he calls, and so if the need arises they will even go through death itself in the fulfilment of their ministry. COMMENTARY ON ACTS 14:5.[4]

IT WAS WISE TO FLEE. THE ENGLISH ANNOTATIONS: Notice later when they are in danger of

---

[2]Spangenberg, *Der Apostel Geschichte*, 127r-v, 128r.

[3]Gwalther, *Homelyes or Sermons upon the Actes*, 559-60* (*In Acta Apostolorum*, 174r).
[4]CNTC 7:4-5* (CO 48:320).

being destroyed they fled according to our Savior's command, thus avoiding the fury of their adversaries. This was wisdom, not inconstancy. ANNOTATIONS ON ACTS 14:6.[5]

14:8-18 Paul and Barnabas Worshiped in Lystra

WHAT WAS PAUL PREACHING? JOHANN SPANGENBERG: He preached, namely, that it is not in our power to walk in the way of the Lord. Thus, we through our works and merits cannot be freed from our sins and finally be saved; instead, God the Father has placed before us—out of his mercy—his dear Son Jesus Christ, in whom, if we heartily believe, we will receive health in body and soul through his help and assistance. This sermon the lame man heard and believed it is so. Now when Paul looked at him and noted that he believed, he wanted to help him. So he spoke in a loud voice, "stand up." . . . With this miracle Paul reinforced his teaching and preaching, as Christ said. BRIEF EXEGESIS OF ACTS 14:8-9.[6]

THE LAME MAN IS AN ILLUSTRATION OF THE GOSPEL. KONRAD PELLIKAN: [The man's] appearance fit with the message, for Paul was teaching the Lycaonians how we, who are too weak by nature to walk in the way of piety, can expiate our sins and obtain salvation, not by our own righteousness, but we have Christ offered to us, in whom and through whom all those who believe are justified and endowed with eternal salvation. COMMENTARY ON ACTS 14:10.[7]

THE CRIPPLED MAN IS HEALED BY FAITH. RUDOLF GWALTHER: Let us see what this crippled man did, before he was made whole. . . . When the crippled man heard Paul preaching the salvation of Christ, he conceived with the good hope that it would be confirmed with many miracles, including

his own restitution, by some secret suggestion of the Holy Spirit. Forasmuch as there are no universal promises that promise bodily health to all who believe in the name of Christ, Luke meant to show the cause of his salvation: "he had faith." For all the Scripture teaches us that by faith we are made partakers both of Christ and of all his benefits, and Christ many times teaches us the same, saying when he healed any, "Be it done to you according to your faith," or "your faith has saved you," or "made you whole." . . . This teaches us through what means faith comes to us. It is obvious that faith is the gift of God and that it consists not in the will, eloquence or wisdom of people. . . . And God uses people as ministers and instruments of his Word when he means to teach people his Word. HOMILY 97, ACTS 14:8-13.[8]

MIRACLES CONFIRM THE WORD. KONRAD PELLIKAN: Miracles of this sort issued through the name of Christ are tokens and confirmations of the veracity of the gospel message concerning the remission of sins. COMMENTARY ON ACTS 14:10.[9]

PAUL'S SERMON HAS UNEXPECTED RESULTS. RUDOLF GWALTHER: When the effect of the miracle is described, it does not result in the way that Paul intended it to. . . . By the miracle, he meant to teach his hearers about Christ. But they take occasion thereby to turn from Christ—being deceived with the old fables of poets, they suppose the apostles are gods, who took on them the form or likeness of human beings, and so came down into the earth. And perhaps they called to mind the coming down of Jupiter and Mercury to Lycaonia, their progenitor. HOMILY 97, ACTS 14:8-13.[10]

PEOPLE SET UP FALSE GODS IN PLACE OF THEIR TRUE SAVIOR. JOHN CALVIN: This story is ample testimony as to how prone people are to

---

[5]Downame, ed., *Annotations*, KKK1r*; alluding to Mt 10:23.
[6]Spangenberg, *Der Apostel Geschichte*, 129v-130r; alluding to Mk 16:16-18.
[7]Pellikan, *In Acta Apostolorum*, 141.
[8]Gwalther, *Homelyes or Sermons upon the Actes*, 565-67* (*In Acta Apostolorum*, 176r); quoting Mt 9:29; Lk 7:50; Mk 5:34.
[9]Pellikan, *In Acta Apostolorum*, 141.
[10]Gwalther, *Homelyes or Sermons upon the Actes*, 567* (*In Acta Apostolorum*, 176v). Cf. Ovid, *Metamorphoses*, 1.

vanity. Paul did not utter the word *arise* abruptly but brought it in as a conclusion to his sermon about Christ. The people, however, ascribe the glory of the miracle to their idols, as if they had not heard a word about Christ. . . .

On seeing unaccustomed power in the healed cripple the people of Lycaonia decide that it is a work of God, and they are right so far. But then they go wrong, because, in keeping with habitual error, they make false gods for themselves in Paul and Barnabas. For what leads them to prefer Barnabas to Paul, except their following the childish fancy about Mercury as the interpreter of the gods, something with which they had long been imbued? We are warned by this example of how evil it is to be habituated to errors in our tender years, because it is by no means easy for them to be eradicated from our minds, so that they tend to become more hardened through the very works of God, by which they ought to have been corrected. Commentary on Acts 14:11.[11]

Even Today We Worship Saints Instead of the One True God. Konrad Pellikan:

Even far more foolishly and with greater impiety have we remained fixated on the saints, and because of the miracles that they performed while still living here on earth some continue to invoke the saints, to devote themselves to the saints and to trust in the saints as saviors. And it has been very widespread among the masses to venerate the saints in this manner and to erect altars, to fashion statues, to offer sacrifices, to adore and worship, to fear their judgments, to go to them as intercessors, as if we are convinced they are more compassionate than our God. Instead, saints have been offered to us by God not so that we might worship them and invoke them but so that we might imitate their examples of piety, whereby we might come to know the good will of God toward us and that we are summoned to follow the calling of God. . . . Therefore, those who esteem the saints in such a way that in them they recognize the mercy and

clemency of God and imitate them in piety, these manifest a kind of adoration that is most pleasing to God as well as to the saints. Commentary on Acts 14:11-13.[12]

The Priest of Jupiter Was Motivated by Greed. John Calvin:

Although Luke does not say what moved the priest to be so diligent, still it is probable that he was driven by greed, since hope of great gain was offered. His future was bright with the hope of wealth if a rumor could be spread all round that Jupiter had appeared there. For it would have been immediately followed by the idea that Jupiter favored the temple of Lystra more than any other. Now, when such a superstition has filled the minds of human beings, no expense is spared in the offering of gifts. Certainly this is the sort of thing that the world tends to do of its own accord, but then the sacrificing priests come on the scene to spur them on. There is also no doubt that ambition drove on the whole multitude, making them so eager in their desire to offer sacrifices to Paul under the name of Jupiter, in order that their city might be the more illustrious in fame and renown. As a result, while the priests are out to net their profits, and the people are truly delighted to be confirmed in their errors, Satan has such freedom to deceive. Commentary on Acts 14:13.[13]

Paul and Barnabas Teach About the One True God. Konrad Pellikan:

The apostles teach them with these specific words, lest glory along with worship and adoration be conferred on themselves rather than to God, who alone is a help in times of need, and lest we worship any human being in place of God, that is, lest we place our confidence in the favor and power, intercession or restoration of some saint. Even today the saints

---

[11]CNTC 7:6, 7* (CO 48:322-23).

[12]Pellikan, *In Acta Apostolorum*, 141-42. Pellikan generally follows Erasmus's *Paraphrases* extremely closely—what today would be considered plagiarism—every now and again going beyond Erasmus. In this passage, however, Pellikan takes up a loud and lengthy anti-Catholic polemic against the invocation of the saints. Compare with CWE 50:92-93 (LB 7:273-74).
[13]CNTC 7:7 (CO 48:323).

who are being adored and invoked are shouting, "What are you people doing? While we were living in a miserable state, we were not invoking other saints but only the true God. You also invoke him, believe in him alone, he alone will reconcile you to the Father."

They also teach a humbleness of the heart, lest we do anything through haughtiness, that we might understand that we are tormented by the same evils by which others are, and likewise that we are enveloped with the fragility of the flesh just as other people. They also indicate what the nature of the apostolic gift is, namely, to proclaim that the world should be turned from the worship of the created to the living God, the Creator of all things.

But Paul and Barnabas did not in this instance make mention of Jesus Christ, only of God. For it would have been foolish for them to foist on them the Son of the one God, given that they were not yet convinced that he is the only true and living God. Therefore gradually they lead them from the beginning into the knowledge of our one Lord Jesus Christ, because knowing not only God the Father but also his Son Jesus Christ leads to true happiness. COMMENTARY ON ACTS 14:14.[14]

"TURN FROM THESE VANITIES." THE ENGLISH ANNOTATIONS: That is, from idolatry, superstistion, and so on. This is according to the Hebrew manner of speech; they called idols *hebel*, vanity. . . . Certainly adoration of senseless idols is the most irrational vanity that Satan ever put in the stupified human heart. "How much more truly do dumb creatures judge your gods," Minucius Felix said in [his] Octavius, "they know they have no sense, they gnaw on them, leap on them, sit on them. The birds breed in the mouth of your gods; spiders hang their slender threads on their heads." ANNOTATIONS ON ACTS 14:15.[15]

THE CREATED ORDER TESTIFIES TO GOD'S PRESENCE. JOHN CALVIN: From the beginning God has indeed made himself known to all humankind through the Word. But Paul and Barnabas show that there was no age on which God did not bestow his blessings, which could testify that the world is ruled by his power. However, because the light of doctrine had been buried for many generations, it is for that reason that they only say that God was manifested by natural evidences. . . . They assume this principle that in the order of nature there is a certain and clear manifestation of God. Because the earth is watered by rain, because the heat of the sun quickens its growth, because fruits in such great abundance are produced year by year, we may surely gather from these things that there is some God who governs all things. For the heaven and the earth are not moved by their own power, much less even by chance. Therefore the conclusion is that this amazing ingenuity of nature plainly points to the providence of God, and that those who have said that the world is eternal have not spoken according to the understanding of their minds but have tried through spiteful and barbarous ingratitude to obliterate the glory of God, and in doing so have betrayed their own impudence. COMMENTARY ON ACTS 14:17.[16]

THE TWOFOLD DUTY OF MINISTERS. RUDOLF GWALTHER: The apostles in this passage comprehended the duty of those who are ministers of the Word, while they affirm that their preaching is for the purpose that people should turn from the vain worshiping of creatures and to the only living God. Therefore the faithful ministers of Christ must join these two things together, that is, they must both overthrow false religion and plant the true one, as the prophet says: "Behold, this day have I appointed you, to root up and destroy, and to build up and plant." For as it is in farming, all the labor taken in plowing and watering is in vain unless the things that hinder the corn's growth are

---

[14]Pellikan, *In Acta Apostolorum*, 143.

[15]Downame, ed., *Annotations*, KKK1r-v*; alluding to Deut 32:21. Minucius Felix, "The Octavius," ANF 4:187-88. This second- or third-century work is a dialogue between a non-Christian, Caecilius, and a Christian, Octavius, in which they debate the truth of Christianity; ultimately Caecilius is convinced of its truth and converts.

[16]CNTC 7:13* (CO 48:328).

rooted up and good seed sown, so it is in cultivating the mind, they have most unfruitfully labored who have not painfully and carefully joined both of these things together.

Therefore the people of our days commit double offense, for there are some people who so abhor the antichrist and his wicked religion that being occupied only in overthrowing the same, they forget to restore again true and sincere religion. Again there are others who teach the true religion by preaching the Word but will not dare touch abuses and superstition, because they do not want all the displeasure of the world. And these latter sorts hope that superstition will fall of its own accord, when people come to the knowledge of the true God. But they do not perceive that there is no place for the knowledge of God in human minds until these superstitions are removed. Therefore who means, profitably and with commendation, to travail in matters of religion must join both these together. HOMILY 98, ACTS 14:14-18.[17]

---

[17]Gwalther, *Homelyes or Sermons upon the Actes*, 572-73* (*In Acta Apostolorum*, 178r); quoting Jer 1:10.

14:19-28 PAUL CONTINUES TO STRENGTHEN THE CHURCH

¹⁹But Jews came from Antioch and Iconium, and having persuaded the crowds, they stoned Paul and dragged him out of the city, supposing that he was dead. ²⁰But when the disciples gathered about him, he rose up and entered the city, and on the next day he went on with Barnabas to Derbe. ²¹When they had preached the gospel to that city and had made many disciples, they returned to Lystra and to Iconium and to Antioch, ²²strengthening the souls of the disciples, encouraging them to continue in the faith, and saying that through many tribulations we must enter the kingdom of God. ²³And when they had appointed elders for them in every church, with prayer and fast-ing they committed them to the Lord in whom they had believed.

²⁴Then they passed through Pisidia and came to Pamphylia. ²⁵And when they had spoken the word in Perga, they went down to Attalia, ²⁶and from there they sailed to Antioch, where they had been commended to the grace of God for the work that they had fulfilled. ²⁷And when they arrived and gathered the church together, they declared all that God had done with them, and how he had opened a door of faith to the Gentiles. ²⁸And they remained no little time with the disciples.

Overview: Despite the initial welcome that Paul and Barnabas receive, their reception turns into animosity. A majority of commentators draw two lessons from this pericope. The first lesson recognizes both the rewards and trials of apostles, pastors and teachers. Ministers and teachers carry on their work based on a calling from God and affirmed by the believing community. As Paul and Barnabas travel to various cities, they select ministers and elders with prayer and fasting, and then confirm them by the laying-on of hands. This practice communicates God's consecration and the congregation's consent. The second lesson, emphasized mostly by Radicals, recognizes persecution as an expected if not necessary aspect of Christian faith. Because Jesus and the early apostles were persecuted, preachers who come after them should not be surprised by similar mistreatment and rejection.

14:19-23 Paul and Barnabas Continue Their Mission Despite Persecution

Satan's Malice Is Restless. The English Annotations: Here we see Satan's restless malice in assaulting the ministers of Christ. Now accusing them of sacrilege and robbing God of his honor, in accepting sacrifices and divine honor, when that failed, he incited the Jews and the people to persecute and stone them. See also the inconstancy of the common people. Just now mad to adore them as gods, then immediately as unsober in the other extreme, persecuting them, as if they had been the worst people, stoning Paul and dragging him out of the city as dead. Annotations on Acts 14:19.[1]

Paul's Miraculous Revival. Heinrich Bullinger: It is abundantly clear from this passage that, by the power of God, Paul was raised up as if from the dead; he was not cured by the remedies of the brothers. For who has ever heard of someone who was stoned walking the next day? Especially someone whom they assumed to be dead! Someone whom they stoned with hatred seething through themselves! Certainly they would not have stopped throwing stones, if they had be-

---

[1]Downame, ed., *Annotations*, KKK1v*.

lieved any living breath remained in him. Anyone who would have come across this wretched man removed from the city limits would not have found a person half-alive, but indeed a corpse! The full power of the Lord displayed itself in Paul's weakness, so that from then on we should not dread in the least the danger of death. . . . For Paul returns to those cites in which he, with his companion Barnabas, had already established churches and consecrated to the faith, so that he might rouse them out of their torpor, [exhorting them] to perseverance and endurance. For perseverance is the pinnacle of all things; its sinew and tendon is suffering. . . . The world hates, rejects and persecutes the truth; piety loves and cherishes the truth, clinging to it tenaciously. Therefore it also clings to suffering. COMMENTARY ON ACTS 14:20.[2]

PAUL THE INDUSTRIOUS FARMER. DESIDERIUS ERASMUS: Paul was much too worried to grieve for his own sake—worried that the hardships he was suffering from the ungodly might provide the occasion by which the weak would be estranged from Christ. Meanwhile, he offers an example to bishops: they should imitate industrious farmers who do not think it enough to plant or sow, but who also watch that what begins to spring up successfully reaches maturity. PARAPHRASE OF ACTS 14:21-22.[3]

SUFFERING MAKES BELIEVERS LIKE CHRIST. BALTHASAR HUBMAIER: No, no! . . . A Christian does not fight, strike or kill unless he is in a seat of authority and is ordered to do it or is called to do it by the properly instituted government. No, instead, sooner than draw a sword, a Christian forfeits his cloak and coat. Yes, he offers the other cheek, even life and limb. Christian conduct is so peaceable because this is the Christian's victory, our faith, which overcomes the world. Accordingly, a Christian's life is set toward suffering in order that he may in some measure become like Christ in suffering, fulfill Christ's suffering in his body, and, with his cross, follow in the path that he has prepared for us and on which he himself has gone before us with his cross and suffering. Then we shall also inherit eternal life with him. APOLOGIA.[4]

"THROUGH MUCH TRIBULATION." MENNO SIMONS: My good reader, examine the Scriptures correctly and you will find that to the free children of God there is no liberty promised for the flesh here on earth, even as Christ says, "You shall be hated of all nations for my name's sake." Again, "if any man will come after me, let him deny himself and take up his cross and follow me." . . . "All who will live godly in Christ Jesus," says Paul, "must suffer persecution, and through much tribulation we must enter into the kingdom of God." For the liberty of the Spirit is to be attested to with much misery, tribulation, persecutions, bonds, fear and death. FOUNDATION OF CHRISTIAN DOCTRINE (1539).[5]

CHRIST'S IS A DIFFICULT CUP TO DRINK. HANS SCHLAFFER AND LEONHARD FRICK: No one can hinder and oppress your Word and work, O mighty God. Those who are highly regarded by the world want to demolish and utterly destroy your Word, but what they do ends up promoting and directing it. You are wonderful, O my God, in your saints.

Therefore it will not come about with sleeping, living comfortably or going about idly, laughing madly, singing, blathering on, ringing bells, burning candles. If one wants to be a Christian, it means risking one's body and life. Yes, to eat the flesh of Christ and drink his blood is a tough meal. Therefore it is also a tough saying for them, just as it was for his disciples when he said, "Unless you eat my flesh and drink my blood, you will have no life in you." Therefore many were troubled, deceived themselves and no longer went about with him.

This is what the entire so-called Christendom,

---

[2]Bullinger, *In Acta Apostolorum*, 173v-174r.
[3]CWE 50:93 (LB 7:724-25).

[4]CRR 5:560* (QGT 9:489-90); alluding to 1 Jn 5:4; Col 1:24.
[5]Simons, *Complete Writings*, 188-89; quoting Mt 24:9; 16:24; alluding to 2 Tim 3:12; Acts 14:22.

along with their scribes and Pharisees, do to this very day. They write copious commentaries on the words of our Lord in John, and they desire to receive the body of Christ or his flesh in bread and his blood in a cup. It is not tough to eat and drink daily; in principle it is a good thing to do; it makes for a good, peaceful day and life to eat plenty and to drink in complete ecstasy—that's the pinnacle of worthiness.

But those who enjoy it once a year and in one kind, as they call it, remain in their fleshly lives from year to year, worldly-minded until they reach the end, even though Christ said, "Whoever eats my flesh and drinks my blood will remain in me and I in him, and as my Father sent me to live and I live by the will of my Father, whoever eats my flesh will live according to my will."

Here one plainly sees that eating and drinking is another, new life, different from the way the world lives. That is, one ought to live in suffering, persecution and death for the sake of the Lord, as it is shown throughout all the blessed Scripture. For everyone who wants to live a life of blessedness must suffer persecution. KUNSTBUCH: A SIMPLE PRAYER.[6]

LIKE A SPRING DOWNPOUR, PERSECUTION BURSTS UNEXPECTEDLY. JOHANN SPANGENBERG: In Christianity with the gospel it is like a storm in the air. Now it rains, soon the sun shines, before we look around a storm gale and downpour comes, again the sun peeks out and it is nice and bright and clear. This is how it is in Christianity, too. Today there is good peace, tomorrow persecution comes, before we look around the persecution is halted, the tyrants are dead and immediately the gospel shines out brightly. Those from Lystra want to heave Paul and Barnabas into heaven and place them on God's throne, but now the Jews from Iconium and Antioch come and stone Paul, dragging him out of the city like a corpse. Here we see how the common rabble think, how erratic, how un-

thankful. The good Paul comes and preaches God's Word to them, would gladly like to help them into heaven and eternal life, but they reward him wickedly, wanting to hurl stones at him until he is dead, so that surely he can say, "Through many tribulations we must enter the kingdom of God." BRIEF EXEGESIS OF ACTS 14:22.[7]

THE CONFIRMATION OF THE WORD. JOHN CALVIN: Paul and Barnabas returned to the churches they had established, in order to confirm the disciples. By this he means that the use of the Word does not consist in mere instruction, by which the hearer is only taught, but that it also avails for the confirmation of faith, in warning, exhorting and convicting. Indeed, Christ commands his ministers not only to teach but also to exhort, and Paul also declares that Scripture is useful not only for teaching but also for exhortation. Accordingly pastors are not to think that they have fulfilled their ministry when they have properly imbued their people with the right knowledge, unless they also devote themselves to this task. [And] believers are not to neglect the Word of God, as if the reading and preaching of it were superfluous, for there is no one who does not need constant confirmation....

This was the principal method of confirmation, using exhortation to encourage the disciples, who had already embraced and professed the gospel, to continue. For we are far from being ready and active, as we ought to be, in doing our duty. For that reason our sloth needs goads, and our coldness needs to be warmed up. But, because God wants his people to be disciplined through various struggles, Paul and Barnabas warn the disciples to be prepared to endure tribulations.... For although God deals more gently with certain people, still he is not so lenient or indulgent to any one of his own that he is altogether immune from tribulation. COMMENTARY ON ACTS 14:20-22.[8]

---

[6]CRR 12:289-91* (QGT 17:362-63); alluding to Ps 68:35; quoting Jn 6:53, 56-57.

[7]Spangenberg, *Der Apostel Geschichte*, 126r-v.
[8]CNTC 7:16-17, 18* (CO 48:330-31, 332); alluding to 2 Tim 3:16.

AN APOSTLE WHEREVER I MAY ROAM. HEINRICH BULLINGER:

Regular election and maintenance of the apostolic office is entrusted to us for the benefit of the church. Some elders (*presbyteri*) were formerly apostles, still with great authority, but now they administered a different office. For an apostle roams freely, preaching the gospel first to these people then to those people. However, an elder (*presbyter*) or bishop (*episcopus*) is placed over one specific church. He is to care for this church alone; he does not roam like apostles do. COMMENTARY ON ACTS 14:23.[9]

THE ELECTION OF MINISTERS IN THE EARLY CHURCH. RUDOLF GWALTHER:

The Evangelist also declares the ceremony or manner of choosing elders, wherein prayer and fasting were first placed. . . . When the Scripture joins both these together, it signifies that the church used to come together in solemn ways. For the primitive church was accustomed, when any great necessity urged or constrained them, to appoint solemn assemblies, giving themselves to prayer and fasting until the evening. . . . The primitive church was moved with weighty considerations to observe these things in the electing of the ministers. For where they thought people might easily be deceived, they would not in such a weighty case attribute anything to human judgment, and therefore they thought it right to seek by godly prayers the inspiration of God's Spirit. Again, where they thought it was requisite to have those furnished with singular gifts for such an office, they implored God by humble supplication. Whenever it was necessary to be more fervent, they joined fasting, as we have elsewhere declared. Moreover, Luke makes mention of the laying on of hands, by which is understood not only consent of voices but also imposition of hands, which was a sacrament and token of consecration. HOMILY 100, ACTS 14:23-28.[10]

FORMERLY MINISTERS OF THE WORD WERE CHOSEN THROUGH PRAYER AND FASTING. JOHANN SPANGENBERG:

In the early church they received bishops, pastors and preachers from God and confirmed them with prayer and fasting, with little ceremony and churchly ostentation. They led well and unlocked heaven, bringing God many souls. But today we elect bishops, prelates and pastors according to connections and power, and we perform many ceremonies and pompous churchly ostentations, but there is very little prayer to God. Thus they try to do what they can to lock others out of heaven, and they themselves also cannot enter. BRIEF EXEGESIS OF ACTS 14:23.[11]

THE DISTINCTION BETWEEN PASTORS AND PRESBYTERS. JOHN CALVIN:

It is apparent from this that it is not enough for people once to have been instructed correctly in godly doctrine and to hold the substance of the faith, if they do not make continual progress. That is why Christ not only sent apostles to spread the gospel but also commanded pastors to be appointed, so that the proclamation of the gospel might be perpetual and in daily practice. Paul and Barnabas observe this order laid down by Christ when they assign pastors to individual churches, so that after their departure teaching may not cease and fall silent. Moreover, this passage teaches us that the church cannot be without the ordinary ministry, and it is only those who are willing disciples through the whole course of life who are considered Christians in the eyes of God. I interpret presbyters here as those on whom the office of teaching had been enjoined, for it is evident from what Paul says that some were only censors of morals. Now when Luke says that they were set over every church, a distinction is drawn from this between their office and that of the apostles. For the apostles did not have a definite station anywhere, but they moved about here and there, continually founding new churches. [But] pastors were appointed individually to their own churches and

---

[9]Bullinger, *In Acta Apostolorum*, 174v.
[10]Gwalther, *Homelyes or Sermons upon the Actes*, 584-85* (*In Acta Apostolorum*, 182r).

[11]Spangenberg, *Der Apostel Geschichte*, 133v-134r.

were placed, so to speak, in charge. COMMENTARY ON ACTS 14:23.[12]

THE CONGREGATION'S CALL OF MINISTERS. DIRK PHILIPS: The calling and election of teachers and ministers occurs from the congregation, through God's inspiration and command with the single voice of the congregation, and with fasting and praying. And the same elected ministers were ordained by the elders through the laying on of hands. . . .

From all this it follows clearly that a true minister must have both this calling and election, that is, the calling from God and the orderly election of the congregation of the Lord. According to the first election and godly calling, he is obligated to the entire church. According to the other election he is the minister of the congregation that has chosen him and in which he was ordained. Thus the congregation at Philippi had bishops and deacons. And every congregation in Asia also had a bishop and a messenger, that is, a teacher.

Again, Paul and Barnabas came to agreement with Cephas, James and John that these three should serve the apostolic office among the Jews and the other two among the heathen, only that they should consider the poor. Therefore it is proper for a minister to have a special place and congregation where he has his career and serves, yet always under the condition that the whole flock is cared for, the congregation is also served and that the entire body of the Lord be built up and improved. 1565 AGREEMENT.[13]

PASTORS, COMMIT YOUR SUCCESS TO GOD. RUDOLF GWALTHER: Moreover, the example of the apostle teaches us what we should do after we have done our duty. Let us commit all the success of it to God, by whose providence we know all things are governed. This is the only means by which we can moderate and quiet our devices, wherein those so who are ignorant are marvel-

ously troubled and often times abandon their duty, supposing to bring matters to pass through their own wisdom and devices. For, standing between hope and dread, they can find no resting place for their devise. But those who know that trust and diligence is required of them in doing their duty and that all success thereof depends on God, when they see they have done their duty, they can ignore all dangers that come to them; no fear of danger can prevent them from doing their duty. HOMILY 100, ACTS 14:23-28.[14]

14:24-28 *Paul and Barnabas Return to Antioch*

GRAMMATICAL OBSERVATIONS ABOUT ACTS 14:27. JOHN CALVIN: As ambassadors returning from a mission usually give an account of their acts, so Paul and Barnabas give to the church a complete account of their travels, in order to show how faithfully they carried out their ministry and at the same time to encourage the believers to give thanks to God, for the actual situation was affording ample grounds for doing so. Accordingly Luke does not say that they extolled their own deeds but all the things that the Lord had carried out through them. Literally it reads "with them," but according to the Hebrew idiom it amounts to much the same thing as if there had been put "in them" or "by means of them" or "toward them," or the simple dative "to them." Therefore Luke does not say σὺν αὐτοῖς but μετ᾿ αὐτῶν. The reason why I say this is so that no ignorant person may ascribe a share of the praise to Paul and Barnabas, as if they had been God's partners in the work, whereas they rather make God the one and only Author of all the things that they had done effectively. COMMENTARY ON ACTS 14:27.[15]

THE SURPRISE OF THE "OPEN DOOR." JOHN CALVIN: Luke adds immediately after that the

---

[12]CNTC 7:18-19* (CO 48:332-33); alluding to 1 Tim 5:17.
[13]CRR 6:485-86* (BRN 10:533).

[14]Gwalther, *Homelyes or Sermons upon the Actes*, 585* (*In Acta Apostolorum*, 182r).
[15]CNTC 7:20-21* (CO 48:334-35).

Lord had opened a door of faith to the Gentiles. For even though they had been sent to the Gentiles, still the novelty of the situation did not fail to surprise. And the sudden change was not the only thing that astonished the Jews. But because it was a monstrous thing to them that those who were unclean and alienated from the kingdom of God should be united with the holy seed of Abraham, so that together they might constitute the one church of God, they are now taught by the actual result that the apostles had not been given to them for nothing. COMMENTARY ON ACTS 14:27.[16]

PAUL AND BARNABAS STAY TO HELP WITH THE HARVEST. DESIDERIUS ERASMUS: Paul and Barnabas, however, stayed for a considerable time with the disciples at Antioch, because in such a populous city a large congregation of believers of different ethnic identities had joined together and the congregation was growing larger every day. There the apostles took pleasure in staying longer where the harvest was more plentiful. PARAPHRASE OF ACTS 14:28.[17]

---

[16]CNTC 7:21 (CO 48:335).

[17]CWE 50:94 (LB 7:725).

15:1-21 THE JERUSALEM COUNCIL

But some men came down from Judea and were teaching the brothers, "Unless you are circumcised according to the custom of Moses, you cannot be saved." ²And after Paul and Barnabas had no small dissension and debate with them, Paul and Barnabas and some of the others were appointed to go up to Jerusalem to the apostles and the elders about this question. ³So, being sent on their way by the church, they passed through both Phoenicia and Samaria, describing in detail the conversion of the Gentiles, and brought great joy to all the brothers.ᵃ ⁴When they came to Jerusalem, they were welcomed by the church and the apostles and the elders, and they declared all that God had done with them. ⁵But some believers who belonged to the party of the Pharisees rose up and said, "It is necessary to circumcise them and to order them to keep the law of Moses."

⁶The apostles and the elders were gathered together to consider this matter. ⁷And after there had been much debate, Peter stood up and said to them, "Brothers, you know that in the early days God made a choice among you, that by my mouth the Gentiles should hear the word of the gospel and believe. ⁸And God, who knows the heart, bore witness to them, by giving them the Holy Spirit just as he did to us, ⁹and he made no distinction between us and them, having cleansed their hearts by faith. ¹⁰Now, therefore, why are you putting God to the test by placing a yoke on the neck of the disciples that neither our fathers nor we have been able to bear? ¹¹But we believe that we will be saved through the grace of the Lord Jesus, just as they will."

¹²And all the assembly fell silent, and they listened to Barnabas and Paul as they related what signs and wonders God had done through them among the Gentiles. ¹³After they finished speaking, James replied, "Brothers, listen to me. ¹⁴Simeon has related how God first visited the Gentiles, to take from them a people for his name. ¹⁵And with this the words of the prophets agree, just as it is written,

¹⁶"'After this I will return,
and I will rebuild the tent of David
        that has fallen;
I will rebuild its ruins,
    and I will restore it,
¹⁷that the remnantᵇ of mankind
        may seek the Lord,
    and all the Gentiles who are called
        by my name,
    says the Lord, who makes these things
        ¹⁸known from of old.'

¹⁹Therefore my judgment is that we should not trouble those of the Gentiles who turn to God, ²⁰but should write to them to abstain from the things polluted by idols, and from sexual immorality, and from what has been strangled, and from blood. ²¹For from ancient generations Moses has had in every city those who proclaim him, for he is read every Sabbath in the synagogues."

a Or brothers and sisters; also verse 22   b Or rest

OVERVIEW: At the Jerusalem Council, the apostles and elders gather to discuss whether Gentile believers must follow the laws and customs of Moses—especially circumcision—in order to receive salvation. James, the brother of Jesus, exhorts the Jerusalem church to include the Gentiles who "turn to God" without burdening them with the Mosaic law. Based on this decision, the commentators collectively stress that at the center of the Christian religion is the reality that salvation is through God's grace, not human works. The central point of the sermons and speeches is the sufficiency of faith for justification before God; all the law and the prophets agree with the apostles concerning this.

The temptation to grant some measure of independent virtue to human action in the work of salvation is strong and common to all human beings, our commentators observe, ever since the fall of Adam and Eve. Hidden in this danger is a consolation. Though sinners are just as weak today as they were in the first century, the Holy Spirit is just as truly present and active.

THE JERUSALEM COUNCIL TEACHES ABOUT TRUE FREEDOM OF CONSCIENCE AND THE PERSISTENCE OF PELAGIANISM. MARTIN LUTHER:

In this chapter the freedom of the conscience is disputed and discussed. We have often talked about this. Namely, that wherever we preach faith and God's grace, there whatever belongs with and is stated by works must be discarded and abandoned. These two—works and grace, faith and law—will not and cannot tolerate being placed side by side. One alone must win as far as the conscience is concerned. Works may and ought to be performed, but as long as the conscience does not depend on them and does not place its trust in them. Instead, works are freely performed to honor God and to help our neighbors. The conscience must depend only on faith, on the Word and on the grace of God.

That is the true, pure teaching and preaching. Now wherever it is, it never fails that heresy and sects spring up. Even from the beginning of the world the archheresy which we call Pelagianism, concerning free will and the merit of our works, has followed this true instruction. It has always interjected itself and sticks to the true preaching like muck on a wheel. So in the beginning Abel taught the pure Word and held it in his conscience. But Cain remained dependent on works and lost faith. The same happened afterwards with Isaac and Ishmael, Esau and Jacob, and many others. All the prophets were determined to lead people away from false works to faith; they vehemently combatted with the false prophets concerning this.

This discord will and must always remain. We must get used to what we see before our eyes: once one sect falls away, immediately many others spring up, so that things will never stay completely pure. The cause is that reason is unable to surrender itself to faith. If someone believes completely and absolutely in God's Word, then the Holy Spirit must have created and worked this [faith] in the heart. By its own powers nature is incapable of this; what we say and do must remain dependent on works. Since not everyone has the Holy Spirit, but rather the great majority remain in their flesh and blood, acting according to reason, it must be that they remain reliant on works and not faith. This is how impossible it is for us to be free of the fanatics and false teachers. SERMON ON ACTS 15.[1]

THE UNLEARNEDNESS OF THE LEARNED ONES. VALENTIN ICKELSHAMER:

All of my days I've heard
a lot said about experience. People justly say
that she's the mistress of all understanding.
So it is not for nothing
that experience is called the mother
of all proverbs, as is well known.
And we're also told
that those of old said:
The more learned you are,
the prouder and the more senseless
    you will be. . . .
Even during Paul's time
there were learned people like this,
concerned especially about circumcision,
who, without sense and without
    the Spirit of God,
simply clung doggedly to the letter of the law,
with which they played around
    in all the churches,
muscled their way in,
and also claimed to be apostles,
advancing their cause with good appearances.
So that they might live in peace,
they preached Moses in addition,
introduced circumcision,
confusing everybody

---

[1]WA 15:578-80.

and stirring up great discord
in all of early Christendom.
Paul argued against them
with the power of God and with miracles,
not solely with Scriptures,
for they had those in common with him,
they studied it day and night,
and with Scripture they carried on pompously.
Otherwise they had neither power nor might
with which to give value to their teaching.
They were nothing but scribes
who perverted all Paul's teachings,
rebelling against Paul,
and indeed, frequently persecuting him,
even calling on secular powers,
the same as the Pharisees did to Christ.
These people had the same spirit.
Everywhere, above all,
they resisted the Holy Spirit,
as Stephen said they did
and as all the prophets lamented.
People like the ones mentioned
from antiquity into our time
stand by the proverb that is true
and you will find much written about it
in books both new and old.
They interpret it in the same way
that I'm telling you here.

KUNSTBUCH: THE LEARNED ONES, THE
WRONGHEADED ONES.[2]

15:1-5 *The Judaizers Debate Paul and Barnabas*

**TRUE ZEAL FOR THE LAW SHOULD LEAD TO
AN EMBRACE OF THE GOSPEL.** DESIDERIUS
ERASMUS: Those who dwelled in the part of Syria
properly called Judea were more tenacious for the
law of Moses than others. Because they had less
contact with Gentiles and were closer to the temple,
they were less willing to have the Gentiles received
into the fellowship of the gospel apart from the

observance of the law. They did not understand
that once the light of truth had been revealed the
law was to be abrogated insofar as it pertained to
shadows, figures and ceremonies—such as circumcision, the Sabbath rest, choice of foods, feast days,
distinctions in clothing, vows, fasts and avoiding
the dead, all of which were imposed for a time on
carnal people to accustom them to obey God until
the shadows flee away under the very bright light
of truth revealed through the gospel.

Accordingly, those who did not understand that
the law was spiritual maintained that what had
been prescribed by God, handed down by the ancestors and observed through so many ages by their
ancestors, ought to be unending. This conviction
arose not so much from malice as from an over-
scrupulous regard for the law, which they destroy
in their zealous effort to keep....

This was the beginning of a fight on the part of
those who clung tenaciously to the flesh of the law
against those who followed the genuine spiritual
liberty of the gospel, a struggle there will always
be among Christians. God permitted this conflict
to arise so that all disciples of Christ might better
understand how deadly is a religion that relies on
ceremonies. PARAPHRASE OF ACTS 15:1-2.[3]

**FALSE TEACHERS OFTEN MAKE MUCH OF AP-
OSTOLIC AUTHORITY.** RUDOLF GWALTHER: The
consideration of this history serves both to instruct
and comfort all congregations. By the example of
the apostles we are taught how to resist false doctrine. So we learn that the doctrine of truth stands
firm and sure against all invasions....

Luke tells who the authors of this strife and dissension were, including certain persons who came
out of Judea and from Jerusalem. Therefore they
must be of great authority, considering Jerusalem
was the mother church of all others and was worthily esteemed by all people, because from there the
gospel of salvation did first issue and spring. Paul
also commends [the true doctrine], saying, It was
right that the Gentiles should minister corporeal

---

[2]CRR 12:41-43 (QGT 17:107-9).

[3]CWE 50:94, 95* (LB 7:725-26).

things to those in Jerusalem, who had given them the spiritual and eternal gifts of salvation. And it is no doubt that those deceivers and seducers did marvelously brag of the name and authority of the apostles and did make light of Paul's name, as one who did not deserve to be counted among the apostles, because he had not been conversant with Jesus Christ while he lived. This we may gather from Paul's epistles, where he is forced to defend earnestly his authority and apostleship against them. Furthermore, we may here see how deceivers breed even in the church but were never true members of the church. HOMILY 101, ACTS 15:1-4.[4]

FALSE TEACHING IS THE SOURCE OF REBELLION. HEINRICH BULLINGER: Just as that evil one sows his bad seed in the field of the Lord, so the Lord constantly tests his people with various afflictions. So far he has tested them with a variety of persecutions; now he tries them with a variety of heresies. Heresy is worse than persecution. For it afflicts and undermines people's souls after their bodies are torn apart. However, since heresy is inserted for the good of the church, thus it is allowed to crop up for the greatest good of both the genuine and the faithful. As Paul said, "It is necessary for heresies to exist in order to reveal those who are genuine." So, then, it was necessary for this error to outlive the apostles, so that their enduring testimony and the primary tenet of our faith, most clearly explicated and confirmed, would bring an end to all future doubts and controversies. COMMENTARY ON ACTS 15:1-2.[5]

SATAN ALWAYS SEEKS TO FAN THE FLAMES OF DISSENSION. JOHN CALVIN: Let us learn that disagreements, no matter what they are, must be resisted at an early stage, so that they may not burst out into the flame of contentions, because all that Satan is after with the fans of dissensions is to kindle just so many fires. But . . . when we see

that the first church was in an uproar and that all the best ministers of Christ were busily engaged in quarrels, if the same thing happens to us today, let us not be alarmed, as if we were involved in something new and unexpected, but, seeking from God a solution like the one he gave on that occasion, let us carry on through stormy disturbances with the same tenor of faith. COMMENTARY ON ACTS 15:2.[6]

SPIRITUAL STRIFE IS WORSE THAN PHYSICAL VIOLENCE. DESIDERIUS ERASMUS: This warfare was much more destructive to the gospel than the violence of Herod or of other princes because it assaulted true godliness under a false image of piety. PARAPHRASE OF ACTS 15:2.[7]

CIRCUMCISION IS A SYNECDOCHE FOR THE ENTIRE LAW. JOHN CALVIN: With these words Luke gives a brief definition of the main question at issue, namely, that those impostors wished to bind consciences with the necessity of keeping the Law. Circumcision is certainly the only thing mentioned here, but it is quite clear from the context that they raised the controversy about the keeping of the whole Law. But because circumcision was, as it were, the solemn initiation into all the other rites of the Law, therefore, by synecdoche, the whole Law is included under one part. Those enemies of Paul were not denying that Christ is the Messiah, but while giving their allegiance to him, they were still retaining the old ceremonies of the Law.

At first glance the error could have given the appearance of being a tolerable one. Why then does Paul not keep quiet, at least for a short time, so as not to shake the church with conflict, for the dispute was about external things, about which Paul himself elsewhere forbids too much bitter quarrelling? In fact there were three important reasons, which forced him to protest. For if the keeping of the Law is a necessary thing, the salvation of people is bound to works, whereas it must be founded only on the grace of Christ, for faith to

---

[4]Gwalther, *Homelyes or Sermons upon the Actes*, 588* (*In Acta Apostolorum*, 183r); alluding to Gal 1.
[5]Bullinger, *In Acta Apostolorum*, 176r; alluding to Mt 13:24-30; quoting 1 Cor 11:19.

[6]CNTC 7:25* (CO 48:338).
[7]CWE 50:95 (LB 7:726).

be peaceful and untroubled. Therefore when Paul saw the cult of the Law being set over against the free righteousness of faith, it was not right for him to be silent, unless he wished to abandon Christ. For when his adversaries denied that anyone will be saved unless he keeps the law of Moses, in this way they snatched away the glory of salvation from Christ and were transferring it to works, and they were troubling and disquieting miserable souls by shaking their confidence. In the second place, it was not a matter of trifling importance to strip faithful souls of the liberty acquired by the blood of Christ. Even if the inward liberty of the Spirit was something common to the fathers and us, we know, however, what Paul says, that is, that they were confined under the childish custody of the Law, so that they were scarcely different from slaves, but that, after the manifestation of Christ, we have been set free from the custodianship of the Law, to act with more freedom, as if our time for being protected has come to an end. The third fault of this teaching was that it poured out darkness on the light of the gospel, or at least interposed something like dark clouds, so that Christ the Sun of Righteousness might not send out his full splendor. In short, it would have been all over with Christianity in a short time if Paul had yielded to such principles. COMMENTARY ON ACTS 15:2.[8]

TRUE TEACHERS ARE TO BE SHOWN DEFERENCE. HEINRICH BULLINGER: Scripture everywhere admonishes the disciples—that is, Christians—to be courteous, kind and friendly. And so I say this obligingly about everyone, but especially about teachers of the truth. Therefore, here, the disciples take care of the apostle as he travels through Phoenicia and Samaria; he is received, without a doubt, most kindly on his way to Jerusalem! There was no enmity among the apostles or in the church itself, but these [men from Judea] spoke falsely about Paul, desiring to plant this deceptive

seed in the hearts of the simple. COMMENTARY ON ACTS 15:3.[9]

THE SPIRIT-GIVEN CONFIDENCE OF PAUL AND BARNABAS. DESIDERIUS ERASMUS: So confident were the apostles of what they had done that of their own accord they spoke of it everywhere. They were not proceeding to Jerusalem to learn from [the other] apostles whether they had thus far acted rightly or not, but to calm the disquietude of the weak with the authority of more eminent persons. PARAPHRASE OF ACTS 15:3.[10]

THE HOLY SPIRIT'S COUNSEL IS THE ONLY TRUSTWORTHY COUNCIL. MARTIN LUTHER: It is important to understand this example well. We praise the early church enthusiastically, how perfect it was and how mightily the Holy Spirit was with them. But when we examine the matter in the light, we see that the Holy Spirit has always been just as strong and just as weak. They had received the Holy Spirit, but they were still so weak that they could wriggle out of knowing that faith alone—not the law—saves. SERMON ON ACTS 15:5.[11]

THIS CONTROVERSY IS THE SAME AS TODAY'S. RUDOLF GWALTHER: This therefore was the whole state of the controversy: "whether people were justified through the grace of God, by faith only in Christ, or whether the righteousness of the Law was necessary for salvation." And if one would weigh and expound this matter well, it would appear that this was the very same controversy which is between us and the papists now in these days, who profess Christ also but still affirm that human beings are justified and saved by their merits and good deeds, except that in this point the papists' case is the weaker and worse, for they do not ground their argument on the law of Moses, which was once given by God, but on human traditions. HOMILY 101, ACTS 15:1-4.[12]

---

[8]CNTC 7:25-26* (CO 48:338-39); alluding to Rom 14:1; 1 Tim 1:3-7; Gal 4:1-2; 3:23-24.

[9]Bullinger, *In Acta Apostolorum*, 177v.
[10]CWE 50:95-96 (LB 7:726).
[11]WA 15:581.
[12]Gwalther, *Homelyes or Sermons upon the Actes*, 589* (*In Acta*

WERE THESE TEACHERS OF WORKS RIGHTEOUSNESS BAD PEOPLE? JOHANN SPANGENBERG: They were not bad people; rather, they were the apostles themselves who were mired in such error, the same who indeed had the Holy Spirit in the highest degree. If these three had not stood so firmly, the entire coterie of Christians would have fallen and held such errant teaching. BRIEF EXEGESIS OF ACTS 15:5.[13]

15:6-11 Peter Testifies to the Council

THE COUNCIL ASSEMBLES ELDERS AND THE LEARNED. THE ENGLISH ANNOTATIONS: To [apostles and elders] pertains the decision of all controversies of faith. Being aware of the current situation, they came together to consider what course to take. By the influence of the Holy Spirit, they were both qualified and authorized to be the most competent judges in such cases. It is possible that they discussed this question in the presence of the laity, but lest any should dream that the common people were allowed to judge this controversy, the apostles and elders—who are ministers—are named here explicitly. ANNOTATIONS ON ACTS 15:6.[14]

EVEN THE LEARNED STRUGGLE TO UNDERSTAND. JOHN CALVIN: Although eminent men and the public teachers of the church were chosen, not even they could agree among themselves at once. It is clear from that how even at that time the Lord troubled the church by the human weakness, so that it might humbly learn to be wise. In addition he allowed the main principle of Christian doctrine to be turned over in different ways in that assembly over which he presided, so that we may not be surprised if it ever happens that otherwise godly and learned people fall into error through ignorance. For some of them were not so acute as to perceive the magnitude of the matter. So, when they are

carried away by an unthinking zeal for the Law and decide that the Law must be kept, they do not see into how dense a labyrinth they are hurling other people's consciences as well as their own. They were thinking that circumcision was an eternal and inviolable symbol of the divine covenant and held the same opinion about the whole Law. Therefore Peter dwells most particularly on this, so as to indicate the main point at issue, for most of them were ignorant of it. COMMENTARY ON ACTS 15:7.[15]

WE MUST ULTIMATELY RELY ON GOD'S GRACE, NOT ON EXPERTS OR EVEN COUNCILS. MARTIN LUTHER: From this passage we learn that each person must himself confirm that he is confident and sure of the true teaching, not shrugging it off on others to sort out and decide, otherwise [hoping] that the Holy Spirit should help you locate someone in a doctor's beret. If you want to be saved, then you must be so certain of the Word of grace yourself that if every other person said otherwise, yes, even if every angel said no, you could stand alone and say, "Still I know that this Word is true." This is important because those who are against us have no stronger argument than that they throw up their hands and say, "Right, should God let the world remain in error for so long with so many learned, devout, holy people?" By this they imply that wherever the largest heap comes down on an issue, we should agree. They insist on this and scream, "On *our* side are so many and such important people, as well as so many years and customs; therefore, we cannot err!" Hold this council before their nose and say, "If the majority and the most learned should decide and rule, then why is it written here that over the principal tenet of the Christian faith everyone, even the absolute best Christians, err, except for three people alone who bravely stand their ground?" And even Saint James stumbles a bit, though he comes to his senses, but he is not so absolute as the other two. . . .

That is what God revealed to us in this first council. He allows it to happen that you

---

Apostolorum, 183r-v).

[13]Spangenberg, Der Apostel Geschichte, 137r.
[14]Downame, ed., Annotations, KKK2r*; alluding to Acts 12:22.

[15]CNTC 7:31* (CO 48:343).

strengthen your faith through devout people who share the faith with you, so long as you do not rely so strongly on this that you think they won't fail you. Accept their help, but do not rely completely on this alone! The Holy Spirit did not promise that he would dwell in councils but in the hearts of Christians whom he knows. SERMON ON ACTS 15:7.[16]

FAITH IN CHRIST IS SELF-DENIAL, NOT SELF-DECEPTION.

HANS SCHLAFFER AND LEONHARD FRICK: My heavenly Father, at the very end you did not look upon my damnable, evil and sinful life, and in your pure grace and compassion drew me to your Son, Christ the crucified. You revealed it to me—yes, I heard it and learned it from you—that I have come to him, which is none other than renouncing the prideful, self-seeking, arrogant world, being released from all creatures, denying myself to take up my cross and follow Christ. That is what faith in Christ means. Through it, not through works of the law (as Peter says) the hearts of believers are purified. KUNSTBUCH: A SIMPLE PRAYER.[17]

WE ARE CLEAN THROUGH FAITH IN THE WORD.

MENNO SIMONS: It is true, Christ has so loved his church that he has given himself for it, and has sanctified it through the power and merits of his innocent blood, and has cleansed it through the power and merits of his innocent blood and has cleansed it by water, which is a proof and sign of a new and penitent life, but not otherwise than in the Word or through the Word preached in the power of the Spirit, accepted in true faith and followed by the baptism as commanded in his ordinance. You are clean through the word which Christ has spoken. They were not clean because it was outwardly spoken to them but because they believed what was spoken to them. For God does not cleanse the hearts through any literal water, word or ceremony but through belief in the Word.

Otherwise all who heard the Word externally and received the sign of the water externally would be holy and clean. This is incontrovertible. REPLY TO GELLIUS FABER (1554).[18]

THE WORLD FINDS FAITH MERELY FOLLY.

HANS SCHLAFFER AND LEONHARD FRICK: Ah! Dear Lord, that is a heavy, unbearable burden for the old Adam. To the world it is a foolish and silly teaching and sermon. To our Jews, that is, those who confess you, your Word and your gospel with their mouth, it is an irritation, but to us believers it is divine power and wisdom. KUNSTBUCH: A SIMPLE PRAYER.[19]

WORKS MUST DRIVE US TO SEEK GRACE.

MARTIN LUTHER: So now it is firmly and strongly demonstrated that no one [or nothing] can console or strengthen the conscience other than faith in pure grace. Thus, Peter concludes that the patriarchs also were not saved in any other way; they too were unable to bear the law. Why couldn't they bear it? What was their deficiency? This: they saw that however many works they did, still their conscience could never have rest. Moses did nothing more than that with so many laws he drove the conscience to [seek] grace. So, each and every law is impossible for the conscience to bear. For the body it is not too harsh, but the conscience underneath is so tired and miserable that if it always tries to depend on works it will never be able to have rest. The more it does, the more tired it becomes. Yes, it is oppressed by even a single work, that for it the world is far too narrow, continually goading it and saying, "Do, do, do." It does not cease to goad until through God's grace we see that this doesn't work. Grace must accomplish this rest; otherwise it will never happen. So, the heart will finally be at peace, bold and brave in God. Let the works fall away, causing no more unrest. This Peter's opponents could not bear: that it is so simple, that we should not impose the law or circumcision. . . . Thus we

---

[16]WA 15:582-83, 584; alluding to Gal 1:8.
[17]CRR 12:284* (QGT 17:356-57).
[18]Simons, *Complete Writings*, 707-8*; alluding to Acts 15:9.
[19]CRR 12:284 (QGT 17:357).

must differentiate between the two: to impose the law and to impose on the conscience. We may indeed impose a law, so long as we leave the conscience free, untethered and unoppressed, so that it remains pure and clings wholly to the bridegroom Christ, knowing no other comfort to adhere to other than God's grace. If the law interferes, God is tested. SERMON ON ACTS 15:10.[20]

INNER LOVE TRUMPS EXTERNAL CEREMONIES. HANS DENCK: You say [that] the apostles walked in the Spirit. Nonetheless, they speak of customs and ceremonies as of a burden, which neither they nor the fathers have been able to bear. How then can the highest commandments be easy? Answer: Ceremonies are an external order, given for their improvement to the common people of Israel to whom all spiritual language is foreign. Thereby they were to be reminded of the simplicity of all laws which had been revealed from the beginning to Adam in paradise, namely, to love God alone and hate all that might hinder love. This then is the apple, which God denied to Adam and all humankind with him. . . . Whoever truly has such simplicity in his heart is free of and unencumbered by all ceremonies. Yet, where it might hasten the advancement of such love in others, he must adhere to ceremonies; where it might hinder, he must refrain from them. THE LAW OF GOD.[21]

THE DIVINE TESTIMONY OF PETER'S WORDS. CARDINAL CAJETAN: Balance these words of Peter. You should weigh this matter carefully, distorting the law neither to the salvation of the Gentiles nor to that of the Jews. For he explicitly states that we believe Jews are saved in the same way as they—Gentiles, of course—through the grace of our Lord Jesus Christ. Peter proceeded cautiously. First, he demonstrates from the divine testimony that the law is not necessary for Gentiles. Finally, he concludes that neither Gentiles nor Jews receive salvation from it. We believe all are saved through the grace of our Lord Jesus Christ. COMMENTARY ON ACTS 15:11.[22]

IS THERE POTENTIAL MISUNDERSTANDING IN JUSTIFICATION BY FAITH ALONE? JOHANN SPANGENBERG: By faith we act toward God, by love toward neighbor, by the killing of the flesh toward ourselves. This is the correct process; whoever inverts this order inverts all of Scripture. . . . Wherever this teaching goes, there you will find sects and fanatics—especially the Pelagians—of free will and the merit of works. These have always cropped up ever since the beginning. . . . What is the cause? Human reason is incapable of relying solely on faith; it always clings to works. . . . And since not all people have the Holy Spirit, instead the great majority live in their flesh and blood according to reason, they continue to cling to works. As impossible as it is that we will lack wicked people, so also it is impossible that we will be free of the sects and fanatics' false teaching. BRIEF EXEGESIS OF ACTS 15.[23]

15:12-21 James Addresses the Council

REVERENT LISTENING IS APPROPRIATE FOR RESOLVING CONTROVERSIES. THE ENGLISH ANNOTATIONS: Paul and Barnabas were met with a reverend silence. This shows how people should act in councils concerning controversies in religion. [The laity should have] a humble silence, so that they may listen and learn from those whom God has appointed to the ministry of his Word. ANNOTATIONS ON ACTS 15:12.[24]

JAMES AS GUARDIAN OF THE CHURCH. JOHN CALVIN: It is easy to gather from this verse that he was held in unusually high regard, seeing that he confirms Peter's words, with his own approval, so that all go over to his opinion. And we shall see again how powerful his authority was at Jerusa-

---

[20]WA 15:590-91, 592-93.
[21]Denck, *Selected Writings of Hans Denck*, 224*.

[22]Cajetan, *In Acta Apostolorum*, 226v.
[23]Spangenberg, *Der Apostel Geschichte*, 135v-136v.
[24]Downame, ed., *Annotations*, KKK2r*.

lem. The ancient writers think that this happened because he was the bishop of the place. But it is not likely that, of their own free will, the faithful changed the order established by Christ. Accordingly I have no doubt that he was the son of Alphaeus and a blood relation of Christ, and in that sense he is also called his brother. I leave it an open question whether he was the bishop of Jerusalem or not, and it is not very relevant, except that the impudence of the pope is clearly refuted by the fact that the decree of the council is determined by the authority of James rather than of Peter. COMMENTARY ON ACTS 15:13.[25]

JAMES CONFIRMS PETER'S ARGUMENT. RUDOLF GWALTHER: James acknowledges here God's counsel and purpose. . . . And lest the apostles only might seem to be of that opinion, he proves the same by the uniform consent of the prophets, although he brings but one testimony out of them. Neither was it needful to bring any more, because all the prophets were inspired with one and the same Spirit and agreed in the declaration of human salvation. It should be diligently noted how the apostles by their mere authority charged the church with nothing, but by Scripture proved all the things that they teach. For they acknowledged themselves to be the servants of Christ and his church, and therefore they thought they ought to establish nothing that was repugnant to the will of Christ and the holy Scripture. HOMILY 103, ACTS 15:13-21.[26]

CHRIST CONQUERS WITH THE JAWBONE OF AN ASS. DIRK PHILIPS: Christ took to himself the heathen, and chose a congregation out of them and gathered it through the preaching of the gospel, which he betrothed to himself by faith. This the Jews did not understand, that it was foreseen and ordained by the Lord. He overcame the young lion, the adversary of Christians, that is, Satan, out of which conquest has come all the sweetness

of divine grace, all comfort and refreshing of the soul. With the jawbone of an ass, that is, with his unlearned apostles who were regarded as asses by the world, he overcame the uncircumcised of heart, the worldly-wise and the scribes, the enemies of the gospel. Out of the poor Word of the cross, God gives to all true worshipers the living water of the Holy Spirit through faith, in order to refresh thirsty souls with it. THE ENCHIRIDION: CONCERNING SPIRITUAL RESTITUTION.[27]

SCRIPTURE JUDGES ALL TRADITIONS. THE ENGLISH ANNOTATIONS: Note here the rule by which the apostles themselves proceeded: the written Word of God. They do not equate any human traditions with it. They do not apply human traditions in order to judge the Scriptures, much less to determine anything against them. For there is but one truth and one Spirit of God, speaking both in the prophets and the apostles. ANNOTATIONS ON ACTS 15:15.[28]

THE PROPHETS TESTIFY TO THE GOSPEL. CARDINAL CAJETAN: James brought up this [prophetic] authority, so that from this he might highlight that the prophets agree that the Gentiles should be received into the people of God, calling out the name of the Lord over them during baptism. COMMENTARY ON ACTS 15:16-18.[29]

AN EXHORTATION FOR OUTWARD ACTIONS. GIOVANNI DIODATI: This is an ecclesiastical ordinance, as they call it, canonical—not so much to rule the conscience and inner person as the external actions, for the peace, unity and order of the church in those days—either in things indifferent like eating blood or strangled meat or in things which the Gentiles abused, as eating flesh which was offered to idols and committing fornication. . . . This sin is here mentioned because the Gentiles

---

[25]CNTC 7:44-45* (CO 48:354); alluding ot Acts 21:18.
[26]Gwalther, *Homelyes or Sermons upon the Actes*, 600* (*In Acta Apostolorum*, 187r).
[27]CRR 6:335* (BRN 10:361); alluding to Rom 11:25; Acts 10:44-45; Gal 2:8; 1 Pet 5:8-9; Heb 2:8; Hos 2:19-20; 1 Cor 1:26-28; 3:19; Acts 7:54; Jn 4:11; 7:38; cf. Judg 14:3, 6; 15:14-15.
[28]Downame, ed., *Annotations*, KKK2v*.
[29]Cajetan, *In Acta Apostolorum*, 226v. James cites Amos 9:11-12 LXX, which repoints *'dm* from "Edom" to "humanity."

made it so common that they no longer understood it as a sin. Annotation on Acts 15:20.[30]

Blood That You Can Drink. Peter Walpot: Ever since the time of Noah until the apostles' time it was not fitting for us to drink or eat blood, be it human or animal blood. This the apostles themselves also instructed out of consideration for love; we should therefore hold ourselves to this. It was also not permitted for the patriarchs of the Jews to drink the blood of the lamb. Nevertheless the blood was given [to them] as a sign, to daub the blood on the lintels of the houses in which they ate the Passover lamb. "And the blood," the Lord said, "will be a sign for you on the houses where you are, so that when I see [the blood], I will pass over and the plague will not befall you when I strike the land of Egypt." Thus, Christ clearly reveals the mystery of his blood in light of this previous figure. He says, "This is my blood," and calls the wine his blood accordingly. As if he had said, "You have seen the sign, namely, the lamb's blood, up on the lintels, which is an indication of the blood poured out long ago. Now focus your eyes on this chalice: it is not a cup of the former ancient lamb's blood, no, it is a memorial of my own blood. That old blood was poured out in Egypt, but my blood was poured out first on the cross, and since we are not permitted to drink blood, thus I have instituted bread in place of the lamb, and now I sanctify a vital remembrance of my blood being poured out in the form of the wine which you can drink." The Great Article Book: On the Eucharist.[31]

The Familiarity of the Law. The English Annotations: James indicates by this that the Jews could not so suddenly bear the abolition of the legal ceremonies to which they had been so long accustomed by the continual hearing of the law read in every synagoge. Annotations on Acts 15:21.[32]

The Difference Between Law and Gospel. Philipp Melanchthon: This difference is one of the main tenets in the church. And if we let it be snuffed out—as it is erased among the papists—savage blindness follows, so that we dream that people are justified through their works and merit the forgiveness of sins with their own works. But at the same time, all people feel sin in themselves, remain in doubt, are unable to call out to God and finally sink into desperation and eternal death—and they do not understand why the Son of God was sent [to them]—just as the Pharisees among the Jews were steeped in such blindness and had lost the true understanding of the Messiah. But God, again and again, raised up prophets, who preached the correct differentiation of law and promises—as also the Lord Christ himself taught, and the apostles after him, taught.

The law is this eternal divine wisdom, as is said, which God in creation incorporated into rational creatures, and after this in the preaching office he reiterated again and again. It teaches and testifies that we must be obedient to him and how this same obedience should be in all our endeavors. Thus, after [the fall into] sin it is a dreadful judgment against all people. For no person, except for the Son of God alone, has been obedient to the entire [law]. Now the law does not grant the forgiveness of sins but only testifies to God's wrath against sin. Although the promises are dependent on the law, the law nevertheless demands complete obedience of the entire law for this. It does not say that God without our merit will forgive and remove sin.

But the gospel is really the gracious, joyous good news about the Son of God Jesus Christ, who in the wonderful counsel of the divine Majesty has been ordained as Mediator and Reconciler and as our righteousness and Savior. This good news punishes all sin immediately, especially this great sin in the entire human race, that the world is unwilling to recognize the Son of God according to the given promise. For this reason the Lord himself says, "The Holy Spirit will convict the world concerning sin, because they do not believe in me." . . . And alongside this conviction of unbelief and every

---

[30]Diodati, *Pious Annotations*, BB2v* (*I Commenti alla Sacra Biblia*, 1108); alluding to 1 Cor 6:12-13; 10:20; Rev 2:14, 20.
[31]QGT 12:132; quoting Ex 12:13.
[32]Downame, ed., *Annotations*, KKK2v*.

other sin, the gospel proclaims this eternal gracious consolation, that to us God on account of his Son Jesus Christ will certainly grant the forgiveness of sins freely by grace, without our merit, and on account of his Son will credit to us righteousness and will accept us. And through his Son Jesus Christ he gives us the Holy Spirit and makes us heirs of eternal salvation. And this we should accept by faith, that this is certainly given to us on account of the Lord Christ without our merit and not on account of the law or our works.

This deep consolation has been preached in the church since the time of Adam, according to which this wonderful promise—which no creature knew before—is revealed. "The seed of the woman will crush the snake's head," and through this consolation Adam and Eve have been rescued from eternal death.

Through this promise God has continually sustained a visible church, in which there have always been many elect. Otherwise there is no assembly on earth that is the true church of God in which this alone, this true teaching of the Son of God, is preached. And it is here very important often to remind the ordained and others that God out of his inexpressible lovingkindness, on account of his Son, accepts people powerfully through the gospel, that is, he works through the preaching office and the meditation of the gospel. Through this the Son of God, who is the eternal Word, himself grants the Holy Spirit and through his instruction kindles a new light and life [in us]. EXAMINATION OF CANDIDATES FOR ORDINATION (1552).[33]

THE YOKE OUR ANCESTORS COULD NOT BEAR.
JOHANN ECK: Scripture says, "The hands of Moses were heavy." But the New Testament was not given in writing; rather, it was poured into the hearts of the first believers, as the Lord promised through Jeremiah: "After those days, I will place my law in the innermost part of their heart, and I will write it on their heart, and I will be their God." "That is the reason why Christ wrote nothing; that is also

why he did not let anyone write anything until the Holy Spirit placed the gospel in the hearts of the apostles and the disciples. . . . And for this reason, I have decided to concentrate more on the living gospel than on what is written on parchment or paper."[34] Now this is enough about why the law of Moses was called the written law and not the gospel. FOURTH SERMON, ON THE FIRST COMMANDMENT OF THE FIRST TABLE.[35]

WHAT DOES THIS COUNCIL TEACH US?
JOHANN SPANGENBERG: Each person must ensure that he is certain of Christ's teaching and not defer this to other people to decide or sort out. It is: "My sheep hear my voice." If you want to be saved, then you must be certain of God's Word, so that even if an angel from heaven came and said otherwise, this would not sway you. For our adversaries have no other defense than that they scream that on their side they have so many important, powerful, holy, learned people, and so many years, such a long time, such ancient custom. Thus they cannot err. In fact, they claim that for God to let so many people for so many years walk and talk in such error would be impossible.

How should we answer such screaming? We must hold this council of the apostles under their nose and say, "Then how is it that here concerning the main tenet of the Christian faith every Christian falls, even the apostles' disciples and every believer except for three people who alone bravely hold their ground, while all the others rule against the Holy Spirit and make this council nothing at all?" BRIEF EXEGESIS OF ACTS 15.[36]

---

[34]Jerome, *A Commentary on the Apostles' Creed*, NPNF 2 3:543. In this section Jerome explains that the creeds are called symbols because they are watchwords, or shibboleths, for distinguishing those who preach Christ for God's glory and those who preach Christ for their belly's glory. "And for this reason, the tradition continues, the creed is not written on paper or parchment but is retained in the hearts of the faithful, that it may be certain that no one has learned it by reading, as is sometimes the case with unbelievers, but by tradition from the apostles."
[35]Eck, *Christenliche Predigen*, 5:6v; quoting Ex 17:12; Jer 31:33 (cf. Heb 10:16).
[36]Spangenberg, *Der Apostel Geschichte*, 137r-138r; quoting Jn 10:27; alluding to Gal 1:8.

---

[33]MWA 6:186-87*; quoting Jn 16:8-9; Gen 3:15.

15:22-35 THE COUNCIL SENDS
A LETTER TO GENTILE BELIEVERS

[22]Then it seemed good to the apostles and the elders, with the whole church, to choose men from among them and send them to Antioch with Paul and Barnabas. They sent Judas called Barsabbas, and Silas, leading men among the brothers, [23]with the following letter: "The brothers, both the apostles and the elders, to the brothers[a] who are of the Gentiles in Antioch and Syria and Cilicia, greetings.[24]Since we have heard that some persons have gone out from us and troubled you[b] with words, unsettling your minds, although we gave them no instructions, [25]it has seemed good to us, having come to one accord, to choose men and send them to you with our beloved Barnabas and Paul, [26]men who have risked their lives for the name of our Lord Jesus Christ. [27]We have therefore sent Judas and Silas, who themselves will tell you the same things by word of mouth. [28]For it has seemed good to the Holy Spirit and to us to lay on you no greater burden than these requirements: [29]that you abstain from what has been sacrificed to idols, and from blood, and from what has been strangled, and from sexual immorality. If you keep yourselves from these, you will do well. Farewell."

[30]So when they were sent off, they went down to Antioch, and having gathered the congregation together, they delivered the letter. [31]And when they had read it, they rejoiced because of its encouragement. [32]And Judas and Silas, who were themselves prophets, encouraged and strengthened the brothers with many words. [33]And after they had spent some time, they were sent off in peace by the brothers to those who had sent them.[c] [35]But Paul and Barnabas remained in Antioch, teaching and preaching the word of the Lord, with many others also.

a Or brother and sisters; also verses 32, 33, 36   b some manuscripts some persons from us have troubled you   c Some manusctripts insert verse 34: But it seemed good to Silas to remain there

---

Overview: A cohort of four representatives receives the task of communicating the decision of the Jerusalem Council. Gentile believers were already learning how to interpret divine laws and temporal customs in the freedom of Christ; the commentators focus on the doctrinal basis of Gentile acceptance into the church. The reformers are not concerned so much with the observance of certain rites and commands, as with why *these* commands, why *these* prohibitions, are handed down by the council. They assume an important distinction between the conscience and the body—applying freedom (gospel) to the conscience and subjugation (law) to the body. In this framework the key is not who has power, but who has love.

A Christian Is Both Lord and Servant of All.[1] Martin Luther: In summary, neither the pope nor an angel from heaven has authority to bind the conscience with a law. But over the body, not only does the pope have power, but even each one of us has power to make a law if it is useful to our neighbor on account of love. Also each person is responsible to his neighbor. Love is the sum of the law. According to the heart you are free; according to the fist you should behave as other people behave. When you enter into a city, conduct yourself like other people. Thus, you are free *and* subject to every person; first in conscience, second in body. Sermon on Acts 15:22-29.[2]

"Unsettling Your Minds." The English Annotations: Ἀνασκευάζοντες comes from the word that, among other things, means to demolish and cast down. It is fitly used here, seeing that the false

---

[1]Cf. LW 31:344 (German, WA 7:21; Latin 7:49).

[2]WA 15:601-2; alluding to Gal 1:8.

apostles by their "superstructions"—or laying other foundations for salvation aside from the free mercy of God in Christ—destroyed souls. He builds to ruin who builds his salvation on any means but the sole merits of Christ. "Another foundation no one can lay other than that which is already laid, that is, Christ Jesus." He subverts and casts down who does not build on Christ alone. ANNOTATIONS ON ACTS 15:24.[3]

"EATING BLOOD" MEANS SHEDDING HUMAN BLOOD. PETER WALPOT: The Holy Spirit did not mean this according to the prohibition in the law of Moses—rather, as the psalmist also says, "I will not offer you drink offerings of blood"—but rather this is first introduced in these last times. As soon as worldly power intermingles itself into the kingdom of Christ, common Christians begin to get involved in eating blood, that is spilling human blood, which the Holy Spirit has clearly forbidden us as children of God, commanding us to guard ourselves from this. If we act accordingly, then we act justly. THE GREAT ARTICLE BOOK: ON THE SWORD.[4]

THESE PROHIBITIONS FLOW FROM VARIOUS MOTIVES. CARDINAL CAJETAN: Pay attention, lest you understand these obligations alone but not the reason for them. The reason for the prohibition of fornication is according to the divine law. The reason for abstaining from what has been sacrificed to idols either from eating blood or from eating what has been strangled is so that you share customs with the Jews while you live together with them. This same restriction expired when Jews and Gentiles ceased to live together. They added to the laws [the ban on] fornication. By this Gentiles who did not believe fornication to be a sin learned to avoid it from the law prohibiting it. The apostles therefore added abstinence from it among the other three prohibitions. COMMENTARY ON ACTS 15:28-29.[5]

LOVE IS THE FULFILLMENT OF THE CEREMONIAL LAW. HANS DENCK: The disciples absolve the Gentiles from the ceremonial law. The disciples believed therefore that the Gentiles had everything. In support of this, take the following parables. One who has gold and silver has enough small change as well, although he may not actually have any of the latter. Anyone who believes in God and loves his neighbor has and does all the ceremonies by keeping the greatest [commandment]. REFLECTIONS ON MICAH.[6]

JUDGE THE FRUIT, NOT THE FOLIAGE. PILGRAM MARPECK: The Holy Spirit of God is the key of heaven, through which sin is retained or forgiven in the communion of saints! For this reason the apostles wrote to the churches and spoke against those who were again introducing the law.... No one is commanded to judge without the Holy Spirit, without whom no certain judgment is possible. That is why the Lord Jesus Christ first gave the Holy Spirit to those whom he empowered to judge, so that they should certainly and truly judge and decide according to the Word of grace and truth, in order that the witness and fruit, good or evil, may precede and be known in the deed.

This is the only way to bind and loose with certainty and, in the external judgment, to judge according to the testimony of the external fruit, and not of the foliage or blossoms that precede the fruit. As mentioned earlier, Christ says, "You shall know them by their fruits." Those who judge in truth may therefore not judge before the time but must wait for the fruit. Otherwise, we take God hostage, [meddling] in his secret, hidden judgments and decisions, judging and punishing before God himself is willing to punish.... In making judgment, one must always distinguish foliage and blossoms from the fruit. KUNSTBUCH: CONCERNING HASTY JUDGMENTS AND VERDICTS.[7]

---

[3]Downame, ed., *Annotations*, KKK2v*; quoting 1 Cor 3:11-12; alluding to Eph 2:20; Gal 1:8.
[4]QGT 12:295; quoting Ps 16:4.
[5]Cajetan, *In Acta Apostolorum*, 226v-227r.

---

[6]Denck, *Selected Writings of Hans Denck*, 158-59*.
[7]CRR 12:162-63* (QGT 17:216-17); quoting Mt 7:16, 20; 21:43.

The Congregation Is Encouraged. Peter Riedemann: When humanity has seen the condition it is in and how deeply it has plunged into death and eternal destruction through sin, then humanity must be shown once more the grace which Christ offers to all people. People must be shown how to find this grace and be grafted into Christ. When humanity has received Christ's grace, it should continually be exhorted to stand firm and grow daily toward perfection. In this way a person is guided onto the right path and made to depend upon God. Confession of Faith.[8]

Rejoicing in Peace with God and One Another. The English Annotations: As the truly religious cannot choose but to be grieved by the divisions of the body of which they are members, so also it must be a great joy to see everyone sweetly in harmony to God's honor. Nor could there be any more comforting news than their assurance by the testimony of the Holy Spirit and the apostles of Christ that they are freely justified by faith in him without the works of the law. For in this alone human beings have peace with God. Annotations on Acts 15:31.[9]

What Kind of Prophets Were Judas and Silas? John Calvin: Those two brothers were sent for the specific purpose of adding their spoken testimony to the letter. Otherwise the apostles would not have sent such a short and concise letter about a matter of such importance, and would have mentioned something about the mysteries of the faith and would have given an exhortation at greater length for devotion to godliness. Luke then relates something else that they did, that is, that, being endowed with the gift of prophecy, they edified the church in a general way, as if he said that not only did they faithfully carry out their duty in the immediate situation but also by teaching and exhorting they did a useful service for the church. But we must note that he says

that they exhorted the church because they were *prophets*, for it is not given to all to discharge such a distinguished function. Therefore care must be taken so that no one rashly oversteps his limits, just as Paul teaches that individuals are to confine themselves within the measure of grace received. Accordingly it is not for nothing that Luke mentions that the task of teaching is a special one, so that nobody who wishes to come on the scene, either out of ambition unaccompanied by ability or thoughtless zeal or other stupid desire may disturb the order of the church. . . .

Although the word [*prophet*] has various meanings it is not taken in this verse for seers, to whom it was given to predict future events, because this phrase would have been inserted quite inappropriately when another situation is being dealt with. But Luke means that Judas and Silas were endowed with an exceptional understanding of the mysteries of God so that they were excellent interpreters of God, just as Paul, when he is dealing with prophecy and prefers it to all other gifts, does not put prophecies or predictions in the center but commends it on account of this result, that it builds up the church by teaching, exhortation and consolation. In this way Luke assigns exhortation to the prophets as if it were the principal duty of their office. Commentary on Acts 15:32.[10]

The Travail of Ministry. Rudolf Gwalther: Silas had more regard for the church of Christ than for his own matters, considering that he preferred Antioch before the city of Jerusalem and his own proper habitation. This example is fitting for all the ministers of Christ to imitate, that they may forsake themselves and all earthly things to be able to give themselves more fully to the ministry of Christ and his church.

The exercise of the apostles is most worthy to be considered, who, as we see, chiefly sought to preach the gospel. They knew that was the message of salvation. They knew that with these weapons, nations were subdued for Christ and the world

---

[8]CRR 9:86-87; alluding to Eph 4:11-15.
[9]Downame, ed., *Annotations*, KKK3r*; alluding to Rom 5:1.
[10]CNTC 7:58* (CO 48:365); alluding to 1 Cor 14:3; 7:20; Eph 4:1.

brought to the obedience of faith. They knew, finally, that our Savior Christ was chiefly concerned about this one thing and did nothing so much as that. . . . But nowadays it has come to pass that bishops abhor nothing so much as the ministry of the Word, thinking it to be more commendable for them to feed hounds and great horses, as well as a sluggish and servile class of underlings, with the revenues of the church, than to feed Christ's sheep with the food of heavenly doctrine. HOMILY 105, ACTS 15:31-41.[11]

---

[11]Gwalther, *Homelyes or Sermons upon the Actes*, 611* (*In Acta Apostolorum*, 190v).

15:36-41 PAUL AND BARNABAS PART WAYS

[36]And after some days Paul said to Barnabas, "Let us return and visit the brothers in every city where we proclaimed the word of the Lord, and see how they are." [37]Now Barnabas wanted to take with them John called Mark. [38]But Paul thought best not to take with them one who had withdrawn from them in Pamphylia and had not gone with them to the work. [39]And there arose a sharp disagreement, so that they separated from each other. Barnabas took Mark with him and sailed away to Cyprus, [40]but Paul chose Silas and departed, having been commended by the brothers to the grace of the Lord. [41]And he went through Syria and Cilicia, strengthening the churches.

OVERVIEW: While upholding the virtue of Christian unity as exemplary, the commentators now contemplate the reality of the internal discord between Paul and Barnabas that resulted in separation rather than resolution. They assure readers that this difference of opinion, while unresolved, does not inhibit a common faith and commitment to furthering the gospel. On the contrary, in God's providence, the gospel could spread even farther as a result of their separation. Additionally, the reformers believe the Holy Spirit instigated Luke to record this quarrel for the consolation of future Christians—even such holy and important apostles as Paul and Barnabas could be consumed with anger and disagreement to the point of open rupture. They too were sinful, just as we are, and the Lord was pleased to bless their ministry—sometimes despite them.

DISAGREEMENT DOES NOT AUTOMATICALLY ENTAIL HOSTILITY. DESIDERIUS ERASMUS: Not that there was any bitterness between such great apostles, but each strove to get what he thought was best for the work of the gospel. And, in the event, an example was furnished for us that we should not immediately suppose something is to be condemned because it is not in accord with our opinion. Difference of opinion does not harm, provided hearts are united in their purpose to advance the gospel. From the disagreement of the apostles God provided that the gospel should be carried even farther with the two leaders separated than if they had persevered in their original association. PARAPHRASE OF ACTS 15:39.[1]

THE EXISTENCE OF THE CHURCH IS A MATTER OF FAITH, NOT REASON. MARTIN LUTHER: That the church exists is an article of faith. For it is perceived by faith, not our eyes. Because of this God conceals the church in strange ways—now under sins, now under disagreements and errors, now under weakness, under stumbling blocks, under the death of the saints and under the great mob of the wicked, etc. In fact, he conceals it to such an extent that there was even disagreement in the apostles' work, as can be seen in Paul's controversy against Peter, and likewise in the disagreement about Mark [between] Barnabas and Paul. Even all of Asia—a most notable region for many reasons—on no other basis fell away from [the teaching of] Paul, as must be believed, than only because the church had been concealed. The church certainly was still in Asia, but consisted of only very few people who knew God. TABLE TALK, KONRAD CORDATUS (1531).[2]

THE WEAKNESS OF THE SAINTS IS THE COMFORT OF THE HOLY SPIRIT. JUSTUS JONAS: The Spirit of God places before us these examples of the imbecility of the saints, so that we may be

---

[1]CWE 50:100 (LB 7:729).
[2]WATR 2:283 no. 1969; alluding to Gal 1:14; 1 Cor 14:3.

comforted from this, not so that we may defend our vices. Therefore, they were foolish who appointed such people as saints for us, as if they endured nothing of humanity, as if they were not people but angels. For this is the particular counsel of the Spirit, so that he may comfort us by these examples and make us alive in this kingdom of Satan and sin, so that he may deposit the fullness of grace with us and show how powerful a thing is faith, which is in the middle of the world. In the middle of sin, among so many snares of Satan, in such unbelievable weakness of the flesh, the Spirit nevertheless sanctifies, nevertheless supports and guards us. For without a doubt, this dissension was a great scandal. ANNOTATIONS ON ACTS 15:36-41.[3]

DISSENSION IS UNFAVORABLE, BUT THIS WAS NOT TOO SEVERE. CARDINAL CAJETAN: What is worse than dissension? Or does an exasperation of this sort lack sin? Let the one who knows be angry. Neveretheless, it is certain that this was not a severe sin. COMMENTARY ON ACTS 15:39.[4]

SOME COMMENTATORS MUFFLE THE SEVERITY OF THE DISSENSION. JUSTUS JONAS: The old translation has here, "A dissension arose among them," for the translator wished to lessen the force of the Greek. But *paroxismos* means more than dissension, as can be seen from the verb *paroxino*, that is, to irritate, to provoke, to exasperate. For Luke wishes to indicate that those men had disagreed to the point of agitation in this matter. ANNOTATIONS ON ACTS 15:36-41.[5]

WHETHER RIGOR OR LENIENCY IS PREFERRED. JOHN CALVIN: Now we must discuss the cause itself. For there are those who lay the blame for the dispute on Paul's excessive rigidity, and, at a first hearing, the reasons which they bring forward are probable. John Mark is rejected because he had withdrawn himself from the company of Paul, but

he had not severed himself from Christ. Being young, and not yet accustomed to bearing the cross, he had returned home from the journey. Some allowance had to be made for his age. As a recruit he had given in to troubles at the beginning, but that did not mean that he was going to be a cowardly soldier all his life. Now if his return to Paul is clear evidence of his penitence, it seems inhuman to reject him. For those who voluntarily accept the punishment for their own wrongs must be dealt with more leniently. There were also other reasons which ought to have moved Paul to clemency. The home of John Mark was a renowned place of hospitality for the church. In the severest persecution his mother had taken in the faithful; when Herod was raging and all the people were in a fury, they were in the habit of holding their sacred meetings there, as Luke has already reported. Surely such a holy and good-hearted woman ought to have been spared, so that excessive rigor might not alienate her. She wished her son to be devoted to preaching the gospel; how very bitter a thing could it have been to her that his services are now rejected on account of one trivial mistake? Now when John Mark not only deprecates his fault but actually makes amends, Barnabas has a plausible excuse for forgiving him.

However, we may gather from the context that Paul's decision was pleasing to the church. For Barnabas hurries off and sails with his companion for Cyprus. No mention is made of the brothers, as if he had gone away in secret, without greeting them. But the brothers commend Paul to the grace of God by their prayers, which makes it evident that the church stood by his side....

And we must note that John Mark was not absolutely rejected by Paul. He was regarding him as a brother, provided that he would be content with the ordinary standing. He was refusing to admit him to the public office of teaching, of which he had been shamefully deprived by his own fault. But it makes a great deal of difference whether a man who has sinned is absolutely debarred from pardon or is merely denied public office. However, it is possible that both men went beyond the score, as

---

[3]Jonas, *Annotationes in Acta*, G6v.
[4]Cajetan, *In Acta Apostolorum*, 227r.
[5]Jonas, *Annotationes in Acta*, G6v-G7r.

things that are nonessential may often spoil an otherwise good situation. Paul was correct and duly acting in accordance with disciplinary authority in being unwilling to accept the companion whose unreliability he had once experienced, but when he saw Barnabas insisting more stubbornly he could have given in to his request. COMMENTARY ON ACTS 15:36-41.[6]

---

[6]CNTC 7:61-62* (CO 48:367-68); alluding to Acts 12:12.

16:1-10 TIMOTHY JOINS PAUL AND SILAS

Paul[a] came also to Derbe and to Lystra. A disciple was there, named Timothy, the son of a Jewish woman who was a believer, but his father was a Greek. [2]He was well spoken of by the brothers[b] at Lystra and Iconium. [3]Paul wanted Timothy to accompany him, and he took him and circumcised him because of the Jews who were in those places, for they all knew that his father was a Greek. [4]As they went on their way through the cities, they delivered to them for observance the decisions that had been reached by the apostles and elders who were in Jerusalem. [5]So the churches were strengthened in the faith, and they increased in numbers daily.

[6]And they went through the region of Phrygia and Galatia, having been forbidden by the Holy Spirit to speak the word in Asia. [7]And when they had come up to Mysia, they attempted to go into Bithynia, but the Spirit of Jesus did not allow them. [8]So, passing by Mysia, they went down to Troas.[9]And a vision appeared to Paul in the night: a man of Macedonia was standing there, urging him and saying, "Come over to Macedonia and help us." [10]And when Paul[c] had seen the vision, immediately we sought to go on into Macedonia, concluding that God had called us to preach the gospel to them.

a Greek He   b Or brothers and sisters; also verse 40   c Greek he

OVERVIEW: In their itinerant work as ambassadors of the Jerusalem Council, Paul and Silas meet Timothy, who joins them in Lystra. From this, some commentators emphasize the importance of Paul's quest to find and call faithful and fit ministers for Christ, presenting them as exemplars for how to plant new Christian communities. The description of Timothy serves as a template for those who are chosen to lead God's people. They must be respected for their reputation, training, and discipline according to the Scriptures. Furthermore, the reformers feel it would be unfaithful to the cause of Christ's suffering to send preachers out before they have been well instructed.

16:1-5 Paul Commissions Timothy

TRUE FAITH IS THE ONLY SURE FOUNDATION OF LOVE. MARTIN LUTHER: We have surely made [the gospel] easily available, so that the common person can grasp it, but he is adeptly prohibited by some wearing bishops' masks who resist and oppose [the gospel] with force. Since they have heard enough preaching and it is not our fault [that they

resist it], we must briskly press on. If there are still some among us who have not heard the gospel, we must continue for the sake of those who believe. If we have to forfeit to one of the two—to yield to the weak or to represent the faith—we must sooner oppose the obdurate, maintaining the Word against those who would like to abolish it than capitulate to the weak and through such capitulation allow freedom to be curtailed and oppressed. So then, if I am among such a group where some have the gospel and some want to restrain it, I am more responsible to obey faith than love. For faith is above love, and love is dependent on faith. Also, if I neglect love it is a sin against my neighbor, but if I desert faith and allow it to be blasphemed then Christ and God are denied. This is much more severe than sinning against my neighbor; there we can return to grace again, but to deny God is too much.

Now where—I say—in one heap there are strong and weak, I must focus more on the strong and commend the weak to God. I must defend the faith with my head, neck and belly, so that it is not dampened and beaten down. If we have faith, then we can come back to love. But whoever takes faith and abandons it has lost Christ and everything, so that there is no longer any help [for that person]. Then it is valid that we risk our neck for freedom. It is indeed a small thing to eat meat, to discard your hat, to take a wife. However, before we allow such rights and freedoms to be torn away and opposed, we should sooner die. We must not deny Christ who with his precious blood has purchased us freedom from all laws. SERMON ON ACTS 16:1-5 (1524).[1]

EVANGELICAL LEADERS MUST BE BEYOND BLAMELESS. DESIDERIUS ERASMUS: Now, Paul longed for only one thing—that the gospel kingdom should through every opportunity be advanced further from day to day, and he was accordingly everywhere on the look-out for persons suitable for this work. He was like ambitious kings bent upon extending the boundaries of their authority, whose greatest concern is the recruitment of leaders and administrators apt in managing affairs. Moreover, it is not enough that the evangelical leader be endowed with modest gifts; it is not enough that he be of a blameless character; he must also be commended by the attestation of all good people, so that no ugly rumor, however false, should obstruct the work of the gospel. It was Timothy, therefore, both singularly upright and fully approved by the testimony of all the approved, whom Paul desired to have as the companion of his journey. PARAPHRASE OF ACTS 16:1-3.[2]

TIMOTHY DEMONSTRATES THE IMPORTANCE OF GOOD PASTORS. RUDOLF GWALTHER: Paul knew that without fit ministers of the Word, the kingdom of Christ and faith in him could not be enlarged. . . . In the calling of Timothy, there are [three] things to be considered, of which we shall speak in order.

First, it is described who and what kind of person he was. His mother was a Jew, and one who believed; but his father was a Greek, that is to say,

a Gentile. And Paul in his later epistle to Timothy does commend the godliness of Eunice his mother and Lois his grandmother . . . because she procured her son to be well brought up in the faith and religion of Christ. And here Luke says that he was a disciple, that is to say, a Christian, before Paul called him to the office of the ecclesiastical ministry. Besides, he says he was well commended by all the brothers and not just by those at Lystra, where he lived, but also by those at Iconium, so that his godliness was perceived and known to those who were abroad also.

[Second,] this description of Timothy teaches us what manner of person ought to be chosen to the ministry of God's Word and church, where it requires the greatest care to be had for religion, lest any who are either utterly devoid of faith or else young students and novices enter into the ministry. For as the latter are commonly uncertain and stand in doubt of all things and are light and inconstant, so the former only uses religion for gain, which they also laugh at up their sleeve and cause others to deride the same. Then respect must be had of their learning, that we may have such to govern the church as are well exercised in the holy Scripture, wherein Paul testifies that the doctrine of the church must be taken out of the holy Scriptures, and it is important for ministers of the church to be well-trained in them. There is no account to be made of them, though they are ever so expert and prompt in philosophy, if they be rude and ignorant in the holy Scripture. For this reason Christ would not suffer the apostles to go abroad to preach before they were well instructed.

Third, it is fitting for them to have the testimony of an approved life and conversation, lest their teaching be condemned, or at the least suspected for their sake. Therefore Paul will have a bishop to be irreproachable. And how much religion and doctrine is defaced by the dishonest life of ministers, through whose concupiscence and sacrilegious boldness it came to pass that all the people for the most part refrained from the worship of God, and by that occasion wickedness so prevailed among all sorts of people that it could

---

[1] WA 15:615-16.
[2] CWE 50:100-101 (LB 7:730).

not be redressed but by public calamity and much bloodshed! HOMILY 106, ACTS 16:1-5.[3]

THE WEAK MUST BE WEANED FROM THE LAW.
DESIDERIUS ERASMUS: And so Paul preferred to accept in the case of Timothy the loss of a little piece of foreskin—which when present does not make one more holy, when removed does not make one worse—than that the Jews should be more estranged from the gospel by this circumstance, for he knew how obstinate they were. The apostolic decree made at Jerusalem in the presence of Paul freed the Gentiles from the burden of the law. But circumcision was an acknowledgment of, and a symbol, as it were, of the obligation to keep the whole law, and the Jews were not yet openly freed from the burden of the law, which had to come to an end gradually. PARAPHRASE OF ACTS 16:3.[4]

THERE IS NO HYPOCRISY IN PAUL'S ACTIONS. JOHN CALVIN: Luke makes it quite clear that Timothy was not circumcised because it was necessary, or because the religion of that sign still continued in existence, but so that Paul might avoid a scandal. Therefore regard was paid to humans, although there was freedom in the matter in the sight of God. Accordingly the circumcision of Timothy was not a sacrament, such as had been given to Abraham and his descendants, but a neutral and indifferent ceremony, which was of use only for the fostering of love, and not for the exercise of godliness.[5] It is now asked whether Paul had the right to usurp the use of an empty sign, the meaning and force of which had been abolished. For it seems to be an ineffective thing when it is separated from the institution of God. But at any rate

circumcision had been commanded by God only until the coming of Christ. To this question I reply that circumcision ceased at the coming of Christ in the sense that its use was not completely abolished all at once; but it remained free until, with the light of the gospel being seen more clearly, all might know that Christ is the end of the law.

And at this point we must notice three stages. The first is that the ceremonies of the law were so abrogated by the revelation of Christ that they pertained to the worship of God no longer, they were not figures of spiritual realities, and there was no necessity to make use of any of them. The second is surely that their use was free until the truth of the gospel would become more clearly known. The third is that the faithful were not permitted to retain them, except so far as their use would make for edification, and no superstition would be encouraged by them. However there was an exception to that power to use them freely, of which I have spoken. For circumcision was not in the same position as the sacrifices which had been ordained for the expiation of sins. Accordingly it was legitimate for Paul to circumcise Timothy; but it would not have been lawful to offer a sacrifice for sin. This is indeed a general principle, that the whole of the worship of the law, because it was a temporary thing, came to an end at the advent of Christ, as far as faith and conscience were concerned. But as to use, we must hold this view, that it was left neutral and in the freedom of the godly, in so far as it was not contrary to the gospel, because certain learned people are confused and wandering in this respect, for to them circumcision seems still to have a place among the Jews, whereas Paul teaches that it is superfluous when we are buried with Christ through baptism. COMMENTARY ON ACTS 16:3.[6]

16:6-10 *The Macedonian Call*

PROHIBITED BY THE WIND OR THE SPIRIT?
MARTIN LUTHER: How this happened Luke does not write. He does not explicitly state whether

---

[3]Gwalther, *Homelyes or Sermons upon the Actes*, 614, 615-16* (*In Acta Apostolorum*, 191v); alluding to 2 Tim 1:5.
[4]CWE 50:101 (LB 7:730).
[5]Calvin understood baptism in the new covenant as correlating to circumcision in the old covenant, succinctly stating that at least what pertains to circumcision must also pertain to baptism. Here Calvin is indicating that this passage should not, however, be understood sacramentally. For Calvin's treatment of circumcision and baptism, see *Institutes* 4.16.1-6, esp. 3-4 (LCC 21:1324-29, esp. 1325-27).

[6]CNTC 7:63-64* (CO 48:370); alluding to Col 2:11-12; Gal 2:3.

Paul was prevented by wind or through the Holy Spirit—in both the Hebrew and Greek languages wind and spirit are the same word. However, that Paul should be opposed by wind I cannot believe; therefore, I have brought this into German as "by the Holy Spirit."[7] SERMON ON ACTS 16:7 (1524).[8]

THE TEXT SHOULD READ "THE SPIRIT OF JESUS." THEODORE BEZA: The Spirit of Jesus, τὸ πνεῦμα Ἰησοῦ. Thus I restore the reading not only of three manuscripts and the oldest of my codices, and in the same manner the Syriac, Arabic and Old Latin translations, but also the reading represented by the authority of Cyril, as found in his *Thesaurus*, book 2, chapter 4, and book 12, chapter 12. ANNOTATIONS ON ACTS 16:7.[9]

PREACHERS MUST OBEY GOD'S WILL, NOT THEIR OWN. MARTIN LUTHER: Here you see that although it is certainly the greatest vocation to preach God's Word and there can be no greater service to God than to retrieve and save souls, still here it is written that Paul was prepared to do this and yet the Spirit would not allow him to do so! Is this not puzzling that a person is more willing and more prepared to help people than God? In fact, we often read the exact opposite: God is always ready to help people and to be present with them,

before they ask him or even think to ask him. If God here in this holy attempt to help people indicates that it is a culpable and fleshly idea to preach the gospel and to help people, who will ever again trust a good idea? . . . What is still more puzzling is that it is certain that Paul was called to preach! It was his office that was commanded to him by God. Paul wants to press on, but God will not let him go. . . . It is not his will that is lacking but rather God's will.

Now this is recorded for this reason: God wants to demolish all presumptuousness, so that we walk in fear and humility, so that no one should brag, "I can do this," or, "I did this out of my own good judgment." Instead, speak in this way, as Paul did: "I would like to do this, if it is God's will, but since it is not yet the time for this . . . I must direct myself according to him and be obedient to him, following his Word, not my will even if I could convert the entire world." Thus, it is forbidden in the very most important task not to follow our will but God's. He will not likely accept our good judgments and our self-selected tasks. This is what a good work is, not that I choose it and have a good opinion about it, but rather that his name is honored through it and that it is according to his will and service. We must stand before God with such hearts: "If it is your will, honors your name and furthers your kingdom, then I will do it, not because it seems so good to me." . . . If we act otherwise, it is from the devil, even if it seems excellent.

Therefore the reason here that Paul was opposed we must surrender to God. Paul's will is good, but it was not yet the time. For he went there later and preached to them; after this he even wrote to them in the Epistle to the Galatians. So here is the sum of this text: However good the work is, even by his command, still God reserves the space, place, time and manner to himself. He does not quash the task of preaching; instead, he prevents and postpones it for a time, for they were not yet ripe. SERMON ON ACTS 16:7 (1524).[10]

---

[7]𝔐 does not include Ἰησοῦ ("of Jesus") in Acts 16:7. Thus, Luther's need to depend on theological rationale for justifying his translation of τὸ πνεῦμα as the Holy Spirit rather than the wind. Mickey Mattox has noted that Luther prefers theological over grammatical explanations when ambiguities need to be explained. See Mickey L. Mattox, *"Defender of the Most Holy Matriarchs": Martin Luther's Interpretation of the Women of Genesis in the* Enarrationes in Genesin, *1535-45* (Leiden: Brill, 2003), 169. Also, it should be observed that the case for the inclusion of Ἰησοῦ is a strong one. 𝔓⁷⁴, ℵ, A, B, plus other uncials include this variant.
[8]WA 15:617.
[9]Beza, *Annotationes Majores*, 1:525. Cardinal Cajetan also correctly renders the text this way; see Cajetan, *In Acta Apostolorum*, 227r. This is the only occurrence of the phrase "the Spirit of Jesus"; modern commentators say very little with regard to this phrase, but for a more in-depth examination, see Gustav Stählin, "Τὸ πνεῦμα Ἰησοῦ (Apostelgeschichte 16:7)," in *Christ and the Spirit in the New Testament: In Honor of Charles Francis Digby Moule*, ed. Barnabas Lindars and Stephen S. Smalley (Cambridge: Cambridge University Press, 1973), 229-52.

[10]WA 15:617-19; alluding to Rom 1:13; Acts 18:18.

THE LORD IS THE MASTER OF THE VINEYARD.
DIRK PHILIPS: As Scripture clearly indicates, one
may not speak about God's Word wherever and
whenever one wills, but alone when and where
God wills. But the Lord wills that his Word shall
be spoken where it bears fruit. Again, where it does
not bear fruit, there it shall not be spoken.... Out
of all these words it is easily observed that God
himself hid his Word from the world, that Christ
spoke to the people in obscure parables, the Holy
Spirit forbade Paul to speak God's Word in Asia,
and God revealed his Word to his saints and not
to the world. How then may the ministers of the
Word be blamed with any reasonableness that they
act according to this example in these dangerous
times, to conceal the mystery of the gospel from
this evil world and in quietness secretly to reveal
and speak what is profitable to the good-hearted
who are receptive to hear them, in order that they
not grieve the Holy Spirit? THE ENCHIRIDION:
THE SENDING OF PREACHERS.[11]

THE MACEDONIAN MAN. CARDINAL CAJETAN:
In that vision of sleep, a man appeared before
Paul, having the demeanor, appearance and other
attributes of a Macedonian. He then appeared,
standing and speaking, pleading that [Paul]
might come into Macedonia to help them. By
chance, Paul discerned the Macedonian man from
his words in the dream, for he spoke in the first
person, "Help us!" meaning Macedonia. COM-
MENTARY ON ACTS 16:9.[12]

THE MACEDONIAN MAN IS AN ANGEL. GEORG
MAJOR: In order that also in Macedonia and
Greece God's congregation would increase and
that through the good news of the holy gospel
people would be called to righteousness and
eternal life, this angel appears to the apostle Paul
in the night at Troas in the form of a Macedonian
man. The angel asks Paul to come to Macedonia
and help the holy angel through his preaching to

gather and call [Macedonians] to the holy Christian church. It is as if he wanted to say, "We angels
who were sent by God to protect Macedonia have
made peace in this land and have moved the hearts
of many devout people, so that they yearn to recognize and serve the one true God, who with the
Son and the Holy Spirit created heaven and earth,
and abandon the idolatry in which they have lived
for so many years. Therefore come help us now, so
that through the preaching of the holy gospel of
Christ Jesus these people would be brought to a
further recognition of God and his Son and might
be saved."...

In this passage we see that the angelic office is
not primarily to protect land and people but to
move the hearts of people to fear God, to love God,
to know and confess God and to every virtue and
good work, to stir up and call apostles, pastors and
preachers, so that through them God's Word might
be spread. Angels are to protect and defend these
same apostles, pastors and preachers, as well as the
entire congregation. Those in distress and misery
they strengthen, console and rescue like Daniel in
the midst of lions, Saint Peter in prison, Paul in
shipwreck. HOW SAINT PAUL WAS CALLED TO
PREACH THE GOSPEL IN MACEDONIA.[13]

**DREAM FREELY, BUT WAIT ON THE LORD FOR
THE INTERPRETATION.** MARTIN LUTHER: We
should not believe dreams or interpret them according to how reason understands them; instead,
we must entrust them to God and let him exegete
them, as Joseph also says: "Does not interpretation
belong to God?" Although dreams are common to
both Christians and non-Christians, nevertheless
no one knows what they mean, but the Spirit alone
interprets them.... So dream here, dream there,
just don't try to interpret it yourself! Trust God
to do so; do not trust yourself. Thus, Paul here
deciphers the dream through the Holy Spirit and
does not fail. It confirms and fits with the matter
at hand and is in accordance with faith. For Paul

---

[11]CRR 6:232, 233-34 (BRN 10:243, 244-45); alluding to Eph 4:30.
[12]Cajetan, *In Acta Apostolorum*, 227r.

[13]Major, *Auslegung der Epistel S. Pauli an die Philipper*, 18r-19r;
alluding to Dan 6; Acts 12; 27. See also RCS NT 11:1-3.

was a preacher, and the dream was concerned with the preaching office, which so far was somewhat neglected because it was not yet time. But then, suddenly a Macedonian man appears and requests help from Saint Paul; this fits with his office, since Paul was in the preaching office. Although this was not sufficient for absolute certainty, the Holy Spirit had to confirm it in his heart. So, the vision was just the medium and vehicle for such a certain understanding. Just as also the Word without the Spirit and faith is not enough for someone to be certain, so it is also the case with the medium through which the Spirit and certain faith comes. For reason by itself would have not have been able to interpret or understand the dream; reason is blind. SERMON ON ACTS 16:9-10 (1524).[14]

---

[14]WA 15:621-22; quoting Gen 40:8; alluding to 2 Pet 1:20-21.

16:11-15 THE CONVERSION OF LYDIA

[11]*So, setting sail from Troas, we made a direct voyage to Samothrace, and the following day to Neapolis, [12]and from there to Philippi, which is a leading city of the[a] district of Macedonia and a Roman colony. We remained in this city some days. [13]And on the Sabbath day we went outside the gate to the riverside, where we supposed there was a place of prayer, and we sat down and spoke to the women who had come together. [14]One who heard us was a woman named Lydia, from the city of Thyatira, a seller of purple goods, who was a worshiper of God. The Lord opened her heart to pay attention to what was said by Paul. [15]And after she was baptized, and her household as well, she urged us, saying, "If you have judged me to be faithful to the Lord, come to my house and stay." And she prevailed upon us.*

a Or that

OVERVIEW: In the premier Macedonian city of Philippi, Paul, Silas and Timothy preach to a group of women gathered for prayer. This example leads some commentators to note that the gospel usually bears the greatest amount of fruit where it is least expected. The commentators understand this as God challenging both the expectations of this first-century missionary team and their own contemporary standards.

The genuineness of Lydia's conversion is evident because of the way she views her possessions and gathers her family to pass along her faith. In one instance, Lydia is compared to Cornelius as a God-fearer, especially in her receptive encounter with Paul and the baptism of her household. Lydia is praised for her piety, but the reformers note that her open mind and heart were dependent on the illumination of the Spirit.

Paul and the others accept Lydia's hospitality but are careful not to see it as an award for preaching the gospel. Through the ministry of Lydia, exegetes see an example of how pastors and parishioners are to treat one another. The acceptance of Lydia's hospitality is an appropriate one and generally demonstrates the rule for preachers that they should not refuse such offers while also not taking undue advantage of the generosity of others.

THE MACEDONIAN MISSION DID NOT GO AS EXPECTED. RUDOLF GWALTHER: The apostle Paul being called by God through the angel passed into Macedonia to preach the gospel to the men of that country . . . to teach them the true reason for salvation. But let us see what he did in Philippi, the premier city of Macedonia. . . . The reason that the apostle remained in this city (as may be gathered from all the circumstances) was that the apostles saw no opportunity to preach—the reason they had come. After a while, they sought to preach outside the city, for they went out of the city on the Sabbath day and preached the gospel to some women, near some river, where they customarily resorted to public prayer. This is a very notable example, teaching us how God uses these women to test and refine the faith and constancy of his servants. For it had been declared that the apostle was called by the angel who spoke on behalf of the entire country, desiring help. We would hope that the Macedonians would have received Paul when he arrived with all kinds of alacrity and declarations of joy and that everyone's mind would have been prepared to receive the light of the gospel. But this hope deceives them—in a most famous and populous city, there is not one person who listens to them. . . . Even outside the city, only women listened to them. But one of them believed the Word, one Lydia who was a foreigner. Who then would not think this calling of Paul to have been a mockery, seeing no results followed? But God often places many obstacles in the way of those who follow his calling, to hinder them, to test their faith, to train them in faithfulness and to teach them to wrestle with and overcome adversity. HOMILY 108, ACTS 16:12B-15.[1]

STUBBORN MEN SPURN GOD'S PROMISES.

JOHN CALVIN: Either that place was intended for women alone to meet, or religion was coldly received among the men, as they were slower to appear at any rate. Be that as it may, we do see that the holy men neglect no opportunity, because they have no reluctance about presenting the gospel only to women. Moreover since to me it is likely that prayer was shared by men and women in that place, I think that Luke made no mention of men, because either they were unwilling to listen, or they did not benefit from what they heard. COMMENTARY ON ACTS 16:13.[2]

LYDIA'S FAITH A GIFT OF THE HOLY SPIRIT.

KONRAD PELLIKAN: The gospel usually bears the greatest amount of fruit where it is least expected. . . . With Lydia we can compare how Paul was cast out of Antioch by religious women who were overly zealous for God but lacking in understanding. This excellent mother and merchant, however, understood the gospel and repented of her sins. And she became repentant not by nature but by grace. The Lord, it says, opened her heart to pay attention to what Paul was saying. For no one can have faith in the gospel by his own strength, but only by the gift of the Holy Spirit, and not because he has faith beforehand. Therefore, on hearing the promises of the gospel, let us despair concerning the power of the flesh, but let us pray to the Lord to open our heart, to give us the gift of the Spirit, to put belief in our heart and to fill us with the work of righteousness. COMMENTARY ON ACTS 16:14.[3]

LYDIA A PIOUS LEADER OF THE CHURCH.

JOHN CALVIN: It is as if Lydia said, "I implore you by the faith, which you have confirmed by the sign of baptism, not to refuse my hospitality." Apart from that, Lydia certainly testified by such an ardent wish how passionate and serious she was in her love for the gospel. At the same time there is no doubt that the Lord granted her such an attitude of mind that Paul might be all the more encouraged to carry on, not so much because he saw himself being generously and kindly received, as because he could form an opinion from that about the success of his teaching. Therefore that invitation to detain Paul and his companions was not only the woman's but also God's. And the same thing also applies to what follows, that Lydia constrained them; it is as if God laid his hand on them by the agency of the woman. COMMENTARY ON ACTS 16:15.[4]

LYDIA'S HOSPITALITY.

KONRAD PELLIKAN: Here the efficacy of the faith residing in the woman is clear, for she embraces Christianity to the peril of herself and her possessions, takes care that her family be gathered to God with a similar faith, and with great entreaties she sees to it that not only Paul but also the many companions with him are supported against the wishes of their enemies. COMMENTARY ON ACTS 16:15.[5]

MUTUAL SUPPORT BETWEEN MATURE CHRISTIANS AND NEW CONVERTS.

DESIDERIUS ERASMUS: An example has been provided for evangelical teachers not to avoid services spontaneously offered by recent converts to Christ, if they extend their offer readily and persistently; otherwise, it might appear that they do not acknowledge the converts as their own. On the other hand, the example shows that they should not thrust themselves upon the converts, lest they appear to demand a reward for communicating evangelical doctrine. But whoever has received a spiritual benefit ought to compel their benefactors to accept a material

---

[1]Gwalther, *Homelyes or Sermons upon the Actes*, 623-24* (*In Acta Apostolorum*, 194r-v).
[2]CNTC 7:72* (CO 48:377).
[3]Pellikan, *In Acta Apostolorum*, 157; alluding to Lk 14:1-11.

[4]CNTC 7:74 (CO 48:379).
[5]Pellikan, *In Acta Apostolorum*, 157.

benefit, should there be a need. PARAPHRASE OF ACTS 16:15.[6]

WHAT DOES THIS STORY TEACH US? JOHANN SPANGENBERG: Nothing other than the wonderful power of the holy gospel. For what we despise as the very lowest, there the greatest fruit is brought forth. This woman was a purveyor of silk and purple; she was very rich. Now Christ says about the rich that, "It is easier for a camel to go through the eye of a needle than for a rich person to enter into the kingdom of God." Now purveyors and vendors have such a reputation in the world that they saunter about with great profit, importance and wealth. Nevertheless it is this vendor Lydia who is the first among all those in Macedonia to accept the gospel! Indeed everyone would agree that if someone were to assail Paul's preaching, it would be this Lydia. And yet, she is the first person to accept the gospel and the Christian faith. BRIEF EXEGESIS OF ACTS 16:11-15.[7]

---

[6]CWE 50:102-3 (LB 7:731).

[7]Spangenberg, *Der Apostel Geschichte*, 143v-144r; quoting Mt 19:24.

16:16-40 DEMONIC POSSESSION,
APOSTOLIC IMPRISONMENT
AND THE HARVEST OF
THE HOLY SPIRIT

[16]As we were going to the place of prayer, we were met by a slave girl who had a spirit of divination and brought her owners much gain by fortune-telling. [17]She followed Paul and us, crying out, "These men are servants[a] of the Most High God, who proclaim to you the way of salvation."[18]And this she kept doing for many days. Paul, having become greatly annoyed, turned and said to the spirit, "I command you in the name of Jesus Christ to come out of her." And it came out that very hour.

[19]But when her owners saw that their hope of gain was gone, they seized Paul and Silas and dragged them into the marketplace before the rulers. [20]And when they had brought them to the magistrates, they said, "These men are Jews, and they are disturbing our city. [21]They advocate customs that are not lawful for us as Romans to accept or practice." [22]The crowd joined in attacking them, and the magistrates tore the garments off them and gave orders to beat them with rods. [23]And when they had inflicted many blows upon them, they threw them into prison, ordering the jailer to keep them safely.[24]Having received this order, he put them into the inner prison and fastened their feet in the stocks.

[25]About midnight Paul and Silas were praying and singing hymns to God, and the prisoners were listening to them, [26]and suddenly there was a great earthquake, so that the foundations of the prison were shaken. And immediately all the doors were opened, and everyone's bonds were unfastened.[27]When the jailer woke and saw that the prison doors were open, he drew his sword and was about to kill himself, supposing that the prisoners had escaped. [28]But Paul cried with a loud voice, "Do not harm yourself, for we are all here." [29]And the jailer[b] called for lights and rushed in, and trembling with fear he fell down before Paul and Silas. [30]Then he brought them out and said, "Sirs, what must I do to be saved?" [31]And they said, "Believe in the Lord Jesus, and you will be saved, you and your household." [32]And they spoke the word of the Lord to him and to all who were in his house. [33]And he took them the same hour of the night and washed their wounds; and he was baptized at once, he and all his family. [34]Then he brought them up into his house and set food before them. And he rejoiced along with his entire household that he had believed in God.

[35]But when it was day, the magistrates sent the police, saying, "Let those men go." [36]And the jailer reported these words to Paul, saying, "The magistrates have sent to let you go. Therefore come out now and go in peace." [37]But Paul said to them, "They have beaten us publicly, uncondemned, men who are Roman citizens, and have thrown us into prison; and do they now throw us out secretly? No! Let them come themselves and take us out." [38]The police reported these words to the magistrates, and they were afraid when they heard that they were Roman citizens. [39]So they came and apologized to them. And they took them out and asked them to leave the city. [40]So they went out of the prison and visited Lydia. And when they had seen the brothers, they encouraged them and departed.

a Greek *bondservants* b Greek *he*

Overview: Reformation commentators demonstrate keen awareness of spiritual warfare, noting demonic forces at work in opposition to the gospel. Some explicitly describe Satan himself as possessing the girl, and leaving her at the moment Paul gives the command in Christ's name (simultaneously entering into the hearts of the girl's masters). Others similarly describe the masters' motivation as arising specifically from a spirit—or a demon—of greed. By accusing Paul and Silas in the way they did, Satan and his angels were acting in typical fashion: under the guise of righteousness and zeal. This spiritual dimension to the events does not preclude human sin and moral responsibility; covetousness itself is pinpointed as an open door to demonic influence.

In the story of the Philippian jailer, the commentators alert us to his faith in and obedience to God after witnessing God's powerful deliverance. Both the boldness of Paul and Silas and the inward inspiration of God are responsible for the jailer's conversion. While at first the jailer is deathly afraid, after being transformed through faith and the indwelling of the Holy Spirit, he courageously invites Paul and Silas—whom he has been assigned to guard—to his home. The jailer's changed disposition enables him to be bound to God in peace instead of being bound to fear.

16:16-24 Paul and Silas Thrown in Prison

The Spirit of Divination. Johannes Brenz: First, we will briefly touch on what this spirit of divination is. . . . The superstitious pagans believed that Apollo was the god of prophecy. When he had come with his mother, Leto, to the Phoecian city of Delphi, he used his arrows to kill a snake named Python that had attacked them from a cave. Afterwards, in that place a sacred temple was built for Apollo where oracles were given. It is said that there was an underground chamber from which a cold spirit that was forced out as some sort of gas into the air above turned the minds of the prophets mad and compelled them to give responses to those who were consulting the oracle. Gentile writers make much mention of this Delphic oracle; its great authority was held in repute, not so much by private individuals as by the greatest kings of the pagans. But this was a mere deceit of Satan, who was fooling the empty minds of the pagans. For neither was Apollo a god of prophecy, nor were the prophets or seers able to issue true oracles, inasmuch as they gave their responses to those who consulted the oracle, filled not with the divine Spirit but with the spirit of Satan. For this reason the responses were generally either obscure or fallacious, as here and there historical writers testify. And those who were prophesying, gifted with such a spirit, were said by most to have the spirit of divination or of "Python,"[1] not of the god Apollo, as the superstitious pagans believed, but of a serpent or dragon, that is, of Satan, who deceives people.

There are those who call such diviners ventriloquists, because the unclean spirits issue forth their responses not from the mouth of those in whom they reside but from their belly. And because any superstition is a mere sport of Satan, divine law forbids the consultation of diviners and punishes by death anyone who engages in prophetic divination. For it is stated that a man or a woman possessed by a Python's spirit or a spirit of divination should be put to death and crushed with stones. . . . So what then? Does this not show unequivocally how twisted and ungodly people's generosity is? This is the norm for people, generally speaking, that they expend a great deal of their money on the worship of demons and learning about curiosities, sparing no expense, but on the true worship of God and looking into and learning about the things of piety, they are scarcely ready to pay a penny or two. Homily 74 on Acts 16.[2]

---

[1]The Greek phrase πνεῦμα πύθωνα translated as "a spirit of divination" is literally "a spirit of a python."
[2]Brenz, *In Acta Apostolorum Homiliae*, 152r-v; alluding to Deut 18:9-14 (cf. Lev 20:27). The NRSV, in contrast to all other English translations, renders this verse with "a way of salvation." Some commentators note that *this* is what irritated Paul. See Bruce Malina and John J. Pilch, *Social-Science Commentary on the Book of Acts* (Minneapolis: Fortress, 2008), 117-18.

THE SLAVE GIRL'S SPIRIT IS FROM THE FATHER OF LIES. KONRAD PELLIKAN: [This girl] followed Paul and his companions and was shouting after them things that were true, but to a pernicious end. And people were paying a great deal of money to the masters for this girl, so that they might hear from her some future event or other or something pleasing, but in doing so they were severely distracting Paul and his companions. Moreover, it is the deceitful genius of Satan, that he is the father of lies, not only because he always speaks through manifest lies but because he also misuses the manifest truth to convince people of lies for the purpose of deceiving them, so that in the end, by the appearance of truth, he convinces people of falsehood.

Satan's cleverness and trickery are of no use to him against Christ, for Christ also cast out demons of this sort and forbade them to speak. In fact, here Paul orders the demon to be silent in the name of Christ, and it departs from the girl. It was an unmistakable sign indicating that, even if Satan speaks the truth from time to time, nevertheless he does so to deceive. Therefore we must close our ears to Satan's voice whether he speaks factually or not, lest we are seduced to the lies of Satan by some version of the truth. Also, the fact that Satan is cast out from this girl in the name of Christ confirms the power of the gospel of Jesus Christ with its message about the remission of sins through him. It possesses such great vitality that whoever believes in it is justified before God and obtains eternal salvation, and it allows us to see that Christ is far more powerful than Satan regardless of how much evil he contrives. COMMENTARY ON ACTS 16:17.[3]

THIS PASSAGE IS A WARNING TO THE CHURCH TODAY. JOHANNES BRENZ: We today exhibit the same behavior. For, although up until now we have most splendidly supported countless priests who teach and engage in impieties, now we are not able to take care of even a few ministers of true piety.

Although we generously filled the coffers of those mendicants who demanded alms in the name of some saint or other, now for the most part we have sent those away empty-handed who ask us for alms in the name of God.

Such was the case in this passage with the Philippians. They paid out a lot of money to the ventriloquist girl that this master owned, just so they could hear from her some marvelous things about the future. Meanwhile, not only did they allow Paul and his companions, teachers of true piety, to go wanting; they also cut them up with rods and locked them in prison, as we find out later. And what generosity is more impious, than to deny to a benevolent God what wealth you possess by the kindness of God and to give it to Satan? What generosity is more accursed? . . . Do you hear the punishment with which the Lord threatens Israel for their impious generosity? The Israelites were directing to the worship of Baal those things which they had received by the kindness of God. HOMILY 74 ON ACTS 16.[4]

SATAN FLIES INTO THE GIRL'S MASTERS. KONRAD PELLIKAN: We are to understand from this that Satan indeed had left the girl but had entered into her masters. At the same time, the formerly tranquil demon that had possessed the masters of the girl now became more disturbed and agitated because of the expulsion and was intent on destroying Paul and his companions completely. It is obvious that these masters were possessed with a spirit of greed, which is placid enough, so long as everything is turning out according to its liking and if it continually grows rich with greater gain and profit. But if it is irritated, there is no wickedness under the sun that it will not dare to keep its advantage. It rages with anger, it robs and plunders, it contemplates murder, just to get what it wants. . . .

They themselves do not say in the accusation, "We are greedy, and up to this point we have made a living from impious soothsaying, but now these heralds of the truth impede us in our deceit." No,

---

[3]Pellikan, *In Acta Apostolorum*, 157-58.

[4]Brenz, *In Acta Apostolica Homiliae*, 152v; alluding to Hos 2:8-9.

they say, "These men are agitating our city and proclaim a new faith that the Romans, who are skeptical about it, and to whom we are subjected and obedient, are not allowed to take up and keep." And it is the practice of Satan to show himself not in his true form but to pass himself off under the guise of righteousness and zeal. COMMENTARY ON ACTS 16:19-24.[5]

THE ROOT OF EVIL IS COVETOUSNESS. RUDOLF GWALTHER: Covetousness therefore was the chief cause of this commotion, which did not only dazzle their eyes so that they could not see the truth but also so set them on fire that they could not but with deadly hatred persecute the apostles. This is a notable example to teach us what a mischievous evil covetousness can be. Paul calls it the root of all evil. And the Scripture in another place teaches us that there is nothing more wicked than a covetous person. There are everywhere examples which prove that through covetousness, law and justice are corrupted, good manners infected, the honesty of maids and matrons assaulted, friendships broken and finally flourishing common welfare overturned. But the force and infection of this evil is nowhere more evidently seen than in matters of religion. HOMILY 110, ACTS 16:19-24.[6]

DISPEL GREED FROM YOUR HEART THROUGH THE POWER OF THE GOSPEL. JOHANNES BRENZ: To describe the depravity of greed more clearly, Paul calls greed "the worship of idols"—and what is more impious than that? Accordingly, everyone must take great care to cast out Satan or the unclean spirit from their mind. I am not admonishing you to cast off the desire for the sustenance of living. We have this desire naturally, and as a sick person will naturally crave health, so a living person naturally craves the sustenance of living. If we did not have this craving in us by nature, we could not seriously pray in the Lord's Prayer, "Give us this day

our daily bread." Christ also had the same disposition of body. When he was hungry and saw the fig tree with leaves from a distance, he started making his way to it with the expectation of finding fruit there. Therefore, the desire for sustenance is not evil, but I admonish you to cast out greed, which is a desire for food coupled with a lack of faith. For to be greedy is to desire sustenance in such a way that you do not believe that God will feed and sustain you or give you possessions, unless you focus on possessions and strive to accumulate them by deceits, lies, shams and other such wickedness. "I exhort you to expel this demon from your heart," that is to say, the faithless worry over sustenance and the impious desire for possessions....

And just as Paul expelled the demon of lies from the soothsaying girl in the name of Christ, so the demon of greed is expelled from the human heart through the gospel of Jesus Christ and through the faith which is placed in that gospel. For the gospel teaches that our sins are remitted through Jesus Christ and that through him we might have peace with God in heaven, who according to his promises aids us in all our afflictions both bodily and spiritual, and he will not abandon anyone to die in hunger. If he feeds the birds of the sky and clothes the flowers of the field, how much more will he provide the same for his people? This gospel is of such great power that whoever believes in it soon expels the demon of greed and thereafter steers clear of those sins to which greed usually drives its devotees. HOMILY 75 ON ACTS 16.[7]

THE GOSPEL ENTERS MACEDONIA THROUGH GREAT ADVERSITY. DESIDERIUS ERASMUS: Such were the beginnings of the preaching in Macedonia. Either gain or ambition or superstition is always at war with the gospel, but when the world rages most fiercely against the members of Christ, then especially is the solace of heaven at hand to help. PARAPHRASE OF ACTS 16:24.[8]

---

[5]Pellikan, *In Acta Apostolorum*, 158.
[6]Gwalther, *Homelyes or Sermons upon the Actes*, 631* (*In Acta Apostolorum*, 196v-197r); alluding to 1 Tim 6:10; Sir 10:9.

[7]Brenz, *In Acta Apostolica Homiliae*, 153v-154r; alluding to Mt 21:18-19.
[8]CWE 50:103 (LB 7:732).

16:25-40 *The Philippian Jailer Converted*

Joy in the Midst of Affliction. The English Annotations: Satan's purpose was to make them blaspheme or to desert or doubt their cause and calling into Macedonia as inauspicious. But the more they are afflicted, the more they rejoice and praise the Lord. . . . There is nothing more vain than violence or plotting against the truth of Christ. The more you labor to suppress it, the more it shines; it flourishes in its wound. Annotations on Acts 16:25.[9]

The Patience of the Afflicted. The English Annotations: By this it is shown that these servants of God were not so solicitous for their own lives and liberties as for the propagation of the gospel and human salvation. Otherwise, once freed and all the doors open, they could have been silent. They could have easily escaped. But informed by the Spirit that God woke up the jailer, so that he could be converted and saved, Paul and Silas do not move, nor did they test God or lose the value of the miracle. The main purpose of this was so that God could identify with this religion which the world then so heartily condemned, and so that this jailer and his family might by saved. Annotations on Acts 16:28.[10]

God's Presence Is Acknowledged. Giovanni Diodati: The jailer was secretly inspired to acknowledge that the miracle happened for the apostles' sakes. Thus, he humbles himself before God in them, seeking to participate in that salvation which he may have heard that the apostles taught. Annotation on Acts 16:29.[11]

After the Threat of Death, the Jailer Is Willing to Listen. John Calvin: This jailer, recognizing the power of God, was not terrified

merely for a short time, soon afterwards to return to his former cruelty, but he shows himself obedient to God and eager for sound teaching. He asks about the way to obtain salvation, and that makes it all the plainer that he was not suddenly shaken merely by a vanishing fear of God but that he was truly humbled to present himself as a pupil to his ministers. For he knew that they had been thrown into prison for no other reason except that they were overthrowing the normal, established religion. Now he is ready to attend to their teaching, which he had previously despised. Commentary on Acts 16:30.[12]

God Gives the Jailer Exactly the Right Question. Rudolf Gwalther: After [the jailer] heard the prisoners had not fled but stayed by the hand of God, he was stricken with the inward inspiration of God and was altogether amazed in his mind, comparing the boldness and plainness of the apostles, which he had not seen in any other people, with the present miracle. And he began to feel in himself how grievously he had sinned by his ungentle acts toward these people whom he saw God so greatly regarded. So, calling out for light, he went to them, fell down at their feet and at length brought them forward (which was contrary to the magistrates' commandment) saying, "Sirs, what must I do to be saved?"

Who will not here acknowledge the mighty hand of God, which brought about all this matter? Surely it must be ascribed to God, that he reverences these men being scourged and put to open shame, that he breaks the wicked and unjust commandment of the magistrate and that he demands to know the right way to be saved. Indeed, he teaches by his example that those things must not lightly or negligently be passed over and that God works miraculously in his servants. For there is nothing more pernicious than that confusion which makes us blind to the manifest works of God. It is evident that this thing in time past

---

[9]Downame, ed., *Annotations*, KKK3v*; alluding to Acts 5:41; Rom 5:3; Col 1:11; 1 Pet 4:13.
[10]Downame, ed., *Annotations*, KKK3v*.
[11]Diodati, *Pious Annotations*, BB3r* (*I Commenti alla Sacra Biblia*, 1110).

[12]CNTC 7:86* (CO 48:388).

brought Pharoah to his destruction, and to this day this hurts many people, that they judge that all things come to pass by fortune and chance and do not search out the judgments of God in the things which they see fall out beyond the course of nature. Let us therefore always diligently search out the right way of salvation, in the same way that we see this jailer did so profitably. HOMILY III, ACTS 16:25-32.[13]

EVEN PRISON IS A SUITABLE TEMPLE OF GOD.

DESIDERIUS ERASMUS: You see that any time and any place is suitable for evangelical devotion. That prison, so terribly foul, was a temple for the apostles; the dead of night did not stand in the way of their hymns. The gospel is preached in the prison and trophies are taken for Christ; the jail is the magisterial chair of the gospel. PARAPHRASE OF ACTS 16:32-34.[14]

THE JAILER'S HOSPITALITY AND JOY REVEAL HIS FAITH.

JOHN CALVIN: Luke again commends the godly zeal of the jailer, because he dedicated his whole household to God. The grace of God is also reflected in that, because he suddenly brought a whole family to godly unanimity. At the same time the extraordinary change must truly be observed. Not long before the jailer intended to kill himself, because he thought that Paul and the others had fled; now, having got rid of his fear, he willingly takes them home. So we see that faith gives a disposition for prompt action to those who previously had no feeling. And certainly when fear and doubt make us do nothing, there is no better source of confidence than being able to cast all our cares on the bosom of God, so that no danger may deter us from performing our duty, while we may expect an advantageous outcome from God, for he himself will see to it that it will be so....

The joy of which Luke speaks here is a singular blessing, which individuals derive from their faith. No torture is more grievous than a bad conscience, for even if unbelievers try by all means to make themselves insensitive, yet, because they do not have peace with God, they are bound to be agitated. But if they do not undergo torments at the present time, if, on the contrary, they indulge in revels with wild and unbridled license, yet they are never at peace and do not obtain unclouded joy. COMMENTARY ON ACTS 16:33-34.[15]

THE GLORY OF GOD.

GIOVANNI DIODATI: Paul does not desire civil satisfaction for himself, much less any worldly honor; rather, he desires public acknowledgment of his innocence for the glory of God and the advancement of the gospel. ANNOTATION ON ACTS 16:37.[16]

INNOCENCE JUSTIFIES HER CHILDREN.

RUDOLF GWALTHER: They well knew the severity of the Romans in defending their laws and privileges, in so much that ... this saying—"I am a Roman citizen"—helped and saved many even in the remotest parts of the world, even among the barbarians. Surely aside from true devotion to religion there is no stronger sinew or cord for the common good than the firm and constant preservation of law and justice. Therefore their fear was not without reason! ...

We see here the condition of the wicked, who have no fear of God, but only fear human beings with more authority than they themselves, and the severity of law. If they are able freely without punishment to sin before others, then they are willing to do anything! This is for no other reason than that they think there is no God who cares about human deeds. Now the godly are quite different. Focusing on God, they so detest the horror of sin, that if at anytime they sin ... they are more afraid of the sin committed than its punishment.... This example teaches us that the power of innocence

---

[13]Gwalther, *Homelyes or Sermons upon the Actes*, 638-39* (*In Acta Apostolorum*, 1991r).
[14]CWE 50:104* (LB 7:733).

[15]CNTC 7:86-87* (CO 48:389).
[16]Diodati, *Pious Annotations*, BB3r* (*I Commenti alla Sacra Biblia*, 1110).

is so great that she totally vanquishes her enemies. Therefore, let us strive for innocence, and let us not doubt that through her we will triumph over our enemies, however fierce they may be. HOMILY 112, ACTS 16:33-40.[17]

THE CONSOLATION OF THE WORD. JOHANN SPANGENBERG: After they visited and consoled the brothers, they departed in peace and preached the Word of life. May Jesus Christ help us to do this also. Amen. BRIEF EXEGESIS OF ACTS 16:40.[18]

NOTHING CAN IMPEDE THE TRIUNE GOD. RUDOLF GWALTHER: This proves that the course of the gospel cannot be hindered by the efforts of the wicked. The ministers of the gospel might be bound, but the Word of God cannot be bound. They who preach the gospel are thrust out and banished, but the Spirit of Christ cannot be banished. He breathes wherever he pleases. Indeed, if human beings are silent, the stones will preach Christ. Let these things make our faith steadfast, that having overcome the world and its prince, we may live and reign in heaven with Jesus Christ our Savior. HOMILY 112, ACTS 16:33-40.[19]

---

[17]Gwalther, *Homelyes or Sermons upon the Actes*, 644-45* (*In Acta Apostolorum*, 201r).
[18]Spangenberg, *Der Apostel Geschichte*, 148r.
[19]Gwalther, *Homelyes or Sermons upon the Actes*, 645* (*In Acta Apostolorum*, 201r); alluding to Lk 19:40.

17:1-15 RESISTANCE IN THESSALONICA AND BEREA

Now when they had passed through Amphipolis and Apollonia, they came to Thessalonica, where there was a synagogue of the Jews. ²And Paul went in, as was his custom, and on three Sabbath days he reasoned with them from the Scriptures, ³explaining and proving that it was necessary for the Christ to suffer and to rise from the dead, and saying, "This Jesus, whom I proclaim to you, is the Christ." ⁴And some of them were persuaded and joined Paul and Silas, as did a great many of the devout Greeks and not a few of the leading women. ⁵But the Jewsᵃ were jealous, and taking some wicked men of the rabble, they formed a mob, set the city in an uproar, and attacked the house of Jason, seeking to bring them out to the crowd. ⁶And when they could not find them, they dragged Jason and some of the brothers before the city authorities, shouting, "These men who have turned the world upside down have come here also, ⁷and Jason has received them, and they are all acting against the decrees of Caesar, saying that there is another king, Jesus." ⁸And the people and the city authorities were disturbed when they heard these things. ⁹And when they had taken money as security from Jason and the rest, they let them go.

¹⁰The brothersᵇ immediately sent Paul and Silas away by night to Berea, and when they arrived they went into the Jewish synagogue. ¹¹Now these Jews were more noble than those in Thessalonica; they received the word with all eagerness, examining the Scriptures daily to see if these things were so.¹²Many of them therefore believed, with not a few Greek women of high standing as well as men.¹³But when the Jews from Thessalonica learned that the word of God was proclaimed by Paul at Berea also, they came there too, agitating and stirring up the crowds. ¹⁴Then the brothers immediately sent Paul off on his way to the sea, but Silas and Timothy remained there. ¹⁵Those who conducted Paul brought him as far as Athens, and after receiving a command for Silas and Timothy to come to him as soon as possible, they departed.

a Greek *Ioudaioi* probably refers here to Jewish religious leaders, and others under their influence, in that time; also verse 13 **b** Or *brothers and sisters*; also verse 14

OVERVIEW: The reformers follow the flow of this passage, contrasting the "knowledgeable" and stubborn response of some in Thessalonica to the curious and humble response of those in Berea. They highlight Paul's motivation due to his love for the kingdom of God as well as his own nation, Israel. Most commentators focus on the positive results of Paul's encounters, such as those who believed and joined them, rather than on the accusations and mobs that formed in response. However, the commentators are quick to laud Paul's constancy and courage in the face of many dangers, even when disorder arises as a result of his preaching. The Bereans also offer our exegetes a ready opportunity to extol the power and primacy of Scripture. They highlight the Bereans' "readiness of mind" to receive the gospel, because even those of noble standing have the desire to study the Word. This desire is seen as an exemplary quality, since this practice will lead readers to the truth. For those who affirm the gospel confession that Jesus is Lord, the reformers insist, Scripture is true soulfood that nourishes faith and love and consoles in tribulations.

17:1-9 Paul and Silas in Thessalonica

DIDN'T PAUL SAY FAREWELL TO THE JEWS? WHY DOES HE RETURN TO THEM HERE? JOHANN SPANGENBERG: Because he was an Israelite from the tribe of Benjamin! He could not abandon the Jews, his brothers; instead, he diligently turns to them wherever he is able, and he would like to lead them to Christ. He continues to hope for this. God preserved many for himself—as during the time of Elijah—who would turn to Christ. BRIEF EXEGESIS OF ACTS 17:1-2.[1]

PREACHERS MUST NOT DISMISS THOSE WHO SEEM HARDENED TO THE GOSPEL. RUDOLF GWALTHER: Perhaps it might seem strange that Paul would offer the doctrine of salvation again to the Jews, whose incurable malice he had so often tried and whom he perceived that God had cast off by many evident arguments. But he was moved partly with the fervent desire he had to set forward the kingdom of God and partly with the constant love that he bore to his nation, for whose sake otherwise he wished to be accursed. And yet we must not think this to be any blind affection, for the Lord had long before prophesied that though the Jews were cast off, certain remnants should be saved. . . . We are taught by this example of Paul that we must not over hastily cease from doing our duty because of many people's ingratitude but rather (as the apostle in other places teaches us) tolerate the evil with meekness, instruct those who resist, if at any time God will give them repentance to know the truth. HOMILY 113, Acts 17:1-4.[2]

CHRIST IS THE TRUE IMAGE OF THE PROPHETS' SKETCHES. DESIDERIUS ERASMUS: He compared these texts with the events that had taken place and showed that it was by the will and determination of God that Christ thus suffered and rose from the dead for the salvation of the world. Accordingly, since everything that had been predicted through the mouths of the prophets about the future Messiah and everything sketched

out in figures found a correspondence in Jesus of Nazareth, he showed the Jews that no other Messiah was to be expected, since the one he was preaching to them was the Christ. PARAPHRASE OF ACTS 17:2-3.[3]

DID THEY NOT KNOW ABOUT THE MESSIANIC PROMISES OF THE LAW AND THE PROPHETS? JOHANN SPANGENBERG: They knew them quite well, but they erred in their understanding of them. They imagined the Messiah would come in royal splendor and would establish the kingdom of Israel like David and Solomon did. They did not believe that Jesus of Nazareth crucified under Pilate was the Messiah but rather a deceiver of the people. BRIEF EXEGESIS OF ACTS 17:2-3.[4]

LUKE IMPROPERLY CALLS THESE GREEKS DEVOUT. JOHN CALVIN: By the wonderful plan of God their wretched dispersal was turned to the opposite purpose, so that it gathered those wandering and lost in errors to the right faith. But even though religion was also spoiled by many vicious fabrications in their midst, yet, because very many of the Gentiles were weary of their folly, they were being attracted to Judaism by this summary, that there is nothing that gives more security than the worship of the one God. Therefore understand by the "devout Greeks" those who had some taste of the true and legitimate worship of God, so that they were no longer devoted to crass idolatries. However, as I have said, it is probable that their taste was only vague and slight, so that it was far removed from true instruction. Accordingly Luke is wrong in giving them such an honorable title. But just as the Spirit of God sometimes thinks some rude first beginning, or the mere preparation of faith deserving of the name of "faith," so here "devout" is applied to those who had taken farewell of idols and were beginning to acknowledge the one God. COMMENTARY ON ACTS 17:4.[5]

---

[1]Spangenberg, *Der Apostel Geschichte*, 148v; alluding to 1 Kings 18.
[2]Gwalther, *Homelyes or Sermons upon the Actes*, 647* (*In Acta Apostolorum*, 201v); alluding to Rom 9:3.
[3]CWE 50:105-6 (LB 7:734).
[4]Spangenberg, *Der Apostel Geschichte*, 149r.
[5]CNTC 7:95 (CO 48:395-96).

"Wicked Men of the Rabble." The English Annotations: That is, idle fellows, who, having no employment at home, would walk lazily up and down markets and public places. They are the dregs of cities, mercenaries, worthless burdens of the earth. Often they watch for opportunities to stir up sedition, hoping to find some advantage in the upheaval. Annotations on Acts 17:5.[6]

The True Israelite Confession. Desiderius Erasmus: True Jews cry out, "We have no king but Jesus of Nazareth!" and, "Whoever has given himself to Caesar is not Christ's friend!" For Christ alone holds sway over the whole earth. Paraphrase of Acts 17:7.[7]

Magistrates in Thessalonica More Responsible Than Those in Philippi. Johann Spangenberg: "After they had received surety from Jason and the others, they released them." These magistrates in Thessalonica act in a more brotherly and wiser fashion than those in Philippi. For they decided the matter without a hearing; they let Paul and Silas be beaten, and they shoved them into prison. These magistrates, however, were not willing to act so arbitrarily. Instead, they heard both sides, and finding no guilt in Jason, released him along with the others. This is the true office of the magistracy: that they protect the pious and release the innocent. Brief Exegesis of Acts 17:8-9.[8]

17:10-15 Paul and Silas in Berea

Your Pastor Is an Ambassador from the King of Heaven. John Donne: Prejudices and disaffections and undervaluations of the abilities of the preacher in the hearer disappoint the purpose of the Holy Spirit, frustrate the labors of the man and injure and defraud the rest of the congregation who would, and justly, like what is said, if they were not misled and shaken by those hearers. Thus they work such jealousies and suspicions that though his abilities are good, still his effect on his audience is not their edification but to work on them to other purposes.

Though we do not require an implicit faith in you, so that you believe because we say it, still we do require a holy nobleness in you, a religious good nature, a conscientious ingenuity, so that you remember from whom we come—the King of heaven—and in what office, as his ambassadors. Therefore, know that since we must return to the One who sent us, giving him a report of our business, we dare not transgress our commission. Sermon on the Sunday After the Conversion of Saint Paul (1627).[9]

Why Does Luke Call the Bereans "More Noble"? John Calvin: There is a threefold reason why Luke mentions superiority of birth in their case. We know how reluctantly people come down from a high position, how rare it is for the great, who are prominent in the world, to lay aside their pride and submit to the ignominy of the cross and to glory in humiliation, as James enjoins.

Therefore, Luke commends the remarkable efficacy of the Spirit of God when he says that the dignity of the flesh was no obstacle to those noble men, but that having embraced the gospel, they prepared themselves to bear the cross and preferred the reproach of Christ to the glory of the world. In the second place Luke wished to make it plain to us that the grace of Christ is open to people of all ranks. That is what Paul means when he says that God wishes all people to be saved, so that those who are poor and of lowly birth, even though Christ did think them deserving of the first place, may not close the door to the rich. Therefore we see that noblemen and common men are gathered together, that people distinguished by a position of honor and those who are despised are growing together into the one body of the church, so that all, without exception, may humble themselves

---

[6]Downame, ed., *Annotations*, KKK4r*.
[7]CWE 50:106 (LB 7:734).
[8]Spangenberg, *Der Apostel Geschichte*, 150r-v.
[9]Donne, *Works*, 1:325*.

and truly extol the grace of God. In the third place Luke seems to be pointing out the reason why so many were added and why the kingdom of Christ increased in such a short time at Thessalonica, that is, because it was no ordinary help that the leading men, and those distinguished by birth, showed the way to others, because the common people are usually influenced by authority. COMMENTARY ON ACTS 17:11.[10]

EAT GOOD SPIRITUAL FOOD. STEPHEN DENISON: This should teach the church of God the wisdom that God's people are not bound to receive every doctrine that they hear, but they must be like good Bereans, searching the Scriptures daily whether these things are so. We ought to be as wary about what we receive into our ears as about what we receive into our mouths; and indeed it is the sin of many, that when they are careful and thoughtful concerning the diet of their bodies and will have a care to eat no food but that which is wholesome and good, in the meantime are careless of the diet of their souls, feeding grossly on the very carrion of human inventions. THE DOCTRINE OF BOTH THE SACRAMENTS.[11]

THE SWEET HONEY OF THE WORD OF GOD. JOHN DONNE: If a man taste a little of this honey at the end of his staff, as Jonathan did, even though he thinks his eyes enlightened, as Jonathan did, he may be in Jonathan's situation: "I tasted a little honey with the tip of my staff, and behold, I will die." If the man read the Scriptures a little, superficially, perfunctorily, his eyes seem to be enlightened immediately. He thinks that he sees everything that he had preconceived and fore-imagined in himself as clear as the sun in the Scriptures. He can find flesh in the sacrament without bread, because he finds "This is my body." . . . So also he can find wormwood in this honey, because he finds in this Scripture "the reward for sin is death." . . . For the Scriptures are made to

agree with one another, but not to agree with your particular taste and humor.

But still the counsel is good on the other hand that "If you have found honey, eat only enough for you, lest you have your fill of it and vomit it." Content yourself with reading those parts of Scriptures which are clear and edify. Do not perplex yourself with prophecies not yet fulfilled. And content yourself with hearing those sermons which rectify you in all those things which you ought to believe and to practice. Do not follow those men who pretend to know those things which God has not revealed to his church. Too little or too much of this honey, of this reading and hearing may be unhealthy. God has chosen ways of moderation. He does not redeem us by God alone nor by man alone, but by him who was both. He instructs us not by the Holy Ghost alone without the ministry of man, nor by the minister alone without the assistance of the Holy Ghost. SERMON 31, PREACHED ON PENTECOST.[12]

A CHRISTIAN IS BIRTHED THROUGH THE PAGES OF THE SACRED WORD. BALTHASAR HUBMAIER: Search the Scriptures. They themselves will give the right witness about Christ and the Christian life. Do as the Thessalonians[13] and you will not go astray or be deceived. And even if your pastors and preachers would offer to give their very souls for you, even that would not be enough. You must believe the Word of God and not them. God alone is truthful, but all human beings are deceitful. For Christ says, When a blind person leads a blind person, both fall into the ditch. It would be a little thing if the shepherd alone fell, but by the authority of the Word of Christ the little sheep would fall also. ON THE CHRISTIAN BAPTISM OF BELIEVERS.[14]

---

[12]Donne, *Works*, 2:23-24; alluding to 1 Sam 14:27; Heb 4:4-6; quoting 1 Sam 14:43; Mt 26:26; Rom 6:23; Ezek 18:31; Prov 25:16.
[13]The QGT editors note that "Hubmaier unquestionably meant the Bereans."
[14]CRR 5:143* (QGT 9:158); alluding to Mt 15:14. Hubmaier uses this same argument in the introduction to his *Summa of the Entire Christian Life*, CRR 5:83-84 (QGT 9:110).

---

[10]CNTC 7:100* (CO 48:399-400); alluding to Jas 1:10; 1 Tim 2:4.
[11]Denison, *Doctrine of Both the Sacraments*, 62*.

NO REST FOR THE DEVIL. JOHANN SPANGEN-
BERG: How restless the devil is! He is absolutely
unable to suffer the preaching of God's Word! So,
he must quickly stir up in other lands and cities
people who will persecute the gospel. BRIEF EX-
EGESIS OF ACTS 17:13.[15]

WHAT DOES THIS STORY TEACH US? JOHANN
SPANGENBERG: Two things. [First], nothing other
than that a Christian's life is a constant soldier's
struggle here on earth, a daily fighting and brawl-
ing, so that it would not be surprising if a Christian
became sluggish and lethargic. If Paul had been a
worldly person, without grace and the Holy Spirit,
he likely would have said, "The devil take this
gospel stuff! For me it is nothing but pure cross,
tribulation and persecution!" But he does not do
that. He knows very well that a Christian must
bear the cross. So, he presses on and lets nothing
trouble him.

[Second], following the example of those
in [Berea], we should gladly read Scripture. For
Scripture is the only rule and foundation of our
faith. If a carpenter or mason is to build something
ably, then he must have a plumbline. If a goldsmith
is to test gold, then he must have a touchstone. So
then, if we Christians are to judge what is God's
Word or human teaching, then we too must have a
touchstone, and this is holy Scripture. From Scripture we must learn about Christ. Whoever teaches
something other than what Scripture states about
him errs and is mistaken. All human teaching
should be tested with Scripture to determine if it is
to be tolerated or discarded. Nothing should be allowed in a Christian congregation other than what
has a sure basis in Scripture. For Scripture is nothing other than the pure sanctified Word of God
delivered through the prophetic Spirit into the
world, as Saint Peter says. Thus, Christ so often
directs us to Scripture; he also exhorts us to search
the Scripture. In Scripture he speaks with us in a
living voice and comforts us in every concern and
there promises us eternal life. BRIEF EXEGESIS OF
ACTS 17:10-15.[16]

---

[15]Spangenberg, *Der Apostel Geschichte*, 151r.

[16]Spangenberg, *Der Apostel Geschichte*, 151r-152v*; alluding to 2
Pet 1:21.

17:16-34 PAUL VISITS ATHENS AND ADDRESSES THE AREOPAGUS

¹⁶*Now while Paul was waiting for them at Athens, his spirit was provoked within him as he saw that the city was full of idols.* ¹⁷*So he reasoned in the synagogue with the Jews and the devout persons, and in the marketplace every day with those who happened to be there.* ¹⁸*Some of the Epicurean and Stoic philosophers also conversed with him. And some said, "What does this babbler wish to say?" Others said, "He seems to be a preacher of foreign divinities"—because he was preaching Jesus and the resurrection.* ¹⁹*And they took him and brought him to the Areopagus, saying, "May we know what this new teaching is that you are presenting?* ²⁰*For you bring some strange things to our ears. We wish to know therefore what these things mean."* ²¹*Now all the Athenians and the foreigners who lived there would spend their time in nothing except telling or hearing something new.*

²²*So Paul, standing in the midst of the Areopagus, said: "Men of Athens, I perceive that in every way you are very religious.* ²³*For as I passed along and observed the objects of your worship, I found also an altar with this inscription, 'To the unknown god.' What therefore you worship as unknown, this I proclaim to you.* ²⁴*The God who made the world and everything in it, being Lord of heaven and earth, does not live in temples made by man,*^a ²⁵*nor is he served by human hands, as though he needed anything,*

since he himself gives to all mankind life and breath and everything. ²⁶*And he made from one man every nation of mankind to live on all the face of the earth, having determined allotted periods and the boundaries of their dwelling place,* ²⁷*that they should seek God, and perhaps feel their way toward him and find him. Yet he is actually not far from each one of us,* ²⁸*for*

'In him we live and move and have our being';^b

as even some of your own poets have said,

'For we are indeed his offspring.'^c

²⁹*Being then God's offspring, we ought not to think that the divine being is like gold or silver or stone, an image formed by the art and imagination of man.* ³⁰*The times of ignorance God overlooked, but now he commands all people everywhere to repent,* ³¹*because he has fixed a day on which he will judge the world in righteousness by a man whom he has appointed; and of this he has given assurance to all by raising him from the dead."*

³²*Now when they heard of the resurrection of the dead, some mocked. But others said, "We will hear you again about this."* ³³*So Paul went out from their midst.* ³⁴*But some men joined him and believed, among whom also were Dionysius the Areopagite and a woman named Damaris and others with them.*

a Greek *made by hands*   b Probably from Epimenides of Crete   c From Aratus's poem "Phainomena"

OVERVIEW: Upon arriving in Athens, Paul acknowledges its great philosophical tradition and religious heritage. While there is common consensus criticizing idolatry, the commentators show varying emphases ranging from outright indignation and renunciation of all forms of idolatry to concentration on the (humble) success that Paul has in his exchange with those to whom he preached. The commentators portray Paul as God's messenger who rescues the wise and learned in their own eyes from their true spiritual blindness.

By highlighting Paul's argument that God cannot be contained by anything made with human hands, the reformers argue that the one, true and holy God has been made generally known through creation—so that all human beings are without excuse—though only savingly known in Christ. Yet the learnedness and wisdom of the Greeks does not correlate to a lesser degree of superstition, since divine wisdom is veiled as foolishness to the world. Hence the commentators expect the ensuing struggle between adherents of God's wisdom and the world's wisdom and accentuate the importance of discipleship in Christian communities. The revealed knowledge of God through Christ is a clean break from wayward pagan religion. In the end, the reformers agree that the same news can be received either as good or as offensive; still, the fruitfulness of Paul's speech encourages believers never to cease proclaiming God's judgment and mercy.

17:16-21 *Paul in Athens*

WISDOM VERSUS FOOLISHNESS: A BATTLE CHRISTIANS CANNOT LIVE WITHOUT. MARTIN LUTHER: Here Luke describes what happened to Paul in Athens, in order to indicate how the wisdom of God and human reason fit together. Athens was the most famous city, and the Athenians believed that the wisdom of God and human reason were not compatible—nor is this even possible. Now according to human reason there were no people more intelligent than these; Plato could not indicate a place which had more wise men than Athens. Thus, he is able to use Athens as a type for all wise men. Divine wisdom comes here and considers how it fits together with human reason. Divine wisdom shows that human reason is foolishness; likewise, human reason believes that divine wisdom is foolishness. Just as even today people wish to teach the gospel in peace; at other times discord happened which is necessitated by a council. Such people want to remove and put to rest the discord that divine wisdom has with human reason, but no one is able to put this discord to rest except God himself. Indeed such harmony can be granted by a council, but falsely. It is necessary for this struggle always to remain. True, but it does this: it hurls Christians into danger, because it entrusts us with preaching. If we preach, we are said to be foolish, and then we are commanded again to rebuke those [who assert this]. Who will unite us? No one, except God alone. A Christian who has the Word

must live in the cross; without discord you will not live. The world has been led away and besieged by the devil. Therefore, when the Lord has mercy on the world and gives light to it, it is necessary that you be a minister of this light. The devil is not able to endure this but sets the whole world in motion against you. Wherever this struggle is not in the world it is a certain sign that the gospel is not there. SERMON ON ACTS 17:16-21 (1524).[1]

ATHENS'S REPUTATION. RUDOLF GWALTHER: The Evangelist Luke has previously described the different journeys and wanderings of Paul the apostle, in which he enlightened so many nations and cities with the preaching of the gospel. In other places, he had drawn ignorant and unlearned people ..., but then he came eventually to the most famous city of Athens, through the certain counsel of God's providence. In antiquity Athens surpassed many.... We have it to thank for Socrates, Plato, Zenophon, Erates and infinite others famous because of their wisdom....

Into this city the Lord sent Paul the apostle to bring it by his ministry into the obedience of faith. This was attempted with good success and profit, as the ending well proves. This is a notable example both of the goodness of God and of the power of the gospel. For who would not acknowledge the unspeakable grace of God when he hears about a city utterly drowned in the darkness of idolatry and human wisdom that is so favorably regarded by God? HOMILY 116, ACTS 17:16-21.[2]

ATHENS, A CITY FILLED WITH LEARNING AND IDOLATRY. MARTIN LUTHER: But it is necessary that divine wisdom be foolishness in the world and against [the world]. This was done in the foremost city of Athens. Paul had not come there so that he could preach but so that he could wait. But when he saw that the city was devoted to the worship of idols, he was not able to be silent, but

---

[1]WA 15:630.
[2]Gwalther, *Homelyes or Sermons upon the Actes*, 658* (*In Acta Apostolorum*, 205r).

the Holy Spirit spurred him on so that he opened his mouth. This city was famous because of its great wisdom; nevertheless, it truly was much more devoted to the worship of idols than to anything else. But those people were influenced just like ourselves; they brought in whatever new god they heard about and worshiped it, just like the Romans brought whatever gods they found into one temple and called it the Pantheon. So also we ourselves listen to any scoundrel: this one lifts up that saint, that one lifts up another for devotion. Paul always preached in the synagogue first, because the Jews had been scattered throughout the whole world. Therefore, he first preached to the Jews, who had the spiritual custom of worshiping God, like the Pharisees, who had an impressive life, as the monks do among us. SERMON ON ACTS 17:16-21 (1524).[3]

EVEN SPLENDID WORSHIP OF ANY OTHER BUT THE TRUE GOD IS MERELY IDOLATRY.

JOHN CALVIN: Wherever the Jews had synagogues it was Paul's normal practice to make a beginning in them and offer Christ to his own nation. After that the next step was to Gentiles who had experienced the teaching of the Law, and, although they were not yet properly imbued with true godliness, were nevertheless worshiping the God of Israel, and, being eager to learn, did not reject the things that they knew to be taken from Moses and the Prophets. But because such docility was an entrance to faith, and indeed, a kind of beginning of faith, the Spirit thought worthy of a title of honor those who, with but a slight smattering of first principles, had drawn nearer to the true God, for they are called devout. But let us remember that they are distinguished from others by this mark, so that the whole of the world's religion might be reduced to nothing. Those who gave their allegiance to the God of Israel are specifically called "worshipers of God"; religion is attributed only to them. Therefore there is nothing left for the rest except the ignominy of atheism, no matter how anxiously

they torture themselves in superstitions. And that is justified, for whatever splendor idolaters may boast of, if their inner attitude is examined, nothing will be found there except a horrible contempt of God, and it will be clear that their pretense of fawning on idols is merely an excuse. COMMENTARY ON ACTS 17:17.[4]

THE ATHENIANS THINK PAUL IS A STREET PERFORMER.

JOHANN SPANGENBERG: Here they call Paul a jester—a person who provides for himself through useless drivel, traveling here and there throughout the land, only concerned that he brings something new to the table and feeds people with words as witch doctors, tricksters and mountebanks do. BRIEF EXEGESIS OF ACTS 17:18.[5]

"FOREIGN DIVINITIES."

DESIDERIUS ERASMUS: But others said, "He seems to be introducing some new kind of daemon [xenōn daimoniōn]," because he preached Jesus the author of salvation and Son of God, and the resurrection of the dead. (From the teaching of Plato, the Athenians called the sons of gods "daemons," to which they indeed assigned bodies, though immortal.) PARAPHRASE OF ACTS 17:18.[6]

WE ARE JUST AS FOOLISH TODAY.

MARTIN LUTHER: Certainly they were wisest with respect to their outward governance and scarcely had equals. They were certainly the wisest and the most foolish. It is the same way today: those who are the wisest in earthly matters are the most foolish in spiritual matters. Clearly the kingdoms in which we rule and are ruled must be separated greatly. We do not find wisdom; it is necessary for us to have another teacher, who says that we are full of idolatry. Let yourself step from darkness into the light. If you wish to become wise, believe that Christ was crucified for you and that he is yours . . . let him who saves, govern [you]. Finally it happens that a human being suffers, speaks or does nothing unless

---

[4]CNTC 7:105* (CO 48:404).
[5]Spangenberg, Der Apostel Geschichte, 154v.
[6]CWE 50:107 (LB 7:735).

[3]WA 15:630-31.

God is in him. The kingdom of God wishes to possess all things alone, wherefore it must not do that, so that a human being may be ruled according to his own interior part. And all precepts of the papists tend toward this point: how the soul ought to act with God. Thus here nothing is strong except the unified and pure Word of God. God is jealous; he does not suffer [fools].

Plainly we are foolish when we wish to raise people up to the heavens by their works. Are we not as foolish as the Epicureans and the Stoics, who said that God does not exist? Here we are not so foolish, because the Christian thinks that he does good, as a funeral band encircles himself, as a dying layman puts on a hooded cloak. We listen to reason; then clearly we are just as foolish. If you do not understand this, do not mix the spiritual kingdom into that lower kingdom now, but wait for the light from heaven to illuminate you. SERMON ON ACTS 17:18 (1524).[7]

MARS HILL: THE STAGE OF LIFE AND DEATH. DESIDERIUS ERASMUS: Since in the marketplace opinions about Paul differed, they decided to take him off to a quarter known as Mars. This was the most celebrated place in Athens wherein cases of life and death were investigated in trials held at night. It was a place appropriate to this debate, which offered salvation to those who believed but death to the unbelieving. PARAPHRASE OF ACTS 17:19.[8]

TWO GROUPS WHO ARE FAR FROM GOD. JOHN CALVIN: Luke places two kinds of people before us. Both are indeed far removed from godliness, yet one of them is far worse than the other. Take those who once more desire to hear what they call "something new." In the first place they are not moved by a proper desire to learn, but by empty curiosity. Second, they do not feel enough respect for the Word of God, for they treat it just like a profane novelty. Yet because they do listen and are indeed open-minded until they would find out more about the matter, they are not absolutely hopeless. The others, however, by proudly rejecting what is offered, and, what is more, by insolently condemning it, close the gate of salvation for themselves. COMMENTARY ON ACTS 17:18.[9]

GOD OFTEN SNARES US THROUGH OUR HOBBIES AND PLEASURES. DESIDERIUS ERASMUS: But God, keen for human salvation, snares each person by taking advantage of the things each especially likes, in the way fishermen or hunters do. And so Paul, who knew how to become all things to all people and how to accommodate his eloquence to the character of any listener, found a theater for himself in the midst of the Martian quarter. PARAPHRASE OF ACTS 17:21.[10]

17:22-34 Paul's Speech to the Areopagus

A SUMMARY OF PAUL'S SERMON. RUDOLF GWALTHER: The argument of Paul's sermon was meant to bring the Athenians from superstition and idolatry to the honor of the only true God through Jesus Christ. First, therefore, he reproves them in a friendly way and accuses them of their abundant and overwrought superstition. After that he reasons about God and the true religion, piercing their foolishness, which taught that God could be worshiped through images or any other human inventions. At length he comes nearer to Christ's cause. HOMILY 117, ACTS 17:22-25.[11]

---

[7]WA 15:632.1-22.
[8]CWE 50:107-8* (LB 7:735). See also Erasmus, *Annotationes* on 17:19, LB 6:500-501. It is disputed what precisely Luke means by "Areopagus" here; usually the choices are between the council that met there or the place itself, though some are incredulous that either could be meant since the council would have excluded the public and the location itself is too small for such a great gather. See Richard I. Pervo, *Acts: A Commentary* (Minneapolis: Fortress, 2009), 428, and Ernst Haenchen, *The Acts of the Apostles: A Commentary*, trans. Bernard Noble and Gerald Shinn (Philadelphia: The Westminster Press, 1971), 518-19.

[9]CNTC 7:107* (CO 48:406).
[10]CWE 50:108* (LB 7:736); alluding to 1 Cor 9:22.
[11]Gwalther, *Homelyes or Sermons upon the Actes*, 664* (*In Acta Apostolorum*, 206v).

PAUL APPEALS TO THE ATHENIANS TO GAIN A HEARING. JOHANN SPANGENBERG: Paul entreats his audience to listen willingly and quietly. He calls them men, which is a magnificent title. Still he also calls them superstitious, which they also accepted as a magnificent title, for they wanted to be praised as greatly honoring the gods. Thus, Paul clarifies that he does not preach new gods but rather the ancient God whom they too, though unknowingly, honor. BRIEF EXEGESIS OF ACTS 17:22-23.[12]

NO TRUE RELIGION WITHOUT PERSONAL KNOWLEDGE OF GOD. RUDOLF GWALTHER: Moreover, let us mark here how the Athenians are at this point chiefly accused of false religion because they worship an unknown god. For it is here that Paul proves that they have nothing certain in their religion. By this it appears that religion cannot stand without the true knowledge of God. For not only Paul but Christ also uses the same argument against the Samaritans, when with one blow he strikes down all their religions saying, "You worship what you do not know." For the whole Scripture teaches us that religion consists chiefly in true faith and invocation of God. . . . But unless we are inspired with the knowledge of the Christ, we can neither believe in God nor call on him. HOMILY 117, ACTS 17:22-25.[13]

"TO THE UNKNOWN GOD." GIOVANNI DIODATI: Many authors mention this inscription, of which its cause and origin is very uncertain. Perhaps it was intended to make even foreign gods favorable to them. Paul only uses it to show them that they had, therefore, absolutely no reason to reject his teaching and the God whom he preached to them, under the pretense of an unknown novelty. ANNOTATION ON ACTS 17:23.[14]

FAITH CANNOT BE FORMED BY COMPULSION. MARTIN LUTHER: Once, when Paul came to Athens, a mighty city, he found in the temple many ancient altars, and he went from one to the other and looked at them all, but he did not kick down a single one of them with his foot. Rather, he stood up in the middle of the marketplace and said they were nothing but idolatrous things and begged the people to forsake them; yet, he did not destroy one of them by force. When the Word took hold of their hearts, they forsook them of their own accord, and in consequence the thing fell of itself. Likewise, if I had seen them holding Mass, I would have preached to them and admonished them. Had they heeded my admonition, I would have won them; if not, I would nevertheless not have torn them from it by the hair or employed any force but simply allowed the Word to act and prayed for them. For the Word created heaven and earth and all things; the Word must do this thing, and not we poor sinners.

In short, I will preach it, teach it, write it, but I will constrain no one by force, for faith must come freely without compulsion. Take myself as an example. I opposed indulgences and all the papists, but never with force. I simply taught, preached and wrote God's Word; otherwise I did nothing. And while I slept or drank Wittenberg beer with my friends Philip and Amsdorf, the Word so greatly weakened the papacy that no prince or emperor ever inflicted such losses on it. I did nothing; the Word did everything. Had I desired to foment trouble, I could have brought great bloodshed on Germany; indeed, at Worms[15] I could have started such a game that even the emperor would not have been safe. But what would it have been? Mere fool's play. I did nothing; I let the Word do its work. SECOND INVOCAVIT SERMON (1522).[16]

---

[12]Spangenberg, *Der Apostel Geschichte*, 155v.

[13]Gwalther, *Homelyes or Sermons upon the Actes*, 665* (*In Acta Apostolorum*, 207r); quoting Jn 4:22.

[14]Diodati, *Pious Annotations*, BB3r* (*I Commenti alla Sacra Biblia*, 1110).

[15]Luther is referring to the Diet of Worms (1521). The diet had taken place nearly a year before the Invocavit sermons, which, due to the dissension Karlstadt had stirred up, were Luther's first public appearance in Wittenberg after being kidnapped by Frederick the Wise.

[16]LW 51:76-78* (WA 10,3:18-19); alluding to Ps 33:6; Mk 4:26-29. For the Invocavit sermons the base text for the LW translation

WORSHIP MEETS OUR NEEDS, NOT GOD'S.
THE ENGLISH ANNOTATIONS: The worship of
God does not consist of external things, human
traditions or the works of human hands—idols,
images—but in Spirit and truth according to the
holy prescript of his own Word. He is self-existent
and all-sufficient, needing nothing from us. He
gives all creatures what they have and are. If he
blesses us with the ability to give (which is an acceptable service to him) and if he rewards what we
do by this, in faith and obedience to him, he only
crowns his own graces in us. ANNOTATIONS ON
ACTS 17:25.[17]

PAUL PROCLAIMS THE FIRST ARTICLE OF THE
CREED. JOHANN SPANGENBERG: Now he reproaches their false worship, which consists in gold,
silver, stone and wooden images, and directs them to
the one living God, who implanted intelligence and
reason in human beings, so that through the visible
things of this world they could learn to acknowledge
the God and Creator of all things, both seen and
unseen. BRIEF EXEGESIS OF ACTS 17:24-27.[18]

"HE MADE OF ONE BLOOD."[19] JOHN CALVIN:
Paul now warns the Athenians of the purpose for
which the human race was created, so that in this
way he may invite and encourage them to consider
the purpose of their own life. It is certainly shameful ingratitude on the part of human beings, when
all enjoy a common life, not to consider why God
has given them life. But still this brute-like stupid-
ity has the majority in its grip, so that they do not
reflect upon why they are placed in the world, and
they do not give a thought to the Creator of heaven

and earth, with whose good things they gorge
themselves. Therefore, after Paul has discussed the
nature of God, he opportunely introduces this admonition, that human beings ought to give careful
consideration to the knowledge of God, because it
was for this reason that they were made, and they
were born for this end. For, briefly, he assigns to
them this reason for living, to seek God. COMMEN-
TARY ON ACTS 17:26.[20]

A TIME OF GRACE. BOHEMIAN CONFESSION OF
1535: [The Scriptures] teach in this chapter that
as long as they are living, people may know a time
granted them by God, which is a time of grace
in which they may seek him and his grace, goodness, mercy and leniency. They should find this in
his promises and thus attain a blessed salvation.
. . . Therefore our people diligently admonish that
one should not fail to make full use of this time
of grace, but that while one is in good health and
is permitted to pass through this time, one should
do penance to attain a higher life, be reconciled to
God, and through his administration in the church
render one's conscience peaceful and tranquil and
secure. One should firmly believe that one's sins
are forgiven and that God is appeased because of
Christ. One should certainly believe that one is
made firm in Christ's grace, walking and going forward in good works. One should also certainly believe that when one's soul is freed from the chains
of the body it will not pass over into any punishment, but like Lazarus will be carried by the angels
into eternal blessing, where it will remain forever
with Christ, in whose presence all things exist and
can be sought. Not even on the Last Day does one
need to fear the judgment of death, for one will
be caught up into heavenly life. Paul wishes us to
strive for this (see Heb 3:13; 4:3). ARTICLE 20, THE
TIME OF GRACE.[21]

REASON IS A GOD-GIVEN GIFT BY WHICH WE
INFER HIS EXISTENCE. DESIDERIUS ERASMUS:

---

is from LWA 7:363-87 (here pp. 369-70); the corresponding WA
text is WA 10, 3:1-64. The only difference between these two editions of the German text is punctuation. The LWA reproduces
the original punctuation and printing abbreviations, while the
WA implements more modern punctuation and fills out the
abbreviations.
[17]Downame, ed., *Annotations*, KKK4v*; alluding to Jn 4:24; Ps
50:8-15; Phil 4:18; Heb 13:16.
[18]Spangenberg, *Der Apostel Geschichte*, 156r-v.
[19]𝔐 adds αἵματος to Acts 17:26, giving "he made from one blood
all nations."

[20]CNTC 7:116-17* (CO 48:414).
[21]Boh 1535, 38*.

Since, however, God cannot in his own nature be grasped by the capacities of human intellect, weighed down, as it is, by the heavy mass of the body, he has endowed human beings with reason so that they might be able to infer one thing from another—the invisible from the visible, the universal from the particular, the eternal from the temporal, the things that are grasped only by the intellect from the things perceived by the senses; and he has set human beings in the midst of the theater of the world so that from the created things which they see with their eyes, touch with their hands, experience through use, they might trace out and search for the Creator. Like the blind who discover by feel what they cannot see, so human beings through reflection on the marvelous creation of the universe might arrive at some knowledge of God, whom truly to know is utmost felicity. PARAPHRASE OF ACTS 17:26-27.[22]

THE GOSPEL IS HIDDEN FROM HUMAN REASON. JOHN CALVIN: There is no reason why the ministers of the gospel should give up the proclaiming of the judgment, with which they have been charged. Although the ungodly may laugh, still this teaching, which they try to elude, will so bind them that at last they may realize that they have struggled with their fetters in vain. And surely it is no wonder that this part of Paul's speech was scoffed at in Athens. For it is a mystery hidden from human minds, a mystery about which not an inkling ever entered the heads of even the greatest philosophers. And it can only be grasped by us when we lift up eyes of faith to the immense power of God. And yet Paul's speech was not fruitless, because there were some of the audience who desired to go further. For when they openly admit that they wish to hear him again, they mean that, although they are not yet fully convinced, they nevertheless have some taste, which makes them eager to learn more. Certainly this desire was a different thing altogether from scornful contempt. COMMENTARY ON ACTS 17:32.[23]

TO WITNESS OUR CREATOR'S WORK, LOOK AT YOURSELF. DESIDERIUS ERASMUS: And yet it is not necessary to seek God in external things, since we may find him in ourselves, if only each person observes himself and sees within himself the power, the wisdom and the goodness of the Creator. Though God has disclosed certain traces of his divinity in the heavenly orbs, on the earth, in the sea and in all living things, yet in none is his divinity more wonderful than in human beings themselves. Even if someone is too dull-witted to be able to comprehend the movements of the stars, the ebb and flow of the sea, the bubbling of springs, the perennial flow of rivers and the hidden causes of other things, God is not far from each of us, for through him we all live and move and have our being. We owe our existence to him alone who created this world from nothing. Our breathing is a benefit bestowed by no other—if he should desert us, we would die on the spot. To no one else do we owe the fact that the limbs of the living body each performs its own function: eyes see, feet walk, hands work. So God is in each of us and works through us, as a craftsman works through the instrument he himself has made.

Human beings, however, reflect God not only as a work reflects the workman but also as a child reflects its parent, by a certain similarity and kinship of nature. It has been handed down to us in sacred books that God fashioned for Adam—who was the first of the human race—a body from wet clay, in which respect he would have kinship with other living creatures; but with his mouth God breathed into this mud image a tiny bit of celestial breath, through which we might resemble more closely our parent God himself and because of the similarity in nature might recognize him more easily. This was not granted to the other animals. You should not find this absurd, for what has been revealed in mystic literature some of the poets of your own race have also said. PARAPHRASE OF ACTS 17:28.[24]

---

[22]CWE 50:109 (LB 7:736-37).
[23]CNTC 7:126-27 (CO 48:422-23).

[24]CWE 50:109-10* (LB 7:737).

HOW INSOLENT IT IS THAT HUMAN BEINGS WORSHIP THEIR OWN HANDIWORK. DESIDERIUS ERASMUS: Now on how many counts is a human being superior to the image to which divine honors are paid? First, he has received from God this very bodily form. Second, he breathes, lives, moves and acts. Finally, in his lively force of mind he has a certain likeness to God, his parent. A statue has none of these. But if it is impious to worship a human being as a god, how much further from true piety is it to worship a figure fashioned from matter at the will of the artisan— from the same matter he could have made a stool too, had he wished. This has no likeness to God who is incorporeal. Far from it! Indeed, apart from a certain exquisite bodily form, the product of the imagination, it possesses nothing resembling human beings, for it does not have even a grain of that part by which a human being bears the image of God. PARAPHRASE OF ACTS 17:29.[25]

PAUL PRESENTS REPENTANCE AND PROPITIATION IN CHRIST. JOHANN SPANGENBERG: He directs them to true worship and to the unknown true God, Jesus Christ. He tempers his words and channels them through his audience's understanding. He does not say that they have behaved ungodly but unknowingly. Therefore, God has had consideration for their unknowingness and tolerated them, but now is the time to repent and rightly acknowledge and accept Christ, so that they do not suffer Sodom and Gomorrah's punishment. BRIEF EXEGESIS OF ACTS 17:27-31.[26]

CHRIST IS BOTH JUDGE AND SAVIOR, BOTH HUMBLE AND GLORIOUS. VALENTIN WEIGEL: It is sure that Christ did not come into the world so that he could judge the world but rather so that the world could be saved through him. . . . These contradictions are immediately understood in the Holy Spirit: Christ must be viewed according to two states. According to the state of his humiliation, of

his cross, of his assumed human nature he did not come to judge, to condemn anyone, but instead to seek those who are lost and to save sinners. In this state he is transformed into the Lamb of God in profound patience, in mild goodness, in meekness, in lovingkindness. And he compels no one neither to good nor to bad, neither to life nor to death. He leaves each person free to choose. Whoever is willing to believe wants to do this through the power of the Spirit. Whoever is unwilling wants to leave it be through the resistance of the Spirit.

But according to the understanding of his glory and majesty, all power in heaven and on earth has been given to him. In this state he will come to judge the world with righteousness. He will judge the living and the dead, that is, he will condemn those who do not believe and thus who are already judged, and he will call saved those who have believed and thus who are already saved. His mild lovingkindness will be transformed into a strict righteousness. He will come in the clouds with great power and majesty. However, he says this in the state of his humility, that he comes to judge is not to be understood that in such a state he judges or condemns someone but that the Word that each person hears will judge and condemn each person. To judge he came into the world, that is, that the unbelieving world is confirmed, that they are in the darkness and are already judged together with their prince the devil. And the believing will be confirmed, that they are in the light, as new creatures, and will not enter into judgment. CHURCH OR HOUSE POSTIL FOR PENTECOST MONDAY.[27]

THE MERCY OF GOD IN LIGHT OF OUR INSOLENCE. DESIDERIUS ERASMUS: Despite this terrible insolence against God, still because of his love toward the human race he has not taken revenge but thus far has, as it were, taken no notice of human ignorance, until the time should come when he has determined to become known to all and to scatter all the gloom and darkness of error. This time is now at hand, when he commands everyone

---

[25]CWE 50:110-11 (LB 7:737).
[26]Spangenberg, *Der Apostel Geschichte*, 157r.
[27]Weigel, *Sämtliche Schriften*, 12,2:273-74; alluding to Jn 3:17; 9:39.

to come to their senses and repent of their former error. To those who so repent he wants forgiveness to be granted, a forgiveness which will not be granted in the future to the insolent, for he has established a day on which he will judge the whole world with a just and unerring judgment, and no one will be allowed to escape it. The reason he has issued his declaration in advance is so that no one might be able to allege ignorance as an excuse, and he offers pardon to the repentant so that no one should find mercy lacking in God. PARAPHRASE OF ACTS 17:30-31.[28]

A MEAGER RETURN FOR PAUL'S LABORS. JOHN CALVIN: Since Luke names only one man and one woman, it appears that at the beginning the number of believers was small. For the others, whom he mentions, remain as it were on the fence, because they were not rejecting Paul's teaching out of hand, but they had not been so seriously affected that they attached themselves to him as disciples. Luke

names Dionysius before the others because he possessed no ordinary authority among his fellow citizens, and in the same way it is very likely that Damaris was a woman of the first rank. COMMENTARY ON ACTS 17:34.[29]

WAS THIS ARTFUL SERMON FOR NOTHING? JOHANN SPANGENBERG: It is puzzling that in such a populous city, so few became Christians. But in Paul's way lay worldly wisdom and the cleverness of the flesh. For the gospel and worldly wisdom will not suffer being next to one another. Where the Holy Spirit works with his grace, there that person must forfeit his reason as captured and [instead] believe, accept and keep holy Scripture. Then in him the word of Christ will be fulfilled, "Blessed are they who hear God's Word and keep it." God help us, Amen. BRIEF EXEGESIS OF ACTS 17:32-34.[30]

---

[28]CWE 50:111* (LB 7:737-38).

[29]CTS 37:178.

[30]Spangenberg, *Der Apostel Geschichte*, 157v-158r; quoting Lk 11:28.

18:1-17 PAUL PREACHES AND TEACHES IN CORINTH

After this Paul[a] left Athens and went to Corinth. [2]And he found a Jew named Aquila, a native of Pontus, recently come from Italy with his wife Priscilla, because Claudius had commanded all the Jews to leave Rome. And he went to see them, [3]and because he was of the same trade he stayed with them and worked, for they were tentmakers by trade. [4]And he reasoned in the synagogue every Sabbath, and tried to persuade Jews and Greeks.

[5]When Silas and Timothy arrived from Macedonia, Paul was occupied with the word, testifying to the Jews that the Christ was Jesus. [6]And when they opposed and reviled him, he shook out his garments and said to them, "Your blood be on your own heads! I am innocent. From now on I will go to the Gentiles." [7]And he left there and went to the house of a man named Titius Justus, a worshiper of God. His house was next door to the synagogue. [8]Crispus, the ruler of the synagogue, believed in the Lord, together with his entire household. And many of the Corinthians hearing Paul believed and were baptized. [9]And the Lord said to Paul one night in a vision, "Do not be afraid, but go on speaking and do not be silent, [10]for I am with you, and no one will attack you to harm you, for I have many in this city who are my people." [11]And he stayed a year and six months, teaching the word of God among them.

[12]But when Gallio was proconsul of Achaia, the Jews[b] made a united attack on Paul and brought him before the tribunal, [13]saying, "This man is persuading people to worship God contrary to the law." [14]But when Paul was about to open his mouth, Gallio said to the Jews, "If it were a matter of wrongdoing or vicious crime, O Jews, I would have reason to accept your complaint. [15]But since it is a matter of questions about words and names and your own law, see to it yourselves. I refuse to be a judge of these things." [16]And he drove them from the tribunal. [17]And they all seized Sosthenes, the ruler of the synagogue, and beat him in front of the tribunal. But Gallio paid no attention to any of this.

a Greek he   b Greek Ioudaioi probably refers here to Jewish religious leaders, and others under their influence, in that time; also verses 14 (twice), 28

OVERVIEW: When Paul arrives in Corinth, his initial contacts are Aquila and Priscilla, a Jewish couple who had relocated from Italy to Corinth because of Emperor Claudius's decree expelling the Jews from Rome. Paul's profession as a tentmaker becomes, for the reformers, a way to reveal his industrious character as one who makes an honest living. In Corinth, it is clear that Paul continues his pattern of preaching the gospel in the synagogues to both the Jews and the Greeks. Reformation commentators highlight this narrative for its historical significance (it records the beginnings of the church in Corinth) and for its theological significance (faith in the gospel is spreading among the Gentile nations).

CORINTH, A CITY STEEPED IN SEXUAL SIN.
JOHANN SPANGENBERG: Corinth is the capital of the district Achaia. It has two ports—one toward Asia, the other toward Italy—and so it was a powerful trading center. There people from every part of the world, traders and merchants, gathered. Now usually wherever there is great wealth, there is also great splendor, haughtiness and everything in abundance. Also where many people from different lands and nations come together, numerous strange sins, iniquities and vices are found. And so it was here in Corinth, too. For we read that in Corinth there was a temple of the goddess Venus, in which more than a thousand women, fashioned in the image of Venus, lived

in open sin.[1] Satan led the Corinthians into such blindness that they considered rampant shame a service to God. Thus the city of Corinth was a groundswell of every sin, iniquity and vice. BRIEF EXEGESIS OF ACTS 18:1.[2]

CORINTH, A DEN OF IMMORALITY. RUDOLF GWALTHER: The Evangelist Luke . . . here relates the history of the conversion of Corinth, one of the richest and most corrupt cities, to Christ in which the power of Christ's Spirit and the efficacy of the gospel begin to shine so brightly and wonderfully that Paul called the church of Corinth the seal of his apostleship. Corinth because of its situation between two seas was very rich and famous, and because of all its merchandise and trade, the baits, enticements and number of merchants resorting there from all regions and coasts infected the city with the most corrupt manners, such that any riotousness was now noted in common proverbs. "They are Corinthians," they would say, "who strive for excessive luxury." This is everywhere commonly said, "It is not granted to everyone to go to Corinth." HOMILY 120, ACTS 18:1-5.[3]

THE BEGINNING OF THE CHURCH IN CORINTH. JOHN CALVIN: This story is indeed a memorable one for the single reason that it contains the beginnings of the church in Corinth. On the one hand, that church was justly renowned, both on account of its great numbers of people and on account of the extraordinary gifts with which they had been endowed, and, on the other, it was troubled by gross and disgraceful faults. Moreover, Luke makes it plain here how great was the labor and how many were the dangers and difficulties by which Paul won them for Christ. It is well enough known how populous a city Corinth was, how rich it was

on account of its fame as a trading center and how devoted it was to pleasure. In fact, the old proverb, "It is not granted to everybody to go to Corinth," testifies that it was extravagant and full of debauchery.[4] When Paul goes into it, what hope, I ask you, can he have in his mind? He is an unknown, little man, lacking eloquence or brilliance, making no show of wealth or power. From the fact that this huge whirlpool did not swallow up his confidence and his eagerness for spreading the gospel, we gather that he was equipped with the extraordinary power of the Spirit of God, and at the same time that God operated through his agency in a heavenly, and in no human, fashion. Accordingly it is not for nothing that he boasts that the Corinthians are "the seal of his apostleship." COMMENTARY ON ACTS 18:1.[5]

WHY CORINTH AND NOT A MORE RECEPTIVE CITY? JOHANN SPANGENBERG: Paul acts like a good doctor. He seeks out the sick. He does not travel to Corinth so that he can trade with merchants but rather so that he can preach the gospel and the kingdom of God to them. BRIEF EXEGESIS OF ACTS 18:1.[6]

CONTRARY TO HUMAN EXPECTATIONS, THE GOSPEL FLOURISHES IN CORINTH. RUDOLF GWALTHER: Paul came into this city after Athens by God's ordinance, as the outcome will show. For the Lord who promised to save his elect out of the dregs of shame, by the preaching of the gospel, had [gathered] there a great many people. This city gives us an example both of the goodness of God toward sinners and of the power of the gospel. For if someone would compare the abject and base status of Paul, who was a stranger and unknown, with the entrenched custom of sin with its glorious show of riches, with the abundance of delights, with the enticements of pleasures on every side and with the pomp and pride of merchants, his

---

[1]"The image of Venus" is an oblique reference to sexual sin. The Latin adjective for describing someone or something as belonging to or associated with Venus (*venerius*) is the root for the German *venerisch* and English *venereal*.

[2]Spangenberg, *Der Apostel Geschichte*, 158v-159r.

[3]Gwalther, *Homelyes or Sermons upon the Actes*, 677* (*In Acta Apostolorum*, 210v-211r).

[4]Calvin is referring to the phrase *non licet omnibus adire*, which is attributed to Horace.

[5]CNTC 7:128* (CO 48:423-24); quoting 1 Cor 9:2.

[6]Spangenberg, *Der Apostel Geschichte*, 159r.

attempt to go about to reform both their life and religion at once would seem altogether ridiculous. But the thing that seems ridiculous in the judgment of the flesh does not lack a most prosperous success given by the Lord. For within a year and a half, by the preaching of the gospel, with the Spirit of Christ working there, Paul set a new face on this city and publicly reformed it: a thing which no lawmaker, no matter how great of an authority, could have been able to have persuaded them. So it is not without cause that Paul rejoiced so much for the converting of this city, considering he nowhere found a more efficacious working of the gospel than there. Homily 120, Acts 18:1-5.[7]

The Lord Brings Great Ends Out of Humble Beginnings.

John Calvin: It was a severe test for Paul to find nobody at Corinth to give him hospitality except Aquila, an exile twice over. Although Aquila was born in Pontus, he had left his native land and crossed the sea to live in Rome. Again, he had been forced to leave there by an edict of Claudius Caesar. Although, I say, the city was so commodious, its wealth was so great, its situation was so pleasant and there were also so many Jews there, still Paul found no more suitable host than a man who was an exile both from his native land and a foreign country. If with such a poor beginning we compare the huge success that emerged as soon as he preached, the power of the Spirit of God will be made much clearer. We may also see how, by his extraordinary purpose, the Lord turns those things which seem to the flesh hostile and unpropitious to his own glory and the salvation of the godly. Nothing is more wretched than exile, according to the understanding of the flesh. But it was far more desirable for Aquila to become Paul's associate than to assume all the high magistracies either at Rome or in his own country. Therefore, that fortunate misfortune of Aquila's tells us that the Lord often has better regard for

our welfare when he afflicts us rather severely than if he were to deal with us with the utmost indulgence, and when he makes us go through the hardships of exile in order to lead us to the peace of heaven. Commentary on Acts 18:2.[8]

Paul Was Not Ashamed to Work at His Trade.

Desiderius Erasmus: As Peter was not ashamed to return to fishing when need required, so Paul—such a great apostle who had done such great things for Christ—was not ashamed to return to the skins he had left behind for the sake of the gospel. Nevertheless he did not in the meantime cease from his evangelical ministry. Paraphrase of Acts 18:3-4.[9]

"Your Blood Be on Your Own Heads!"

The English Annotations: This is a Hebrew manner of speaking. . . . This phrase seems to be taken from the Jewish custom of laying hands on the head of the guilty person by which they intimated that the witnesses laid that crime which they testified to on the head or to the charge of the accused person. And thus they devoted him to punishment in the same way that their [priest's] hand was on the head of the beast to be sacrificed. So, that blood is said to be laid on the head when one is guilty of the sin which deserves death. The meaning of Paul's words is, "you are guilty for your own destruction." Annotations on Acts 18:6.[10]

We Must Preach Without Fear.

John Calvin: This exhortation shows that Paul had some grounds for being afraid. For it would be superfluous to correct fear when things were quiet and favorable, and especially in the case of a man so willing and eager. Moreover when, in order to have his servant carry out his task faithfully and strenuously, the Lord begins by checking fear, we gather from that, that nothing is more unfavorable to the pure and free preaching of the gospel than the per-

---

[7]Gwalther, *Homelyes or Sermons upon the Actes*, 677-78* (*In Acta Apostolorum*, 211r).

[8]CNTC 7:129* (CO 48:424).
[9]CWE 50:112 (LB 7:738).
[10]Downame, ed., *Annotations*, LLL1r*; alluding to Josh 2:19; 2 Sam 1:16; Mt 27:25 Josh 2:19; 2 Sam 1:16; Lev 1:4; 3:2; Ex 29:10.

plexities of a petty spirit. And experience certainly shows that none of those who are hindered by this fault are faithful and whole-hearted ministers of the Word, and indeed that the only ones who are properly prepared for teaching are those to whom it has been given to overcome any sort of danger with fortitude of mind. That is why he writes to Timothy that "a spirit of timidity has not been given" to preachers of the gospel, but one "of power and love and self-control." Therefore we must note this connection of the words, *Do not fear, but speak*, for it amounts to the same thing as if he said, "Do not let fear keep you from speaking." Finally, because timidity does not deprive us of speech altogether but puts a restraint on us, so that we do not say what needs to be said, clearly and frankly, Christ mentioned both briefly. "Speak," he says, "and do not be silent," that is, "Do not speak just with half your mouth," as the common proverb goes. Besides, in these words a general rule is prescribed for ministers of the Word, that they explain simply, and without pretense or deceit, whatever the Lord wishes to be known to his church, yes, and that they do not conceal anything that is of value for the building or growth of faith. COMMENTARY ON ACTS 18:9.[11]

GOD IS WITH US WHEN NO ONE ELSE IS. THE ENGLISH ANNOTATIONS: God often permits his ministers to suffer the violence of their enemies, but still he is with them in life and death; indeed, then most when they are wholly destitute of human assistance. ANNOTATIONS ON ACTS 18:10.[12]

GALLIO THOUGHT JEWS AND CHRISTIANS WORSHIP DIFFERENT NAMES. GIOVANNI DIODATI: Gallio seems to agree with that Roman belief that the Jews worshiped a mere name because, having no corporeal image of the deity, they held the mighty, essential name of God in great reverence, which therefore they also kept secret, not daring to utter it. It is as if Gallio should say, "You Jews

worship one name, and the Christians another," the conceit of an ignorant and profane man. ANNOTATION ON ACTS 18:15.[13]

THE ROMANS HATED THE JEWS. JOHN CALVIN: Such non-interference ought to be attributed not so much to the sloth of the proconsul as to hatred of the Jewish religion. The Romans would have wished for the memory of the true God to be buried; and so, because it was lawful for them to offer and pay vows to all the idols of Asia and Greece, it was a capital offense to perform religious rites to the God of Israel. In a word, when common license was given to all superstitions, the only exception was the true religion. That is why it comes about that Gallio takes no notice of the injuries to Sosthenes. He had just acknowledged that he would avenge injuries if any were inflicted; now he allows an innocent man to be beaten before his judgment seat. What gave rise to such tolerance, except that he wished all the Jews to perish from wounds they inflicted on each other, so that their religion might be destroyed along with them? But when, through the mouth of Luke, the Spirit condemns Gallio's negligence, because he does not assist and protect a man who is afflicted unjustly, let our own magistrates realize that there will be far less excuse for them if they close their eyes to injuries and wrongs, if they do not restrain the impudence of the wicked, if they do not reach out a hand to the oppressed. But if a just condemnation awaits the lazy and idle, how terrible is the judgment that threatens the treacherous and malicious who countenance bad causes and are indulgent to crimes, as if they are under a standard raised to impunity and so are fans for encouraging people to be bold in inflicting injury. COMMENTARY ON ACTS 18:17.[14]

DID GALLIO ACT JUSTLY? JOHANN SPANGENBERG: In the first part he acts justly; in the second part he acts unjustly. Because he is a proconsul and

---

[11]CNTC 7:134* (CO 48:428-29); quoting 2 Tim 1:7.
[12]Downame, ed., *Annotations*, LLL1r*; alluding to 2 Tim 4:16-18.

[13]Diodati, *Pious Annotations*, BB3v* (*I Commenti alla Sacra Biblia*, 1112).
[14]CNTC 7:138-39* (CO 48:432-33).

does not know who worships God correctly, the Jews or Paul, he acts wisely because in a questionable matter he does not want to be judge. He does not act like many magistrates today who want to judge and rule in religious matters but who know just as much about them as an ass knows about bagpipes. But Gallio acts unjustly in that he allows the innocent man Sosthenes to be beaten before his eyes. It is fitting indeed for the magistracy to be sure that no one suffers violence or injustice, whether he is a Jew or Christian. BRIEF EXEGESIS OF ACTS 18:12-17.[15]

---

[15]Spangenberg, *Der Apostel Geschichte*, 163r-v.

18:18-28 PAUL'S ITINERANCY AND THE MINISTRY OF APOLLOS

[18]After this, Paul stayed many days longer and then took leave of the brothers[a] and set sail for Syria, and with him Priscilla and Aquila. At Cenchreae he had cut his hair, for he was under a vow.[19]And they came to Ephesus, and he left them there, but he himself went into the synagogue and reasoned with the Jews. [20]When they asked him to stay for a longer period, he declined. [21]But on taking leave of them he said, "I will return to you if God wills," and he set sail from Ephesus.

[22]When he had landed at Caesarea, he went up and greeted the church, and then went down to Antioch. [23]After spending some time there, he departed and went from one place to the next through the region of Galatia and Phrygia, strengthening all the disciples.

[24]Now a Jew named Apollos, a native of Alexandria, came to Ephesus. He was an eloquent man, competent in the Scriptures. [25]He had been instructed in the way of the Lord. And being fervent in spirit,[b] he spoke and taught accurately the things concerning Jesus, though he knew only the baptism of John. [26]He began to speak boldly in the synagogue, but when Priscilla and Aquila heard him, they took him aside and explained to him the way of God more accurately. [27]And when he wished to cross to Achaia, the brothers encouraged him and wrote to the disciples to welcome him. When he arrived, he greatly helped those who through grace had believed, [28]for he powerfully refuted the Jews in public, showing by the Scriptures that the Christ was Jesus.

a Or brothers and sisters; also verse 27　b Or in the Spirit

OVERVIEW: For Reformation commentators, Paul's extensive travels credibly display his zeal for the truth of the gospel, even in willing to accommodate his home and habits to others. This extensive journey also shows his enduring interest in seeking God's provision for other teachers and preachers who sustain these ministerial duties after he moves on. In this passage, Apollos is the exemplary colleague of Paul who demonstrates great knowledge of the Scriptures, faithfulness, and eloquence. The commentators applaud Apollos for using his speaking gifts to preach, teach and illuminate others for the service of God.

18:18-23 Paul in Antioch

PAUL, A PRACTICAL PASTOR, ACCOMMODATES HIMSELF TO HIS AUDIENCE. DESIDERIUS ERASMUS: This was not a fraudulent pretense on Paul's part, but the indulgence of love. He desired that everyone should be drawn to the gospel, and on this account he accommodated himself, as far as permitted, to the feelings of all so that he might gain all for Christ—he became a Jew to the Jews, to the uncircumcised, uncircumcised. This was granted for a time to the unconquerable superstition of certain people until the evangelical truth should appear more clearly. To shave the head as a result of a vow is not in itself bad, but it is bad to rely on Jewish ceremonies of this sort. In the same way circumcision does not harm one who trusts in Christ, nor does uncircumcision. To submit to these things is sometimes a matter of charity, but only for a time, and while speaking against them whenever the opportunity arises. In other things which are evil in themselves, there must be no concession to the weakness of anyone. On the issue of fornication or idolatry Paul never made concessions to the Gentiles. In associating with them, in disregarding choice of foods, in citing their poets he sometimes accommodates himself to them. PARAPHRASE OF ACTS 18:18.[1]

A NAZARITE-LIKE VOW THAT WAS PART OF EARLY CHURCH TRADITION. GIOVANNI DIODATI: Though some understand this of Aquila, still it is more likely to be applied to Saint Paul. Nor is it very likely that it is related to the Nazarite vow, but by the Jewish history it seems that it was a kind of vow brought in by ecclesiastical custom or tradition, by which a person in great sickness or danger made a vow similar to the Nazarite vow— to abstain from wine for a time and to shave one's head for purification or cermonial preparation for the principal part of the vow, which consisted in sacrifices and offerings. Now we do not read that Paul actually performed this last act of offerings, but it may be assumed that he left those who knew about it with the opinion that he would do this in Jerusalem, where such offerings ought to be made, not elsewhere. He had no other intent in all this than solely by these indifferent actions to insinuate with the Jews who were very zealous for the ceremonies of Moses; he himself had no religious or superstitious thought in this. But through the same wisdom and charity, Paul joins himself with others who offered such offerings in the temple. ANNOTATION ON ACTS 18:18.[2]

18:24-28 *Apollos Preaches Christ Boldly*

APOLLOS KNEW THE CHRIST, BUT ONLY THROUGH JOHN. RUDOLF GWALTHER: Now Apollos was born at Alexandria, where a most famous church and school were erected, even in the time of the apostles. For from there comes this Apollos furnished with so many diverse gifts, whose labor and travail afterward appeared so great in the building up of the congregation. Luke in very few words attributes to him singular qualities, saying he is eloquent, that is to say, had a gift

aptly and in due manner to speak or reason about any topic. He is also powerful or mighty in the Scriptures, that is, possessing dexterity in handling or entreating of them, as one who had not learned them only for ostentation's sake. Moreover, he declares he was brought up in the way of the Lord, thereby attributing to him the knowledge of Christ, yet mentioning he lacked some points, when he says he knew only of John's baptism. . . .

Yet this place must not so be understood as though John had had no knowledge of Christ or had taught his disciples any doctrine contrary to Christ. For John's doctrine and Christ's was all one. For as Christ commands the apostles to preach repentance and forgiveness of sins in his name, so we read that John moved his hearers to repentance and showed them that the grace of God and salvation was to be had in Christ only. HOMILY 124, ACTS 18:24-28.[3]

ELOQUENCE IS NOT TO BE DESPISED. JOHN CALVIN: Luke first commends Apollos with two descriptions, that "he was eloquent and mighty in the Scriptures"; then he adds his zeal, faith and steadfastness. But even if Paul truly denies that the kingdom of God depends on speaking and he himself lacked the commendation of eloquence, yet skill in discussion, such as Luke praises here, is not to be despised, especially when ostentatious display is not striven after with a splendor of words. But whoever maintains the responsibility of teaching has enough to do to give a clear statement of the matter which is in question, without pretence or ambition, without bombastic words and cultivated artifice. Paul lacked eloquence; evidently the Lord intended the chief apostle to be without this virtue, so that the power of the Spirit might shine with greater brilliance in his clumsy and uncouth speech. And still he was endowed with that ability of speaking which sufficed to make the name of Christ renowned and to declare the doctrine of salvation. Finally, as the gifts of the Spirit are distrib-

---

[1]CWE 50:114 (LB 7:740); alluding to 1 Cor 9:20-21; 7:18-19.
[2]Diodati, *Pious Annotations*, BB3v* (*I Commenti alla Sacra Biblia*, 1113); alluding to Num 6:18; Acts 21:24.

[3]Gwalther, *Homelyes or Sermons upon the Actes*, 697-98* (*In Acta Apostolorum*, 217r-v).

uted in numerous and varied ways, Paul's inability to speak, if one likes to use such an expression, did not prevent God from choosing fluent ministers for himself. Moreover, so that no one might think Apollos's eloquence was profane, or empty and futile, Luke says that it was united with a greater power, that is, that he was mighty in the Scriptures. I take that expression to mean not only that he was well and soundly versed in the Scriptures but that he had a grip of their power and efficacy, so that, armed with them, he was victorious in all contests. COMMENTARY ON ACTS 18:24.[4]

ALL GIFTS ARE FROM GOD. JOHANN SPANGENBERG: What purpose does this praise serve? Many things, especially as a reminder to Christians that according to this example, they too receive their goods, graces and gifts from God and should use them rightly and well to the honor of God and for the salvation and redemption of their neighbor. It is not enough to have God's gifts; we must correctly use them to honor God and to serve and help our neighbor with them, be they riches, power, knowledge or wisdom. It is, "To whom much is given, from him much will be expected." BRIEF EXEGESIS OF ACTS 18:24-28.[5]

THE GIFTS OF APOLLOS. RUDOLF GWALTHER: We have two things to consider in the description of this person. First is the order and linking together of gifts, with which God thought good to adorn Apollos. Among these things eloquence occupies the first rank, which is a thing necessary for all persons, as well in the ministry as in the commonwealth, as daily experience declares. But whether this gift comes to a person by nature or is received by art, labor, study and travail, we know it has been a thing long since argued by the fine-witted orators and philosophers. But we follow the apostle's attributing of this gift of utterance among the gifts of the Holy Spirit. By this inspiration we say that Apollos had this gift. Second, Luke says that he was

mighty in the Scriptures and imbued with an efficacious dexterity of handling them. Thus he makes a difference between this man's godly eloquence and profane eloquence. For unless the matter entreated of be taken out of the holy Scriptures or from the mouth of God, eloquence is worthless which is occupied by trifles and ostentation rather than about things needful to be known and done. Truly the orators of the Gentiles are not to be called eloquent, who disputed and debated things well and neatly, but not pertaining to the leading of a godly and Christian life. HOMILY 124, ACTS 18:24-28.[6]

APOLLOS, WITHOUT BAPTISM, WAS ONLY HALF A CHRISTIAN. DESIDERIUS ERASMUS: This Apollos was half a Christian. He had learned from Christians the rudiments of evangelical doctrine, communicated to others with fervent zeal what he had learned and diligently taught what he knew about Jesus. But he had not yet been baptized with the baptism of Christ, which conferred a richer grace; he knew only the baptism of John, which taught repentance. He thought this enough, as he had not been fully instructed about the things Christ had taught. PARAPHRASE OF ACTS 18:24-25.[7]

THE AID OF APOLLOS. JOHN CALVIN: This had been foreseen by the brothers, who had already experienced it, when they encouraged him to undertake the journey that he had planned. But his statement that he benefited the faithful can be taken in two ways. First, he brought help to those who were less well equipped and supported them in breaking down the stubbornness of enemies; for it did not belong just to anyone to have weapons ready for sustaining a difficult battle against experienced enemies who would never have given in unless forced to do so. Or, second, he gave support to them so that their faith might not be struck down by the contra-

---

[4]CNTC 7:143* (CO 48:436); alluding to 1 Cor 4:20; 2 Cor 11:6.
[5]Spangenberg, *Der Apostel Geschichte*, 164v-165r; quoting Lk 12:48.

[6]Gwalther, *Homelyes or Sermons upon the Actes*, 698-99* (*In Acta Apostolorum*, 217v).
[7]CWE 50:115 (LB 7:740).

diction of enemies and collapse as happens very often to the weak. I take it to mean that they were helped in both ways, so that having a skilled and experienced leader they might be victorious in the conflict; second, that their faith was established on a new base, so that it was no longer in danger of tottering. Moreover, Luke seems to hint that the brothers were helped by his activity and determination, when he mentions that he disputed publicly with the Jews. For it was a sign of zeal and confidence not to avoid the public. COMMENTARY ON ACTS 18:27.[8]

SCRIPTURE IS MIGHTY FOR TEACHING AND DEFEATING THE STUBBORN. JOHN CALVIN:

This makes it clear what purpose Apollos's ability of being mighty in the Scriptures served, that is, that powerful and effectual proof was available to him for refuting enemies. The main theme of the disputation is also briefly set down, that Jesus was the Christ. For there was no controversy among the Jews that the Christ, the Deliverer, was promised, but it was not easy to persuade them that Jesus, the Son of Mary, was this Christ, through whom salvation had been offered. Therefore it was necessary for Apollos to deal with the office of Christ, so as to prove that the testimonies of Scripture have been fulfilled in the Son of Mary, and to deduce from this that he is the Christ.

Moreover, this verse is evidence that Scripture is useful not only for teaching but also for breaking down the stubbornness of those who do not give their willing assent. For our faith would not be strong enough, if there did not exist in it a clear description of those things that we need to know for salvation. Certainly if the Law and the Prophets had so much light that Apollos proved clearly from them that Jesus was the Christ, as if he pointed out the fact with his finger, the addition of the gospel ought to prove at least this, that the full knowledge of Christ is to be sought from the whole of Scripture. COMMENTARY ON ACTS 18:28.[9]

THE NEW TESTAMENT IS SIMPLY THE OLD TESTAMENT PREACHED. MARTIN LUTHER:

Christ has two witnesses to his birth and his realm. The one is Scripture or the Word composed in letters. The other is the Voice or the words proclaimed by mouth; Saint Paul and Saint Peter call this same Word a light and lamp. We cannot understand Scripture until the light shines. For by the gospel the prophets are illuminated, so that star must rise first and be seen. In the New Testament, preaching must be done orally and publicly, with the living voice, to produce in speech and hearing what earlier lay hidden in the letter and in secret vision. For the New Testament is nothing but an uncovering and a revelation of the Old Testament, as is shown when the Lamb of God opens the book with the seven seals. We also see this in the preaching of the apostles. All their preaching was simply setting forth Scripture and building on it. Thus Christ never did write his teaching himself, as Moses did his, but transmitted it orally, and commanded that it should be orally continued giving no command that it should be written. Likewise the apostles wrote little, and not all of them at that, but only Peter, Paul, John and Matthew. From the other apostles we have nothing except James and Jude, and many do not consider them apostolic writings. Those who did write do no more than point us to the old Scripture, just as the angel pointed the shepherds to the manger and the swaddling clothes, and the star pointed the Magi to Bethlehem. So it is not at all in keeping with the New Testament to write books on Christian doctrine. Rather, in all places there should be good, learned, Spirit-filled, diligent preachers without books, who extract the living Word from the old Scripture and unceasingly inculcate it into the people, just as the apostles did. For before they wrote, they first of all preached to the people by word of mouth and converted them, and this was their real apostolic and New Testament work. That is the right star which points to Christ's birth and the angelic message which tells of the swaddling clothes and the crib.

---

[8]CNTC 7:145-46* (CO 48:438).
[9]CNTC 7:146* (CO 48:439).

THE GOSPEL POSTIL FOR THE FESTIVAL OF THE HOLY THREE KINGS.[10]

CHRIST'S COMPULSION MAKES US FREE AND WILLING. PETER WALPOT: Through the Word of God they must and ought to be compelled in heart and conscience to come to his congregation, and they are called from the paths and behind the fences of their falsely twisted love and hope, to leave this behind them. . . . No other compulsion is Christ willing to have. But the devil compels and forces people into his kingdom with hangmen and henchmen, turrets, anguish and murder, with swords and pikes. Christ, however, wants to have a free and willing heart. THE GREAT ARTICLE BOOK: ON THE SWORD.[11]

---

[10]LW 52:205-6* (WA 10, 1.1:625-26); alluding to 2 Cor 4:4; 2 Pet 1:19; Rev 5:3-5 .

[11]QGT 12:282; alluding to Lk 14:21-24.

19:1-20 PAUL IN EPHESUS

And it happened that while Apollos was at Corinth, Paul passed through the inland*a* country and came to Ephesus. There he found some disciples. ²And he said to them, "Did you receive the Holy Spirit when you believed?" And they said, "No, we have not even heard that there is a Holy Spirit." ³And he said, "Into what then were you baptized?" They said, "Into John's baptism." ⁴And Paul said, "John baptized with the baptism of repentance, telling the people to believe in the one who was to come after him, that is, Jesus." ⁵On hearing this, they were baptized in*b* the name of the Lord Jesus. ⁶And when Paul had laid his hands on them, the Holy Spirit came on them, and they began speaking in tongues and prophesying. ⁷There were about twelve men in all.

⁸And he entered the synagogue and for three months spoke boldly, reasoning and persuading them about the kingdom of God. ⁹But when some became stubborn and continued in unbelief, speaking evil of the Way before the congregation, he withdrew from them and took the disciples with him, reasoning daily in the hall of Tyrannus.*c* ¹⁰This continued for two years, so that all the residents of Asia heard the word of the Lord, both Jews and Greeks.

¹¹And God was doing extraordinary miracles by the hands of Paul, ¹²so that even handkerchiefs or aprons that had touched his skin were carried away to the sick, and their diseases left them and the evil spirits came out of them. ¹³Then some of the itinerant Jewish exorcists undertook to invoke the name of the Lord Jesus over those who had evil spirits, saying, "I adjure you by the Jesus whom Paul proclaims." ¹⁴Seven sons of a Jewish high priest named Sceva were doing this. ¹⁵But the evil spirit answered them, "Jesus I know, and Paul I recognize, but who are you?" ¹⁶And the man in whom was the evil spirit leaped on them, mastered all*d* of them and overpowered them, so that they fled out of that house naked and wounded. ¹⁷And this became known to all the residents of Ephesus, both Jews and Greeks. And fear fell upon them all, and the name of the Lord Jesus was extolled. ¹⁸Also many of those who were now believers came, confessing and divulging their practices. ¹⁹And a number of those who had practiced magic arts brought their books together and burned them in the sight of all. And they counted the value of them and found it came to fifty thousand pieces of silver. ²⁰So the word of the Lord continued to increase and prevail mightily.

a Greek *upper* (that is, highland)   b Or *into*   c Some manuscripts add *from the fifth hour to the tenth* (that is, from 11 a.m. to 4 p.m.)   d Or *both*

OVERVIEW: For Reformation commentators who desire to uphold the inspiration and authority of Scripture, the details and even minutia of the sacred Scriptures are taken seriously. Often the seemingly small details connect to larger theological considerations. One of the key questions arising at the beginning of this chapter involves the relationship between John's baptism and Jesus' baptism—whether they are in essence one baptism or two. This question relates to the broader continuity between the old covenant and the new. Another theme is the role of exorcism and the reality of evil spirits working in the world in tangible ways. Preachers and ministers like Paul are the proponents of true religion against all evil spiritual forces and human sinfulness, because they stand in contrast to those who preach for the sake of material gain or the ostentatious demonstration of power.

19:1-7 Ephesian Disciples Are Baptized and Receive the Spirit

THE "SPIRIT" THEY HAD NOT HEARD OF WAS SPIRITUAL GIFTS. JOHN CALVIN: The conclusion of the story shows that here Paul is not speaking about the Spirit of regeneration but of the special gifts, which God distributed, at the beginning of the gospel and in a variety of ways, on those whom he pleased, for the general edification of the church. But now the question arises from Paul's inquiry, whether all, everywhere, had the Spirit in common at that time. For if he was being given to a certain few, why does he link him with faith, as if the connection were inseparable? Perhaps the men did not belong to the flock, or, because their number, that is, twelve, was a modest one, Paul asks whether they are all without the gifts of the Spirit. However, my own judgment is this, that so many Jews, and indeed disciples, that is, members of the flock of the faithful, were presented to the Gentiles' view at one time, not by chance but by the purpose of God, to confess, nevertheless, that previously the supreme glory of the gospel, which was conspicuous in spiritual gifts, had been unknown to them, so that luster might be given to Paul's ministry through them. For it is not likely that so few disciples were left at Ephesus by Apollos; and they would have been instructed more correctly by him, seeing that he himself had learned the way of the Lord precisely from Aquila and Priscilla. Yes, moreover, I do not doubt that the brothers whom Luke mentioned previously were different from these particular men.

To sum up, when Paul sees that these men are confessing the name of Christ, he asks whether they have received the Holy Spirit, in order to find out more precise information about their faith. For Paul himself makes it clear that this method was a sign of the grace of God, for establishing the trustworthiness of doctrine, "I wish to know whether you received the Holy Spirit by works of the Law or by the hearing of faith." . . . Paul clearly shows that [John's baptism] was a baptism of regeneration and renewal, as is ours. But because both cleansing and newness of life flow from Christ alone, he says that it has been founded on his faithfulness. We are also taught by these words that because of faith in Christ we may lay hold of all that it figures, it being far from the case that the

outward sign diminishes the grace of Christ in any way. Commentary on Acts 19:2.[1]

They Had Scriptural but Not Personal Knowledge of the Holy Spirit. Johann Spangenberg: These disciples are not talking about the being or nature of the Holy Spirit or about the common gifts that he works in human beings but rather about the extraordinary, remarkable gifts that he worked in the apostles and the believers after Christ's resurrection and ascension. It is as if they wanted to say, "That the Holy Spirit exists, *this* we obviously know from Scripture; but that he appeared visibly in fiery tongues on believers, *that* we have not heard." For this question of Paul's—"Into what were you baptized?"—is nothing other than as if he wanted to say, "Who were your preachers and baptizers? Through whom did you come to Christian faith?" Brief Exegesis of Acts 19:1-3.[2]

John's Baptism Fulfilled in Christian Baptism. Rudolf Gwalther: "In whose name were you baptized?" That is to say, what did you profess, when you first received the gospel and joined yourselves to the church of Christ? . . . They testified that they professed that doctrine and religion of which John was a minister and teacher, and thereby they plainly show they care little for any other than that. Now Paul here catches them and holds them fast, and . . . teaches that John required a very different thing of his disciples than a bare profession of his name and of the gospel. For first he appointed repentance, to which with great earnestness he exhorted all degrees of persons, as it appears. Nor does he require only repentance, but also he shows remission of sins, preaching Jesus Christ whose forerunner he was appointed by God to be. He taught people to embrace Christ by true faith, to follow him, to give themselves wholly to him, because in him only those things were to be

---

[1]CNTC 7:148-49, 150* (CO 48:440, 441); alluding to Acts 18:27; Gal 3:2.
[2]Spangenberg, *Der Apostel Geschichte*, 167r.

found which are figured by outward baptism. For who is able to perform them without the operation of the Holy Spirit? Therefore the glory you have in John your teacher is of so little sufficiency that his doctrine and baptism with which you were baptized compels you to go further and so to cling to Christ, that being grafted in him through a lively faith, and made alive in his Spirit, you may declare by the very effects of the Holy Spirit that you are true Christians.

That this is the very plain and unfettered meaning of Paul's words the whole order of the history proves. Those who are foolish err when they go about to prove that John's baptism and Christ's are not the same, but different. For this is so far from Paul's meaning that it rather proves how people are sent by John's baptism of water to Christ, in whom the tokens we receive in baptism are grasped. Here a general rule is also confirmed: how it is not to be accepted that they who are true worshipers of God should stay or rest on human authority but that they ought to be urged to give themselves wholly to Christ, to live in him by the quickening of his Spirit, lest while they profess him with their mouth, they declare by their deeds, how they be farthest away from him. Homily 125, Acts 19:1-7.[3]

John's Baptism Incomplete. Hans Hut: The baptism by John with water is incomplete and can free no one from sin, for it is only a symbol, a preparation and a pattern of the true baptism in Christ. Therefore, all of [the elect] have to be baptized differently in Christ. Christ enters [the soul] symbolically in baptism, in that he destroys his true form in favor of his true essence. Thus Christ had to be baptized first, as an example for us, that in him everything came true. For in the death of Christ we are all members of one body in the equality of dying which is consented to under the sign. . . . Christ came to be baptized by John in order to humble himself beyond other human beings, to retake on himself our proud nature which

had deviated from God and to make it obedient to God again through baptism, which he shows and in which each must be baptized into a new creature through the killing of our evil, disobedient, insolent nature in order to wash away all sins and human weakness. . . . So everyone will live to Christ who dies to Adam. But whoever does not want this baptism always remains in the dead Adam. Therefore baptism is a struggle to kill sin throughout our whole life. On the Mystery of Baptism.[4]

John's Baptism Only Dressed the Wound. Desiderius Erasmus: "No sin has been committed because some time ago, before the light of the gospel appeared, you received the baptism of John. But this does not suffice for eternal salvation. The teaching of John was not an end in itself, but only witnessed to Jesus, the true author of salvation who would come after John. It was a teaching that prepared people's minds so that they might believe in the one who was coming. Likewise the baptism of John did not confer perfect righteousness but only encouraged people to prepare their hearts by repenting of their former life for the physician soon to come, who by his baptism would through faith abolish all sins, and through his own Spirit would enrich the souls of believers with celestial gifts. The Lord Jesus handed down to his apostles this command, to baptize in the name of the Father and of the Son and of the Holy Spirit those who had believed in the Gosepl word." This is the way those deserve to be taught who have in all sincerity gone astray. Paraphrase of Acts 19:5.[5]

Baptism by Water Not to Be Repeated. John Calvin: [John's baptism] was a token and pledge of the same adoption and the same newness of life which we receive in our baptism today. Therefore we do not read that Christ baptized afresh those who came over to him from John. . . . And indeed there is no need of a long refutation,

---

[3]Gwalther, *Homelyes or Sermons upon the Actes*, 706-7* (*In Acta Apostolorum*, 220r).

[4]Hans Hut, "On the Mystery of Baptism," in *The Radical Reformation*, ed. and trans. Michael G. Baylor (Cambridge: Cambridge University Press, 1991), 168*.

[5]CWE 50:116* (LB 7:741).

because in order that [our opponents] may convince us that the baptisms are different, they must necessarily show, first of all, how the one differs from the other. But the resemblance and correspondence to each other is excellent, and there is a symmetry and similarity of all parts, which forces us to admit that it is the same baptism.

But now the question is asked whether it was right to repeat it. And fanatical people of our day, relying on this evidence, have tried to introduce Anabaptism. Some take the word *baptism* for new instruction; and I do not agree with them for the reason that their explanation, forced as it is, smacks of evasion. Others deny that baptism was repeated, because they had been baptized wrongly by some foolish imitator of John. But because their conjecture has no substance, and, what is more, because Paul's words suggest that they were true and genuine disciples of John, and Luke does them the honor of calling them disciples of Christ, I do not subscribe to this opinion also; and yet I do deny that the baptism of water was repeated, because Luke's words imply nothing else but that they were baptized with the Spirit. COMMENTARY ON ACTS 19:5.[6]

JOHN'S BAPTISM IS INSUFFICIENT. JOHANN ECK: Further it should be known that John's baptism was not a mighty sign of divine grace; it did not grant grace. It functioned as the intent to be baptized, just like in other good works.[7] This is clear from John's words in the prologue, "I baptize with water, but the One who is coming will baptize with the Holy Spirit." John washed the body alone; he accomplished nothing in the soul. Thus, as we heard earlier, it was called a baptism of John. Now when Saint Peter baptized it was not Saint Peter's baptism. So, Saint John alone baptized. Nowhere

do we read or find that John's disciples baptized [see Biel]; in contrast, Christ himself did not baptize, but his disciples did baptize. It follows from this that John's baptism is no sacrament of the new law, because it was not a mighty sign of divine grace, nor does it correspond to the old covenant. Therefore, it was a foreshadowing of and preparation for the new covenant.

It follows from this why someone baptized with John's baptism had to be baptized again with Christ's baptism, as Saint Paul baptized the Ephesians. . . . It is as Saint Augustine says: "Those whom Judas baptized should not be baptized again, for Christ baptized them; however, those baptized by John should be baptized again, for Christ did not baptize them." I am not against [John's baptism]; if John had kept the same form of baptism as the apostles who baptized next to him, then they were correctly baptized and no one should be allowed to baptize them again. THE SEVENTH SERMON, ON THE BAPTISM OF JOHN.[8]

IF JOHN'S BAPTISM IS INSUFFICIENT, THEN INFANT BAPTISM IS INSUFFICIENT. PETER WALPOT: Now then, if John's baptism is insufficient, though it was indeed from God, and Paul baptizes [these Ephesians] again and correctly, then how much more is infant baptism absolutely insufficient, which was introduced, conceived and established not by God but by the devil and by human beings. Infants or nursing children know much less about the Holy Spirit, have received him much less than the twelve here received and who never understood that there is even a Holy Spirit. Thus, all believers who were muddied with infant bap-

---

[6]CNTC 7:150-51* (CO 48:441-42).
[7]Eck's reference to intent here is analogous to what the Roman Catholic Church refers to as "the desire for baptism," namely, that if someone dies, clinging to Christ, although not baptized, "their intention of receiving [baptism] and their repentance for past sins will avail them to grace and rigteousness" (*The Catechism of the Council of Trent*, 124-25).

[8]Eck, *Christenliche Predigen*, 4:11v; quoting Mk 1:8; Mt 3:11; alluding to Jn 4:2; citing Augustine, "Tractate 5 on John 1:33" (NPNF 7:38). Biel agrees with Thomas Aquinas that John's baptism does not confer grace; instead, it points to Christ. As well it only preached the remission of sin; it did not actually effect such remission. Gabriel Biel, *Epitome et collectorium ex Occamo circa quatuor sententiarum Libros* (Tübingen, 1501; reprint, Frankfurt am Main: Minerva, 1965), 4.2.2 (unpaginated); see also John L. Farthing, *Thomas Aquinas and Gabriel Biel: Interpretations of St. Thomas Aquinas in German Nominalism on the Eve of the Reformation* (Durham, NC: Duke University Press, 1988), 134.

tism, which is no baptism, must and ought to allow themselves to be baptized again and correctly. As little as Paul is a rebaptizer in this passage, much less the believers today. THE GREAT ARTICLE BOOK: ON BAPTISM.[9]

THESE EPHESIANS SHOW THE CHIEF TENET OF BAPTISM. DIRK PHILIPS: John, in his baptizing, taught the people whom he baptized repentance, confession of their sins and faith in Jesus Christ. How much more appropriate it is then at baptism to teach those being baptized in such a manner and to require this of them. It is also important to note and remember that some disciples who were already baptized with the baptism of John knew nothing about the baptism of the Holy Spirit. These Paul baptized again or commanded that they be baptized in the name of the Lord Jesus. How much more then is it appropriate that those who were baptized under the papacy, without any knowledge or awareness of the difference between good and evil, yes, without the true knowledge of the almighty God and his only begotten Son and the Holy Spirit in ignorance, according to the papal manner, that they should not allow themselves to be satisfied with that, but receive Christian baptism orderly in the pure knowledge of the Holy Trinity and on the confession of their faith, according to the word and command of the Lord. THE ENCHIRIDION: THE BAPTISM OF OUR LORD JESUS CHRIST.[10]

THE PAEDOBAPTISTS REVEL IN THEIR LIES. PETER WALPOT: There are some who are willing to be content with infant baptism and will not [let themselves] be baptized again or correctly.... But whoever believes that he is correctly baptized having been baptized as an infant does not believe in God but rather in the pope, priests and liars! Infant baptism is not founded on God's Word but is founded completely on falsified Scripture, that is,

on straw and stubble. How can someone teach me the goldsmith craft who is not himself a goldsmith? Thus, no one can make me a Christian who is not himself a Christian....[11]

Since we until now have unknowingly submitted ourselves to antichrist, our Lord and Master Christ Jesus will have no pleasure until we submit to his command and allow ourselves to be correctly baptized, since infant baptism is no baptism but a feast of the great harlot, the pope. For if someone tries to spend a gold coin and finds out it is actually a wooden token, he will certainly be disappointed. THE GREAT ARTICLE BOOK: ON BAPTISM.[12]

BAPTISM DEPENDS ON CHRIST'S PROMISE. MARTIN LUTHER: How can we think that God's Word and ordinances should be wrong and invalid because we use it wrongly! Therefore, I say, if you did not believe before, then believe now and confess, "The baptism indeed was right, but unfortunately I did not receive it rightly." I myself, and all who are baptized, must say before God: "I come here in my faith and in the faith of others; nevertheless, I cannot build on the fact that I believe and many people are praying for me. Instead, I build on this, that it is your Word and command." In the same way I go to the Sacrament not on the strength of my own faith but on the strength of Christ's Word. I may be strong or weak; I leave that for God to decide. This I know, however: that he has commanded me to go, eat and drink, and that he gives me his body and blood; he will not lie or deceive me.

Thus we do the same with infant baptism. We bring the child with the intent and hope that it may believe, and we pray God to grant it faith. But we do not baptize on this basis but solely on the command of God. Why? Because we know that God does not lie. My neighbor and I—in short, all people—may deceive and mislead, but God's Word cannot deceive.

---

[9]QGT 12:68. Peter Riedemann uses the same argument; see CRR 9:191-92.
[10]CRR 6:98-99* (BRN 10:98).

[11]The editors of the QGT note that this is a "fundamental principle" for the Radicals. See Leonhard Schmeier, "The Twelve Articles of the Christian Faith: Concerning the True Baptism of Christ [1527]," CRR 12:259-61 (QGT 17:298-340).
[12]QGT 12:101-2; alluding to 1 Cor 3:10-15.

Therefore only presumptuous and stupid spirits draw the conclusion that where there is no true faith, there also can be no true baptism. Likewise I might argue, "If I have no faith, then Christ is nothing." Or again, "If I am not obedient, then father, mother and magistrates are nothing." Is it correct to conclude that when people do not do what they should, the thing they misuse has no existence or value? Friend, rather reverse the argument and conclude in this way: Baptism does have existence and value, precisely because it is wrongly received. For if it were not right in itself, no one could misuse it or sin against it. The saying goes, "Misuse does not destroy the substance but confirms its existence."[13] Gold remains no less gold if a harlot wears it in sin and shame. The Large Catechism.[14]

In Baptism the Heavenly Priest Pours Out the Fullness of Grace. Johann Eck:

Everything that took place in the baptism of John, Saint John himself did, but Saint Peter, or any other priest who baptizes, does the smallest part of this act, merely the external pouring of the water. But God completes it; he pours grace into the soul and purifies it from sin. Therefore it does not matter who the minister of the Sacrament is, whoever he may be or however he may act. We should look to Christ alone, who baptizes all who are baptized. The Seventh Sermon, On the Baptism of John.[15]

We Believe in One Baptism, One Word, One Spirit. Johann Spangenberg: When we speak of the baptism of John, we do not merely mean the dipping in water but everything that belongs to baptism—teaching, preaching and baptizing. So then, there is one baptism of John and Christ—one water, one Spirit, one Word. John preaches exactly what Christ preaches, namely, the law and the gospel, repentance and the forgiveness

of sins. John said, "Repent! The kingdom of heaven is near." Christ said, "Repent and believe in the gospel." . . . To speak tersely, John baptizes and forgives sins just as well as Christ and the apostles, but to give the Holy Spirit visibly in fiery tongues, as he was given to the apostles, this John is not able to do. For at the time Christ was not yet transfigured through the resurrection and ascension but still walked the earth in the form and figure of a servant in order to die on the cross and to save us from the devil, death, sin and hell. To him be the praise, honor and glory forever and ever, Amen. Brief Exegesis of Acts 18:25-26.[16]

Were These Twelve Rebaptizers? Johann Spangenberg: Far from it! That Luke says, "They were baptized in the name of Christ," we should not understand concerning water baptism but rather concerning fire baptism. That is, Paul preached to them about Jesus Christ, how he suffered, was crucified and died, rose again from the dead, ascended to heaven and obtained the Holy Spirit for us. Such a sermon they had never heard. Now, after they heard the good news and Paul laid his hands on them, the Holy Spirit comes on them, and they speak with tongues and prophesy. Brief Exegesis of Acts 19:6-7.[17]

Cling to the Forgiveness Sealed to You in Baptism. Martin Luther: In Christ—indeed, in our baptism, since we are baptized into Christ—we have the forgiveness of sins without ceasing. So even if you fall and sin out of weakness—as happens, alas, too much and too often, without ceasing—then run and crawl to your baptism, in which all your sins are forgiven and washed away; draw comfort; lift yourself up again; and believe that in baptism you were washed not only from one sin but from all your sins. For just as the baptized Jesus Christ does not die but lives and remains in eternity, so the forgiveness of sin is also

---

[13]*Abusus non tollit, sed confirmat substantiam.* See also LW 40:248* (WA 26:161).
[14]BoC 463-64* (WA 30, 1:219-20).
[15]Eck, *Christenliche Predigen*, 4:11v.

[16]Spangenberg, *Der Apostel Geschichte*, 165r-166r; alluding to Eph 4:4-6; quoting Mt 3:2; Mk 1:15.
[17]Spangenberg, *Der Apostel Geschichte*, 167v-168r.

eternal, [the forgiveness] that he won for you and gave you as a gift. Therefore, baptism is a glorious washing, one that washes away sins and purifies. Whatever is not washed away and remains left in us is forgiven. Accordingly, whatever baptism does not purge altogether is nevertheless completely purified through the forgiveness of sins that we receive in baptism. . . . If I stumble and fall into sin, then I should repent and crawl to the cross, go there and fetch my pure and white robe with which I was clothed in baptism, where all my sins, if they are not completely washed away, are nonetheless forgiven, because the forgiveness is altogether pure! That is what I cling to! SERMON ON THE DAY OF CHRIST'S EPIPHANY (1546).[18]

19:8-10 Paul's Ministry in Ephesus

THE IMPORTANCE OF THE SABBATH FOR CHRISTIANS. JOHN DONNE: As our being itself comes before all degrees of well-being, so is the Sabbath, which reminds us of our being, before all other festivals which present to and refresh for us the memory of our well-being. This is especially true for us to whom it is not only a Sabbath—as a day of rest in respect to creation—but *Dies Dominicus*, the Lord's Day, in respect of the redemption of the world. This is because the consummation of the work of redemption for all accomplished in the world, the resurrection of our Lord and Savior Christ Jesus, was accomplished on that day—*that* is our Sabbath. SERMON ON THE SUNDAY AFTER THE CONVERSION OF SAINT PAUL (1627).[19]

THE REPROBATE ARE HARDENED BY THE TRUTH. JOHN CALVIN: We do not read that Paul was heard by Jews anywhere so quietly and with such forbearance as he was when he first came to Ephesus. For while others raised an uproar and drove him out, he was asked by them to stay longer. Now, after he has tried for three months to set up the kingdom of God among them, the ungodliness

and stubbornness of many reveals itself. For Luke says that they were hardened. And the heavenly doctrine has this particular power, that it either turns the reprobate into a fury or makes them more obstinate; and it does so not because of its own nature but accidentally, as people say, because, when the truth presses hard on them, their hidden venom breaks out. COMMENTARY ON ACTS 19:9.[20]

BELIEVERS SEPARATE THEMSELVES FROM THE WORLD. PETER RIEDEMANN: Paul . . . separates the faithful from the unbelievers. Accordingly, we also wish in this matter and in all things, to be worthy to receive with him the promise of the inheritance. This is possible, insofar as it is in us to follow Christ as our Master. With his help we will keep his command and covenant, not turning aside from it to the right or to the left. May he give us and all others who wholeheartedly want it, his grace to do this, through Jesus Christ our Lord. Amen. CONFESSION OF FAITH.[21]

19:11-20 The Seven Sons of Sceva

HEALING THROUGH HANDKERCHIEFS AND APRONS PROVES CHRIST'S POWER. THE ENGLISH ANNOTATIONS: This does not support the superstitious use of relics. God's providence did this, so that by such cures he might prepare the absent and those who had never seen the face of Paul to a reverend esteem and opinion of the gospel and truth of Christ, in whose name they were cured; also, so that in these means—so slender and improbable themselves—the power of Jesus healing them might be demonstrated more clearly. ANNOTATIONS ON ACTS 19:12.[22]

ABUSE OF THE LORD'S NAME. JOHANN SPANGENBERG: There were Jews who through the name Tetragrammaton practiced a great deal of superstition and magic, and they imagined that they drove

[18]LW 58:3667-68 (WA 51:116).
[19]Donne, *Works*, 2:316-17*.
[20]CNTC 7:153* (CO 48:444).
[21]CRR 9:180.
[22]Downame, ed., *Annotations*, LLL2r*.

out the devil [in this way], but in truth they accomplished nothing. The devil deceived these people by a mirage, as if they drove one [demon] out, but really in its place a hundred flew back in. For how could such people who abuse God's name drive out the devil? Brief Exegesis of Acts 19:13.[23]

But Aren't They Using a Holy Name? Johann Spangenberg: All the worse! For who will say that it is right to use God's Word for magic and devilry! Then a drunkard could defend himself, saying, "That I'm drunk is no sin! I'm using the pure and good creation of God: beer and wine." Again, a Mass priest would want to say, "Mass is good; I'm using the pure and good Word." Is the matter answered by this? Not at all! We must consider the reasons and purposes why they hold Mass—when this is done, it will quickly be seen that such a papist Mass-in-a-nook[24] is far worse than any magic or blasphemy. The reason: They abuse God's Word, deny Christ's ministry and attribute to their own works what should only be attributed to the precious blood of Christ. Brief Exegesis of Acts 19:13.[25]

God Possesses Those Who Possess the Possessed. The English Annotations: The possessed man fell violently on them, and, by the power of the evil spirit in him, mastered them, tearing their cloths and wounding them. Sometimes the devil willingly cooperates with the conjurers and witches, allowing himself to be mastered, perhaps even driven out. . . . He does this so that he can enter men or women to conspire with him for mischief, holding them—and others through them—in superstition. But here he had some other purpose, and God thus defeated their mischievous practices, making everything serve the advancement of the gospel that Paul preached. Annotations on Acts 19:16.[26]

The Power of Saying "Amen." Valentin Weigel: Now "Amen" is as much as [saying], "The Lord is a true King," according to Jewish Kabbalah, to pray in the name of Christ, to pray in his Spirit, to walk in his life. When we remain in Christ and he in us, we pray in his name, for daily we experience anguish and suffering because of our sin and blindness. O how many there are who place the name of Christ in their mouth and recite the Our Father, as the seven [sons of Sceva] employed the name of Christ, using it on the possessed. . . . Whoever does not pray "hallowed be your name" commits blasphemy against the divine name and desecrates the One who remains forever sacred. But whoever prays this [petition] protects himself from such desecration. Church or House Postil for the Fifth Sunday After Easter.[27]

The Sacred Name of Jesus Is Exalted. The English Annotations: Here we see the fruit of this divine revenge on those who impiously profane the holy name of Jesus. First, by their example, others were afraid to condemn this teaching that God so mightily supported. Second, everyone began to magnify the sacred name of Jesus. The report of this incident made everyone afraid, not only to blaspheme his name as some of the Jews did, but even to place the words in their profane mouths, to abuse it as these sons of Sceva did. Annotations on Acts 19:17.[28]

The High Price of the Gospel Grants Priceless Salvation. Desiderius Erasmus: Money was lost but the gospel gained, for by these means the Word of the Lord grew exceedingly and prevailed—a saving word to those who embraced it with unfeigned faith, but terrible for those who took it up less honestly. Paraphrase of Acts 19:19-20.[29]

---

[23]Spangenberg, *Der Apostel Geschichte*, 170r; alluding to Mt 12:43-45.
[24]*Winckelmess*. Spangenberg is mocking the practice of saying private Masses.
[25]Spangenberg, *Der Apostel Geschichte*, 170r-v.
[26]Downame, ed., *Annotations*, LLL2r-v*.

[27]Weigel, *Sämtliche Schriften*, 12, 2:252.
[28]Downame, ed., *Annotations*, LLL2v*.
[29]CWE 50:118 (LB 7:743).

19:21-41 THE RIOT AT EPHESUS

²¹Now after these events Paul resolved in the Spirit to pass through Macedonia and Achaia and go to Jerusalem, saying, "After I have been there, I must also see Rome." ²²And having sent into Macedonia two of his helpers, Timothy and Erastus, he himself stayed in Asia for a while.

²³About that time there arose no little disturbance concerning the Way. ²⁴For a man named Demetrius, a silversmith, who made silver shrines of Artemis, brought no little business to the craftsmen. ²⁵These he gathered together, with the workmen in similar trades, and said, "Men, you know that from this business we have our wealth. ²⁶And you see and hear that not only in Ephesus but in almost all of Asia this Paul has persuaded and turned away a great many people, saying that gods made with hands are not gods. ²⁷And there is danger not only that this trade of ours may come into disrepute but also that the temple of the great goddess Artemis may be counted as nothing, and that she may even be deposed from her magnificence, she whom all Asia and the world worship."

²⁸When they heard this they were enraged and were crying out, "Great is Artemis of the Ephesians!" ²⁹So the city was filled with the confusion, and they rushed together into the theater, dragging with them Gaius and Aristarchus, Macedonians who were Paul's companions in travel. ³⁰But when Paul wished to go in among the crowd, the disciples would not let him. ³¹And even some of the Asiarchs,ᵃ who were friends of his, sent to him and were urging him not to venture into the theater. ³²Now some cried out one thing, some another, for the assembly was in confusion, and most of them did not know why they had come together. ³³Some of the crowd prompted Alexander, whom the Jews had put forward. And Alexander, motioning with his hand, wanted to make a defense to the crowd. ³⁴But when they recognized that he was a Jew, for about two hours they all cried out with one voice, "Great is Artemis of the Ephesians!"

³⁵And when the town clerk had quieted the crowd, he said, "Men of Ephesus, who is there who does not know that the city of the Ephesians is temple keeper of the great Artemis, and of the sacred stone that fell from the sky?ᵇ ³⁶Seeing then that these things cannot be denied, you ought to be quiet and do nothing rash. ³⁷For you have brought these men here who are neither sacrilegious nor blasphemers of our goddess. ³⁸If therefore Demetrius and the craftsmen with him have a complaint against anyone, the courts are open, and there are proconsuls. Let them bring charges against one another. ³⁹But if you seek anything further,ᶜ it shall be settled in the regular assembly. ⁴⁰For we really are in danger of being charged with rioting today, since there is no cause that we can give to justify this commotion." ⁴¹And when he had said these things, he dismissed the assembly.

a That is, high-ranking officers of the province of Asia   b The meaning of the Greek is uncertain   c Some manuscripts *seek about other matters*

OVERVIEW: During Paul's stay in Ephesus, a great disturbance breaks out because of his vehement preaching against idolatry. Because of the temple of Artemis in Ephesus (one of the seven wonders of the ancient world), silver shrines generated a great deal of revenue for local businesses. The commentators see much contemporary relevance for their own day; their critique of excessive dependence on idols and images is meant to denounce ultimate reliance on any created object or ritual. In most cases, they themselves adopt Luke's tone of critique that links idolatry to wrong motivations of profit and greed. The commentators agree that the Ephesus riot, like other controversies in their own time, was prompted primarily by inordinate desire for money and wealth, and only secondarily by religious zeal (although piety often serves as a plausible pretext).

19:21-27 Demetrius and the Trade in Silver Shrines

PAUL'S TRAVEL PLANS ARE SCRIPTURE, TOO.
JOHANNES BRENZ: Although many things in divine literature seem not to relate to us and to be written nonchalantly, nonetheless, because sacred Scripture is the work of the Holy Spirit, let us not think that anything in it, even the most minute and unessential thing, is so useless that it does not reward someone who scrutinizes it carefully. For although in the natural world many things are found which, even if they seem as if they are created as a bane for the human race, such as snakes and poisonous bramble toads and other things of that sort, when studied more carefully and collected for the right use offer significant benefits. All the more, those things that in Scripture appear to be superfluous and nonchalant hold their own fruit. If the Holy Spirit, who is the author of Scripture, creates something out of nothing, how is he not able to give enormous blessings to believers through the minutiae of Scripture? Wherefore, that which follows, that Paul proposed that he should set forth into Macedonia, Achaia, Jerusalem and afterwards Rome, although it seems not to relate to us, nevertheless, once scrutinized and explicated, it can only be of great advantage to us....

So why are these details related to us? What value do they hold for us? All sorts of value. For we are presented with Paul's immense and tireless diligence in administrating his apostolic gift. First, this is done that we might see how true faith in the gospel of Jesus Christ is not in the least nonchalant and just how great is the efficacy of faith in believers; and second, that we might also be invited by the example of Paul to serve diligently and faithfully, each one in his own calling. HOMILY 91 ON ACTS 19.[1]

DEMETRIUS AND THE TEMPLE IN EPHESUS.
JOHANNES BRENZ: Before we explain this oration of Demetrius, we have to indicate who Diana was and what sort of temple she had in Ephesus. For these things shed some light on this passage.

Diana was believed by the Greeks to be a goddess of hunting and of pathways, likewise the nourisher of all the wild beasts and living creatures. For this reason she also has the name Polymasthon, that is, the many-breasted. And with this name a temple was set up in her honor, which was by far the most celebrated of all, acclaimed in the whole world and counted among the chief wonders of the world, as pagan writers testify. And although everyone was amazed at the wonderful structure, so much so that even enemies who were ravaging Asia Minor with sword and fire were sparing it, still it was not able to escape a fire.... Once it had perished by this fire, it was restored again by the Ephesians and by all the Asians with greater expense and workmanship, and it lasted for four hundred years. In it was placed a wooden image of Diana, which an Ephesian writer later said fell from heaven. ... When we know the details of the case, we can understand more easily what is going on in this passage. HOMILY 91 ON ACTS 19.[2]

DEMETRIUS IS AN EXAMPLE OF THE GREEDY AMONG US TODAY. JOHN CALVIN: But in the case of Demetrius it is plain how injurious the plague of avarice is. For one man, in the interests of his own private gain, does not hesitate to throw a great city into an upheaval with sedition. But the artisans, who are like torches set alight by him and spreading fire everywhere, are a warning to us, how easy it is to incite sordid people, who are devoted to their bellies, to any sort of crime, especially if their living comes from an unrewarding occupation and their expectation of making money is snatched away....

Accordingly, with the warning of such examples, let us learn to choose the kind of life that is consistent with the teaching of Christ, so that eagerness for gain may not incite us to take up arms in an impious and wicked battle. But let those who, through ignorance or error, have fallen into some bad occupation, or have become entangled in some other vicious and impure way of life, nevertheless be on their guard against such rash sacrilege. But

---

[1]Brenz, *In Acta Apostolica Homiliae*, 183r-v.

[2]Brenz, *In Acta Apostolica Homiliae*, 184r-v.

as far as godly teachers are concerned, let them learn by this example that they will never lack adversaries until the whole world procures peace by self-denial, and *that*, we know, will never happen. Commentary on Acts 19:24.[3]

Demetrius Sold Trinkets of This Landmark. The English Annotations: "Silver temples" ... were made in some such form.[4] These silver shrines or medals of silver with the form of their idol Diana's  temple impressed or wrought on it Demetrius sold to those who came to Ephesus either due to superstition to worship or curiosity to see the magnificent structure of that temple. Annotations on Acts 19:24.[5]

Demetrius Appears Prudent and Pious. Johannes Brenz: By this speech Demetrius wants to seem pious and prudent. For prudent people work for the provision of their family and see to it that they do not go hungry. Pious people have regard for the public religion over and above their own vocation. But if you shake out the character of Demetrius, you will find, instead of true prudence and piety, in reality a seditious and impious character. For he did not formulate the piece that he delivered about defending the majesty of Diana from the zeal of his religious fervor but a zeal for his profit and from greed.

Furthermore, even if the religion of Diana were true, though it is very false, still Demetrius would be defending her impiously, given that he was pleading his case for his own gain under the pretext of religion. Pious prudence and prudent

piety in obtaining provision and preserving profit make an effort, first, to learn a craft or business that is in accord with the Word of God. Second, it makes an effort to handle this craft or business to no one's detriment but is engaged in it with a love toward one's neighbor. When a craft is engaged in out of faith and love, it is naturally followed by the Lord's blessing. Therefore, whoever desires piously to pursue profit, let him not do it to accumulate by his business or craft much employment at the expense of his neighbor but to give attention to piety and to be content with a little. A great profit is piety together with a mind content with its own lot. That this may be the case for us, we will pray to our Lord Jesus Christ, who as God together with the Father and the Holy Spirit must be praised forever, Amen. Homily 91 on Acts 19.[6]

Do Not Pay Too Much Attention to Finances. John Calvin: A man is entitled to pay a certain amount of attention to his own private source of income. But it is certainly a thoroughly disgraceful thing to disturb the public peace, to pervert human and divine justice, to stoop to violence and slaughter, to make a serious attempt at destroying what is just and right, for his own interest. Demetrius admits that the heart of the matter is that Paul says that gods made by human hands are not gods at all. He does not inquire whether that is true or not, but, blinded by his passion for money making, he is driven to destroy the true teaching. The same blindness rushes him into violent remedies. Also, because the workmen are afraid that they will suffer poverty and hunger, they are just as violent in their haste. For the belly is deaf and blind, so that it permits no fairness. Accordingly each one of us ought to be all the more critical of himself, when his personal gain and advantage are in question, so that that cupidity, which drove those men to madness, may not remove all distinction between the just and the unjust and the disgraceful and the honest. Commentary on Acts 19:25.[7]

---

[3]CNTC 7:160-61* (CO 48:450).
[4]The *English Annotations* take this image from Beza's annotations; see Beza, *Annotationes Majores*, 1:541. For some contemporary thoughts on the wares of Demetrius and his associates, see Bruce J. Malina and John J. Pilch, *Social-Science Commentary on the Book of Acts* (Minneapolis: Fortress, 2008), 140-41.
[5]Downame, ed., *Annotations*, LLL2v*.

[6]Brenz, *In Acta Apostolica Homiliae*, 184v.
[7]CNTC 7:162* (CO 48:451).

19:28-41 *"Great Is Artemis of the Ephesians!"*

TRUST IN GOD SHOULD NOT MAKE US RECK-LESS. DIRK PHILIPS: The Christians at Ephesus also knew and indeed believed that God is almighty and could certainly protect Paul from all his enemies. Nevertheless they would not permit Paul to go among the people and give them a reply. But now some wish to expel the teachers into the midst of their enemies, even when it has been shown before their eyes how extremely bloodthirsty the world is and with abominable tyrannies persecutes the teachers unto death. But what kind of a spirit, disposition and love these people have may be seen and understood [when compared with] the example of these disciples . . . at Ephesus. THE ENCHIRIDION: THE SENDING OF PREACHERS.[8]

PAUL FILLS HIS MOUTH DAILY WITH THE SAVOR OF DEATH. JOHN DONNE: Who dies more than once? Yet Paul dies often. How often? Death that is every other man's everlasting fast and fills his mouth with earth was Saint Paul's *panis quotidianus*, his daily bread. "I protest," he says, "by your rejoicing which I have in Christ, I die daily." SERMON ON THE SUNDAY AFTER THE CONVERSION OF SAINT PAUL (1627).[9]

WHO ARE ASIARCHS? GIOVANNI DIODATI: This name is sometimes attributed to certain public people who were sent from the cities of Asia Minor as procurators in public business for the Greek cities in Asia, to Ephesus which was the chief of them, sometimes also to certain priests which oversaw public plays and sports which were shown in public theaters in honor of the gods. ANNOTATION ON ACTS 19:31.[10]

PEOPLE ARE PROVOKED AS EASILY AND VIOLENTLY AS THE SEA. THE ENGLISH

ANNOTATIONS: People, like great waters, are easily enraged but seldom well-informed why. False rumors fill their ears and ungoverned passion their hearts with disdain and vehement desire of some new unconsidered undertakings, the purpose of which they neither prudently foresee nor cautiously examine. ANNOTATIONS ON ACTS 19:24.[11]

WHY DID THE JEWS PUT ALEXANDER FORWARD? GIOVANNI DIODATI: It is likely that the Ephesians were equally agitated against the Jews and the Christians. This Alexander was brought in by the Jews to defend their nation against any occasion of hatred which might be perceived against them and to lay all the blame on the Christians. Or, since the pagans often conflated the Christians and the Jews, taking one for the other, this Alexander was supposed to show them the great difference between them. ANNOTATION ON ACTS 19:33.[12]

WHY DID THE EPHESIANS REFUSE ALEXANDER? JOHANN SPANGENBERG: When they see Alexander,[13] who motions with his hand and who wants to make a defense before the people, knowing he is a Jew, they believe that he too will mock their goddess Diana as idolatry. Therefore they all cried out with a single voice and chanted for about two hours, "Great is Diana of the Ephesians." It is as if they wanted to say, "If someone should mock our goddess in this way, who will tolerate it? Diana is a goddess of such majesty and might, of such honor and grandeur, that not only throughout Asia but also throughout the entire world spiritual people rush here and worship her. What good can follow from [her denial]? What sort of misfortune do you mean to bring over us? We would much rather die than to tolerate such a heavenly image being despised." BRIEF EXEGESIS OF ACTS 19:34.[14]

---

[8]CRR 6:229 (BRN 10:240).
[9]Donne, *Works*, 2:319-20*.
[10]Diodati, *Pious Annotations*, BB4r* (*I Commenti alla Sacra Biblia*, 1115).
[11]Downame, ed., *Annotations*, LLL2v*.
[12]Diodati, *Pious Annotations*, BB4v* (*I Commenti alla Sacra Biblia*, 1115).
[13]Spangenberg identifies this Alexander as the coppersmith who caused Paul such harm (2 Tim 4:14).
[14]Spangenberg, *Der Apostel Geschichte*, 176v-177r.

WHAT DOES THE TOWN CLERK TEACH US?

JOHANN SPANGENBERG: Luke here shows us an example of civic intelligence and tactfulness, namely, how in such cases a friendly instruction is more useful than angrily threatening, chiding and chastising. After everything that happened, this town clerk with his friendly words calmed the uproar and everyone went home. BRIEF EXEGESIS OF ACTS 19:35-41.[15]

IS THE TOWN CLERK'S WISDOM USEFUL IN THE CHURCH?

JOHANN SPANGENBERG: Certainly. Such civic intelligence is a gift from God. Just as we should ask God for common peace, so also we should ask for this gift from God, so that God would grant such civic wisdom, tactfulness and friendliness to rulers and magistrates; thus they may rule their subjects in peace. See here, this town clerk is not angry, he does not rage, he does not hurl back some insult, but instead with friendly exhortation he measures his words and speech, so that they must be quiet to hear and not instigate anything further. BRIEF EXEGESIS OF ACTS 19:35-41.[16]

THE LORD'S PROVIDENT CARE.

RUDOLF GWALTHER: Luke demonstrates the effect of this speech by showing that this crowd that was so unruly just moments before, dispersed peacefully. As common folk are easily stirred into an uproar, so also they are easily pacified again, if someone deals with them through reason and good sense rather than through violence. And here we see the provident care of God by which he delivers and defends his children. As this same God is accustomed to raise the waves of the sea with sudden blasts of wind and suddenly quiets them again, in the same way he tests his children with dreadful storms of dangers, and when he sees fit he still restores them without any harm. Therefore, trusting his goodness and power, let us persevere with stout courage, assuring ourselves that through Christ Jesus our Lord and most faithful and invincible Defender, we have the upper hand against the efforts of the wicked. HOMILY 130, ACTS 19:35-41.[17]

---

[15]Spangenberg, *Der Apostel Geschichte*, 178v.
[16]Spangenberg, *Der Apostel Geschichte*, 178v-179r.
[17]Gwalther, *Homelyes or Sermons upon the Actes*, 728* (*In Acta Apostolorum*, 226v).

20:1-16 PAUL'S JOURNEY
TO MACEDONIA, GREECE AND TROAS

After the uproar ceased, Paul sent for the disciples, and after encouraging them, he said farewell and departed for Macedonia. ²When he had gone through those regions and had given them much encouragement, he came to Greece. ³There he spent three months, and when a plot was made against him by the Jews[a] as he was about to set sail for Syria, he decided to return through Macedonia.⁴Sopater the Berean, son of Pyrrhus, accompanied him; and of the Thessalonians, Aristarchus and Secundus; and Gaius of Derbe, and Timothy; and the Asians, Tychicus and Trophimus. ⁵These went on ahead and were waiting for us at Troas, ⁶but we sailed away from Philippi after the days of Unleavened Bread, and in five days we came to them at Troas, where we stayed for seven days.

⁷On the first day of the week, when we were gathered together to break bread, Paul talked with them, intending to depart on the next day, and he prolonged his speech until midnight. ⁸There were many lamps in the upper room where we were gathered. ⁹And a young man named Eutychus, sitting at the window, sank into a deep sleep as Paul talked still longer. And being overcome by sleep, he fell down from the third story and was taken up dead. ¹⁰But Paul went down and bent over him, and taking him in his arms, said, "Do not be alarmed, for his life is in him." ¹¹And when Paul had gone up and had broken bread and eaten, he conversed with them a long while, until daybreak, and so departed. ¹²And they took the youth away alive, and were not a little comforted.

¹³But going ahead to the ship, we set sail for Assos, intending to take Paul aboard there, for so he had arranged, intending himself to go by land. ¹⁴And when he met us at Assos, we took him on board and went to Mitylene. ¹⁵And sailing from there we came the following day opposite Chios; the next day we touched at Samos; and[b] the day after that we went to Miletus. ¹⁶For Paul had decided to sail past Ephesus, so that he might not have to spend time in Asia, for he was hastening to be at Jerusalem, if possible, on the day of Pentecost.

a Greek *Ioudaioi* probably refers here to Jewish religious leaders, and others under their influence, in that time; also verse 19 b Some manuscripts add *after remaining at Trogyllium*

OVERVIEW: Just as traveling marks the passing of long distances, so also the experiences of ministry mark the passing of time. Now as an older, senior apostle, Paul travels throughout Macedonia and Greece to visit and encourage fellow believers. The reformers highlight Paul's work in spite of his own weariness and suffering as a model for Christian mission, finding true peace in Christ through the fellowship of the Holy Spirit among other Christians as they frequently gather for worship. Finally, the miraculous resuscitation of the young man Eutychus affirms and commends the work of Paul's ministry and the preaching of the gospel as truly life-giving.

20:1-6 Paul in Macedonia and Greece

TIMING OF PAUL'S LETTERS AND TRAVELS.
GEORG MAJOR: In the twenty-second year of Paul's conversion, the fifty-fifth year after Christ's birth and the thirteenth year of Claudius's reign—after the Ephesian tumult had been sedated—Paul traveled to Macedonia, visiting the cities and churches where he had taught before. In the city of Philippi, having written the second letter to the Corinthians, which he sent through Titus and Luke, whom he sent ahead to collect alms in Corinth and Achaia and coming soon after them, he remained in Greece and particularly in Corinth for three months. At that time the Epistle to the

Romans, written in Corinth, was sent through Phoebe the minister of the church at Cenchreae. Now Paul had spent his time continually proclaiming the gospel to all from Jerusalem to Illyricum, as he reports in Romans 15, where he says, "Now I must travel to Jerusalem to minister to the saints." For it seems that to Macedonia and Achaia . . . he sent ahead Titus and Luke from Corinth to collect alms in order to share fellowship with the poor saints who were in Jerusalem. LIFE OF PAUL.[1]

IN THE MIDST OF TRAGEDY, WE MUST SUPPORT EACH OTHER. JOHN CALVIN: The church at Ephesus was still young and feeble. Having once experienced an unexpected tumult the faithful could have been justifiably afraid of similar storms springing up from time to time. There is no doubt that Paul was reluctant to leave them, yet because greater need calls him elsewhere, he is forced to leave his recently begotten children in a heaving sea, hardly yet clear of one shipwreck as they are. . . . Although Paul's departure is a sad and bitter experience, still they do not keep him back or detain him, in case they might do harm to other churches. So we see that they were not self-centered, but that they honored the kingdom of Christ by their care and devotion, so that they had regard for the brothers as well as for themselves. This example ought to be carefully noted, so that we may take pains to help each other in this lamentable dispersion of ours. COMMENTARY ON ACTS 20:1.[2]

PAUL TENDS TO THE CHURCH LIKE A GARDENER OR A FATHER. JOHANN SPANGENBERG: Paul came to Greece and spent three months there. Here you see Paul's diligence. The congregations which he planted and built at Philippi, Thessalonica, Athens and other places, he wants to water and console them so that they do not wither but instead grow much stronger. The church is like a garden or a vineyard. A garden must be watered

with dew or rain; otherwise it will go to ruin from heat and drought. In the same way Christian congregations also wither through tribulation, affliction and persecution. So then, they must be watered and sustained with the water and consolation of the Holy Spirit. . . .

It is a merciless father who does not give his children physical sustenance, but how much more merciless is a preacher who deprives his people of the spiritual sustenance of God's Word! Through Christ Paul had given birth to many spiritual children; thus, he wants to nourish them with spiritual sustenance. So he testifies in Greece for three months. BRIEF EXEGESIS OF ACTS 20:3.[3]

NO GOOD COMES FROM WICKEDNESS. JOHANNES BRENZ: Paul is pressed on every side by adversities because of his diligent administration of his office. He lacks friends. The hostile Jews, when they are not able to kill him openly and legally on land, devise plots against him on the sea to kill him and throw him overboard into the deep sea. They were imagining that they would finally be at peace and happy if they should kill Paul, who alone was a splinter in their eyes, and they obviously thought they would extinguish the gospel, if only they could extinguish him. . . . But you see, no one ever has obtained peace and happiness through wicked deeds, but instead extreme misery and affliction. The gospel is more watered by the blood of the apostles than it is choked off and extinguished. . . . Thus the Pharisees imagined they would attain some sort of blessedness if they killed Christ. But all these people realized their wishes in casting out and killing did not achieve peace of mind; [instead,] they were overwhelmed by much greater disasters after realizing their wishes. Therefore, no one should hope that they will acquire anything good through wickedness, but rather learn from the Word of the Lord that wickedness is the source of every curse and all devastation. HOMILY 94 ON ACTS 20.[4]

---

[1]Major, *Vita S. Pauli Apostoli*, C7v-C8r; alluding to Rom 16:1-2; quoting Rom 15:25.
[2]CNTC 7:167* (CO 48:455).

[3]Spangenberg, *Der Apostel Geschichte*, 181v, 182v.
[4]Brenz, *In Acta Apostolica Homiliae*, 188v-189r; alluding to Mt 7:3-5.

**IF PREACHING IS SO DANGEROUS AND
THANKLESS, WHY DOES PAUL CONTINUE TO
DO IT?** JOHANN SPANGENBERG: How could he
quit? Cross and persecution should frighten no
one away from his vocation in civic matters, much
less in divine matters. However, Paul does not
tempt God; he slips away from present danger.
Because he observed that his trip to Syria was not
safe, he turned back to Macedonia. From this we
should learn that each person should maintain his
vocation despite any present danger. For God is a
trustworthy God who can transform all things for
the best. BRIEF EXEGESIS OF ACTS 20:3.[5]

PAUL'S CONSTANCY IN AFFLICTION. JOHN
CALVIN: God disciplined his servant in a variety of ways and incessant struggles, so that he
might present to us an indefatigable example of
steadfastness. As if it were not enough that he is
exhausted by the effort and irksomeness of a long
and difficult journey, there is also the added threat
of a plot for his life. Let all the servants of Christ
place this mirror before their eyes so that irksome
difficulties may never cause them to faint. However,
when Paul turns his steps in another direction and
avoids the ambush prepared for him, he is showing,
at the same time, that we must have regard for our
own lives to the extent that we do not rashly rush
into the midst of dangers. Surely the companions
who accompany him give no ordinary proof of
their loyalty; and we see how precious his life was
to the faithful when several chosen associates from
different nations undertake a hard, rough journey
at great expense for his sake. COMMENTARY ON
ACTS 20:3.[6]

**GOD PROVIDES HUMAN EMOTIONAL SUP-
PORT.** JOHANNES BRENZ: So that we might see
that God is faithful and does not allow anyone to
be tested beyond their capabilities (yes, he makes
the outcome along with the temptation such that
it can be endured), although many of his friends

failed Paul and his enemies were plotting for his
life, still God joined to him certain companions,
the best of men, by whose company he was considerably invigorated amid his afflictions. . . . It is
not for nothing that Luke mentions such devoted
companionship for Paul. First, he tacitly commends the clemency of God, because although
Paul had many false friends and true enemies, still
God endowed him with many sincere friends and
brothers, from whose intimacy he found some
consolation in his adverse situations. Second, he
indicates with how much concern the churches
of Christ attended to Paul. For these companions
seem to have accompanied Paul under the name
and support of their own church. . . .

But here notice the diverse judgments and
inclinations of people. Some were judging Paul as
rubbish for throwing out, but others were treating
him as an angel of God. Some night and day were
plotting for his life, but others were guarding him
as if he were the most precious pearl. . . . What is
the source of this diversity of judgments? It is definitely from the fact that the gospel which Paul was
preaching is for some the smell of death to death,
for others the smell of life to life. Accordingly, for
those whom the gospel is the smell of death, they
seek the destruction and death of the evangelist.
But for those whom it is the smell of life, they
attend to those who proclaim the gospel as if they
are the ministers of their own life, not bodily, but
spiritual and eternal. HOMILY 94 ON ACTS 20.[7]

20:7-16 Eutychus Raised from the Dead

CHRIST IS THE LAMP OF THE CHURCH. RU-
DOLF GWALTHER: [Luke] says there were diverse
candles lighted in the chamber to put away the
darkness of the night and for avoiding the suspicion of dishonesty. . . . For here it is plainly night
time when it is necessary for candles to be lit. For
the same reason afterward, Christians used candles
in their assemblies, because they could not meet
together but in the morning before day because

---

[5]Spangenberg, Der Apostel Geschichte, 183v-184r.
[6]CNTC 7:168* (CO 48:456).

[7]Brenz, In Acta Apostolica Homiliae 189r; alluding to 2 Cor 2:16.

of their enemies, as appears in the letters of Pliny the Younger.[8] . . . This cause being taken away, it is but foolishness to help the daylight with artificial lights. It is evident there was another meaning of the candlestick in Leviticus. For as all the ceremonies of that priesthood were figures of things that Christ should perform and were ordained only until the time of correction, so the candlestick also was a figure of Christ, who is the true and eternal Light of the world, and who by the ministry of the gospel lightens his church, for this reason the apostles and they who are their true and lawful successors are called the light of the world. HOMILY 132, ACTS 20:7-16.[9]

A PITHY SUMMARY OF PUBLIC WORSHIP.

GIOVANNI DIODATI: The ecclesiastical assembly [came together] . . . to celebrate the sacrament of the holy supper, together with the meal of charity. Now under this principle part which terminates and ends all the rest, we must understand all those parts that went before, namely, prayers, expounding of the Word, praise. ANNOTATION ON ACTS 20:7.[10]

THE IMPORTANCE OF CORPORATE WORSHIP.

RUDOLF GWALTHER: By this passage we learn that such days as God has appointed for service or religion ought not to be neglected by Christians. They are necessary not only because of outward worship but also inward, which consists mainly in the study of God's Word and in the diligent meditation of his benefits. The body and mind for the time would be cleanly separated from all profane mat-

ters, which was the reason that God commanded the breakers of the Sabbath to be punished with death. The breaking of the Sabbath is accounted by the prophets among the most heinous sins and causes of the Babylonian captivity. It was not without cause that Nehemiah thought it was his duty to see that day kept holy when the people returned from their captivity. [Consider] also the example of Christ, who as he oftentimes on the Sabbath day went into the synagogues, so he at different times disputed diligently of the right use of that day to deliver it both from superstition and from contempt. Then he shows also the place where this company or assembly met. This was a loft or chamber in the private house of one of the faithful, who appointed it for the church or congregation, because the Christians, for good reason, abhorred the temples of the idolaters, and they had no public place permitted them because the Roman procurators ruled in every place, who either did not favor the Christian religion or else were open enemies of it. HOMILY 132, ACTS 20:7-16.[11]

THROUGH SYNECDOCHE, BREAD INDICATES THE BODY AND BLOOD.

JOHANNES BRENZ: Let us hear now what miraculous thing happened in Troas. . . . Now, assuming they came together to partake of the Lord's Table, . . . it is evident both from the institution of the Lord's Table, whereby it was ordained that both bread and wine, that is, the body and blood, be received, and from the Hebrew phrase, by which, under the term "bread," both food and drink are meant, that the disciples in Troas consumed not only the body of Christ but also his blood. . . .

From this story first it must be observed what should be done during the breaking of the bread of the Lord's Table. "Paul was talking to them," he says. Therefore, there should be talking and preaching of the gospel of Jesus Christ. For even Christ himself commands it, saying, "Do this in remembrance of me," that is, in Paul's interpretation, "As often as

[8]Pliny the Younger (62–113) was the governor of Bithynia-Pontus during the reign of the Emperor Trajan (53–117). Gwalther is referring to Pliny's correspondence with the emperor concerning what to do with Christians; see Henry Bettenson and Chris Maunder, eds., *Documents of the Christian Church*, 3rd. ed. (Oxford: Oxford University Press, 1999), 3-5, here 4. For background and analysis of Pliny and this letter, see Robert L. Wilken, *The Christians as the Romans Saw Them* (New Haven, CT: Yale University Press, 1984), 1-30.

[9]Gwalther, *Homelyes or Sermons upon the Actes*, 734* (*In Acta Apostolorum*, 228r); alluding to Lev 24:1-4.

[10]Diodati, *Pious Annotations*, BB4v* (*I Commenti alla Sacra Biblia*, 1115); alluding to Acts 2:42.

[11]Gwalther, *Homelyes or Sermons upon the Actes*, 733-34* (*In Acta Apostolorum*, 228r).

you come together to eat this bread and drink of the cup, you will proclaim the death of the Lord until he comes." Therefore, it is not a correct use of the Lord's Table when in some corner the Mass is muttered in a private little rite, so that those who are standing near see nothing except gesturing and the raising and waving of the hands, but they do not hear any word of the gospel of Jesus Christ, to say nothing meanwhile about the impious opinion whereby the Mass is celebrated as if it were a work that gives satisfaction for sins. But if indeed the disciples in Troas broke the bread of communion, it can easily be inferred with how much diligence and majesty of the preaching of the gospel they conducted the rite of the Lord's Table, who with such great piety consumed the bread of communion. HOMILY 94 ON ACTS 20.[12]

ANCIENT PRACTICE CHASTISES CONTEMPORARY EXPECTATIONS. RUDOLF GWALTHER: The manner that Paul used in his preaching pertains to the description of the assembly of the church, which we may conjecture based on the time. First he prolonged his sermon until midnight. Then, when supper was done, he discoursed until daybreak of things pertaining to religion. Therefore his teaching was not for presentation's sake, or careless as to whether or not he made the most of this opportunity, but with great zeal and diligence. As he had a right judgment of his ministry and knew he was sent by God to be an ambassador for Christ, he therefore was very fervent in zeal, because he would not be counted as an untrustworthy ambassador for God. It is evident that the hearers had as good a judgment of Paul's ministry as of his doctrine, because they intended to bear with him so patiently all night long.

By this example the sloth of our age is reproved and the great contempt of God's Word. For in the ministers appear not those tokens of the apostolic zeal, because many of them are occupied more in vain studies than in the meditation of God's Word and think they have well discharged their duty if

they make one or two cold collations in a week. Again, the people that cannot stand long to hear think every minute of an hour that they spend in hearing of God's Word is a whole day, whereas in trifling studies, yes, in filthy and dishonest, they think no time, no cost, no labor too much. Here it comes to pass that the authority of the ministry is despised and the Word of God kept from a great many. HOMILY 132, ACTS 20:7-16.[13]

DO NOT SLEEP DURING SERMONS. JOHANNES BRENZ: Take note of the unshakable perseverance of Paul in preaching the gospel. He does not think that he has failed in his duty, if for a long time he speaks only of divine Scriptures but protracts his sermon all the way to midnight. Even then, he did not grow weary and cease, but he spoke together with the disciples, surely concerning matters of piety, all the way until dawn. But the longer Paul teaches piety, the more a certain young man by the name Eutychus, who is sitting in the window, is overcome by deep sleep. Because he was overcome by sleep, he fell from the third story and was lifted up dead. Those who often sleep during the delivery of divine sermons should keep this example in mind. Because this young man so carelessly and so lazily paid attention to Paul's sermon that he fell asleep, by God's just judgment he collapsed and died. Yes, those who do not hear the Word of God with the greatest care and vigilance not only show that they have no regard for their own salvation but also have the highest contempt and disdain for the majesty of God. Those who do not care about their salvation and disdain the divine majesty certainly are worthy of extreme punishment. Therefore, we must stay awake during divine sermons and diligently pay attention, lest we be overcome by sleep and earn death by our sleep. Homily 94 on Acts 20.[14]

NO REASON TO CONDEMN EUTYCHUS. JOHN CALVIN: I see no reason why certain com-

---

[13]Gwalther, *Homelyes or Sermons upon the Actes*, 735* (*In Acta Apostolorum*, 228v).

[14]Brenz, *In Acta Apostolica Homiliae*, 189v.

[12]Brenz, *In Acta Apostolica Homiliae*, 189r-v.

mentators condemn the young man's sleepiness so strongly and sharply by saying that he was punished for his lethargy with death. For what is strange about his struggling with sleep at the dead of night and finally succumbing? One may gather from the fact that he was attacked and overpowered by sleep against his will and contrary to his expectation, that he had not settled down to rest. It would have been a sign of laziness to try to get a suitable place for sleeping. But what else is his being overwhelmed by sleep, when sitting in the window, but innocently yielding to natural weakness, just as if someone lost consciousness from fasting or excessive fatigue? COMMENTARY ON ACTS 20:9.[15]

IF PAUL BROUGHT EUTYCHUS BACK TO LIFE, THEN SURELY HE DID NOT SIN BY SLEEPING?

JOHANN SPANGENBERG: Paul resurrected this boy from death, so that by this miracle he might show that the preaching of the gospel is not the voice of death but rather of life, not of destruction but rather of salvation; and that the gospel leads no one to destruction other than those who scorn it, hear and treat it inattentively. BRIEF EXEGESIS OF ACTS 20:9-11.[16]

REMARKABLE DILIGENCE IN BOTH AUDITOR AND AUDIENCE.

THE ENGLISH ANNOTATIONS: This was an extraordinary occasion; Paul was pressed for time in light of his upcoming departure and zealous for their edification and confirmation in faith. This was a singular example of Paul's unwearied diligence and his audience's vigilance, patience and willingness to hear the Word. It will once rise in judgment to condemn negligent speakers and drowsy, secure and impatient hearers of today who might deservedly hear what Christ once said to his weak disciples, "So, you could not watch with me one hour?" ANNOTATIONS ON ACTS 20:11.[17]

ANOTHER MIRACLE CONFIRMS THE WORD.

JOHN CALVIN: When Paul embraces the body of the dead man, he is indicating by this gesture that he is offering it to God to be restored to life. And one may gather from the context that he did not give up his embrace until he knew that life was given back to it. . . . We must observe that the chief cause of Paul's concern was that this sad event might not shake the faith of the godly and trouble their minds. At the same time, the Lord ratified the last sermon that Paul delivered at Troas, as if with a seal impressed before their eyes. When he says that his soul is in him, he is not denying that he was dead, because he would be obliterating the glory of the miracle in that way, but the meaning is that life was restored to him by the grace of God. I do not restrict the subsequent statement that they felt greatly comforted to the joy that they had at the young man's recovery, but at the same time I include the confirmation of their faith, because God had given them such a remarkable token of his love. COMMENTARY ON ACTS 20:10.[18]

PAUL RUSHES TO JERUSALEM TO ENCOURAGE THE CHURCH.

JOHN CALVIN: There is no doubt that Paul had strong and important reasons for hurrying to Jerusalem, not because the sacredness of the day meant such a lot to him but because foreigners were in the habit of flocking to Jerusalem from all directions for the feast days. Because he hoped that he would do some effective work in such a great multitude, he did not wish to miss the opportunity. Let us therefore realize that worship according to law did not enter into the reason for his making such great haste, but that what he had in mind was the upbuilding of the church, partly by reporting to the faithful that the kingdom of Christ had been extended, partly by winning any who were still unfamiliar with Christ, partly by repelling the calumnies of impudent people. COMMENTARY ON ACTS 20:16.[19]

[15]CNTC 7:170* (CO 48:457).
[16]Spangenberg, *Der Apostel Geschichte*, 187r.
[17]Downame, ed., *Annotations*, LLL3r*; quoting Mt 26:40.
[18]CNTC 7:170-71* (CO 48:458).
[19]CNTC 7:172* (CO 48:459).

20:17-38 PAUL'S FAREWELL TO THE EPHESIAN ELDERS

[17]Now from Miletus he sent to Ephesus and called the elders of the church to come to him. [18]And when they came to him, he said to them:

"You yourselves know how I lived among you the whole time from the first day that I set foot in Asia, [19]serving the Lord with all humility and with tears and with trials that happened to me through the plots of the Jews; [20]how I did not shrink from declaring to you anything that was profitable, and teaching you in public and from house to house, [21]testifying both to Jews and to Greeks of repentance toward God and of faith in our Lord Jesus Christ. [22]And now, behold, I am going to Jerusalem, constrained by[a] the Spirit, not knowing what will happen to me there, [23]except that the Holy Spirit testifies to me in every city that imprisonment and afflictions await me. [24]But I do not account my life of any value nor as precious to myself, if only I may finish my course and the ministry that I received from the Lord Jesus, to testify to the gospel of the grace of God. [25]And now, behold, I know that none of you among whom I have gone about proclaiming the kingdom will see my face again. [26]Therefore I testify to you this day that I am innocent of the blood of all, [27]for I did not shrink from declaring to you the whole counsel of God. [28]Pay careful attention to yourselves and to all the flock, in which the Holy Spirit has made you overseers, to care for the church of God,[b]which he obtained with his own blood.[c] [29]I know that after my departure fierce wolves will come in among you, not sparing the flock; [30]and from among your own selves will arise men speaking twisted things, to draw away the disciples after them. [31]Therefore be alert, remembering that for three years I did not cease night or day to admonish every one with tears. [32]And now I commend you to God and to the word of his grace, which is able to build you up and to give you the inheritance among all those who are sanctified. [33]I coveted no one's silver or gold or apparel. [34]You yourselves know that these hands ministered to my necessities and to those who were with me. [35]In all things I have shown you that by working hard in this way we must help the weak and remember the words of the Lord Jesus, how he himself said, 'It is more blessed to give than to receive.'"

[36]And when he had said these things, he knelt down and prayed with them all. [37]And there was much weeping on the part of all; they embraced Paul and kissed him, [38]being sorrowful most of all because of the word he had spoken, that they would not see his face again. And they accompanied him to the ship.

a Or *bound in*   b Some manuscripts *of the Lord*   c Or *with the blood of his Own*

Overview: Based on Paul's departing speech to the Ephesian elders, Reformation commentators focus on the qualities of a good minister. In summary, Paul is the quintessential model of a faithful teacher, demonstrating a thorough grasp of the gospel as well as a life lived in strong faith. His tireless effort to serve believers in the midst of trials emerges, for our commentators, as a constant encouragement to others to repent and believe. Instead of serving God halfheartedly, ministers of the Word ought to live a purposeful life. By instructing others in the Scriptures and exposing ignorance, they are building up the kingdom of God with their wholehearted devotion to God's calling. The commentators also describe the traits of bad ministers—wolves, disguised as shepherds, who ravage the sheep for their meat and fleece.

Paul's Sermon Is an Exhortation to Bishops. Heinrich Bullinger: The speech of Paul, which Luke described in this place, is elegant beyond measure and not any less useful, espe-

cially . . . to those who, as prefects of the churches, sufficiently uphold a perilous office. If they are wise, they will want to reflect night and day on Paul's speech. In most other passages exhortation and advice are mixed together throughout. But all [essential] things are reported here, so that they may continue in the correct doctrine of truth and may faithfully distribute this to the churches. They do not dread labors or seek their own gain but separate themselves from the heretics; they are very attentive in all their responsibilities. Everywhere, however (according to his own custom), he blends pleas and spurs to persuade. Truly through his deep and sure fatherly love and care the entire oration gives the impression of a heart aflame [through the Spirit]. Therefore, just as we have said, in his whole speech, Paul teaches nothing other than what sort of people should be bishops, that is, ministers of the gospel, to whom the salvation of souls is entrusted. From this they have an example set before them to imitate. So he explains his own affairs with a brief enumeration, so that they might view things properly, as he leaves with them successors in the work of God's Word. COMMENTARY ON ACTS 20:17-21.[1]

MINISTERS MUST SET THEIR MINDS ON THE RIGHT COURSE.
JOHN CALVIN: He commends his own faithfulness and diligence in teaching in three particulars, that he gave the disciples sound and thorough instruction, so that he omitted nothing which made for their salvation, that, not satisfied with general preaching, he also took pains to be of service to individuals. In the third place he summarizes the whole of his teaching saying that he urged them to have faith in Christ and to repent. Now, since he is portraying for us the model of a good and faithful teacher, the proper course for all who wish to make their labor acceptable to the Lord is to have the upbuilding of the church set before their eyes. . . .

But Paul prescribes such zeal for edifying, so that a pastor may omit nothing, as far as he is

concerned, that it is beneficial to know. For teachers who keep their pupils at first principles, so that they never attain to knowledge of the truth, are bad teachers. And surely the Lord does not instruct us by half measures in his Word but teaches wisdom that is perfect and complete in every way. That makes it plain that those who not only conceal and encourage the ignorance of the people by their silence but also take no notice of gross errors and impious superstitions, are impudent in their boasts that they are ministers of the Word. COMMENTARY ON ACTS 20:20.[2]

WHAT BELONGS TO CHRISTIAN TEACHING?
JOHANN SPANGENBERG: Repentance and faith. Repentance embraces the law; faith, the gospel. These things a Christian must know, namely, what the law is, what purpose it serves and how we should use it. Likewise [a Christian should] also [know] what the gospel is, what purpose it serves and how we should use it. Through this Saint Paul wants to show what traits the minister of the Word should have, namely, humility, kindness, studiousness. And when tribulation and persecution occur, they should console people and conceal nothing that belongs to salvation. BRIEF EXEGESIS OF ACTS 20:20-21.[3]

THE GOSPEL OF REPENTANCE AND FAITH.
HEINRICH BULLINGER: There are two things that the gospel teaches: contrition (*poenitentia*), which is repentance of mind and life, and faith, which is founded on Christ Jesus' death and stirs up courage (*fidutia*). Indeed these things should be proclaimed not only to Jews, but also to all Gentiles. COMMENTARY ON ACTS 20:21.[4]

BUILD YOUR TOLERANCE FOR DEATH BY DRINKING IT DAILY.
JOHN DONNE: As cordials lose their virtue and become no cordials if they are taken every day, so poisons do their venom too. If a man adapts himself to them in small proportions

---
[1]Bullinger, *In Acta Apostolorum*, 252v-253r.

[2]CNTC 7:174* (CO 48:461); alluding to 1 Tim 4:6-10.
[3]Spangenberg, *Der Apostel Geschichte*, 188v-189r.
[4]Bullinger, *In Acta Apostolorum*, 253v.

at first, he may grow to take any quantity. He who takes a dram of death today may take an ounce tomorrow, and a pound the next. He who begins with that mortification of denying himself his delights (which is a dram of death) shall be able to suffer the tribulations of this world (which is a greater measure of death) and then death itself, not only patiently but cheerfully. And to such a man death is not a dissolution but a restoration, not a divorce of body and soul but a sending of both ways (the soul upward to heaven, the body downward to the earth) to an indissoluble marriage to him who, for the salvation of body and soul, assumed body and soul—our Lord and Savior Jesus Christ. SERMON ON THE SUNDAY AFTER THE CONVERSION OF SAINT PAUL (1627).[5]

CHRIST'S PROMISES SOOTHE THE BELIEVERS' FEARS. HEINRICH BULLINGER: Now, however, lest they be excessively grieved, Paul adds words of consolation: "I don't worry about the chains at all, or even about death. For my temporal life is not more beloved to me than Christ and the truth, in whom I will live eternally, if in the end I do not fail in the function placed on me. There is nothing dearer to my heart than for me to follow faithfully in the duty assigned to me. Just as I have shown the grace of God exhibited through Christ in the world, I set forth with the greatest persistence and readiness of my soul. I beseech the bishops to read these things, [especially] they who are frightened by the fear of death, so that they may with all truth be resilient." Death is indeed harsh, and more horrible for the body than is able to be said, but the mind is to be comforted by the goodness of heavenly things, which will undoubtedly follow those who have scorned earthly things. . . . Your salvation is dearer to you than life, just as his ministry was dearer to Paul than even his own life. He preferred to risk his life rather than not to follow that ministry strenuously. COMMENTARY ON ACTS 20:24.[6]

LIVE FOR GOD, NOT FOR LIFE. JOHN CALVIN: All the godly, and especially ministers of the Word, ought to be composed in their minds like this, so that setting aside everything else, they may hasten to obey God in the right course of action. Certainly life is too remarkable a gift of God that it ought to be despised, seeing that in it we have been created after the image of God, so that we may meditate on that blessed immortality that is reserved for us in heaven, and that in it God now shows himself a Father to us by many proofs. But because it has been arranged for us like a race course, it is proper always to make haste to the winning post and to overcome obstacles, so that nothing may impede or delay us on the course. For it is a shameful thing for us to be so gripped by a blind love of living that, because of life, we lose the reasons for living. And Paul's words bring that out. For he does not simply esteem his life as of no value, but he puts consideration of it out of his mind, so that he may finish his course and complete his ministry that he received from Christ. It is as if he said that he is not possessed by any desire to live, except to satisfy the call of God, and, for that reason, that the loss of life will not be a serious thing for him, provided that he is coming near, by death, to the goal of the function that God had prescribed for him. COMMENTARY ON ACTS 20:24.[7]

SHOULD A PREACHER JUST LET EVERYTHING BE? JOHANN SPANGENBERG: Dear friends, do you think that it does not pain a preacher when he hears that in his congregation among his sheep there is open blasphemy, usurers, usurpers, prostitutes, adulterers, drunkards and similar scoundrels? Do you think that he should be calm and quiet? Have you not heard what God said to the prophet? God will demand their blood from the hands of those who did not punish sin. BRIEF EXEGESIS OF ACTS 20:26.[8]

---

[5]Donne, *Works*, 2:327-28*.
[6]Bullinger, *In Acta Apostolorum*, 254r.

[7]CNTC 7:179* (CO 48:465).
[8]Spangenberg, *Der Apostel Geschichte*, 190r; alluding to Ezek 3:18, 20; 33:6, 8.

WE ARE BLESSED WITH AN ABUNDANCE OF PREACHING. JOHN DONNE: "The principal office of the bishop is to preach."[9] And as there is no church in Christendom—no, let us glorify God in the fullness of an obvious truth—not all the churches of God in Christendom have more or more useful preaching than ours has from those to whom the cure of souls belongs. So neither were there ever any times in which more men were preferred for former preaching or that continued it more after their preferments than in these our times. There may be, there should be a *transiverunt*, a passing from place to place, but still it is as it should be, *praedicando*, a passing for preaching and a passing to preaching, and then a preaching conditioned so, as Saint Paul's was. "I have gone among you preaching the kingdom of God." SERMON ON THE SUNDAY AFTER THE CONVERSION OF SAINT PAUL (1627).[10]

THE CREEDS AND THE WORD OF GOD ARE INEXTRICABLY CONNECTED. GALLICAN CONFESSION: We believe that the Word contained in these books has proceeded from God and receives its authority from him alone, and not from human beings. And inasmuch as it is the rule of all truth, containing all that is necessary for the service of God and for our salvation, it is not lawful for human beings, or even for angels, to add to it, to take away from it or to change it. Whence it follows that no authority, whether of antiquity, or custom, or numbers, or human wisdom, or judgments, or proclamations, or edicts, or decrees, or councils, or visions or miracles should be opposed to these holy Scriptures, but, on the contrary, all things should be examined, regulated and reformed according to them. And therefore we confess the three creeds, to wit: the Apostles', the Nicene and the Athanasian, because they are in accordance with the Word of God. ARTICLE 5.[11]

THE PROPER ROLE OF BISHOPS. JOHN CALVIN: About the word *bishops* we must briefly note that Paul calls all the Ephesian presbyters this, without distinction. From that we gather that, according to the usage of Scripture, bishops do not differ from presbyters in any way. But through vice and corruption it came about that those who held the leading place in individual cities began to be called bishops. I say "vice" not because it is a bad thing for any one person to be prominent in every college, but because it is an intolerable presumption when human beings twist the words of Scripture to their own customs and do not hesitate to change the language of the Holy Spirit. COMMENTARY ON ACTS 20:28.[12]

CHERISH THE FLOCK PURCHASED BY THE INVALUABLE BLOOD OF OUR SAVIOR. PETER RIEDEMANN: Christ gives us a twofold command. First, we should gather with him as those who have been sent by him. Second, we should do our utmost to keep those who are gathered, so that they do not again become scattered and torn apart by wolves. Christ's sheep are very dear to him, for he has bought them dearly. He wants his shepherds to cherish them; he commits them to none but those who love him. CONFESSION OF FAITH.[13]

"WHICH HE OBTAINED WITH HIS OWN BLOOD." JOHANN SPANGENBERG: As if he wanted to say, "If you are lazy and negligent, you do not merely sin against mortal human beings but against the Holy Spirit, which is a terrifying sin, that will not be forgiven here or there." . . . Paul says, "Christ purchased, procured and redeemed the Christian congregation through his own blood. This was costly. Therefore, he demands that they are held in honor." Pay attention here, preachers, magistrates and fathers, so that you do not treat, provoke and abuse those in your care like cattle and ignorant beasts. BRIEF EXEGESIS OF ACTS 20:28.[14]

---

[9]From the Council of Trent, Session Five, Chapter 2, "Preachers of the Word of God and Questors of Alms," see H. J. Schroeder, *Canons and Decrees of the Council of Trent: Original Text with English Translation* (New York: B. Herder Book Co., 1960), 26; Latin, 305.
[10]Donne, *Works*, 2:323-24*.
[11]*Creeds*, 3:362*.
[12]CNTC 7:183* (CO 48:468).
[13]CRR 9:185.
[14]Spangenberg, *Der Apostel Geschichte*, 190v-191r; alluding to 1 Jn 5:16.

BELIEVERS JUDGE CLEARLY BY THE WORD.
MENNO SIMONS: If now you are of a pious mind
and not led by the blind spirit of spiritual adultery,
then judge our cause according to the Word and
truth of the Lord. If you do not understand it,
then fear God and pray. All those who are born of
God and inclined to the Word of the Lord must
acknowledge that our doctrine is of God and the
end has eternal life; but whosoever rejects them
does not reject us, but Christ Jesus himself who
has taught us from the mouth of his Father and
sealed it with his own blood. [May] the gracious
Father through his beloved Son Jesus Christ, our
Lord, enlighten you and all hungry hearts by the
gift of his Holy Spirit and lead you by his strength
in this eternal, saving truth. CONFESSION OF THE
DISTRESSED CHRISTIANS (1552).[15]

CHRIST HAS NO NEED FOR ANY VICAR. THE
SECOND HELVETIC CONFESSION: Therefore we
do not allow the doctrine of the Romish prelates,
who would make the pope the general pastor and
supreme head of the church militant here on earth,
and the very vicar of Jesus Christ, who has (as they
say) all fullness of power and sovereign authority
in the church. For we hold and teach that Christ
our Lord is, and remains still, the only universal
pastor, and highest bishop, before God his Father;
and that in the church he performs all the duties
of a pastor or bishop, even to the world's end; and
therefore stands not in need of any other to supply
his room. For he is said to have a substitute, who is
absent; but Christ is present with his church, and
is the head that gives life thereunto. He did strictly
forbid his apostles and their successors all superiority or dominion in the church. Those, therefore,
who by gainsaying set themselves against so manifest a truth, and bring another kind of government
into the church, who does not see that they are to
be counted among those apostles of whom Christ
prophesied? CHAPTER 17, OF THE CATHOLIC AND
HOLY CHURCH OF GOD.[16]

MINISTERS ARE SALT AND LIGHT. DIRK
PHILIPS: Out of this it follows forcefully that the
ministers of Christ, the teachers and bishops in his
congregations, must have the Holy Spirit through
whom they first and before all things must be well
instructed in God's Word. The common people
will err and walk in darkness if the teachers themselves are unwise. The reason? Christ calls teachers
a light of the world and salt of the earth. How shall
the world see correctly whenever those to whom
it belongs to be a light of the world are themselves
darkness? Again, how shall the world correctly
understand and know the holy Scriptures and the
power of God when those who should be the salt
of the earth have lost the power of the divine Word
and themselves do not know what it is fitting for
a good Christian to know? Again, how should the
world not err when those who properly and with
truth should be the city (built on a high mountain)
and show all erring ones the right way are themselves those lead astray? Therefore, I say again, that
the teachers themselves must before all things be
well instructed and taught in God's Word. THE
ENCHIRIDION: THE SENDING OF PREACHERS.[17]

**THE GOD OF THESE WOLVES IS THEIR STOM-
ACH.** JOHANN SPANGENBERG: Here Paul proph-
esies of the "belly saints" and enemies of Christ's
cross, whom he calls ravenous wolves, because they
voraciously scatter and tear to shreds Christ's little
sheep. BRIEF EXEGESIS OF ACTS 20:29-30.[18]

BEWARE OF WOLVES, CLING TO THE LAMB.
KATARINA SCHÜTZ ZELL: Indeed an evil teaching
is more dangerous than a wicked life. Teaching affects many others, but with a wicked life the greatest harm is to the self. I must also say a little about
the teaching . . . for the whole multitude of those
who preach the gospel, such as Luther, along with
all those who serve the gospel with him—whose
names are too many to count. I say then to the

---

[15]Simons, *Complete Writings*, 522.
[16]*Creeds*, 3:871* (Latin, 273-74).

[17]CRR 6:203-4* (BRN 10:212-13); alluding to Mt 5:13-14; Mal 2:7;
  Tit 1:9.
[18]Spangenberg, *Der Apostel Geschichte*, 191r.

poison brewers, yes, to those who pour out all the worst kinds of poison, who are still in Strasbourg and in all the lands, whether they still wear gray hoods or black hoods, or used to wear them, "If the teaching of Luther and his followers is false, why have you not shown its falsity and overcome it with clear godly Scripture?" It is as if they want to build beautiful houses and tall cathedrals with clay and straw, while the others build them with good lime and stone....

Paul often spoke of such people and finally with weeping to the Philippians in the third chapter. And in the book of the Acts of the Apostles he says that he has proclaimed to us all the counsel of God; therefore we should pay heed to and take care of the community of God. For Paul knows that after his departure there will come bad wolves who will not spare the flock.... Therefore I exhort all Christians, by the promise they made to God in their baptism, not to allow [such] poison [spewers] to corrupt them, but to choose to remain with the wholesome, life-giving teaching of Christ Jesus, who alone is our wisdom, righteousness, sanctification and redemption. APOLOGIA FOR MASTER MATTHEW ZELL.[19]

AMBITION IS THE MOTHER OF ALL HERESIES. JOHN CALVIN: For the purity of the Word of God flourishes when pastors gain disciples for Christ with a common zeal, because the state of the church is sound only when he is the one Master that is heard. Accordingly it is inevitable that both the teaching of salvation is destroyed and the safety of the flock goes for nothing when the passion for mastery prevails. But just as this verse teaches that nearly all corruptions of doctrine flow from human pride, when each one eagerly desires to be more prominent than is allowed, so again we gather from the same source that it is hardly possible that the ambitious will not turn aside from the proper purity and adulterate the Word of God. For since the pure handling of Scriptures has this for its

aim, that Christ alone may be preeminent, and since . . . human beings cannot arrogate anything to themselves without taking away just so much from the glory of Christ, it follows that those who are devoted to themselves and strive after their own glory, which obscures Christ completely, are corrupters of the sound teaching. And the Lord himself confirms this. Moreover, by his use of the word *arise* he means that those wolves are now fostering destruction secretly, until they may break out when an opportunity is given them. COMMENTARY ON ACTS 20:30.[20]

"WHO IS ABLE TO BUILD YOU UP." JOHN CALVIN: The participle δυνάμενος, which Paul uses, refers to God and not to his Word.[21] Now this consolation is added for this reason, that they may not despair out of an awareness of their weaknesses. For as long as we are beset by the vices of the flesh, we are like an unfinished building. Indeed, all the godly must be founded on Christ, but their faith is a very long way from being perfect and complete. On the contrary, although the foundation remains firm, certain parts of the building sometimes totter and fall. Accordingly there is need both of constant building and, from time to time, of fresh supports. At the same time Paul is also saying that they must not lose hope, because the Lord does not wish to leave his work incomplete....

What he adds at once about the inheritance of life refers to the actual enjoyment of it. As soon as Christ has dawned on us, we indeed pass from death to life, and faith is the entrance into the king-

---

[19]Zell, *Church Mother*, 69, 70-71, 72*; alluding to Mt 7:24-27; Phil 3:18-19.

[20]CNTC 7:185-86* (CO 48:470-71); alluding to Jn 7:18.
[21]The structure of the Greek here is ambiguous—τῷ θεῷ καὶ λόγῳ τῆς χάριτος αὐτοῦ τῷ δυναμένῳ. The participle (τῷ δυναμένῳ) can refer to both τῷ θεῷ ("God") and λόγῳ ("word"). All modern English translations understand τῷ δυναμένῳ to refer to "the word of grace." However, many Reformation commentators agreed with Calvin. Luther and the Vulgate both signal that God is being referred to, not the Word. See WADB 6:500-501, Vg in loco. Erasmus managed to mantain the ambiguity of the Greek by translating λόγῳ as *sermoni*, not *verbo*. Some modern commentators do admit that this could be a hendiadys; see Richard I. Pervo, *Acts: A Commentary* (Minneapolis: Fortress, 2009), 526-27, and C. K. Barrett, *The Acts of the Apostles: A Shorter Commentary* (London: T & T Clark, 2002), 318.

dom of heaven; and the Spirit of adoption has not been given to us in vain. But here Paul promises the faithful a continuous increase of grace until they see and possess the inheritance to which they have been called and which is now laid up for them in heaven.

He mentions "the power of God," not as we are accustomed to imagine it, without effect, but as something that is commonly described as active. The faithful ought to lay hold of it, so that they may have it ready, like a shield, to hold before all the onslaughts of Satan. Just as Scripture teaches that we have protection enough in the power of God, so let us remember that the only ones who are strong in the Lord are those who renounce confidence in their own free will and rest on him, and Paul is quite right in asserting that he alone can build up. COMMENTARY ON ACTS 20:32.[22]

THE MASTER BUILDER WILL ASSUREDLY SUSTAIN YOU.
THE ENGLISH ANNOTATIONS: That is, the gospel which declares his grace and free mercy. It is as if he had said, "I know it is a difficult thing and beyond all human ability, but God whose cause and work it is, in which you labor, is all-sufficient. He who has laid the foundation can and will perfect all, enabling you to perform your duties which he has committed to you." ANNOTATIONS ON ACTS 20:32.[23]

MINISTERS MUST NOT BE GREEDY.
JOHN CALVIN: We gather that nobody will be a good minister of the Word without being, at the same time, one who puts little value on money. We certainly see that there is nothing more common than all who are shamefully devoted to riches corrupt the Word of God to please others. . . .

He is not using these words to impose an absolute law, which all ministers of the Word must always, necessarily, keep, for he did not conduct

himself so imperiously that he himself took away what the Lord granted to his servants. On the contrary, in many places he affirms his own right, for them, so that they may be maintained at public expense. Add to this that he allowed food and clothing to be supplied to himself by many churches. In fact not only did he gladly accept wages for the work in hand, but when he was in need at Corinth he says that "he robbed other churches" to relieve his poverty. Therefore he does not simply order pastors to make their living by manual labor, but immediately afterwards he makes it plain to what extent he urges them to follow his example, that is, to support the weak. COMMENTARY ON ACTS 20:33-34.[24]

ABLE PASTORS MUST TILL SOIL AND SOULS.
BOHEMIAN CONFESSION OF 1535: [The Scriptures] also teach that those who are able and are not occupied in great labor in the interests of their people, or impeded in some other way, should provide food for themselves with [the labor of] their own hands, lest they become a burden and become lazy and unfaithful, for sloth too is a fault, and thus they may become a burden to the church. ARTICLE 9, ECCLESIASTICAL ORDER.[25]

DO NOT ALLOW MONEY TO TRANSFORM THE SHEEP INTO THE SHEPHERD.
DESIDERIUS ERASMUS: Thus no one would become more averse to the gospel because he was compelled to support his own evangelist; nor would he be the less inclined to obey the admonitions of the pastors because he supposed they had been put under obligation to himself on account of the benefits received. For it is human nature that we somehow have less respect for those on whom we have conferred a benefit. True, it is fair that for those who have imparted to you the riches of the gospel you should provide in turn far cheaper resources. PARAPHRASE OF ACTS 20:34-35.[26]

---

[22]CNTC 7:187-88* (CO 48:472-73); alluding to Phil 1:6; Ps 138:8. In referring to the power of God, Calvin's meaning is that God's "power" (cf. δύναμαι) is not to be interpreted as his potential or ability to act, but his powerful activity.
[23]Downame, ed., *Annotations*, LLL3v*.

[24]CNTC 7:189* (CO 48:473-74); quoting 2 Cor 11:8.
[25]Boh 1535, 20.
[26]CWE 50:125 (LB 7:748-49).

WHERE DOES JESUS SAY "IT IS MORE BLESSED TO GIVE THAN TO RECEIVE"?

JOHANN SPANGENBERG: We do not find this word for word in the Gospels, but only the idea. For what [in them]—"Give and it will be given to you" and "Whoever gives a cup of water in my name, I tell you the truth, it will not remain unrewarded"—is contrary to "to give is more blessed than to receive"? BRIEF EXEGESIS OF ACTS 20:35.[27]

A UNIQUE SAYING OF CHRIST.

JOHN CALVIN: This sentence is not to be found, word for word, anywhere else, but the Evangelists record others that are not unlike it, from which Paul could have elicited this one. Now we do know that not all of Christ's sayings were committed to writing. On the other hand, he does repeat that general teaching about the despising of money, of which there is a genuine proof, if someone is readier to give than to receive. And Christ not only spoke about what was prudent, as if the liberal are blessed simply because they hold others in their debt by their benefits, and, on the other hand, it is a form of slavery to owe anything, but he was mindful of something deeper, that he who gives money to the poor is lending to the Lord, that the faithful and honest stewards of God are those who share with their brothers the riches entrusted to themselves. Nothing brings people nearer to God than beneficence.

These sayings about liberality are also to be read in the works of secular authors, and a large part of the world admit that they are true, but they nod with a donkey's ears, as the proverb goes. For common life shows how few are convinced that there is nothing more desirable than to devote our goods to helping our brothers. That is why the disciples of Christ must meditate on this felicity with greater zeal, so that by keeping away from someone else's property as far as they can, they may accustom themselves to giving, and to do so not with a proud spirit, as if it is a wretched thing for them to be indebted to anyone, or out of a perverse ambition to lay others under obligation to them, but only to

exercise themselves in the services of love, and, in this way, make the grace of their adoption manifest. COMMENTARY ON ACTS 20:35.[28]

DIVIDE AND CHEW WELL THE HOOVES OF SCRIPTURE BEFORE ASSERTING IT CONTRADICTS ITSELF.

BALTHASAR HUBMAIER: You ask, dear Christian, how can [both] stand [together] . . . to be poor and to be more blessed to give rather than to receive? . . . As the Father and Christ are one and yet the Father is more than Christ and many other passages which seem on the surwface to be contradictory—like the wings of the cherubim—however, in Christ they all fit together perfectly. Therefore we should divide the hooves of the Scriptures and chew them well before we swallow, that is, believe them. Otherwise we will swallow death instead, and through half-truths and half-judgments deviate far, very far from the whole truth and seriously go astray. ON THE SWORD.[29]

THREE EXHORTATIONS TO PREACHERS.

STEPHEN DENISON: Since ministers should be careful to preach in the first place, this condemns the practice of such as press and intrude into the ministry merely for gain, being in no sort furnished with ability to preach to or to instruct the people, which kind of men the Spirit of God in a holy contempt describes as dumb dogs and will not intend to call them ministers. Second, this serves to condemn the gross negligence of all idle ministers who look for the fleece but starve the flock, who have talents but not a heart to use them for the good of the people committed to their charge. The people committed as lambs to the keeping of such wolves shall die in their sin, but surely their blood shall be required at the hands of such unconscionable ministers. Third, the ministers ought to preach God's Word with all diligence. Then the people ought by their diligent hearing, and by their conscionable obedience and by comfortable maintenance

---

[27]Spangenberg, *Der Apostel Geschichte*, 192r-v; quoting Lk 6:38; Mk 9:41; Mt 10:42.

[28]CNTC 7:190* (CO 48:474); alluding to Prov 19:17.
[29]CRR 5:512, 514* (QGT 9:449, 450); alluding to Acts 20:35; Mt 5:3; Jn 10:30; 14:10; Lev 11:3.

encourage their ministers to the performance of this duty. For it is as well required of the people to hear as of the minister to preach, and of the people to obey, as well as of the minister to instruct. THE DOCTRINE OF BOTH SACRAMENTS.[30]

WEEP FOR THE REMOVAL OF THE GOSPEL.

JOHN DONNE: Consider the difference between the candle and the candlestick, between the preacher of the gospel and the gospel itself, between a religious person and religion itself. The removing of the candlestick and the withdrawing of the gospel and the profaning of religion is infinitely a greater loss than if hundreds of the present laborers should be taken away from us. SERMON ON THE SUNDAY AFTER THE CONVERSION OF SAINT PAUL (1627).[31]

OUR BODY REVEALS THE ATTITUDE OF OUR HEART.

JOHN CALVIN: The inward attitude certainly holds first place in prayer, but outward signs, kneeling, uncovering the head, lifting up the hands, have a twofold use. The first is that we may employ all our members for the glory and worship of God; second, that we are, so to speak, jolted out of our laziness by this help. There is also a third use in solemn and public prayer, because in this way the children of God profess their piety, and they inflame each other with reverence of God. But just as the lifting up of the hands is a symbol of confidence and longing, so in order to show our humility we fall down on our knees. COMMENTARY ON ACTS 20:36.[32]

SEEK THE FACE OF CHRIST IN THE WORD AND SACRAMENTS.

JOHN DONNE: If it is a sad thing to you to hear a Paul, a holy man say, "You will see my face no more" on this side . . . there cannot be so sad a voice as to hear Christ Jesus say, "You will see my face no more." . . . God manifests himself to us in the Word and in the sacraments. If we do not see them in their true lines and colors—the Word and sacraments sincerely and religiously preached and administered—we do not see them but place masks over them. If we do not see them, we do not see the face of Christ. I could as well stand under his "I do not know," said to the negligent virgins, or his "I never knew you," said to those who boast of their works, as under this fearful thunder from his mouth, "You will see my face no more." [That is,] I will absolutely withdraw or I will suffer desecration to enter into those means of your salvation, Word and sacraments, which I have so long continued in their sincerity toward you, and you have so long abused.

Blessed God, do not say this to us yet! Let the tree grow another year before you cut it down. As you dig around it, by judging our neighbors, so water it with your former rain, the dew of your grace, and with your latter rain, the tears of our contrition, so that we may still see your face, here and hereafter. Here, in your kingdom of grace; hereafter in your kingdom of glory, which you have purchased for us with the inestimable price of your incorruptible blood. Amen. SERMON ON THE SUNDAY AFTER THE CONVERSION OF SAINT PAUL (1627).[33]

---

[30]Denison, *Doctrine of Both the Sacraments*, 65*; alluding to Is 56:10; Ezek 3:20.
[31]Donne, *Works*, 2:331*.
[32]CNTC 7:190* (CO 48:474-75).

[33]Donne, *Works*, 2:332-33*; quoting Mt 25:12; 7:23; alluding to Lk 13:6-9; Joel 2:23.

21:1-16 PAUL JOURNEYS TO JERUSALEM

And when we had parted from them and set sail, we came by a straight course to Cos, and the next day to Rhodes, and from there to Patara.*a* *2*And having found a ship crossing to Phoenicia, we went aboard and set sail. *3*When we had come in sight of Cyprus, leaving it on the left we sailed to Syria and landed at Tyre, for there the ship was to unload its cargo. *4*And having sought out the disciples, we stayed there for seven days. And through the Spirit they were telling Paul not to go on to Jerusalem. *5*When our days there were ended, we departed and went on our journey, and they all, with wives and children, accompanied us until we were outside the city. And kneeling down on the beach, we prayed *6*and said farewell to one another. Then we went on board the ship, and they returned home.

*7*When we had finished the voyage from Tyre, we arrived at Ptolemais, and we greeted the brothers*b* and stayed with them for one day. *8*On the next day we departed and came to Caesarea, and we entered the house of Philip the evangelist, who was one of the seven, and stayed with him. *9*He had four unmarried daughters, who prophesied. *10*While we were staying for many days, a prophet named Agabus came down from Judea. *11*And coming to us, he took Paul's belt and bound his own feet and hands and said, "Thus says the Holy Spirit, 'This is how the Jews*c* at Jerusalem will bind the man who owns this belt and deliver him into the hands of the Gentiles.'" *12*When we heard this, we and the people there urged him not to go up to Jerusalem. *13*Then Paul answered, "What are you doing, weeping and breaking my heart? For I am ready not only to be imprisoned but even to die in Jerusalem for the name of the Lord Jesus." *14*And since he would not be persuaded, we ceased and said, "Let the will of the Lord be done."

*15*After these days we got ready and went up to Jerusalem. *16*And some of the disciples from Caesarea went with us, bringing us to the house of Mnason of Cyprus, an early disciple, with whom we should lodge.

---

a Some manuscripts add *and Myra* b Or *brothers and sisters*; also verse 17 c Greek *Ioudaioi* probably refers here to Jewish religious leaders, and others under their influence, in that time

---

OVERVIEW: As Paul continues his final journey to Jerusalem he is hounded by prophecies and fears about what will happen to him, culminating in Agabus's illustrative belt-prophecy that Paul will be delivered to the Romans. The reformers wonder why Paul is given this forewarning (and why Luke writes with such painstaking detail). They suggest that both the prophetic foreboding and Luke's precision help the reader to understand better Paul's bravery and determination to obey the commission God had given him. Once God's purposes have been made clear by the Word and Spirit, Christians must fully submit themselves.

The statement that Philip had "four unmarried daughters who prophesied" elicits a lengthy digression from our commentators. During the early modern period there was a heated debate about the status of women (*querelle des femmes*); the reformers were not idle spectators. There was a spectrum of views ranging from female superiority to questioning whether women should properly be considered fully human. The scholarship is not in agreement as to how the reformers may have improved or stifled the status of women. Their comments on verse 9 can be divided into John Thompson's four views of New Testament prophecy: passive, privately active, publicly active and opaque.[1] It can be strange to see some of these

---

[1]John L. Thompson, *John Calvin and the Daughters of Sarah: Women in Regular and Exceptional Roles in the Exegesis of Calvin, His Predecessors and His Contemporaries* (Geneva: Droz, 1992), 188-206.

ostensibly literal-grammatical commentators argue that an active participle (προφητεύουσαι, "those who prophesy") should be taken as a passive participle (προφητεύμενοι, "those who listened to prophecy") because the subjects are women. Even Peter Martyr Vermigli, who affirms that Philip's daughters held a public office, concedes that this was an (extraordinary) exception to the rule.[2] Still, it is important to recall their historical context. There was after all no ordained office open to women in their day, and except for certain nobility and royalty, women were not highly educated. In any case, Reformation exegetes were not nearly as concerned or interested about the role of women in ordained ministry as the contemporary church is.[3]

WHY DOES LUKE DESCRIBE PAUL'S VOYAGE WITH SUCH PAINSTAKING PRECISION? JOHANN SPANGENBERG: He wants to display Paul's constancy. He allowed no danger—neither by water nor by land—to deter him; instead, he continually pressed on in his preaching office given to him by God. Surely it must baffle every Christian that Paul hurries so quickly to Jerusalem! Although he hears again and again what the prophets through the Holy Spirit proclaimed to him, namely, that in Jerusalem he will be captured and bound, nevertheless he hurries nowhere else but there, as if he were approaching blissful living where he would encounter every joy and charity. And what he says with words—"I desire to depart and be with Christ"—he proves here with this action. BRIEF EXEGESIS OF ACTS 21:1-6.[4]

GOD'S PROVIDENCE EVEN IN DANGER. RUDOLF GWALTHER: The Holy Spirit retells the painful and dangerous voyages of the apostles so that we might learn the exceeding goodness of God toward us . . . and that we should more fervently embrace the doctrine of the gospel. . . . We are taught how

Paul, passing through many seas through many hazards, came into Syria, and from there to Jerusalem, where, being courteously received by the godly but betrayed by the seditious and apprehended, he was committed to the power of the tribune or the guard of the Romans. HOMILY 137, ACTS 21:1-7.[5]

THE VOYAGE SHOWS PAUL'S BRAVERY. JOHN CALVIN: Luke surveys the course of the voyage briefly, and he does so not only to give a faithful account, so that we may know what happened in each place, but also so that readers may ponder, along with himself, the invincible and heroic bravery of Paul. He preferred to experience the upheavals from such long, tortuous and troublesome journeys in order to labor for Christ, rather than be concerned for a quiet life for himself. His statement that they were parted, or pulled away, is not to be referred simply to spatial distance but to the fact that the brothers stood on the shore as long as their eyes could follow the ship in which Paul and his companions were sailing. He names the ports at which the ship moored, so that we may know that the voyage was easy and calm. For the location of the cities that he lists, the [works of] geographers should be consulted. It is enough for me to have pointed out Luke's intention. COMMENTARY ON ACTS 21:1.[6]

THE LORD PREPARES PAUL FOR THE AFFLICTIONS TO COME. RUDOLF GWALTHER: In every city and congregation, the Lord tells Paul how he shall be imprisoned. Now others come with the spirit of prophecy and warn him not to go. What purpose do these things serve? Truly God meant to prepare his apostle for the cross by continual premeditation. . . . Also he teaches us here an example of Christian constancy and obedience, which we must so earnestly labor to have, such that we must not obey people, although we see rare examples of God's Holy Spirit in them, if they counsel us

[2]Ibid., 193-97.
[3]Mickey L. Mattox, "Defender of the Most Holy Matriarchs": Martin Luther's Interpretation of the Women of Genesis in the Enarrationes in Genesin, 1535-45 (Leiden: Brill, 2003), 84.
[4]Spangenberg, Der Apostel Geschichte, 193v-194r; quoting Phil 1:23.

[5]Gwalther, Homelyes or Sermons upon the Actes, 759, 760* (In Acta Apostolorum, 236r).
[6]CNTC 7:192* (CO 48:475). See Geneva Bible map on lxiv-lxv of this volume.

anything contrary to the will and commandment of God. HOMILY 137, ACTS 21:1-7.[7]

PROPHETS DO NOT ALWAYS HAVE GOOD DISCRETION. JOHN CALVIN: There are different gifts of the Spirit, so that it is no wonder that those who are strong in the gift of prophecy are sometimes lacking in judgment or courage. The Lord revealed to those brothers, whom Luke mentions, what was to be; but at the same time, they do not know what is expedient and what Paul's calling demands, because the measure of their gifts does not stretch so far. But the Lord deliberately intended his servant to be warned, partly that he might approach whatever he had to undergo better prepared by long meditation, partly that his perseverance might be plainer, when, having been informed of a sad outcome by the prophecies, he nevertheless willingly and knowingly hastens to suffer anything. COMMENTARY ON ACTS 21:4.[8]

THE PRAISEWORTHY COMPASSION OF THE BELIEVERS. JUSTUS JONAS: Luke expresses the very dear affection of those who had heard the gospel [from Paul] for their most faithful shepherd. They could scarcely have been wrenched away, since out of great charity they together with their wives and children accompanied him to the ship. For they had just heard from him that perhaps "you will not see my face [again]." Truly these brothers deserve great praise, because they treated him so respectfully, even though the world completely despised him and spat on him. For no one is able to support the true ministers of the Word, unless he is willing to have the entire world as an enemy, risking his life and all good things. Paul commends the Galatians excellently, saying "You did not despise me," etc. Do not doubt that in Tyre there were Jews and many other powerful people who were intensely

displeased by this and who considered Paul unworthy of life. ANNOTATIONS ON ACTS 21:5.[9]

THE BELIEVERS' LOVE AND DETERMINATION. JOHN CALVIN: It was no ordinary testimony of love that they accompanied Paul out of the city even with their wives and children. Luke has recorded this, partly for the purpose that he might praise their loyalty in fitting terms, partly to show that Paul was given honor, which he deserved. We also gather from this that nothing was further from his mind than looking to his own advantage, seeing that he was not deterred from his course by such great good will, which could have been a pleasant inducement to stay. We must also note the common habit of praying over more important matters, and that, having been informed about the danger, they are the more eager to pray. COMMENTARY ON ACTS 21:5.[10]

HOW DIFFICULT TO LEAVE THE COMPANY OF LOVED ONES. RUDOLF GWALTHER: For three years, Paul, conversing with them, had engendered a mutual love between them. This love was apparent by fresh tears and common grief shared by all. Moreover, Paul knew that he would not come again to those who loved him so dearly and that he left them in danger of wolves. All these things would have been able to move even a heart of iron. Likewise, we see parents mourn when their children are pulled from them by death, when they could not yet help themselves. Yet Paul overcomes all grief, because he wants to obey the calling of God, which drew him to Jerusalem. By this example, we are taught that God's will and calling must be preferred before all affections. It is impossible for us to be wholly void of these affections, as long as we live in the flesh, and it is evident that they affect even the godly. But moderation must be used to bring them under the obedience of faith. This must be observed in all cases, but especially when our friends are pulled from us by death, or we from

---

[7]Gwalther, *Homelyes or Sermons upon the Actes*, 762* (*In Acta Apostolorum*, 236v).
[8]CNTC 7:193* (CO 48:476).

[9]Jonas, *Annotationes in Acta*, I2v; quoting Acts 20:38; Gal 4:14.
[10]CNTC 7:193 (CO 48:476).

them, whose good counsel and help we found to be very profitable for us. Let us then remember that we are urged with God's calling, so that whoever may strive against it is in a very rash enterprise, which is both foolish and dangerous. HOMILY 137, ACTS 21:1-7.[11]

THE GOSPEL EVOKES PROFOUND LOVE AND BRAVERY. JOHANN SPANGENBERG: Here you see and hear the great love the disciples had for Paul: not only the men, but even the women and children accompanied him to the sea. And in fact, considering all the circumstances of this event, these Christians placed themselves in no small danger. For both the Jews and Gentiles were determined to persecute not only the preachers of the gospel but also those who listened to the gospel—especially those associated with Paul. What is accompanying Paul through the city of Tyre other than freely and publicly confessing the gospel and by such confession placing themselves along with wife and child in complete danger?

What made these disciples so joyful, brave and strong-hearted? Faith in Jesus Christ. They thought accordingly, "Look, if we have to submit on account of our local government—who merely keep temporal peace—to every danger, yes, even death, because they order it, why wouldn't we also do this on account of our Lord Christ and his dear apostles, who provide us eternal peace, yes, in fact, eternal life?" This example all Christians should wholeheartedly follow. BRIEF EXEGESIS OF ACTS 21:5-6.[12]

THE OFFICE OF DEACON IS TEMPORARY. JOHN CALVIN: Luke says that at Caesarea they enjoyed the hospitality of Philip, whom he calls an evangelist, although he was one of the seven deacons. From this it is easy to gather that the diaconate was a temporary office, because otherwise Philip would not have been free to

leave Jerusalem and move to Caesarea. But he is not set before us as a voluntary deserter of office but as one to whom a more important charge has been committed. In my opinion evangelists were halfway between apostles and teachers. For they used to discharge a function very close to that of the apostles, in that they preached the gospel everywhere and were not appointed to a fixed station; only their standing carries less honor. In his description of the order of the church Paul puts them after the apostles, so as to show that they were given a wider field for teaching than the pastors, whose labor was devoted to definite places. Therefore Philip exercised his diaconate at Jerusalem for a while, and after that the church considered him suitable to have the treasure of the gospel entrusted to him. COMMENTARY ON ACTS 21:8.[13]

LUKE EXALTS MARRIAGE. JOHANN SPANGENBERG: [That Philip had four daughters who prophesied] Luke wrote against those filthy and marriage-profaning people, the papists, who blaspheme and profane the marriage of priests. Saint Luke gags these charlatans and states that Philip the evangelist, the preacher, had four legitimate daughters, prophetesses, certainly filled with the Holy Spirit, raised in the fear of God since childhood, who also prophesied to Paul what would happen to him in Jerusalem. Here these despisers of marriage, the papists—open fornicators and adulterers—will blush in shame before God and the entire world and will never again have peace in conscience. BRIEF EXEGESIS OF ACTS 21:8-9.[14]

FOUR PROPHESYING DAUGHTERS. JOHN CALVIN: This has been added in commendation of Philip, so that we might know that his house was very suitable and that it was famous and renowned by the blessing of God. It was no ordinary gift to have four daughters, all endowed

---

[11]Gwalther, *Homelyes or Sermons upon the Actes*, 760* (*In Acta Apostolorum*, 236r).

[12]Spangenberg, *Der Apostel Geschichte*, 195r-196r.

[13]CNTC 7:194* (CO 48:477); alluding to Acts 6:5; Eph 4:11.

[14]Spangenberg, *Der Apostel Geschichte*, 197r-v.

with the spirit of prophecy. But God wished to give luster to the beginnings of the gospel by this method of raising men and women to predict coming events. For very many years now prophecies had almost ceased among the Jews, so that their minds might be more attentive or more alert to hear the new voice of the gospel. Therefore when prophecy returned, as if by restoration, it was a sign of a more complete situation. Yet the reason why it ceased a little later appears to have been the same. For God sustained the people of old by various predictions until, by his advent, Christ put an end to all prophecies. Therefore it was fitting for the new reign of Christ to be distinguished and adorned in this way, so that all would know that the promised visitation of God was a present reality. On the other hand, it was proper for it to flourish only for a short time, so that believers might not always be in a state of uncertainty, or so that an opportunity might not be given to those of a curious turn of mind to be looking repeatedly for or devising something new. We know that when that power had already been taken away, there were, nevertheless, many fanatics who boasted that they were prophets. And it is also possible that human perverseness deprived the church of this gift. COMMENTARY ON ACTS 21:9.[15]

THESE WOMEN ARE ABLE ONLY TO TELL THE FUTURE. THEODORE BEZA: Understand this as a private gift to predict the future, not as the teaching office in the church. ANNOTATIONS ON ACTS 21:9.[16]

WOMEN MUST HAVE THE COURAGE TO PREACH WHEN MEN WILL NOT. BALTHASAR HUBMAIER: Where the men are afraid and have become women, then the women should speak up and become manly, like Deborah, Hulda, Anna the prophetess, the four daughters of the evan-

gelist Philip, and in our times Argula.[17] THESES AGAINST ECK.[18]

WHEN APPLIED TO WOMEN, PROPHESYING IS PASSIVE. HEINRICH BULLINGER: We do not understand [this to mean] that they would have prophesied, that is, taught, which was forbidden by a precept of Paul—no, indeed, by the Lord! Thus they are prophetesses who, wholly devoted to prophecy, that is, to the Word of the Lord, practice true piety.... And Paul plainly uses the word *prophesying* for "listening to prophecy." COMMENTARY ON ACTS 20:9.[19]

SCRIPTURE IS CLEAR: WHEN APPLIED TO WOMEN, PROPHESYING IS ACTIVE. PETER MARTYR VERMIGLI: Others say that these words about women are interpreted to mean that they either pray or prophesy privately (which is not forbidden to them). We may also be able to explain this command of the apostle in another way. It was agreed that women were silent in the customary order: whence any public role which is ordinary and perpetual in the church was not entrusted to them. Nevertheless, if now and then the Spirit of the Lord had passed through women, [a public role] was not altogether forbidden to them, if they should happen to speak something.

---

[17]Argula of Grumbach (c. 1492–1554), a Bavarian noblewoman who defended a student ejected from the University of Ingolstadt for his evangelical beliefs. Argula maintained epistolary contact with Luther—they met once. Unfortunately, all her letters have been lost. See Thompson, *John Calvin and the Daughters of Sarah*, 198-202; Ingetraut Ludolphy, "Die Frau in der Sicht Martin Luthers," in *Vierhundertfünfzig Jahre lutherische Reformation, 1517–1967: Festschrift für Franz Lau sum 60. Geburtstag*, eds. Helmar Junghans, Ingetraut Ludolphy and Kurt Meier (Göttingen: Vandenhoeck & Ruprecht, 1967), 212-14. Luther makes similar statements about women preaching: "If no man were to preach, then it would be necessary for a woman to preach" (LW 36:151-52; WA 8:497).

[18]CRR 5:56 (Latin, QGT 9:90; German, QGT 9:94); alluding to Judg 4-5; 2 Chron 34:22-28; Lk 2:36-38; Acts 21:9. The only difference between the Latin and German copies of Hubmaier's thesis here is that in Latin he included Priscilla (Acts 18).

[19]Thompson, *John Calvin and the Daughters of Sarah*, 189-90* (Bullinger, *In Acta Apostolorum*, 260v); alluding to 1 Cor 14:33-35; 1 Tim 2:11-12; 1 Cor 11:5.

---

[15]CNTC 7:194-95* (CO 48:477-78).
[16]Beza, *Annotationes Majores*, I:546.

... Nevertheless, those people who think that these words pertain not only to those who prophesy or pray publicly but also to their hearers—since "men should have an uncovered head and women a covered head"—more quickly misunderstand this passage. The words of Paul do not seem to agree with their opinion, since he clearly made claims about a woman praying or prophesying. COMMENTARY ON 1 CORINTHIANS 11:5.[20]

WOMEN OUGHT TO EXEGETE AND TEACH SCRIPTURE, BUT NOT AS PART OF PUBLIC WORSHIP.

MARTIN LUTHER: The four daughters were all prophets, that is, they knew how to prophesy. Women and girls are also able to console, indeed, to preach the Word. That is, they truly know how to exegete and interpret Scripture and how to console and teach people so that they might be saved. Even though "prophesying" here does not mean that they preach as I do, nevertheless a mother should teach her daughter and her household, because she has the Word and God gives the Holy Spirit so that she can understand [Scripture]. SERMON ON PENTECOST MONDAY (1531).[21]

PROPHECY IS FOR THE BENEFIT OF OTHERS, NOT PAUL.

JOHN CALVIN: Now we must see why the threatening persecution was made known once again by Agabus. As far as Paul was concerned, he had already been given more than enough warning. Therefore, I have no doubt that this confirmation was added for the sake of others, because the Lord wished to make his servant's bonds famous everywhere, partly so that all might know that he entered the fight of his own free will, partly so that they might learn that God had appointed him a champion to fight for the gospel. It was surely a useful example of invincible steadfastness, when, knowingly and willingly, he offered himself to the violence of his enemies. It is just as much to our advantage today that his apostleship is confirmed by this voluntary and equally steadfast devotedness of life. COMMENTARY ON ACTS 21:10-11.[22]

WHAT DID THE PEOPLE SAY TO PAUL?

JOHANN SPANGENBERG: Certainly these and the very same words: "Dear Paul, since certain harm and destruction is prepared for you in Jerusalem, you should not test God and deliberately place yourself in danger. Besides, there are still many lands and people that should be turned to faith through you! So that the newly begun Christian congregations here and there, built and established through you, may receive consolation and exhortation to stand firm, especially in these dangerous times, remain with us—even if you indeed do not want to spare yourself—do so for the poor newly initiated Christians." BRIEF EXEGESIS OF ACTS 21:12.[23]

COME DEATH!

RICHARD CRASHAW:

> Come death, come bands, nor do you shrink,
>   my ears,
> At those hard words man's cowardice calls fears.
> Save those of fear, no other bands fear I;
> Nor other death than this; the fear to die.
>
> STEPS TO THE TEMPLE.[24]

REBUKE FELLOW BELIEVERS LOVINGLY.

JOHN CALVIN: When Paul takes the brothers to task, because they are breaking his heart by their weeping, he makes it quite plain that he was not made of iron but that he was moved by love to sympathy. Therefore the tears of the godly were wounding his heart, but that tenderness did not turn him aside; he continued to follow God with an even tenor. Therefore, we ought to be gentle in our behavior toward the brothers in such a way that God's will always has the upper hand. Now in his reply Paul once again declares that it is only by contempt of death that the servants of Christ will be prepared to discharge their duty, and that only those who

---

[20]Martyr, *In selectissimam D. Pauli priorem ad Corinthios Epistolam*, 285r-v; alluding to 1 Cor 11:4-5. Martyr cites the examples of Anna, Deborah, Miriam, Huldah, Mary and Mary Magdalene.
[21]WA 34,1:483.

[22]CNTC 7:195* (CO 48:478).
[23]Spangenberg, *Der Apostel Geschichte*, 198r-v.
[24]Crashaw, *Complete Works of Richard Crashaw*, 28.

will freely lay down their own lives as a testimony to the truth will ever be properly disposed to live for the Lord. COMMENTARY ON ACTS 21:13.[25]

WHY IS PAUL SO ADAMANT HERE WHEN HE WILLINGLY EVADED DEATH BEFORE? JOHANN SPANGENBERG: This is not some stubbornness or overconfidence of Paul, but much more a steadfast obedience to the divine will. These disciples ask for nothing improper and for nothing wicked, but the work and will of the Holy Spirit must proceed. What Paul did before—fleeing and avoiding—he did because at this time he had still not received a clear word from the Lord concerning his death. For

that reason he was unwilling for the time to place himself in danger. Now, however, he hears the will of God everywhere, in cities and congregations, shown to him through the Holy Spirit, so he willingly submits himself to this. BRIEF EXEGESIS OF ACTS 21:13-14.[26]

TRUE BELIEVERS ENTRUST ALL THINGS TO GOD'S PROVIDENCE. DESIDERIUS ERASMUS: An expression belonging to those truly Christian, one that ought always to be in everyone's heart, even if it is not on the lips, no matter what is imminent, whether joy or sorrow: the will of the Lord be done. PARAPHRASE OF ACTS 21:14.[27]

---

[25]CNTC 7:196-97* (CO 48:479).

[26]Spangenberg, *Der Apostel Geschichte*, 199r.
[27]CWE 50:127 (LB 7:750).

21:17-36 PAUL VISITS JAMES

¹⁷When we had come to Jerusalem, the brothers received us gladly. ¹⁸On the following day Paul went in with us to James, and all the elders were present. ¹⁹After greeting them, he related one by one the things that God had done among the Gentiles through his ministry. ²⁰And when they heard it, they glorified God. And they said to him, "You see, brother, how many thousands there are among the Jews of those who have believed. They are all zealous for the law, ²¹and they have been told about you that you teach all the Jews who are among the Gentiles to forsake Moses, telling them not to circumcise their children or walk according to our customs. ²²What then is to be done? They will certainly hear that you have come. ²³Do therefore what we tell you. We have four men who are under a vow; ²⁴take these men and purify yourself along with them and pay their expenses, so that they may shave their heads. Thus all will know that there is nothing in what they have been told about you, but that you yourself also live in observance of the law. ²⁵But as for the Gentiles who have believed, we have sent a letter with our judgment that they should abstain from what has been sacrificed to idols, and from blood, and from what has been strangled,ᵃ and from sexual immorality." ²⁶Then Paul took the men, and the next day he purified himself along with them and went into the temple, giving notice when the days of purification would be fulfilled and the offering presented for each one of them.

²⁷When the seven days were almost completed, the Jews from Asia, seeing him in the temple, stirred up the whole crowd and laid hands on him, ²⁸crying out, "Men of Israel, help! This is the man who is teaching everyone everywhere against the people and the law and this place. Moreover, he even brought Greeks into the temple and has defiled this holy place." ²⁹For they had previously seen Trophimus the Ephesian with him in the city, and they supposed that Paul had brought him into the temple. ³⁰Then all the city was stirred up, and the people ran together. They seized Paul and dragged him out of the temple, and at once the gates were shut. ³¹And as they were seeking to kill him, word came to the tribune of the cohort that all Jerusalem was in confusion. ³²He at once took soldiers and centurions and ran down to them. And when they saw the tribune and the soldiers, they stopped beating Paul. ³³Then the tribune came up and arrested him and ordered him to be bound with two chains. He inquired who he was and what he had done. ³⁴Some in the crowd were shouting one thing, some another. And as he could not learn the facts because of the uproar, he ordered him to be brought into the barracks. ³⁵And when he came to the steps, he was actually carried by the soldiers because of the violence of the crowd, ³⁶for the mob of the people followed, crying out, "Away with him!"

a Some manuscripts omit *and from what has been strangled*

OVERVIEW: Paul and his companions arrive in Jerusalem and receive a warm reception; however, he again must defend himself against accusations of abandoning Moses and circumcision. The reformers are interested in Paul's pastoral willingness to submit himself to the elders and even to former old covenant ceremonies. Aside from Karlstadt's anomalous view that Paul abhorred the weak, the commentators agree that Paul exemplifies that gradual change is wisest, so that those who still cling to "shadows" can be properly taught that these shadows are cast by their Savior Jesus Christ. Why chase shadows when the thing itself, the substance, can be had?

DO NOT LET FAITHFUL MINISTERS BE SLANDERED. JOHN CALVIN: Luke mentions this in order to commend the fair-mindedness of the brothers who had not relied on unfavorable rumors and misrepresentations. Although many spiteful and wicked people, one after the other, daily loaded Paul with odium, yet, because James and his colleagues were fully convinced of his integrity, they were not hostile to him. Therefore, they now receive him as a servant of Christ in a brotherly and courteous fashion and make it plain that his coming gives them pleasure. And we must pay diligent attention to this moderation, so as not to be too ready to believe vicious accusations, especially when those who have given us some evidence of their uprightness and whom we have found by experience to be serving the Lord faithfully are burdened with charges that are doubtful or unexamined. Because Satan knows that nothing will suit better for overthrowing the kingdom of Christ than the disagreements and jealousies of the faithful, he does not cease spreading indirect rumors, which make them suspicious of each other. Therefore, we must close our ears to accusations, so as not to believe anything about faithful ministers of Christ except on good information. COMMENTARY ON ACTS 21:17.[1]

Should We Glorify Our Good Works? JOHANN SPANGENBERG:

Paul glorifies his actions not for his own sake but so that before the entire world he might make known and praise God's goodness and lovingkindness, that God has incorporated the Gentiles into faith. When Paul speaks of himself, he speaks completely humbly. "I am," he says, "the least among the apostles." Again, "Last of all Christ appeared to me as one untimely born," and other such similar passages. But when he speaks of God's wonders and power, goodness and lovingkindness, he knows no limit to how highly he should praise [God], for this all words are insufficient. BRIEF EXEGESIS OF ACTS 21:19.[2]

How Did the Apostles and Disciples Respond to Paul's Report? JOHANN SPANGENBERG:

Because they heard what great acts God accomplished through Paul, they praised the Lord. Listen to that. They did not praise Paul but the Lord. And this is indeed the true form and manner to honor the dear saints and children of God, namely, whenever we hear the wonders and mighty deeds that God accomplishes through his dear saints, we should not introduce them as gods, pray and call to them and rob God of his proper honor and grant it to [his] creatures. Instead, we should praise God who works in them, who also had flesh and blood, that God raised them up so mercifully and bestowed on them true faith, love, patience and other Christian virtues. That they were children of God should cause us also to ask God for such grace, that he would willingly impart on us even a spark of their faith, love and patience. As well, according to their example we should act and live toward God and the world as they lived and followed Christ. BRIEF EXEGESIS OF ACTS 21:20.[3]

Do Not Show Leniency for the Weak. ANDREAS VON KARLSTADT:

Paul had no concern for the few who took offense or for those who were sick, ignorant and weak.... In this you see that Paul ignored the offense which so many thousand Jews had taken, and he freely preached without regard for the weak. You may want to respond, "I think preaching and doing are two different things." To that I say that preaching is a work like any other and does not happen for nothing. Furthermore, Paul actively prevented circumcision from happening, so how can we say that we want to be Pauline when we do not actively undertake anything that might go against fraternal love? What Paul does later by which he silences some of the clamor against him does not compel me to state that Paul therefore did not physically stop circumcision. His epistle to the Galatians is too revealing to be concealed by anyone. And from that epistle one can see that Paul did not have any concern for the weak. Rather, in sharp words he pulled them away from Moses when he said, "You foolish people, are you having yourselves circumcised?"

---

[1]CNTC 7:198* (CO 48:480-81).
[2]Spangenberg, *Der Apostel Geschichte*, 200v; quoting 1 Tim 1:15; 1 Cor 15:8.
[3]Spangenberg, *Der Apostel Geschichte*, 201r-v.

Here then you have clear grounds that we are not obliged, either in word or deed, to hold back in doing God's commandments until our neighbors and those gluttons at Wittenberg are prepared to follow suit. WHETHER WE SHOULD GO SLOWLY AND AVOID OFFENDING THE WEAK.[4]

PAUL HAS SYMPATHY FOR THE WEAK. JOHN CALVIN: Although these four men may be reckoned in the number of the faithful, still their vow was superstitious. From that it is plain that the apostles had a great deal of difficulty with that nation, which not only had become hardened by daily practice in the discipline of the Law but also was naturally very obstinate and almost intractable. However, it is possible that those men were still novices, and therefore their faith was tender and not yet well formed. Accordingly, the teachers were permitting them to fulfill the vow, which they had rashly made in public through ignorance. As far as Paul is concerned, his reason was different, because he did not submit to this vow because of his own conscience but for the sake of those men to whose error he was indulgent, his reason was different. COMMENTARY ON ACTS 21:23.[5]

PAUL'S DOCTRINE IS AT PEACE WITH MOSES. THE ENGLISH ANNOTATIONS: This was an odious and false accusation. For the doctrine of the gospel which Paul preached was according to Moses' testimony of Christ. However, he taught how we must pass from the shadows and representations to the substance which is in Christ, the end of the law, and how they must use all those indifferent things in wisdom and charity, knowing our freedom in Christ. ANNOTATIONS ON ACTS 21:21.[6]

THE MULTITUDE MUST CERTAINLY COME TOGETHER.[7] JOHN CALVIN: The verb is neutral (δεῖ), as if they said, "It is inevitable that the multitude come together." For it would have been absurd for an apostle with such a great reputation not to appear before the whole assembly of the faithful. If he had avoided the light and the eyes of the people, the sinister suspicion would have increased. At the same time we see how the elders conducted themselves with moderation in fostering harmony, when they quickly anticipate the displeasure of the people, except that they are perhaps too indulgent to their weakness in requiring a vow from Paul. COMMENTARY ON ACTS 21:22.[8]

CEREMONIES ARE EMPTY WITHOUT CHRIST. JOHN CALVIN: Ceremonies would be empty things, if the effect of them had not been exhibited in Christ. Therefore, those who teach that they were abolished by the coming of Christ, far from being abusive of the Law, are rather confirming the truth of it. Close attention must be paid to two things in regard to ceremonies, the truth to which efficacy is linked, second, their outward use. Moreover, the abrogation of the outward use which Christ brought depends on the fact that he himself is the true body[9] and that nothing was foreshadowed in earlier times in which the fullness did not become visible in him. It is a very different thing than defection from the Law, to show its proper aim, that, with figures coming to an end, their spiritual truth may always prevail. Accordingly we see that those who were branding Paul with the charge of apostasy, although he was recalling the faithful from the external worship of the Law, were perverse and unjust in their interpretation. But their ordering Paul to make a public vow with the particular object of proving himself as one who reverences the Law has no other purpose except that he might testify

---

[4]CRR 8:253 (Hertzsch, ed., *Karlstadts Schriften aus den Jahren 1523-25*, 80); quoting Gal 3:1-5.
[5]CNTC 7:202* (CO 48:484).
[6]Downame, ed., *Annotations*, LLL4r*; alluding to Gal 5:1; see also Col 2:17.
[7]Calvin's Greek text differs from the ESV's base text here. He is

here commenting on δει πληθος συνελθειν, "the multitude must come together." This variant is supported by Codex D, Ψ, and 𝔐; modern translations elide this variant on the basis of older manuscripts, namely, Codex B and C, in addition to several miniscules.
[8]CNTC 7:201* (CO 48:483).
[9]See Col 2:17; see also the note above on Calvin's comment at Acts 6:14.

that he does not abhor the Law, like an impious apostate, who would shake off the yoke of the Lord himself and urge others to similar contumacy. COMMENTARY ON ACTS 21:20.[10]

HUMAN TRADITIONS ARE MADE TO BE BROKEN. BOHEMIAN CONFESSION OF 1535: Christ also threatened severely those who were burdening the people with a great number of traditions, saying, "Woe to you lawyers! For you load people with burdens which cannot be borne" (Lk 11:46). Concerning this [the Scriptures] teach that human traditions ought not to be taken as inviolable and eternal laws. Indeed, just as they are kept for certain sure and just reasons, so when other reasons and matters arise and needs are different, they can be violated without sin. Indeed the apostles transgressed against the traditions of the elders when they ate bread with unwashed hands, or again when they did not fast with the rest, but both times they were without sin since they had been excused by Christ. And again in the primitive church, the apostles, gathered together as one with the other saints, led by the Holy Spirit, decreed that the faithful should abstain from meat offered to idols, and from blood, and from things that had been strangled (Acts 15:29; 21:25). But afterward when the reasons for which this had been decreed had disappeared, the command also disappeared (1 Cor 8:1-13). ARTICLE 15, HUMAN TRADITIONS.[11]

THE BLINDNESS OF PREJUDICE. JOHN CALVIN: [The Jews from Asia] cry out as if they are in extreme danger and call on all to bring help, as if their whole religion is in peril. That lets us see how inflamed they were with fierce hatred against Paul, simply because in warning that the full and genuine truth is found in Christ, he was teaching that an end has been put to the figures of the Law. Now because they jump to a false supposition at the sight of Trophimus [the Ephesian], they make it all the plainer, by this hasty and superficial judgment, how virulent they are. They accuse Paul of sacrilege. On what pretext? Because he brought an uncircumcised man into the temple. But on the basis of a false belief they have raised a most serious charge against an innocent man. The audacity of those who are driven by a preconceived opinion is usually preposterous like that. Let us learn from such examples to beware of uncontrolled passions and not to give free reign to unfounded and prejudiced opinions, so as not to rush blindly in an assault on the innocent. COMMENTARY ON ACTS 21:28.[12]

THE RELIGIOUS HYPOCRISY OF THOSE WHO ATTACKED PAUL. RUDOLF GWALTHER: They complained that Paul had brought Gentiles into the temple and thereby had polluted that holy place. But this was a most false and slanderous reproach, yet it found credit with all the people because they had seen one Trophimus, an Ephesian, in the city among Paul's companions. Thus they suspected that he had brought him into the temple. Again this place teaches us how common it is that ministers are accused of being the ones who wickedly sin against the chosen people of God, who impudently condemn the laws and traditions of the church and who are the subverters of the church and of all ancient religion. Thus we read Christ was accused, and the enemies of truth did likewise to Stephen. Certain persons in these days object the very same things against us also: who are motivated no whit by respect for God's church, or by the authority of God's law or even with any care or desire for true religion.

Moreover, being not contented to have apprehended Paul and to load him with false accusations, they use plain force against him. They drag him out of the temple, first shutting the temple gates because they would have the temple by no means polluted. . . . For they had great care that they did not pollute the temple with blood, and therefore they shut the doors. But meanwhile,

---

[10]CNTC 7:200* (CO 48:482).
[11]Boh 1535, 30-31.

[12]CNTC 7:205-6* (CO 48:486).

they did not fear to shed innocent blood. Christ upbraids these things in the Gospel, where he says they strain out a gnat and swallow a camel. So the priests would not go into the judgment hall, because they would not profane their feast day, but they could deliver an innocent person to Pilate and with all manner of unrighteousness and importunacy require his blood. HOMILY 140, ACTS 21:26-32.[13]

---

[13]Gwalther, *Homelyes or Sermons upon the Actes*, 775-76* (*In Acta Apostolorum*, 240v-241r); alluding to Mt 23:24; Jn 18:28.

21:37—22:29 PAUL SPEAKS TO THE CROWD

[37]As Paul was about to be brought into the barracks, he said to the tribune, "May I say something to you?" And he said, "Do you know Greek? [38]Are you not the Egyptian, then, who recently stirred up a revolt and led the four thousand men of the Assassins out into the wilderness?" [39]Paul replied, "I am a Jew, from Tarsus in Cilicia, a citizen of no obscure city. I beg you, permit me to speak to the people." [40]And when he had given him permission, Paul, standing on the steps, motioned with his hand to the people. And when there was a great hush, he addressed them in the Hebrew language,[a] saying:

22 "Brothers and fathers, hear the defense that I now make before you."

[2]And when they heard that he was addressing them in the Hebrew language,[b] they became even more quiet. And he said:

[3]"I am a Jew, born in Tarsus in Cilicia, but brought up in this city, educated at the feet of Gamaliel[c] according to the strict manner of the law of our fathers, being zealous for God as all of you are this day. [4]I persecuted this Way to the death, binding and delivering to prison both men and women, [5]as the high priest and the whole council of elders can bear me witness. From them I received letters to the brothers, and I journeyed toward Damascus to take those also who were there and bring them in bonds to Jerusalem to be punished.

[6]"As I was on my way and drew near to Damascus, about noon a great light from heaven suddenly shone around me. [7]And I fell to the ground and heard a voice saying to me, 'Saul, Saul, why are you persecuting me?' [8]And I answered, 'Who are you, Lord?' And he said to me, 'I am Jesus of Nazareth, whom you are persecuting.' [9]Now those who were with me saw the light but did not understand[d] the voice of the one who was speaking to me. [10]And I said, 'What shall I do, Lord?' And the Lord said to me, 'Rise, and go into Damascus, and there you will be told all that is appointed for you to do.' [11]And since I could not see because of the brightness of that light, I was led by the hand by those who were with me, and came into Damascus.

[12]"And one Ananias, a devout man according to the law, well spoken of by all the Jews who lived there, [13]came to me, and standing by me said to me, 'Brother Saul, receive your sight.' And at that very hour I received my sight and saw him. [14]And he said, 'The God of our fathers appointed you to know his will, to see the Righteous One and to hear a voice from his mouth; [15]for you will be a witness for him to everyone of what you have seen and heard. [16]And now why do you wait? Rise and be baptized and wash away your sins, calling on his name.'

[17]"When I had returned to Jerusalem and was praying in the temple, I fell into a trance [18]and saw him saying to me, 'Make haste and get out of Jerusalem quickly, because they will not accept your testimony about me.' [19]And I said, 'Lord, they themselves know that in one synagogue after another I imprisoned and beat those who believed in you. [20]And when the blood of Stephen your witness was being shed, I myself was standing by and approving and watching over the garments of those who killed him.' [21]And he said to me, 'Go, for I will send you far away to the Gentiles.'"

[22]Up to this word they listened to him. Then they raised their voices and said, "Away with such a fellow from the earth! For he should not be allowed to live." [23]And as they were shouting and throwing off their cloaks and flinging dust into the air, [24]the tribune ordered him to be brought into the barracks, saying that he should be examined by flogging, to find out why they were shouting against him like this. [25]But when they had stretched him out for the whips,[e] Paul said to the centurion who was standing by, "Is it lawful for you to flog a man who is a Roman citizen and uncondemned?" [26]When the centurion heard this, he went to the tribune and said to him, "What are you about to do? For this man is a Roman citizen." [27]So the tribune came and said to him, "Tell me, are you a Roman citizen?" And he said, "Yes." [28]The tribune

answered, "I bought this citizenship for a large sum." Paul said, "But I am a citizen by birth." ²⁹So those who were about to examine him withdrew from him *immediately, and the tribune also was afraid, for he realized that Paul was a Roman citizen and that he had bound him.*

a Or *the Hebrew dialect (probably Aramaic)*   b Or *the Hebrew dialect (probably Aramaic)*   c Or *city at the feet of Gamaliel, educated*   d Or *hear with understanding*   e Or *when they had tied him up with leather strips*

OVERVIEW: Once inside the less raucous barracks, Paul realizes that not only the soldiers but probably also the crowds believe he is an Egyptian insurrectionist. To rectify the misunderstanding Paul addresses the crowd, narrating, for the second time in Luke's account, his own biography. The reformers, somewhat puzzled by Luke's preference for redundancy—after all in Acts 26 Paul will chronicle his life once more—explain that this repetitive narrative serves a worthy Spirit-inspired purpose: to inscribe the most important parts of this book on the readers' minds, and to comfort them that God is faithful even in hostile circumstances.

Reformation exegetes note that Paul's address follows typical rhetorical form, flattering the audience so that they will listen, promising to resolve the issue at hand, and then doing so. Though Paul is unable to finish his defense, he demonstrates proper Christian charity in forgiving and showing kindness even though he had just been flogged by the Jewish rulers. An important engine for this charity is to meditate on the union believers share with Christ. Just as the head suffers when a limb is injured, so our Lord suffers with his people and so fellow believers should suffer with one another.

For the reformers, the response of the crowd to Paul's call to the Gentiles reveals their misunderstanding of God's grace and benefits, which do not belong by right to human beings but to the Lord, who can and will distribute them as he sees fit.

21:37-40 *Paul Allowed to Make His Case*

PAUL IS RIGHT TO DEFEND HIMSELF. JOHN CALVIN: Because it is something that all the

servants of God must do, Paul offered to defend his own case personally. For as far as we can we must take pains to make our integrity known to all, so that no discredit may redound on the name of God from our bad name. When the tribune asks whether Paul is not that Egyptian brigand who, a little earlier, had incited a band of men to insurrection, let us learn that no matter how modestly and quietly ministers of Christ conduct themselves, and no matter how free from blame they are, still they cannot avoid the insults of the world. Therefore we must take note of this, so that we may accustom ourselves to reproaches and be prepared to be blamed for doing well. COMMENTARY ON ACTS 21:37.[1]

PAUL SEEKS TO SHED LIGHT ON THEIR PRESUMPTION. JOHANN SPANGENBERG: "I beg you, allow me to speak to the people." It is as if he wanted to say, "Because not only you but all the people believe that I am an Egyptian, I want to defend myself publicly before everyone." BRIEF EXEGESIS OF ACTS 21:39.[2]

DID PAUL ADDRESS THE PEOPLE IN ARAMAIC OR HEBREW? THE ENGLISH ANNOTATIONS: Whether he spoke in pure Hebrew—used before the captivity, but around the time of Christ this language was dying—or in Syriac, it is not certain.[3] For Syriac was called Hebrew because of its derivation from Hebrew and because it was then the mother tongue of those who were Hebrews. ANNOTATIONS ON ACTS 21:40.[4]

---

[1]CNTC 7:208 (CO 48:488).
[2]Spangenberg, *Der Apostel Geschichte*, 205r.
[3]By Syriac, Aramaic is meant.
[4]Downame, ed., *Annotations*, LLL4v*.

22:1-21 *Paul Recounts His Apostolic Call*

**Why Does Luke Describe This Event
with So Much Detail?** Johann Spangenberg: [First,] in order to show that there are none
on earth who act more detestably—raging and
clamoring—against Christ and his Word and
against Christians than the work-righteousness
and hypocrites. [Second,] we should not despair,
even if we are already in the hands of our enemies;
they are unable to and must not do us any harm
until it is the very hour and it is the Father's will.
These godless [people] would have gladly killed
Paul, but they could not. They had to tolerate
him still longer than three years, while he openly
preached, even by the permission of the emperor!
So God works, who dearly wants to help the entire
world and to bring all people to salvation. Brief
Exegesis of Acts 22.[5]

**Paul's Putative Crimes Demand an Expla-
nation.** Johannes Brenz: We notice that Paul
was accused or falsely suspected of two crimes in
particular. First, by the Jews, because he supposedly instructs everyone everywhere against the
law of Moses, the people of Israel, the holy city of
Jerusalem and its temple—and this is a crime of
heresy.[6] Second, by the tribune, because supposedly
he is that Egyptian bandit who recently led several
thousand assassins out into the desert, and when
his followers were killed by the Roman garrison, he
sought safety for himself by flight—and this is the
crime of sedition. These two crimes are almost as
a matter of course leveled against teachers of piety
and the gospel truth....

[Here] Paul refutes these charges and defends
himself, showing that he neither is that seditious
Egyptian nor teaches heresies against the law and
the prophets of God. And although several things
in this oration concerning the calling of Paul were
described by Luke above in Acts 9 and likewise
will be brought back up later in Acts 26, still the

author of this book had his reasons for relating
the calling of Paul in this passage also, undoubtedly to highlight the most important details of the
story and so that we would never forget them. For
he gives us plenty that we can use, both for grasping the teaching of Paul and for confirming our
faith from the enormous mercy by which Christ
embraced his own persecutor. Homily 101 on
Acts 22.[7]

**Do Not Condemn an Entire Nation for
the Crimes of a Few.** Rudolf Gwalther:
He calls them brothers and fathers in order to gain
their good will. For the same reason he uses the
Hebrew language, in which he knew they greatly
delighted.... His modesty is worth noting. He
is so careful to call those who were in so many
ways his explicit enemies, who had injured him,
brothers and fathers. He does not do this out of
flattery or fear, but in part because he himself is
of the same nation and in part because he hopes
that in so great a multitude there would be found
those ... who would be converted and won by the
teaching of the Word. Therefore, by Paul's example
here they are reproved who condemn the lawful
and accepted honors which the apostle elsewhere
commands us to use: he instructs us to treat one
another honorably....

Now here we are taught that because of a few
who have harmed us, we should not condemn the
entire nation. For what more grievous injuries
can be imagined than those which the Jews did
to Paul? And yet he loves them and respectfully
speaks to them. He longs for their health and
salvation and would redeem their lives by the loss
of his own life. Indeed, still sore from his most
recent wounds and floggings, and in chains, he
accepts them as brothers and fathers. Now, those
who are blinded with impulsive anger for a trifling
injury done by some rascal and who therefore
heap slander and other evils on an entire nation,
let them test themselves by this rule. For if it is
not lawful for a Christian to seek revenge on his

[5]Spangenberg, *Der Apostel Geschichte*, 206v-207r.
[6]See Luther's comment above on Acts 3:17-22.
[7]Brenz, *In Acta Apostolica Homiliae*, 201v-202r.

enemies, what madness is it to indict a whole country or nation for the wickedness of one person! Homily 142, Acts 22:1-5.[8]

PAUL SHOWS RHETORICAL TACT. JOHANNES BRENZ: Rhetoricians teach that someone who is about to give a speech should, at the beginning of the oration, win over the listener to himself and draw his attention. In this exordium of Paul many things serve to render the Jews attentive and well disposed. First, Paul, inasmuch as he was shackled, sought a place for speaking. He was not accustomed to giving speeches while being in chains. Second, he addresses the Jews in the Hebrew language, which they all understood and which they held in great esteem, even considering it sacred. Furthermore, although the Jews had seized and beaten him and tried to kill him, nevertheless he attributed solemn titles to them, calling them brothers and fathers. It is a mark of civility when in the midst of war an enemy attributes solemn titles to his enemy. Also by these titles Paul declares his own gentleness and clemency, no doubt signaling that his heart was far removed from thoughts of revenge and bitterness. Last, when he says, "Hear my defense," with one word he renders the listeners well-disposed to him, promising that he would make clear that he is not guilty of the thing for which he is accused. For naturally we favor a defendant who promises a complete rebuttal of the charge. Therefore, at the beginning Paul refutes the charge of sedition and says, "I am a Jewish man born in Tarsus of Cilicia. There are many among you who think that I am that Egyptian bandit who recently slipped away and fled. So lest they err, let them know that I am not at all Egyptian but Cilician, born in the city of Tarsus, not of Egypt but of Cilicia. And how far Egypt and Cilicia are apart from one another, anyone who has a mind for geography knows." HOMILY 101 ON ACTS 22.[9]

OUR DEEP DEBT TO THOSE WHO TAUGHT US. RUDOLF GWALTHER: It is not without reason that he mentions both the city of Jerusalem and his teacher. For in this city was the most famous university of the entire nation, and his master among the lawyers and doctors was of the greatest authority. Therefore, it cannot be that he—who had been raised since childhood in that city, in the middle of their sacrifices and under such a man—could be rude and ignorant in the Scriptures and [their] religion. Moreover, Paul's example serves well for our instruction, who deal with faith and religion. First, he removes all suspicion of ignorance and inability, demonstrating that no one ought to be ignorant in religion and that they are wrong who assert it is enough only to believe and will not allow diligent study in matters of religion....

Furthermore, it is a great sign of modesty and love in Paul that he mentions so reverently Gamaliel his master, even though he knew that he still erred in many points and even though it was through him that he learned that preposterous zeal for the law. Nevertheless he acknowledges his indebtedness to him because, at the very least, he learned great literature. Now then, how much more do we owe to such masters who not only teach us wisdom but also godliness and the path to true salvation? HOMILY 142, ACTS 22:1-5.[10]

WHY DOES PAUL MENTION HIS STUDIES SO OFTEN? JOHANNES BRENZ: We should not think that Paul, who was extremely sharp, would arbitrarily repeat the same exact thing over and over again. And so, first, he recounts his studies in Judaism so that by antithesis he can illustrate his calling to the preaching of the gospel of Jesus Christ and render it more commendable, to the degree that he shows it could not have happened except by divine power. For Paul was trained with such great erudition in the law of his fathers that in knowledge and doctrine he surpassed many peers among his people. Therefore, it is not because of

---

[8]Gwalther, *Homelyes or Sermons upon the Actes*, 781-82* (*In Acta Apostolorum*, 242v); alluding to Rom 12:10.
[9]Brenz, *In Acta Apostolica Homiliae*, 202r.

[10]Gwalther, *Homelyes or Sermons upon the Actes*, 782, 783* (*In Acta Apostolorum*, 242v); alluding to Acts 5:34.

lack of knowledge or simplicity that he now follows the gospel that he once persecuted. Additionally, he excelled with such great righteousness in works of the law that in accordance with the exacting sect of the Pharisees he was blameless, and he led a life praised by all. Therefore, it was not some malice perpetrated against the law that drove him to forsake the study of the law and to commit himself to the profession of the gospel. It usually happens that they, who on account of their own sins cannot remain in some religion, turn to following another one; but Paul was so far removed from any outward indication of sin in his own religion that he was reckoned to be extremely holy.

Furthermore, he was devoted and bound with such a great passion for his law that he was persecuting all Christians with an excessive amount of zeal, and not lightly but very heavily, not to flight, exile or shackles only, but all the way up to death. And he was persecuting not just men but even women, and not only in Jerusalem but also in foreign cities, in Damascus and other places. And he preferred to risk his life, and even three hundred times to face death, than to desert the inheritance of his law. Therefore, when such a great and devoted follower of the law suddenly begins to profess that which formerly with all his might he persecuted, surely it is obvious that he was changed not by some human power but by a celestial and divine force. Moreover, if he was changed by divine force, who is Paul to be able to resist such a divine force?

Second, Paul recounts his studies also for the following reason, that by his authority he might show that the preaching of the gospel is not contrary to the law and the prophets; rather, it fulfills that which the law required and the prophets prophesied. For someone who was not a scholar in the law and the prophets were to teach these things, surely he would hear, "Why are you talking nonsense about things you know nothing about?" Now Paul was meticulously instructed in the law and advanced beyond his peers, but at the same time he teaches that the gospel without question fulfills what the law requires, namely, righteousness; who would not put their trust in this scholarly man?

There is an additional reason why so many times he recounts his studies in Judaism, to wit, so that by his example he might show that what seems right to us is not necessarily right, nor is what seems to us impious in our good (as they term it) intentions always impious in the future. For to such an extent did it seem to Paul as he persecuted the church that he was doing the right thing that he thought he was exhibiting a particularly special obedience to God and figured that he was so certain that the gospel message was the height of impiety that he dared even with his death to affirm that; yet, later, illumined by divine revelation, he held a far different opinion. What then? Do not be a stubborn campaigner in your own discoveries, but listen also to the opinion of others, and judge free from emotions. And after you ascertain what is right and just, then it will be time to confess what is just, even if a sword threatens your neck. As, for example, we are now sure that the teaching of Paul concerning Jesus Christ and the justification of faith as opposed to the justification of works is the true and divine doctrine. Consequently, even if the world should collapse and come to an end, the truth of this doctrine must be held to and confessed. Homily 101 on Acts 22.[11]

God's Faithful Voice Drowns Out the Foolish Advice of the Flesh. Rudolf Gwalther: By this Paul declares that he had such a fervent zeal that he could not have been converted so suddenly without the work of God. He was called by God, compelled to embrace the faith of Christ. . . . This example of Paul teaches us that in religion we must chiefly seek not our own advantage by taking the advice of the affections of the flesh. For they who do are carried about with every wind, and even though they sometimes seize true religion, still they eventually fall away from it again, as soon as they feel it does not agree with their desires. Let us therefore cast away the blind desires of the world and the flesh and obey the voice of God—which we must follow—and

---

[11]Brenz, *In Acta Apostolica Homiliae*, 202v.

embrace Christ, so that established in him we my stand tall against all tempests and storms, growing in him so that we may reign and live with him in heaven: to whom be praise, honor, power and glory forever. Amen. HOMILY 142, ACTS 22:1-5.[12]

JESUS TAKES OUR PERSECUTION PERSONALLY.
RUDOLF GWALTHER: By these words Jesus plainly testifies that whatever had been done against his faithful people was done to him. For there is such a connection between Christ and us as there is between the head and its members. Who would have imagined that Christ cared at all for his church when Stephen was put to death in such an unworthy manner? Or when Saul burst open the doors and carried away both men and women to prison? Indeed, not only did Christ see these things and not only was he saddened by the afflictions of his people, but he suffered in such a way as if he himself had been beaten and carried to prison.

With this belongs that saying in the prophet: "He who touches you touches the pupil of my[13] eye." This should console the godly and terrify those who think it a light thing to persecute the members of Christ. . . . For he hears the cry of his servants and proves himself to be a mighty defender. In the meanwhile, Christ's example teaches us what kind of sympathy should be among us who glory in Christ our head: we declare that we are members of one and the same body. Let us therefore rejoice with those who rejoice and weep with those who weep. HOMILY 143, ACTS 22:6-11.[14]

SCRIPTURE IS NOT CONTRADICTED. CARDINAL CAJETAN: "Paul's companions heard a certain voice." This conversation reported by Luke in Acts 9:7 is not contradicted, because Luke speaks about the voice of Paul to Jesus; this, however, is the speech of the voice of Jesus to Paul. COMMENTARY ON ACTS 22:9.[15]

HIS COMPANIONS COULD HEAR ONLY PAUL.
THE ENGLISH ANNOTATIONS: In Acts 9:7, it is said they heard a voice, that is, the voice of Saul speaking to someone they could not see. They did not hear the voice of Christ. Some think they heard only a confused sound—so they might perceive it was from heaven—as the people did when some said it thundered, some said an angel spoke but did not understand what was said. ANNOTATIONS ON ACTS 22:9.[16]

A PREACHER'S MESSAGE MUST COME FROM THE WORD OF GOD. STEPHEN DENISON: It has been the practice of all good ministers not to preach their own dreams and fancies but to receive their message from God. . . The Word of God for the excellence of it far surpasses any other words: yes, the excellence of a person's wit is but chaff in comparison with it. And therefore if ministers would excel at the edification of the church, they must deliver God's Word. Second, as the Word excels in quality, so it excels in power; it is able to cast down strongholds through God. It is able to save the soul. . . . Therefore if ministers desire to do good by their ministry, they must preach the Word. Third, if any out of a newfangled humor shall neglect the Word, and instead of God's truth preaches his own fancies, he is liable to great rebuke.

But how do ministers receive their messages from God in these days? Not immediately by extraordinary revelation, as the prophets and apostles did, but mediated by the Word, and in this respect the Scriptures are fitly termed oracles of God. From them, as from an oracle, we receive the mind and will of God. THE DOCTRINE OF BOTH THE SACRAMENTS.[17]

---

[12]Gwalther, *Homelyes or Sermons upon the Actes*, 783-84* (*In Acta Apostolorum*, 243r).

[13]Zech 2:8. ESV uses "his" here, following the scribal emendation of "my" to clarify that God's eye, not Zechariah's, is the object. The NRSV is the only major modern English translation to use "my."

[14]Gwalther, *Homelyes or Sermons upon the Actes*, 786* (*In Acta Apostolorum*, 244r); alluding to 1 Cor 12:26; Rom 12:15.

[15]Cajetan, *In Acta Apostolorum*, 232r-v.

[16]Downame, ed., *Annotations*, LLL4v*; alluding to Jn 12:29.

[17]Denison, *Doctrine of Both the Sacraments*, 58, 59-60*; alluding to Lam 1:21; Rom 2:3.

PAUL IS CARRIED INTO DAMASCUS AS A VICTIM. THE ENGLISH ANNOTATIONS: He who brought servants and others to assist him in carrying away the servants of Christ from Damascus bound to Jerusalem is pleased to use their help in leading him blind into Damascus. Thus God made him an example of his justice, punishing him and, out of his mercy, converting him. ANNOTATIONS ON ACTS 22:11.[18]

THE EARLIEST IS THE PUREST. STEPHEN DENISON: Certainly things in their first institutions were the purest; doctrine was purest in the first preaching, to wit, out of the mouths and from the pens of the prophets and apostles: the sacraments were freest from corruption at their first administration. How innocent was the baptism of John, and how perfect was the Supper of Christ when they first administered these. What shall we say, the old way is the good way, as the prophet speaks, and therefore it is fit we should walk in a similar manner. But here it may be demanded to what copies we must have recourse in order to find out the true institutions of things. . . . We must proceed to the canonical Scriptures, for they of all other writings most perfectly and faithfully describe to us the first institution of all things which are necessary for us to believe or practice. THE DOCTRINE OF BOTH THE SACRAMENTS.[19]

ANANIAS IS DEVOUT "ACCORDING TO THE LAW." THE ENGLISH ANNOTATIONS: He inserts this phrase to show them that the gospel is not contrary or destructive to the law, but merely the fulfillment of it. For a man zealous for and learned in the law by God's appointment persuaded him to embrace the gospel. ANNOTATIONS ON ACTS 22:12.[20]

THE RESTORATION OF PAUL'S PHYSICAL VISION CONFIRMS ANANIAS'S SPIRITUAL VISION. RUDOLF GWALTHER: The chief point God used this for seems to be this: that Paul might know that Ananias was indeed sent to him by God. For who would accuse him of vanity who—after being admonished by a heavenly oracle, indeed, utterly amazed—following the oracle changed his religion? Paul's example teaches us that of all things we must flee levity in religion. We should not rashly believe everyone. For as in religion consists the sum of our salvation, so it appears that there have been deceivers in all ages who have laid snares to trap the minds of the simple. Both Christ and the apostles abundantly show us that such would arise in the church after them. Therefore, the ideas of some today should be lamented, who in the clearest light of the gospel believe every spirit contrary to the command of John the apostle. Indeed, they take them to be true followers of the apostles who, with scurrilious abuses, secretly castigate both the ministers of the Word and the magistrates while they themselves are neither learned nor honest. HOMILY 144, ACTS 22:12-16.[21]

PAUL SHOWS THE CONTINUITY BETWEEN THE OLD COVENANT AND THE NEW. JOHN CALVIN: In calling him the God of our fathers, he renews the memory of the promises, so that the Jews may know that Paul's recent call is connected with them and that those who make the transition to Christ are not abandoning the Law. Therefore by these words Paul confirms what he has previously asserted in person, that he has not deserted the God of Abraham and the God who had already been worshiped by the Jews in times past, but that he is continuing in the ancient worship of their ancestors, which he had learned from the Law. COMMENTARY ON ACTS 22:14.[22]

ANANIAS EXHORTS PAUL TO EXPERIENCE THE GRACE OF BAPTISM. JOHN CALVIN: There is no doubt that Ananias faithfully instructed Paul in the rudiments of the faith. He would not have baptized him if he lacked true faith. But Luke leaves

---

[18]Downame, ed., *Annotations*, LLL4v*.
[19]Denison, *Doctrine of Both the Sacraments*, 53*.
[20]Downame, ed., *Annotations*, LLL4v*.

[21]Gwalther, *Homelyes or Sermons upon the Actes*, 789* (*In Acta Apostolorum*, 244v-245r); alluding to 1 Jn 4:1.
[22]CNTC 7:216* (CO 48:494-95).

out many things and only gives a brief summary. Therefore since Paul understands that the promised redemption has now been procured in Christ, Ananias is quite right in saying that nothing ought to cause his baptism to be delayed. But when he says, "What are you waiting for?" he is not rebuking Paul and is not accusing him of being slow, but he is further amplifying the grace of God by the addition of baptism. COMMENTARY ON ACTS 22:16.[23]

IN BAPTISM THE HOLY SPIRIT APPLIES THE BLOOD OF CHRIST TO OUR SOULS. GIOVANNI DIODATI: The Holy Spirit ratifies your external baptism by the inward application of the blood and satisfaction of Christ for the purification of your soul before God and for regeneration to newness of life. ANNOTATION ON ACTS 22:16.[24]

BAPTISM COMES AFTER CONVERSION. FELIX MANZ: Just as they were purified internally by the descent of the Holy Spirit, so too water was also poured over them externally as a symbol of their inner cleansing and dying to sin. And as evidence that this is the meaning of baptism, . . . Paul tells what happened to him on the road to Damascus. . . . We see very clearly from these words what baptism is and when baptism should be practiced. That is, a person should be baptized if he has been converted through God's Word, if he has changed his mind and wants to live henceforth a renewed life, as Paul clearly shows, if he is dead to his old life and his heart has been circumcised, and if he has died to sin with Christ. Then he should be buried with Christ in baptism and be resurrected with him to new life. PROTEST AND DEFENSE.[25]

BAPTISM COVERS OUR WHOLE LIFE. GALLIC CONFESSION: Baptism is given as a pledge of our adoption; for by it we are grafted into the body of Christ, so as to be washed and cleansed by his blood, and then renewed in purity of life by his Holy Spirit. We hold, also, that although we are baptized only once, still the gain that it symbolizes to us reaches over our whole lives and to our death, so that we have a lasting witness that Jesus Christ will always be our justification and sanctification. Nevertheless, although it is a sacrament of faith and penitence, still as God receives little children into the church with their fathers, we say, on the authority of Jesus Christ, that the children of believing parents should be baptized. ARTICLE 35.[26]

GOD DOES NOT NEEDLESSLY GIVE COMMANDS TO HIS PEOPLE. RUDOLF GWALTHER: Here we must observe how Ananias speaks about the sacrament, which declares the dignity and purpose of baptism. For Ananias did not mean that he thought sins were washed away by water. The Scriptures everywhere teach that sins are cleansed and purged only by the blood of Christ. But, because that washing which is made of the blood of Christ is externally shadowed and expressed by baptism, it comes to pass, so that by this phrase of Scripture, sins are said to be washed away by baptism. And so that Paul does not think it a strange or difficult kind of saying, Ananias adds, "by calling on the name of the Lord." For by these words he is sent to Christ, who being grasped and called on by faith bestows the gifts of salvation on us that the sacraments figure and shadow unto us. If we are to profit from the sacraments, we must focus on Christ. Thus, we are taught that they must not be condemned as superfluous in any way. For God has ordained nothing without great consideration; his intent is not to have his church oppressed in any way. HOMILY 144, ACTS 22:12-16.[27]

PAUL WRESTLES WITH THE LORD IN PRAYER. JOHN CALVIN: But the question is raised whether it was right for Paul to bring forward these objections to Christ. For it is just as if he contends that

---

[23]CNTC 7:217 (CO 48:496).

[24]Diodati, *Pious Annotations*, CCIv* (*I Commenti alla Sacra Biblia*, 1118).

[25]Felix Manz, "Protest and Defense," in *The Radical Reformation*, ed. and trans. Michael G. Baylor (Cambridge: Cambridge University Press, 1991), 98*, alluding to Acts 22:14-16; Rom 6:4.

[26]*Creeds* 3:379-80*.

[27]Gwalther, *Homelyes or Sermons upon the Actes*, 791-92* (*In Acta Apostolorum*, 245v).

what Christ said would not happen, probably would. I reply that God allows his saints to unburden their feelings on his bosom in an intimate way, especially when all that they are seeking is the confirmation of their faith. If anyone relies on his own wisdom or stubbornly rejects what God orders, his arrogance will be justifiably condemned. But God thinks his faithful people worthy of the unique privilege that they may humbly put before him things that could call them back or detain them when they are eager to obey, so that, freer and readier, they may commit themselves wholly to God. We find an example of it here, for after Paul has been instructed to please the Lord in this way, he does not reply and does not make any further assertion, but content with that one objection and desisting from it, he prepares himself for the journey, which he had appeared to be avoiding. Commentary on Acts 22:19.[28]

Like a Good Pastor, Paul Prays for the People. Rudolf Gwalther: What he prayed may easily be gathered when he says that he often prayed for the Jews, that they would obtain salvation. . . . Now ministers are here admonished concerning their duties, that is, with continual prayers to help procure and advance the salvation of the people. For as the rule of faith and charity, by which they are bound to the flock committed to them, commands the same, so also necessity requires it, because it is evident that their labors are in vain unless God grants the growth. Homily 145, Acts 22:17-22.[29]

Martyrs Are Special Suffering Servants. The English Annotations: *Martyr* is a Greek word meaning "witness." It is used in a special way to indicate those who in constant profession, in grievous punishment or violent death give testimony to the truth of the gospel. Annotations on Acts 22:20.[30]

22:22-29 Paul Rejected and Almost Flogged

The People Could Not Bear to Share God s Grace with Sinners. The English Annotations: They could not endure to hear about Paul going to the Gentiles. Therefore, here they interrupt him with tumultuous clamors. They had such a proud confidence in themselves that they could not bear that God would grant his own benefits on anyone other than themselves; and yet they themselves refused them! We should not be grieved that sinners partner with us in repentance and mercy, since we belong to Christ who for the redemption of his people did not refuse to be crucified between thieves and evildoers. Annotations on Acts 22:22.[31]

When It Comes to Religious Arguments, Many Lose All Restraint. Rudolf Gwalther: This example teaches us how much hatred of the truth is able to do. Those whose minds it has seized forget all modesty, equity and charity. For what is here done against Paul was earlier done before Pilate against Christ. . . . Furthermore, this passage shows us what kind of arguments are commonly used against the servants of Christ today—as well as in their own quarrel, as in Christ's. That is to say, shouting, threatening, punishments, fire, sword. With these weapons they have fought even from the beginning of the world, and with the same they fight still today. This is a miserable blindness and perverseness of the world, that while in profane and worldly matters everyone prays and holds advised deliberation, in matters of religion and the common case of eternal salvation, many think the matter should be handled and dispatched with unreasonable noise, furious braids, uproars and rebellion. Homily 146, Acts 22:23-29.[32]

What Is Flogging? Giovanni Diodati: It was a kind of Roman torture or rack on which they

---

[28]CNTC 7:221* (CO 48:499).

[29]Gwalther, *Homelyes or Sermons upon the Actes*, 793* (*In Acta Apostolorum*, 246r); alluding to Rom 10:1; 1 Cor 3:5-9 (cf. Ps 127:1).

[30]Downame, ed., *Annotations*, LLL4v*.

[31]Downame, ed., *Annotations*, MMMIr*.

[32]Gwalther, *Homelyes or Sermons upon the Actes*, 796* (*In Acta Apostolorum*, 247r).

were laid naked, bound with strong cords and then harshly scourged with leather lashes until they confessed the truth. ANNOTATION ON ACTS 22:24.[33]

THE BLOOD OF THE INNOCENT WILL BE REQUIRED FROM THE GUILTY. RUDOLF GWALTHER: This was a grievous sin in the tribune. And by this all who are in authority should learn not to be excessively rash or cruel in interrogating and punishing. For it is a great sin to disgrace the innocent with punishment, and it is not rare that, overcome by pain, they confess to doing what they would never even contemplate.... Therefore, all who are in authority should strive to fulfill justice, for the judgments of God are commited to them, and one day the Lord will require the blood of his servants from their hands.... We are also taught by this example in what state the saints are in this world. They are counted among the wicked and judged as the vilest of all humans. Everyone freely scorns and mocks their body and life, as they please. This was true of the prophets and Christ.... Therefore let it not grieve us to be counted with these people or be offended with the unjust judgments of this world, knowing that God will remember his servants and will not allow the slanders against the innocent to remain hidden for long. HOMILY 146, ACTS 22:23-29.[34]

PAUL'S CITIZENSHIP HIS MOST USEFUL DEFENSE. JOHN CALVIN: In the first place Paul brings forward the right to the privileges of citizenship and then pleads a general right in his defense. But although the second point was the more important, namely, that it is not right for a man to be scourged without a hearing, still it would have been useless if the centurion had not been more disturbed about the honor of the Roman Empire. For at that time there was no greater crime than the violation of the liberty of the Roman people. The laws of Valerius, Porcius, Sempronius and

others like them forbade anyone to inflict punishment on the body of a Roman citizen without the command of the people.[35] The privilege was so sacred that they considered it not only a capital but also an inexpiable offense for a Roman citizen to be beaten. Therefore Paul escaped because of a privilege, rather than common justice; but he did not hesitate to use, in a good cause, this shield of citizenship to ward off the injury that was prepared for him. COMMENTARY ON ACTS 22:25.[36]

LUKE OMITS THE PROCESS OF CONFIRMING PAUL'S ROMAN CITIZENSHIP. JOHN CALVIN: Somebody may wonder why the man who was in charge of holding the examination was so credulous that he makes a firm assertion, as if about something of which he had certain knowledge. For if he was bound to give credence to Paul's statement, then any criminal could have avoided punishment by this artifice. But this was their method of acting: a man who was asserting that he was a Roman citizen was punished, unless he produced someone who knew him, or proved legally that he was a citizen; for it was a capital offense to lay false claim to the right of citizenship. Accordingly the centurion refers the matter to the tribune, as if it were in doubt, but the tribune, as we have said, immediately hastens to investigate. But even if Luke does not tell what evidence Paul used to prove himself a Roman citizen, yet there is no doubt that the tribune obtained full knowledge of the truth before he untied him. COMMENTARY ON ACTS 22:26.[37]

---

[33]Diodati, *Pious Annotations*, CCIv* (*I Commenti alla Sacra Biblia*, 1119).
[34]Gwalther, *Homelyes or Sermons upon the Actes*, 796-97* (*In Acta Apostolorum*, 247r).

[35]The laws of Valerius and Porcius are earlier versions of the Lex Julia on the lawful use of force against Roman citizens. See Richard I. Pervo, *Acts: A Commentary* (Minneapolis: Fortress, 2009), 413-14, and John Clayton Lentz, Jr., *Luke's Portrait of Paul* (Cambridge: Cambridge University Press, 1993), 120-30. For a general description of the legal use of force see "Vis," in BNP 15:462-63. The Sempronian law to which Calvin is referring is *lex de capite civis*, which "prohibited the Senate from instituting criminal courts and provided for capital punishment for the killing of citizens who had not been condemned by a court instituted by the people" (BNP 13:246).
[36]CNTC 7:221-22* (CO 48:500).
[37]CNTC 7:223 (CO 48:500-501).

HOW CAN PAUL BE ROMAN IF HE HAS NEVER BEEN TO ROME? JOHN CALVIN: The tribune makes this objection in order to refute him, as if he said that the right of citizenship is not such a common thing and is not open to all. He says, "How can it be that an obscure fellow of the Cilician people like you acquired this honor, which cost me a great deal of money?" When Paul replies that he was born (a Roman citizen), he, who had never seen the city, and, furthermore, whose father had perhaps never gone near it, there is no reason for that to upset anyone. For those who are acquainted with Roman history know that certain men in the provinces were granted citizenship if they served the state well either in war or in other important affairs and requested this reward for themselves from the proconsuls; so there is nothing absurd about a man having been born a Roman citizen, although, being a native of a remote province, he might never have yet set foot in Italy. COMMENTARY ON ACTS 22:28.[38]

---

[38]CNTC 7:223-24* (CO 48:501).

22:30—23:11 PAUL BEFORE THE JEWISH COUNCIL

[30]*But on the next day, desiring to know the real reason why he was being accused by the Jews, he unbound him and commanded the chief priests and all the council to meet, and he brought Paul down and set him before them.*

23 *And looking intently at the council, Paul said, "Brothers, I have lived my life before God in all good conscience up to this day."* [2]*And the high priest Ananias commanded those who stood by him to strike him on the mouth.* [3]*Then Paul said to him, "God is going to strike you, you whitewashed wall! Are you sitting to judge me according to the law, and yet contrary to the law you order me to be struck?"* [4]*Those who stood by said, "Would you revile God's high priest?"* [5]*And Paul said, "I did not know, brothers, that he was the high priest, for it is written, 'You shall not speak evil of a ruler of your people.'"*

[6]*Now when Paul perceived that one part were Sadducees and the other Pharisees, he cried out in the council, "Brothers, I am a Pharisee, a son of Pharisees. It is with respect to the hope and the resurrection of the dead that I am on trial."* [7]*And when he had said this, a dissension arose between the Pharisees and the Sadducees, and the assembly was divided.* [8]*For the Sadducees say that there is no resurrection, nor angel, nor spirit, but the Pharisees acknowledge them all.* [9]*Then a great clamor arose, and some of the scribes of the Pharisees' party stood up and contended sharply, "We find nothing wrong in this man. What if a spirit or an angel spoke to him?"* [10]*And when the dissension became violent, the tribune, afraid that Paul would be torn to pieces by them, commanded the soldiers to go down and take him away from among them by force and bring him into the barracks.*

[11]*The following night the Lord stood by him and said, "Take courage, for as you have testified to the facts about me in Jerusalem, so you must testify also in Rome."*

OVERVIEW: Paul's defense before the Jewish council offers the reformers an irresistible dichotomy: the newly minted, pure apostolic office in contrast to the ancient but deeply corrupted priesthood. All the commentators agree that the temple priesthood is a legitimate office ordained by God and ultimately rooted in his Word and command. But what happens when those in office are corrupted and unscrupulous? The reformers acknowledge that Paul is a sinner, but one in good conscience who has been faithful to his calling. Thus Paul exemplifies the difficult station of the preaching office: Paul, a sinner, can only preach faithfully to other sinners on the basis of God's holy Word, not his own moral goodness or wisdom. In the end Paul and Ananias, or any church leader, are for our commentators only parables of God's love, as it were; they too will fail to model this properly, as both Jewish and Christian

schisms demonstrate.[1] Therefore, believers should cherish and respect their leaders and peers in Christ, but the true example is found in Christ— in the Father's love for his Son, and the Son's love for his Father.

Jesus' comfort to Paul in verse 11 provokes further questions about the nature of Christian suffering. Each commentator groans at the difficulty of this "comfort"; for Gwalther it is like telling a sick person they are well only to tell them they have a new, more potent disease. No one offers explanations of *how* the Lord's consolation works, they merely state that Christian faith is not based on experience or feelings—which fluctuate—but on God's faithfulness to his promises.

---

[1]The idea of being a parable of God's love comes from David Hansen's language in *The Art of Pastoring: Ministry Without All the Answers*, rev. ed. (Downers Grove, IL: InterVarsity Press, 2012).

How Can Paul Say He Has Lived a Good Life Before God? JOHANN SPANGENBERG:
Paul is not here talking about his corrupt nature and inherent sin, which he has in common with all people—this is also true of those who accused him, since we are all together stuck in [original sin]; rather, he is talking about the preaching office, concerning which he is accused. It is as if he wanted to say, "God charged me with the preaching office. To this I am called by God and chosen by the Holy Spirit: to preach the gospel. I have preached with such diligence both among Jews and Gentiles that I hope to stand before God with a good conscience." This is a good lesson for preachers. BRIEF EXEGESIS OF ACTS 23:1.[2]

Paul Knows He Is a Sinner but Not Concerning the Temple Rulers' Accusations. RUDOLF GWALTHER: These words are not to be understood as if he gloried in himself, that he is free of all sin and able to stand on his own righteousness before the judgment seat of God. He means in the present matter. For his adversaries accused him of deviating from the ancient religion, of impiety against God and that, like a public enemy, he had wickedly violated the law and the temple and the entire Levitical worship—bringing the unclean Gentiles into contact with God's people. Since no one should be prevented with these false accusations and be denied a hearing, therefore, Paul clears himself of all charges at the beginning of his defense, saying he has done all things in a good conscience in his office as apostle. For he was able to call God to witness to his integrity and honor. HOMILY 147, ACTS 23:1-5.[3]

Paul Refutes His Accusers with Audacious Claims. THE ENGLISH ANNOTATIONS:
Paul said this to refute the calumnies of those who accused him of profanation. Not that he was free from all sin, but to show that they wrongfully accused him of contempt of God's law or the profanation of the temple. ANNOTATIONS ON ACTS 23:1.[4]

The Importance of a Good Conscience.
RUDOLF GWALTHER: The beginning of Paul's speech teaches us that in matters of religion we must first have regard for our conscience, lest we act through wicked trickery or hypocrisy. Because the issue is between God, "who tests hearts and kidneys,"[5] and us, there is no room for deception and hypocrisy. It is lawful for us to rejoice in the integrity of our conscience, if we order our religion according to the Word of God, walking diligently in his calling and not according to our desire and pleasure. If we endeavor to do this, God will leniently pardon those daily lapses of life—which we commit through the infirmity of our flesh—because we turn to Christ to whom we are joined in repentance. HOMILY 147, ACTS 23:1-5.[6]

Paul's Insult. GIOVANNI DIODATI: "Whitewashed wall," that is, false hypocrite in your feigned zeal under which you cloak the corruption of your injustice and cruelty. ANNOTATION ON ACTS 23:3.[7]

Civil Versus Ecclesiastical Authority. JOHN MAYER: It may seem that Paul forgot Christ's precept, "If he strike you on the left cheek turn to him the right also." However, the solution is easy. The Lord does not by these words exact silence, whereby the malice and wickedness of enemies is nourished, but he bridles people's minds from impatience, when wrongs are offered, teaching to overcome evil with goodness. . . .

---

[4]Downame, ed., *Annotations*, MMMIr*; alluding to Rom 7:23.
[5]See Ps 7:9. Formerly, the kidneys were understood as the seat of the conscience. All modern translations render this verse as "hearts and minds"—except the KJV, which uses "hearts and reins," an archaic synonym for kidneys—still the Hebrew literally is "hearts and kidneys."
[6]Gwalther, *Homelyes or Sermons upon the Actes*, 800* (*In Acta Apostolorum*, 248r).
[7]Diodati, *Pious Annotations*, CCIv* (*I Commenti alla Sacra Biblia*, 1119); alluding to Ezek 13:10; Mt 23:27.

---

[2]Spangenberg, *Der Apostel Geschichte*, 208r-v.
[3]Gwalther, *Homelyes or Sermons upon the Actes*, 799-800* (*In Acta Apostolorum*, 248r).

I hold this to be unworthy of the reverence of a ruler seeing that he has corrupted and perverted the whole order of the church of God. If it is said this is to give an example of refusing to obey princes who are wicked, I answer there is a difference between civil magistrates and ecclesiastical prelates. To the first, obedience and reverence must be yielded, though their government be confused and wicked, because the Lord wills to have their dominion still remain safe, but when the spiritual government is degenerate, the consciences of the godly are loosed from obeying their unjust domination, because they falsely pretend the sacerdotal title when they use it to pervert true doctrine. On these grounds, it is lawful, even necessary, for the faithful to shake off the yoke of the pope. TREASURY OF ECCLESIASTICAL EXPOSITIONS.[8]

PREACHERS MUST EXHORT EVERY SORT OF PERSON. JOHANN SPANGENBERG: He knew of his tyranny, hypocritical nature and life, as well that he did not fulfill a single task of his office. Therefore, Paul called him an external mask, a hypocrite, so that Paul fulfilled his own office and reminded him of his godless life, since there was no one who could or was willing to discipline such great authorities and prelates. Whoever is in the preaching office is commanded by God to discipline all estates, spiritual and worldly, poor and rich. BRIEF EXEGESIS OF ACTS 23:3.[9]

THE OLD AND CORRUPTED PRIESTHOOD WOULD SOON BE DESTROYED. DESIDERIUS ERASMUS: To such a pitch of tyranny had the Jewish priesthood come that they demanded to be allowed to harm someone contrary to justice and right, and did not permit free speech in others. This was a sign, surely, of the abolition, soon to come of the priesthood, after it had descended to the lowest depths of wickedness. PARAPHRASE OF ACTS 23:3-4.[10]

HOW DOES PAUL NOT KNOW ANANIAS IS THE HIGH PRIEST? JOHANN SPANGENBERG: He wants to say so much as this: "The high priest should be kind and merciful to those who cry out to him, listening, protecting and sheltering poor, innocent people. But now he allows me, a poor man, to be hit in the face, here in public council on account of a truthful word that I said, namely, that I have walked in all good conscience before God up to this day. Thus, I do not consider him the high priest. He is not so before God but is a true tyrant, a whitewashed wall, an external mask, a hypocrite, who should be sitting sooner in a pigsty among pigs than here in the priestly chair among rational people. Yes, he should lie in the abyss of hell in the hellish fire." As Paul here disciplines this high priest without consideration for his lofty title and office, so must every preacher of the gospel by God's command also do, not leaving undisciplined any who does evil and acts unjustly, be he spiritual or worldly. BRIEF EXEGESIS OF ACTS 23:5.[11]

PAUL'S IRONY IS A WAY TO REBUKE UNWORTHY RULERS. RUDOLF GWALTHER: Now Paul elegantly reproves through irony this tyrannous hypocrisy, saying, "I did not know, brothers, that he is the high priest." It is as if he were saying, "Truly, who would acknowledge *him* as the high priest— in whom there is nothing discernibly worthy of such a name and title? For if he is the high priest, why does he not listen to petitions peaceably and equitably? Why does he bellow impudently? Why does he command the uncondemned to be struck? Aside from this I am not ignorant that God's law stipulates that no one shall curse a legitimate magistrate." By Paul's irony magistrates are instructed that their authority is inviolable and sound if they act in their office and demonstrate themselves to be worthy of honor, able to judge anyone honestly. For unless they promote the glory of God, refrain from violence, defend good laws and be an example of honest living, the same may be said to them that Paul here objects to Ananias.

---

[8]John Mayer, *A Treasury of Ecclesiastical Expositions, vpon the difficult and doubtfull places of the Scriptures* (London: John Bellamie, 1622), 692-93*; quoting Mt 5:39.
[9]Spangenberg, *Der Apostel Geschichte*, 209v.
[10]CWE 50:133 (LB 7:755).
[11]Spangenberg, *Der Apostel Geschichte*, 210v-211r.

For who wants to have people who are blasphemers, bloodthirsty oppressors, desecrators of the law, drunkards, adulterers, buffoons and other such flaky [farinae] people as senators and rulers? We know indeed that God, of his just judgment, sometimes ordains those whose misgovernance the godly must patiently suffer in temporal matters. But if they are not honored as they desire, let them not marvel but acknowledge their sin and repent. For in so doing, they will have Jesus Christ, the King of kings and Lord of lords, as the defender of their authority. HOMILY 147, ACTS 23:1-5.[12]

TREAT OFFICES WITH DIGNITY, BUT ALWAYS OBEY GOD. JOHN CALVIN: Every office of dignity which has been instituted for the preservation of the civil order ought to be respected scrupulously and held in honor. For whoever rises in rebellion against the magistrate and those endowed with authority or official standing is striving after anarchy. But a passion of that sort tends to the disruption of order and deals a shattering blow to humanity itself. Therefore, Paul clears himself of this charge, but in such a way as to deny that Ananias, who has corrupted and ruined the whole order of the church, is to be regarded as a priest of God.

But here the question arises whether we must obey a ruler, even when the ruler exercises tyranny. If a person who discharges one's office badly is not to be stripped of honor, Paul has sinned in robbing the high priest of his honor. I reply that there is a certain distinction between civil magistrates and leaders of the church. Although the administration of earthly or civil sovereignty is disorderly and corrupt, yet the Lord wishes submission. But when the spiritual rule degenerates, the consciences of the godly are released from obedience to an unjust domination, especially if impious and profane enemies of holiness make a false pretense to the title of the priesthood to destroy the doctrine of salvation and arrogate to themselves a lordship by which God himself is reduced to order. Thus today it is not only permissible but also necessary for the faithful to shake off the yoke of the pope, since they can obey his laws only if they revolt from God. COMMENTARY ON ACTS 23:5.[13]

JUST AS GOD IS GRACIOUS TO PAST SINNERS, SO ALSO TO YOU. JOHN DONNE: The benefit that we are to make of the errors of holy people is not that "that person did this, therefore I may do it," but this, "God suffered that holy person to fall and still loved that good soul well; God therefore has not cast me away; he suffers me to fall, too." Bread is a person's best sustenance, but still there may be a dangerous overabundance of bread; charity is the bread that the soul lives by, but still there may be an overabundance of charity. I may mislead myself shrewdly if I say, "Surely my father is a good person, my master a good person, my pastor a good person, people who have the testimony of God's love by his manifold blessings on them. Therefore I may be bold to do whatever I see them do." Be perfect even as your Father in heaven is perfect is the example that Christ gives you. Be followers of me as I am of Christ is the example that the apostle gives you. Good examples are good assistances, but no human example is sufficient to constitute a certain and constant rule. SERMON ON THE CONVERSION OF SAINT PAUL (1629).[14]

THE THREE PRINCIPAL SECTS OF JUDAISM. JOHANN SPANGENBERG: There were three principal sects: Pharisees, Sadducees and Essenes. Pharisees were set apart from others, keeping the commands of the elders along with the law of Moses. They went about in special clothes, they had long tassels [on their garments] and wrote the commandments of God on them. They believed that human souls are immortal, that the dead will be raised and that there is a life after this one.

The Sadducees denied the resurrection of the dead. They claimed that the soul dies with the body like animals. They also held that there were

---

[12]Gwalther, *Homelyes or Sermons upon the Actes*, 801-2* (*In Acta Apostolorum*, 248v); alluding to Ex 22:28.

[13]CNTC 7:229-30* (CO 48:505-6).
[14]Donne, *Works*, 2:359*; alluding to Mt 5:48; 1 Cor 11:1.

no angels or spirits, that God is unconcerned with terrestrial creatures and that the law was given only so that humans could lead a peaceful life here on earth.

Essenes, "doers," because they saw that other sects glorified themselves greatly concerning righteousness and nevertheless did not act accordingly, adopted a difficult and strict life: they held all things in common, they did not marry, they had no family, they also did not sacrifice with other [communities]. This was their life: before the rising of the sun they did not speak, but they prayed assiduously, then they worked, they ate in total silence like monks. (This Jewish spirit has flown into the rebaptizers.) . . .

God did not institute [these sects], nor did Moses command them, but rather they came into existence during the time of the Maccabees. Then there was no Jewish king, and the high priests made alliances with the Gentile kings, princes, lands and cities, so that they could establish a passive priesthood. So, [the priests] neglected their office and let Scripture lie. They did not teach. They did not preach. Thus, such sects arose in Judaism, as also the numerous spiritual orders of monks and nuns came into Christianity, because bishops, prelates and preachers were lazy and drowsy, allowing the enemy to sow tares among the good wheat. BRIEF EXEGESIS OF ACTS 23:6.[15]

PAUL MENTIONS RESURRECTION IN ORDER TO ESCAPE. THE ENGLISH ANNOTATIONS: Paul said this not to gain the favor of the Pharisees or to approve all their traditions but out of a prudent policy to set divison among his accusers, so that he might escape more easily. ANNOTATIONS ON ACTS 23:6.[16]

IS PAUL BEING DECEITFUL? JOHN CALVIN: Paul's stratagem, which Luke reports, seems out of keeping with a servant of Christ. For the astuteness which he used was closely related to a bluff

that was not far removed from lying. He says that the circumstances of his case turn on the resurrection of the dead. But we know that the issue was about other matters, that he abrogated the ceremonies and admitted the Gentiles to the covenant of salvation. I reply that even if those things are true, yet he did not lie. For he does not deny that he was accused of other things, and he does not resolve the dispute on this one issue but truly acknowledges that the Sadducees are hostile to him because he affirms the resurrection of the dead. He knew that those who had conspired against him suffered from internal disagreements. Certainly his own conscience was perfectly clear, and it would have been easy for him to present a good case to fair judges. However, because he sees that they are in an uproar and clamoring against him and that no opening is being allowed for his defense, he sets his enemies to fight among themselves. It is also made clear from that, that they are being carried away by ignorance and blind zeal. Therefore, we must note that Paul began by wishing to explain his whole situation frankly and sincerely and that he did not cunningly avoid a clean and honest confession, such as the servants of Christ should have given. But we must also observe that, because an opening was barred and no hearing was granted to him, he used an extreme remedy to make it plain that his adversaries were being swept off their feet by a blind hatred. COMMENTARY ON ACTS 23:6.[17]

PAUL STRIVES TO WIN SOME TO THE GOSPEL EVEN AS HE DIVIDES THEM. JUSTUS JONAS: For the sake of the gospel, the apostle suddenly mentions his Phariseeism. Because in other situations the Pharisees persistently defended the resurrection of the dead against the Sadducees, perhaps some might thus be drawn to accept the gospel. ANNOTATIONS ON ACTS 23:7.[18]

I AM BY NATURE A SADDUCEE AND A PHARISEE. JOHN DONNE: My "Sadducee"—my presump-

---

[15]Spangenberg, *Der Apostel Geschichte*, 212r-213r; alluding to Num 15:37-41.
[16]Downame, ed., *Annotations*, MMM1r*.

[17]CNTC 7:230-31* (CO 48:506).
[18]Jonas, *Annotationes in Acta*, K2r.

tion—suggests that there is no spirit, no soul to suffer for sin. And my "Pharisee"—my desperation—suggests that my soul must perish irremediably, irrecoverably, for every sin that my body commits. Now if I go Saint Paul's way—to put a dissension between these my Sadducees and my Pharisees, to put jealousy between my presumption and my desperation, to make my presumption see that my desperation lies in wait for it and to consider seriously that my presumption will end in desperation—I may, as Saint Paul did in the text, escape the better for it. But if, without further troubling these Sadducees and these Pharisees, I am content to let them agree and to divide my life between them, so that my presumption shall possess all my youth and desperation my age, then I have heard my sentence already: The end of this man will be worse than his beginning. SERMON ON THE CONVERSION OF SAINT PAUL (1629).[19]

"Spirit" Has a Wide Semantic Range.

GIOVANNI DIODATI: This word ["spirit"] has a larger range of meaning than the word *angel*, which follows it. "Spirit" can be applied to the Spirit of God speaking to the prophets by internal revelation, or to some spirit or soul of some deceased person, according to the error of those times. ANNOTATION ON ACTS 23:9.[20]

The Pharisees Are Correct but Not Right.

RUDOLF GWALTHER: Indeed, they speak piously and even truthfully; nevertheless, before God they deserve no praise, because [this confession was] not due to devotion for the truth or justice, but rather crooked desires wrenched this confession out of them. This is a noteworthy example of how quickly sectarian devotion rages to extremes; suddenly those who only a little earlier thirsted for his blood now have become Paul's defenders. This frequently happens both in religion and in other controversies. But, because such judg-

ments usually tend to a more wicked purpose, it is fitting that we diligently avoid the same.

There are two other things which it will be beneficial to note. First, the harmony of the wicked cannot last very long. For, as they are tossed here and there like the sea with uncertain affections, so God on high ridicules and scatters their plans. He is able to do this with such dexterity that sometimes he even co-opts the works of his most wicked enemies to save his people. . . . Therefore, do not allow the conspiracies of the wicked offend anyone, but let us firmly fix our certain trust of salvation in God.

The other thing is that those who besiege divinely revealed instruction fight against God. This is a horrible crime, but all too common today. For in the midst of the gospel being besieged both the leaders and the antistes[21] of the church labor tremendously, while the Son of God still fittingly reveals the gospel by his own mouth to all the world. Still, in the end, those giants will experience, to their great misfortune, how much more powerful God is than they, and how horrible it is to fall into his hands. HOMILY 148, ACTS 23:6-10.[22]

How Can Paul "Take Courage"?

JOHANN SPANGENBERG: It can be seen in this passage, from this consolation of God, that Paul was deeply grieved in heart. Certainly he reflected on what happened to him in Asia, Greece and other places. Now here in Jerusalem he is seized in the temple, dragged before the council of the Jews, struck in the face, lastly here he is almost torn apart by the crowds. Who would not become limp and fainthearted from such swift tribulations? Is there no God in heaven who sees this? Who feels compassion over this? Yes, the true God who allows no one to be tested beyond the limit of what he can bear. He does not abandon those who place their hope in him. He stood by Paul in the night and said, "Be comforted, Paul, for as you testified about me in

---

[19]Donne, *Works*, 2:373-74*; alluding to Lk 11:26.
[20]Diodati, *Pious Annotations*, CC1v* (*I Commenti alla Sacra Biblia*, 1120); alluding to Acts 12:15.

[21]This was the title for the head of Zurich's Reformed church.
[22]Gwalther, *Homelyes or Sermons upon the Actes*, 805-6* (*In Acta Apostolorum*, 249v).

Jerusalem, in the capital of the Jews, now you must also testify about me in Rome, in the capital of the entire world. Therefore, do not be afraid; no one can harm you." BRIEF EXEGESIS OF ACTS 23:10-11.[23]

TRUST EVEN GOD'S DIFFICULT WORDS. JOHN CALVIN: The main point is that Paul is to bear himself with confidence, because he is going to be a witness for Christ at Rome also. But this seems to be cold and empty comfort. It is as if he said, "Do not be afraid, because a far harder situation is awaiting you." For, according to the flesh, it would have been preferable to die once and for all, getting it over quickly, than to languish in chains for a long period of time. The Lord does not promise him freedom, not even a favorable outcome. He is merely protracting for a long time the troubles, which already press on him more than enough. But from this we gather better how very important in itself is this confidence, that in our afflictions God cares for us, although he may not put out his hand at once to help us. Therefore let us learn even in the very worst afflictions to rest on the Word of God alone, and let us never be disheartened as long as he revives us by the testimony of his fatherly love. But because oracles are not sent from heaven now, and the Lord himself does not appear by visions, we must meditate on his innumerable promises, by which he affirms that he will always be near us. If it is to our advantage for an angel to come down to us, the Lord will not deny this kind of confirmation even now. Meanwhile, we must pay this honor to the Word, that, content with it alone, we patiently anticipate the help which it promises to us. Besides, some people received no benefit from hearing angels sent from heaven. But it is not in vain that the Lord seals the promises given by him on the hearts of believers by his Spirit. COMMENTARY ON ACTS 23:11.[24]

WHAT SORT OF CONSOLATION IS THIS? RUDOLF GWALTHER: The Lord warns him of new toils and new struggles, just as if a physician were to say to a sick patient, "Be of good cheer, friend, for you have a new sickness coming! Within the next few days you will be tormented by fresh pains." Or, if someone provoked a soldier wearied by a recent battle into a more grievous fight. Indeed, who would say this is a consolation or comfort? How is such a thing said to Paul here? For by mentioning Rome, he reminds him of the annoyances of travels, the dangers of the voyages and of a number of the cruelest kinds of torture. Claudius was now emperor—a frenzied and cruel man, too ready to punish the innocent.

But if we examine the thing itself more closely, then two things become clear which would have deeply consoled Paul. First, he saw that God took care of him. Second, he heard that he will be a vessel and instrument of glory to declare the name of Christ among the Romans, who were lords over the entire world. In this passage, therefore, we are taught where to find comfort in adversity. Not in the fortunate success of worldly affairs or in hope of living idly and easily, but in the providence of God. HOMILY 149, ACTS 23:11-16.[25]

CHRIST IS PRESENT, ESPECIALLY DURING AFFLICTIONS. JUSTUS JONAS: Here is another passage where Christ is particularly present with Paul, when the most violent trial is seething. Therefore, after the raging of the trial is past, the voice of Christ is heard in his conscience: "Endure, be of good courage. Come now, what creature can deter you?" ANNOTATIONS ON ACTS 23:11.[26]

---

[23]Spangenberg, *Der Apostel Geschichte*, 214r-v; alluding to 1 Cor 10:13.
[24]CNTC 7:237* (CO 48:511).

[25]Gwalther, *Homelyes or Sermons upon the Actes*, 807-8* (*In Acta Apostolorum*, 250r-v).
[26]Jonas, *Annotationes in Acta*, K2v.

23:12-35 PAUL ESCAPES
THE PLOT TO ASSASSINATE HIM

¹²*When it was day, the Jews made a plot and bound themselves by an oath neither to eat nor drink till they had killed Paul. ¹³There were more than forty who made this conspiracy. ¹⁴They went to the chief priests and elders and said, "We have strictly bound ourselves by an oath to taste no food till we have killed Paul. ¹⁵Now therefore you, along with the council, give notice to the tribune to bring him down to you, as though you were going to determine his case more exactly. And we are ready to kill him before he comes near."*

¹⁶*Now the son of Paul's sister heard of their ambush, so he went and entered the barracks and told Paul. ¹⁷Paul called one of the centurions and said, "Take this young man to the tribune, for he has something to tell him." ¹⁸So he took him and brought him to the tribune and said, "Paul the prisoner called me and asked me to bring this young man to you, as he has something to say to you." ¹⁹The tribune took him by the hand, and going aside asked him privately, "What is it that you have to tell me?"²⁰And he said, "The Jews have agreed to ask you to bring Paul down to the council tomorrow, as though they were going to inquire somewhat more closely about him. ²¹But do not be persuaded by them, for more than forty of their men are lying in ambush for him, who have bound themselves by an oath neither to eat nor drink till they have killed him. And now they are ready, waiting for your consent." ²²So the tribune dismissed the young man, charging him, "Tell no one that you have informed me of these things."*

²³*Then he called two of the centurions and said, "Get ready two hundred soldiers, with seventy horsemen and two hundred spearmen to go as far as Caesarea at the third hour of the night.^a ²⁴Also provide mounts for Paul to ride and bring him safely to Felix the governor." ²⁵And he wrote a letter to this effect:*

²⁶*"Claudius Lysias, to his Excellency the governor Felix, greetings. ²⁷This man was seized by the Jews and was about to be killed by them when I came upon them with the soldiers and rescued him, having learned that he was a Roman citizen. ²⁸And desiring to know the charge for which they were accusing him, I brought him down to their council. ²⁹I found that he was being accused about questions of their law, but charged with nothing deserving death or imprisonment. ³⁰And when it was disclosed to me that there would be a plot against the man, I sent him to you at once, ordering his accusers also to state before you what they have against him."*

³¹*So the soldiers, according to their instructions, took Paul and brought him by night to Antipatris. ³²And on the next day they returned to the barracks, letting the horsemen go on with him. ³³When they had come to Caesarea and delivered the letter to the governor, they presented Paul also before him. ³⁴On reading the letter, he asked what province he was from. And when he learned that he was from Cilicia, ³⁵he said, "I will give you a hearing when your accusers arrive." And he commanded him to be guarded in Herod's praetorium.*

a That is, 9 p.m.

OVERVIEW: In this passage the reformers strongly emphasize the Triune God's providence over all things. The Lord delights when others participate in his actions. So that the Acts 1:8 program might be carried out in Rome, God governs and trans- forms the actions of those who want to murder Paul, as well as the alleged pride of a Roman tribune and the curiosity of the typically harsh Felix. And the catalyst for these events? An adolescent boy! God is of course able to communicate, act and react via extraordinary means, but far more often he delights in ordinary, mundane means. In this the commentators see a prime example of Paul's words to the Corinthians, that he "planted, Apollos watered, but God gave the growth" (1 Cor 3:6). While human beings have real responsibility, the progress and outcome of events is ultimately dependent on the Lord.

23:12-15 The Plan to Murder Paul

How Does This New Threat Harmonize with God's Consolation to Paul? Johann Spangenberg: God does not console his people in this way, nor does he promise to them that they will not suffer at all; rather, much more that they should be prepared and ready for the coming tribulations and persecutions. For God's children must be tried like gold in fire. Brief Exegesis of Acts 23:12.[1]

God Ordains the Actions of the Wicked for Our Good. Hans Has von Hallstatt: This and many other examples happened so that we could learn to recognize that it rests in God's might and power alone to rescue his own from these things, regardless of how great and how terrible the enemy and the persecution might be. Even today God moves the hearts, courage and intentions of tyrants to inflict all manner of plagues and misfortunes on his elect. . . . As David says, he transforms the hearts of those who are harmful to his people and act maliciously to his servants. Of what good is that blind and miserable people on this earth than that they behave as God's rods and instruments to be used on his Christians, as God ordains them to do, and reveal his glory through them? Kunstbuch: Concerning the Comfort of Christians.[2]

Never Try to Defend the Faith by Force. Rudolf Gwalther: With regard to their crime

not unjustly do you hesitate, whether you should marvel at their audacity or their bloodythirsty minds. Beside this—that contrary to the law of God they are prepared to murder an innocent person—they also devote themselves to a vow, disregarding how many things could happen that might hinder their efforts. But by their example, we learn to judge the audacity of the wicked and of all who believe they will defend the religion they profess by force rather than by Scripture. Homily 149, Acts 23:11-16.[3]

Public Authority Greatly Increases Evil's Power. The English Annotations: It seems [the plotters] knew that the council too were intent to destroy Paul with them. The most pernicious impiety loves the veil of public authority; Satan never does more wickedness than when he gains councils to his side. Annotations on Acts 23:15.[4]

God Sees Every Secret Plot. Johann Spangenberg: Here you have an example that the counsel of the godless does not remain secret or hidden but rather comes to light at the right time. Even if people plot together in absolute secrecy, still God is above in heaven, who sees and makes known everything. God cares for his own who trust in him with their heart and cry out to him in truth; he saves them from every threat. Brief Exegesis of Acts 23:16.[5]

Paul Trusts God and Takes Advantage of This Opportunity. John Calvin: Paul was certainly not so eager for life that he would not have gladly hastened to die if the Lord had wished him to do so. But since he knows that he serves Christ on this condition, that he lives to him just as much as he dies to him, he does not disregard the danger that has been made known to him. And indeed he has no doubt whatsoever that God is the Guardian of his life, but he does not wait until he

---

[1]Spangenberg, *Der Apostel Geschichte*, 215r.
[2]CRR 12:450-51* (QGT 17:472); alluding to Ps 105:25.

[3]Gwalther, *Homelyes or Sermons upon the Actes*, 808* (*In Acta Apostolorum*, 250v).
[4]Downame, ed., *Annotations*, MMMir*.
[5]Spangenberg, *Der Apostel Geschichte*, 216r-v.

put out his hand from heaven to perform a miracle. On the contrary, he uses the remedy presented to him, having no doubt that it is ordained for him by God. All the ministers of Christ must act in this way, so that, provided with invincible perseverance, as far as their calling demands, they do not fear dangers, and yet do not yield themselves to death with heedless temerity. Let them quietly call on the Lord in the midst of difficulties, and yet do not let them despise the aids that come to hand. Otherwise they will be insulting God, not only by being deaf to his promises, but also by rejecting the means of liberation set before them by God. COMMENTARY ON ACTS 23:17.[6]

GOD PROVIDES, BUT DO NOT FAIL TO SEEK HIS PROVISION. RUDOLF GWALTHER: By this

example we are first taught how we should use the providence and promises of God in adversity. For there should be no doubt that God, by his eternal providence and counsel, indeed rules all things, and that nothing can even be hampered by any of his enemies' efforts. For God scatters the counsel of the nations, but his counsel, as David testifies, endures forever. He promises to be with his people and to assist them in all adversities. We must firmly believe his promises! In the meanwhile the means which are legal and offered by God must not be despised or neglected, lest by putting ourselves too rashly in danger we seem to tempt God. For the same must be observed in all our actions as in agriculture. Although all the growth comes from God alone, still no one ought to neglect their duties without profound contempt of God. . . .

Therefore, it is repulsive and impious, this error of those who exploit God's providence for the benefit of their own impudence and their blind license in all things. Under this pretext they flamboyantly scorn not only good sense but, worse yet, divinely bestowed means. Instead, we must shun the evil of unbelief, lest we be overcome by it and turn to unlawful means. Now, using the lawful means provided by God, let us commit every result to the

good and holy will of God. For we will travel the safest path when we strive to shun unbelief and overconfidence. HOMILY 150, ACTS 23:17-24.[7]

THE PATIENCE AND HUMILITY OF THE TRIBUNE. JOHN CALVIN: We ought to ascribe it to

the grace of God that the tribune showed such courtesy and kindness to the youth, that he took him by the hand and led him aside, that he heard him willingly and patiently. For God promised that he would give favor to his people in the eyes of the Egyptians; he is accustomed to softening hearts of iron, taming fierce spirits and making those whom he has decided to use to help his own people considerate in every way. For the soldier could have cast aside an unknown youth, just as he could have rejected the pleas of Paul himself. Therefore, the Lord, who has human hearts in his power, moved this worldly man to listen to him. It was also an advantage that he knew beforehand how fiercely they were raving against Paul, so that he might be more willing to help the man in his wretchedness and abandonment. Finally, let those who are in positions of authority over others learn from this example, what a great virtue considerateness is. If he had been a difficult man to approach, then, through ignorance, he would have given Paul to the Jews to be killed. Thus magistrates often rush into many serious offenses because of their pride, simply because they do not deign to receive warnings from others. COMMENTARY ON ACTS 23:19.[8]

THE TRIBUNE REFLECTS THE RECEPTIVENESS ALL RULERS SHOULD HAVE. RUDOLF GWAL-

THER: This example should be imitated by all those in authority, considering that this is not the least of their responsibilities: to ensure open access for all people and to hear their subjects' pleas mercifully and patiently. For they correspond to the character of God, who voluntarily invites us and who is always willing to listen to the prayers of the afflicted. And

---

[6]CNTC 7:240 (CO 48:514).

[7]Gwalther, *Homelyes or Sermons upon the Actes*, 810-11* (*In Acta Apostolorum*, 251r-v); alluding to Ps 33:10-11; 1 Cor 3:5-9.
[8]CNTC 7:240-41* (CO 48:514); alluding to Ex 3:21.

because bashfulness or fear hampers many who are less able to clearly present their thoughts before those in authority, it is important for the authorities to demonstrate signs of benevolence and humanity clearly, lest the people's amplified bashfulness or fear deceive them. Homily 150, Acts 23:17-24.[9]

23:23-35 Paul Sent to Felix

Not Even Minutiae, Inspired by the Spirit, Are Superfluous. Rudolf Gwalther: To some the diligence of Luke the Evangelist might seem superfluous—this diligence by which he records how Paul through the might of Roman soldiers escaped the ambush set by those scheming crooks, by recounting the most trifling details which he emphasizes ad nauseam. But because it is well-known that he wrote by the prompting of the Holy Spirit, nothing reported by *that* author ought to be considered superfluous. For he places before our eyes the infallible loyalty of God, that is, the truth, and his invincible power by which he sets his people free. Homily 151, Acts 23:25-35.[10]

The Tribune Is Worried About His Reputation. Desiderius Erasmus: The tribune exercised such great care not because he had regard for the life of one man (for he was not that scrupulous), but he wished to be free of Paul, for he could not have protected him against such obstinate hatred from the whole council, nor did he dare to hand a Roman citizen over to their hatred. For this reason he ordered Paul to be led forth by night with a large company of soldiers, fearing that if Paul left during the day or in the company of only a few soldiers, the Jews would seize him on the way and slay him, and the criticism from this would thereafter fall on him who had perfidiously surrendered a Roman citizen. Paraphrase of Acts 23:23-24.[11]

The Tribune as God's Vessel. John Calvin: Here indeed the providence of God is seen still more clearly. For even if the tribune's plan were to seek to avert a public disturbance of which account would have had to be given before the governor, still he executes God's plan in delivering Paul. For soldiers had to be collected, the city stripped of its garrison, and the expedition demanded some expense. Therefore, we must reflect on the prudence of the tribune, so that faith may lift up its eyes to heaven and perceive that God is directing the heart of this worldly man by a secret inspiration and that he also is the leader for the journey for Paul and the soldiers, so that he may reach Caesarea in safety. Commentary on Acts 23:23.[12]

No Expense or Effort Should Be Spared When Protecting Pastors. Rudolf Gwalther: All these things could not have been done without great effort and expense. But, remembering his office, the tribune spares neither pain nor cost to deliever a prisoner—still convicted of no crime—out of the hands of murderers. It is imperative that Christian authorities employ similar diligance to defend good people; obviously that is their chief responsibility for which they were ordained. But the example of this pagan reproves both the negligence and inquity of many people who would rather deliver a hundred ministers of the Word to be mutilated by the enemy than to suffer pain and expense for their sake. Still the ingratitude of our age should not discourage anyone from faithfully discharging their office. For people cease fulfilling their office, and there seems to be no hope of help from them, still in no circumstance will God desert his promise. He is accustomed to delivering his worshipers unexpectedly from the midst of a thousand dangers. In the end he will transfer them to the inheritance of the kingdom of heaven through his Son Jesus Christ, to whom be praise, honor, power and glory forever. Amen. Homily 150, Acts 23:17-24.[13]

[9]Gwalther, *Homelyes or Sermons upon the Actes*, 812* (*In Acta Apostolorum*, 251v-252r).
[10]Gwalther, *Homelyes or Sermons upon the Actes*, 814* (*In Acta Apostolorum*, 252r-v).
[11]CWE 50:135 (LB 7:756).
[12]CNTC 7:241* (CO 48:514-15).
[13]Gwalther, *Homelyes or Sermons upon the Actes*, 813* (*In Acta Apostolorum*, 252r).

PAUL'S INNOCENCE PROCLAIMED BY A PAGAN.
JOHANN SPANGENBERG: In this passage you
hear the magnificent testimony of a Gentile
tribune! He records that he finds in Paul nothing deserving death or imprisonment. Such
testimony Pilate and the centurion also gave
concerning our Lord Christ. BRIEF EXEGESIS OF
ACTS 23:25-30.[14]

**OUR ANCESTORS' BREVITY SHAMES OUR
VERBOSITY.** RUDOLF GWALTHER: This letter
[to Felix] teaches us, among other things, what
brevity our ancestors used in the most important
matters, while today in the most whimsical matters we use an excessive mountain of words, of
which no other cause can be asserted than that
trust in anything is extinguished. In its place
dishonesty and empty pretense rule everywhere
HOMILY 151, ACTS 23:25-35.[15]

GOD WORKS ALL THINGS FOR OUR GOOD.
RUDOLF GWALTHER: Let us remember that all
these things happened according to God's administration. For it was his work, that soldiers—without grumbling—served Paul, that for the sake of
his safety they were willing to do anything, that
Felix received him in a more civilized and friendly
manner than he usually did and that he arranged
to keep Paul in custody in Herod's praetorium
rather than some ignoble prison. These things are
intended to teach us that we should not concern
ourselves with human enterprises; instead, we
should strive to please the one God, who is able
to bring peace to barbaric minds, tame savage behavior and even to transform our enemies so that
they love us. Let these things refresh us, so that
with invincible perserverance of faith we overcome
the tyranny of the world, living eternally in heaven
with Jesus Christ our Savior to whom be praise,
honor, glory and power forever. Amen. HOMILY 151,
ACTS 23:25-35.[16]

---

[14]Spangenberg, *Der Apostel Geschichte*, 217r; alluding to Mt 27:24, 54.
[15]Gwalther, *Homelyes or Sermons upon the Actes*, 814* (*In Acta Apostolorum*, 252v).

[16]Gwalther, *Homelyes or Sermons upon the Actes*, 816* (*In Acta Apostolorum*, 253r).

24:1-27 PAUL'S TRIAL BEFORE
FELIX IN CAESAREA

And after five days the high priest Ananias came down with some elders and a spokesman, one Tertullus. They laid before the governor their case against Paul. ²And when he had been summoned, Tertullus began to accuse him, saying:

"Since through you we enjoy much peace, and since by your foresight, most excellent Felix, reforms are being made for this nation, ³in every way and everywhere we accept this with all gratitude.⁴But, to detain* you no further, I beg you in your kindness to hear us briefly. ⁵For we have found this man a plague, one who stirs up riots among all the Jews throughout the world and is a ringleader of the sect of the Nazarenes. ⁶He even tried to profane the temple, but we seized him.ᵇ ⁸By examining him yourself you will be able to find out from him about everything of which we accuse him."

⁹The Jews also joined in the charge, affirming that all these things were so.

¹⁰And when the governor had nodded to him to speak, Paul replied:

"Knowing that for many years you have been a judge over this nation, I cheerfully make my defense.¹¹You can verify that it is not more than twelve days since I went up to worship in Jerusalem, ¹²and they did not find me disputing with anyone or stirring up a crowd, either in the temple or in the synagogues or in the city. ¹³Neither can they prove to you what they now bring up against me. ¹⁴But this I confess to you, that according to the Way, which they call a sect, I worship the God of our fathers, believing everything laid down by the Law and written in the Prophets, ¹⁵having a hope in God, which these men themselves accept, that there will be a resurrection of both the just and the unjust. ¹⁶So I always take pains to have a clear conscience toward both God and man. ¹⁷Now after several years I came to bring alms to my nation and to present offerings. ¹⁸While I was doing this, they found me purified in the temple, without any crowd or tumult. But some Jews from Asia—¹⁹they ought to be here before you and to make an accusation, should they have anything against me. ²⁰Or else let these men themselves say what wrongdoing they found when I stood before the council, ²¹other than this one thing that I cried out while standing among them: 'It is with respect to the resurrection of the dead that I am on trial before you this day.'"

²²But Felix, having a rather accurate knowledge of the Way, put them off, saying, "When Lysias the tribune comes down, I will decide your case." ²³Then he gave orders to the centurion that he should be kept in custody but have some liberty, and that none of his friends should be prevented from attending to his needs.

²⁴After some days Felix came with his wife Drusilla, who was Jewish, and he sent for Paul and heard him speak about faith in Christ Jesus. ²⁵And as he reasoned about righteousness and self-control and the coming judgment, Felix was alarmed and said, "Go away for the present. When I get an opportunity I will summon you." ²⁶At the same time he hoped that money would be given him by Paul. So he sent for him often and conversed with him. ²⁷When two years had elapsed, Felix was succeeded by Porcius Festus. And desiring to do the Jews a favor, Felix left Paul in prison.

a Or weary b Some manuscripts add *and we would have judged him according to our law.* ⁷*But the chief captain Lysias came and with great violence took him out of our hands,* 8*commanding his accusers to come before you.*

OVERVIEW: Now that their violent plans have been foiled, the temple rulers attempt to defeat Paul through words. The reformers note the dichotomy between Paul's plain and courteous rhetoric, demonstrated here and in Acts 22, and Tertullus's verbose and pandering speech. Both

---

are able speakers, but Paul's case stands on the solid foundation of truth and honesty. Again our commentators ask: Why is Luke so detailed in his account? This is by the intention and guidance of the Holy Spirit, they have no doubt; in reading this account believers are reminded that no temptation or affliction is unique to them. Also, the Holy Spirit shows an even hand—the words of Paul's opponent are recorded credibly and faithfully.

Finally, Felix's greed and Drusilla's curiosity present disguised opportunities for gospel proclamation. Paul preaches boldly to this august audience, and during Paul's time in custody, surely many people—the reformers reason—are converted to faith in Christ.

24:1-9 *The Jews Accuse Paul*

The Temple Rulers Hire a Scandalmonger to Ensnare Paul. Johann Spangenberg: What do we witness in the heart of these bloodthirsty Jews? They will not leave any option unattempted in order to kill Paul: they use all sorts of deceptive methods and fraudulent practices. First they seized Paul in the temple and dragged him out, wanting to kill him. When this did not work, they gathered together a false trial, though with a pious appearance; when this trial also did not succeed, they thought they could kill him through secret trickery. Now this roguishness is also discovered, so they want to bolster their agenda with hearsay. They hire a speaker, a tongue-slinger [*Zugendrescher*] and scandalmonger, Tertullus, who is to do his best and defeat Paul with words. And so that the governor, Felix, understands the importance of the matter to them, they do not delay long but in five days arrive in Caesarea: the high priest himself with the elders and the speaker Tertullus. They had no other intent than to crush Paul. Brief Exegesis of Acts 24:1.[1]

Do Not Be Surprised If You Find Yourself in Paul's Place. Rudolf Gwalther:

Now Christ prophesied these things will take place . . . so that we would be less troubled if at any time something similar happens to us, too. As the apostles suffered all kinds of persecution and adversities, so they teach by their example what is fitting for us to do when we are tested by persecutions and temptations. This is the chief use and purpose of all this present matter and of the entire story that follows. Homily 152, Acts 24:1-9.[2]

Is What Tertullus Says About Felix True? Johann Spangenberg: How can it be true? Josephus writes that Felix secretly had Jonathan the high priest killed; he also ordered mercenaries to kill the Jews not only in the streets but also in the temple. He also looked the other way when his soldiers in Caesarea rummaged through the Jews' houses, plundering and wreaking havoc. On account of this wicked act he was indicted before the emperor Nero and was removed from his office. Still, in this passage he seems to be a pure saint and does nothing terrible; so it was also when Pilate and Herod became friends over Christ. Brief Exegesis of Acts 24:2-4.[3]

Here the Vulgate Is More Reliable Than Erasmus. John Calvin: Where Erasmus translates, "many things are done properly," the Vulgate seems to come closer to Luke's intention, for it reads, "things are being successfully achieved," which amounts to the same things as "reforms" or "improvements."[4] Therefore Tertullus commends Felix's activity because he purged Judaea of many corruptions and changed many things for the better, which otherwise were going to ruin. Tertullus clearly did so in order that Felix may be the more eager to gain for himself, by the death of one man,

---

[1]Spangenberg, *Der Apostel Geschichte*, 219r-v.

[2]Gwalther, *Homelyes or Sermons upon the Actes*, 818* (*In Acta Apostolorum*, 253v).
[3]Spangenberg, *Der Apostel Geschichte*, 219v-220r; alluding to Lk 23:12. See Josephus, *Antiquities*, 20.8.
[4]The CNTC editors note: "Erasmus: *multa recte gerantur*. Calvin: *multa restituantur*. Vg: *multa corrigantur*. Greek: διορθωμάτων γινομένων ('reforms are being carried out'), but a great many mss have κατορθωμάτων."

the favor of a nation, which he knew was otherwise hostile to him. COMMENTARY ON ACTS 24:2.[5]

PREACHERS MUST NOT BECOME FASHION-ABLY DOMESTICATED. JOHN DONNE: Birds that are kept in cages may learn some notes which they should never have sung in the woods or fields, but still they may forget their natural notes, too. Preachers that bind themselves always to cities and courts and great audiences may learn new notes; they may become occasional preachers and make the emergent affairs of the time their text and the humors of the hearers their Bible. But they may lose their natural notes—both the simplicity and the boldness that belong to the preaching of the gospel. SERMON ON ACTS 1:8.[6]

TERTULLUS SLANDERS PAUL AS SEDITIOUS, BUT WHY AS A NAZARENE? JOHN CALVIN: Tertullus has a double aim. In the first place he strives to get Paul handed over to the Jews, because they have the right to make a judicial inquiry into questions concerning the worship of God and the law of Moses. Should this, however, be denied, he brings forward a capital charge, that Paul stirred up sedition among the common people. For they were aware that no crime was more offensive to the Romans, and therefore they particularly burdened Paul with the disgrace of it. Tertullus expands on the point when he says that Paul stirs up the Jews all over the world.

But it is strange why he adds that he is leader of the sect of the Nazarenes (*Nazaraeorum*),[7] because we know that the Jews regarded that as praiseworthy rather than blameworthy. But I do not think that he meant those who used to conse-crate themselves to God according to a legitimate and ancient rite of the Law, but those turbulent assassins who took on a worthy name and boasted that they were zealots. That faction emerged around that time, and indeed one gathers from

Josephus's history that they were already active then. Others think that the word *Nazarenes* (*Naz-ernos*) is used here for Christians, and I am quite willing to accept that. But if the first explanation is acceptable, he cunningly alleges that Paul belongs to a sect hateful to the Romans. COMMENTARY ON ACTS 24:5.[8]

PAUL'S ACCUSERS TRY TO TAR HIM WITH A BAD NAME. RUDOLF GWALTHER: They call him a champion of the sect of the Nazarenes. Thus, they are accusing him of schism and heresy—consid-ered the most serious indictment by the church in all ages. Tertullus seems to speak with contempt of the Christians as Nazarenes, intimating that they have an obscure and ignobile origin as this sect. For Nazareth was a small town of no regard, as it is shown when, to Philip's proclamation of Jesus of Nazareth, Nathanael responds, "Can anything good come out of Nazareth?" Now this is an ancient strategy of the devil: to cause true religion to be distrusted by an ignoble name. By this same provocation Julian the Apostate formerly called Christ "the Galilean" and Christians "Galileans." HOMILY 152, ACTS 24:1-9.[9]

WHY DOES GOD ALLOW THE GODLESS TO LIE ABOUT HIS SERVANTS? JOHANN SPANGEN-BERG: It is a poor, miserable fact about the world that whoever does good to the world and means it with their heart is the most terrible, but whoever drags the world about by the nose is the dearest and the best. This high priest Ananias along with the Pharisees were the cause of all the misfortunes of the Jews, but here [according to the world] they must be pure saints, while Paul and the dear apostles who upheld God's discipline must be the

---

[5]CNTC 7:245-46* (CO 48:518).
[6]Donne, *Works*, 6:236-37*.
[7]*Nazaraeorum*: It is ambiguous whether a Nazirite or a Nazarene is being referred to by this term.

[8]CNTC 7:246* (CO 48:518).
[9]Gwalther, *Homelyes or Sermons upon the Actes*, 820* (*In Acta Apostolorum*, 254r); quoting Jn 1:46. Julian the Apostate was a Roman emperor (331–363) who tried to revive paganism, against the policies of previous emperors who, since Constantine, had promoted Christianity. Theodoret records Julian's putative last words as "You have conquered, O Galilean!" See *Historia Ecclesi-astica* 3.25.

bane and refuse[10] of the world. Even to this very day the world still believes that gospel preachers are the most harmful people on earth; if it were free of them, then everything would be fine and because of this every misery would be repudiated.

Why does God allow this to happen? He keeps watch until the time [of judgment]. First, he waits, so that by his longsuffering and patience he might call the sinful to repentance. Second, he might sift and purify the devout, showing them that a very different blessedness follows after this life than is found here on earth. BRIEF EXEGESIS OF ACTS 24:5-6.[11]

PAUL SUFFERS WITH CHRIST, AND CHRIST IN HIM. LEONHARD SCHIEMER: That's what happens to all Christians! . . . It is surely true that Christ's sufferings destroy sin, even as he suffers in me. As water quenches my thirst only if I drink it, and bread does not still my hunger unless I eat it, even so Christ does not keep me from sin unless he suffers in me. . . . Therefore the Lord says: "Without me you can do nothing." KUNSTBUCH: THE TWELVE ARTICLES OF THE CHRISTIAN FAITH.[12]

THE TEMPLE RULERS NOW TURN ON THE TRIBUNE.[13] RUDOLF GWALTHER: Here we must examine this example of great audacity and impudence. For they dare to accuse the tribune and complain that they were restrained by him from shedding Paul's blood. The tribune deserved great praise for this. So little the wicked repent of their wicked deeds that they continually hate any who hamper or prevent their wicked acts. HOMILY 152, ACTS 24:1-9.[14]

TERTULLUS'S LIES ARE RECORDED PRECISELY TO BOLSTER THE TRUTH OF SCRIPTURE. RUDOLF GWALTHER: We heard the details of the most serious accusation made against Paul in Tertullus's speech, which the Holy Spirit desired to be recorded most diligently, partly so that the truth of the apostolic story would not be suspected—because we see that the words of enemies are reported so accurately—and partly so that we should not be offended when we hear similar objections against us or others who follow the true faith. HOMILY 153, ACTS 24:10-16.[15]

24:10-21 *Paul's Defense Before Felix*

HOW DOES FELIX RESPOND TO THIS ACCUSATION? JOHANN SPANGENBERG: As he listened diligently to the prosecutors and [their] witnesses, in the same way he wants to listen to the accused Paul. Therefore he nodded to him in order to begin his defense. It is an excellent virtue in judges and councils to be kind and gentle, to hear gladly the poor, the widows and the orphans. . . . "One person's argument is no argument; hear also the counterargument." BRIEF EXEGESIS OF ACTS 24:10.[16]

TWO OR THREE DAYS NOT ENOUGH TO INSTIGATE A FULL-SCALE REBELLION. RUDOLF GWALTHER: Paul very diligently refutes [Tertullus's] charges. Establishing an argument based on his timetable, he says it is impossible for him to have stirred up a riot: it was only twelve days ago that he came to Jerusalem. From this number subtract the time he lay in prison and hardly a day or two remain. Now, who, after unexpectedly showing up, could agitate the entire city population into a riot in the span of only two or three days? . . .

It serves for our instruction that Paul so diligently refutes the charge of sedition against him. For by this ministers learn that they must guard themselves, lest they throw the commonwealth

---

[10]See 1 Cor 4:13; Lam 3:45. The Greek word περίψημα describes the scraps and burned-up remains from a sacrifice or fire.
[11]Spangenberg, *Der Apostel Geschichte*, 220v-221r.
[12]CRR 12:247 (QGT 17:314, 315-16); quoting Jn 15:5.
[13]Modern translations deem the witnesses for Acts 24:6b-8a in Erasmus's *textus receptus*—translated "and we would have judged him according to our law. [7]But the chief captain Lysias came and with great violence took him out of our hands, [8]commanding his accusers to come before you"; [7]παρελθων δε Λυσιας ο χιλιαρχος μετα πολλης βιας εκ των χειρων ημων απηγαγεν [8]κελευσας τους κατηγορους αυτου ερχεσθαι επι σε—as too late and therefore inauthentic.
[14]Gwalther, *Homelyes or Sermons upon the Actes*, 820* (*In Acta Apostolorum*, 254r).

[15]Gwalther, *Homelyes or Sermons upon the Actes*, 821* (*In Acta Apostolorum*, 254v).
[16]Spangenberg, *Der Apostel Geschichte*, 221v, 222r.

into confusion through sedition—there is nothing more destructive than this. And God delights in concord and unity above all things. HOMILY 153, ACTS 24:10-16.[17]

DID PAUL REALLY COME TO JERUSALEM TO WORSHIP? JOHN CALVIN: In the first place it is certain that he came for other reasons, and afterwards he acknowledged that the principal reason was to bring alms for the assistance of the needy brothers. But he is easily excused, because there was no need for him to give any reason for his coming. He merely wished, in passing, to clear himself of violating religion. Accordingly, although there was another purpose for undertaking the expedition, it is always true that he came with no other intention except to profess himself as a worshiper of God and to endorse the sacredness of the temple by his worship. There is another, more perplexing question, how he says that he came in order to worship, when the religion of the temple had already been abolished and all distinction in the temple taken away. Here I also reply that although he does not explain his purpose, he does not make any false pretension. For worship in the temple was not forbidden to believers in Christ, so long as they did not attach sacredness to the place but lifted up pure hands freely and with no distinction of places. When Paul had come to Jerusalem, he was at liberty to enter the temple in order to give evidence of his piety and there engage in the customary rites of the worship of God, because he was undefiled by superstition as long as he undertook no expiations contrary to the gospel. Yet religion did not impel him to come to Jerusalem as the Law laid down, as if the sanctuary were the face of God, as it had been in the past; yet he did not shrink from outward worship, which people looked on as evidence of piety. COMMENTARY ON ACTS 24:11.[18]

PAUL'S ORTHODOX PROFESSION OF FAITH. RUDOLF GWALTHER: From this it is indeed clear what Paul's faith was. By this he proves that he cannot be taken for some heretic. Therefore, according to his example, whoever according to faith in Christ worships the God of their ancestors based in the Scriptures, clings to the hope of the resurrection and strives to keep a pure conscience toward God and human beings, as best they can, is truly Pauline and apostolic, indeed Christian and orthodox, so that the wretched world rages against them. Let us therefore cling to this faith, brothers and sisters, and through the steadfast hope of the future resurrection stoutly pass through all tribulations, certain that we will one day have an eternal reward with Jesus Christ our Savior to whom be praise, honor, glory, and power forever. Amen. Homily 153, Acts 24:10-16.[19]

BE DESPISED BECAUSE OF THE TRUTH. RUDOLF GWALTHER: It is worth noting Paul's confidence and frank speech, which provide clear evidence of his innocence. All Christ's ministers should strive after this example, so that they are certain that the world is hostile toward them on account of the truth alone. For this will make them undaunted and constant against all dangers. HOMILY 154, ACTS 24:17-23.[20]

24:22-27 Felix's Delayed Response

FELIX SAW THROUGH THE JEWS' ACCUSATIONS. JOHN CALVIN: It is apparent that although Felix gave no decision on the case, he sensed that Paul was being charged through no fault of his own, but by the ill will of the priests. For when Luke narrates that the action was deferred until the arrival of Lysias, he inserts at the same time, as if instead of a reason, that the governor had precise knowledge about the things pertaining to the Way. By these words I think is meant either that long

---

[17]Gwalther, *Homelyes or Sermons upon the Actes*, 822-23* (*In Acta Apostolorum*, 255r).
[18]CNTC 7:249* (CO 48:520-21); alluding to 1 Tim 2:8.

[19]Gwalther, *Homelyes or Sermons upon the Actes*, 823* (*In Acta Apostolorum*, 255r-v).
[20]Gwalther, *Homelyes or Sermons upon the Actes*, 826* (*In Acta Apostolorum*, 256r); alluding to 1 Pet 3–4.

experience had already made him familiar with the practice of the priests and how they were accustomed to behaving; or that he perceived, from the things that had been said on both sides, how trivial the accusation was. And that is confirmed by the more considerate and more indulgent treatment given to Paul himself. For he commits him to the charge of a centurion, so that he may have, so to speak, greater freedom in custody. Commentary on Acts 24:22.[21]

Paul's Accusers Obviously Defeated. Johann Spangenberg: It is as if Felix wanted to say, "Do you have no other charges against this person? To make such accusations against him, you might as well have stayed home. I am no judge over these accusations that you level against him. I cannot make a ruling in this case. If you have something against him on account of Scripture, then defeat him with Scripture, as is right; if not, then leave him in peace." Thus, the Jews had to withdraw; all their attacks were now lost, so they stumbled home to Jerusalem as if stone drunk. Brief Exegesis of Acts 24:22.[22]

Felix Allows Paul to Be Kept "in Custody." Giovanni Diodati: [That is,] to be kept out of a confined prison or hard bonds, instead only wearing a little chain around his wrist, according to the Roman custom with their freest kind of prisoners. Annotation on Acts 24:23.[23]

Drusilla Still Somewhat Interested in Pure Religion. John Calvin: Now as far as his wife Drusilla is concerned, readers must be reminded that she was the daughter of Agrippa the Elder, of whose loathsome death Luke gave an account in Acts 12. . . . Captivated by her matchless beauty, Felix instigated a certain Jew, called Simon, a native of Cyprus, to allure and entice her to a new marriage. The upshot therefore was that the lust-

ful woman broke her marriage vow and married an uncircumcised man, contrary to the Law. But although she had defiled herself by a profane marriage, still it is easy to conjecture from this verse that the feeling for religion that she had imbibed from infancy had not been completely obliterated from her mind. For Felix would neither have desired to hear Paul, nor deigned to speak with him, except to please his wife. Certainly Luke does not say so explicitly, but in naming Drusilla he gives enough of a hint that Paul was called to speak about the gospel for her sake. However, apostates of that sort are tickled by a certain curiosity rather than moved by a sincere desire to learn. Commentary on Acts 24:24.[24]

God Desires the Salvation of All. Rudolf Gwalther: It is fitting that we mark the goodness of God, who allowed the Word of the gospel—by which life and salvation are offered to people—to be preached to those polluted with such filthy lust. He is therefore truly that God who desires to save people and who does not desire the death of a sinner but rather that he should repent and live. With this belong many examples from the Gospels, where we read that Christ out of a special favor and intimacy offered salvation to tax collectors and prostitutes. As this ought to serve for our consolation when we are jolted by satanic trials which call the certainty of our salvation into doubt, so also it should remind us of our office, lest we wickedly despise God's grace which he so lovingly offers to us. As the preaching of the gospel is the source of salvation for whoever believes and repents, so also they are inexcusable before God who, unwilling to repent, impiously condemn the grace offered to them. Homily 155, Acts 24:24-27.[25]

Paul Shares with Felix the True Way of Salvation. Desiderius Erasmus: Paul disclosed to Felix what he had before concealed—the

[21]CNTC 7:254 (CO 48:525).
[22]Spangenberg, Der Apostel Geschichte, 223r-v.
[23]Diodati, Pious Annotations, CC2r* (I Commenti alla Sacra Biblia, 1120).
[24]CNTC 7:255* (CO 48:526).
[25]Gwalther, Homelyes or Sermons upon the Actes, 828-29* (In Acta Apostolorum, 256v); alluding to Ezek 18:23. See Josephus, Antiquities, 20.7.

way of salvation. This way does not consist in the observances of the law, as the Jews thought, but in trust in Jesus Christ, whom the Jews had crucified though they had awaited him so many centuries. Through baptism all the sins of our former life are once for all abolished, so that those who have been reborn into him may henceforth live pure and holy lives according to the rule of the gospel, doing so until the same Jesus who gave himself for the salvation of the human race returns in exultation with the glory of the Father, judge of the living and the dead. PARAPHRASE OF ACTS 24:24-25.[26]

TRUE TEACHERS PREACH THE LAW, THEN THE GOSPEL. DIRK PHILIPS: In order to cultivate and prepare the field of the heart, the law of God serves [well]. Therefore, true preachers must also first and before all things proclaim and preach repentance to the people (even as Christ and the apostles did) and teach them out of the law God's wrath and severe judgment on sin, but out of the gospel rightly know that God the Father in his eternal love and fathomless mercy, Christ Jesus in his grace and merits, through the cooperation of the Holy Spirit in order that the hearts, smitten and broken through the law, may again be comforted and strengthened through the gospel. For this is the nature, character and power of the divine Word. Where it is spoken orderly and through the motivating of the Spirit flinty hearts are smitten, the cold made fervent and the sorrowful are comforted thereby. This is also the true teacher's office and work, according to the command of Christ; first to preach the law, thereafter the gospel. THE ENCHIRIDION: THE SENDING OF PREACHERS.[27]

NOT WANTING TO LOSE DRUSILLA, FELIX SENDS PAUL AWAY. JOHANN SPANGENBERG: Because Paul spoke of righteousness and of chastity and of the future judgment, Felix became fright-

ened. . . . Felix feared that Drusilla might leave him because of Paul's preaching and return to her actual husband.[28] BRIEF EXEGESIS OF ACTS 24:25.[29]

THE IRRATIONALITY OF THE GREEDY. JOHN CALVIN: Although Paul's integrity was obvious to Felix, so that he felt ashamed to condemn him for payment by the Jews, yet, because he was an avaricious man, given to corrupt practices, he was not willing to acquit him for nothing. That is why he sent for Paul again and again, to speak to him in flattering terms and raise his hopes of obtaining his freedom. For mercenary judges ingratiate themselves like that when they wish to open up the way for corrupt methods. From this we gather that the fear, which seized Felix when he heard Paul's discussion, vanished, seeing that hope of gain gives him a compelling urge to call the man whom he had been forced to remove from his presence because of his alarm. How did Felix expect money from a man who was penniless and destitute? For a handful of plunder would not have satisfied that abyss. As those who have justice for sale are sharp and shrewd, I have no doubt that when he saw the Jews pressing so vigorously for Paul to be destroyed, he got a vague inkling about him, namely, that he was no ordinary man but one whom many held in the highest esteem. Accordingly he had no doubt that many of his friends would gladly meet the cost of releasing him. . . .

Because Paul knew that the mercenary judge would show favor to him on handing over money, and he had plenty of time to collect it, it is probable that he not only spared the brothers but also shrank in horror from that sort of trafficking by which the sanctity of the civil order is shamefully defiled. Now, although governors, on departing from a province, are in the habit of releasing from captivity prisoners whom they know to be guilty

---

[26]CWE 50:138 (LB 7:759).
[27]CRR 6:207-8 (BRN 10:217).

[28]Herod Agrippa II betrothed his sister to the king of Emesa after the death of his father, who had failed to betroth Drusilla previously because of the suitor's refusal to be circumcised. Josephus, *Antiquities*, 20.7. On distinguishing the Herods, see figure 1 on page 162.
[29]Spangenberg, *Der Apostel Geschichte*, 223v-224r.

of no crime, Felix took the opposite course, to gain favor. COMMENTARY ON ACTS 24:27.[30]

FELIX'S SELF-SERVING GESTURE FAILED TO PROMOTE ANYTHING EXCEPT THE GOSPEL.
JOHANN SPANGENBERG: Felix intended with Paul here to feign to do the Jews a favor and friendly gesture, so he leaves Paul behind in prison. However, his attempt misses the mark, for in the end he was still removed from office. Paul remained there around three years unharmed and preached the gospel of Christ, bringing many people to the confession of Christ and to eternal life. BRIEF EXEGESIS OF ACTS 24:27.[31]

---

[30]CNTC 7:257-58* (CO 48:527-28).

[31]Spangenberg, *Der Apostel Geschichte*, 224v.

25:1-12 PAUL'S TRIAL BEFORE FESTUS AND APPEAL TO CAESAR

Now three days after Festus had arrived in the province, he went up to Jerusalem from Caesarea. *²And the chief priests and the principal men of the Jews laid out their case against Paul, and they urged him, ³asking as a favor against Paul*ᵃ *that he summon him to Jerusalem—because they were planning an ambush to kill him on the way. ⁴Festus replied that Paul was being kept at Caesarea and that he himself intended to go there shortly. ⁵So," said he, "let the men of authority among you go down with me, and if there is anything wrong about the man, let them bring charges against him."*

⁶After he stayed among them not more than eight or ten days, he went down to Caesarea. And the next day he took his seat on the tribunal and ordered Paul to be brought. ⁷When he had arrived, the Jews who had come down from Jerusalem stood around him, bringing many and serious charges against him that they could not prove. *⁸Paul argued in his defense, "Neither against the law of the Jews, nor against the temple, nor against Caesar have I committed any offense." ⁹But Festus, wishing to do the Jews a favor, said to Paul, "Do you wish to go up to Jerusalem and there be tried on these charges before me?" ¹⁰But Paul said, "I am standing before Caesar's tribunal, where I ought to be tried. To the Jews I have done no wrong, as you yourself know very well. ¹¹If then I am a wrongdoer and have committed anything for which I deserve to die, I do not seek to escape death. But if there is nothing to their charges against me, no one can give me up to them. I appeal to Caesar." ¹²Then Festus, when he had conferred with his council, answered, "To Caesar you have appealed; to Caesar you shall go."*

a Greek *him*

OVERVIEW: Following his trial before Felix, Paul must stand trial for the good news twice more before finally heading to Rome: once before Festus, and then again before King Agrippa and Bernice. (Luke's repetition here elicits terse commentary from the reformers.) Again a distinction between the *person* in public office and the *office* itself is highlighted. The Lord desires for the office to be respected—whether ecclesial or temporal—as something he has ordained. Yet the person still must hear God's Word concerning sin and salvation, for God is a God without partiality. The injustice of his accusers and inaction of his judges drives Paul to appeal to Caesar. He must press on to Rome. Our commentators underscore God's faithfulness to his promises despite Paul's circumstances, and that the Holy Spirit is fully capable of commandeering the actions of the wicked for his own good purposes.

TRIALS AND TEMPTATONS ARE OPPORTUNITIES FOR GOD TO EXPRESS HIS FAITHFULNESS. RUDOLF GWALTHER: In this chapter and the next are described two very grave trials of the apostle Paul, the first of which he endures before Festus, the new governor, the other in which he articulates the reason for his faith before King Agrippa and Queen Bernice. The first account is the most memorable, because through the pretext [of this trial] the Jews place Paul in immense danger which he, however, escaped through God's favor. God promised him that he will be unharmed, so that he would be able to testify concerning Jesus Christ in Rome before Caesar, as it was stated above in Acts 23. The main purpose of all these things is to teach us the concern God has for his people. Indeed, he allows them to be tempted in various ways, but still he faithfully delivers them from every temptation, as long as they remember their calling and place all their hope and trust in him. Homily 156, Acts 25:1-8.[1]

25:1-5 The Jewish Rulers Speak to Festus

The Lord's Will Is Done on Earth as in Heaven. Johann Spangenberg: Human reason and wisdom would never be able to conclude anything other than that Paul here has certainly met his end. Now he must sacrifice himself and die. But does it happen? No. God in heaven watches over his people. Paul in Caesarea has no idea how treacherously they want to treat him, how heinously they want to kill him. But because Paul trusts God, God guides his path, so that it must not happen according to the Jews' will but according to God's will. Brief Exegesis of Acts 25:1-5.[2]

Paul Again Endures and Answers False Charges. John Calvin: Here there is described for us the second action, in which Paul underwent just as severe and difficult a struggle as in the first. Because he had been left in prison, Festus could have suspected that the case was an intricate one, and as a result could have prejudged it unfairly. But another aspect of the situation brought a more serious danger. We know that new governors, seeking to win the favor of provincials, are in the habit of granting them many things on their arrival. One might therefore well believe that the death of Paul would not be unacceptable to Festus, as a preliminary way of grasping at favor. Therefore the faith of the holy man is assailed and tested all over again, as if the promise of God, on which he had rested so far, had been empty. But the grace of God reveals itself all the more clearly in liberating him, because, contrary to expectation, he is snatched out of the jaws of death. Commentary on Acts 25:1-12.[3]

The Rage of the Wicked Often Focuses on Pastors. Rudolf Gwalther: In this passage it can be seen how restless the minds of the impious are after they are inflamed with hatred of the truth. For wherever their wicked works are disclosed by the light, it cannot be that they easily lay aside their hatred once it is conceived. But rather they boil and froth in their minds like the raging sea, busily watching every small opportunity in which they can extinguish the light of that truth that they hate so much. Often the force of this hatred is such that without any regard to their personal benefit, they strive for and desire this one thing: to remove from their midst the ministers of the Truth, whose teaching they perceive to be such torment. Homily 156, Acts 25:1-8.[4]

The Grave Danger Paul Faces. Johann Spangenberg: Here again Paul's life stands in the greatest danger. For if Festus had acquiesced to the Jews' request, then it certainly would have been finished with Paul. Festus knew nothing of Paul's innocence; thus, he did not anticipate that such powerful people—high priests, Pharisees—would use lies and deception. For that reason, this was the first request of the Jews to the new governor, who could not deny them. Paul was not present so that Festus could investigate the truth from him. So it seemed that Festus did not value Paul very highly, because he welcomed the Jews' hatred and hostility against Paul. Brief Exegesis of Acts 25:4-5.[5]

25:6-12 Paul Appeals to Caesar

The Tired Song Against the Way. Heinrich Bullinger: Now Paul was led forward and exposed to the Jews' accusations as if he were attacked by spears. First, of course, he was led to Jerusalem by the tribune Claudius Lysias. Next he was handed over to Caesar's jurisdiction by Felix when Tertullus accused him. Finally, he was led here by Festus. Luke, however, glances over these events in the shortest possible manner here,

[1]Gwalther, *Homelyes or Sermons upon the Actes*, 832* (*In Acta Apostolorum*, 258r).
[2]Spangenberg, *Der Apostel Geschichte*, 227r.
[3]CNTC 7:259 (CO 48:529).
[4]Gwalther, *Homelyes or Sermons upon the Actes*, 833* (*In Acta Apostolorum*, 258r).
[5]Spangenberg, *Der Apostel Geschichte*, 226v-227r.

because he had already laid out the same matter in Acts 24. For here are the same points of the accusation, which he recounted there, and the defense of Paul is also the same, except the mention of Caesar, which perhaps seems to be new. They truly thought that Paul was transgressing against Caesar in this matter, because he had stirred up a crowd in Jerusalem or because he preached another king, namely, Jesus. This slander was mentioned in Acts 17. Now, the apostles were not preaching that Jesus was King or Messiah so that they could reject Caesar, for the Lord himself had said, "Give to Caesar what is Caesar's, and to God what is God's." Besides these things, Paul argued enough about the temple and the Law elsewhere. The Jews brought nothing new but sang the same old song. COMMENTARY ON ACTS 25:6-8.[6]

PAUL'S WISE DEFENSE. JOHN CALVIN: As long as Paul had lived under the Law his integrity had been known and renowned. Then, after his conversion to Christ, he had been a remarkable exemplar of a blameless life. Yet we see that he submits to many insults and severe misrepresentations. But the situation of the servants of Christ is nearly always like that. Therefore, they ought to be the more courageous, so that they may advance firmly through bad and good repute, and so that it may not be strange to them to be blamed when they have done well. In the meantime they must take care not only that their own consciences are clear before God, but also that they are equipped with a proper defense before humans, when the opportune moment is given. Paul does not neglect his own advantage but wisely opposes their false charges with the defense of his own innocence. However, let us note that the ungodly can never be restrained from slandering good people and reviling them impudently. COMMENTARY ON ACTS 25:7.[7]

THE LAW DIRECTS US TO THE GOSPEL. JOHANN SPANGENBERG: Paul did not preach against the law, for he said, "We do not overthrow the law, but rather establish it correctly for the first time." Thus, Paul says, we preach the law so that people have a mirror in which to see themselves, what they lack, what their sickness is. Thus, they are induced to begin yearning for God's grace. If a person does not know he is sick, he does not ask for a doctor. The law causes recognition of sin; the gospel, however, through faith and God's Word removes [sin] completely. BRIEF EXEGESIS OF ACTS 25:8.[8]

HOW CAN PAUL, WHO PREACHED AGAINST IDOLATRY, CLAIM NOT TO HAVE OFFENDED NERO? JOHANN SPANGENBERG: It is two different things to preach against the majesty of the emperor and against the person of the emperor. With regard to the majesty of the emperor, it is fitting that we pay tribute, tariffs and honor to the emperor; whoever teaches against this, acts against the emperor. Paul never did this; rather, he openly taught: "Pay to everyone what you owe, taxes to whom taxes are owed, tariffs to whom tariffs are owed." With regard to the person of the emperor, it is fitting that he execute his vocation, not acting contrary to natural laws or against civic laws, and not against religion. If he does and if the preacher rebukes him for it, then the preacher does not sin against the imperial majesty but rather fulfills his office, which is to rebuke sinners without showing partiality to the person. BRIEF EXEGESIS OF ACTS 25:8.[9]

THE CORRUPTION OF THOSE WITHOUT THE SPIRIT OF GOD. JOHN CALVIN: Whether Festus had learned something about their ambush, and it is easy to conjecture that he had, or whether he was completely ignorant of it, nevertheless he deals with Paul unfairly. And we see how all who are not led by the Spirit of God are swayed towards all corruption. For Festus does not intentionally

---

[6]Bullinger, *In Acta Apostolorum*, 299v-300r; quoting Mt 22:21; Mk 12:17; Lk 20:25.
[7]CNTC 7:260-61* (CO 48:530).

[8]Spangenberg, *Der Apostel Geschichte*, 228v; quoting Rom 3:31.
[9]Spangenberg, *Der Apostel Geschichte*, 228v-229r; quoting Rom 13:7.

treat Paul as of no consequence or hate him, but ambition, perhaps also the passion for gain, has the upper hand, so that to please the opposing side, he exposes him unjustly to the danger of death. For it is probable that he was attracted by the suggestion of a reward also, with the result that he was so ready to gratify the priests. However, it is strange how he gives Paul the choice and does not rather order him, by virtue of his authority, to be led away against his will. Certainly we gather that he was held back by fear of infringing his right to obtain the privileges of a Roman citizen, and that was a very odious offense. However, he deceitfully desires to persuade Paul not to refuse to be tried at Jerusalem. For he knew quite well what did happen, that a Roman citizen had the right to appeal, with the result that he himself would not be allowed to proceed further. COMMENTARY ON ACTS 25:9.[10]

GREED SULLIES FESTUS'S JUDGMENT. JOHANN SPANGENBERG: From these words we can discern that the governor Festus's palms have been greased. He has completely changed his mind! He is willing to push Paul's case back to Jerusalem, so that Paul might be killed underway, and then Festus can excuse himself, because it happened without his knowledge and will. Here you see what money does, that it often turns a pious person into a scoundrel. Now Paul's innocence is completely forgotten. BRIEF EXEGESIS OF ACTS 25:9.[11]

JESUS' COMMAND DOES NOT NEGATE PAUL'S LAWFUL APPEAL. JUSTUS JONAS: Paul, they say, appealed, so it is right for them to appeal and to bring charges, but in fact they do not understand these terms. Truly, you agree that it is not possible for Christians to bring charges without sin. But if the accused Christian is brought before the court it is permissible for him to defend himself and explain his case clearly and simply. For injustice

committed against the devout should be endured but not in such a way that you approve and praise your adversaries' false accusations. Thus Paul here appeals to Caesar not to bring charges, but to protect and defend himself, as he says in the final chapter, "I was compelled to appeal to Caesar." ANNOTATIONS ON ACTS 25:11.[12]

CHRISTIANS CAN JUSTLY APPEAL TO A MERCIFUL JUDGE. JOHANN SPANGENBERG: Paul recognized in the Spirit that the governor Festus wanted to deliver him to the Jews, so he appealed to the emperor. By this he gives an example to all Christians, that they may in good conscience save their life and appeal if they believe they have false accusers and unmerciful judges. BRIEF EXEGESIS OF ACTS 25:11.[13]

FESTUS ACTS OUT OF PETTY SELF-IMPORTANCE. RUDOLF GWALTHER: As if he is saying, "Are you so bold to take Caesar for your judge rather than me? All right then, you will go to Caesar himself!" [Luke] indeed excellently portrays the behavior of the wicked, who are properly aware of their own iniquity but who nevertheless behave shamefully if someone mildly insults them or objects to their decrees. HOMILY 157, ACTS 25:9-12.[14]

THE SPIRIT OF GOD IS AT WORK IN THE WORDS OF FESTUS. JOHANN SPANGENBERG: These words God certainly placed in the mouth of Festus, so that the Word of the Lord would be fulfilled that was spoken to Paul: "Be comforted, Paul, for as you testified of me in Jerusalem, so also must you testify in Rome." BRIEF EXEGESIS OF ACTS 25:12.[15]

---

[10]CNTC 7:261-62* (CO 48:530-31).
[11]Spangenberg, *Der Apostel Geschichte*, 229v.

[12]Jonas, *Annotationes in Acta*, K4v; alluding to 1 Cor 6:1-11; Mt 5:10-11; quoting Acts 28:19.
[13]Spangenberg, *Der Apostel Geschichte*, 230r.
[14]Gwalther, *Homelyes or Sermons upon the Actes*, 839* (*In Acta Apostolorum*, 259v).
[15]Spangenberg, *Der Apostel Geschichte*, 230v; quoting Acts 23:11.

25:13-27 PAUL BROUGHT
BEFORE KING AGRIPPA

[13]Now when some days had passed, Agrippa the king and Bernice arrived at Caesarea and greeted Festus. [14]And as they stayed there many days, Festus laid Paul's case before the king, saying, "There is a man left prisoner by Felix, [15]and when I was at Jerusalem, the chief priests and the elders of the Jews laid out their case against him, asking for a sentence of condemnation against him. [16]I answered them that it was not the custom of the Romans to give up anyone before the accused met the accusers face to face and had opportunity to make his defense concerning the charge laid against him. [17]So when they came together here, I made no delay, but on the next day took my seat on the tribunal and ordered the man to be brought. [18]When the accusers stood up, they brought no charge in his case of such evils as I supposed. [19]Rather they had certain points of dispute with him about their own religion and about a certain Jesus, who was dead, but whom Paul asserted to be alive. [20]Being at a loss how to investigate these questions, I asked whether he wanted to go to Jerusalem and be tried there regarding them. [21]But when Paul had appealed to be kept in custody for the decision of the emperor, I ordered him to be held until I could send him to Caesar." [22]Then Agrippa said to Festus, "I would like to hear the man myself." "Tomorrow," said he, "you will hear him."

[23]So on the next day Agrippa and Bernice came with great pomp, and they entered the audience hall with the military tribunes and the prominent men of the city. Then, at the command of Festus, Paul was brought in. [24]And Festus said, "King Agrippa and all who are present with us, you see this man about whom the whole Jewish people petitioned me, both in Jerusalem and here, shouting that he ought not to live any longer. [25]But I found that he had done nothing deserving death. And as he himself appealed to the emperor, I decided to go ahead and send him. [26]But I have nothing definite to write to my lord about him. Therefore I have brought him before you all, and especially before you, King Agrippa, so that, after we have examined him, I may have something to write. [27]For it seems to me unreasonable, in sending a prisoner, not to indicate the charges against him."

OVERVIEW: Despite how often Paul has now had to defend himself publicly, Festus still is unsure what charge should accompany this prisoner to Rome. As Luke prepares the stage for Paul's long defense before Agrippa, the reformers praise God's loving-kindness and mercy. That the Lord has assembled such a privileged yet depraved audience to hear the life-giving good news firmly establishes his promise to Ezekiel (Ezek 18:23): "Have I any pleasure in the death of the wicked, declares the LORD God, and not rather that he should turn from his way and live?" This again highlights the importance of the preaching office and its complete dependence on the Trinity; human beings can and must faithfully teach the Father's Word concern-

ing his Son, but only the Spirit can plant it in the human heart to produce faith.

25:13-22 Festus Lays Paul's Case Before Agrippa

WHO ARE AGRIPPA AND BERNICE? JOHANN SPANGENBERG: The son of Herod Agrippa who had James the brother of John killed and allowed Peter to fall into the hands of the Jews who placed him in prison.[1] The emperor Claudius loved this Agrippa so much that he gave him an entire nation, Syria, as well as Philip's land in Idumea and

---

[1]Acts 12:1-5. See figure 1, p. 162.

several cities in Judea. At this time Jerusalem was destroyed. If the Jews had obeyed this Agrippa, things may have gone better with them. Bernice was Agrippa's sister, and Poleme the king of Lycia's wife. BRIEF EXEGESIS OF ACTS 25:13.[2]

LUKE RECORDS EVERY DETAIL OF THIS UN-USUAL EVENT. RUDOLF GWALTHER: Because it was such an anomalous event for kings to listen to a person in chains deliver a speech, Luke believed nothing that happened here should be passed over in silence. HOMILY 158, ACTS 25:13-22.[3]

GOD'S GRACE IS HELD OUT TO THE VILEST OF SINNERS. RUDOLF GWALTHER: This is a singular example of God's goodness by which he offers the salvation that is purchased by Christ to be preached by Paul to two people born of such wicked stock and polluted with incest. For their great-grandfather was Herod the Great, who laid in wait for Christ, being newborn, and commanded the most cruel murder of the infants of Bethlehem. . . . Their father, Agrippa, we already mentioned, who killed James and cast the apostle Peter into prison, meaning to have him put to death as well, but he was delivered by the help of an angel. Agrippa and Bernice, born . . . of such progenitors as these, hear Paul preach the gospel of salvation. By this it is clear that God is not so wayward nor desirous of revenge as to punish the children for the wickedness of their ancestors; instead, his grace is stretched out to all who will truly repent and turn to him. . . . Christ was especially sent to those whose ancestors were unfaithful to God and who slayed the prophets sent to them.

Now we see today that the grace of God and the merit of Christ is most courteously offered to many who have sinned atrociously. Therefore, those who Satan has taught to doubt God's grace and mercy—as if our sins were greater than these!—let them learn consolation through this.

Also, let these things serve to instruct us so that we condemn no one rashly because of his ancestors, seeing that in the genealogy of Christ are numbered many defamed people, so that no one should doubt that Christ belongs chiefly to sinners. HOMILY 158, ACTS 25:13-22.[4]

FESTUS'S REPORT EXEMPLIFIES JUST JUDG-MENT. JOHANN SPANGENBERG: In these words Festus sufficiently demonstrates the traits a just judge should have, namely, that he is God-fearing, does not do anyone violence or injustice, is truthful, tells no lies, is not greedy, is not money-hungry, does not accept gifts [for the benefit of the rich] over the poor. He should not judge anyone unless he is present for the accusation and is sufficiently convinced [of their guilt]. If he has no understanding of the matter and it is not under his authority, then he should give no judgment. BRIEF EXEGESIS OF ACTS 25:14-21.[5]

THE SPIRIT ENABLES FAITHFUL HEARING. JOHN CALVIN: There is no doubt that Paul spoke seriously, and with the earnestness it deserved, about the resurrection of Christ, but, because of his own pride, Festus did not think it a fitting subject to which to turn his mind. Certainly he does not openly mock Paul, but he makes it plain enough how heedless he was when he heard him speaking about Christ. We perceive from that how little effect preaching has, indeed how it has no effect at all, unless the Spirit of the Lord affects hearts inwardly; for the ungodly take no notice of all that is said, just as if someone were telling fairy tales. Accordingly there is no cause for the heedlessness of many today to disturb us, when Paul accomplished nothing with Festus. COMMENTARY ON ACTS 25:19.[6]

FESTUS IS CONCERNED ABOUT HIMSELF. THE ENGLISH ANNOTATIONS: Or, "I was doubtful to

---

[2]Spangenberg, *Der Apostel Geschichte*, 231r.
[3]Gwalther, *Homelyes or Sermons upon the Actes*, 840* (*In Acta Apostolorum*, 260r).

[4]Gwalther, *Homelyes or Sermons upon the Actes*, 841* (*In Acta Apostolorum*, 260v); alluding to Ezek 18.
[5]Spangenberg, *Der Apostel Geschichte*, 232r.
[6]CNTC 7:266 (CO 48:534).

ask further." This was Festus's pretense, but the truth was that he sought to gain favor with the Jews. Here he betrays his own injustice. For why did he not acquit Paul against whom nothing was proved? ANNOTATIONS ON ACTS 25:20.[7]

THE MULTIPLICITY OF TESTIMONIES CONFIRMS PAUL'S INNOCENCE. RUDOLF GWALTHER: Let us observe how Paul's innocence is confirmed by many testimonies. First we had Lysias the tribune as a witness, then Felix, now Festus, and soon enough we will have Agrippa, too. Even though the wicked priests go on in their accusation, still they confirm Paul's innocence all the more, because they are able to prove none of their accusations against him. Similar situations happened with the other apostles, too, as we have often seen—just as the Evangelists declare that Pilate and Herod bear witness to Christ's innocence. HOMILY 158, ACTS 25:13-22.[8]

25:23-27 Festus Addresses Agrippa and Bernice

GOD ORCHESTRATES THESE EVENTS FOR THE GLORY OF HIS NAME. JOHANN SPANGENBERG: God wants this particular lowly person, Paul, to be led here and there before kings, princes, judges and councils, so that the Word of the Lord about Paul to Ananias would be fulfilled, when he said, "Go, for this person is a chosen vessel of mine; he will carry my name before the Gentiles and before kings and before the children of Israel." BRIEF EXEGESIS OF ACTS 25:23.[9]

THE LORD GRANTS PAUL A PROMINENT AUDIENCE. JOHN CALVIN: Agrippa and his sister do not come as humble disciples of Christ but bring pomp and splendor that would close their ears and blind their eyes. And one may well believe that arrogance of mind was the exact counterpart of that magnificent show. It is therefore no wonder if they were not

won over to obedience to Christ. However, it seems that Luke mentioned the magnificence so that we may know that, in a great gathering, and before the most select witnesses who carried great influence, Paul was given the opportunity and the freedom not only to plead his case, as if a prisoner defending himself, but also to promulgate the gospel. For he appears in the role of teacher and nothing else, so that he may give luster to the name of Christ. The truth of God therefore broke out from his bonds and soon spread everywhere by a free and unimpeded course, yes, and what is more, has flowed even to us. COMMENTARY ON ACTS 25:23.[10]

HUMAN PRIDE IS THE LARGEST BARRIER TO THE EFFICACY OF THE WORD. RUDOLF GWALTHER: This desire [to hear Paul's case] proceeds more from a certain vain curiosity of mind than from any love for truth or salvation. In this way he resembles Herod Antipas, his grandfather's brother, who also wanted to see Christ, but for no other reason than because he heard his miracles praised by so many. He gives us proof of this when he approaches Paul's sermon not like a disciple or student, nor lays aside his princely pomp but brings all his court with great ostentation into the auditorium. . . . It happens many times that some come to hear the Word, not led by the desire of salvation but by the affections of the flesh—that is to say, by curiosity, or with hope of some gain, or from hatred of the popish doctrine or because they would not be thought to be ungodly or enemies of religion. But because such come not as students but as judges and censors and bring with them their preconceived ideas, it cannot be that the gospel benefits them at all. As Paul says, the purpose of faith is to take captive all the wisdom of the flesh and bring it into obedience to faith. Therefore, we must bring with us humble and lowly minds, willing to learn, if we will receive any benefit from the Word. HOMILY 159, ACTS 25:23-27.[11]

[7]Downame, ed., *Annotations*, MMM2v*; alluding to Acts 25:9.
[8]Gwalther, *Homelyes or Sermons upon the Actes*, 843* (*In Acta Apostolorum*, 261r); alluding to Mt 27:24-26; Lk 23:13-16; Jn 19:4.
[9]Spangenberg, *Der Apostel Geschichte*, 232v; quoting Acts 9:15.

[10]CNTC 7:268* (CO 40:535-36).
[11]Gwalther, *Homelyes or Sermons upon the Actes*, 844-45* (*In Acta Apostolorum*, 261v); alluding to 2 Cor 10:1-5.

26:1-23 PAUL'S DEFENSE BEFORE KING AGRIPPA

So Agrippa said to Paul, "You have permission to speak for yourself." Then Paul stretched out his hand and made his defense:

²"I consider myself fortunate that it is before you, King Agrippa, I am going to make my defense today against all the accusations of the Jews, ³especially because you are familiar with all the customs and controversies of the Jews. Therefore I beg you to listen to me patiently.

⁴"My manner of life from my youth, spent from the beginning among my own nation and in Jerusalem, is known by all the Jews. ⁵They have known for a long time, if they are willing to testify, that according to the strictest party of our religion I have lived as a Pharisee. ⁶And now I stand here on trial because of my hope in the promise made by God to our fathers, ⁷to which our twelve tribes hope to attain, as they earnestly worship night and day. And for this hope I am accused by Jews, O king! ⁸Why is it thought incredible by any of you that God raises the dead?

⁹"I myself was convinced that I ought to do many things in opposing the name of Jesus of Nazareth. ¹⁰And I did so in Jerusalem. I not only locked up many of the saints in prison after receiving authority from the chief priests, but when they were put to death I cast my vote against them. ¹¹And I punished them often in all the synagogues and tried to make them blaspheme, and in raging fury against them I persecuted them even to foreign cities.

¹²"In this connection I journeyed to Damascus with the authority and commission of the chief priests.

¹³At midday, O king, I saw on the way a light from heaven, brighter than the sun, that shone around me and those who journeyed with me. ¹⁴And when we had all fallen to the ground, I heard a voice saying to me in the Hebrew language,ᵃ 'Saul, Saul, why are you persecuting me? It is hard for you to kick against the goads.' ¹⁵And I said, 'Who are you, Lord?' And the Lord said, 'I am Jesus whom you are persecuting. ¹⁶But rise and stand upon your feet, for I have appeared to you for this purpose, to appoint you as a servant and witness to the things in which you have seen me and to those in which I will appear to you, ¹⁷delivering you from your people and from the Gentiles—to whom I am sending you ¹⁸to open their eyes, so that they may turn from darkness to light and from the power of Satan to God, that they may receive forgiveness of sins and a place among those who are sanctified by faith in me.'

¹⁹"Therefore, O King Agrippa, I was not disobedient to the heavenly vision, ²⁰but declared first to those in Damascus, then in Jerusalem and throughout all the region of Judea, and also to the Gentiles, that they should repent and turn to God, performing deeds in keeping with their repentance. ²¹For this reason the Jews seized me in the temple and tried to kill me. ²²To this day I have had the help that comes from God, and so I stand here testifying both to small and great, saying nothing but what the prophets and Moses said would come to pass: ²³that the Christ must suffer and that, by being the first to rise from the dead, he would proclaim light both to our people and to the Gentiles."

a Or *the Hebrew dialect* (probably Aramaic)

OVERVIEW: For the third time Paul recounts his credentials, conversion and calling. The reformers have sufficiently commended Paul's rhetoric and message, so they turn again to a beloved topic, the efficacy of the Word. Worship and ministry are to be established in the Word alone; it might be tempting to try to change or add to it, but this, our commentators assert, can only end in idolatry. God's Word does not return empty (Is 55:11); for our commentators, there are only two possible ways of receiving the Word: with increasing hostility or increasing receptivity.

PAUL TESTIFIES THROUGH TEACHING. JOHN CALVIN: We have mentioned the purpose for which Paul was brought before that gathering, namely, so that Festus might write to Caesar in accordance with the advice of Agrippa and the others. He therefore does not use the simple or usual form of defense but rather adapts his speech to teaching. Luke certainly records an expression of apology, but one that suits quite well where an account is being given of teaching. Moreover, because Paul knew from experience that Festus was indifferent to, and despised, anything taken from the Law and the Prophets, he turns to the king, who, he hoped, would be more attentive, as he was no stranger to the Jewish religion. And because he had so far been pouring out words on deaf ears, he now rejoices since he has a man who, because of his knowledge and experience, may judge properly. But as he praises Agrippa's experience, because he is a legitimate judge of the matters in question, so, on the other hand, he asks that he may be willing to hear him patiently, for otherwise neglect and aversion would be less excusable in him. COMMENTARY ON ACTS 26:2.[1]

FAITH HAS DECLINED TO THE POINT THAT "THE FAITHFUL" REJECT THE GOSPEL. JOHN CALVIN: He complains before Agrippa that the circumstances of the church have declined so far that the priests are fighting against the common hope of the faithful. It is as if he said, "Look at those of our nation who worship God punctiliously and devote nights and days to the offices of piety. What is the object of their sighing out their prayers, except that at last they may attain to everlasting life? But that is precisely the goal of all my teaching, because, when the grace of redemption is presented, at the same time the gate of the kingdom of heaven is opened. And when I preach that the Author of salvation has been raised up from the dead, I am offering the first fruits of blessed immortality in his person." Thus, the first confirmation of his teaching was taken from the Word of God when he publicly cited the promise made to the ancestors.

Now, in the second place he adds the agreement of the church. And this is the proper way to affirm the doctrines of the faith, the authority of God taking the lead and the approval of the church coming after. At the same time, however, we must wisely distinguish the true church, as Paul teaches here by his own example. For although he knew that the priests were bringing the charge of a false church against him, still he fearlessly declares that the sincere worshipers of God are on his side, and he is content with their support. COMMENTARY ON ACTS 26:7.[2]

ON INTENTIONS, GOD'S WORD AND IDOLATRY. MARTIN LUTHER: They instituted and established [worship], out of their own notions and opinions, and without God's command. They concocted new forms and persons and times for worship, even though Moses had strictly forbidden this, especially in Deuteronomy 12, and was always pointing them to the place that God had chosen for his tent and tabernacle. This false thinking was their idolatry. Yet they regarded it as a fine and precious thing and relied upon it as if they had done it well, though it was outright disobedience and apostasy from God and his commands. . . .

This is the real committing of idolatry, to set up a form of divine worship and service without God's bidding simply out of one's own pious inclination. For God will not have us teach him how he is to be served. He wills to teach us and to prescribe for us. His Word is supposed to be there; it is supposed to enlighten and guide us. Without this Word everything is idolatry and outright lies, however devout and beautiful it may appear to be. . . .

Therefore it does not help our clergy at all to allege that in their churches and chapters they serve no idol, but only God, the true Lord. For here you learn that it is not enough to say or think, "I am doing it to God's glory; I have in mind the true God; I mean to be worshiping and serving the only God." All idolaters say and intend the same thing.

---

[1]CNTC 7:269* (CO 48:537).

[2]CNTC 7:271-72* (CO 48:538-39).

The thinking and intending is not what counts, otherwise those who martyred the apostles and the Christians would also have been God's servants. For they too thought that they were offering a service to God, as Christ says in John 16; and Saint Paul in Romans 10 bears witness to the Jews that they have a zeal for God, and adds in Acts 26 that with their worship night and day they hope to attain to the promised salvation.

On the contrary, let everyone see to it that he is certain his worship and service of God has been instituted by God's Word, and not invented by his own pious notions or good intentions. Whoever engages in a form of worship to which God has not borne witness ought to know that he is serving not the true God but an idol that he has concocted for himself. That is to say, he is serving his own notions and false ideas, and thereby the devil himself; and the words of the prophets are against him. For the God who would have us establish worship and service of him according to our own choice and inclination—without his commission and Word—does not exist. There is only one God, he who through his Word has abundantly established and commissioned all the various stations of life and the forms of worship and service in which it is his will to be served. We should abide by this and not turn aside from it either to the right or to the left, doing neither more nor less, making it neither worse nor better. Otherwise there will be no end of idolatry, since all have the true God in mind, and all use his true Name. PREFACE TO THE PROPHETS.[3]

PAUL RECOUNTS HIS CONVERSION TO REFUTE HIS OPPONENTS' ARGUMENTS. THE ENGLISH ANNOTATIONS: He anticipates an objection. Some might say, "Were you raised a Pharisee? You never taught them to believe that Jesus was the Messiah." True indeed, he says, I was an adversary to Christians, as much as any of them, and thought myself bound in conscience to try to suppress them. No one persuaded me otherwise, but God revealed to me from heaven the truth of Christ and redirected my course. Therefore here he inserts the history of his admirable conversion. ANNOTATIONS ON ACTS 26:9.[4]

THE HAND OF GOD REDIRECTED PAUL'S PATH. JOHN CALVIN: He repeats the story of his conversion, not only to remove the reproach of fickleness from himself but also to testify that he was called by God and was not even urged to action by a commandment from heaven. For, seeing that he was suddenly transformed from a wolf to a sheep against his own will, such a violent change is most effective for gaining confidence in his teaching. Accordingly, he magnifies his eagerness to inflict injury, which drove him against the members of Christ and the pertinacity to which he yielded himself completely. If he had been imbued with the faith of Christ from his earliest childhood, or having been instructed by some man he had embraced it of his own free will and with no resistance, his call would indeed have been certain to him personally, but it would not have been so illustrious in the eyes of others. But now, when this man who was burning with stubborn, inflexible fury, who was not prompted by any motive and not persuaded by any mortal man, underwent a change of heart, it is clear that he was subdued by the hand of God. Therefore that contrast has great importance, because he recalls that he was inflated with perverse self-confidence, so that he thought that he would be the one to conquer Christ; and he wished to teach by it that it was not by any means in accordance with the inclination of his own mind that he became a disciple of Christ. COMMENTARY ON ACTS 26:9.[5]

"IT WILL BE HARD FOR YOU TO KICK AGAINST THE GOADS."[6] MARTIN LUTHER: This is a warning which everyone should take to heart who intends to persecute this teaching. But they do not

---

[3]LW 35:269-70, 272-73 (WADB 11,1:9, 11, 15); alluding to Deut 12:4, 8, 28, 32; 12:5, 11, 13-14, 17-18, 21, 26; Jn 16:2; Rom 10:2; Acts 26:7; Deut 5:32; 28:14; Josh 1:7; Prov 4:27.

[4]Downame, ed., *Annotations*, MMM2v*.
[5]CNTC 7:273-74* (CO 48:540).
[6]A goad is a sharp, pointed tool used to prod oxen when they are unwilling to plow.

have the grace to believe it, so, they do not convert like Paul but instead continue in their sins, until they must die and decay—here temporally and there eternally. "It is a costly thing," Christ says, "for you to rage in this way; what do you think is going to come from it? Nothing other than that through me you run into a skewer. But is this not only a ridiculous but also a harmful battle, that someone is so angry that in his anger he kicks a goad with his foot and wants to vent his anger in this way, [resulting in] self-harm?"

So this is a very noteworthy and comforting word for the poor, persecuted Christians, that we understand that whoever persecutes Christ is kicking against a sharp goad. Their foot will either become maimed or at the very least they certainly won't have much success. This, too, should be advised to those who rage against Christ. Many powerful princes, and especially the pope and his godless heap, think they will tear Christ out of heaven, that is, smother his teaching and Word. But we should see immediately how this will go for them. For the skewer is not made for us to charge against but rather for us to jab with. Thus, these blind people who kick their feet against it will certainly leap up in the air in pain. This warning was sufficient for Paul, and he yielded immediately. HOUSE POSTIL FOR SAINT PAUL'S CONVERSION (1544).[7]

PAUL'S PREACHING ACCOMPLISHES GOD'S WORK. JOHN CALVIN: Paul seems to be putting himself on too high a level in arrogating to himself what properly belongs to God. We know that the eyes of the mind are enlightened only by the Holy Spirit. We know that Christ is the one and only Liberator who snatches us out of the tyranny of Satan. We know that it is God alone, who, having destroyed our sins, admits us into the lot of the saints. But it is a common thing for God to transfer to his ministers the honor due to himself alone, not in order to take anything away from himself but to commend the efficacy of his Spirit, which he puts forth in them. God does not send them to work

so that they may be dead instruments or as if they were play actors, but so that God may work powerfully with their assistance. But the effectiveness of their preaching depends on the secret power of him who "works all things in all people" and who alone "gives the increase."

Therefore, teachers are sent not to strew their words uselessly on the air or to beat others' ears merely with empty sound but to bring life-giving light to the blind, to transform their hearts into the righteousness of God and to confirm the grace of salvation, which has been procured by the death of Christ. But they do not carry out any of these things, except in so far as God works through them, so that their labor may not be in vain, with the result that all the praise remains with God alone, as the effect comes from God.

Accordingly, we must note that as often as Scripture gives such honor and praise to the outward ministry, it must not be separated from the Spirit, who gives life to it just as the soul quickens the body. For in other passages it teaches how human activity achieves nothing, and, what is more, confers nothing by itself. For it is their responsibility to "plant" and "water," but it lies with God alone to "give the increase." COMMENTARY ON ACTS 26:18.[8]

THE GOSPEL BEAUTIFULLY DESCRIBED. JOHN CALVIN: Because their own ignorance and ill will stand in the way of a great many, so that they do not obtain from the gospel the fruit that they ought to get, we must note this description, which briefly and splendidly sets that incomparable treasure before our eyes. Therefore this is the goal of the gospel that, delivered from mental blindness, we may become sharers of the heavenly light. Snatched out of the dominion of Satan, we may be turned to God, and having received the free forgiveness of sins, we may obtain a share in the eternal inheritance among the saints. All who desire to make proper progress in the gospel ought

---

[7]WA 52:614.

[8]CNTC 7:276-77* (CO 48:542-43); quoting 1 Cor 12:6; 3:6-9; alluding to 2 Tim 4:3.

to have their sense turned intently toward it. COM-
MENTARY ON ACTS 26:18.[9]

**PAUL WAS RIGHT TO OBEY THE HEAVENLY VI-
SION.** RUDOLF GWALTHER: Now he declares what
he did and what happened to him and takes an
occasion to preach to those who were present. First,
he confesses plainly the obedience that he showed
to the heavenly vision, which thing is diligently to
be noted. For if we compare the commandment
of God with the precept that Paul received from
the priests, we shall perceive they differed very
much one from another. For the priests sent him to
Damascus with public commission and authority
to bring those faithful of Christ there to be put in
bonds and prison. But God commanded him not
only to cease from doing this but also to preach the
gospel. Therefore, he says he obeyed the calling of
God and that speedily and without all delay, and
he is not ashamed to confess the same before those
with whom he knew the priests were of more authority than he was. Therefore, he teaches us by his
example that we must obey God more than people
and that we must make no delay or put off, as soon
as we are certain what his will is. Whoever follows
this rule frees himself from great anxiety and care.
HOMILY 164, ACTS 26:19-23.[10]

"TURNING" DESCRIBES REPENTANCE. JOHN
CALVIN: To repentance there is added turning
to God, not as something different, but so that
we may know what repenting means, just as, also,
on the other hand, corruption and depravity are
nothing else but alienation from God. But because
repentance is an inward thing and depends on the
disposition of the heart, Paul, in the second place,
demands works to prove it, and this is in accordance with the exhortation of John the Baptist,
"Bring forth fruits worthy of repentance." COMMEN-
TARY ON ACTS 26:20.[11]

**PAUL'S MESSAGE FULFILLS MOSES AND THE
PROPHETS.** HEINRICH BULLINGER: After Paul
had answered each point of the accusation, he was
freer to preach Jesus Christ to the leaders, testifying that Christian teaching was not new but that
this very teaching the prophets once handed down
by divine inspiration. Nevertheless he begins with
these greater things in this way: "The Jews, on
account of the truth of the gospel, want to put me
to death, but the Lord does not want me to perish
prematurely. Further, he has protected me so that I
would be able to offer testimony to the divine truth.
Therefore, preserved by his grace and protection, I
know that I am free to declare the truth. I preach
to all without partiality, that truly the God of the
human race—all of whom were already dead in
sin and error—had compassion, sent his Son as
atonement for sin and to be the Light and Teacher
of the entire world. For this reason he died. For
this reason he rose again. He ascended into heaven
and he sent ambassadors as witnesses about this
not only to Jews but to all nations." It seemed
incredible to many (as is shown in John 7) that the
Messiah would be capable of suffering or that the
light of truth would be shared with the Gentiles.
COMMENTARY ON ACTS 26:22-23.[12]

---

[9]CNTC 7:277* (CO 48:543); alluding to Col 1:11-14.
[10]Gwalther, *Homelyes or Sermons upon the Actes*, 863* (*In Acta
Apostolorum*, 256v-266r).

[11]CNTC 7:278 (CO 48:544); quoting Mt 3:8.
[12]Bullinger, *In Acta Apostolorum*, 308r-v; alluding to Eph 2:1-9.

26:24-32 THE RESPONSES OF FESTUS AND AGRIPPA

²⁴*And as he was saying these things in his defense, Festus said with a loud voice, "Paul, you are out of your mind; your great learning is driving you out of your mind." ²⁵But Paul said, "I am not out of my mind, most excellent Festus, but I am speaking true and rational words. ²⁶For the king knows about these things, and to him I speak boldly. For I am persuaded that none of these things has escaped his notice, for this has not been done in a corner. ²⁷King Agrippa, do you believe the prophets? I know that you believe." ²⁸And Agrippa said to Paul, "In a short time would* you persuade me to be a Christian?"ᵃ ²⁹*And Paul said, "Whether short or long, I would to God that not only you but also all who hear me this day might become such as I am—except for these chains."*

³⁰Then the king rose, and the governor and Bernice and those who were sitting with them. ³¹And when they had withdrawn, they said to one another, "This man is doing nothing to deserve death or imprisonment." ³²And Agrippa said to Festus, "This man could have been set free if he had not appealed to Caesar."

a Or *In a short time you would persuade me to act like a Christian!*

OVERVIEW: Festus's interruption of Paul's defense elicits deliberation from Reformation exegetes on the adage that the wisdom of God is foolishness to human beings. The reactions of Festus and Agrippa evince the radically counterintuitive nature of the gospel. Humanity is so thoroughly corrupted by sin that a willingness to look foolish and silly is required to accept the good news of Jesus' death and resurrection. While there is disagreement about the nature of grace (whether resistible or not), the commentators agree that the pastor personally has no control over a person's response to the preached Word; regardless, each pastor must preach in the confidence that the Word and the power of the Spirit are inseparable. God alone must grant the growth.

ALLOW YOURSELF TO BE INVERTED AND REDEFINED BY THE GOSPEL. MARTIN LUTHER: The gospel inverts everything and goes against our senses. What [our senses] call shameful is actually honorable, what they call honorable is actually shameful, and those who burn others at the stake are worthy of the fire, while those who are burned are worthy of the judgment seat, which they will possess on Judgment Day. On that day it will be made quite plain how things actually are, which the prophet says: "With the inverted God inverts himself." Because they forge ahead against their senses and judge unjustly, so God forges ahead and judges justly against their senses. DEDICATION TO COUNT MANSFELD.[1]

GOD'S WORD VERSUS HUMAN REASON. RUDOLF GWALTHER: Festus listened to Paul, declaring his visions and proving all the mysteries of the Christian faith and human salvation by the testimonies of the Scriptures, of which he had never heard anything at all as a Gentile—as someone who likely had more understanding in matters of wars than in religion. He supposes that Paul, in reasoning of such profound and difficult matters, was mad . . . and very importunately he interrupts Paul in his speaking.

This example teaches us how little the Word of God prevails with those who are led only with human reason. For this is their common property: to consider it a mockery which passes the reach of their capacity and reason. In the meantime, there is nothing they understand less than the things belonging to the Spirit of God. . . . They must

---

[1]WA 10, 1.1:6-7; cf. LW 52:6; quoting Ps 18:26.

think the gospel of Jesus Christ crucified to be the greatest foolishness in the world, because there is nothing so absurd and void of reason as to ask and hope for salvation in him who was hanged and died on a cross between thieves and murderers. Homily 165, Acts 26:24-32.[2]

Paul Fears Christ and No Other. Rudolf Gwalther: What happened to Paul as he was preaching before Festus is the same as what happened before to the prophets, and afterward to the successors of the apostles also, namely, that they were considered to be people out of their wits. Even Christ himself was mocked by Pilate, at which time he confessed that he came into the world to preach the truth. For Pilate thought he was one of those people who had labored long in vain to find out the truth, because all things among people are doubtful and uncertain. Therefore, why are we offended that the gospel prevails so little in these days, seeing there is such a multitude of human beings everywhere who are blinded by reason of the flesh and distracted in their minds?

But what does Paul do? Is he so afraid of Festus's importunate interruption that he holds his peace, and so through his silence confirms the sinister suspicion that he was out of his wits? No, rather, he boldly defends the authority both of his ministry and of the gospel: "I am not mad," he says, "most dear Festus, but I speak the words of truth and sobriety." Therefore, he boldly puts such slander away, yet modestly and with such reverence as is due to magistrates, lest through impatience and ire he should have been declared out of his wits indeed. Therefore, in a wiser way, he utterly denies he was mad, and those words which seemed to Festus to be of a madman he declared to be most true and uttered by him with as much sobriety as could be. He proves this by very credible witnesses, among whom first he produces a king who could not be ignorant about these things concerning Christ,

because they were not done in a corner or in secret but in the most famous city of all nations and at the greatest and most principal feast of all. Homily 165, Acts 26:24-32.[3]

What Does Agrippa Mean by "in a Short Time"? John Calvin: Interpreters give different explanations of the phrase ἐν ὀλίγῳ. Valla thought that it ought to be translated like this, "You are very near to making me a Christian." Erasmus renders it, "in a small degree." The Vulgate has the simpler reading, "in a little," because in rendering it word for word, it has left readers free to make up their own minds. And it certainly can be made to apply to time well, as if Agrippa had said, "You will make me a Christian all at once, or in a single moment." If anyone objects that Paul's reply does not fit in with that, there is an easy solution. Because his words were ambiguous, Paul skillfully referred what had been said about time to the situation. Therefore, when Agrippa meant that he was almost made a Christian in a short time, Paul added that he wished that both he and his companions might ascend from small beginnings to higher levels of progress. Yet it is quite suitable to take ἐν ὀλίγῳ as amounting to the same thing as "almost."

But this reply is evidence of how greatly the holy man's breast was inflamed with zeal for increasing the glory of Christ, when, patiently carrying the fetters put on him by the governor, he desires that the governor be rescued from the deadly snares of the devil and to make both him and the others sharers and partners in the same grace as himself, at the same time being content with his own irksome and ignominious lot. It must be observed that he does not make a simple wish, but wished by God, as it is his part to draw us to the Son, because outward teaching will always be coldly received unless his Spirit is teaching within. Commentary on Acts 26:28.[4]

---

[2]Gwalther, *Homelyes or Sermons upon the Actes*, 865-66* (*In Acta Apostolorum*, 267v-268r).

[3]Gwalther, *Homelyes or Sermons upon the Actes*, 866* (*In Acta Apostolorum*, 268v); alluding to Jn 18:33-38.
[4]CNTC 7:283-84* (CO 48:548).

Grace Is Resistible. The Remonstrance
of 1610: That this grace of God is the beginning,
continuance, and accomplishment of all good, even
to this extent, that the regenerate person himself,
without prevenient or assisting, awakening, following and cooperative grace, can neither think, will
or do good, or withstand any temptations to evil;
so that all good deeds or movements that can be
conceived must be ascribed to the grace of God in
Christ. But as respects the mode of the operation
of this grace, it is not irresistible, inasmuch as it is
written concerning many that they have resisted
the Holy Spirit (Acts 7 and elsewhere in many
places). Article 4.[5]

Irresistible Grace. The Canons of Dordrecht: To whom so great and so gracious a
blessing is communicated, above their merit, or
rather notwithstanding their demerits, are bound
to acknowledge it with humble and grateful hearts,
and with the apostle to adore, not curiously to pry
into the severity and justice of God's judgments
displayed in others, to whom this grace is not given.

As many as are called by the gospel are un-
feignedly called; for God has most earnestly and
truly declared in his Word what will be acceptable to him, namely, that all who are called should
comply with the invitation. He, moreover, seriously
promises eternal life and rest to as many as shall
come to him and believe on him.

It is not the fault of the gospel, or of Christ
offered therein, or of God, who calls human beings
by the gospel and confers on them various gifts,
that those who are called by the ministry of the
Word refuse to come and be converted. The fault
lies in themselves; some of whom when called, do
not accept the security of the Word of life; others,
though they receive it, suffer it not to make a lasting impression on their heart; therefore, their joy,
arising only from a temporary faith, soon vanishes,
and they fall away; while others choke the seed of
the Word by perplexing cares and the pleasures of
this world and produce no fruit. This our Savior

teaches in the parable of the sower (Mt 13).

But that others who are called by the gospel obey the call and are converted is not to
be ascribed to the proper exercise of free will,
whereby one distinguishes himself above others
equally furnished with grace sufficient for faith
and conversion (as the proud heresy of Pelagius
maintains); but it must be wholly ascribed to God,
who, as he has chosen his own from eternity in
Christ, so he [calls them effectually in time] confers on them faith and repentance, rescues them
from the power of darkness and translates them
into the kingdom of his own Son, that they may
show forth the praises of him who has called them
out of darkness into his marvelous light; and may
glory not in themselves but in the Lord, according
to the testimony of the apostles in various places.
Of Human Corruption, Conversion and Its
Manner, Articles 7-10.[6]

Outward Versus Inward Teaching. John
Calvin: The apostle accomplished at least this,
that he wrested an involuntary confession out of
King Agrippa, just as those who cannot resist the
truth any longer are in the habit of nodding or at
any rate giving some sign of assent. Agrippa indeed
means that he will not be a Christian willingly, and
what is more, has no intention of becoming one,
yet that he is unable to resist but is somehow being
drawn in spite of himself. That goes to show how
great the stubbornness of human nature is until
the Spirit of God reduces it to obedience. Commentary on Acts 26:28.[7]

**No Matter the Result, the Word Must
Be Preached and Believed.** Heinrich Bullinger: Though Paul saw that the rest of his work
and its cost would go to waste among these leaders
of the world, nevertheless with noble charity of his
fervent mind, he who thirsted for nothing except
the salvation of human beings proved [this], saying
"Indeed I would to God that not only [you but also

---

[5]*Creeds*, 3:547*.

[6]*Creeds*, 3:589-90* (Latin, 565-66).
[7]CNTC 7:283* (CO 48:548).

all]," etc. So then it is not enough if you believe only partially or temperately. For indeed, it should be believed correctly and completely with all your heart, unless you prefer lamps without oil. Those who prefer lamps without oil have the appearance of faith without faith itself. In the end to these people the Lord says, "I do not know you." Therefore we cry out with the disciples, "Increase our faith, Lord!" COMMENTARY ON ACTS 26:29.[8]

DESIRE THE CONSOLATION OF THE CROSS.
JOHN DONNE:

> Since Christ embrac'd the Cross itself, dare I
> His image, th'image of his Cross deny?
> Would I have profit by the sacrifice,
> And dare the chosen Altar to despise?

It bore all other sins, but is it fit
That it should bear the sin of scorning it?
Who from the picture would avert his eye,
How would he fly his pains, who there did die?
From me, no Pulpit, nor misgrounded law,
Nor scandal taken, shall this Cross withdraw,
It shall not, for it cannot; for, the loss
Of this Cross, were to me another Cross;
Better were worse, for, no affliction,
No Cross is so extreme as to have none.
Who can blot out the Cross,
    which th'instrument
Of God, dew'd on me in the Sacrament?
Who can deny me power and liberty
To stretch mine arms, and mine own Cross
    to be?

THE CROSS.[9]

---

[8]Bullinger, *In Acta Apostolorum*, 310r-v; alluding to Mt 25:1-13; quoting Mt 25:12; Lk 17:5. [9]Donne, *Poems of John Donne*, 331-33.

27:1-12 PAUL SAILS FOR ROME AND ENCOUNTERS A STORM

And when it was decided that we should sail for Italy, they delivered Paul and some other prisoners to a centurion of the Augustan Cohort named Julius. ²And embarking in a ship of Adramyttium, which was about to sail to the ports along the coast of Asia, we put to sea, accompanied by Aristarchus, a Macedonian from Thessalonica. ³The next day we put in at Sidon. And Julius treated Paul kindly and gave him leave to go to his friends and be cared for. ⁴And putting out to sea from there we sailed under the lee of Cyprus, because the winds were against us. ⁵And when we had sailed across the open sea along the coast of Cilicia and Pamphylia, we came to Myra in Lycia. ⁶There the centurion found a ship of Alexandria sailing for Italy and put us on board. ⁷We sailed slowly for a number of days and arrived with difficulty off Cnidus, and as the wind did not allow us to go farther, we sailed under the lee of Crete off Salmone. ⁸Coasting along it with difficulty, we came to a place called Fair Havens, near which was the city of Lasea.

⁹Since much time had passed, and the voyage was now dangerous because even the Fast[a] was already over, Paul advised them, ¹⁰saying, "Sirs, I perceive that the voyage will be with injury and much loss, not only of the cargo and the ship, but also of our lives." ¹¹But the centurion paid more attention to the pilot and to the owner of the ship than to what Paul said. ¹²And because the harbor was not suitable to spend the winter in, the majority decided to put out to sea from there, on the chance that somehow they could reach Phoenix, a harbor of Crete, facing both southwest and northwest, and spend the winter there.

a That is, the Day of Atonement

OVERVIEW: The reformers only briefly comment on this passage, preparing for the more exciting shipwreck passage that follows. They again remind us that though the Christian life is marked by suffering, still the Lord providently provides friends and cosufferers to comfort us. The centurion's rejection of Paul's advice again highlights how unwilling human beings are to listen to the Word of God and his Spirit, preferring instead their own fantasies.

What Does This Journey of Paul Teach Us? JOHANN SPANGENBERG: That a Christian's life is nothing other than a pilgrimage, a daily journey and trek, a daily fighting and struggling—like [Solomon] says. As Saint Paul suffered diverse affliction, persecution, grief and offense, both by water and by land, so each Christian must expect that he will not have a kingdom of heaven or para-

dise here. For it is [written]: "All who desire to live a godly life in Christ Jesus must suffer persecution." BRIEF EXEGESIS OF ACTS 27.[1]

This Passage Is a Comfort. RUDOLF GWALTHER: Luke describes the painful and dangerous navigation of Paul the apostle sent to Rome to appear before Caesar. At first sight such great diligence of the Holy Spirit might seem vain and superfluous, but if you would weigh everything thoroughly, you should perceive many things in the passage that are worth knowing and considering. For this history teaches us what the state of the godly is in this world. In Paul, it shows us examples of patience and constancy and teaches us the infallible truth of God's promises. For although all

---

[1]Spangenberg, *Der Apostel Geschichte*, 237r-v; alluding to Eccl 2:17; quoting 2 Tim 3:12.

things in the world seemed to go wrong with Paul and to hinder him from coming to Rome, the truth of God, which had promised he should be brought before Caesar, bursts through all these impediments. HOMILY 166, ACTS 27:1-8.[2]

PAUL INSTRUCTS BELIEVERS AS JESUS ALREADY HAD. RUDOLF GWALTHER: Now a diligent and long description of their navigation or sailing follows, so let them who are desirous to know everything about the course search in the geographers' tables. We have to consider how it was a painful and dangerous voyage, seeing it is expressly declared that the winds were against them. God could have easily remedied these encumbrances; by many examples he has declared himself to be the Lord and Ruler of the seas. But thus it pleased him to have his chosen vessel tried that the glory both of his truth and power might seem the more evident. In the meantime, it appears what state our life is in: truly a troublesome state and likened to a pilgrimage wherein we see new travails and dangers appear every day. But chiefly this is to be seen in the life of those who are godly: they are continually assaulted with new troubles and anxieties. . . .

[Just as] the Son of God, our Savior Jesus Christ, while he lived on the earth, constantly endured diverse and daily afflictions, so Paul, both by his example here and by eloquent words elsewhere, teaches all those who follow his path to remain steadfast. For two whole years he had suffered to lay in bonds and to feel the grief of imprisonment, daily experiencing his enemies' new plots against him, now he is cast to a most brutal element, namely, the dangerous tempests of the sea and eventually he suffers the misfortunes of shipwreck. HOMILY 166, ACTS 27:1-8.[3]

THE SOLACE OF FRIENDS. JOHANN SPANGENBERG: God gave Paul two good companions, Luke and Aristarchus, who were no little

consolation to him on such a trip. The centurion Julius treated him kindly and allowed him to go to his friends and to be cared for. It is not a small refreshment to a poor, deserted person when in the midst of stress and grief he finds people who befriend him and treat him well. BRIEF EXEGESIS OF ACTS 27.[4]

WHY IS ARISTARCHUS SINGLED OUT FOR PRAISE? JOHN CALVIN: Luke appears to be praising the constancy of Aristarchus in order to censure others. For a great many companions had followed him to Jerusalem, but we see that only two of them are now left. But because it is possible that good reasons kept the others back, or even that Paul refused their services, I affirm nothing either way. In fact, it is not absurd that Luke had a special reason for commending this man in comparison with others, although he was nevertheless one out of many. Surely it is quite likely that he was a wealthy man who was able to bear the expense of being away from his home for three years. For we read earlier that many of the leading families of Thessalonica embraced Christ. However, Luke recounted that Aristarchus and Secundus accompanied Paul to Asia in order to show honor to him. Therefore, let it suffice to grasp what is certain and useful to know, that an example of holy patience is set before us, because Aristarchus is not wearied by any irksomeness or trouble but of his own accord submits to the same lot as Paul, and, after he had shared his imprisonment for two years, is now crossing the sea in order to look after him in Rome also; however, not without the disapproval and reproaches of many, apart from the loss of his home and possessions and the inconveniences of so much expense. COMMENTARY ON ACTS 27:2.[5]

"THE FAST" WAS ADDED TO SHOW THE TIME OF YEAR. JOHN CALVIN: He means not only that the winds were then contrary but that it was also

---

[2]Gwalther, *Homelyes or Sermons upon the Actes*, 869-70* (*In Acta Apostolorum*, 269r).
[3]Gwalther, *Homelyes or Sermons upon the Actes*, 871, 872* (*In Acta Apostolorum*, 269v, 270r).
[4]Spangenberg, *Der Apostel Geschichte*, 238v.
[5]CNTC 7:286* (CO 48:550); alluding to Acts 17:11; 20:4.

an unsuitable time of year, and he then brings that out more clearly by saying that the fast was past; for I think that this clause was added by way of explanation to indicate the end of autumn. And it does not matter that the centurion and the rest of the passengers, and the sailors, knew nothing about that annual time of fasting, which Luke indicates, for he describes the seasons of the year according to the custom of the Jews. Moreover, there is no doubt that it was the autumn fast. However, I do not agree with the opinion of those who think that it was one of the four fasts which the Jews instituted for themselves after their exile to Babylon.[6] For Luke would not simply have cited the third one without adding some distinguishing mark, since it was no more celebrated than the rest, inasmuch as it was appointed on account of the death of Gedaliah and the destruction of the rest of the people. COMMENTARY ON ACTS 27:9.[7]

IN DANGER PEOPLE OFTEN LISTEN TO REASON BUT NOT THE HOLY SPIRIT. JOHANN SPANGENBERG: In this month winter usually begins, and so then it is difficult to navigate at sea. This danger Paul pointed out to the centurion and the sailors. . . . What Paul said by the Holy Spirit meant nothing to these people, but what the sailors said from their own mind, this everyone followed. So it is still! If we preach the truth even from a sound [passage of] Scripture, everyone despises it, but if we suggest something based on our reason, our good thinking or from old custom, then this is a very precious and pleasing thing. BRIEF EXEGESIS OF ACTS 27:9-11.[8]

LISTEN TO THE PHYSICIANS OF THE SOUL. RUDOLF GWALTHER: Paul's wholesome counsel is not accepted, but to the great hindrance and loss of them all. It behooves us to consider the proceeding of the matter, so that we may learn how it comes to pass that a great many despise wholesome counsel and procure their own loss and sometimes destruction. The first cause alleged in this place is that the centurion thought it good to believe the governor and master of the ship rather than Paul. And in doing so, if a man would consider the reason of the flesh, it seems he did so very wisely. Yet he errs because he esteems and regards the counsel not according to the cause but according to human authority. Otherwise, he would easily have perceived that it was not without a cause that Paul said it was jeopardous sailing, considering the winter was drawing near.

And this is a very common error, especially if God gives counsel by the ministers of his Word. For many, listening to them seems to be not only a grievous but also a very heinous offense. There are nowadays everywhere Ahabs and Zedekiahs, which disdain to hear the Micahs and Jeremiahs and think they themselves can give the best counsel, or else take other counselors whom they find more agreeable with their humors and conditions.

Usually it comes to pass that in dangers of war, we flee to barbarous nations and bloody soldiers, to the treaties and fortifications of kings, in sicknesses to physicians only, in need and poverty to unlawful arts, and we give ear to them, whom we suppose to have had good success up to now in similar enterprises. Such persons are wrapped in many evils and encumbrances which they might easily eschew if they would admit the Word of God and the advice and counsels taken from it. HOMILY 167, ACTS 27:9-20.[9]

---

[6]Calvin is referring to Tisha B'Av, the Fast of Tevet, the Fast of Gedaliah and the Fast of Tammuz.
[7]CNTC 7:287-88* (CO 48:551); alluding to Zech 8:19; 7:5; 2 Kings 25:25.
[8]Spangenberg, *Der Apostel Geschichte*, 239v-240r.

[9]Gwalther, *Homelyes or Sermons upon the Actes*, 873-74* (*In Acta Apostolorum*, 270v).

27:13-44 A STORM AT SEA LEADS TO SHIPWRECK

¹³*Now when the south wind blew gently, supposing that they had obtained their purpose, they weighed anchor and sailed along Crete, close to the shore.* ¹⁴*But soon a tempestuous wind, called the northeaster, struck down from the land.* ¹⁵*And when the ship was caught and could not face the wind, we gave way to it and were driven along.* ¹⁶*Running under the lee of a small island called Cauda,ᵃ we managed with difficulty to secure the ship's boat.* ¹⁷*After hoisting it up, they used supports to undergird the ship. Then, fearing that they would run aground on the Syrtis, they lowered the gear,ᵇ and thus they were driven along.* ¹⁸*Since we were violently storm-tossed, they began the next day to jettison the cargo.* ¹⁹*And on the third day they threw the ship's tackle overboard with their own hands.* ²⁰*When neither sun nor stars appeared for many days, and no small tempest lay on us, all hope of our being saved was at last abandoned.*

²¹*Since they had been without food for a long time, Paul stood up among them and said, "Men, you should have listened to me and not have set sail from Crete and incurred this injury and loss.* ²²*Yet now I urge you to take heart, for there will be no loss of life among you, but only of the ship.* ²³*For this very night there stood before me an angel of the God to whom I belong and whom I worship,* ²⁴*and he said, 'Do not be afraid, Paul; you must stand before Caesar. And behold, God has granted you all those who sail with you.'* ²⁵*So take heart, men, for I have faith in God that it will be exactly as I have been told.* ²⁶*But we must run aground on some island."*

²⁷*When the fourteenth night had come, as we were being driven across the Adriatic Sea, about midnight the sailors suspected that they were nearing land.* ²⁸*So they took a sounding and found twenty fathoms.ᶜ A little farther on they took a sounding again and found fifteen fathoms.ᵈ* ²⁹*And fearing that we might run on the rocks, they let down four anchors from the stern and prayed for day to come.* ³⁰*And as the sailors were seeking to escape from the ship, and had lowered the ship's boat into the sea under pretense of laying out anchors from the bow,* ³¹*Paul said to the centurion and the soldiers, "Unless these men stay in the ship, you cannot be saved."* ³²*Then the soldiers cut away the ropes of the ship's boat and let it go.*

³³*As day was about to dawn, Paul urged them all to take some food, saying, "Today is the fourteenth day that you have continued in suspense and without food, having taken nothing.* ³⁴*Therefore I urge you to take some food. For it will give you strength,ᵉ for not a hair is to perish from the head of any of you."* ³⁵*And when he had said these things, he took bread, and giving thanks to God in the presence of all he broke it and began to eat.* ³⁶*Then they all were encouraged and ate some food themselves.* ³⁷*(We were in all 276ᶠ persons in the ship.)* ³⁸*And when they had eaten enough, they lightened the ship, throwing out the wheat into the sea.*

³⁹*Now when it was day, they did not recognize the land, but they noticed a bay with a beach, on which they planned if possible to run the ship ashore.* ⁴⁰*So they cast off the anchors and left them in the sea, at the same time loosening the ropes that tied the rudders. Then hoisting the foresail to the wind they made for the beach.* ⁴¹*But striking a reef,ᵍ they ran the vessel aground. The bow stuck and remained immovable, and the stern was being broken up by the surf.* ⁴²*The soldiers' plan was to kill the prisoners, lest any should swim away and escape.* ⁴³*But the centurion, wishing to save Paul, kept them from carrying out their plan. He ordered those who could swim to jump overboard first and make for the land,* ⁴⁴*and the rest on planks or on pieces of the ship. And so it was that all were brought safely to land.*

---

a Some manuscripts *Clauda*   **b** That is, the sea-anchor (or possibly the mainsail)   **c** About 120 feet; a fathom (Greek *orguia*) was about 6 feet or 2 meters
d About 90 feet (see previous note)   **e** Or *For it is for your deliverance*   **f** Some manuscripts *seventy-six,* or *about seventy-six*   **g** Or *sandbank,* or *crosscurrent;* Greek *place between two seas*

OVERVIEW: The ship that began such a lengthy journey so late into autumn—whose captain ignored God's Word spoken through Paul—meets grave trouble. The reformers revisit their strong emphasis on the true character and purposes of suffering, on God's sovereign providence (over both the faithful and unfaithful), and on the "foolish wisdom" of trinitarian faith. After those on the ship are worn out from their hopeless efforts to save themselves, Paul, almost at the last minute, stands up and offers them physical and spiritual bread, proclaiming God's free promise of grace to each one on the ship. Even amid the ingratitude of the sailors—who plot to kill all the prisoners—the Lord delivers each precious life, provoking the reformers to marvel at God's secret counsel in which he delays punishment of the ungodly, hoping that they might turn and repent. Though it might seem like sea and sky are united against believers (whether in ancient or contemporary times, the reformers insist), in the midst of the storm they may find peace in Christ.

27:13-38 *The Storm at Sea*

PAUL THE STEADFAST. JOHN CALVIN: For only people who are themselves examples of steadfastness and fortitude are qualified to encourage others. Moreover, Paul put off this exhortation until they were all lying almost at death's door. It is easy to gather from the way that unbelievers usually behave that at first they were in a state of violent and uncontrolled uproar. In the midst of their shouting and clamoring, a moderate voice would never have been heard. Now, when, worn out by their wailing and commotion, they sit down like men thunderstruck, and Paul addresses them. Therefore it was necessary for them to flag, as if half-dead, before they would be calm for a little while and listen quietly and in silence to someone giving good advice. COMMENTARY ON ACTS 27:21.[1]

THE CONSTANCY OF PAUL'S FAITH. RUDOLF GWALTHER: First, the time is noted and what dire situation they faced when Paul made his oration. It was not without a cause that he did not speak to them before this time, for while they were troubled about their business, he would have had no audience. But now, they being wearied both in body and mind and being weighed down without hope of any help, he shows them both counsel and comfort at the right time. Whereby we gather that he did not despair and was not overcome with fear in the middle of dangers instead through prayer he fled to God, who comforted him, so that he was able to comfort and strengthen others. By this example we are taught that we must not by and by despair in time of danger but put our whole hope and trust in God, who never forsakes those who are his according to his promises, and as many human beings abundantly declare. Therefore, this is a shameful error of those who, as soon as they see no more hope in other human beings, utterly despair or else turn them into saints, in order to seek counsel and help at their hands. HOMILY 168, ACTS 27:21-26.[2]

THE SUFFICIENCY OF GOD'S PROVIDENCE. THE SECOND HELEVETIC CONFESSION: We do not condemn the means whereby the providence of God works as though they were unprofitable; but we teach that we must apply ourselves to them, so far as they are commended to us in the Word of God. Wherefore we dislike the rash speeches of such as say that if all things are governed by the providence of God, then all our studies and endeavors are unprofitable. It shall be sufficient if we leave or permit all things to be governed by the providence of God; we shall not need hereafter to behave or act with carefulness in any matter. For though Paul did confess that he did sail by the providence of God, who had said to him, "You must testify also in Rome" (Acts 23:11); who, moreover, promised and said, "There will be no loss of life among you, not even a hair is to perish from the head of any of you" (Acts 27:22, 34);

---

[1]CNTC 7:290* (CO 48:553-54).

[2]Gwalther, *Homelyes or Sermons upon the Actes*, 877-78* (*In Acta Apostolorum*, 271v).

the mariners devising how they might find a way to escape, the same Paul says to the centurion and to the soldiers, "Unless these men stay on the ship, you cannot be saved" (Acts 27:31). For God, who has appointed everything its end, has also ordained the beginning and the means by which we must attain unto the end. The heathens ascribe things to blind fortune and uncertain chance. But Saint James would not have us say, "Today or tomorrow we will go into such and such a town, and there trade and make profit," but he adds, "Instead you ought to say, 'If the Lord wills, we will live, and do this or that'" (Jas 4:13, 15). CHAPTER 6, THE PROVIDENCE OF GOD.[3]

MINISTERS MUST OFFER TRUE CONSOLATION. HEINRICH BULLINGER: In the midst of these dangers, the spirits of all have fallen, except Paul alone—the minister of the most high God—who comforts the saddened. From this it is easily proven what it is to serve God: the saints exert such great confidence through God, or, if you prefer, God expresses his kindness and care through his faithful. Paul's speech by which the people are consoled is more than cheerful and sensible. For it was by his sensibility that these men were earlier warned. Nevertheless he rebukes them with the fewest words, then immediately he stoops to a position of consolation. Sensible men are the least likely to turn a blind eye to error whenever an opportunity is presented to them to censure it. Others are insensible who in the midst of calamities recall distant negligent acts and long-gone wrongs. So, Paul rebukes, but not too harshly, their foolishness which had dragged them into this danger. . . .

Now immediately with the briefest words, but full of consolation, he explains that all will be delivered from this tribulation. He says, "Do not despair of your health and well-being! For this reason, none of you will perish, only the ship will be lost." Again he confirms his statement by the revelation [of the angel], by which he sought there to be more hope and less sadness. . . . God is truthful and

powerful who is able to fulfill what he promises. Also the power of sound and steady faith is great. Now so that it would be even more sure, he also describes the manner in which they will be saved, saying, "We will run aground on some island; we will be saved from the shattered ship by divine power." This is the consolation of Paul. COMMENTARY ON ACTS 27:21-26.[4]

ENCOURAGEMENT IN THE SPIRIT COMES IN THE MIDST OF DESPAIR. JOHANNES BRENZ: Yet, in such a great calamity, Paul warns them with cheerful enthusiasm that they should definitely now take food and restore their spirits, lest evading the storm they die from starvation, since none of them would lose even a hair on their head, but all would escape safely. You have here in Paul an example of the nature of faith and what the works of it are. For no other rationale was evident to Paul why he should be able to promise safety other than the Word and promise of God, namely, that he must stand before Caesar, and that God would give to him all those sailing with him. For, if he looked at the sea, the storm was very great. If he looked at the ship, it was now stripped of all its protections and was not able to survive much longer in the face of such great blasts of wind. If he looked to the shore, it was night; and although the sailors thought that they saw land, this was still uncertain. If he looked to his companions and fellow shipmates, they had all despaired for their lives. The Word of God was promising safety. Therefore, Paul averted his eyes from all those obstacles and directed them toward the Word of the Lord alone, confident that the one who made the promise was also powerful enough to fulfill it (for he had already indicated with words what his will was). HOMILY 118 ON ACTS 27.[5]

GOD SHOWS FAVOR TO HIS SAINTS BY SPARING THE WICKED. JOHN CALVIN: Here the question is asked, "To what extent does the integrity of

---

[3]*Creeds*, 3:840-81*.

[4]Bullinger, *In Acta Apostolorum*, 315r-316r.
[5]Brenz, *In Acta Apostolica Homiliae*, 223v.

the saints benefit the ungodly?" In the first place we must remove the superstition of the papists, who, when they hear that the bad are blessed for the sake of the godly, imagine that the latter are mediators, who obtain salvation for the world by their own merits. But they are foolish and preposterous twice over, because they refer these descriptions that belong to the living, to the dead, and hope that God will be favorable to themselves simply by his consideration of the dead, and therefore they adopt them as their patrons. I pass over the fact that they obscure the gracious goodness of God by extolling the merits of the saints.

Now to answer the question raised, it must be considered briefly in this way. Since the good and bad are mixed up together, adverse and favorable things befall them both, without distinction, and yet it sometimes happens that, when the Lord spares his own, he preserves the ungodly for a time along with them. In the second place there are many reasons why he blesses the wicked and reprobate for the sake of the faithful. "He blessed Potiphar's house for Joseph's sake," in order to move his heart to show kindness to that holy man. He showed favor toward Paul by saving the many people who were with him, in order that he might bear witness to his godliness and that, as a result, the majesty of the gospel might shine forth. Finally, we must grasp that all the blessings that God lavishes on the ungodly finally make for their destruction, just as, on the other hand, the punishments which the faithful suffer in common with the reprobate are to their advantage. In the meantime it is a remarkable pledge of God's love toward us that he makes some drops of his kindness flow from us to others. COMMENTARY ON ACTS 27:24.[6]

HOW DID THEY SURVIVE SO LONG WITHOUT FOOD? JOHANNES BRENZ: In this exhortation, Paul, though on the surface it seems otherwise, clues us in to the fact that there is such a huge amount of peril in this voyage that almost nothing more horrible can be said. For

he says that they have fasted and done without food continuously up until the fourteenth day, clearly not wanting food because they were expecting death at any moment. Now those who are experts in the way that the natural world works write that going without food is fatal for a person after the seventh day, and that a large number of people have just barely held out beyond the eleventh day. But in this passage you hear that those who are on the sea voyage have sustained the fast beyond the thirteenth day and still survive. Therefore, whether you understand it to mean that, in the stated time frame, just as would be normal in the face of danger, they ate nothing together, but each one by himself consumed a little food, as much as was permitted given the depressing situation and struggle for survival, or you understand that they were seized by such a great fear of death that, because they were expecting death, they neglected to take up food altogether (for affections often overcome affections), certainly the whole affair suggests that because of the opposing storm, their spirits were sinking very low. People who are afflicted with extreme punishments and who see death now placed before their eyes still usually have appetite for food and even water. But, clearly, for so many days they took no thought for food, or at least very little. Therefore, it must be that their spirits have been shaken more strongly than by the horror of death, to the point that this affection has completely surpassed other natural affections. HOMILY 118 ON ACTS 27.[7]

THE MEANING OF FOURTEEN DAYS WITHOUT FOOD. JOHN CALVIN: But his statement that they fasted continuously for fourteen days could appear absurd. Some individual will be found who may endure fasting longer, but one can hardly believe it of such a great crowd. The reply is easy, that unaccustomed abstinence from food is improperly called fasting, because they had

---

[6]CNTC 7:292* (CO 48:555); quoting Gen 39:5.

[7]Brenz, *In Acta Apostolica Homiliae*, 233v.

never been revived by a proper meal for the whole of that time, as those who are in trouble and sorrow are almost nauseated by food. But because despair was the cause of their distaste, he again affirms that they will survive, provided that they recover their spirits. For a faithful minister of the Word ought not only to make promises publicly known, but at the same time to add advice, so that people may follow the call of God and not remain idle and listless. Moreover, what the words mean is this, "God has determined to save you. This assurance ought to encourage you and make you eager not to neglect yourselves." COMMENTARY ON ACTS 27:33.[8]

IN THE FACE OF DEATH, TRUST GOD'S WORD.

JOHANN SPANGENBERG: From this admonition we can discern that they were not in minor danger. Fourteen days of fasting, neither eating nor drinking, yes, every hour and every minute they saw death before their eyes, undulating and oscillating on the wild sea, between water and cloud, in rain, snow and storm, seeing nothing, neither heaven nor earth, neither sun nor stars, this is surely such a cruel, terrifying thing that it can be no more horrible. For all the experts of nature write that a person cannot live longer than nine days without food and drink. Some have lived until the eleventh day, but here they have fasted for fourteen days and are still alive! They were totally and completely in shock and fright due to the fear of present death, so that they did not even think about food. But Paul consoles them in this fear.

From where does Paul get consolation in the midst of such horrible images of death? From God's Word and promises. From where else should he have gathered such consolation? If he looked into the sea, there was nothing other than pure violence—wind, swells and waves. If he looked at the ship, it was overflowing with every danger, under, above and on every side—it could not last long. If he looked to land, it was night and dark. If he looked to his companions, they were all despon-

dent, pale and vapid like dead people. In sum, Paul could look only to God's Word, which gave him such consolation that he could also console others. BRIEF EXEGESIS OF ACTS 27:33-34.[9]

NOTHING DRIVES US TO THE GOSPEL BETTER THAN TRIALS.

HANS HAS VON HALLSTATT: For persecution and oppression make genuine Christians and strengthen them, so that they become truly experienced and well practised in true faith and strong reliance on God. Indeed, they become truly educated and experienced, more bold and unwavering, since one learns and studies more of the gospel through a little tribulation than in any other way in one's entire life. Thus the elect must undergo all misfortunes as best they can. For no persecution or tribulation will come on them that is not entirely profitable for their salvation. They will become even stronger and more faithful in their faith in God and boldly trust him. For one sees, notices and acknowledges how all of this together rests solely on God's power, might and strength. Indeed, not a hair will fall or perish from the heads of the truly faithful against his will. KUNSTBUCH: CONCERNING THE COMFORT OF CHRISTIANS.[10]

BREAKING BREAD BRINGS REST.

JOHANNES BRENZ: By his example, he exhorts them not so much to take up food as to take up courage. For when he had said these things, after receiving bread, he gave thanks in everyone's presence, and, breaking it, began to eat. What made Paul act with such cheerful enthusiasm, and what made him so sure of his safety? It is certainly nothing but the Word of the Lord and the faith that comes through it. Let us learn by this example, that in the face of obstacles we do not fix our eyes on superficialities and adverse appearances but on the Word of the Lord, wherein safety is promised to us. Through this our soul is rendered so tranquil and full of good cheer

[8]CNTC 7:294-95* (CO 48:557).

[9]Spangenberg, Der Apostel Geschichte, 243r-244r.
[10]CRR 12:441-42* (QGT 17:465); alluding to 2 Tim 3:12; Rom 8:28.

that we cannot conduct ourselves otherwise than as if we were already holding salvation and liberation in our hand. Homily 118 on Acts 27.[11]

The Gratitude of the Godly. John Calvin:

In order to encourage them better by setting an example, he takes bread and eats. Luke says that he gave thanks, not only because that was his daily custom but because it was of great value as evidence of his confidence. Indeed, there is no doubt that in taking food Paul was being careful to do what he was enjoining on the others. But now not only does he bear witness to his own gratitude, and not only does he ask God to bless the food which he is about to eat, but he boldly calls on God, the source of life, that those wretched people who were in the grip of despair might be given some element of good hope. At least he accomplished this, namely, that these people, who through fear had forgotten to look after themselves, recovered their spirits and took food. Commentary on Acts 27:35.[12]

Prayer, the Perfect Seasoning for Every Meal. Johannes Brenz: Dishes of food or vegetables are not sufficiently oiled or seasoned if they are prepared with external butter or salt, but they must also be prepared by the Lord's Prayer. This is the heavenly condiment, whereby food that is otherwise of very poor quality is yet rendered very delicious for a pious person. We should add here that, even if now we have placated our belly with food, nevertheless a little later again it insists on more, as a wicked creditor, and hunger pangs come frequently during the day, so that our present satisfaction always gives way to the need for food shortly afterwards. But thanksgiving not only gives thanks for present food but honestly and reverently asks for food in the future. Therefore, the act of thanksgiving is necessary before God, not only because he gave to us the present food but also that in the future he might give it to us generously. Homily 118 on Acts 27.[13]

Never Despise the Lowly. Johannes Brenz:

This passage also teaches modesty. When Paul first embarked on this ship, it appeared he had no help to offer to those who were sailing; instead, it seemed on the surface that it was on his account that they are exposed to danger on the high seas, and because he is bound, that rather he is the one who needs consolation amid the trouble rather than that he himself should console others. But now we see him being very useful, so that not only were the rest saved on his account, though they did not realize it because of their disbelief, but also their minds were filled with great hope and consolation, which was an undeniable fact of their experience. Therefore, no one, however useless they might seem, should be despised. Whether someone is weak in body, or a prisoner, or poor or unimportant, still the Lord our God administers his affairs so that the person who seems completely unfit in the eyes of the world nevertheless becomes the most apt instrument for helping people. Homily 118 on Acts 27.[14]

All People on the Ship Are Saved. Rudolf

Gwalther: The number of those who were with Paul in the same ship was 276 souls. It is declared pleasing to the Holy Spirit to have this number plainly expressed, partly because the truth of God might appear the more certainly to us and partly that the miracle of the deliverance might seem the more evident. Because the number of people is certain, not one of them is able to claim that they were ignorant of these things or that it was a mystery. And where in the danger of shipwreck even a few used to hinder and let one another, while each man provides for his own safety with the peril of another, God evidently put forward his hand in that he brought so many together safe and sound to the shore. Here we see that it is easy for God to save many or a few. He has numbered all things, and his providence extends even over the hairs [on your head] and the little sparrows. His power is infinite and immeasurable. He is not overwhelmed by the multitude of those who need his

---

[11]Brenz, *In Acta Apostolica Homiliae*, 222v-224r.
[12]CNTC 7:295* (CO 48:557).
[13]Brenz, *In Acta Apostolica Homiliae*, 234r.
[14]Brenz, *In Acta Apostolica Homiliae*, 234r.

help nor by the intensity of their affliction. HOMILY 170, ACTS 27:37-44.[15]

27:39-44 The Shipwreck

THE INGRATITUDE OF THE WORLD. JOHANNES BRENZ: What could be called crueler than this plan or more impious? Everyone who is sailing on this ship is saved because of Paul, and previously they were greatly encouraged in their spirits by Paul, and in exchange for this favor the soldiers were plotting to repay him with murder—what could be more wicked than this? But this is the gratitude of this age, that the more favors you confer on people of this age, the more appalling are the evil deeds with which they repay you.

So should we not do good to our neighbors? Dispel such thoughts! For the ingratitude of this age is not set before our eyes so that we might do evil deeds to the ungrateful but so that, learning and coming to know this established custom of this age, we might compose ourselves to tolerate it patiently and not in the least desert the calling of God because of it. For, although the world is ungrateful, no, unworthy of the one who does it a favor, nevertheless, the Lord our God is worthy of being obeyed by us and is so grateful that he will forget even a cup of cold water offered to someone who was thirsty. Paul here again is in danger for his life, because the Word of the Lord is not able to be false. The Lord furnishes the means for keeping Paul safe. HOMILY 118 ON ACTS 27.[16]

GOD'S GRACE IN THE FACE OF INGRATITUDE. JOHN CALVIN: The soldiers' ingratitude was far too cruel. Although they owed their lives to Paul on two or three occasions, they plan to kill him; the proper thing would have been to spare the others for his sake. Safety had been brought to them by him, just as if by an angel of God; they had heard salutary advice from his lips; that very day he had revived them when they were half dead with fear. Now they do not hesitate cruelly to destroy the man by whom they had been delivered so often and in so many ways. Accordingly, if it happens that we are repaid unjustly for our good deeds, that is no reason why human ingratitude ought to disturb us, for it is an exceedingly common disease. But they are not only ungrateful to Paul, the minister of their life, but at the same time they display shameful unbelief and forgetfulness of God's grace....

Therefore, they have now forgotten the grace which they had been forced to taste in the utmost despair, and they have no longer any taste for it after a haven appears near. But it is fitting that we ponder the wonderful purpose of God, both in saving Paul and in fulfilling his promise, when he brings to land the very men to whom no thanks were due, for the fact that the promise was not nullified. His goodness is very often in conflict with the malice of people like that. Yet he is merciful to the ungodly in such a way that, while he puts off their punishment to a suitable time, he does not absolve them of guilt; yes, moreover, he makes up for such a great delay, that is due to his tolerance, with the severity of the punishment. COMMENTARY ON ACTS 27:42.[17]

FEAR ROBS THE SOLDIERS OF HOPE IN GOD'S PROMISES. RUDOLF GWALTHER: These men at first are delighted with the promises of God and frame themselves accordingly, that is, when the success of things agree with the promises and when they think everything will go forward and well. But as soon as dangers begin to appear and dash their hope of success, they plainly renounce their faith and turn to the counsels of the flesh and show themselves most dishonest persons both toward God and others. HOMILY 169, ACTS 27:27-36.[18]

BELIEVE IN CHRIST, AND HE IS NEAR. JOHANNES BRENZ: You can understand now that

---

[15]Gwalther, *Homelyes or Sermons upon the Actes*, 884-85* (*In Acta Apostolorum*, 273v-274r); alluding to Lk 12:4-7.
[16]Brenz, *Acta Apostolica Homiliae*, 234v; alluding to Mt 10:42.

[17]CNTC 7:296-97* (CO 48:558-59).
[18]Gwalther, *Homelyes or Sermons upon the Actes*, 881* (*In Acta Apostolorum*, 272v).

the truth of the word and promise of God is so great that no storm of the sea, no plotting of the wicked, no adverse misfortune is so powerful as to thwart it. Therefore, from the story of this shipwreck, let us strengthen our faith in the face of all opposing storms. For this age in which we live is the sea, and the states and conditions of our life are the ship. And in this ship now we are buffeted by the dangerous blasts of wind. What then? Does the Lord allow us to be submerged? Not at all; he has promised to all who invoke him in truth that he is the port of safety. Furthermore, the Lord our God has such great power and clemency that he is able and he is willing besides to do abundantly all things that we ask or think. . . .

Truly if you believe in him, he is very much present. For, he says, "If anyone loves me, he will keep my Word, and my Father will love him, and we will come to him, and we will make our home with him." Therefore, since you have such a powerful and gracious helper present, take heed that you bear your afflictions with great courage, persuaded in your heart that the one who promised liberation is also powerful to deliver it through our Lord Jesus Christ, who together with the Father and the Holy Spirit must be praised as God forever to the ages, Amen. Homily 118 on Acts 27.[19]

AN ALLEGORY OF THE STORM AND THE SHIPWRECK. JOHANN SPANGENBERG: The ship in which Paul sits is Christendom; the sea is the turbulent world. Swells and storm winds are diverse afflictions. Paul is the preacher of the gospel. Those in the ship are the audience. The sailors are prelates and rulers. Now if in important matters we will not believe the preacher of the divine Word and instead follow whatever idea comes out of each person's head, then it goes as it must and God imposes on us so much misfortune, fear and trouble that we are driven to him, screaming to high

heaven for help and assistance. God's Word should be our light and lamp in this dark world. But if we want to use the light of our reason and good thinking, then we will certainly go backwards like crabs do—as we see in all human efforts when we do not ask God for his counsel. So then, we should learn from this passage that in our misfortunes, fears and troubles—whether we are in water or on land—we should always place our trust and confidence in God. For "he alone is the hope of the entire world and the distant seas."

Here no human or creaturely help was present. The water and air were one. The light of the sky was extinguished. The earth and land was far away from them. Finally the boat began to fall apart, but still Paul remained steadfast in faith. We should act in the same way. If we think that the world and all creatures have abandoned us, we see nothing before our eyes other than grisly death, and we cannot turn to the right or to the left, even then we should not despair. For God is such a marvelous God that before we look around he has found some means and rescues us from every fear and trouble, as he did for the children of Israel at the Red Sea. Also for Samson when the Philistines assaulted him, hoping to kill him, but he had neither sword nor shield, but he called on God and turned around, found a donkey's jawbone and killed with it a thousand men. Also, Shamgar, who killed six hundred men with an oxgoad. In summary, when human help is at an end, then divine help begins— wherever there is steadfast faith. For to a believer all things are possible. God is the true Holy Helper,[20] who can and will help us in both body and soul, temporally and eternally. BRIEF EXEGESIS OF ACTS 27:13-44.[21]

---

[19]Brenz, *In Acta Apostolica Homiliae*, 234v-235r; quoting Jn 14:23.

[20]Spangenberg here is referring to the Fourteen Holy Helpers, fourteen saints—Agatha, Barbara, Blaise, Catherine of Alexandria, Christopher, Cyriacus, Denis, Erasmus, Eustace, George, Giles, Margaret of Antioch, Pantaleon, and Vitus—vaunted for their putative healing powers.

[21]Spangenberg, *Der Apostel Geschichte*, 245v-247r; quoting Ps 65:5; alluding to Ex 14; Judg 15:14-17; 3:31.

28:1-16 PAUL'S STAY ON MALTA
AND HIS ARRIVAL AT ROME

After we were brought safely through, we then learned that the island was called Malta. ²The native people[a] showed us unusual kindness, for they kindled a fire and welcomed us all, because it had begun to rain and was cold. ³When Paul had gathered a bundle of sticks and put them on the fire, a viper came out because of the heat and fastened on his hand. ⁴When the native people saw the creature hanging from his hand, they said to one another, "No doubt this man is a murderer. Though he has escaped from the sea, Justice[b] has not allowed him to live." ⁵He, however, shook off the creature into the fire and suffered no harm. ⁶They were waiting for him to swell up or suddenly fall down dead. But when they had waited a long time and saw no misfortune come to him, they changed their minds and said that he was a god.

⁷Now in the neighborhood of that place were lands belonging to the chief man of the island, named Publius, who received us and entertained us hospitably for three days. ⁸It happened that the father of Publius lay sick with fever and dysentery. And Paul visited him and prayed, and putting his hands on him healed him. ⁹And when this had taken place, the rest of the people on the island who had diseases also came and were cured. ¹⁰They also honored us greatly,[c] and when we were about to sail, they put on board whatever we needed.

¹¹After three months we set sail in a ship that had wintered in the island, a ship of Alexandria, with the twin gods[d] as a figurehead. ¹²Putting in at Syracuse, we stayed there for three days. ¹³And from there we made a circuit and arrived at Rhegium. And after one day a south wind sprang up, and on the second day we came to Puteoli. ¹⁴There we found brothers[e] and were invited to stay with them for seven days. And so we came to Rome. ¹⁵And the brothers there, when they heard about us, came as far as the Forum of Appius and Three Taverns to meet us. On seeing them, Paul thanked God and took courage. ¹⁶And when we came into Rome, Paul was allowed to stay by himself, with the soldier who guarded him.

a Greek barbaroi (that is, non–Greek speakers); also verse 4   b Or justice   c Greek honored us with many honors   d That is, the Greek gods Castor and Pollux   e Or brothers and sisters; also verses 15, 21

OVERVIEW: Somehow, despite schemes, slanders and squalls, Paul has made it to Rome just as Jesus promised him; the final leg of the Acts 1:8 program ("to the end of the earth") has begun. And yet Reformation exegetes remind us that Paul's suffering was not finished. Though just before he reaches Rome it seems that his life might be taken by a poisonous snake, God transforms the sudden tragedy into redemption for the Maltese people. The reformers are greatly impressed by the swift acceptance of the gospel by the islanders. They exhort their audiences likewise to suspend judgment regarding those who seem to be afflicted by God's displeasure.

GOD TEMPERS ADVERSITY WITH PROSPERITY. RUDOLF GWALTHER: It has been declared how God cared for Paul and his companions as he promised him in the midst of the dangers and tempests of the sea. It follows how he delivered them afterward from drowning and how he ministered an occasion for Paul to preach the gospel, first to those of Malta and then to the Romans. We are taught that God's works are perfect. Although we are tried every day with new dangers, still we must not cast away all hope but look every day for new benefits from God's hands, which tempers adversity with prosperity to raise up discouraged minds with effective consolation. HOMILY 171, ACTS 28:1-6.[1]

28:1-10 Paul on the Island of Malta

THE LORD TRAINED PAUL FOR EVERY SITUA-TION. JOHN DONNE: Almighty God had bred up Saint Paul in this way: so he had catechized him all the way with vicissitudes and revolutions from extreme to extreme. He had taught him how to want and how to abound; how to bear honor and dishonor. He permitted an angel of Satan to buffet him (so he gave him some sense of hell), he gave him a rapture, an ecstasy, and in that a drawing near or an approximation to himself, and so some possession of heaven in this life. So God proceeded with him here in Malta, too. He passed him in their mouths from extreme to extreme. A viper seizes him and they condemn for a *murderer*; he shakes off the viper and they change their minds and say he is a *god*. SERMON ON THE SUNDAY OF SAINT PAUL'S CONVERSION (1628).[2]

THE ISLANDERS' GENEROSITY IS A GIFT FROM GOD. JOHN CALVIN: Luke then narrates that the barbarians received them kindly, that a fire was kindled so that they might dry their clothes and warm their limbs, powerless with the cold, and, finally, that they were given shelter from the rain. Therefore, Paul shows his gratitude by praising these acts of kindness; such great generosity toward strangers deserves to be praised, when examples of it are rare in the world. Although ordinary human nature forces some feeling of pity from the barbarians, there is no doubt that God moved the minds of the Maltese to sympathy, so that his promise might be firmly fulfilled, for it could have appeared to have been shattered if the shipwreck had proved fatal to anyone. COMMENTARY ON ACTS 28:2.[3]

MALTA'S LOVINGKINDNESS FULFILLS CHRIST'S TEACHING. RUDOLF GWALTHER: The island was Malta, ... the place where the Knights of Saint John's order have their residence, lying between Sicilia and Africa. Luke commends the singular humanity of the people of Malta, who received them and showed them all kinds of pleasantries as the time and place required. Here a notable example of love and hospitality is set for us to follow. For without a doubt, those shipwrecked were unknown to the people of Malta, and there was no hope of recompense to be looked for at their hands, whom they saw spoiled of all their goods. Yet because they see that they have need of their help, they show them this courtesy. This is what Christ teaches us in the parable of the Samaritan. It behooves us all to do without any respect of persons or hope of reward to come to be loving and charitable to those whom God sends to us to be assisted and helped. We must primarily remember to be hospitable to strangers because they are in need of many things and because, as the apostle testifies, "in so doing many have received angels into their homes in the likeness of human beings." But this is a far more excellent and profitable thing that they who offer to take strangers into their houses make much of Christ and receive him in them. HOMILY 171 AND HOMILY 172, ACTS 28:1-6.[4]

NO WORK IS TOO LOWLY FOR GODLY MINISTERS. HEINRICH BULLINGER: We see Paul work with his own hands to gather twigs—which the Latins called "the rubbish of the vine" ... and which among us are commonly called "shavings" and "sprigs." He vehemently condemns leisure and laziness, especially considering such a man is unashamed to collect twigs. As he did not rashly perform miracles anywhere, so here he had hardly

---

[1]Gwalther, *Homelyes or Sermons upon the Actes*, 887* (*In Acta Apostolorum*, 274v).
[2]Donne, *Works*, 2:334*; alluding to Phil 4:11-13; 2 Cor 12:1-10.
[3]CNTC 7:298* (CO 48:559).

[4]Gwalther, *Homelyes or Sermons upon the Actes*, 887-88* (*In Acta Apostolorum*, 274v-275r); quoting Heb 13:2. The Knights of Saint John or the Knights Hospitaller is a lay order established during the Crusades. They were tasked to take care of the poor and sick in Jerusalem; eventually they established their headquarters in Malta over which they were sovereign until the nineteenth century.

begun to do anything, but necessity itself and the providence of God compel a miracle to be performed. Indeed he credits himself with nothing, but praises God who works through him along with the spectators. Therefore all the glory is God's. COMMENTARY ON ACTS 28:3.[5]

GOD'S ANGER: ONE DOCTRINE THAT NEEDS NO REVEALING.

JOHN DONNE: For this doctrine a man does not need to be preached to, a man does not need to be catechized, a man does not need to read the fathers or the councils or the schoolmen or the ecclesiastical story or summists or casuists or canonists—no, nor the Bible itself for this doctrine. For this doctrine—that when God strikes he is angry, and when he is angry he strikes—the natural man has as full a library in his bosom as the Christians. SERMON ON THE SUNDAY OF SAINT PAUL'S CONVERSION (1628).[6]

THE JUDGMENT OF THE FLESH VERSUS THAT OF THE SPIRIT.

JUSTUS JONAS: Immediately the flesh judges as wicked anyone who suffer-s from affliction or evil; conversely, the Spirit judges correctly. For that reason Christ condemns the judgment of flesh and reason, saying, "Do you think that these Galileans alone are sinners?" ANNOTATIONS ON ACTS 28:4.[7]

EVEN BARBARIANS KNOW MURDER IS DESPICABLE.

HEINRICH BULLINGER: The viper had been numb with cold, but now roused with the heat of the fire and stirred into a frenzy it tenaciously clamps down on Paul's hand. Pliny says that "the teeth of the viper are sheathed in its gums. The viper by penetrating [the skin] with its poison filled teeth and then withdrawing them pours venom into the bite." Now the poison of this beast is very deadly. Thus, Luke says that the barbarians predict what will happen next: he would swell up and suddenly fall over dead once the poison penetrated his heart. It should be observed that at first

all the barbarians cried out altogether, "This person is a murderer who was saved out of the sea, but justice [dikē]"—that is, vengeance—"will not allow him to live." By this we understand that murder, even among the fiercest people and the most savage tribes, is considered among the most depraved and extreme outrages. Today they are punished insufficiently who shed the blood of so many Christians by mercenaries. But the Word of the Lord stands, "Your brother's blood cries out to me from the earth!" Therefore, God will find the criminal. For, as the proverb goes, "even a mouse will bite the wicked man." COMMENTARY ON ACTS 28:4.[8]

GOD WILL JUDGE, BUT OFTEN NOT HOW WE EXPECT.

JOHN CALVIN: Everywhere, and in every generation, it was the accepted opinion that those who suffered rather severely were involved in some dreadful crime. There was, in fact, some justification for that opinion, yes, and one might say that it sprang from a proper sense of piety. For in order to make the world inexcusable, God wished it to be impressed on the minds of all that troubles and adversities but extraordinary disasters in particular are examples of his wrath and just vengeance on sins. Therefore, whenever some memorable calamity occurs, at the same time it comes into people's minds that God is deeply offended, when he exercises judgment so severely and harshly. And in fact impiety never prevailed to such an extent that all did not retain this principle, that in order to show that he is the judge of the world, God inflicts conspicuous punishments on the wicked.

But at this point an error has also nearly crept in, that people condemn as wrongdoers whoever is being mistreated severely—without exception. But even if God always punishes sins with adversities, in this present life he does not take vengeance strictly according to what each one deserves; and sometimes the afflictions of the godly are not so much punishments as tests of their faith and exercises in endurance. Therefore, those who make

---

[5]Bullinger, *In Acta Apostolorum*, 321r-v; quoting Gen 4:10.
[6]Donne, *Works*, 2:336*.
[7]Jonas, *Annotationes in Acta*, K7r; quoting Lk 13:2.

[8]Bullinger, In *Acta Apostolorum*, 321r-v; quoting Pliny, *Natural History*, 11.62; Gen 4:10; Erasmus, *Adages*, 1.8.96 (CWE 32:176; LB 2:332).

a general rule for themselves to judge every single individual according to prosperous or adverse circumstances are mistaken. That was the point of the debate between Job and his friends, when they thought that a man whom God afflicted was reprobate and hateful to God. He, however, took the opposite view, that the godly are sometimes humbled by affliction.

Therefore, in order not to talk nonsense in this connection, we must beware of two things. The first is that we do not make a blind and hasty judgment about unknown people based on their lot alone. For seeing that God afflicts the good and bad indiscriminately, yes, and even spares the reprobate and scourges his own with greater severity, in order to make a proper judgment, we must begin from something other than punishments, that is, we must inquire about life and deeds. If any adulterer, or blasphemer, or perjurer or robber, if anyone given over to lust, if a defrauder, if any bloodthirsty person is punished, God is pointing out his judgment as if with his finger. If no offense is apparent to us, the best thing is for us to suspend judgment about punishment. The other caution is to wait for the final outcome. For God's purpose is not plain to us as soon as he begins to strike; on the contrary, a different outcome finally makes it plain that those who seem to be sharing in the same punishment in the eyes of people are quite different in the sight of God. COMMENTARY ON ACTS 28:4.[9]

IGNORANT OF JESUS AND THE POWER OF HIS NAME. DESIDERIUS ERASMUS: The Maltese had not yet heard of Jesus, who grants to the confessors of his name that no poison will have potency and power to harm them, no matter how rapidly it works. PARAPHRASE OF ACTS 28:6.[10]

THE WORLD FLIES FROM ONE CRIME TO ANOTHER. JOHN CALVIN: Such an astonishing and unexpected change ought to have moved the Maltese in earnest to give glory to the mercy of God, as they

had previously given it to vengeance. But as human reason always wrongly rushes to extremes, they suddenly make Paul a god instead of a vicious murderer; but if it was necessary to choose one or the other, it was better to be regarded a murderer than a god. Paul would certainly have preferred not only to be condemned for one crime but also to be loaded with infamy of every kind and be plunged into the depths of the underworld rather than appropriate the glory of God to himself; and all those who had heard him preaching in the midst of the storms were quite well aware of that. However, it is possible that later on, after they received instruction, the Maltese realized that God was responsible for the miracle....

Let us learn from this how prone the world is to superstition. Yes, and what is more, we are almost born with this perverse attitude of gladly embellishing created things with the spoils stripped from God. Accordingly, it is no wonder if new errors have repeatedly appeared in all generations, when each one of us, from his mother's womb, is wonderfully adept at devising idols. But so that the chance of an excuse may not be sought from this incident, it bears witness that the source of superstition lies in the fact that humans are ungrateful to God and transfer his glory to another person or thing. COMMENTARY ON ACTS 28:6.[11]

PUBLIUS, HIS HOSPITALITY AND HIS REWARD. JOHN CALVIN: Because Publius is a Roman name, I rather suspect that the man who is mentioned here was a Roman citizen rather than an islander. For Greeks and other foreigners, apart from insignificant men, were not in the habit of borrowing names from the Latins. And it is possible that one of the leading men of Rome was visiting his estates at that time and is called the chief of the island not because he stayed there but because no one would equal him in wealth and abundance of possessions.

But it is hardly possible that the whole crowd of Greeks was given hospitality for three days. I rather suspect that when he received the centurion, he also

---

[9]CNTC 7:299-300* (CO 48:550).
[10]CWE 50:148 (LB 7:768); alluding to Mk 16:18; Lk 10:19.

[11]CNTC 7:301* (CO 48:561-62); alluding to Ps 51:5.

showed honor to Paul and his companions, because the miracle had prompted him to believe that Paul was a man pleasing to God. However, be that as it may, his hospitality did not go unrewarded. For a little later the Lord had restored his father to health from a grave and dangerous illness by the hand of Paul. And in this way he wished to make it plain how much the kindness which is shown to the wretched and needy is pleasing to him. Although those who are given some help are often ungrateful and forgetful of kindness, or they lack the means to make recompense, still God himself abundantly repays whatever has been expended on human beings at his command; but sometimes he has appointed some of his servants to the kind and hospitable, to bring a blessing with them. It was already a great honor that Publius had received Christ as a guest in the person of Paul. However, the crowning feature was that Paul came endowed with the gift of healing, so that he was able not only to repay him in his turn but also to give far more than he had received. COMMENTARY ON ACTS 28:7.[12]

PUBLIUS, AN EXAMPLE OF HOSPITALITY FOR THE WEALTHY. RUDOLF GWALTHER: [Publius,] the chief man or governor of the island, [is] a singular example of hospitality. At his farms which were nearby, he courteously entertained them for three days. His humanity is the more notable, for being a ruler and a rich man, he did not disdain strangers in such manifold afflictions, as rich people for the most part are accustomed to do, who think that other people's mishaps appertain nothing to them. Then next he receives them all together, which could not be without some trouble and very great cost. For we heard how there were in that ship 276 people, and all escaped safe to land. Let the rich and those with authority learn what is their duty and not think that God has given to them alone such great gifts. But let them remember that they are appointed as stewards. Let them be liberal to those who have need, so that their plenty may relieve the others' scarcity. This is doubtlessly

a great offense to them who, forgetting their duty, have compassion on nobody but pass over the cry of the poor with deaf ears, who at length, according to the sayings of Solomon, shall find the ears of God shut to their prayers. On the Last Day they shall have Christ to accuse them. HOMILY 172, ACTS 28:7-14.[13]

PAUL REWARDS THE GENEROSITY OF HIS HOSTS. RUDOLF GWALTHER: Furthermore, the people of Malta receive notable recompense and amends for their hospitality by the ministry of Paul. We learn that there is no one so vile that they cannot be the author of some good toward us, if we present ourselves as beneficent to them. For God can reward us by anyone, and such resources are not to be lost, but for God's sake, or for Christ's, ought to be used to benefit everybody. In this passage are declared two rewards which these men received from Paul himself. First, the father of Publius, being sick from a fever and dysentery, a disease utterly incurable, was restored to health by Paul. No one can deny that this was a great benefit and pleasure, if we consider the body; but more importantly, we see how by this occasion he was brought to the faith. We must note how in this cure Paul observed the manner and order prescribed by Christ. In both instances, he uses prayer and laid his hands on the sick body. We are taught that this miracle was not wrought through the power of Paul but of God.... For the apostles did not perform their miracles except through Christ, who by the absolute power of his Word drove away devils and diseases. But the apostles and other holy servants of Christ did the same by calling on the name of Christ. Here is the error of those confused people, who because of the miracles that holy people wrought, think they ought to be invocated and do not regard how God is the author of them whose honor and glory the saints chiefly sought. HOMILY 172, ACTS 28:7-14.[14]

---

[12]CNTC 7:302* (CO 48:562-63).

[13]Gwalther, *Homelyes or Sermons upon the Actes*, 891* (*In Acta Apostolorum*, 275r-276r); alluding to Prov 21:13.

[14]Gwalther, *Homelyes or Sermons upon the Actes*, 891-92* (*In Acta Apostolorum*, 276r).

GIVE GLORY FOR HEALING TO GOD ALONE.
JOHN CALVIN: By praying Paul makes it plain
that he is not the one responsible for the miracle,
but only the minister, so that God may not be
defrauded of his glory. He also confirms that by
the outward sign. For as we have seen earlier in
other passages, the laying on of hands was nothing
else but a solemn rite of presentation. Accordingly, when Paul presented the man to God with
his own hands, he showed that he was humbly
asking for his life from God. By this example not
only is a warning given to those who are so strong
in the extraordinary graces of God that they must
take very great care not to obscure the glory of
God by extolling themselves, but also we are all
taught in general that gratitude must be shown to
the ministers of God in such a way that the glory
remains with him alone. Paul is certainly said to
have healed a man suffering from dysentery, but
the added details bring out that this blessing was
given by God through him. COMMENTARY ON
ACTS 28:8.[15]

**THE PEOPLE OF MALTA WILL WITNESS
AGAINST US ON THE LAST DAY.** JOHANN
SPANGENBERG: In this brief time Paul converted
the entire island. And Luke did not place this
here without reason. For how will we, especially
those [of us] in Germany, stand before God? Since
childhood we have been instructed by our parents
and school teachers in the Creed, the Ten Commandments and the Our Father, and now for many
years we have heard the pure teaching of the holy
gospel. God's Word has been preached, read aloud,
carved, painted for us, but still no one matures in
faith, much less in the fruits of faith! These people
only heard Paul's preaching for three months,
and they believed! Yes, such faith that they soon
demonstrated to Paul, doing many good works. As
the people of Nineveh will rise up on the Last Day
and condemn the Jews for their unbelief, so these
people will also stand against us, condemning us

because they converted after so few sermons and
repented, but we, inundated with so many sermons,
are unwilling to convert and repent. BRIEF EXEGE-
SIS OF ACTS 28:10.[16]

28:11-16 *Paul Arrives in Rome*

PAUL SHOWED NO SIGNS OF SUPERSTITION.
JOHN CALVIN: But he clearly says that the ship of
Alexandria, in which they were conveyed to Rome,
had the sign of Castor and Pollux, so that we may
know that Paul was not given the choice to sail
with people like himself but was forced to board a
ship that was dedicated to two idols. The ancient
poets imagined that Castor and Pollux were the
offspring of Jupiter and Leda, as a result of which
they were also called in Greek Διόσκουροι ("the
twin gods"), the word which Luke uses in this verse,
as if you might say "the sons of Jupiter." In the second place they said that they are the Gemini in the
zodiac. Another superstition also prevailed among
sailors that the same two are the fiery exhalations
which appear in tempests. Therefore, long ago they
were supposed to be gods of the sea and invoked,
as Nicholas, Clement and the like are today. COM-
MENTARY ON ACTS 28:11.[17]

**PAUL IGNORES CASTOR AND POLLUX, RELY-
ING ON GOD'S WORD.** MARTIN LUTHER: Saint
Paul . . . sat in a ship on which the twin gods were
painted or carved. He went on board and did not
bother about them at all. He did not tear them
down. Why must Luke describe the twin gods at
this point? Without a doubt he wanted to show
that outward things can do no harm to faith, if
only the heart does not cleave to them or put its
trust in them. This we must preach and teach, and
let the Word alone do the work, as said before. The
Word must first capture people's hearts and enlighten them; we will not be the ones who will do
it. Therefore, the apostles magnified their ministry

---

[16]Spangenberg, *Der Apostel Geschichte*, 249r-v; alluding to Mt
12:41; Lk 11:32.
[17]CNTC 7:303-4 (CO 48:564).

[15]CNTC 7:303 (CO 48:563); alluding to Acts 6:6; 8:17-18; 13:3;
19:6.

and not its results. SECOND INVOCAVIT SERMON (1522).[18]

WHY DOES LUKE DESCRIBE THIS SHIP? JOHANN SPANGENBERG: For this reason: he highlights the superstition and idolatry of the pagans, who produced and selected a throng of gods for themselves. Sky gods like Jupiter, air gods like Juno, fire gods like Vulcan, earth gods like Pluto, sea gods like Neptune, house gods like Lares, field gods like Terminus, power gods like Diana of the forest, war gods like Mars, food gods like Ceres, wine gods like Bacchus. Human beings crafted so many gods! Lucina helped in childbirth, Vagitanus in rocking children to sleep, Levana raised the child, Laverna washed it, Rumina nursed it, Educa provided it food, Potina provided it drink, Lachesis sustained it. Atropos cut the thread and brought the child to its end. It is completely ridiculous! They gave the entrance to the house alone three gods: Forculus, Cardea and Limentinus for doors, hinges and thresholds.[19] Thus, the pagans made these twins—Castor and Pollux, the sons of Jupiter—the gods of ships. They were so vaunted among the gods that people even swore by their names. Accordingly, these people from Alexandria built a ship in honor of these gods, so that voyages by it would be that much safer.

Were the pagans really so foolish that they held such false gods for the true God? It seems foolish to us, but if we consider our times and the times of our ancestors, we discover that we have acted far more foolishly. For we have fabricated and pray to even more gods than the pagans. Indeed, there is no fortune or misfortune, poverty or wealth, even no sickness that we have not contrived a specific idol for! The pagans did not have God's Word, nor did they know Christ; therefore, they should not be blamed. We, however, boast ourselves to be Christians and we have the Word of God in abundance, but we are still fabricating many idols—not merely golden, silver, wooden and stone images but also our piety, works and merits, that in this matter we are far more repugnant than the pagans. BRIEF EXEGESIS OF ACTS 28:11.[20]

CEREMONIES SHOULD BE NEITHER ABHORRED NOR ABUSED. JOHN DONNE: Because pictures have been adored, we do not abhor a picture; nor do we sit during the sacrament, because idolatry has been committed in kneeling. That church which they call Lutheran has retained more of these ceremonies than ours; and ours more than that which they call Calvinist. But both the Lutheran and ours have done so without danger, because in both places we are diligent to preach to the people the right use of these indifferent things. For this is a true way of shutting out superstition, not always to abolish the thing itself—because, in the right use of it, the spiritual profit and edification may exceed the danger. SERMON ON THE SUNDAY OF SAINT PAUL'S CONVERSION (1628).[21]

GOD GIVES US COMFORT IN THE COMMUNION OF SAINTS. RUDOLF GWALTHER: Although Paul was bold enough and ready to suffer not only bonds but death also for the name of Christ, still he was a man and suffered his temptations. Surely he might have feared that he should have labored in vain in Christ's cause in such a city where ungodliness and tyranny reigned. God therefore to pluck this care out of his mind moves these brothers to go and meet him, so that he might see that they lacked nothing and that by his steadfast example he was to strengthen them, and they would help him with their prayers in this conflict. Let us therefore be encouraged by this example and constantly hold on in our vocation. For neither shall the godly zeal of God's Word lack fruit, nor will God himself fail us. HOMILY 173, ACTS 28:15-22.[22]

---

[18]LW 51:83* (WA 10, 3:29-30; cf. LWA 7:374); alluding to Rom 11:13. See footnote on earlier Invocavit selection, Acts 17:23.

[19]Augustine is Spangenberg's source on these three gods; only Cardea is known to have been worshiped by the Romans. See Augustine, *De Civitate Dei*, 4 §8; NPNF 1 2:68-69. Tertullian also mentions this triad; see ANF 3:70, 102, 145.

[20]Spangenberg, *Der Apostel Geschichte*, 250r-251r.
[21]Donne, *Works*, 2:353*.
[22]Gwalther, *Homelyes or Sermons upon the Actes*, 894* (*In Acta Apostolorum*, 277r).

BETTER TO HAVE COMPANY, EVEN WITH PIGS, THAN TO BE ALONE. MARTIN LUTHER: This is especially so when the devil turns the gospel into law. The teachings of law and gospel are altogether necessary, but they must be distinguished even when they are conjoined; otherwise, human beings will despair or become presumptuous. Consequently Moses describes these teachings well when he speaks of an upper and lower millstone. The upper millstone rumbles and pounds. This is the law. It is very well set up by God so that it only grinds. On the other hand, the lower millstone is quiet, and this is the gospel. Our Lord has suspended the upper millstone in such a way that the grain is crushed and ground only on the lower stone.

This is my only and best advice: Do not remain alone when you are assailed! Flee solitude! Do as that monk did who, when he felt tempted in his cell, said, "I won't stay here; I'll run out of the cell to my brothers." So it is reported of Paul in the book of Acts that he suffered for fourteen days from severe hunger and from shipwreck and afterward was received by his brothers and took courage. This is what I do too. I'd rather go to my swineheard John, or even to the pigs themselves, than remain alone. TABLE TALK, ANTON LAUTER-BACH (1538).[23]

THE ROMAN BELIEVERS WERE BRAVE. RUDOLF GWALTHER: It was a dangerous thing among the Romans to profess the Christian faith and religion, which during the reign of Tiberius (as Tertullian writes[24]) was condemned by public statute and decree. Furthermore, those who met him were not only in danger, but also the whole congregation at Rome was in danger, for whom by this occasion more diligent and earnest search and inquisition might have been made. But however these matters went, they thought it right to declare their duty of love to such an apostle who travailed so earnestly on behalf of all. To deny him would have been a sin, thus they were willing to endure any danger rather than abandon their duty. These things teach us what we owe to the ministers of Christ by whose ministry we are brought to salvation, if at any time they happen to be in danger for their faith and doctrine. Let us not be ashamed of them being in bonds, for we know that Christ was bound, and that the Word of God cannot be bound. HOMILY 173, ACTS 28:15-22.[25]

FREEDOM IN THE MIDST OF IMPRISONMENT. JOHN CALVIN: Luke means that Paul was given more than rest, for his circumstances were different and special. He was allowed to live in a private house with one guard to whom he was bound, while others were confined in the public prison. For the commander of the Praetorian Guard knew from Festus's official report that Paul had no part in any crime. And it is likely that the centurion faithfully reported things that had the effect of procuring favor for him. However, let us realize that God, from heaven, mitigated the imprisonment of his servant, not only to lessen his troubles but also so that the faithful might have freer access to him. For he did not wish the treasure of his faith to be held confined within the walls of a prison but to be kept free and open, to enrich many on all sides. Yet Paul was not given the freedom of house custody in such a way that he did not always carry a chain. COMMENTARY ON ACTS 28:16.[26]

[23]LW 54:276-77* no. 3799 (WATR 3:625-26); alluding to Deut 26:4.
[24]Tertullian, "Apologetic," ANF 3:21-22.

[25]Gwalther, *Homelyes or Sermons upon the Actes,* 895* (*In Acta Apostolorum,* 277r).
[26]CNTC 7:306* (CO 48:566).

28:17-31 PAUL'S GOSPEL MINISTRY IN ROME

[17]After three days he called together the local leaders of the Jews, and when they had gathered, he said to them, "Brothers, though I had done nothing against our people or the customs of our fathers, yet I was delivered as a prisoner from Jerusalem into the hands of the Romans. [18]When they had examined me, they wished to set me at liberty, because there was no reason for the death penalty in my case. [19]But because the Jews objected, I was compelled to appeal to Caesar—though I had no charge to bring against my nation. [20]For this reason, therefore, I have asked to see you and speak with you, since it is because of the hope of Israel that I am wearing this chain." [21]And they said to him, "We have received no letters from Judea about you, and none of the brothers coming here has reported or spoken any evil about you. [22]But we desire to hear from you what your views are, for with regard to this sect we know that everywhere it is spoken against."

[23]When they had appointed a day for him, they came to him at his lodging in greater numbers. From morning till evening he expounded to them, testifying to the kingdom of God and trying to convince them about Jesus both from the Law of Moses and from the Prophets. [24]And some were convinced by what he said, but others disbelieved. [25]And disagreeing among themselves, they departed after Paul had made one statement: "The Holy Spirit was right in saying to your fathers through Isaiah the prophet:

[26]"'Go to this people, and say,
"You will indeed hear but never understand,
and you will indeed see but never perceive."
[27]For this people's heart has grown dull,
and with their ears they can barely hear,
and their eyes they have closed;
lest they should see with their eyes
and hear with their ears
and understand with their heart
and turn, and I would heal them.'

[28]Therefore let it be known to you that this salvation of God has been sent to the Gentiles; they will listen."[a]

[30]He lived there two whole years at his own expense,[b] and welcomed all who came to him,[31]proclaiming the kingdom of God and teaching about the Lord Jesus Christ with all boldness and without hindrance.

a Some manuscripts add verse 29: *And when he had said these words, the Jews departed, having much dispute among themselves*   b Or *in his own hired dwelling*

OVERVIEW: In the closing vignette of Luke's account of the acts of the risen Christ and the apostles, the proclamation of the Word is lifted high by Reformation commentators once more. Inviting the Roman Jews to his temporary home, Paul preaches again the gospel of salvation through faith in Christ. This message is not something one can be indifferent to; it forces a response, either acceptance or rejection. The Lord is present with his ministers by his Spirit, sustaining and empowering them for this difficult task. The reformers draw their exegesis of Acts to a close by praising God's grace and provision, praying that Christ will abide with them to the end.

THE GATHERINGS OF THE FIRST CHURCHES.
RUDOLF GWALTHER: They returned to Paul's lodging on the appointed day. In those days it was not permitted for Christians to have any churches, although even if they had had churches, it would have been unlawful for Paul to have taught in them, being a prisoner and in bonds. Therefore, as in other places, the apostles preached in private houses. So here Paul also assembles them in his rented house that the worship and doctrine of God ought not so to be tied to any place, as though it helped or availed anything to salvation. For it is evident that the Word of God has authority in itself.

God hears prayers in every place, so that we can pray in faith and lift up clean hands to him. If necessity urges us, we need not to be careful for time or place. When we enjoy peace and have Christian magistrates, then we must have a regard to order, which requires both time and place. Therefore, the examples of the primitive church do nothing to defend the furious clamors of the Anabaptists, because necessity in previous times compelled them in their assemblies to do diverse things contrary to our usage. Homily 174, Acts 28:23-29.[1]

The Gist of Paul's Sermon to the Roman Jews. Johann Spangenberg: What is the sum of this sermon? That no one is righteous and saved from his own works and efforts; rather, our righteousness and salvation come from faith in Jesus Christ. This sermon is not a new teaching, freshly contrived today; rather, it is the first, yes, the most ancient sermon and teaching ever to have come to earth. It is the same as when God said to the snake, "I will place enmity between you and the woman, between your seed and her seed; her seed will crush your head." This Word was the first gospel ever heard on earth. By it Adam abided along with his children and their progeny until Abraham. What else is taught and instructed from this teaching and sermon other than that the teaching of the idolatrous Gentiles, the Pharisaical Jews, the accursed Turks, the hypocritical papists and the unholy fanatics and sects is all absolute false teaching, concocted human dreams, lies and chains for the soul. Brief Exegesis of Acts 28:23.[2]

Paul Preaches the Kingdom and Its True King. John Calvin: But we must note the essential feature of the speech, which Luke makes twofold. In the first place Paul taught what was the nature of the kingdom of God among them, and particularly of the supreme happiness and glory promised them, which the prophets every-

where praise so much. For since most of them had dreams of the kingdom of God having a transitory state in the world and wrongly made it consist in ease, pleasures and an abundance of present goods, it was necessary for the right definition to be established, so that they might know that the kingdom of God is spiritual, and that the beginning of it was newness of life, and the end, blessed immortality and the glory of heaven. In the second place Paul strongly urged them to receive Christ, the source of the promised happiness. And once again this second point had two parts. For it could not have been dealt with profitably and thoroughly without an explanation of the office of the promised Redeemer; and second, without showing that he has already been revealed, and that the Son of Mary is the One for whom the ancestors had hoped.

Indeed, the principle was accepted among all the Jews that the Messiah would come to restore all things to the order of perfection. But Paul gave attention to another aspect which was not so well known, that the Messiah was promised to make atonement for the sins of the world by the sacrifice of his death, to reconcile God to humans, to procure eternal righteousness, to regenerate humans by his Spirit and fashion them according to the image of God, and, finally, to make his faithful ones heirs with him of the life of heaven; and that all these things have been fulfilled in the person of Jesus Christ, crucified. Commentary on Acts 28:23.[3]

Why Does the Gospel of Christ Experience Such Opposition? Johann Spangenberg: There are two causes. The first is that Satan is a prince of the world and rules in it with absolute pride, greed, indecency, hatred, drunkenness, murder and similar perversions and vices. Now Christ enters the world with his gospel; his kingdom destroys the devil. For in place of pride, in the gospel Christ teaches humility; in place of greed, gentleness; in place of indecency, chastity; in place of wrath and hatred, friendliness. This the devil cannot tolerate, so he instigates the entire

---

[1]Gwalther, *Homelyes or Sermons upon the Actes*, 899* (*In Acta Apostolorum*, 278v).
[2]Spangenberg, *Der Apostel Geschichte*, 259r-v; quoting Gen 3:14-15.

[3]CNTC 7:309* (CO 48:568-69).

world against Christ and his Word, but he is incapable of accomplishing anything. He is already in checkmate. He is already conquered.

The second cause is that the world asserts that through its piety, righteousness, works and efforts it will be saved. Then the gospel of Christ comes, teaches contrary to this and says that all human piety, righteousness, works and efforts cannot stand before God's judgment; rather, whoever wants to be saved through faith must clasp on to Christ Jesus, the Son of God, and cling tightly to his Word and die in it. This the world cannot tolerate. It is willing neither to see nor to hear such preaching. It revolts and rages and raves against Christ and his Word, but they are incapable of accomplishing anything. For they are already conquered by Christ. BRIEF EXEGESIS OF ACTS 28:24.[4]

THE RESULTS OF THE WORD IN ROME. JOHN CALVIN: Luke records that in the end the outcome of the disputation was that by no means did they all derive equal benefit from the same teaching. We know that the apostle was endowed with such grace of the Spirit that he ought to have moved stones; yet, by arguing a great deal for a long time and by testifying, he did not manage to win them all to Christ. Accordingly, do not let us wonder if today the unbelief of many resists the clear teaching of the gospel; many remain inflexible, although the truth of Christ is just as plain to them as the sun shining at noon. Moreover, those who had come willingly to Paul, as if with a mind to learn, go away from him blind and stupid. If there was such obstinacy in willing listeners, is there any wonder if those who are swollen with pride and bitterness deliberately avoid the light and reject Christ with a bitter mind? COMMENTARY ON ACTS 28:24.[5]

PAUL'S USE OF ISAIAH'S PROPHECY. JOHN CALVIN: In fact, Paul has not carefully repeated the exact words of the prophet himself but rather has adapted his words to his own purpose. Therefore, whereas the prophet attributed their blindness to the secret judgment of God, he ascribes it to their ill will. For the prophet is ordered to close the eyes of his listeners; here Paul reproaches the unbelievers of his own day because they have shut their own eyes. However, he distinctly states both things, that God is responsible for their blindness, and yet they have closed their own eyes and are blind of their own accord, since these two agree with each other very well. COMMENTARY ON ACTS 28:25-27.[6]

CHRISTIANS ARE ALIVE THROUGH CHRIST'S BAPTISM. MARTIN LUTHER: We who are Christians and have the Holy Spirit in us—who awakens us and makes us vigilant—do not say, "It seems to me." Rather, a Christian says, "I know certainly and truly that it is so: that Christ for my sake and for my benefit was born and became human, and through baptism washed me of my sins. That is why I cherish my baptism and hold it dear. For it is not only my baptism but also Christ's baptism, and Christ's baptism is my baptism. For if it helps Christ and washes from sin and makes entirely pure, then it helps me also and purifies me, too, from sin." SERMON ON THE DAY OF CHRIST'S EPIPHANY (1546).[7]

"THE SALVATION OF GOD." RUDOLF GWALTHER: Our Lord and Savior Jesus Christ comforts his disciples many times with this argument, saying that he will not leave them destitute but will be present with them until the end of the world. The truth of this promise appears everywhere, as well at all other times, also chiefly in adversities, for there Christ is so near to his servants that not only does he defend them mightily and faithfully but also directs those things which seem doleful and unfortunate to their salvation and to his glory. In this matter Paul's captivity is as good as numerous

---

[4]Spangenberg, *Der Apostel Geschichte*, 256v-257v; alluding to Jn 16:33.
[5]CNTC 7:310* (CO 48:569).

[6]CNTC 7:312-13* (CO 48:571)
[7]LW 58:366* (WA 51:115).

testimonies for us! At first his captivity might have seemed to have stopped the course of the gospel completely, but the Lord guided it so that even through these obstacles the teaching of the gospel flourished rather than being hindered. For through this it happened that both the Roman guard and soldiers heard the gospel. In the end the preaching of the gospel filled Rome, indeed even the imperial court and Caesar's chambers! HOMILY 175, ACTS 28:30-31.[8]

THE APOSTLE'S EXAMPLE ENCOURAGES US.

JUSTUS JONAS: By this we too are rightly refreshed and roused to faith, because Paul—even in the midst of such a number of his enemies' snares—is protected, in fact, so much so that for the entire two years he preached. From this we should always know that we are not in the hands of our enemies, even as they harm us, but instead we are completely in the hands of the Father. Therefore we know that all the power and wisdom of the world, even all the gates of hell wage war against us for nothing unless the Father has given us into their hands. ANNOTATIONS ON ACTS 28:30-31.[9]

PAUL'S MINISTRY THE SAME IN FREEDOM OR IN BONDS.

RUDOLF GWALTHER: He did then the same in bonds which he had done before being at his liberty, because he understood he was now the apostle and servant of Jesus Christ, as well as before. And he did not only preach but also sent letters, now to one place, and then to another, and both instructed and comforted the congregations abroad, insomuch that if we considered those times, we shall confess we have received more profit and benefit by Paul's bonds than of all his doings and sayings beside, while he went at liberty over all the world. For those times may we give thanks for those distinguished epistles, written as the Holy Spirit directed them to the Ephesians, to the Philippians, to the Colossians, to the Hebrews, to

Philemon and the second to Timothy. The church until this day has kept and preserved these epistles as precious jewels. HOMILY 175, ACTS 28:30-31.[10]

CHRIST PARTICIPATES WITH US IN AFFLICTION.

RUDOLF GWALTHER: We know that they that are partakers of Christ's afflictions in this world shall reign with him hereafter in heaven. Here appears also the infinite goodness of God, which preserved Paul for so long in open confines, verily for his elect's sake to whom he would reveal his gospel. Therefore the hope of both Paul and all the other faithful was passed on—even though under Nero, a most vicious and cruel tyrant—no one could possibly have had any hope. Therefore, let as many who walk in God's calling fetch counsel. For as long as we are occupied in God's affairs, and so as it is requisite for our salvation, God will easily defend us among the most cruel enemies. He was able to save Noah in the midst of the waves of the flood, which overflowed all the world, and Jonah that lay hidden in the belly of the huge whale. And truly when the time comes he will transfer all those free from evil into the eternal kingdom of his Son. . . .

And this is truly a wonderful example whereby we are taught how much we owe to God, if at any time we perceive to be helped and defended by him in the midst of dangers and adversity. For then we must not fear either dangers past or dangers present or to come but must be inflamed with greater zeal that by our bold defense of the glory of God, we may show ourselves accordingly thankful to him. Therefore, that reason of fleshly wisdom that many in these days follow is plainly foolish and perverse; they think we should hold our peace because of enemies and dangers on every side appearing, as though it were in the enemies' power to hinder or further the course of the gospel. In fact we must boldly promote God's cause since we demonstrate his truth and power in the midst of looming dangers. HOMILY 175, ACTS 28:30-31.[11]

---

[8]Gwalther, *Homelyes or Sermons upon the Actes*, 904* (*In Acta Apostolorum*, 280r).
[9]Jonas, *Annotationes in Acta*, K7v-K8r.

[10]Gwalther, *Homelyes or Sermons upon the Actes*, 905-6* (*In Acta Apostolorum*, 280r-v).
[11]Gwalther, *Homelyes or Sermons upon the Actes*, 905, 906* (*In Acta Apostolorum*, 280r, 280v); alluding to Col 1:13-14.

DILIGENTLY PURSUE YOUR CALLING TO THE END, BY THE GRACE OF GOD. JOHANN SPANGENBERG: From this example of Paul we should learn that God the Almighty wants all devout Christians to attend to their calling and diligently carry out their vocation, placing all their trust and confidence in him, knowing that in every affliction and danger he will sustain and save them in the end. Such affliction, opposition, fear and misery not only will not harm them, but even better God will transform them for the best. . . .

If in life you have diligently attended to your calling, then you cannot die a wicked or disdainful death. After a good Christian life, no wicked or untimely death can follow. For Christians, because they have been buried with Christ through baptism, are prepared to die—any year, any day, even any hour and moment. Death, as grisly, as terrifying, as traumatic as it may be, can do them no harm; rather, it sanctifies them. For it helps them out of this wicked world, yes, out of this valley of misery into eternal life. . . .

A Christian should press on in his calling and not fear death, but instead he should be like those people waiting on their Lord, waiting for him to commence the wedding, so that when he comes and knocks they can let him in immediately. And the Lord, the heavenly Father, will accept them as devout, faithful servants, drawing them into his joy, into eternal life. Help us to this, dear Father, through Christ your dear Son by the Holy Spirit. Amen. BRIEF EXEGESIS OF ACTS 28:30-31.[12]

LORD JESUS CHRIST, WITH US ABIDE. PHILIPP MELANCHTHON AND NIKOLAUS SELNECKER:

Lord Jesus Christ with us abide,
For round falls the eventide.
O let your Word that saving light,
Shine forth undimmed into the night.

In these last days of great distress
Grant us, dear Lord, true steadfastness

That we keep pure till life is spent
Your Word and Sacrament.

To hope grown dim, to hearts turned cold
Speak tongues of fire and make us bold
To shine your Word of saving grace
Into each dark and loveless place.

May glorious truths that we have heard
The bright sword of your mighty Word
Spurn Satan that your church be strong
Bold, unified in act and song.

Restrain, O Lord, the human pride
That seeks to thrust your truth aside
Or with some manmade thoughts or things
Would dim the words your Spirit sings.

Stay with us, Lord, and keep us true
Preserve our faith our whole life through
Your Word alone our heart's defense,
The church's glorious confidence.

LORD JESUS CHRIST, WITH US ABIDE.[13]

---

[12]Spangenberg, *Der Apostel Geschichte*, 267v-268v; alluding to Rom 8:28; Mt 25:1-13.

[13]The Commission on Worship, ed., *Lutheran Service Book*, no. 585.

Map of Europe at the time of the Reformation

Legend: Boundary of Holy Roman Empire

SWEDEN

NORWAY

ESTONIA

LIVONIA

TEUTONIC ORDER

SCOTLAND

IRELAND

ENGLAND

DENMARK

North Sea

Baltic Sea

BRANDENBURG

LITHUANIA

RUSSIA

POLAND

NETHERLANDS

SAXONY

BOHEMIA

GERMAN TERRITORIES

BAVARIA

AUSTRIA

HUNGARY

MOLDAVIA

UKRAINE

CRIMEA

Black Sea

WALLACHIA

OTTOMAN EMPIRE

FRANCE

SWISS CANTONS

SAVOY

VENICE

PAPAL STATES

KINGDOM OF NAPLES

SICILY

Mediterranean Sea

RHODES

CYPRUS

CRETE

Bay of Biscay

Atlantic Ocean

SPAIN

PORTUGAL

ARAGON

MAJORCA

SARDINIA

CORSICA

Timeline of the Reformation

	German Territories	France	Spain	Italy	Switzerland	Netherlands	British Isles
1337-1453		Hundred Years' War					Hundred Years' War
1378-1415		Western Schism (Avignon Papacy)		Western Schism			
1384							d. John Wycliffe
1414-1418							
1415				Council of Constance; d. Jan Huss			
1450	Invention of printing press						
1452				b. Leonardo da Vinci (d. 1519)			
1453				Fall of Constantinople			
1455-1485							War of Roses; Rise of House of Tudor
1456	Gutenberg Bible						
1460							
1466		b. Jacques Lafèvres d'Étaples (d. 1536)					
1467						b. Desiderius Erasmus (d. 1536)	b. John Colet (d. 1519)
1475				b. Michelangelo (d. 1564)			
1478	b. Wolfgang Capito (d. 1541)		Ferdinand and Isabella				b. Thomas More (d. 1535)
1480	b. Balthasar Hubmaier (d. 1528); b. Andreas Bodenstein von Karlstadt (d. 1541)						
1481-1530			Spanish Inquisition				
1482					b. Johannes Oecolampadius (d. 1531)		
1483	b. Martin Luther (d. 1546)						
1484					b. Huldrych Zwingli (d. 1531)		
1485	b. Johannes Bugenhagen (d. 1554)						b. Hugh Latimer (d. 1555)

	German Territories	France	Spain	Italy	Switzerland	Netherlands	British Isles
1486	r. Frederick the Wise, Elector (d. 1525); b. Johann Eck (d. 1543)						
1488							b. Miles Coverdale (d. 1568)
1489	b. Thomas Müntzer (d. 1525); b. Kaspar von Schwenckfeld (d. 1561)						b. Thomas Cranmer (d. 1556)
1491	b. Martin Bucer (d. 1551)		b. Ignatius Loyola (d. 1556)				
1492			Defeat of Moors in Grenada; Columbus discovers America; Explusion of Jews from Spain				
1494							b. William Tyndale (d. 1536)
1496	b. Andreas Osiander (d. 1552)					b. Menno Simons (d. 1561)	
1497	b. Philipp Melanchthon (d. 1560); b. Wolfgang Musculus (d. 1563)						
1498				d. Girolamo Savonarola	b. Conrad Grebel (d. 1526)		
1499	b. Johannes Brenz (d. 1570)			b. Peter Martyr Vermigli (d. 1562)			
1500			b. Charles V (-1558)				
1501	b. Erasmus Sarcerius (d. 1559)						
1502	Founding of University of Wittenberg						
1504					b. Heinrich Bullinger (d. 1575)		
1505	Luther joins Augustinian Order						
1506				Restoration to St. Peter's begins			
1507				Sale of indulgences approved to fund building			
1509		b. John Calvin (d. 1564)					r. Henry VIII (-1547)

	German Territories	France	Spain	Italy	Switzerland	Netherlands	British Isles
1510	Luther moves to Rome						b. Nicholas Ridley (d. 1555)
1511	Luther moves to Wittenberg						
1512				Sistene Chapel completed			
1512-1517				Fifth Lateran Council; rejection of conciliarism			
1513	Luther lectures on Psalms			r. Pope Leo X (-1521)			b. John Knox (d. 1572)
1515	Luther lectures on Romans	r. Francis I (-1547); b. Peter Ramus (d. 1572)					
1516		Est. French National Church (via Concordat of Bologna)		Concordat of Bologna		publication of Erasmus's Greek New Testament	
1517	Tetzel sells indulgences in Saxony; Luther's Ninety-five Theses						
1518	Heidelberg Disputation; Luther examined by Eck at Diet of Augsburg			Diet of Augsburg			
1519	Leipzig Disputation	b. Theodore Beza (d. 1605)	Cortés conquers Aztecs; Portuguese sailor Magellan circumnavigates the globe		Zwingli appointed pastor of Grossmünster in Zurich; b. Rudolf Gwalther (d. 1576)		
1520	Publication of Luther's "Three Treatises"; Burning of papal bull in Wittenberg		Coronation of Charles V	Papal Bull v. Luther: *Exsurge Domine*			
1521	Luther excommunicated; Diet/Edict of Worms—Luther condemned; Luther in hiding; Melanchthon's *Loci Communes*	French-Spanish War (-1526)	French-Spanish War; Loyola converts	Papal excommunication of Luther			Henry VIII publishes *Affirmation of the Seven Sacraments* against Luther; awarded title "Defender of the Faith" by Pope
1521-1522	Disorder in Wittenberg; Luther translates New Testament						

	German Territories	France	Spain	Italy	Switzerland	Netherlands	British Isles
1521-1525		First and Second Habsburg–Valois War					
1522	Luther returns to Wittenberg; Luther's NT published; criticizes Zwickau prophets; b. Martin Chemnitz (d. 1586)		Publication of Complutensian Polyglot Bible under Cisneros		Sausage Affair & reform begins in Zurich under Zwingli		
1523	Knight's Revolt	Bucer begins ministry in Strasbourg	Loyola writes Spiritual Exercises	r. Pope Clement VII (-1534)	Iconoclasm in Zurich		
1524-1526	Peasants' War						
1524	Luther criticizes peasants					Erasmus's disputation on free will	
1525	Luther marries; execution of Thomas Müntzer				Abolition of mass in Zurich; disputation on baptism; first believers' baptism performed in Zurich		
1526					Zurich council mandates capital punishment of Anabaptists	Publication of Tyndale's English translation of NT	
1527	d. Hans Denck (b. c. 1500) d. Hans Hut (b. 1490)			Sack of Rome by mutinous troops of Charles V	First Anabaptist executed in Zurich; drafting of Schleitheim Confession		
1528	Execution of Hubmaier						
1529	Second Diet of Speyer; evangelical "protest"; publication of Luther's catechisms; Marburg Colloquy; siege of Vienna by Turkish forces	Abolition of mass in Strasbourg			d. Georg Blaurock (b. 1492)		Thomas More appointed chancellor to Henry VIII
1530	Diet of Augsburg; Confession of Augsburg	d. Francois Lambert (Lambert of Avignon) (b. 1487)		Charles V crowned Holy Roman Emperor			
1531	Formation of Schmalkaldic League				d. H. Zwingli; succeeded by H. Bullinger		

	German Territories	France	Spain	Italy	Switzerland	Netherlands	British Isles
1532		Publication of Calvin's commentary on Seneca; conversion of Calvin					
1533		Nicholas Cop addresses University of Paris; Cop and Calvin implicated as "Lutheran" sympathizers					Thomas Cranmer appointed as Archbishop of Canterbury; Henry VIII divorces
1534	First edition of Luther's Bible published	Affair of the Placards; Calvin flees d. Guillame Briçonnet (b. 1470)		Jesuits founded; d. Cardinal Cajetan (Thomas de Vio) (b. 1469)			Act of Supremacy; English church breaks with Rome
1535	Bohemian Confession of 1535; Anabaptist theocracy at Münster collapses after eighteen months						d. Thomas More; d. John Fisher
1536	Wittenberg Concord; b. Kaspar Olevianus (d. 1587)				First edition of Calvin's *Institutes* published; Calvin arrives in Geneva (-1538); First Helvetic Confession	Publication of Tyndale's translation of NT; d. W. Tyndale	d. A. Boleyn; Henry VIII dissolves monasteries (-1541)
1537					Calvin presents ecclesiastical ordinances to Genevan Council		
1538					Calvin exiled from Geneva; arrives in Strasbourg (-1541)		
1539		Calvin publishes second edition of *Institutes* in Strasbourg					Statute of Six Articles; publication of Coverdale's Wheat Bible
1540				Papal approval of Jesuit order			d. Thomas Cromwell
1541	Colloquy of Regensberg	French translation of Calvin's *Institutes* published	d. Juan de Valdés (b. 1500/1510)		d. A. Karlstadt; Calvin returns to Geneva (-1564)		
1542	d. Sebastian Franck (b. 1499)			Institution of Roman Inquisition			War between England and Scotland; James V of Scotland defeated; Ireland declared sovereign kingdom

	German Territories	France	Spain	Italy	Switzerland	Netherlands	British Isles
1543	Copernicus publishes *On the Revolutions of the Heavenly Spheres*; d. Johann Eck (Johann Maier of Eck) (b. 1486)						
1545-1547	Schmalkaldic Wars; d. Martin Luther			First session of Council of Trent			
1547	Defeat of Protestants at Mühlberg	d. Francis I; r. Henri II (-1559)					d. Henry VIII; r. Edward VI (-1553)
1548	Augsburg Interim (-1552) d. Caspar Cruciger (b. 1504)						
1549	d. Paul Fagius (b. 1504)				Consensus Tigurinus between Calvin and Bullinger		First Book of Common Prayer published
1551-1552				Second session of Council of Trent			Cranmer's Forty-Two Articles
1552	d. Sebastian Münster (b. 1488)						
1553	d. Johannes Aepinus (b. 1449)						Book of Common Prayer revised; d. Edward VI; r. Mary I (1558)
1554							Richard Hooker (d. 1600)
1555	Diet of Augsburg; Peace of Augsburg; establishes legal territorial existence of Lutheranism and Catholicism	First mission of French; pastors trained in Geneva				b. Sibbrandus Lubbertus (d. 1625)	b. Robert Rollock (d. 1599); d. Hugh Latimer; d. Nicholas Ridley
1556	d. Pilgram Marpeck (b. 1495) d. Konrad Pellikan (b. 1478) d. Peter Riedemann (b. 1506)		Charles V resigns			d. David Joris (b. c. 1501)	d. Thomas Cranmer
1557					Michael Servetus executed in Geneva		Alliance with Spain in war against France
1558			d. Charles V				b. William Perkins (d. 1602); d. Mary I; r. Elizabeth I (-1603)

	German Territories	France	Spain	Italy	Switzerland	Netherlands	British Isles
1559		d. Henry II; r. Francis II (-1560); first national synod of French reformed churches (1559) in Paris; Gallic Confession		First index of prohibited books issued	Final edition of Calvin's *Institutes*; founding of Genevan Academy	b. Jacobus Arminius (d. 1609)	Elizabethan Settlement
1560	d. P. Melanchthon	d. Francis II; r. Charles IX (1574); Edict of Toleration created peace with Huguenots			Geneva Bible		Kirk of Scotland established; Scottish Confession
1561-1563				Third session of Council of Trent			
1561						Belgic Confession	
1562	d. Katharina Schütz Zell (b. 1497/98)	Massacre of Huguenots begins French Wars of Religion (-1598)					The Articles of Religion—in Elizabethan "final" form (1562/71)
1563	Heidelberg Catechism						
1564				b. Galileo (d. 1642)	d. J. Calvin		b. William Shakespeare (d. 1616)
1566	d. Johann Agricola (b. 1494)			Roman Catechism	Second Helvetic Confession		
1567						Spanish occupation	Abdication of Scottish throne by Mary Stuart; r. James VI (-1603)
1568						d. Dirk Phillips (b. 1504) Dutch movement for liberation (-1645)	
1570		d. Johannes Mercerus (Jean Mercier)		Papal Bull *Regnans in Excelsis* excommunicates Elizabeth I			Elizabeth I excommunicated
1571	b. Johannes Kepler (d. 1630)		Spain defeats Ottoman navy at Battle of Lepanto				
1572		Massacre of Huguenots on St. Bartholomew's Day		r. Pope Gregory XIII (-1583)		William of Orange invades	
1574		d. Charles IX; r. Henri III (d. 1589)					
1575	d. Georg Major (b. 1502); Bohemian Confession of 1575						

	German Territories	France	Spain	Italy	Switzerland	Netherlands	British Isles
1576		Declaration of Toleration; formation of Catholic League		b. Giovanni Diodati (d. 1649)		Sack of Antwerp; Pacification of Ghent	
1577	Lutheran Formula of Concord						England allies with Netherlands against Spain
1578			Truce with Ottomans				Sir Francis Drake circumnavigates the globe
1579			Expeditions to Ireland			Division of Dutch provinces	
1580	Lutheran Book of Concord						
1581			d. Teresa of Avila				Anti-Catholic statutes passed
1582				Gregorian Reform of calendar			
1583							b. David Dickson (d. 1663)
1584		Treaty of Joinville with Spain	Treaty of Joinville; Spain inducted into Catholic League; defeats Dutch at Antwerp			Fall of Antwerp; d. William of Orange	
1585		Henri of Navarre excommunicated		r. Pope Sixtus V (-1590)			
1586							Sir Francis Drake's expedition to West Indies; Sir Walter Raleigh in Roanoke
1587	d. Johann Wigand (b. 1523)	Henri of Navarre defeats royal army					d. Mary Stuart of Scotland
1588		Henri of Navarre drives Henri III from Paris; assassination of Catholic League Leaders	Armada destroyed				English Mary defeats Spanish Armada
1589		d. Henri III; r. Henri (of Navarre) IV (-1610)	Victory over England at Lisbon				Defeated by Spain in Lisbon
1590		Henri IV's siege of Paris		d. Girolamo Zanchi (b. 1516)			Alliance with Henri IV
1592	d. Nikolaus Selnecker (b. 1530)						
1593		Henri IV converts to Catholicism					

	German Territories	France	Spain	Italy	Switzerland	Netherlands	British Isles
1594		Henri grants toleration to Huguenots					
1595		Henri IV declares war on Spain; received into Catholic Church		Pope Sixtus accepts Henri IV into Church			Alliance with France
1596		b. René Descartes (d. 1650)					
1598		Edict of Nantes; toleration of Huguenots; peace with Spain	Treaty of Vervins; peace with France				
1600	d. David Chytraeus (b. 1531)						
1602					d. Daniel Toussain (b. 1541)		
1603							d. Elizabeth I; r. James I (James VI of Scotland) (-1625)
1604	d. Cyriacus Spangenberg (b. 1528)						d. John Whitgift (b. 1530)
1605						b. Rembrandt (d. 1669)	Guy Fawkes and gunpowder plot
1606							Jamestown Settlement
1607							b. John Milton (d. 1674)
1608							
1610		d. Henri IV; r. Louis XIII (-1643)	d. Benedict Pererius (b. 1535)			The Remonstrance	
1611							Publication of Authorized English Translation of Bible (AV/KJV)
1616							b. John Owen (d. 1683)
1617							b. Ralph Cudworth (d. 1689)
1618-1648	Thirty Years' War						
1618-1619						Synod of Dordrecht	
1620							English Puritans land in Massachusetts
1621							d. Andrew Willet (b. 1562)

	German Territories	France	Spain	Italy	Switzerland	Netherlands	British Isles
1633	d. Christoph Pelargus (b. 1565)						Laud becomes Archbishop of Canterbury
1637	d. Johann Gerhard (b. 1582)						
1638							d. Joseph Mede (b. 1638)
1640				Diodati's Italian translation of Bible published			
1642-1649							English civil wars; d. Charles I; r. Oliver Cromwell (1660)
1643-1649							Westminster Assembly
1643		d. Louis XIII; r. Louis XIV (-1715)					
1645							d. William Laud (b. 1573)
1648		Treaty of Westphalia ends Thirty Years' War					
1656	d. Georg Calixtus (b. 1586)						
1660							English Restoration; d. Oliver Cromwell; r. Charles II (-1685)
1662							Act of Uniformity
1664						d. Thieleman Jans van Braght (b. 1625)	d. John Mayer (b. 1583)
1671							d. William Greenhill (b. 1591)
1677							d. Thomas Manton (b. 1620)
1678						d. Anna Maria von Schurman (b. 1607)	
1688							Glorious Revolution; r. William and Mary (-1702); d. John Bunyan (b. 1628)
1691							d. Richard Baxter (b. 1615)

BIOGRAPHICAL SKETCHES OF
REFORMATION-ERA FIGURES AND WORKS

For works consulted, see "Sources for Biographical Sketches," p. 407.

Johannes Aepinus (1499–1553). German Lutheran preacher and theologian. Aepinus studied under Martin Luther,* Philipp Melanchthon* and Johannes Bugenhagen* in Wittenberg. Because of his Lutheran beliefs, Aepinus lost his first teaching position in Brandenburg. He fled north to Stralsund and became a preacher and superintendent at Saint Peter's Church in Hamburg. In 1534, he made a diplomatic visit to England but could not convince Henry VIII to embrace the Augsburg Confession. His works include sermons and theological writings. Aepinus became best known as leader of the Infernalists, who believed that Christ underwent torment in hell after his crucifixion.

Johann Agricola (c. 1494–1566). German Lutheran pastor and theologian. An early student of Martin Luther,* Agricola eventually began a controversy over the role of the law, first with Melanchthon* and then with Luther himself. Agricola claimed to defend Luther's true position, asserting that only the gospel of the crucified Christ calls Christians to truly good works, not the fear of the law. After this first controversy, Agricola seems to have radicalized his views to the point that he eliminated Luther's *simul iustus et peccator* ("at the same time righteous and sinful") paradox of the Christian life, emphasizing instead that believers have no need for the law once they are united with Christ through faith. Luther re-

sponded by writing anonymous pamphlets against antinomianism. Agricola later published a recantation of his views, hoping to assuage relations with Luther, although they were never personally reconciled. He published a commentary on Luke, a series of sermons on Colossians, and a massive collection of German proverbs.

Henry Airay (c. 1560–1616). English Puritan professor and pastor. He was especially noted for his preaching, a blend of hostility toward Catholicism and articulate exposition of English Calvinism. He was promoted to provost of Queen's College Oxford (1598) and then to vice chancellor of the university in 1606. He disputed with William Laud* concerning Laud's putative Catholicization of the Church of England, particularly over the practice of genuflection, which Airay vehemently opposed. He also opposed fellow Puritans who wished to separate from the Church of England. His lectures on Philippians were his only work published during his lifetime.

Moïse Amyraut (1596–1664). French Reformed pastor and professor. Originally intending to be a lawyer, Amyraut turned to theology after an encounter with several Huguenot pastors and having read Calvin's* *Institutes*. After a brief stint as a parish pastor, Amyraut spent the majority of his career at the Saumur Academy. He was well known for his irenicism and ecumenicism (for example, in advocating intercommunion with

Lutherans). Certain aspects of his writings on justification, faith, the covenants and especially predestination proved controversial among the Reformed. His doctrine of election is often called hypothetical universalism or Amyraldianism, stating that Christ's atoning work was intended by God for all human beings indiscriminately, although its effectiveness for salvation depends on faith, which is a free gift of God given only to those whom God has chosen from eternity. Amyraut was charged with grave doctrinal error three times before the National Synod but was acquitted each time. Aside from his theological treatises, Amyraut published paraphrases of almost the entire New Testament and the Psalms, as well as many sermons.

Jacobus Arminius (1559–1609). Dutch Remonstrant pastor and theologian. Arminius was a vocal critic of high Calvinist scholasticism, whose views were repudiated by the synod of Dordrecht. Arminius was a student of Theodore Beza* at the academy of Geneva. He served as a pastor in Amsterdam and later joined the faculty of theology at the university in Leiden, where his lectures on predestination were popular and controversial. Predestination, as Arminius understood it, was the decree of God determined on the basis of divine foreknowledge of faith or rejection by humans who are the recipients of prevenient, but resistible, grace.

Articles of Religion (1562; revised 1571). The Articles underwent a long editorial process that drew from the influence of Continental confessions in England, resulting in a uniquely Anglican blend of Protestantism and Catholicism. In their final form, they were reduced from Thomas Cranmer's* Forty-two Articles (1539) to the Elizabethan Thirty-nine Articles (1571), excising polemical articles against the Anabaptists and Millenarians as well as adding articles on the Holy Spirit, good works and Communion. Originating in a 1535 meeting with Lutherans, the Articles retained a minor influence from the Augsburg Confession (1530) and Württemberg Confession (1552), but showed significant revision in accordance with

Genevan theology, as well as the Second Helvetic Confession.*

Augsburg Confession (1530). In the wake of Luther's* stand against ecclesial authorities at the Diet of Worms (1521), the Holy Roman Empire splintered along theological lines. Emperor Charles V sought to ameliorate this—while also hoping to secure a united European front against Turkish invasion—by calling together another imperial diet in Augsburg in 1530. The Evangelical party was cast in a strongly heretical light at the diet by Johann Eck.* For this reason, Philipp Melanchthon* and Justus Jonas* thought it best to strike a conciliatory tone (Luther, as an official outlaw, did not attend), submitting a confession rather than a defense. The resulting Augsburg Confession was approved by many of the rulers of the northeastern Empire; however, due to differences in eucharistic theology, Martin Bucer* and the representatives of Strasbourg, Constance, Lindau and Memmingen drafted a separate confession (the Tetrapolitan Confession). Charles V accepted neither confession, demanding that the Evangelicals accept the Catholic rebuttal instead. In 1531, along with the publication of the Augsburg Confession itself, Melanchthon released a defense of the confession that responded to the Catholic confutation and expanded on the original articles. Most subsequent Protestant confessions followed the general structure of the Augsburg Confession.

Richard Baxter (1615–1691). English Puritan minister. Baxter was a leading Puritan pastor, evangelist and theologian, known throughout England for his landmark ministry in Kidderminster and a prodigious literary output, producing 135 books in just over forty years. Baxter came to faith through reading William Perkins,* Richard Sibbes* and other early Puritan writers and was the first cleric to decline the terms of ministry in the national English church imposed by the 1662 Act of Uniformity; Baxter wrote on behalf of the more than 1700 who shared ejection from the national church. He hoped for restoration to national church ministry, or toleration, that would allow lawful preaching and pastoring. Baxter sought unity in theological, ecclesiastical, sociopolitical and personal terms and is regarded as a forerunner of Noncomformist ecumenicity, though he was defeated in his efforts at the 1661 Savoy Conference to take seriously Puritan objections to the revision of the 1604 Prayer Book. Baxter's views on church ministry were considerably hybrid: he was a paedo-baptist, Nonconformist minister who approved of synodical Episcopal government and fixed liturgy. He is most known for his classic writings on the Christian life, such as *The Saints' Everlasting Rest* and *A Christian Directory*, and pastoral ministry, such as *The Reformed Pastor*. He also produced *Catholick Theology*, a large volume squaring current Reformed, Lutheran, Arminian and Roman Catholic systems with each other.

Thomas Becon (1511/1512–1567). English Puritan preacher. Becon was a friend of Hugh Latimer,* and for several years chaplain to Archbishop Thomas Cranmer.* Becon was sent to the Tower of London by Mary I and then exiled for his controversial preaching at the English royal court. He returned to England upon Elizabeth I's accession. Becon was one of the most widely read popular preachers in England during the Reformation. He published many of his sermons, including a postil, or collection of sermon helps for undertrained or inexperienced preachers.

Belgic Confession (1561). Written by Guy de Brès (1523–1567), this statement of Dutch Reformed faith was heavily reliant on the Gallic Confession,* although more detailed, especially in how strongly it distances the Reformed from Roman Catholics and Anabaptists. The Confession first appeared in French in 1561 and was translated to Dutch in 1562. It was presented to Philip II (1527–1598) in the hope that he would grant toleration to the Reformed, to no avail. At the Synod of Dordrecht* the Confession was revised, clarifying and strengthening the article on election as well as sharpening the distinctives of Reformed theology against the Anabaptists, thus situating the Dutch Reformed more closely to the international Calvinist movement. The Belgic Confession

in conjunction with the Heidelberg Catechism* and the Canons of Dordrecht were granted official status as the confessional standards (the Three Forms of Unity) of the Dutch Reformed Church.

Theodore Beza (1519–1605). French pastor and professor. Beza was compatriot and successor to John Calvin* as moderator of the Company of Pastors in Geneva during the second half of the sixteenth century. He was a noteworthy New Testament scholar whose *Codex Bezae* formed the basis of the New Testament section of later English translations. A leader in the academy and the church, Beza served as professor of Greek at the Lausanne Academy until 1558, at which time he moved to Geneva to become the rector of the newly founded Genevan Academy. He enjoyed an international reputation through his correspondence with key European leaders. Beza developed and extended Calvin's doctrinal thought on several important themes such as the nature of predestination and the real spiritual presence of Christ in the Eucharist.

Georg Blaurock (1492–1529). Swiss Anabaptist. Blaurock (a nickname meaning "blue coat," because of his preference for this garment) was one of the first leaders of Switzerland's radical reform movement. In the first public disputations on baptism in Zurich, he argued for believer's baptism and was the first person to receive adult believers' baptism there, having been baptized by Conrad Grebel* in 1525. Blaurock was arrested several times for performing mass adult baptisms and engaging in social disobedience by disrupting worship services. He was eventually expelled from Zurich but continued preaching and baptizing in various Swiss cantons until his execution.

Bohemian Confession (1535). Bohemian Christianity was subdivided between traditional Catholics, Utraquists (who demanded Communion in both kinds) and the *Unitas Fratrum*, who were not Protestants but whose theology bore strong affinities to the Waldensians and the Reformed. The 1535 Latin edition of this confession—an earlier Czech edition had already been drafted—was an attempt to clarify and redefine the beliefs of the

Unitas Fratrum. This confession purged all earlier openness to rebaptism and inched toward Luther's* eucharistic theology. Jan Augusta (c. 1500–1572) and Jan Roh (also Johannes Horn; c. 1490–1547) presented the confession to King Ferdinand I (1503–1564) in Vienna, but the king would not print it. The *Unitas Fratrum* sought, and with slight amendments eventually obtained, Luther's advocacy of the confession. It generally follows the structure of the Augsburg Confession (1530).

Bohemian Confession (1575). This confession was an attempt to shield Bohemian Christian minorities—the Utraquists and the *Unitas Fratrum*—from the Counter-Reformation and Habsburg insistence on uniformity. The hope was that this umbrella consensus would ensure peace in the midst of Christian diversity; anyone who affirmed the 1575 Confession, passed by the Bohemian legislature, would be tolerated. This confession was, like the Bohemian Confession of 1535, patterned after the Augsburg Confession. It emphasizes both justification by faith alone and good works as the fruit of salvation. Baptism and the Eucharist are the focus of the sacramental section, although the five traditional Catholic sacraments are also listed for the Utraquists. Though it was eventually accepted in 1609 by Rudolf II (1552–1612), the Thirty Years' War (1618–1648) rendered the confession moot.

Book of Common Prayer (1549; 1552). After the Church of England's break with Rome, it needed a liturgical manual to distinguish its theology and practice from that of Catholicism. Thomas Cranmer* drafted the Book of Common Prayer based on the medieval Roman Missal, under the dual influence of the revised Lutheran Mass and the reforms of the Spanish Cardinal Quiñones. This manual details the eucharistic service, as well as services for rites such as baptism, confirmation, marriage and funerals. It includes a matrix of the epistle and Gospel readings and the appropriate collect for each Sunday and feast day of the church year. The 1548 Act of Uniformity established the Book of Common Prayer as *the* authoritative liturgical manual for the Church of England,

to be implemented everywhere by Pentecost 1549. After its 1552 revision, Queen Mary I banned it; Elizabeth reestablished it in 1559, although it was rejected by Puritans and Catholics alike.

Thieleman Jans van Braght (1625–1664). Dutch Radical preacher. After demonstrating great ability with languages, this cloth merchant was made preacher in his hometown of Dordrecht in 1648. He served in this office for the next sixteen years, until his death. This celebrated preacher had a reputation for engaging in debate wherever an opportunity presented itself, particularly concerning infant baptism. The publication of his book of martyrs, *Het Bloedigh Tooneel of Martelaersspiegel* (1660; *Martyrs' Mirror*), proved to be his lasting contribution to the Mennonite tradition. *Martyrs' Mirror* is heavily indebted to the earlier martyr book *Offer des Heeren* (1562), to which Braght added many early church martyrs who rejected infant baptism, as well as over 800 contemporary martyrs.

Johannes Brenz (1499–1570). German Lutheran theologian and pastor. Brenz was converted to the reformation cause after hearing Martin Luther* speak; later, Brenz became a student of Johannes Oecolampadius.* His central achievement lay in his talent for organization. As city preacher in Schwäbisch-Hall and afterward in Württemberg and Tübingen, he oversaw the introduction of reform measures and doctrines and new governing structures for ecclesial and educational communities. Brenz also helped establish Lutheran orthodoxy through treatises, commentaries and catechisms. He defended Luther's position on eucharistic presence against Huldrych Zwingli* and opposed the death penalty for religious dissenters.

Guillaume Briçonnet (1470–1534). French Catholic abbot and bishop. Briçonnet created a short-lived circle of reformist-minded humanists in his diocese under the sponsorship of Marguerite d'Angoulême. His desire for ecclesial reform developed throughout his prestigious career (including positions as royal chaplain to the queen, abbot at Saint-Germain-des-Prés and bishop of Meaux), influenced by Jacques Lefèvre d'Étaples.*

Briçonnet encouraged reform through ministerial visitation, Scripture and preaching in the vernacular and active study of the Bible. When this triggered the ire of the theology faculty at the Sorbonne in Paris, Briçonnet quelled the activity and departed, envisioning an ecclesial reform that proceeded hierarchically.

Otto Brunfels (c. 1488–1534). German Lutheran botanist, teacher and physician. Brunfels joined the Carthusian order, where he developed interests in the natural sciences and became involved with a humanist circle associated with Ulrich von Hutten and Wolfgang Capito.* In 1521, after coming into contact with Luther's* teaching, Brunfels abandoned the monastic life, traveling and spending time in botanical research and pastoral care. He received a medical degree in Basel and was appointed city physician of Bern in 1534. Brunfels penned defenses of Luther and Hutten, devotional biographies of biblical figures, a prayer book, and annotations on the Gospels and the Acts of the Apostles. His most influential contribution, however, is as a Renaissance botanist.

Martin Bucer (1491–1551). German Reformed theologian and pastor. A Dominican friar, Bucer was influenced by Desiderius Erasmus* during his doctoral studies at the University of Heidelberg, where he began corresponding with Martin Luther.* After advocating reform in Alsace, Bucer was excommunicated and fled to Strasbourg, where he became a leader in the city's Reformed ecclesial and educational communities. Bucer sought concord between Lutherans and Zwinglians and Protestants and Catholics. He emigrated to England, becoming a professor at Cambridge. Bucer's greatest theological concern was the centrality of Christ's sacrificial death, which achieved justification and sanctification and orients Christian community.

Johannes Bugenhagen (1485–1558). German Lutheran pastor and professor. Bugenhagen, a priest and lecturer at a Premonstratensian monastery, became a city preacher in Wittenberg during the reform efforts of Martin Luther* and Philipp Melanchthon.* Initially influenced by

his reading of Desiderius Erasmus,* Bugenhagen grew in evangelical orientation through Luther's works; later, he studied under Melanchthon at the University of Wittenberg, eventually serving as rector and faculty member there. Bugenhagen was a versatile commentator, exegete and lecturer on Scripture. Through these roles and his development of lectionary and devotional material, Bugenhagen facilitated rapid establishment of church order throughout many German provinces.

Heinrich Bullinger (1504–1575). Swiss Reformed pastor and theologian. Bullinger succeeded Huldrych Zwingli* as minister and leader in Zurich. The primary author of the First and Second Helvetic Confessions* (1536; 1566), Bullinger was drawn toward reform through the works of Martin Luther* and Philipp Melanchthon.* After Zwingli died, Bullinger was vital in maintaining adherence to the cause of reform; he oversaw the expansion of the Zurich synodal system while preaching, teaching and writing extensively. One of Bullinger's lasting legacies was the development of a federal view of the divine covenant with humanity, making baptism and the Eucharist covenantal signs.

John Bunyan (1628–1688). English Puritan preacher and writer. His *Pilgrim's Progress* is one of the best-selling English-language titles in history. Born to a working-class family, Bunyan was largely unschooled, gaining literacy (and entering the faith) through reading the Bible and such early Puritan devotional works as *The Plain Man's Pathway to Heaven* and *The Practice of Piety*. Following a short stint in Cromwell's parliamentary army, in which Bunyan narrowly escaped death in combat, he turned to a preaching ministry, succeeding John Gifford as pastor at the Congregational church in Bedford. A noted preacher, Bunyan drew large crowds in itinerant appearances and it was in the sermonic form that Bunyan developed his theological outlook, which was an Augustinian-inflected Calvinism. Bunyan's opposition to the Book of Common Prayer and refusal of official ecclesiastical licensure led to multiple imprisonments, where he wrote many of his famous allegorical works, including *Pilgrim's Progress, The Holy City, Prison Meditations* and *Holy War*.

Jeremiah Burroughs (c. 1600–1646). English Puritan pastor and delegate to the Westminster Assembly (1643–1649). Burroughs left Emmanuel College, Cambridge, as well as a rectorate in Norfolk, because of his nonconformity. After returning to England from pastoring an English congregation in Rotterdam for several years (1637–1641), he became one of only a few dissenters from the official presbyterianism of the Assembly in favor of a congregationalist polity. Nevertheless, he was well known and respected by presbyterian colleagues such as Richard Baxter* for his irenic tone and conciliatory manner. The vast majority of Burroughs's corpus was published posthumously, although during his lifetime he published annotations on Hosea and several polemical works.

Cardinal Cajetan (Thomas de Vio) (1469–1534). Italian Catholic cardinal, professor, theologian and biblical exegete. This Dominican monk was the leading Thomist theologian and one of the most important Catholic exegetes of the sixteenth century. Cajetan is best-known for his interview with Martin Luther* at the Diet of Augsburg (1518). Among his many works are polemical treatises, extensive biblical commentaries and most importantly a four-volume commentary (1508–1523) on the *Summa Theologiae* of Thomas Aquinas.

Georg Calixtus (1586–1656). German Lutheran theologian. Calixtus studied at the University of Helmstedt where he developed regard for Philipp Melanchthon.* Between his time as a student and later as a professor at Helmstedt, Calixtus traveled through Europe seeking a way to unite and reconcile Lutherans, Calvinists and Catholics. He attempted to fuse these denominations through use of the Scriptures, the Apostles' Creed, and the first five centuries, interpreted by the Vincentian canon. Calixtus's position was stamped as syncretist and yielded further debate even after his death.

John Calvin (1509–1564). French Reformed pastor and theologian. In his *Institutes of the Christian Religion*, Calvin provided a theological dogmatics for the Reformed churches. Calvin's gradual conversion to the cause of reform occurred through his study with chief humanist scholars in Paris, but he spent most of his career in Geneva (excepting a three-year exile in Strasbourg with Martin Bucer*). In Geneva, Calvin reorganized the structure and governance of the church and established an academy that became an international center for theological education. He was a tireless writer, producing his *Institutes*, theological treatises and Scripture commentaries.

Wolfgang Capito (1478?–1541). German Reformed humanist and theologian. Capito, a Hebrew scholar, produced a Hebrew grammar and published several Latin commentaries on books of the Hebrew Scriptures. He corresponded with Desiderius Erasmus* and fellow humanists. Capito translated Martin Luther's* early works into Latin for the printer Johann Froben. On meeting Luther, Capito was converted to Luther's vision, left Mainz and settled in Strasbourg, where he lectured on Luther's theology to the city clergy. With Martin Bucer,* Capito reformed liturgy, ecclesial life and teachings, education, welfare and government. Capito worked for the theological unification of the Swiss cantons with Strasbourg.

Thomas Cartwright (1535–1606). English Puritan preacher and professor. Cartwright was educated at St. John's College, Cambridge, although as an influential leader of the Presbyterian party in the Church of England he was continually at odds with the Anglican party, especially John Whitgift.* Cartwright spent some time as an exile in Geneva and Heidelberg as well as in Antwerp, where he pastored an English church. In 1585, Cartwright was arrested and eventually jailed for trying to return to England despite Elizabeth I's refusal of his request. Many acknowledged him to be learned but also quite cantankerous. His publications include commentaries on Colossians, Ecclesiastes, Proverbs and the Gospels, as well as a dispute against Whitgift on church discipline.

Martin Chemnitz (1522–1586). German Lutheran theologian. A leading figure in establishing Lutheran orthodoxy, Chemnitz studied theology and patristics at the University of Wittenburg, later becoming a defender of Philipp Melanchthon's* interpretation of the doctrine of justification. Chemnitz drafted a compendium of doctrine and reorganized the structure of the church in Wolfenbüttel; later, he led efforts to reconcile divisions within Lutheranism, culminating in the Formula of Concord*. One of his chief theological accomplishments was a modification of the christological doctrine of the *communicatio idiomatium*, which provided a Lutheran platform for understanding the sacramental presence of Christ's humanity in the Eucharist.

David Chytraeus (1531–1600). German Lutheran professor, theologian and biblical exegete. At the age of eight Chytraeus was admitted to the University of Tübingen. There he studied law, philology, philosophy, and theology, finally receiving his master's degree in 1546. Chytraeus befriended Philipp Melanchthon* while sojourning in Wittenberg, where he taught the *Loci communes*. While teaching exegesis at the University of Rostock Chytraeus became acquainted with Tilemann Heshusius,* who strongly influenced Chytraeus away from Philippist theology. As a defender of Gnesio-Lutheran theology Chytraeus helped organize churches throughout Austria in accordance with the Augsburg Confession. Chytraeus coauthored the Formula of Concord* with Martin Chemnitz,* Andreas Musculus (1514–1581), Nikolaus Selnecker* and Jakob Andreae (1528–1590). He wrote commentaries on most of the Bible, as well as a devotional work titled *Regula vitae* (1555) that described the Christian virtues.

John Colet (1467–1519). English Catholic priest, preacher and educator. Colet, appointed dean of Saint Paul's Cathedral by Henry VII, was a friend of Desiderius Erasmus,* on whose classical ideals Colet reconstructed the curriculum of Saint Paul's school. Colet was convinced that the foundation of moral reform lay in the education of children. Though an ardent advocate of reform, Colet, like Erasmus, remained loyal to the Catholic Church throughout his life. Colet's agenda of reform was oriented around spiritual and ethical themes, demonstrated in his commentaries on select books of the New Testament and the writings of Pseudo-Dionysius the Areopagite.

Gasparo Contarini (1483–1542). Italian statesman, theologian and reform-minded cardinal. Contarini was an able negotiator and graceful compromiser. Charles V requested Contarini as the papal legate for the Colloquy of Regensburg (1541), where Contarini reached agreement with Melanchthon* on the doctrine of justification (although neither the pope nor Luther* ratified the agreement). He had come to a similar belief in the priority of faith in the work of Christ rather than works as the basis for Christian life in 1511, though unlike Luther, he never left the papal church over the issue; instead he remainied within it to try to seek gentle reform, and he adhered to papal sacramental teaching. Contarini was an important voice for reform within the Catholic Church, always seeking reconciliation rather than confrontation with Protestant reformers. He wrote many works, including a treatise detailing the ideal bishop, a manual for lay church leaders, a political text on right governance, and brief commentaries on the Pauline letters.

Miles Coverdale (1488–1568). Anglican bishop. Coverdale is known for his translations of the Bible into English, completing William Tyndale's* efforts and later producing the Great Bible commissioned by Henry VIII (1539). A former friar, Coverdale was among the Cambridge scholars who met at the White Horse Tavern to discuss Martin Luther's* ideas. During Coverdale's three terms of exile in Europe, he undertook various translations, including the Geneva Bible*. He was appointed bishop of Exeter by Thomas Cranmer* and served as chaplain to Edward VI. Coverdale contributed to Cranmer's first edition of the Book of Common Prayer (1549).

Thomas Cranmer (1489–1556). Anglican archbishop and theologian. Cranmer supervised church reform and produced the first two editions of the Book of Common Prayer (1549; 1552). As a doctoral student at Cambridge, he was involved in the discussions at the White Horse Tavern. Cranmer contributed to a religious defense of Henry VIII's divorce; Henry then appointed him Archbishop of Canterbury. Cranmer cautiously steered the course of reform, accelerating under Edward VI. After supporting the attempted coup to prevent Mary's assuming the throne, Cranmer was convicted of treason and burned at the stake. Cranmer's legacy is the splendid English of his liturgy and prayer books.

Richard Crashaw (1612–1649). English Catholic poet. Educated at Cambridge, Crashaw was fluent in Hebrew, Greek and Latin. His first volume of poetry was *Epigrammatum sacrorum liber* (1634). Despite being born into a Puritan family, Crashaw was attracted to Catholicism, finally converting in 1644 after he was forced to resign his fellowship for not signing the Solemn League and Covenant (1643). In 1649, he was made a subcanon of Our Lady of Loretto by Cardinal Palotta.

Caspar Cruciger (1504–1548). German Lutheran theologian. Recognized for his alignment with the theological views of Philipp Melanchthon,* Cruciger was a scholar respected among both Protestants and Catholics. In 1521, Cruciger came Wittenberg to study Hebrew and remained there most of his life. He became a valuable partner for Martin Luther* in translating the Old Testament and served as teacher, delegate to major theological colloquies and rector. Cruciger was an agent of reform in his birthplace of Leipzig, where at the age of fifteen he had observed the disputation between Luther and Johann Eck.*

Jean Daillé (1594–1670). French Huguenot pastor. Born into a devout Reformed family, Daillé studied theology and philosophy at Saumur under the most influential contemporary lay leader in French Protestantism, Philippe Duplessis-Mornay (1549–1623). Daillé held to Amyraldianism—the belief that Christ died for all humanity inclusively, not particularly for the elect who would inherit salvation (though only the elect are in fact saved). He wrote a controversial treatise on the church fathers that aggravated many Catholic and Anglican scholars because of Daillé's apparent demotion of

patristic authority in matters of faith.

John Davenant (1576–1641). Anglican bishop and professor. Davenant attended Queen's College, Cambridge, where he received his doctorate and was appointed professor of divinity. During the Remonstrant controversy, James I (1566–1625) sent Davenant as one of the four representatives for the Church of England to the Synod of Dordrecht.* Following James's instructions, Davenant advocated a *via media* between the Calvinists and the Remonstrants, although in later years he defended against the rise of Arminianism in England. In 1621, Davenant was promoted to the bishopric of Salisbury, where he was generally receptive to Laudian reforms. Davenant's lectures on Colossians are his best-known work.

Defense of the Augsburg Confession (1531). See *Augsburg Confession*.

Hans Denck (c. 1500–1527). German Radical theologian. Denck, a crucial early figure of the German Anabaptist movement, combined medieval German mysticism with the radical sacramental theology of Andreas Bodenstein von Karlstadt* and Thomas Müntzer.* Denck argued that the exterior forms of Scripture and sacrament are symbolic witnesses secondary to the internally revealed truth of the Sprit in the human soul. This view led to his expulsion from Nuremberg in 1525; he spent the next two years in various centers of reform in the German territories. At the time of his death, violent persecution against Anabaptists was on the rise throughout northern Europe.

Stephen Denison (unknown). English Puritan pastor. Denison received the post of curate at St. Katherine Cree in London sometime in the 1610s, where he ministered until his ejection from office in 1635. During his career at St. Katherine Cree, Denison waded into controversy with both Puritans (over the doctrine of predestination) and Anglicans (over concerns about liturgical ceremonies). He approached both altercations with rancor and rigidity, although he seems to have been quite popular and beloved by most of his congregation. In 1631, William Laud* consecrated the newly renovated St. Katherine Cree, and as part of the festivities Denison offered a sermon on Luke 19:27 in which he publicly rebuked Laud for fashioning the Lord's house into a "den of robbers." Aside from the record of his quarrels, very little is known about Denison. In addition to *The White Wolf* (a 1627 sermon against another opponent), he published a catechism for children (1621), a treatise on the sacraments (1621) and a commentary on 2 Peter 1 (1622).

David Dickson (1583?–1663). Scottish Reformed pastor, preacher, professor and theologian. Dickson defended the Presbyterian form of ecclesial reformation in Scotland and was recognized for his iteration of Calvinist federal theology and expository biblical commentaries. Dickson served for over twenty years as professor of philosophy at the University of Glasgow before being appointed professor of divinity. He opposed the imposition of Episcopalian measures on the church in Scotland and was active in political and ecclesial venues to protest and prohibit such influences. Dickson was removed from his academic post following his refusal of the oath of supremacy during the Restoration era.

Giovanni Diodati (1576–1649). Italian Reformed theologian. Diodati was from an Italian banking family who fled for religious reasons to Geneva. There he trained under Theodore Beza;* on completion of his doctoral degree, Diodati became professor of Hebrew at the academy. He was an ecclesiastical representative of the church in Geneva (for whom he was a delegate at the Synod of Dordrecht*) and an advocate for reform in Venice. Diodati's chief contribution to the Italian reform movement was a translation of the Bible into Italian (1640–1641), which remains the standard translation in Italian Protestantism.

John Donne (1572–1631). Anglican poet and preacher. Donne was born into a strong Catholic family. However, sometime between his brother's death from the plague while in prison in 1593 and the publication of his *Pseudo-Martyr* in 1610, Donne joined the Church of England. Ordained to the Anglican priesthood in 1615 and already widely recognized for his verse, Donne quickly

rose to prominence as a preacher—some have deemed him the best of his era. His textual corpus is an amalgam of erotic *and* divine poetry (e.g., "Batter My Heart"), as well as a great number of sermons.

John Downame (c. 1571–1652). English Puritan pastor and theologian. See *English Annotations*.

Johann Eck (Johann Maier of Eck) (1486–1543). German Catholic theologian. Though Eck was not an antagonist of Martin Luther* until the dispute over indulgences, Luther's Ninety-five Theses (1517) sealed the two as adversaries. After their debate at the Leipzig Disputation (1519), Eck participated in the writing of the papal bull that led to Luther's excommunication. Much of Eck's work was written to oppose Protestantism or to defend Catholic doctrine and the papacy; his *Enchiridion* was a manual written to counter Protestant doctrine. However, Eck was also deeply invested in the status of parish preaching, publishing a five-volume set of postils. He participated in the assemblies at Regensburg and Augsburg and led the Catholics in their rejection of the Augsburg Confession.

English Annotations (1645; 1651; 1657). Under a commission from the Westminster Assembly (1643–1649), the editors of the English Annotations—John Downame* along with unnamed colleagues—translated, collated and digested in a compact and accessible format several significant Continental biblical resources, including Calvin's* commentaries, Beza's* *Annotationes majores* and Diodati's* *Annotations*.

Desiderius Erasmus (1466–1536). Dutch Catholic humanist and pedagogue. Erasmus, a celebrated humanist scholar, was recognized for translations of ancient texts, reform of education according to classical studies, moral and spiritual writings and the first printed edition of the Greek New Testament. A former Augustinian who never left the Catholic Church, Erasmus addressed deficiencies he saw in the church and society, challenging numerous prevailing doctrines but advocating reform. He envisioned a simple, spiritual Christian life shaped by the teachings of Jesus and ancient wisdom. He was often accused of collusion with Martin Luther* on account of some resonance of their ideas but hotly debated Luther on human will.

Paul Fagius (1504–1549). German Reformed Hebraist and pastor. After studying at the University of Heidelberg, Fagius went to Strasbourg where he perfected his Hebrew under Wolfgang Capito.* In Isny im Allgäu (Baden-Württemberg) he met the great Jewish grammarian Elias Levita (1469–1549), with whom he established a Hebrew printing press. In 1544 Fagius returned to Strasbourg, succeeding Capito as preacher and Old Testament lecturer. During the Augsburg Interim, Fagius (with Martin Bucer*) accepted Thomas Cranmer's* invitation to translate and interpret the Bible at Cambridge. However, Fagius died before he could begin any of the work. Fagius wrote commentaries on the first four chapters of Genesis and the deutero-canonical books of Sirach and Tobit.

First Helvetic Confession (1536). Anticipating the planned church council at Mantua (1537, but delayed until 1545 at Trent), Reformed theologians of the Swiss cantons drafted a confession to distinguish themselves from both Catholics and the churches of the Augsburg Confession.* Heinrich Bullinger* led the discussion and wrote the confession itself; Leo Jud, Oswald Myconius, Simon Grynaeus and others were part of the assembly. Martin Bucer* and Wolfgang Capito* had desired to draw the Lutheran and Reformed communions closer together through this document, but Luther* proved unwilling after Bullinger refused to accept the Wittenberg Concord (1536). This confession was largely eclipsed by Bullinger's Second Helvetic Confession.*

John Flavel (c. 1630–1691). English Puritan pastor. Trained at Oxford, Flavel ministered in southwest England from 1650 until the Act of Uniformity in 1662, which reaffirmed the compulsory use of the Book of Common Prayer. Flavel preached unofficially for many years, until his congregation was eventually allowed to build a meeting place in 1687. His works were numerous, varied and popular.

Formula of Concord (1577). After Luther's* death, intra-Lutheran controversies between the Gnesio-Lutherans (partisans of Luther) and the Philippists (partisans of Melanchthon*) threatened to cause a split among those who had subscribed to the Augsburg Confession (1530). In 1576, Jakob Andreae (1528–1590), Martin Chemnitz,* Nikolaus Selnecker,* David Chytraeus* and Andreas Musculus (1514–1581) met with the intent of resolving the controversies, which mainly regarded the relationship between good works and salvation, the third use of the law, and the role of the human will in accepting God's grace. In 1580, celebrating the fiftieth anniversary of the presentation of the Augsburg Confession to Charles V (1500–1558), the *Book of Concord* was printed as the authoritative interpretation of the Augsburg Confession; it included the three ancient creeds, the Augsburg Confession, its Apology (1531), the Schmalkald Articles,* Luther's *Treatise on the Power and Primacy of the Pope* (1537) and both his Small and Large Catechisms (1529).

Sebastian Franck (1499–1542). German Radical theologian. Franck became a Lutheran in 1525, but by 1529 he began to develop ideas that distanced him from Protestants and Catholics. Expelled from Strasbourg and later Ulm due to his controversial writings, Franck spent the end of his life in Basel. Franck emphasized God's word as a divine internal spark that cannot be adequately expressed in outward forms. Thus he criticized religious institutions and dogmas. His work consists mostly of commentaries, compilations and translations. In his sweeping historical *Chronica* (1531), Franck supported numerous heretics condemned by the Catholic Church and criticized political and church authorities.

Leonhard Frick (d. 1528). Austrian Radical martyr. See *Kunstbuch.*

Gallic Confession (1559). This confession was accepted at the first National Synod of the Reformed Churches of France (1559). It was intended to be a touchstone of Reformed faith but also to show to the people of France that the Huguenots—who faced persecution—were not seditious. The French Reformed Church presented this confession to Francis II (1544–1560) in 1560, and to his successor, Charles IX (1550–1574), in 1561. The later Genevan draft, likely written by Calvin,* Beza,* and Pierre Viret (1511–1571), was received as the true Reformed confession at the seventh National Synod in La Rochelle (1571).

Geneva Bible (originally printed 1560). During Mary I's reign many English Protestants sought safety abroad in Reformed territories of the Empire and the Swiss Cantons, especially in Calvin's* Geneva. A team of English exiles in Geneva led by William Whittingham (c. 1524–1579) brought this complete translation to press in the course of two years. Notable for several innovations—Roman type, verse numbers, italics indicating English idiom and not literal phrasing of the original languages, even variant readings in the Gospels and Acts—this translation is most well known for its marginal notes, which reflect a strongly Calvinist theology. The notes explained Scripture in an accessible way for the laity, also giving unlearned clergy a new sermon resource. Although controversial because of its implicit critique of royal power, this translation was wildly popular; even after the publication of the Authorized Version (1611) and James I's (1566–1625) 1616 ban on its printing, the Geneva Bible continued to be the most popular English translation until after the English Civil Wars (1642–1651).

Johann Gerhard (1582–1637). German Lutheran theologian, professor and superintendent. Gerhard is considered one of the most eminent Lutheran theologians, after Martin Luther* and Martin Chemnitz.* After studying patristics and Hebrew at Wittenberg, Jena and Marburg, Gerhard was appointed superintendent at the age of twenty-four. In 1616 he was appointed to a post at the University of Jena, where he reintroduced Aristotelian metaphysics to theology and gained widespread fame. His most important work was the nine-volume *Loci Theologici* (1610–1625). He also expanded Chemnitz's harmony of the Gospels (*Harmonia Evangelicae*), which was finally published by Polykarp Leyser* in 1593. Gerhard was well-known for an irenic spirit and an ability to communicate clearly.

Conrad Grebel (c. 1498–1526). Swiss Radical theologian. Grebel, considered the father of the Anabaptist movement, was one of the first defenders and performers of believers' baptism, for which he was eventually imprisoned in Zurich. One of Huldrych Zwingli's* early compatriots, Grebel advocated rapid, radical reform, clashing publicly with the civil authorities and Zwingli. Grebel's views, particularly on baptism, were influenced by Andreas Bodenstein von Karlstadt* and Thomas Müntzer.* Grebel advocated elimination of magisterial involvement in governing the church; instead, he envisioned the church as lay Christians determining their own affairs with strict adherence to the biblical text, and unified in volitional baptism.

William Greenhill (1591–1671). English Puritan pastor. Greenhill attended and worked at Magdalen College. He ministered in the diocese of Norwich but soon left for London, where he preached at Stepney. Greenhill was a member of the Westminster Assembly of Divines and was appointed the parliament chaplain by the children of Charles I. Oliver Cromwell included him among the preachers who helped draw up the Savoy Declaration. Greenhill was evicted from his post following the Restoration, after which he pastored independently. Among Greenhill's most significant contributions to church history was his *Exposition of the Prophet of Ezekiel.*

Rudolf Gwalther (1519–1586). Swiss Reformed preacher. Gwalther was a consummate servant of the Reformed church in Zurich, its chief religious officer and preacher, a responsibility fulfilled previously by Huldrych Zwingli* and Heinrich Bullinger.* Gwalther provided sermons and commentaries and translated the works of Zwingli into Latin. He worked for many years alongside Bullinger in structuring and governing the church in Zurich. Gwalther also strove to strengthen the connections to the Reformed churches on the Continent and England: he was a participant in the Colloquy of Regensburg (1541) and an opponent of the Formula of Concord.

Hans Has von Hallstatt (d. 1527). Austrian Reformed pastor. See *Kunstbuch*.

Heidelberg Catechism (1563). This German Reformed catechism was commissioned by the elector of the Palatinate, Frederick III (1515–1576) for pastors and teachers in his territories to use in instructing children and new believers in the faith. It was written by theologian Zacharias Ursinus (1534–1583) in consultation with Frederick's court preacher Kaspar Olevianus* and the entire theology faculty at the University of Heidelberg. The Heidelberg Catechism was accepted as one of the Dutch Reformed Church's Three Forms of Unity—along with the Belgic Confession* and the Canons of Dordrecht—at the Synod of Dordrecht,* and became widely popular among other Reformed confessional traditions throughout Europe.

Richard Hooker (c. 1553–1600). Anglican priest. Shortly after graduating from Corpus Christi College Oxford, Hooker took holy orders as a priest in 1581. After his marriage, he struggled to find work and temporarily tended sheep until Archbishop John Whitgift* appointed him to the Temple Church in London. Hooker's primary work is *The Laws of Ecclesiastical Polity* (1593), in which he sought to establish a philosophical and logical foundation for the highly controversial Elizabethan Religious Settlement (1559). The Elizabethan Settlement, through the Act of Supremacy, reasserted the Church of England's independence from the Church of Rome, and, through the Act of Uniformity, constructed a common church structure based on the reinstitution of the Book of Common Prayer. Hooker's argumentation strongly emphasizes natural law and anticipates the social contract theory of John Locke (1632–1704).

Balthasar Hubmaier (1480/5–1528). German Radical theologian. Hubmaier, a former priest who studied under Johann Eck,* is identified with his leadership in the peasants' uprising at Waldshut. Hubmaier served as the cathedral preacher in Regensberg, where he became involved in a series of anti-Semitic attacks. He was drawn to reform through the early works of Martin Luther*; his contact with Huldrych Zwingli* made Hubmaier a defender of more radical reform, including believers' baptism and a memorialist account of the Eucharist. His involvement in the Peasants' War led to his extradition and execution by the Austrians.

Hans Hut (1490–1527). German Radical leader. Hut was an early leader of a mystical, apocalyptic strand of Anabaptist radical reform. His theological views were shaped by Andreas Bodenstein von Karlstadt,* Thomas Müntzer* and Hans Denck,* by whom Hut had been baptized. Hut rejected society and the established church and heralded the imminent end of days, which he perceived in the Peasants' War. Eventually arrested for practicing believers' baptism and participating in the Peasants' War, Hut was tortured and died accidentally in a fire in the Augsburg prison. The next day, the authorities sentenced his corpse to death and burned him.

Valentin Ickelshamer (c. 1500–1547). German Radical teacher. After time at Erfurt, he studied under Luther,* Melanchthon,* Bugenhagen* and Karlstadt* in Wittenberg. He sided with Karlstadt against Luther, writing a treatise in Karlstadt's defense. Ickelshamer also represented the Wittenberg guilds in opposition to the city council. This guild committee allied with the peasants in 1525, leading to Ickelshamer's eventual exile. His poem in the Marpeck Circle's *Kunstbuch* is an expansion of a similar poem by Sebastian Franck.*

Justus Jonas (1493–1555). German Lutheran theologian, pastor and administrator. Jonas studied law at Erfurt, where he befriended the poet Eobanus Hessus (1488–1540), whom Luther* dubbed "king of the poets"; later, under the influence of the humanist Konrad Muth, Jonas focused on theology. In 1516 he was ordained as a priest, and in 1518 he became a doctor of theology and law. After witnessing the Leipzig Disputation, Jonas was converted to Luther's* cause. While traveling with Luther to the Diet of Worms,

Jonas was appointed professor of canon law at Wittenberg. Later he became its dean of theology, lecturing on Romans, Acts and the Psalms. Jonas was also instrumental for reform in Halle. He preached Luther's funeral sermon but had a falling-out with Melanchthon* over the Leipzig Interim. Jonas's most influential contribution was translating Luther's *The Bondage of the Will* and Melanchthon's *Loci communes* into German.

David Joris (c. 1501–1556). Dutch Radical pastor and hymnist. This former glass painter was one of the leading Dutch Anabaptist leaders after the fall of Münster (1535), although due to his increasingly radical ideas his influence waned in the early 1540s. Joris came to see himself as a "third David," a Spirit-anointed prophet ordained to proclaim the coming third kingdom of God, which would be established in the Netherlands with Dutch as its *lingua franca*. Joris's interpretation of Scripture, with his heavy emphasis on personal mystical experience, led to a very public dispute with Menno Simons* whom Joris considered a teacher of the "dead letter." In 1544 Joris and about one hundred followers moved to Basel, conforming outwardly to the teaching of the Reformed church there. Today 240 of Joris's books are extant, the most important of which is his *Twonder Boek* (1542/43).

Andreas Bodenstein von Karlstadt (Carlstadt) (1486–1541). German Radical theologian. Karlstadt, an early associate of Martin Luther* and Philipp Melanchthon* at the University of Wittenberg, participated alongside Luther in the dispute at Leipzig with Johann Eck.* He also influenced the configuration of the Old Testament canon in Protestantism. During Luther's captivity in Wartburg Castle in Eisenach, Karlstadt oversaw reform in Wittenberg. His acceleration of the pace of reform brought conflict with Luther, so Karlstadt left Wittenberg, eventually settling at the University of Basel as professor of Old Testament (after a sojourn in Zurich with Huldrych Zwingli*). During his time in Switzerland, Karlstadt opposed infant baptism and repudiated Luther's doctrine of Christ's real presence in the Eucharist.

John Knox (1513–1572). Scottish Reformed preacher. Knox, a fiery preacher to monarchs and zealous defender of high Calvinism, was a leading figure of reform in Scotland. Following imprisonment in the French galleys, Knox went to England, where he became a royal chaplain to Edward VI. At the accession of Mary, Knox fled to Geneva, studying under John Calvin* and serving as a pastor. Knox returned to Scotland after Mary's death and became a chief architect of the reform of the Scottish church (Presbyterian), serving as one of the authors of the Book of Discipline and writing many pamphlets and sermons.

Kunstbuch. In 1956, two German students rediscovered this unique collection of Anabaptist works. Four hundred years earlier, a friend of the recently deceased Pilgram Marpeck*—the painter Jörg Probst—had entrusted this collection of letters, tracts and poetry to a Zurich bindery; today only half of it remains. Probst's redaction arranges various compositions from the Marpeck Circle into a devotional anthology focused on the theme of the church as Christ incarnate (cf. Gal 2:20).

François Lambert (Lambert of Avignon) (1487–1530). French Reformed theologian. In 1522, after becoming drawn to the writings of Martin Luther* and meeting Huldrych Zwingli,* Lambert left the Franciscan order. He spent time in Wittenberg, Strasbourg, and Hesse, where Lambert took a leading role at the Homberg Synod (1526) and in creating a biblically based plan for church reform. He served as professor of theology at Marburg University from 1527 to his death. After the Marburg Colloquy (1529), Lambert accepted Zwingli's symbolic view of the Eucharist. Lambert produced nineteen books, mostly biblical commentaries that favored spiritual interpretations; his unfinished work of comprehensive theology was published posthumously.

Hugh Latimer (c. 1485–1555). Anglican bishop and preacher. Latimer was celebrated for his sermons critiquing the idolatrous nature of Catholic practices and the social injustices visited on the underclass by the aristocracy and the individualism of Protestant government. After his support for Henry's petition of divorce he served as a court preacher under Henry VIII and Edward VI. Latimer became a proponent of reform following his education at Cambridge University and received license as a preacher. Following Edward's death, Latimer was tried for heresy, perishing at the stake with Nicholas Ridley* and Thomas Cranmer.*

William Laud (1573–1645). Anglican archbishop, one of the most pivotal and controversial figures in Anglican church history. Early in his career, Laud offended many with his highly traditional, anti-Puritan approach to ecclesial policies. After his election as Archbishop of Canterbury in 1633, Laud continued to strive against the Puritans, demanding the eastward placement of the Communion altar (affirming the religious centrality of the Eucharist), the use of clerical garments, the reintroduction of stained-glass windows, and the uniform use of the Book of Common Prayer. Laud was accused of being a crypto-Catholic—an ominous accusation during the protracted threat of invasion by the Spanish Armada. In 1640 the Long Parliament met, quickly impeached Laud on charges of treason, and placed him in jail for several years before his execution.

Jacques Lefèvre d'Étaples (Faber Stapulensis) (1460?–1536). French Catholic humanist, publisher and translator. Lefèvre d'Étaples studied classical literature and philosophy, as well as patristic and medieval mysticism. He advocated the principle of *ad fontes*, issuing a full-scale annotation on the corpus of Aristotle, publishing the writings of key Christian mystics, and contributing to efforts at biblical translation and commentary. Although he never broke with the Catholic Church, his views prefigured those of Martin Luther,* for which he was condemned by the University of Sorbonne in Paris. He then found refuge in the court of Marguerite d'Angoulême, where he met John Calvin* and Martin Bucer.*

Lucas Lossius (1508–1582). German Lutheran teacher and musician. While a student at Leipzig and Wittenberg, Lossius was deeply influenced by Melanchthon* and Luther,* who found work for him as Urbanus Rhegius's* secretary. Soon after

going to work for Rhegius, Lossius began teaching at a local gymnasium (or secondary school), *Das Johanneum*, eventually becoming its headmaster. Lossius remained at *Das Johanneum* until his death, even turning down appointments to university professorships. A man of varied interests, he wrote on dialectics, music and church history, as well as publishing a postil and a five-volume set of annotations on the New Testament.

Sibrandus Lubbertus (c. 1555–1625). Dutch Reformed theologian. Lubbertis, a key figure in the establishment of orthodox Calvinism in Frisia, studied theology at Wittenburg and Geneva (under Theodore Beza*) before his appointment as professor of theology at the University of Franeker. Throughout his career, Lubbertis advocated for high Calvinist theology, defending it in disputes with representatives of Socinianism, Arminianism and Roman Catholicism. Lubbertis criticized the Catholic theologian Robert Bellarmine and fellow Dutch reformer Jacobus Arminius*; the views of the latter he opposed as a prominent participant in the Synod of Dordrecht.

Martin Luther (1483–1546). German Lutheran priest, professor and theologian. While a professor in Wittenberg, Luther reinterpreted the doctrine of justification. Convinced that righteousness comes only from God's grace, he disputed the sale of indulgences with the Ninety-five Theses. Luther's positions brought conflict with Rome; his denial of papal authority led to excommunication. He also challenged the Mass, transubstantiation and communion under one kind. Though Luther was condemned by the Diet of Worms, the Elector of Saxony provided him safe haven. Luther returned to Wittenberg with public order collapsing under Andreas Bodenstein von Karlstadt;* Luther steered a more cautious path of reform. His rendering of the Bible and liturgy in the vernacular, as well as his hymns and sermons, proved extensively influential.

Georg Major (1502–1574). German Lutheran theologian. Major was on the theological faculty of the University of Wittenberg, succeeding as dean Johannes Bugenhagen* and Philipp Melanchthon.* One of the chief editors on the Wittenberg edition of Luther's works, Major is most identified with the controversy bearing his name, in which he stated that good works are necessary to salvation. Major qualified his statement, which was in reference to the totality of the Christian life. The Formula of Concord* rejected the statement, ending the controversy. As a theologian, Major further refined Lutheran views of the inspiration of Scripture and the doctrine of the Trinity.

Thomas Manton (1620–1677). English Puritan minister. Manton, educated at Oxford, served for a time as lecturer at Westminster Abbey and rector of St. Paul's, Covent Garden, and was a strong advocate of Presbyterianism. He was known as a rigorous evangelical Calvinist who preached long expository sermons. At different times in his ecclesial career he worked side-by-side with Richard Baxter* and John Owen.* In his later life, Manton's Nonconformist position led to his ejection as a clergyman from the Church of England (1662) and eventual imprisonment (1670). Although a voluminous writer, Manton was best known for his preaching. At his funeral in 1677, he was dubbed "the king of preachers."

Pilgram Marpeck (c. 1495–1556). Austrian Radical elder and theologian. During a brief sojourn in Strasbourg, Marpeck debated with Martin Bucer* before the city council; Bucer was declared the winner, and Marpeck was asked to leave Strasbourg for his views concerning paedobaptism (which he compared to a sacrifice to Moloch). After his time in Strasbourg, Marpeck travelled throughout southern Germany and western Austria, planting Anabaptist congregations. Marpeck criticized the strict use of the ban, however, particularly among the Swiss brethren. He also engaged in a Christological controversy with Kaspar von Schwenckfeld.*

John Mayer (1583–1664). Anglican priest and biblical exegete. Mayer dedicated much of his life to biblical exegesis, writing a seven-volume commentary on the entire Bible (1627–1653). Styled after Philipp Melanchthon's* *locus* method, Mayer's work avoided running commentary, focusing instead on textual and theological problems. He was a parish priest for fifty-five years. In the office of priest Mayer also wrote a popular catechism, *The English Catechisme, or a Commentarie on the Short Catechisme* (1621), which went through twelve editions in his lifetime.

Joseph Mede (1586–1638). Anglican biblical scholar, Hebraist and Greek lecturer. A man of encyclopedic knowledge, Mede was interested in numerous fields, varying from philology and history to mathematics and physics, although millennial thought and apocalyptic prophesy were clearly his chief interests. Mede's most important work was his *Clavis Apocalyptica* (1627, later translated into English as *The Key of the Revelation*). This work examined the structure of Revelation as the key to its interpretation. Mede saw the visions as a connected and chronological sequence hinging around Revelation 17:18. He is remembered as an important figure in the history of millenarian theology. He was respected as a mild-mannered and generous scholar who avoided controversy and debate, but who had many original thoughts.

Philipp Melanchthon (1497–1560). German Lutheran educator, reformer and theologian. Melanchthon is known as the partner and successor to Martin Luther* in reform in Germany and for his pioneering *Loci Communes*, which served as a theological textbook. Melanchthon participated with Luther in the Leipzig disputation, helped implement reform in Wittenberg and was a chief architect of the Augsburg Confession. Later, Melanchthon and Martin Bucer* worked for union between the reformed and Catholic churches. On account of Melanchthon's more ecumenical disposition and his modification of several of Luther's doctrines, he was held in suspicion by some.

Johannes Mercerus (Jean Mercier) (d. 1570). French Hebraist. Mercerus studied under the first Hebrew chair at the Collège Royal de Paris, François Vatable (d. 1547), whom he succeeded in 1546. John Calvin* tried to recruit Mercerus to the Genevan Academy as professor of Hebrew, once in 1558 and again in 1563; he refused both times. During his lifetime Mercerus published grammatical helps for Hebrew and Chaldean, an aid to the Masoretic symbols in the Hebrew text, and translated the commentaries and grammars of several medieval rabbis. He himself wrote commentaries on Genesis, the wisdom books, and most of the Minor Prophets. These commentaries—most of them only published after his death—were philologically focused and interacted with the work of Jerome, Nicholas of Lyra,* notable rabbis and Johannes Oecolampadius.*

Sebastian Münster (1488–1552). German Reformed Hebraist, exegete, printer, and geographer. After converting to the Reformation in 1524, Münster taught Hebrew at the universities of Heidelberg and Basel. During his lengthy tenure in Basel he published more than 70 books, including Hebrew dictionaries and rabbinic commentaries. He also produced an evangelistic work for Jews titled *Vikuach* (1539). Münster's *Torat ha-Maschiach* (1537), the Gospel of Matthew, was the first published Hebrew translation of any portion of the New Testament. Despite his massive contribution to contemporary understanding of the Hebrew language, Münster was criticized by many of the reformers as a Judaizer.

Thomas Müntzer (c. 1489–1525). German Radical preacher. As a preacher in the town of Zwickau, Müntzer was influenced by German mysticism and, growing convinced that Martin Luther* had not carried through reform properly, sought to restore the pure apostolic church of the New Testament. Müntzer's radical ideas led to expulsions from various cities; he developed a highly apocalyptic theology, in which he heralded the last days that would establish the pure community out of suffering, prompting Müntzer's proactive role in the Peasants' War, which he perceived as a crucial apocalyptic event. Six thousand of Müntzer's followers were annihilated by magisterial troops; Müntzer was executed.

Wolfgang Musculus (1497–1563). German Reformed pastor and theologian. Musculus produced translations, biblical commentaries and an influential theological text, *Loci Communes Sacrae Theologiae* (*Commonplaces of Sacred Theology*), out-lining a Zwinglian theology. Musculus began to study theology while at a Benedictine monastery; he departed in 1527 and became secretary to Martin Bucer* in Strasbourg. He was later installed as a pastor in Augsburg, eventually performing the first evangelical liturgy in the city's cathedral. Though Musculus was active in the pursuit of the reform agenda, he was also concerned for ecumenism, participating in the Wittenberg Concord (1536) and discussions between Lutherans and Catholics.

Nicholas of Lyra (1270–1349). French Catholic biblical exegete. Very little is known about this influential medieval theologian of the Sorbonne aside from the works he published, particularly the *Postilla litteralis super totam Bibliam* (1322–1333). With the advent of the printing press this work was regularly published alongside the Latin Vulgate and the *Glossa ordinaria*. In this running commentary on the Bible Nicholas promoted literal interpretation as the basis for theology. Despite his preference for literal interpretation, Nicholas also published a companion volume, the *Postilla moralis super totam Bibliam* (1339), a commentary on the spiritual meaning of the biblical text. Nicholas was a major conversation partner for many reformers though many of them rejected his exegesis as too literal and too "Jewish" (not concerned enough with the Bible's fulfillment in Jesus Christ).

Johannes Oecolampadius (Johannes Huszgen) (1482–1531). Swiss-German Reformed humanist, reformer and theologian. Oecolampadius (an assumed name meaning "house light") assisted with Desiderius Erasmus's* Greek New Testament, lectured on biblical languages and exegesis and completed an influential Greek grammar. After joining the evangelical cause through studying patristics and the work of Martin Luther,* Oecolampadius went to Basel, where he lectured on biblical exegesis and participated in ecclesial reform. On account of Oecolampadius's effort, the city council passed legislation restricting preaching to the gospel and releasing the city from compulsory Mass. Oecolampadius was a chief ally of Huldrych Zwingli,* whom he supported at the Marburg Colloquy (1529).

Kaspar Olevianus (1536–1587). German Reformed theologian. Olevianus is celebrated for composing the Heidelberg Catechism and producing a critical edition of Calvin's *Institutes* in German. Olevianus studied theology with many, including John Calvin,* Theodore Beza,* Heinrich Bullinger* and Peter Martyr Vermigli.* As an advocate of Reformed doctrine, Olevianus oversaw the shift from Lutheranism to Calvinism throughout Heidelberg, organizing the city's churches after Calvin's Geneva. The Calvinist ecclesial vision of Olevianus entangled him in a dispute with another Heidelberg reformer over the rights of ecclesiastical discipline, which Olevianus felt belonged to the council of clergy and elders rather than civil magistrates.

John Owen (1616–1683). English Puritan theologian. Owen trained at Oxford University, where he was later appointed dean of Christ Church and vice chancellor of the university, following his service as chaplain to Oliver Cromwell. Although Owen began his career as a Presbyterian minister, he eventually departed to the party of Independents. Owen composed many sermons, biblical commentaries (including seven volumes on the book of Hebrews), theological treatises and controversial monographs (including disputations with Arminians, Anglicans, Catholics and Socinians).

Christoph Pelargus (1565–1633). German Lutheran pastor, theologian, professor and superintendent. Pelargus studied philosophy and theology at the University of Frankfurt an der Oder, in Brandenburg. This irenic Philippist was appointed as the superintendent of Brandenburg and later became a pastor in Frankfurt, although the local authorities first required him to condemn Calvinist theology, because several years earlier he had been called before the consistory in Berlin under suspicion of being a crypto-Calvinist. Among his most important works were a four-volume commentary on *De orthodoxa fide* by John of Damascus (d. 749), a treatise defending the breaking of the bread during communion, and a volume of funeral sermons. He also published commentaries on the Pentateuch, the Psalms, Matthew, John and Acts.

Konrad Pellikan (1478–1556). German Reformed Hebraist and theologian. Pellikan attended the University of Heidelberg, where he mastered Hebrew under Johannes Reuchlin. In 1504 Pellikan published one of the first Hebrew grammars that was not merely a translation of the work of medieval rabbis. While living in Basel, Pellikan assisted the printer Johannes Amerbach, with whom he published some of Luther's* early writings. He also worked with Sebastian Münster* and Wolfgang Capito* on a Hebrew Psalter (1516). In 1526, after teaching theology for three years at the University of Basel, Huldrych Zwingli* brought Pellikan to Zurich to chair the faculty of Old Testament. Pellikan's magnum opus is a seven-volume commentary on the entire Bible (except Revelation) and the Apocrypha; it is often heavily dependent upon the work of others (esp. Desiderius Erasmus and Johannes Oecolampadius*).

Benedict Pererius (1535–1610). Spanish Catholic theologian, philosopher and exegete. Pererius entered the Society of Jesus in 1552. He taught philosophy, theology, and exegesis at the Roman College of the Jesuits. Early in his career he warned against neo-Platonism and astrology in his *De principiis* (1576). Pererius wrote a lengthy commentary on Daniel, and five volumes of exegetical theses on Exodus, Romans, Revelation and part of the Gospel of John (chs. 1–14). His four-volume commentary on Genesis (1591–1599) was lauded by Protestants and Catholics alike.

William Perkins (1558–1602). English Puritan preacher and theologian. Perkins was a highly regarded Puritan Presbyterian preacher and biblical commentator in the Elizabethan era. He studied at Cambridge University and later became a fellow of Christ's Church college as a preacher and professor, receiving acclaim for his sermons and lectures. Even more, Perkins gained an esteemed reputation for his ardent exposition of Calvinist reformed doctrine in the style of Petrus Ramus,* becoming one of the first English reformed theologians to achieve international recognition. Perkins influenced the federal Calvinist shape of Puritan theology and the vision of logical, practical expository preaching.

Dirk Philips (1504–1568). Dutch Radical elder and theologian. This former Franciscan monk, known for being severe and obstinate, was a leading theologian of the sixteenth-century Anabaptist movement. Despite the fame of Menno Simons* and his own older brother Obbe, Philips wielded great influence over Anabaptists in the Netherlands and northern Germany where he ministered. As a result of Philips's understanding of the apostolic church as radically separated from the children of the world, he advocated a very strict interpretation of the ban, including formal shunning. His writings were collected and published near the end of his life as *Enchiridion oft Hantboecxken van de Christelijcke Leere* (1564).

Petrus Ramus (1515–1572). French Reformed humanist philosopher. Ramus was an influential professor of philosophy and logic at the French royal college in Paris; he converted to Protestantism and left France for Germany, where he came under the influence of Calvinist thought. Ramus was a trenchant critic of Aristotle and noted for his method of classification based on a deductive movement from universals to particulars, the latter becoming branching divisions that provided a visual chart of the parts to the whole. His system profoundly influenced Puritan theology and preaching. After returning to Paris, Ramus died in the Saint Bartholomew's Day Massacre.

Remonstrance (1609). See *Synod of Dordrecht*.

Urbanus Rhegius (1489–1541). German Lutheran pastor. Rhegius, who was likely the son of a priest, studied under the humanists at Freiburg and Ingolstadt. After a brief stint as a foot soldier, he received ordination in 1519 and was made cathedral preacher in Augsburg. During his time in Augsburg he closely read Luther's* works, becoming an enthusiastic follower. Despite his close friendship with Zwingli* and Oecolampadius,*

Rhegius supported Luther in the eucharistic debates, later playing a major role in the Wittenberg Concord (1536). He advocated for peace during the Peasants' War and had extended interactions with the Anabaptists in Augsburg. Later in his career he concerned himself with the training of pastors, writing a pastoral guide and two catechisms. About one hundred of his writings were published posthumously.

Lancelot Ridley (d. 1576). Anglican preacher. Ridley was the first cousin of Nicholas Ridley,* the bishop of London who was martyred during the Marian persecutions. By Cranmer's* recommendation, Ridley became one of the six Canterbury Cathedral preachers. Upon Mary I's accession in 1553, Ridley was defrocked (as a married priest). Ridley returned to Canterbury Cathedral after Mary's death. He wrote commentaries on Jude, Ephesians, Philippians and Colossians.

Nicholas Ridley (c. 1502–1555). Anglican bishop. Ridley was a student and fellow at Cambridge University who was appointed chaplain to Archbishop Thomas Cranmer* and is thought to be partially responsible for Cranmer's shift to a symbolic view of the Eucharist. Cranmer promoted Ridley twice: as bishop of Rochester, where he openly advocated Reformed theological views, and, later, as bishop of London. Ridley assisted Cranmer in the revisions of the Book of Common Prayer. Ridley's support of Lady Jane Grey against the claims of Mary to the throne led to his arrest; he was tried for heresy and burned at the stake with Hugh Latimer.*

Peter Riedemann (1506–1556). German Radical elder, theologian and hymnist. While traveling as a Silesian cobbler, Riedemann came into contact with Anabaptist teachings and joined a congregation in Linz. In 1529 he was called to be a minister, only to be imprisoned soon after as part of Archduke Ferdinand's efforts to suppress heterodoxy in his realm. Once he was released, he moved to Moravia in 1532 where he was elected as a minister and missionary of the Hutterite community there. His *Account of Our Religion, Doctrine and Faith* (1542), with its more than two thousand biblical references, is Riedemann's most important work and is still used by Hutterites today.

Robert Rollock (c. 1555–1599). Scottish Reformed pastor, educator and theologian. Rollock was deeply influenced by Petrus Ramus's* system of logic, which he implemented as a tutor and (later) principal of Edinburgh University and in his expositions of the Bible. Rollock, as a divinity professor and theologian, was instrumental in diffusing a federalist Calvinism in the Scottish church; he lectured on theology using the texts of Theodore Beza* and articulated a highly covenantal interpretation of the biblical narratives. He was a prolific writer of sermons, expositions, commentaries, lectures and occasional treatises.

Erasmus Sarcerius (1501–1559). German Lutheran superintendent, educator and pastor. Sarcerius served as educational superintendent, court preacher and pastor in Nassau and, later, in Leipzig. The hallmark of Sarcerius's reputation was his ethical emphasis as exercised through ecclesial oversight and family structure; he also drafted disciplinary codes for regional churches in Germany. Sarcerius served with Philipp Melanchthon* as Protestant delegates at the Council of Trent, though both withdrew prior to the dismissal of the session; he eventually became an opponent of Melanchthon, contesting the latter's understanding of the Eucharist at a colloquy in Worms in 1557.

Michael Sattler (c. 1490–1527). Swiss Radical leader. Sattler was a Benedictine monk who abandoned the monastic life during the upheavals of the Peasants' War. He took up the trade of weaving under the guidance of an outspoken Anabaptist. It seems that Sattler did not openly join the Anabaptist movement until after the suppression of the Peasants' War in 1526. Sattler interceded with Martin Bucer* and Wolfgang Capito* for imprisoned Anabaptists in Strasbourg. Shortly before he was convicted of heresy and executed, he wrote the definitive expression of Anabaptist theology, the Schleitheim Articles.*

Leupold Scharnschlager (d. 1563). Austrian Radical elder. See *Kunstbuch*.

Leonhard Schiemer (d. 1528). Austrian Radical martyr. See *Kunstbuch*.

Hans Schlaffer (c. 1490–1528). Austrian Radical martyr. See *Kunstbuch*.

Schleitheim Articles (1527). After the death of Conrad Grebel* in 1526 and the execution of Felix Manz (born c. 1498) in early 1527, the young Swiss Anabaptist movement was in need of unity and direction. A synod convened at Schleitheim under the chairmanship of Michael Sattler,* which passed seven articles of Anabaptist distinctives—likely defined against both magisterial reformers and other Anabaptists with less orthodox and more militant views (e.g., Balthasar Hubmaier*). Unlike most confessions, these articles do not explicitly address traditional creedal interests; they explicate instead the Anabaptist view of the sacraments, church discipline, separatism, the role of ministers, pacifism and oaths. Throughout the document there is a resolute focus on Christ's example. The Schleitheim Articles are considered the definitive statement of Anabaptist theology, particularly regarding separatism.

Schmalkald Articles (1537). In response to Pope Paul III's (1468–1549) 1536 decree ordering a general church council to solve the Protestant crisis, Elector John Frederick (1503–1554) commissioned Martin Luther* to draft the sum of his teaching. Intended by Luther as a last will and testament—and composed with advice from well-known colleagues Justus Jonas,* Johann Bugenhagen,* Caspar Cruciger,* Nikolaus von Amsdorf (1483–1565), Georg Spalatin (1484–1545), Philipp Melanchthon* and Johann Agricola*—these articles provide perhaps the briefest and most systematic summary of Luther's teaching. The document was not adopted formally by the Lutheran Schmalkald League, as was hoped, and the general church council was postponed for several years (until convening at Trent in 1545). Only in 1580 were the articles officially received, by being incorporated into the *Book of Concord* defining orthodox Lutheranism.

Anna Maria van Schurman (1607–1678). Dutch Reformed polymath. Van Schurman cultivated talents in art, poetry, botany, linguistics and theology. She mastered most contemporary European languages, in addition to Latin, Greek, Hebrew, Arabic, Farsi and Ethiopian. With the encouragement of leading Reformed theologian Gisbertus Voetius (1589–1676), van Schurman attended lectures at the University of Utrecht—although she was required to sit behind a wooden screen so that the male students could not see her. In 1638 van Schurman published her famous treatise advocating female scholarship, *Amica dissertatio . . . de capacitate ingenii muliebris ad scientias*. In addition to these more polemical works, van Schurman also wrote hymns and poems, including a paraphrase of Genesis 1–3. Later in life she became a devotee of Jean de Labadie (1610–1674), a former Jesuit who was also expelled from the Reformed church for his separatist leanings. Her *Eucleria* (1673) is the most well known defense of Labadie's theology.

Kaspar von Schwenckfeld (1489–1561). German Radical reformer. Schwenckfeld was a Silesian nobleman who encountered Luther's* works in 1521. He traveled to Wittenberg twice: first to meet Luther and Karlstadt,* and a second time to convince Luther of his doctrine of the "internal word"—emphasizing inner revelation so strongly that he did not see church meetings or the sacraments as necessary—after which Luther considered him heterodox. Schwenckfeld won his native territory to the Reformation in 1524 and later lived in Strasbourg for five years until Bucer* sought to purify the city of less traditional theologies. Schwenckfeld wrote numerous polemical and exegetical tracts.

Scots Confession (1560). In 1560, the Scottish Parliament undertook to reform the Church of Scotland and to commission a Reformed confession of faith. In the course of four days, a committee—which included John Knox*—wrote this confession, largely based on Calvin's* work, the Confession of the English Congregation in Geneva (1556) and the Gallic Confession.* The articles were not ratified until 1567 and were displaced by the Westminster Confession (1646), adopted by the Scottish in 1647.

Second Helvetic Confession (1566). Believing he would soon die, Heinrich Bullinger* penned a personal statement of his Reformed faith in 1561 as a theological will. In 1563, Bullinger sent a copy of this confession, which blended Zwingli's and Calvin's theology, to the elector of the Palatinate, Frederick III (1515–1576), who had asked for a complete explication of the Reformed faith in order to defend himself against aggressive Lutheran attacks after printing the Heidelberg Confession.* Although not published until 1566, the Second Helvetic Confession became the definitive sixteenth-century Reformed statement of faith. Theodore Beza* used it as the organizing confession for his *Harmonia Confessionum* (1581), which sought to emphasize the unity of the Reformed churches. Bullinger's personal confession was adopted by the Reformed churches of Scotland (1566), Hungary (1567), France (1571) and Poland (1571).

Nikolaus Selnecker (1530–1592). German Lutheran theologian, preacher, pastor and hymnist. Selnecker taught in Wittenberg, Jena and Leipzig, preached in Dresden and Wolfenbüttel, and pastored in Leipzig. He was forced out of his post at Jena because of suspicions that he was a crypto-Calvinist. He sought refuge in Wolfenbüttel, where he met Martin Chemnitz* and Jakob Andreae (1528–1590). Under their influence Selnecker was drawn away from Philippist theology. Selnecker's shift in theology can be seen in his *Institutio religionis christianae* (1573). Selnecker coauthored the Formula of Concord* with Chemnitz, Andreae, Andreas Musculus (1514–1581), and David Chytraeus.* Selnecker also published lectures on Genesis, the Psalms, and the New Testament epistles, as well as composing over a hundred hymn tunes and texts.

Short Confession (1610). In response to some of William Laud's* reforms in the Church of England—particularly a law stating that ministers who refused to comply with the Book of Common Prayer would lose their ordination—a group of English Puritans immigrated to the Netherlands in protest, where they eventually embraced the practice of believer's baptism. The resulting Short Confession was an attempt at union between these Puritans and local Dutch Anabaptists ("Waterlanders"). The document highlights the importance of love in the church and reflects optimism regarding the freedom of the will while explicitly rejecting double predestination.

Richard Sibbes (1577–1635). English Puritan preacher. Sibbes was educated at St. John's College, Cambridge, where he was converted to reforming views and became a popular preacher. As a moderate Puritan emphasizing interior piety and brotherly love, Sibbes always remained within the established Church of England, though opposed to some of its liturgical ceremonies. His collected sermons constitute his main literary legacy.

Menno Simons (c. 1496–1561). Dutch Radical leader. Simons led a separatist Anabaptist group in the Netherlands that would later be called Mennonites, known for nonviolence and renunciation of the world. A former priest, Simons rejected Catholicism through the influence of Anabaptist disciples of Melchior Hoffmann and based on his study of Scripture, in which he found no support for transubstantiation or infant baptism. Following the sack of Anabaptists at Münster, Simons committed to a nonviolent way of life. Simons proclaimed a message of radical discipleship of obedience and inner purity, marked by voluntary adult baptism and communal discipline.

Cyriacus Spangenberg (1528–1604). German Lutheran pastor, preacher and theologian. Spangenberg was a staunch, often acerbic, Gnesio-Lutheran. He rejected the Formula of Concord* because of concerns about the princely control of the church, as well as its rejection of Flacian language of original sin (as constituting the "substance" of human nature after the fall). He published many commentaries and sermons, most famously seventy wedding sermons (*Ehespiegel* [1561]), his sermons on Luther* (*Theander Luther* [1562–1571]) and Luther's hymns (*Cithara Lutheri* [1569–1570]). He also published an analysis of the Old Testament (though he only got as far as Job), based on a methodology that anticipated the

logical bifurcations of Peter Ramus.*

Johann Spangenberg (1484–1550). German Lutheran pastor and catechist. Spangenberg studied at the University of Erfurt, where he was welcomed into a group of humanists associated with Konrad Muth (1470–1526). There he met the reformer Justus Jonas,* and Eobanus Hessius (1488–1540), whom Luther* dubbed "king of the poets." Spangenberg served at parishes in Stolberg (1520–1524), Nordhausen (1524–1546) and, by Luther's recommendation, Eisleben (1546–1550). Spangenberg published one of the best-selling postils of the sixteenth century, the *Postilla Teütsch*, a six-volume work meant to prepare children to understand the lectionary readings. It borrowed the question-answer form of Luther's *Small Catechism* and was so popular that a monk, Johannes Craendonch, purged overt anti-Catholic statements from it and republished it under his own name. Among Spangenberg's other pastoral works are *ars moriendi* ("the art of dying") booklets, a postil for the Acts of the Apostles and a question-answer version of Luther's *Large Catechism*. In addition to preaching and pastoring, Spangenberg wrote pamphlets on controversial topics such as purgatory, as well as textbooks on music, mathematics and grammar.

Swiss Brethren Confession of Hesse (1578). Anabaptist leader Hans Pauly Kuchenbecker penned this confession after a 1577 interrogation by Lutheran authorities. This confession was unusually amenable to Lutheran views—there is no mention of pacifism or rejection of oath taking.

Synod of Dordrecht (1618–1619). This large Dutch Reformed Church council—also attended by English, German and Swiss delegates—met to settle the theological issues raised by the followers of Jacobus Arminius.* Arminius's theological disagreements with mainstream Reformed teaching erupted into open conflict with the publication of the *Remonstrance* (1610). This "protest" was based on five points: that election is based on foreseen faith or unbelief; that Christ died indiscriminately for all people (although only believers receive salvation); that people are thoroughly sinful by nature apart from the prevenient grace of God that enables their free will to embrace or reject the gospel; that humans are able to resist the working of God's grace; and that it is possible for true believers to fall away from faith completely. The Synod ruled in favor of the Contra-Remonstrants, its Canons often remembered with a TULIP acrostic—total depravity, unconditional election, limited atonement, irresistible grace, perseverance of the saints—each letter countering one of the five Remonstrant articles. The Synod also officially accepted the Belgic Confession,* Heidelberg Catechism* and the Canons of Dordrecht as standards of the Dutch Reformed Church.

Thomas Thorowgood (1595–1669). English Puritan pastor. Thorowgood was a Puritan minister in Norfolk and the chief financier of John Eliot (1604–1690), a Puritan missionary among the Native American tribes in Massachusetts. In 1650, under the title *Jews in America, or, Probabilities that Americans be of that Race*, Thorowgood became one of the first to put forward the thesis that Native Americans were actually the ten lost tribes of Israel.

Daniel Toussain (1541–1602). Swiss Reformed pastor and professor. Toussain became pastor at Orléans after attending college in Basel. After the third War of Religion, Toussain was exiled, eventually returning to Montbéliard, his birthplace. In 1571, he faced opposition there from the strict Lutheran rulers and was eventually exiled due to his influence over the clergy. He returned to Orléans but fled following the Saint Bartholomew's Day Massacre (1572), eventually becoming pastor in Basel. He relocated to Heidelberg in 1583 as pastor to the new regent, becoming professor of theology at the university, and he remained there until his death.

John Trapp (1601–1669). Anglican biblical exegete. After studying at Oxford, Trapp entered the pastorate in 1636. During the English Civil Wars he sided with Parliament, which later made it difficult for him to collect tithes from a congregation whose royalist pastor had been evicted. Trapp published commentaries on all the books of

the Bible from 1646 to 1656.

William Tyndale (Hychyns) (1494–1536). English reformer, theologian and translator. Tyndale was educated at Oxford University, where he was influenced by the writings of humanist thinkers. Believing that piety is fostered through personal encounter with the Bible, he asked to translate the Bible into English; denied permission, Tyndale left for the Continent to complete the task. His New Testament was the equivalent of a modern-day bestseller in England but was banned and ordered burned. Tyndale's theology was oriented around justification, the authority of Scripture and Christian obedience; Tyndale emphasized the ethical as a concomitant reality of justification. He was martyred in Brussels before completing his English translation of the Old Testament, which Miles Coverdale* finished.

Juan de Valdés (1500/10–1541). Spanish Catholic theologian and writer. Although Valdés adopted an evangelical doctrine, had Erasmian affiliations and published works that were listed on the Index of Prohibited Books, Valdés rebuked the reformers for creating disunity and never left the Catholic Church. His writings included translations of the Hebrew Psalter and various biblical books, a work on the Spanish language and several commentaries. Valdés fled to Rome in 1531 to escape the Spanish Inquisition and worked in the court of Clement VII in Bologna until the pope's death in 1534. Valdés subsequently returned to Naples, where he led the reform- and revival-minded Valdesian circle.

Peter Martyr Vermigli (1499–1562). Italian Reformed humanist and theologian. Vermigli was one of the most influential theologians of the era, held in common regard with such figures as Martin Luther* and John Calvin.* In Italy, Vermigli was a distinguished theologian, preacher and advocate for moral reform; however, during the reinstitution of the Roman Inquisition Vermigli fled to Protestant regions in northern Europe. He was eventually appointed professor of divinity at Oxford University, where Vermigli delivered acclaimed disputations on the Eucharist. Vermigli was widely noted for his deeply integrated biblical commentaries and theological treatises.

Peter Walpot (d. 1578). Moravian Radical pastor and bishop. Walpot was a bishop of the Hutterite community after Jakob Hutter, Peter Riedemann* and Leonhard Lanzenstiel. Riedemann's *Confession of Faith* (1545; 1565) became a vital authority for Hutterite exegesis, theology and morals. Walpot added his own *Great Article Book* (1577), which collates primary biblical passages on baptism, communion, the community of goods, the sword and divorce. In keeping with Hutterite theology, Walpot defended the community of goods as a mark of the true church.

Valentin Weigel (1533–1588). German Lutheran pastor. Weigel studied at Leipzig and Wittenberg, entering the pastorate in 1567. Despite a strong anti-institutional bias, he was recognized by the church hierarchy as a talented preacher and compassionate minister of mercy to the poor. Although he signed the Formula of Concord, Weigel's orthodoxy was questioned so openly that he had to publish a defense. He appears to have tried to synthesize several medieval mystics with the ideas of Sebastian Franck,* Thomas Müntzer* and others. His posthumously published works have led some recent scholars to suggest that Weigel's works may have deeply influenced later Pietism.

John Whitgift (1530–1604). Anglican archbishop. Though Whitgift shared much theological common ground with Puritans, after his election as Archbishop of Canterbury (1583) he moved decisively to squelch the political and ecclesiastical threat they posed during Elizabeth's reign. Whitgift enforced strict compliance to the Book of Common Prayer, the Act of Uniformity (1559) and the Articles of Religion.* Whitgift's policies led to a large migration of Puritans to Holland. The bulk of Whitgift's published corpus is the fruit of a lengthy public disputation with Thomas Cartwright,* in which Whitgift defines Anglican doctrine against Cartwright's staunch Puritanism.

Johann Wigand (1523–1587). German Lutheran theologian. Wigand is most noted as one of the compilers of the *Magdeburg Centuries*, a German ecclesiastical history of the first thirteen centuries of the church. He was a student of Philipp Melanchthon* at the University of Wittenburg and became a significant figure in the controversies dividing Lutheranism. Strongly opposed to Roman Catholicism, Wigand lobbied against innovations in Lutheran theology that appeared sympathetic to Catholic thought. In the later debates, Wigand's support for Gnesio-Lutheranism established his role in the development of confessional Lutheranism. Wigand was appointed bishop of Pomerania after serving academic posts at the universities in Jena and Königsburg.

Andrew Willet (1562–1621). Anglican priest, professor, and biblical expositor. Willet was a gifted biblical expositor and powerful preacher. He walked away from a promising university career in 1588 when he was ordained a priest in the Church of England. For the next thirty-three years he served as a parish priest. Willet's commentaries summarized the present state of discussion while also offering practical applications for preachers. They have been cited as some of the most technical commentaries of the early seventeenth century. His most important publication was *Synopsis Papismi, or a General View of Papistrie* (1594), in which he responded to many of Robert Bellarmine's critiques. After years of royal favor, Willet was imprisoned in 1618 for a month after presenting to King James I his opposition to the "Spanish Match" of Prince Charles to the Infanta Maria. While serving as a parish priest, he wrote forty-two works, most of which were either commentaries on books of the Bible or controversial works against Catholics.

Girolamo Zanchi (1516–1590). Italian Reformed theologian and pastor. Zanchi joined an Augustinian monastery at the age of fifteen, where he studied Greek and Latin, the church fathers and the works of Aristotle and Thomas Aquinas. Under the influence of his prior, Peter Martyr Vermigli,* Zanchi also imbibed the writings of the Swiss and German reformers. To avoid the Inquisition, Zanchi fled to Geneva where he was strongly attracted to the preaching and teaching of John Calvin.* Zanchi taught biblical theology and the *locus* method at academies in Strasbourg, Heidelberg, and Neustadt. He also served as pastor of an Italian refugee congregation. Zanchi's theological works, *De tribus Elohim* (1572) and *De natura Dei* (1577), have received more attention than his commentaries. His commentaries comprise about a quarter of his literary output, however, and display a strong typological and Christological interpretation in conversation with the church fathers, medieval exegetes, and other reformers.

Katharina Schütz Zell (1497/98–1562). German Reformed writer. Zell became infamous in Strasbourg and the Empire when in 1523 she married the priest Matthias Zell, and then published an apology defending her husband against charges of impiety and libertinism. Longing for a united church, she called for toleration of Catholics and Anabaptists, famously writing to Martin Luther* after the failed Marburg Colloquy of 1529 to exhort him to check his hostility and to be ruled instead by Christian charity. Much to the chagrin of her contemporaries, Zell published diverse works, ranging from polemical treatises on marriage to letters of consolation, as well as editing a hymnal and penning an exposition of Psalm 51.

Huldrych Zwingli (1484–1531). Swiss Reformed humanist, preacher and theologian. Zwingli, a parish priest, was influenced by the writings of Desiderius Erasmus* and taught himself Greek. While a preacher to the city cathedral in Zurich, Zwingli enacted reform through sermons, public disputations and conciliation with the town council, abolishing the Mass and images in the church. Zwingli broke with the lectionary preaching tradition, instead preaching serial expository biblical sermons. He later was embroiled in controversy with Anabaptists over infant baptism and with Martin Luther* at the Marburg Colloquy (1529) over their differing views of the Eucharist. Zwingli, serving as chaplain to Zurich's military, was killed in battle.

SOURCES FOR
BIOGRAPHICAL SKETCHES

General Reference Works

Allgemeine Deutsche Biographie. 56 vols. Leipzig: Duncker & Humblot, 1875–1912; reprint, 1967–1971. Accessible online via deutsche-biographie.de/index.html.

Hillerbrand, Hans J., ed. *Oxford Encyclopedia of the Reformation.* 4 vols. New York: Oxford University Press, 1996.

Kolb, Robert, and Timothy J. Wengert, eds. *The Book of Concord: The Confessions of the Evangelical Lutheran Church.* Translated by Charles Arand et al. Minneapolis: Fortress, 2000.

McKim, Donald K., ed. *Dictionary of Major Biblical Interpreters.* Downers Grove, IL: InterVarsity Press, 2007.

Müller, Gerhard, et al., ed. *Theologische Realenzyklopädie.* Berlin: Walter de Gruyter, 1994.

Neue Deutsche Biographie. 28 vols. projected. Berlin: Duncker & Humblot, 1953–. Accessible online via deutsche-biographie.de/index.html.

New Catholic Encyclopedia. 15 vols. New York: McGraw-Hill, 1967; 2nd ed., Detroit: Thomson-Gale, 2002.

Oxford Dictionary of National Biography. 60 vols. Oxford: Oxford University Press, 2004.

Stephen, Leslie, and Sidney Lee, eds. *Dictionary of National Biography.* 63 vols. London: Smith, Elder and Co., 1885–1900.

Additional Works for Individual Sketches

Akin, Daniel L. "An Expositional Analysis of the Schleitheim Confession." *Criswell Theological Review* 2 (1988): 345-70.

Bald, R. C. *John Donne: A Life.* Oxford: Oxford University Press, 1970.

Doornkaat Koolman, J ten. "The First Edition of Peter Riedemann's 'Rechenschaft.'" *Mennonite*

Quarterly Review 36, no. 2 (1962): 169-70.

Friedmann, Robert. "Second Generation Anabaptism as Illustrated by the Walpot Era of the Hutterites." *Mennonite Quarterly* 44, no. 4 (1970): 390-93.

Furcha, Edward J. "Key Concepts in Caspar von Schwenckfeld's Thought, Regeneration and the New Life." *Church History* 37, no. 2 (1968): 160-73.

Hvolbek, Russell H. "Being and Knowing: Spiritualist Epistelmology and Anthropology from Schwenckfeld to Böhme." *Sixteenth Century Journal* 22, no. 1 (1991): 97-110.

Lake, Peter. *The Boxmaker's Revenge: 'Orthodoxy', 'Heterodox' and the Politics of the Parish in Early Stuart London.* Stanford, CA: Stanford University Press, 2001.

Packull, Werner O. "The Origins of Peter Riedemann's Account of Our Faith." *Sixteenth Century Journal* 30, no. 1 (1999): 61-69.

Papazian, Mary Arshagouni, ed. *John Donne and the Protestant Reformation: New Perspectives.* Detroit: Wayne State University Press, 2003.

Synder, C. Arnold. "The Schleitheim Articles in Light of the Revolution of the Common Man: Continuation or Departure?" *Sixteenth Century Journal* 16, no. 4 (1985): 419-30.

———. "The Confession of the Swiss Brethren in Hesse, 1578." In *Anabaptism Revisited: Essays on Anabaptist/Mennonite Studies in Honor of C. J. Dyck.* Edited by Walter Klaassen, 29-49. Waterloo, ON; Scottdale, PA: Herald Press, 1992.

Wengert, Timothy J. "'Fear and Love' in the Ten Commandments." *Concordia Journal* 21, no. 1 (1995): 14-27.

Voogt, Gerrit. "Remonstrant-Counter-Remonstrant Debates: Crafting a Principled Defense of Toleration after the Synod of Dordrecht (1619–1650)." *Church History and Religious Culture* 89, no. 4 (2009): 489-524.

BIBLIOGRAPHY

Primary Sources and Translations Used in the Volume

Agricola, Johannes. *Die Sprichwörtersammlungen.* 2 vols. Edited by Sander L. Gilman. Berlin: Walter de Gruyter, 1971.

Amyraut, Moïse. *Paraphrase sur les Actes des Saints Apostres.* 2 vols. Samur: Jean Lesnier, 1653. Digital copy online at archive.org.

Die Bekenntnisschriften der evangelisch-lutherischen Kirche. 12th ed. Göttingen: Vandenhoeck & Ruprecht, 1998.

Beza, Theodore. *Theodori Bezae Annotationes Majores in Novum Dn. Nostri Jesu Christi Testamentum.* 2 vols. Geneva: Jeremie des Planches, 1594. Digital copy online at e-rara.ch.

Bibliotheca Reformatoria Neederlandica. 10 vols. Edited by S. Cramer and F. Pijper. The Hague: Martinus Nijhoff, 1903–1914. Digital copy online at babel.hathitrust.org.

The Book of Common Prayer (1549). In *The Two Liturgies,* A.D. *1549 and* A.D. *1552.* Edited by Joseph Ketley, 9-158. Cambridge: Cambridge University Press, 1844. Digital copy online at books.google.com.

Brenz, Johannes. *In Acta Apostolica Homiliae Centvm Viginti Duas.* Haganau: Peter Braubach, 1535. Digital copy online at gateway-bayern.de.

———. *Acta Apostolorum: Das Buch der Apostelgeschicht; Die recht und Haubthistoria der ersten heyligen Christlichen Kirchen.* Nuremberg: Berg & Newber, 1551. Digital copy online at books.google.com.

Brunfels, Otto. *Annotationes Othonis Brunfelsii, Rei Medices Doctoris Pertissimi Theologiae, Trium Linguarum, Variarumque Artium Insignite Eruditi, in quatuor Euangelia et Acta Apostolorum, ex Orthodoxis Sacrarum Literarum Scriptoribus Congestae, Plusquam Credi Potest: Divinarum Rerum Candidatis, Usui Futurae.* Strasbourg: Georg Ulricher, 1535. Digital copy online at gateway-bayern.de.

Bullinger, Heinrich. *In Acta Apostolorum.* Zurich: Christoph Froschauer, 1533. Digital copy online at e-rara.ch.

Cajetan, Cardinal (Thomas de Vio). *Evangelia cum Commentariis.* Venice: Luccantonii, 1530. Digital copy online at gateway-bayern.de.

Calvin, John. *Ioannis Calvini Opera quae supersunt omnia.* 59 vols. Corpus Reformatorum 29-88. Edited by G. Baum, E. Cunitz and E. Reuss. Brunswick and Berlin: C. A. Schwetschke, 1863–1900. Digital copy online at archive-ouverte.unige.ch/Calvin.

———. *The Acts of the Apostles.* 2 vols. Translated by John W. Fraser and W. J. G. McDonald. Edited by David W. Torrance and Thomas F. Torrance. Calvin's New Testament Commentaries 6-7. Grand Rapids: Eerdmans, 1965–1966.

———. *Institutes of the Christian Religion* (1559). Edited by John T. McNeill. Translated by Ford Lewis Battles. Library of Christian Classics 20-21. Philadelphia: Westminster, 1960. Latin text availble in CO 2 (1864). Digital copy online at archive-ouverte.unige.ch/Calvin.

———. *Commentariorum Joannis Calvini in Acta Apostolorum.* 2 vols. Geneva: Jean Crispin, 1552–1554. Modern edition, CO 48 (1892). Digital copy online at archive-ouverte.unige.ch/Calvin.

———. *Ioannis Calvini Commentarii integri In Acta Apostolorum*. 2nd ed. Geneva: Jean Crispin, 1560. Modern edition, CO 18 (1878). Digital copy online at archive-ouverte.unige.ch/Calvin. Note that this edition was only used in this volume for the Dedicatory Epistle to the Second Edition.

Cochrane, Arthur C., ed. *Reformed Confessions of the Sixteenth Century*. Philadelphia: Westminster Press, 1966.

The Commission on Worship for the Lutheran Church—Missouri Synod, ed. *Lutheran Service Book*. St. Louis: Concordia, 2006.

Crashaw, Richard. *The Complete Works of Richard Crashaw, Canon of Loretto*. Edited by William B. Turnbull. London: John Russell Smith, 1858. Digital copy online at books.google.com.

Denck, Hans. *Selected Writings of Hans Denck 1500–1527*. Edited and translated by E. J. Furcha. Lewiston, NY: Edwin Mellen Press, 1989.

Denison, Stephen. *The Doctrine of Both the Sacraments: To Witte, Baptisme and the Supper of the Lord, or A Commentary upon the 16 verse of the 22 of the Acts of the Apostles*. London: Augustine Mathewes, 1621. Accessed digitally via EEBO.

Diodati, Giovanni. *I Commenti alla Sacra Bibbia*. 2 vols. Florence: Barbera, 1880. Digital copy online at archive.org.

———. *Pious Annotations upon the Holy Bible*. London: Nicolas Fussell, 1651. Accessed digitally via EEBO.

Donne, John. *The Works of John Donne*. 6 vols. Edited by Henry Alford. London: John Parker, 1839. Digital copy online at archive.org.

———. *The Poems of John Donne*. Edited by Herbert J. C. Grierson. Oxford: Clarendon Press, 1912. Digital copy online at books.google.com.

Downame, John, ed. *Annotations upon All the Books of the Old and New Testament*. London: Evan Tyler, 1657. Accessed digitally via EEBO.

Eck, Johann. *Christenliche Predigen*. 5 vols. Ingolstadt: Apian, 1530–1539. Digital copy online at gateway-bayern.de.

Erasmus, Desiderius. *In Acta Apostolorum Paraphrasis*. Basel: J. Froben, 1524. Modern edition in LB 7 (1706; reprint, 1962). Digital copy online at gateway-bayern.de.

———. *Desideri Erasmi Roterodami Opera Omnia*. 10 vols. Edited by Jean LeClerc. Leiden: Van der Aa, 1704–1706; reprint, Hildesheim: Georg Olms, 1961–1962.

———. *Paraphrase on the Acts of the Apostles*. Edited by John J. Bateman. Translated by Robert D. Sider. Collected Works of Erasmus 50. Toronto: University of Toronto Press, 1995.

Fast, Heinold, and Gottfried Seebaß, eds. *Briefe und Schriften oberdeutscher Täufer 1527–1555: Das 'Kunstbuch' des Jörg Probst Rotenfelder gen. Maler (Burgerbibliothek Bern, Cod. 464)*. Quellen zur Geschichte der Täufer 17. Gütersloh: Gütersloher Verlagshaus, 2007.

Friedmann, Robert, ed. *Glaubenszeugnisse oberdeutscher Taufgesinnter II*. Quellen zur Geschichte der Täufer 12. Gütersloh: Gerd Mohn, 1967.

Gwalther, Rudolf. *In Acta Apostolorum per Divum Lucam Descripta Homiliae CLXXIIII*. Zurich: Christoph Froschauer, 1557. Digital copy online at e-raca.ch.

———. *An Hundred, Threescore and Fiftene Homelyes or Sermons, uppon the Actes of the Apostles*. Translated by John Bridges. London: Henrie Denham, 1572. Accessed digitally via EEBO.

Hubmaier, Balthasar. *Schriften*. Edited by Gunnar Westin and Torsten Bergsten. Quellen zur Geschichte der Täufer 9. Gütersloh: Gerd Mohn, 1962.

———. *Balthasar Hubmaier: Theologian of Anabaptism*. Translated and edited by H. Wayne Pipkin and John H. Yoder. Classics of the Radical Reformation 5. Scottdale, PA: Herald Press, 1989.

Hut, Hans. "On the Mystery of Baptism." In *The Radical Reformation*. Edited by Michael G. Baylor, 152-71. Cambridge: Cambridge University Press, 1991.

Jonas, Justus. *Annotationes Iusti Ionae in Acta Apostolorum*. Wittenberg: Nickel Schirlentz, 1524. Digital copy online at gateway-bayern.de.

Joris, David. *The Anabaptist Writings of David Joris, 1535–1543*. Edited and translated by Gary K. Waite. Classics of the Radical Reformation 7. Scottdale, PA: Herald Press, 1993.

Karlstadt, Andreas Bodenstein von. *The Essential Carlstadt: Fifteen Tracts by Andreas Bodenstein (Carlstadt) from Karlstadt*. Edited and translated by E. J. Furcha. Classics of the Radical Reformation 8. Scottdale, PA: Herald Press, 1995.

———. *Karlstadts Schriften aus den Jahren 1523–25*. Edited by Erich Hertzsch. Halle: Veb Max Niemeyer Verlag, 1956.

Kolb, Robert, and Timothy J. Wengert, eds. *The Book of Concord: The Confessions of the Evangelical Lutheran Church*. Translated by Charles Arand et al. Minneapolis: Fortress, 2000.

Koop, Karl, ed. *Confessions of Faith in the Anabaptist Tradition 1527–1660*. Translated by Cornelius J. Dyck et al. Classics of the Radical Reformation 11. Kitchener, ON: Pandora Press, 2006.

Lossius, Lucas. *Annotationum Lucae Lossii in Novum Testamentum*. 5 vols. Frankfurt: Christian Egenolff, 1553–1562. Digital copy online at gateway-bayern.de.

Luther, Martin. *D. Martin Luthers Werke, Kritische Gesamtausgabe: [Schriften]*. 73 vols. Weimar: Hermann Böhlaus Nachfolger, 1883–2009. Digital copies online at archive.org.

———. *D. Martin Luthers Werke, Kritische Gesamtausgabe: Tischreden*. 6 vols. Weimar: Hermann Böhlaus Nachfolger, 1912–1921. Digital copies online at archive.org.

———. *D. Martin Luthers Werke, Kritische Gesamtausgabe: Deutsche Bibel*. 12 vols. Weimar: Böhlaus Nachfolger, 1906–1961.

———. *Luther's Works* [American edition]. 82 vols. planned. St. Louis: Concordia; Philadelphia: Fortress, 1955–1986; 2009–.

———. "'This Is My Son, the Beloved': Sermon on the Baptism of Jesus, The Epiphany of Our Lord (January 6, 1534)." Translated by Frederick J. Gaiser. *Word & World* 16, no. 1 (1996): 7-10.

Major, Georg. *Vita S. Pauli Apostoli*. Wittenberg: Hans Lufft, 1555. Digital copy online at gateway-bayern.de.

———. *Auslegung der Epistel S. Pauli an die Philipper in acht predigt: den Dorffpfarhern und Hausvetern zu dienst einfeltiglichen verfasset*. Wittenberg: Hans Lufft, 1560. Digital copy online at gateway-bayern.de.

Manz, Felix. "Protest and Defense." In *The Radical Reformation*. Edited by Michael G. Baylor, 95-100. Cambridge: Cambridge University Press, 1991.

Marpeck, Pilgram. *The Writings of Pilgram Marpeck*. Translated and edited by William Klassen and Walter Klaassen. Classics of the Radical Reformation 2. Scottdale, PA: Herald Press, 1978.

Martyr [Vermigli], Peter. *In Selectissimam D. Pauli Priorem ad Corinthios Epistolam*. Zurich: Christoph Froschauer, 1551. Digital copy online at e-rara.ch.

Melanchthon, Philipp. *Philippi Melanthonis Opera quae supersunt omnia*. 28 vols. Corpus Reformatorum 1-28. Edited by C. G. Bretschneider. Halle: C. A. Schwetschke, 1834–1860. Digital copy online at archive.org and books.google.com.

———. *Melanchthons Werke in Auswahl [Studienausgabe]*. Edited by R. Stupperich. 7 vols. Gütersloh: Gerd Mohn, 1951–1975.

———. *Verlegung etlicher unchristlicher Artikel: Welche die Widerteuffer furgeben*. Wittenberg: Georg Rhau, 1534. Digital copy online at gateway-bayern.de.

Müller, Lydia, ed. *Glaubenszeugnisse oberdeutscher Taufgesinnter*. Quellen zur Geschichte der Täufer 3. Leipzig: M. Heinsius Nachfolger, 1938; reprint, New York: Johnson Reprint Corporation, 1971.

Müntzer, Thomas. *Schriften und Briefe: Kritische Gesamtausgabe*. Edited by Paul Kirn and Günther Franz. Gütersloh: Gerd Mohn, 1968.

———. "Sermon to the Princes." In *The Radical Reformation*. Edited by Michael G. Baylor, 11-32. Cambridge: Cambridge University Press, 1991.

Pellikan, Konrad. *In Sacrosancta Quatuor Euangelia et Apostolorum Acta*. Zurich: Christoph Froschauer, 1537. Digital copy online at e-rara.ch.

Philips, Dirk. *The Writings of Dirk Philips 1504–1568*. Edited by Cornelius J. Dyck, William E. Keeney and Alvin J. Beachy. Classics of the Radical Reformation 6. Scottdale, PA: Herald Press, 1992.

Plass, Ewald, ed. *What Luther Says: An Anthology*. 3 vols. St. Louis: Concordia, 1959.

Rempel, John D., ed. *Jörg Maler's Kunstbuch: Writings of the Pilgram Marpeck Circle*. Classics of the Radical Reformation 12. Kitchener, ON: Pandora Press, 2010.

Riedemann, Peter. *Peter Riedemann's Hutterite Confession of Faith: Translation of the 1565 German Edition of* Confession of Our Religion, Teaching and Faith by the Brothers Who Are Known as the Hutterites. Edited and translated by John J. Friesen. Classics of the Radical Reformation 9. Scottdale, PA: Herald Press, 1999.

Sattler, Michael. *The Legacy of Michael Sattler*. Translated and edited by John H. Yoder. Classics of the Radical Reformation 1. Scottdale, PA: Herald Press, 1973.

Schaff, Philip. *The Creeds of Christendom: With a Critical History and Notes*. 3 vols. New York: Harper & Row, 1877; reprint, Grand Rapids: Baker Books, 1977. Accessible online at ccel.org.

Simons, Menno. *The Complete Writings of Menno Simons*. Edited by John Christian Wenger. Scottdale, PA: Herald Press, 1956.

Spangenberg, Johann. *Der Apostel Geschichte: Kurtze auslegung Fur die jungen Christen inn Frage verfasset*. Wittenberg: Georg Rhau, 1545. Digital copy online at gateway-bayern.de.

Thompson, John L. *John Calvin and the Daughters of Sarah: Women in Regular and Exceptional Roles in the Exegesis of Calvin, His Predecessors and His Contemporaries*. Geneva: Droz, 1992.

Trapp, John. *A Commentary or Exposition upon the Four Evangelists and the Acts of the Apostles*. London: John Bellamie, 1647. Accessed digitally via EEBO.

Weigel, Valentin. *Valentin Weigel Sämtliche Schriften*. 14 vols. Stuttgart-Bad Cannstatt: Frommann-Holzboog, 1996–.

Zell, Katharina Schütz. *Church Mother: The Writings of a Protestant Reformer in Sixteenth-Century Germany*. Edited and translated by Elsie McKee. Chicago: University of Chicago Press, 2006.

Zwingli, Huldrych. *Huldreich Zwinglis Sämtliche Werke*. 14 vols. Corpus Reformatorum 88-101. Edited by E. Egli et al. Berlin: C. A. Schwetschke, 1905–1959; reprint, Zürich: Theologischer Verlag Zürich, 1983. Accessed digitally via Institut für Scweizerische Reformationsgeschichte at www.irg.uzh.ch.

———. *Zwingli and Bullinger*. Edited and translated by G. W. Bromiley. Library of Christian Classics 24. Philadelphia: Westminster Press, 1953.

Author and Writings Index

Subject Index

Scripture Index